Laugh Again

Publications by Charles R. Swindoll

Books:

Come Before Winter
Compassion: Showing We Care in a Careless World
Dropping Your Guard
Encourage Me
For Those Who Hurt
The Grace Awakening
Growing Deep in the Christian Life
Growing Strong in the Seasons of Life
Hand Me Another Brick
Improving Your Serve
Killing Giants, Pulling Thorns
Leadership: Influence That Inspires
Living Above the Level of Mediocrity
Living Beyond the Daily Grind, Books 1 and 2
Living on the Ragged Edge
Make Up Your Mind
The Quest for Character
Recovery: When Healing Takes Time
Rise and Shine
Sanctity of Life
Simple Faith
Standing Out
Starting Over
Strengthening Your Grip
Stress Fractures
Strike the Original Match
The Strong Family
Three Steps Forward, Two Steps Back
Victory: A Winning Game Plan for Life
You and Your Child

Minibooks:

Abraham: A Model of Pioneer Faith
David: A Model of Pioneer Courage
Esther: A Model of Pioneer Independence
Moses: A Model of Pioneer Vision
Nehemiah: A Model of Pioneer Determination

Booklets:

Anger
Attitudes
Commitment
Dealing with Defiance
Demonism
Destiny
Divorce
Eternal Security
Fun Is Contagious
God's Will
Hope
Impossibilities
Integrity
Leisure
The Lonely Whine of the Top Dog
Moral Purity
Our Mediator
Peace . . . in Spite of Panic
Prayer
Sensuality
Singleness
Stress
Tongues
When Your Comfort Zone Gets the Squeeze
Woman

LAUGH AGAIN

CHARLES R. SWINDOLL

W PUBLISHING GROUP™
www.wpublishinggroup.com
A Division of Thomas Nelson, Inc.
www.ThomasNelson.com

LAUGH AGAIN

Unless otherwise indicated, Scripture quotations used in this book are from the New American Standard Bible (NASB) © 1960, 1962, 1963, 1968, 1971, 1972, 1973, 1975, 1977 by The Lockman Foundation. Used by permission.

Other Scripture quotations are from the following sources:

The Holy Bible, New International Version (NIV). Copyright © 1973, 1978, 1984 International Bible Society. Used by permission of Zondervan Bible Publishers.

The New Testament in Modern English (PHILLIPS) by J. B. Phillips, published by The Macmillan Company, © 1958, 1960, 1972 by J. B. Phillips.

The Good News Bible, Today's English Version (TEV)—Old Testament: Copyright © American Bible Society 1976; New Testament: Copyright © American Bible Society 1966, 1971, 1976.

The Living Bible (TLB), copyright 1971 by Tyndale House Publishers, Wheaton, Ill. Used by permission.

Library of Congress Cataloging-in-Publication Data

Swindoll, Charles R.
Laugh again / Charles R. Swindoll.
p. cm.
ISBN 0-8499-0957-0
1. Joy—Religious aspects—Christianity. 2. Laughter—Religious aspects—Christianity. I. Title.
BV4647.J68S95 1992
248.4—dc20 92-17825
CIP

Printed in the United States of America

00 01 02 PHX 17 18 19 20

This book is affectionately dedicated to
Al and Margaret Sanders
and
Jon and Peggy Campbell
with gratitude for their unselfish devotion
to the radio ministry of
Insight for Living.
It was the Sanderses' vision that launched the broadcasts and
the Campbells' commitment that sustained it during its infancy.
Because of their tireless involvement in and appreciation for the
ministry, I find myself encouraged and invigorated.
And because of their spirit of outrageous joy,
our times together are often punctuated
with fun and laughter.

Contents

Acknowledgments

The closest a man can come to understanding childbirth is by writing a book. Passing a kidney stone ranks right up there. I've had four of those, but that's another story.

The process of this particular bookbirth has been unusually delightful and relatively free of pain. Maybe after my many literary "kids," I'm getting the hang of it.

Those who have served as midwives are among the best in the business. Byron Williamson, Kip Jordon, Ernie Owen, and David Moberg of Word Publishing not only rejoiced to know I was "expecting," but they also helped name the baby and provided a colorful jacket for it to wear. In fact the whole atmosphere they brought to the delivery center was so pleasant, I found myself forgetting that it was supposed to be a difficult process.

Once again I want to express my gratitude to Helen Peters, who cleaned the baby up after it was born. Thanks also to Judith Markham and Ed Curtis, who again gave me wise editorial counsel and helpful ideas that would keep this newborn healthy and strong. As all my immediate family members either came by to visit or phoned to see how I was feeling as I was moving closer to the delivery date, my spirits were lifted. And, as always, Cynthia was especially encouraging, knowing how concerned I was that this be a happy baby and free of needless complications. Her supportive presence proved crucial.

Finally, I want to declare my gratitude to my Great Physician who allowed me to meet with Him regularly without a scheduled appointment, provided excellent checkups, demonstrated compassionate care, and assisted me in the birth with gentleness and joy. I knew that everything was going to be all right because immediately after it was born, something most unusual happened. Unlike all the others I have had, when this one finally came, it laughed.

I am grateful for you too. As you hold it close and enjoy its company, may its happy disposition bring you hours of delight. All I ask is that when it smiles at you, smile back. If you do, you will soon discover a bond forming between the two of you that will lighten your load and help you relax. It is a funny thing about babies—the way they curl up in our arms and become a part of our lives the longer we spend time with them. Who knows? At some unguarded moment when you two are all alone and no one else is watching, you might even break down and laugh again. Feel free. As a proud parent, I can't think of anything that would please me more.

Introduction

This is a book about joy.

It's about relaxing more, releasing the tension, and refusing to let circumstances dominate our attitudes.

It's about looking at life from a perspective other than today's traffic report or the evening news.

It's about giving the child within us permission to look at life and laugh again.

Can you remember when life was joyful? I certainly can. Without any knowledge of the Dow index or the drop in the gross national product or the accelerating crime rate in twenty-five of America's largest cities or the decreasing health-care benefits in our country's major companies, I was happy as a clam. I neither expected much nor needed much. Life was meant to be enjoyed, not endured, and therefore every day I found something—anything—to laugh about.

Through my childlike eyes people were funny. (When did they stop being funny?) When school was out and those lazy, hazy months of summer were mine to enjoy, there was usually enough water somewhere to swim in or a basketball to dribble and shoot hoops with or old roller skates to make a sidewalk scooter from or a crazy joke to laugh at. (When did everything get so serious?)

Our family of five had no wealth whatsoever. My dad was a machinist, often holding down more than one job to make ends meet. My mom stayed home and did all the stuff moms do at home with three strong-willed, very normal kids. Since there was a war raging on both sides of our nation, we had a truckload of reasons not to laugh . . . but I never got that message back then. I was a child and I did what children did. We made music in our family, another relaxing pastime. Some of it was pretty scary music, but we laughed that off too. And why not? I mean, it wasn't like we were rehearsing for Carnegie Hall or hoping to get a scholarship to the Juilliard School of Music. We were just having fun . . . and music was the creative avenue we chose to enjoy. Boy, did we ever! (Why have families stopped making music together?)

While flying back from Germany in the fall of 1990, I met a delightful man with an infectious laugh. It was fascinating talking with him, and as we talked, I learned that he speaks all around the world and brings joy to thousands, from prisoners to presidents. As you can imagine, he had one great story after another, most of them true and each one absolutely hilarious. Our multiple-hour flight passed all too quickly.

One of my favorites makes me smile every time I recall it. This incident actually happened to the woman who passed the story on to my fellow passenger.

Grandmother and granddaughter, a very precocious ten-year-old, were spending the evening together when the little girl suddenly looked up and asked, "How old are you, Grandma?"

The woman was a bit startled at the question, but knowing her granddaughter's quick little mind, she wasn't completely shocked.

"Well, honey, when you're my age you don't share your age with anybody."

"Aw, go ahead, Grandma . . . you can trust me."

"No, dear, I never tell anyone my age."

Grandmother got busy fixing supper and then she suddenly realized the little darling had been absent for about twenty minutes—much too long! She checked around upstairs in her bedroom and found that her granddaughter had dumped the contents of her grandmother's purse on top of her bed and was sitting in the midst of the mess, holding her grandmother's driver's license.

When their eyes met, the child announced: "Grandma, you're seventy-six."

"Why, yes, I am. How did you know that?"

"I found the date of your birthday here on your driver's license and subtracted that year from this year . . . so you're seventy-six!"

"That's right, sweetheart. Your grandmother is seventy-six."

The little girl continued staring at the driver's license and added, "You also made an F in sex, Grandma."[1]

Sometime between that age of childhood innocence and right now, life has become a grim marathon of frowns—a major downer for far too many adults. I suppose some would justify the change by saying, "When you become an adult, you need to be responsible." I couldn't agree more.

I had that drilled into my cranium. (Remember, my middle name starts with an R!) Furthermore, the same ones would say, "Being responsible includes living in a world of reality, and not everything in the real world is funny. Some things are extremely difficult." Again, you're speaking my language. Having been engaged in real-world responsibilities for well over thirty of my adult years, I am painfully aware that this old earth is not a giant bowl of cherries. They continue, "So then, since adulthood is a synonym for responsibility, and since reality certainly includes difficulties, we have no business laughing and enjoying life." It's at that point of the logic I balk. I simply do not accept the notion that responsible people in touch with the real world must wear a perpetually serious countenance and adopt a grim-reaper mind-set.

My question is this: When did a healthy, well-exercised sense of humor get sacrificed on the altar of adulthood? Who says becoming a responsible adult means a long face and an all-serious attitude toward life?

My vocation is among the most serious of all professions. As a minister of the gospel and as the senior pastor of a church, the concerns I deal with are eternal in dimension. A week doesn't pass without my hearing of or dealing with life in the raw. Marriages are breaking, homes are splitting, people are hurting, jobs are dissolving, addictions of every description are rampant. Needs are enormous, endless, and heartrending.

The most natural thing for me to do would be to allow all of that to rob me of my joy and to change me from a person who has always found humor in life—as well as laughed loudly and often—into a stoic, frowning clergyman. No thanks.

Matter of fact, that was my number-one fear many years ago. Thinking that I must look somber and be ultraserious twenty-four hours a day resulted in my resisting a call into the ministry for several years. Most of the men of the cloth I had seen looked like they held down a night job at the local mortuary. I distinctly remember wrestling with the Lord over all this before He pinned me to the mat and whispered a promise in my ear that forced me to surrender: "You can faithfully serve Me, but you can still be yourself. Being My servant doesn't require you to stop laughing." That did it. That one statement won me over. I finally decided I could be one of God's spokesmen and still enjoy life.

Not too many years ago when I started the radio program, "Insight for Living," I flashed back to that original call, and I decided to be myself, no matter what. Whether the broadcasts succeeded or fizzled, I wasn't about to come across as some superpious religious fanatic, intense about everything. When things struck me funny, I would laugh.

One of the listeners wrote in and commented: "I appreciate your program. The teaching has helped a lot . . . but I have one major request: Don't stop laughing! You can stop teaching and you can make whatever other changes you wish on your broadcasts, but *don't stop laughing!*" And then she added: "Yours is the only laughter that comes into our home."

Her ten concluding words have been ringing in my ears for years. What a sad commentary on our times! In many homes—dare I say most?—laughter has left. Joy that was once a vital ingredient in family life has departed, leaving hearts that seldom sing, lips that rarely smile, eyes that no longer dance, and faces that say no. Tragically, this is true in Christian homes as well as non-Christian . . . maybe more so.

It is my firm conviction that a change is urgently needed—which is precisely why I have taken up my pen to write again. A couple of years ago I warned of grace killers and urged my readers to be courageous as they joined the ranks of the grace-awakening movement. Many have done so. Later, I became concerned about all the complicated busywork many were adding to the life of faith, so I exposed the faith crushers as I encouraged folks to cultivate a simple-faith lifestyle. Many have done that as well. Maybe you are one of them. Now, within the last few months, I have felt an urgent need to take on the joy stealers who have been growing in number, especially since recessionary times have hit. Bad news has become the only news.

Tough times are upon us, no question. The issues we all face are both serious and real. But are they so intense, so all-important, so serious and all-consuming that every expression of joy should be eclipsed? Sorry, I can't buy that.

This book will tell you why. Hopefully, as a result of traveling through its pages with me, you will gain a new perspective on how to view these harsh days. Best of all, many of your childlike qualities will emerge and soften the blows of your intensity. Your attitude will change. You will find yourself changing. How will you know? There is one telltale sign. You'll begin to laugh again.

Chuck Swindoll
Fullerton, California

Where there is no belief in the soul, there is very little drama. . . . Either one is serious about salvation or one is not. And it is well to realize that the maximum amount of seriousness admits the maximum amount of comedy. Only if we are secure in our beliefs can we see the comical side of the universe.

Flannery O'Connor

1

Your Smile Increases Your Face Value

I KNOW OF NO GREATER NEED today than the need for joy. Unexplainable, contagious joy. Outrageous joy.

When that kind of joy comes aboard our ship of life, it brings good things with it—like enthusiasm for life, determination to hang in there, and a strong desire to be of encouragement to others. Such qualities make our voyage bearable when we hit the open seas and encounter high waves of hardship that tend to demoralize and paralyze. There is nothing better than a joyful attitude when we face the challenges life throws at us.

Someone once asked Mother Teresa what the job description was for anyone who might wish to work alongside her in the grimy streets and narrow alleys of Calcutta. Without hesitation she mentioned only two things: the desire to work hard and a joyful attitude. It has been my observation that both of those qualities are rare. But the second is much rarer than the first. Diligence may be difficult to find, but compared to an attitude of genuine joy, hard work is commonplace.

Unfortunately, our country seems to have lost its spirit of fun and laughter. Recently, a Brazilian student studying at a nearby university told me that what amazes him the most about Americans is their lack of laughter. I found myself unable to refute his criticism.

Just look around. Bad news, long faces, and heavy hearts are everywhere—even in houses of worship (especially in houses of worship!). Much of today's popular music, which many consider a voice for the nation's conscience, promotes misery, sorrow, and despair. If sex and violence are not the pulsating themes of a new film, some expression of unhappiness is. Newspapers thrive on tragedies and calamities, lost jobs and horrible accidents. The same can be said of televised newscasts. Even the weather reports give their primary attention to storms, droughts, and blizzards. Tomorrow is usually "partly cloudy with a 20 percent chance of rain," never "mostly clear with an 80 percent chance of sunshine." If you do find laughter on the tube, either it is a recorded laugh track on some stupid sitcom or a stand-up comedian telling filthy jokes.

This long-faced, heavy-hearted attitude has now invaded the ranks of Christianity. Visit most congregations today and search for signs of happiness and sounds of laughter and you often come away disappointed. Joy, "the gigantic secret of the Christian,"[1] is conspicuous by its absence. I find that *inexcusable.* The one place on earth where life's burdens should be lighter, where faces should reflect genuine enthusiasm, and where attitudes should be uplifting and positive is the place this is least likely to be true.

When I was a teenager, the most popular business advertisements in magazines read: SEND ME A MAN WHO READS. As much as I value reading and applaud the resourcefulness of those who pore over the pages of good books, I think today's slogan should be: SEND ME ONE WHOSE ATTITUDE IS POSITIVE, WHOSE HEART IS FULL OF CHEER, WHOSE FACE SHOUTS YES!

Some critics would be quick to point out that our times do not lend themselves to such an easygoing philosophy. They would ask, "Under these circumstances how could I be anything but grim?" To which I reply, "What are you doing *under* the circumstances?" Correct me if I'm wrong, but isn't the Christian life to be lived *above* the circumstances?

A good sense of humor enlivens our discernment and guards us from taking everything that comes down the pike too seriously. By remaining lighthearted, by refusing to allow our intensity to gain the mastery of our minds, we remain much more objective. Ogden Nash believed this so strongly that he claimed that if the German people had had a sense of humor, they would never have let Adolf Hitler deceive them. Instead, the first time they saw some fellow goose-stepping and raising a stiff arm to shout, "Heil Hitler," they'd have keeled over in sidesplitting laughter.[2]

People who live above their circumstances usually possess a well-developed sense of humor, because in the final analysis that's what gets them through. I met such a person at a conference in Chicago several years ago. We shared a few laughs following a session at which I had spoken. Later she wrote to thank me for adding a little joy to an otherwise ultraserious conference. (Why are most Christian conferences ultraserious?) Her note was a delightfully creative expression of one who had learned to balance the dark side of life with the bright glow of laughter. Among other things she wrote:

> Humor has done a lot to help me in my spiritual life. How could I have reared twelve children, starting at age 32, and not have had a sense of humor?
>
> After your talk last night I was enjoying some relaxed moments with friends I met here. I told them I got married at age 31. I didn't worry about getting married; I left my future in God's hands. But I must tell you, every night I hung a pair of men's pants on my bed and knelt down to pray this prayer:
>
> Father in heaven, hear my prayer,
> And grant it if you can;
> I've hung a pair of trousers here,
> Please fill them with a man.

The following Sunday I read that humorous letter to our congregation, and they enjoyed it immensely. I happened to notice the different reactions of a father and his teenaged son. The dad laughed out loud, but the son seemed preoccupied. On that particular Sunday the mother of this family had stayed home with their sick daughter. Obviously neither father nor son mentioned the story, because a couple of weeks later I received a note from the mother:

> Dear Chuck:
>
> I am wondering if I should be worried about something. It has to do with our son. For the last two weeks I have noticed that before our son turns the light out and goes to sleep at night, he hangs a woman's bikini over the foot of his bed. . . . Should I be concerned about this?

I assured her there was nothing to worry about. And I am pleased to announce that the young man recently married, so maybe the swimsuit idea works.

Perhaps you find yourself among those in the if-only group. You say you would laugh *if only* you had more money . . . *if only* you had more talent or were more beautiful . . . *if only* you could find a more fulfilling job? I challenge those excuses. Just as more money never made anyone generous and more talent never made anyone grateful, more of *anything* never made anyone joyful.

> The happiest people are rarely the richest, or the most beautiful, or even the most talented. Happy people do not depend on excitement and 'fun' supplied by externals. They enjoy the fundamental, often very simple, things of life. They waste no time thinking other pastures are greener; they do not yearn for yesterday or tomorrow. They savor the moment, glad to be alive, enjoying their work, their families, the good things around them. They are adaptable; they can bend with the wind, adjust to the changes in their times, enjoy the contests of life, and feel themselves in harmony with the world. Their eyes are turned outward; they are aware, compassionate. They have the capacity to love.[3]

Without exception, people who consistently laugh do so *in spite of*, seldom *because of* anything. They pursue fun rather than wait for it to knock on their door in the middle of the day. Such infectiously joyful believers have no trouble convincing people around them that Christianity is real and that Christ can transform a life. Joy is the flag that flies above the castle of their hearts, announcing that the King is in residence.

MEET A MAN WHO SMILED IN SPITE OF . . .

There once lived a man who became a Christian as an adult and left the security and popularity of his former career as an official religious leader to follow Christ. The persecution that became his companion throughout the remaining years of his life was just the beginning of his woes. Misunderstood, misrepresented, and maligned though he was, he pressed on joyfully. On top of all that, he suffered from a physical ailment so severe he called it a "thorn in my flesh"—possibly an intense form of migraine that revisited him on a regular basis.

By now you know I am referring to Saul of Tarsus, later called Paul. Though not one to dwell on his own difficulties or ailments, the apostle did take the time to record a partial list of them in his second letter to his friends in Corinth. Compared to his first-century contemporaries, he was—

> . . . in far more imprisonments, beaten times without number, often in danger of death. Five times I received from the Jews thirty-nine lashes. Three times I was beaten with rods, once I was stoned, three times I was shipwrecked, a night and a day I have spent in the deep. I have been on frequent journeys, in dangers from rivers, dangers from robbers, dangers

> from my countrymen, dangers from the Gentiles, dangers in the city, dangers in the wilderness, dangers on the sea, dangers among false brethren; I have been in labor and hardship, through many sleepless nights, in hunger and thirst, often without food, in cold and exposure. Apart from such external things, there is the daily pressure upon me of concern for all the churches.
>
> *2 Corinthians 11:23–28*

Although that was enough hardship for several people, Paul's journey got even more rugged as time passed. Finally he was arrested and placed under the constant guard of Roman soldiers to whom he was chained for two years. While he was allowed to remain "in his own rented quarters" (Acts 28:30), the restrictions must have been irksome to a man who had grown accustomed to traveling and to the freedom of setting his own agenda. Yet not once do we read of his losing patience and throwing a fit. On the contrary, he saw his circumstances as an opportunity to make Christ known as he made the best of his situation.

Read a Letter with a Surprising Theme

Interestingly, Paul wrote several letters during those years of house arrest, one of which was addressed to a group of Christians living in Philippi. It is an amazing letter, made even more remarkable by its recurring theme—joy. Think of it! Written by a man who had known excruciating hardship and pain, living in a restricted setting chained to a Roman soldier, the letter to the Philippians resounds with joy! Attitudes of joy and contentment are woven through the tapestry of these 104 verses like threads of silver. Rather than wallowing in self-pity or calling on his friends to help him escape or at least find relief from these restrictions, Paul sent a surprisingly lighthearted message. And on top of all that, time and again he urges the Philippians (and his readers) to be people of joy.

Let me show you how that same theme resurfaces in each of the four chapters.

- When Paul prayed for the Philippians, he smiled!

> I thank my God in all my remembrance of you, always offering prayer *with joy* in my every prayer for you all.
>
> *Philippians 1:3–4*

- When he compared staying on earth to leaving and going to be with Jesus, he was joyful.

> For to me, to live is Christ, and to die is gain. But if I am to live on in the flesh, this will mean fruitful labor for me; and I do not know which to choose. But I am hard-pressed from both directions, having the desire to depart and be with Christ, for that is very much better; yet to remain on in the flesh is more necessary for your sake. And convinced of this, I know that I shall remain and continue with you all for your progress and *joy in the faith.*
>
> *Philippians 1:21–25*

- When he encouraged them to work together in harmony, his own joy intensified as he envisioned that happening.

> If therefore there is any encouragement in Christ, if there is any consolation of love, if there is any fellowship of the Spirit, if any affection and compassion, *make my joy complete* by being of the same mind, maintaining the same love, united in spirit, intent on one purpose.
>
> *Philippians 2:1–2*

- When he mentioned sending a friend to them, he urged them to receive the man joyfully.

> But I thought it necessary to send to you Epaphroditus, my brother and fellow worker and fellow soldier, who is also your messenger and minister to my need; because he was longing for you all and was distressed because you had heard that he was sick. For indeed he was sick to the point of death, but God had mercy on him, and not on him only but also on me, lest I should have sorrow upon sorrow. Therefore I have sent him all the more eagerly in order that when you see him again you may *rejoice* and I may be less concerned about you. Therefore *receive him in the Lord with all joy,* and hold men like him in high regard.
>
> *Philippians 2:25–29*

- When he communicated the "core" of what he wanted them to hear from him, he was full of joy.

> Finally, my brethren, *rejoice in the Lord.* To write the same things again is no trouble to me, and it is a safeguard for you.
>
> *Philippians 3:1*

- When he was drawing his letter to a close, he returned to the same message of joy:

  Rejoice in the Lord always; again I will say, rejoice!

  Philippians 4:4

- Finally, when Paul called to mind their concern for his welfare, the joy about which he writes is (in my opinion) one of the most upbeat passages found in Scripture.

  But I *rejoiced* in the Lord greatly, that now at last you have revived your concern for me; indeed, you were concerned before, but you lacked opportunity. Not that I speak from want; for I have learned to be content in whatever circumstances I am. I know how to get along with humble means, and I also know how to live in prosperity; in any and every circumstance I have learned the secret of being filled and going hungry, both of having abundance and suffering need. I can do all things through Him who strengthens me. Nevertheless, you have done well to share with me in my affliction. And you yourselves also know, Philippians, that at the first preaching of the gospel, after I departed from Macedonia, no church shared with me in the matter of giving and receiving but you alone; for even in Thessalonica you sent a gift more than once for my needs. Not that I seek the gift itself, but I seek for the profit which increases to your account. But I have received everything in full, and have an abundance; I am amply supplied, having received from Epaphroditus what you have sent, a fragrant aroma, an acceptable sacrifice, well-pleasing to God. And my God shall supply all your needs according to His riches in glory in Christ Jesus.

  Philippians 4:10–19

Needed: A Joy Transfusion

I strongly suspect that after the Philippians received this delightful little letter from Paul, their joy increased to an all-time high. They had received a joy transfusion from someone they dearly loved, which must have been all the more appreciated as they remembered Paul's circumstance. If he, in that irritating, confining situation, could be so positive, so full of encouragement, so affirming, certainly those living in freedom could be joyful.

Life's joy stealers are many, and you will need to get rid of them if you hope to attain the kind of happiness described by Paul's pen. If you don't, all attempts to receive (or give) a joy transfusion will be blocked. One of the ringleaders you'll need to do battle with sooner rather than later is that sneaky thief who slides into your thoughts and reminds you of something from the past that demoralizes you (even though it is over and done with and fully forgiven) or conjures up fears regarding something in the future (even though that frightening something may never happen). Joyful people stay riveted to the present—the here and now, not the then and never.

Helen Mallicoat made a real contribution to your life and mine when she wrote:

> I was regretting the past
> And fearing the future . . .
> Suddenly my Lord was speaking:
> "MY NAME IS I AM." He paused.
> I waited. He continued,
>
> "WHEN YOU LIVE IN THE PAST,
> WITH ITS MISTAKES AND REGRETS,
> IT IS HARD. I AM NOT THERE.
> MY NAME IS NOT *I WAS.*
>
> "WHEN YOU LIVE IN THE FUTURE,
> WITH ITS PROBLEMS AND FEARS,
> IT IS HARD. I AM NOT THERE.
> MY NAME IS NOT *I WILL BE.*
>
> "WHEN YOU LIVE IN THIS MOMENT,
> IT IS NOT HARD.
> I AM HERE.
> MY NAME IS *I AM.*"[4]

IF GOD IS GOD . . . THEN LAUGHTER FITS LIFE

As I attempt to probe the mind of Paul, trying to find some common denominator, some secret clue to his joy, I have to conclude that it was his confidence in God. To Paul, God was in full control of everything. Everything! If hardship came, God permitted it. If pain dogged his steps, it was only because God allowed it. If he was under arrest, God still remained the sovereign director of his life. If there seemed to be no way out, God knew he was pressed. If things broke open and all pressure was relieved, God was responsible.

My point? God is no distant deity but a constant reality, a very present help whenever needs occur. So? So live like it. And laugh like it! Paul did. While he lived, he drained every drop of joy out of every day that passed. How do I know? This little letter to the Philippians says so—as we shall see in the following chapters.

- In the first chapter of Philippians we learn *there is laughter in living*—whether or not we get what we want, in spite of difficult circumstances, and even when there are conflicts.
- In the second chapter we learn *there is laughter in serving*. It starts with the right attitude (humility), it is maintained through right theology (God is God), and it is encouraged by right models and mentors (friends like Timothy and Epaphroditus).
- In the third chapter, we learn *there is laughter in sharing* as Paul shares three happy things: his testimony, his goal of living, and his reason for encouragement.
- Finally, in the fourth chapter we learn *there is laughter in resting*. These have to be some of the finest lines ever written on the principle of personal contentment.

What a treasure house of joy! Frankly, I'm excited—and I know you will be too. Before we are very far along, you will begin to realize that joy is a choice. You will discover that each person must choose joy if he or she hopes to laugh again.

Jesus gave us His truth so that His joy might be in us. And when that happens, our joy is full (John 15:11). The tragedy is that so few choose to live joyfully.

Will you? If you will, I can make you a promise: laughter and enthusiasm will follow.

I came across a story in one of Tim Hansel's books that points this out in an unforgettable way. It's the true account of an eighty-two-year-old man who had served as a pastor for over fifty of those years. In his later years he struggled with skin cancer. It was so bad that he had already had fifteen skin operations. Tim writes:

Besides suffering from the pain, he was so embarrassed about how the cancer had scarred his appearance, that he wouldn't go out. Then one day he was given *You Gotta Keep Dancin'* in which I tell of my long struggle with the chronic, intense pain from a near-fatal climbing accident. In that book, I told of the day when I realized that the pain would be with me forever. At that moment, I made a pivotal decision. I knew that it was up to me to choose how I responded to it. So I chose joy. . . .

After reading awhile, the elderly pastor said he put the book down, thinking, "He's crazy. I can't choose joy."

So he gave up on the idea. Then later he read in John 15:11 that joy is a gift. Jesus says, "I want to give you my joy so that your joy may be complete."

A *gift!* he thought. He didn't know what to do, so he got down on his knees. Then he didn't know what to say, so he said, "Well, then, Lord, *give it to me.*"

And suddenly, as he described it, this incredible hunk of joy came from heaven and landed on him.

"I was overwhelmed," he wrote. "It was like the joy talked about in Peter, a 'joy unspeakable and full of glory.' I didn't know what to say, so I said, 'Turn it on, Lord, turn it on!'" And before he knew it, he was dancing around the house. He felt so joyful that he actually felt born again—again. And this astonishing change happened at the age of 82.

He just had to get out. So much joy couldn't stay cooped up. So he went out to the local fastfood restaurant and got a burger. A lady saw how happy he was, and asked, "How are you doing?"

He said, "Oh, I'm wonderful!"

"Is it your birthday?" she asked.

"No, honey, it's better than that!"

"Your anniversary?"

"Better than that!"

"Well, what is it?" she asked excitedly.

"It's the joy of Jesus. Do you know what I'm talking about?"

The lady shrugged and answered, "No, I have to work on Sundays."[5]

Every time I read Tim's story, I shake my head. What a ridiculous response! But not unusual. Basically there are two kinds of people: people who choose joy and people who don't. People who choose joy pay no attention to what day of the week it is . . . or how old they are . . . or what level of pain they are in. They have deliberately decided to laugh again because they have chosen joy. People who do not choose joy miss the relief laughter can bring. And because they do not, they cannot. And because they can't, they won't.

Which one are you?

2

Set Your Sails for Joy

THIS YEAR I TURN FIFTY-EIGHT. Thought I might as well let the whole world know.

When you're my age you discover that your closest friends are the most unmerciful in the cards they send you. Last year, at fifty-seven, it was one insult after another! Like, "Confound your enemies. Amaze your friends. Blow out *all* your candles!"

Another said on the front: "Wish I could be there to help you light your birthday candles . . . ," and on the inside, "but I'll be watching the glow in the sky and thinking of you."

That one was from Helen Peters, my longtime executive assistant who has typed every book I have written . . . someone you would expect to be compassionate and caring toward a guy my age, right? Wrong.

Several more mentioned the cake and candles, one warning me of two dangers: the candles would melt the frosting in fifteen seconds, so blow them out as fast as possible. Once that happens, however, the smoke alarm is likely to go off.

Garfield, the ornery cat, appears on the front of another. He is lying down (naturally) and thinking (with one eye open), "You can tell you're getting older when you wake up with that awful 'morning after' feeling . . . and you didn't do anything the night before!"

When you are this age—matter of fact, when you are *any* age—a sense of humor is essential. I once heard a great talk from a veteran missionary who spoke on "What I Would Pack in My Suitcase If I Were to Return to the Mission Field." The first item he named? A sense of humor. A friend of mine who once served the Lord for several years on foreign soil has a similar saying: "You need two things if you want to be happy in God's work overseas: a good sense of humor and no sense of smell!"

I have discovered that a joyful countenance has nothing to do with one's age or one's occupation (or lack of it) or one's geography or education or marital status or good looks or circumstances. As I wrote earlier—and will continue to write throughout this book—joy is a choice. It is a matter of attitude that stems from one's confidence in God—that He is at work, that He is in full control, that He is in the midst of whatever has happened, is happening, and will happen. Either we fix our minds on that and determine to laugh again, or we wail and whine our way through life, complaining that we never got a fair shake. We are the ones who consciously determine which way we shall go. To paraphrase the poet:

> One ship sails east
> One ship sails west
> Regardless of how the winds blow.
> It is the set of the sail
> And not the gale
> That determines the way we go.[1]

Laughing one's way through life depends on nothing external. Regardless of how severely the winds of adversity may blow, we set our sails toward joy.

I witnessed a beautiful example of this several months ago. Being one of the members of Dallas Seminary's Board of Regents, I have the privilege of interviewing new faculty members. At that particular time we were meeting with four of their newest faculty members, one of whom was a woman. Not just any woman, but the *first* woman ever invited to join the distinguished ranks of the faculty of Dallas Theological Seminary.

Lucy Mabery is her name, and several of us on the board flashed back as she told us of her pilgrimage. We have known Lucy for years.

This delightful, intelligent woman was rearing a family, teaching Bible classes, and busily engaged in a dozen other involvements while happily married to Dr. Trevor Mabery, a successful physician who was at the zenith of his career. Then her whole world caved in.

Trevor was flying back to Dallas with three other men from a Montana retreat, where they had been with Dr. James Dobson, discussing and praying about the Focus on the Family ministry. Their plane crashed, and all four of the men perished in the accident.

Shock waves stunned the city of Dallas. All four men were public figures and highly respected. Their widows were left to pick up the pieces of their own lives and begin again.

Lucy chose to do it with joy. Without a moment's warning, her beloved Trevor was gone. Grief, one of the most vicious of all the joy stealers, tore into the Mabery family like a tornado at full force. But, determined not to be bound by the cords of perpetual grief, Lucy remained positive, keen thinking, and joyful.

As we interviewed Lucy that day, her eyes sparkled with a delightful sense of humor, and her smile was contagious.

We asked what it was like to be the first woman serving on the faculty. With a smile she answered, "I have had great warmth and reception from the faculty members. Now the student body," she added, "is another story." We asked how she handled the more conservative male students who didn't agree with her being in that position. She said, "Oh, I take them to lunch and we talk about things. They soften a bit." After a brief pause, she added, "It's been a joyous experience. As a matter of fact, I was given an award from the student body recently for being the best-dressed woman faculty member!"

How can a person in Lucy's situation recover, pick up the pieces, and go on? How does anyone press on beyond grief? How do you still laugh at life? How do you put your arms around your children as a new single parent and help them laugh at the future? It comes from deep within—because people like Lucy Mabery set their sails for joy regardless of how the wind blows.

Lucy has a quiet confidence. Not in the long life of a husband and not in the fact that external circumstances always will be placid, peaceful, and easy, but in God, who is at work, who is in control, and who is causing all things to result in His greater glory. When you and I focus on that, we too discover we can laugh again, even after the horror of an airplane crash and the loss of our life's partner. Everything, I repeat, is determined by how we set our sails.

A Small But Powerful Letter

All of this leads us quite naturally into the magnificent though brief letter to the Philippians. Although it contains only 104 verses, this delightful piece of inspired mail brings a smile to the faces of all who read it. Why? Because of the one who wrote it! In customary first-century manner he signs his name at the beginning rather than at the end—Paul. What memories must have swirled in the minds of his friends in Philippi when they read that name. Ten years ago this man had been in their midst, founding their church. Ten years ago he had been tossed into jail, though he had committed no crime. Ten years ago they had seen God work in pulling together a small group of young Christians in this unique Roman colony. And now, a decade later, they read the name again. It must have thrilled them just to see that name resurface. Like art-loving Italians . . . thrilled by the works of Michelangelo, like sixteenth-century German believers who were inspired by a spokesman named Martin Luther, like nineteenth-century black Americans who grasped at every word from Abraham Lincoln, like twentieth-century patriotic Britons who needed a Winston Churchill to help them hold fast, the people of the church at Philippi respected and needed Paul. He was their founder and friend. He was their teacher, their able and much-admired leader.

But Paul doesn't simply sign his name to this letter. He also mentions Timothy, a name that means "he who honors God." Timothy is mentioned alongside Paul, not because he wrote the letter, but because he was known to the Philippians, loved by them, and would soon visit them. The first-century dynamic duo: Paul and Timothy! I would imagine the Philippians could not wait to hear what Paul had to say.

From Servants to Saints

Instead of introducing themselves as "Paul and Timothy, hotshot celebrities," or "Paul and Timothy, superleaders," or "Paul and Timothy, men whom you must respect," the apostle writes, "Paul and Timothy, *servants.*" Don't you like that? That's why Paul was great. He didn't act like a prima donna who had to be worshiped, or a fragile hero who had to be treated with kid gloves. He saw himself as a servant.

The Greek term translated *servant* means many things: One bound to another . . . by the bands of constraining love . . . one in such close relationship to another that only death could break the bond . . . one whose will is swallowed up in the sweet will of God . . . one who serves another [Christ] . . . with reckless abandon, not regarding his or her own interests.[2] Those words defined Paul and Timothy.

Interestingly, this is a letter from servants to saints. "Paul and Timothy . . . to all the saints in Christ Jesus in Philippi, including overseers and deacons"(1:1). Today we might say, "to pastors and deacons" or to "elders and deacons."

Saints is a very interesting term. If you've traveled in Europe, you have seen a lot of stone saints in and around huge cathedrals. If you worship in a liturgical church, you have seen them in icons—plaster or marble statues representing people whose lives have become famous in the long and colorful history of the church.

In my reading I came across a fascinating article entitled "On Making Saints." It was not referring to the manufacture of oversize statues, but of the process whereby people today are "sainted."

"Pope John Paul II has been sainting more men and women than all of his predecessors in the 20th century taken together,"[3] writes the author, who goes on to explain the lengthy process behind naming someone as an official saint. You have to know who to contact and what steps to take. I should also add, you need a pretty good slug of money to saint people.

But the saints Paul was writing to were not those kinds of saints. The saints in Philippi were ordinary people. They were everyday, normal folks like you and me. We seldom put common names in that light, but we could! Saint Chuck. Saint Frank. Saint Shirley. Saint Cynthia. Saint Sylvester. Saint Margaret. Saint Bob. Saint You. That's right—you!

The Greek term translated *saint* is from a word that means "set apart and consecrated for the purpose of God's service." Isn't that a great idea? That's why you are a saint. When you were born into God's family by faith in the Lord Jesus Christ, you got that title. You were set apart for God's special purpose. Consecration is at the core of the word.

"Paul and Timothy, servants of the living Christ, to all those set apart for the purpose of serving God, who live in the city of Philippi"; that's the idea.

Both Grace and Peace

And what does Paul offer these saints? "Grace and peace." (I love that.) Grace is something that comes to us which we don't deserve. Peace is something that happens within us which is not in any way affected by our external circumstances. With grace from above and peace within, who wouldn't have cause for rejoicing?

In its earliest form the word *peace* meant "to bind together" and came to include the whole idea of being bound so closely together with something or someone that a harmony resulted. The right woman who is joined in harmony with the right man in marriage begins a "peaceful" companionship. One friend who is joined in heart and soul to another friend sustains a "peaceful" relationship where harmony exists. When there is such grace-and-peace harmony, choosing joy flows naturally. And that certainly explains why Paul remained joyful. He had every reason not to. But he deliberately chose joy. Paul set his sails on the very things he offered his friends in Philippi, grace and peace.

JOYFUL THANKSGIVING

What was it about those folks in Philippi that brought Paul so much joy?

First, *he had happy memories of the people.*

> I thank my God in all my remembrance of you, always offering prayer with joy in my every prayer for you all, in view of your participation in the gospel from the first day until now.
>
> *Philippians 1:3–5*

His memory of them made him smile. Meaning what? What were Paul's happy memories? He had no regrets, he nursed no ill feelings, he struggled through no unresolved conflicts. When he looked back over a full decade and thought of the Philippians, he laughed!

I wonder how many pastors can say that about former churches they have served? Could you say that about former friends you have had? Or places where you have worked? Are yours happy memories? Unfortunately, the memory of certain people makes us churn. When we call them to mind, they bring sad or disappointing mental images. Paul knew no such memories from his days in Philippi. Amazingly, he could not remember one whom he would accuse or feel ill toward, not even those who threw him in prison or those who stood in a courtroom and made accusations against him. He entertained only good memories of Philippi. Positive memories make life so much lighter.

Another reason he was joyful? *He had firm confidence in God.*

> For I am confident of this very thing, that He who began a good work in you will perfect it until the day of Christ Jesus. For it is only right for me to feel this way about you all, because I have you in my heart, since

both in my imprisonment and in the defense and confirmation of the gospel, you all are partakers of grace with me.

Philippians 1:6–7

Paul's confidence in God was a settled fact. He knew that God was at work and in control. He was confident that God was bringing about whatever was happening for His greater glory. When we possess that kind of confidence, we have a solid platform built within us—a solid platform upon which joy can rest.

Look back at the words *began* and *perfect.* They represent opposite ends or, if you will, the *bookends* of life. The One who *started* (began) a good work in your life will *complete* (perfect) it.

The work You have in me begun
Will by Your grace be fully done.[4]

That's what gives us confidence. That's what helps us laugh again.

Focus on the word *perfect.* I doubt that we have imagined the true meaning of it. Travel back in your mind to the cross where Christ was crucified. See the Savior lifted up, paying for the sins of the world. Listen to His words. There were seven sayings that Christ uttered from the cross, commonly called the seven last words of Christ. One of them our Lord cried out was a single word, *Tetelestai!* Translated, it means, "It is finished!" *Telos* is the root Greek term, the same root of the word translated *perfect.* Paul was saying, "He who began a good work in you when you were converted ten years ago, Philippians, will bring it to completion. It will be finished! Jesus will see to it. And that gives me joy."

You want a fresh burst of encouragement? You may have a good friend who is not walking as close to the Lord as he or she once was. Here is fresh hope. Rest in the confidence that God has neither lost interest nor lost control. The Lord has not folded His arms and looked the other way. That person you are concerned about may be your son or daughter. Find encouragement in this firm confidence: The One who began a good work in your boy or in your girl will bring it to completion; He will finish the task. I repeat, that firm confidence in God's finishing what He started will bring back your joy.

I have mentioned joy stealers several times already. Perhaps this is a good place for me to identify three of these most notorious thieves at work today. All three, by the way, can be resisted by firm confidence, the kind of confidence we've been thinking about.

The first joy stealer is *worry.* The second is *stress.* And the third is *fear.* They may seem alike, but there is a distinct difference.

Worry is an inordinate anxiety about something that may or may not occur. It has been my observation that what is being worried about usually does not occur. But worry eats away at joy like slow-working acid while we are waiting for the outcome. I'll say much more about this thief in chapter 12.

Stress is a little more acute than worry. Stress is intense strain over a situation we cannot change or control—something out of our control. (Occasionally the safest place for something to be is out of *our* control.) And instead of releasing it to God, we churn over it. It is in that restless churning stage that our stress is intensified. Usually the thing that plagues us is not as severe as we make it out to be.

Fear, on the other hand, is different from worry and stress. It is dreadful uneasiness over the presence of danger, evil, or pain. As with the other two, however, fear usually makes things appear worse than they really are.

How do we live with worry and stress and fear? How do we withstand these joy stealers? Go back to Paul's words:

> For I am confident of this very thing, that He who began a good work in you will perfect it until the day of Christ Jesus.
>
> *Philippians 1:6*

Let me be downright practical and tell you what I do. First I remind myself early in the morning and on several occasions during the day, "God, You are at work, and You are in control. And, Lord God, You know this is happening. You were there at the beginning, and You will bring everything that occurs to a conclusion that results in Your greater glory in the end." And then? Then (and *only* then!) I relax. From that point on, it really doesn't matter all that much what happens. It is in God's hands.

I love the story of the man who had fretted for fifteen years over his work. He had built his business from nothing into a rather sizable operation. In fact, he had a large plant that covered several acres. With growth and success, however, came ever-increasing demands. Each new day brought a whole new list of responsibilities. Weary of the worry, the stress, and the fear, he finally decided to give it *all* over to God. With a smile of quiet contentment, he prayed, "Lord God, the business is Yours. All the worry, the stress, and the fears I release to You and Your sovereign will. From this day forward, Lord, You own this business." That night he went to bed earlier than he had since he started the business. Finally . . . peace.

In the middle of the night the shrill ring of the phone awoke the man. The caller, in a panicked voice, yelled, "Fire! The entire place is going up in smoke!" The man calmly dressed, got into his car and drove to the plant. With his hands in his pockets he stood there and watched, smiling slightly. One of his employees hurried to his side and said, "What in the world are you smiling about? How can you be so calm? Everything's on fire!" The man answered, "Yesterday afternoon I gave this business to God. I told Him it was His. If He wants to burn it up, that's His business."

Some of you read that and think, *That's insane!* No, that is one of the greatest pieces of sound theology you can embrace. Firm confidence in God means that it is in His hands. He who started something will bear the pressure of it and will bring the results exactly as He planned for His greater glory. How could a business burned to the ground be of glory to God? you may ask. Well, sometimes the loss of something very significant—perhaps something we are a slave to—is the only way God can get our attention and bring us back to full sanity. The happiest people I know are the ones who have learned how to hold everything loosely and have given the worrisome, stress-filled, fearful details of their lives into God's keeping.

We have seen that Paul remained joyful because he had great memories and because he lived with firm confidence.

Third, *he felt a warm affection toward his fellow believers.*

> For it is only right for me to feel this way about you all, because I have you in my heart, since both in my imprisonment and in the defense and confirmation of the gospel, you all are partakers of grace with me. For God is my witness, how I long for you all with the affection of Christ Jesus.
>
> *Philippians 1:7–8*

The term Paul uses for affection is, literally, the Greek word for "bowels." In the first century it was believed that the intestines, the stomach, the liver, even the lungs, held the most tender parts of human emotions. That explains why this joyful man would use "bowels" in reference to "affection." He says, in effect, "As I share with you my feelings, I open my whole inner being to you and tell you that the level of my affection is deep and tender." Too many people live with the inaccurate impression that Paul was somewhat cold and uncaring. Not according to this statement; in fact, quite the contrary! When he was with those he loved, Paul went to the warmest depths in conversation and affection.

If you have not yet read John Powell's *Why Am I Afraid to Tell You Who I Am?* you are missing a great experience. There is a section in the book that is worth a great deal of your time and attention. It is where the author presents the five levels of communication, which, he says, are like concentric circles—from the most shallow and superficial level (outer circle) to the deepest, most intimate level (smallest circle at the core).

Level five, the outer circle of superficiality, is the level he calls "cliché conversation."

> On this level, we talk in clichés, such as: "How are you? . . . How is your family? . . . Where have you been?" We say things like: "I like your dress very much." "I hope we can get together real soon." "It's really good to see you." [Which might really mean, "We may not see each other for a year, and I'm not going to sweat it."] . . . If the other party were to begin answering our question, "How are you?" in detail, we would be astounded. Usually and fortunately the other party senses the superficiality and conventionality of our concern and question, and obliges by simply giving the standard answer, "Just fine, thank you."[5]

That's cliché communication. Tragically, that is the deepest many people choose to go.

Level four is where we "report facts" about each other.

> We remain contented to tell others what so-and-so has said or done. We offer no personal, self-revelatory commentary on these facts, but simply report them.[6]

This is the realm of gossip and petty, meaningless little tales about others.

Level three leads us into the area of ideas and judgments. Rarely do people communicate at this deeper level. They are able, but they're not willing.

> As I communicate my ideas, etc., I will be watching you carefully. I want to test the temperature of the water before I leap in. I want to be sure that you accept me with my ideas, judgments, and decisions. If you raise your eyebrows or narrow your eyes, if you yawn or look at your watch, I will probably retreat to safer ground. I will run for the cover of silence, or change the subject of conversation.[7]

Because this begins to get below the "skating" level, those who go to the depths of ideas and judgments are quite courageous.

Level two moves into "feelings."

> If I really want you to know who I am, I must tell you about my stomach (gut-level) as well as my head. My ideas, judgments, and decisions are quite conventional. If I am a Republican or a Democrat by persuasion, I have a lot of company. If I am for or against space exploration, there will be others who will support me in my conviction. But the *feelings* that lie under my ideas, judgments and convictions are uniquely mine. . . .
>
> It is these feelings, on this level of communication, which I must share with you, if I am to tell you who I really am.[8]

I would hazard a guess that less than 10 percent of us ever communicate on that "feeling" level. To my disappointment, I have discovered that husbands and wives can live for years under the same roof without reaching this level.

Level one is the most personal, intimate form of communication.

> All deep and authentic friendships, and especially the union of those who are married, must be based on absolute openness and honesty. . . .
>
> Among close friends or between partners in marriage there will come from time to time a complete emotional and personal communion.[9]

Such depth of communication, which Paul seems to have practiced on a regular basis, brings a satisfaction—and joy—like few things on earth. And when we are free to express our feelings this deeply, we have little difficulty offering up prayers that are meaningful and specific. Which is precisely what Paul mentions next.

Specific Praying

He names two things that are of equal importance: abounding love and keen discernment. Verse 9 says, "I pray that your love may abound." Verse 10, "I pray that you may approve things that are excellent."

To begin with, love—abounding love—needs to flow freely, somewhat like a river. But that river must be kept within its banks or it swells and overflows. And when that happens, disaster! If you have ever been in a region that has been flooded, you know the calamity floodwaters can create.

When love floods indiscriminately, we love everything, even the wrong things. Paul said it well. It is knowledge—*real* knowledge—and discernment—*keen* discernment—that keep love within its banks.

He concludes this opening paragraph on a high note when he writes of . . .

> . . . having been filled with the fruit of righteousness which comes through Jesus Christ, to the glory and praise of God.
>
> *Philippians 1:11*

What a prayer! I realize how much he loved those folks at Philippi when I read words like this.

When was the last time you wrote somebody and mentioned what you were praying for on their behalf? You and I may frequently pray for individuals, but seldom do we sit down and write a note, "Dear So-and-So, I want you to know I'm praying for these three things to take place in your life: one . . . two . . . three. . . ." Paul's model is worth duplicating. You quickly move beyond level five when you begin to communicate like that, and I challenge you to do it.

PRACTICAL APPLICATION

We begin to laugh again when we rest our full confidence in God. More specifically, according to what we have just read in Philippians 1:

- Confidence brings joy when we fix our attention on the things for which we are thankful.
- Confidence brings joy when we let God be God.
- Confidence brings joy when we keep our love within proper limits.

Even though we are just getting started, we have covered a lot of important territory. As I think about the practical side of all this, it occurs to me that joy is ours to claim. In fact, no one on earth can invade and redirect our life of joy unless we permit them to do so.

Hudson Taylor put it like this:

> It doesn't matter, really, how great the pressure is; it only matters *where the pressure lies.* See that it never comes *between* you and the Lord—then, the greater the pressure, the more it presses you to His breast.[10]

The pressure on you may be intense. A half-dozen joy stealers may be waiting outside your door, ready to pounce at the first opportunity. However, nothing can rob you of your hold on grace, your claim to peace, or your confidence in God without your permission. Choose joy. Never release your grip!

I have lived almost fifty-eight years on this old earth, and I am more convinced than ever that the single most important choice a follower of Christ can make is his or her choice of attitude. Only you can determine that. Choose wisely . . . choose carefully . . . choose confidently.

Earlier I paraphrased a poem by Ella Wheeler Wilcox. I want to close this chapter by quoting it as she wrote it.

The Winds of Fate

One ship drives east and another drives west
 With the selfsame winds that blow.
  'Tis the set of the sails
  And not the gales
 Which tells us the way to go.

Like the winds of the sea are the ways of fate,
 As we voyage along through life:
  'Tis the set of a soul
  That decides its goal,
 And not the calm or the strife.[11]

My advice? Set your sails for joy! You will never regret it.

3

What a Way to Live!

As a boy I spent my leisure hours in the evening listening to various radio shows. In those days before television, action-packed dramas, murder mysteries, and comedy programs—all on radio in the evening hours—were the ticket to adventure and imagination.

There were many to choose from in the 1940s: "The Green Hornet," "Captain Midnight," "Lum 'n' Abner," "The Lone Ranger," "Gang Busters," "Inner Sanctum," "Jack Armstrong (the All-American Boy)," "Fibber McGee and Molly," "Edgar Bergen and Charlie McCarthy," and my all-time favorite, "Mr. District Attorney." I listened to that program so often I memorized the announcer's words of introduction, which always concluded with "defender of our right to life, liberty, and the pursuit of happiness." I used to strut around the house mouthing those lines.

I didn't know it at the time but that part of the announcer's script was borrowed from Thomas Jefferson's immortal words in our nation's Declaration of Independence:

> We hold these Truths to be self-evident; that all Men are created equal, that they are endowed by their Creator with certain unalienable Rights; that among these are Life, Liberty, and the Pursuit of Happiness.

Those final words still intrigue me. One of our unalienable rights is to pursue happiness—to seek out a life of joy and to find peaceful satisfaction. For many, however, happiness is a forgotten pursuit. A dream that has died.

For the longest time I wondered why. Why has a joyful life, an attitude of happiness, eluded so many? Within the past few years I have come to realize why. It's because most people think that happiness is something that happens to them rather than something they deliberately and diligently pursue. Circumstances seldom generate smiles and laughter. Joy comes to those who determine to pursue it in spite of their circumstances.

A good reminder of this is the short story by G. W. Target entitled "The Window," which tells of two men, both seriously ill, who occupied the same small hospital room. One man was allowed to sit up in his bed for an hour each afternoon to help drain the fluid from his lungs. His bed was next to the room's only window. The other man had to spend all his time flat on his back.

The men talked for hours on end. They spoke of their wives and families, their homes, their jobs, their involvement in the military service, where they had been on vacation. And every afternoon when the man in the bed by the window could sit up, he would pass the time by describing to his roommate all the things he could see outside the window. The man in the other bed began to live for those one-hour periods where his world would be broadened and enlivened by all the activity and color of the outside world.

The window overlooked a park with a lovely lake, the man said. Ducks and swans played on the water while children sailed their model boats. Lovers walked arm in arm amid flowers of every color of the rainbow. Grand old trees graced the landscape, and a fine view of the city skyline could be seen in the distance. As the man by the window described all this in exquisite detail, the man on the other side of the room would close his eyes and imagine the picturesque scene.

One warm afternoon the man by the window described a parade passing by. Although the other man couldn't hear the band, he could see it in his mind's eye as the gentleman by the window portrayed it with descriptive words. Unexpectedly, an alien thought entered his head: *Why should he have all the pleasure of seeing everything while I never get to see anything?* It didn't seem fair.

As the thought fermented the man felt ashamed at first. But as the days passed and he missed seeing more sights, his envy eroded into resentment and soon turned him sour. He began to brood and he found himself unable to sleep. *He* should be by that window—that thought now controlled his life.

Late one night as he lay staring at the ceiling, the man by the window began to cough. He was choking on the fluid in his lungs. The other man watched in the dimly lit room as the struggling man by the window groped for the button to call for help. Listening from across the room, he never moved, never pushed his own button which would have brought the nurse running. In less than five minutes the coughing and choking stopped, along with the sound of breathing. Now there was only silence—deathly silence.

The following morning the day nurse arrived to bring water for their baths. When she found the lifeless body of the man by the window, she was saddened and called the hospital attendants to take it away—no words, no fuss. As soon as it seemed appropriate, the other man asked if he could be moved next to the window. The nurse was happy to make the switch, and after making sure he was comfortable, she left him alone.

Slowly, painfully, he propped himself up on one elbow to take his first look. Finally, he would have the joy of seeing it all himself. He strained to look out the window beside the bed.

It faced a blank wall.[1]

The pursuit of happiness is a matter of choice . . . it is a positive attitude we choose to express. It is not a gift delivered to our door each morning, nor does it come through the window. And it is certain that our circumstances are not the things that make us joyful. If we wait for them to get just right, we will never laugh again.

Needed: A Positive Mind-set

Since the pursuit of happiness is an inward journey, it might be helpful to see the two options available to us. Maybe if I put them into opposing columns, the contrast will leave a lasting impression.

Negative Mind-set	**Positive Mind-set**
• The need for certain things before there can be joy	• The need for virtually nothing tangible to be joyful
• A strong dependence on others to provide joy	• The ability to create one's own reasons for joy
• Focusing on joy as being "out there," always in the future . . . waiting for something to happen and thereby bring happiness	• Choosing joy now, making it a present pursuit . . . never waiting for everything to fall into place or for some "ship" to come in

These minds of ours are like bank vaults awaiting our deposits. If we regularly deposit positive, encouraging, and uplifting thoughts, what we withdraw will be the same. And the interest paid will be joy.

One day I came across a fat little book on a friend's desk, and the title grabbed my attention: *14,000 Things to Be Happy About.* As I thumbed through the contents, I realized that each of those 14,000 things was a happy thought, and each one could make the reader happy. However, there isn't one of those 14,000 things that will make us laugh again unless we give ourselves permission to do so. The secret lies in our mind-set—in the things we fix our minds on. As Paul wrote to the Philippians:

> And now, brothers . . . let me say this one more thing: Fix your thoughts on what is true and good and right. Think about things that are pure and lovely, and dwell on the fine, good things in others. Think about all you can praise God for and be glad about.
>
> *Philippians 4:8* TLB

PAUL: A CLASSIC EXAMPLE OF HOW TO LIVE

Speaking of Paul, let me reintroduce you. This is the man who wanted to go to Rome as a preacher in order to testify of his faith before the emperor, Nero. Instead, he wound up in Rome as a prisoner. He was a Roman citizen with every right to appeal to Caesar and await an audience before him. Instead, he was illegally arrested in Jerusalem, misrepresented before the court, incorrectly identified as an Egyptian renegade, entangled in the red tape of political machinery, and finally granted a trip across the Mediterranean, only to encounter a storm and be shipwrecked. When he finally arrived in Rome, he was incarcerated and virtually forgotten for two years. If we looked up *victim* in the dictionary, Paul's picture should appear beside the word!

And yet he is the man who wrote his friends the most joyous letter in the entire New Testament.

Confident, Even Though a Victim

Read his words slowly and see if you find even a hint of resentment or negativism:

> Now I want you to know, brethren, that my circumstances have turned out for the greater progress of the gospel, so that my imprisonment in the cause of Christ has become well known throughout the whole

praetorian guard and to everyone else, and that most of the brethren, trusting in the Lord because of my imprisonment, have far more courage to speak the word of God without fear.

Philippians 1:12–14

Doesn't sound to me like a guy licking his wounds or attending a pity party in honor of himself. On the contrary, he reminds me of the man by the window in that hospital room, looking at a bleak, blank wall but determined to see the unseen. Sitting there with an iron cuff and chain on one arm, bound to a Roman soldier, Paul wrote of his circumstances as having turned out "for the greater *progress* of the gospel."

What a grand, positive statement! After all the man had been through, he considered the things most people would call setbacks as progress. The Greek term Paul selected is colorful. It was used in ancient times to describe a group of pioneer woodcutters who preceded an advancing army, clearing the way through an otherwise impenetrable forest of trees and underbrush. Paul viewed his circumstances as having cleared the way "for the greater progress of the gospel" of Christ to be released.

Instead of seeing the soldier on duty next to him as a galling restriction to the gospel, Paul saw him as a captive audience. What an opportunity to share Christ with one soldier after another, who would, in turn, take the same message back to the barracks so others in the elite praetorian guard might hear and believe. Instead of feeling frustrated and victimized, Paul laughed at the open window of unique opportunity offering numerous possibilities. Paul's joy was outrageous!

How can a person think like that? The answer is neither difficult nor complicated—but it all depends on the question we ask ourselves. Either we ask the negative: Why did this have to happen to me? Or we choose the positive: How has this resulted for some benefit God had in mind?

Like Joseph said many years earlier to his brothers who had ripped him off, "You meant evil against me, but God meant it for good" (Gen. 50:20). With that same positive mind-set, Paul chose to count his blessings rather than list his disappointments. Looking at everything from that perspective, he realized that what seemed a waste or a detour was, in fact, God's divine alchemy. What seemed like a delay had proven to be a divinely appointed opportunity for the message of Christ.

Joyful in Spite of Others

> Some, to be sure, are preaching Christ even from envy and strife, but some also from good will; the latter do it out of love, knowing that I am appointed for the defense of the gospel; the former proclaim Christ out of selfish ambition, rather than from pure motives, thinking to cause me distress in my imprisonment. What then? Only that in every way, whether in pretense or in truth, Christ is proclaimed; and in this I rejoice, yes, and I will rejoice.
>
> *Philippians 1:15–18*

Even back in that first-century era, in the earliest, dynamic days of the church, not everyone who spoke for God was a vessel of pure motive and guileless proclamation. Some deliberately tried to cause Paul distress. Spiritual dynamo though he was, Paul was not perpetually above pain or personal hurt. The man must have had a few dog days like the rest of us. In fact, I like the way Stuart Briscoe describes Paul:

> Whatever we may think of Paul, he was no alabaster saint on a pedestal. The statue and the pedestal are the products of our own lack of reality. The real Paul had a temper that got heated and feelings that got hurt. He was no computerized theological machine churning out inspired writings, but a very warm human individual who needed as much love as the next man, and then some.
>
> You can't hurt a computer's feelings or grieve a theological concept, but you can destroy a man. Paul was destructible, but he wasn't destroyed. And it wasn't for lack of somebody trying! The perspective that he had discovered allowed him to say that he didn't really mind what happened to him so long as nothing happened to stop the gospel, because in his understanding the message preached mattered more than the man preaching.[2]

A large part of learning how to laugh again is being broad-shouldered enough to let things be . . . to leave room for differences . . . to applaud good results even if the way others arrive at them may not be our preferred method. It takes a lot of grace not to be petty, but, oh, the benefits!

Let's see if I can paraphrase what the apostle is communicating here:

> So what if some preach with wrong motives? Furthermore, some may be overly impressed with themselves . . . and take unfair shots at me.

> Who cares? What really matters is this: *Christ is being proclaimed* . . . and that thought alone intensifies my joy! All the other stuff, I leave to God to handle.

To do otherwise is to clutter our minds with judgmental and borderline legalistic thoughts which become joy stealers. They rob us of a positive mind-set. And what happens then? We become petty, cranky, grim people who must have everyone poured into our mold before we are able to relax.

It is important that we understand what is worth our passionate concern and what is not. Most things are not worth the trouble. But some things are. For example, when Paul wrote to the Galatians, he was so concerned about what was happening there that he exclaimed:

> But even though we, or an angel from heaven, should preach to you a gospel contrary to that which we have preached to you, *let him be accursed.* As we have said before so I say again now, if any man is preaching to you a gospel contrary to that which you received, *let him be accursed.*
>
> *Galatians 1:8–9 (italics mine)*

I don't think there is any disagreement . . . the man was hot! But here in Philippians Paul looked at what was going on around him and said, "So what?" The difference is that in Galatia the gospel was being tampered with—some people were preaching a false message of salvation. But in Philippi the truth was being proclaimed even though Paul, personally, was being attacked. When people mess with the message, they need to be rebuked, exposed, and corrected. But when they mess with the messenger, they need to be ignored. No big deal. Not even Paul wasted his time or burnt up a lot of energy nitpicking his way through all that. He was just thrilled that the gospel was being declared.

I have learned over the years that only a few things are worth going to the mat for, and those things always center on the clear gospel message and its surrounding truths. They do not have to do with defending oneself or trying to straighten out other preachers' motives or changing their style. Grace says to let them be. If Paul could shrug it off and say, "So what?" so should we. We will live a lot longer, and we'll start to laugh again.

Hopeful, Regardless of Uncertainties

> For I know that this shall turn out for my deliverance through your prayers and the provision of the Spirit of Jesus Christ, according to my earnest expectation and hope, that I shall not be put to shame in anything, but that with all boldness, Christ shall even now, as always, be exalted in my body, whether by life or by death.
>
> *Philippians 1:19–20*

Those are the words of a man whose image was secure and whose reputation was not in need of being protected, massaged, or defended. His mind was firmly fixed on essentials, so much so that nothing brought him anxiety. "Whether by life or by death," his focus was concentrated. He concerned himself only with things that mattered. For all he knew, death might be right around the corner.

That thought alone provides an excellent filtering system, enabling us to separate what is essential from what is not. As dear old Samuel Johnson once stated, "When a man knows he is to be hanged in a fortnight, it concentrates his mind wonderfully."[3]

Paul was hopeful, regardless of the uncertainties he faced. His quiet confidence is revealed in such phrases as "this shall turn out" and "my earnest expectation." In other words, what he was experiencing was not the end—things would turn out exactly as God directed. That brought the man a rush of mind-calming *peace.* And what may have temporarily brought him pain and discomfort would ultimately result in "Christ . . . exalted in my body." That gave him *hope.* Sandwiched between those two statements was his determination not to feel uneasy or ashamed: "I shall not be put to shame in anything." That brought him *confidence.*

Refusing to be crippled by other people's words, refusing to submerge himself in self-pity, and refusing to take criticism and attacks personally, Paul remained strong, positive, and sure. How could he be so strong? No question about that answer. The man was—

Contented Because Christ Was Central

> For to me, to live is Christ, and to die is gain.
>
> *Philippians 1:21*

This is a well-known statement in Christian circles. We have heard it frequently and quoted it often. Since it is so familiar, perhaps if we try to reword the verse we will discover how any other statement lacks the significance of the authentic words of Paul.

- For me to live is *money* . . . and to die is to leave it all behind.
- For me to live is *fame* . . . and to die is to be quickly forgotten.
- For me to live is *power and influence* . . . and to die is to lose both.
- For me to live is *possessions* . . . and to die is to depart with nothing in my hands.

Somehow, they all fall flat, don't they? When money is our objective, we must live in fear of losing it, which makes us paranoid and suspicious. When fame is our aim, we become competitive lest others upstage us, which makes us envious. When power and influence drive us, we become self-serving and strong-willed, which makes us arrogant. And when possessions become our god, we become materialistic, thinking enough is never enough, which makes us greedy. All these pursuits fly in the face of contentment . . . and joy.

Only *Christ* can satisfy, whether we have or don't have, whether we are known or unknown, whether we live or die. And the good news is this: Death only sweetens the pie! That alone is enough to make you laugh again!

The Living Bible states: "For to me, living means opportunities for Christ, and dying—well, that's better yet!" The New Testament in Modern English, J. B. Phillips's paraphrase, reads: "For living to me means simply 'Christ,' and if I die I should merely gain more of Him." The Good News Bible asks: "For what is life? To me, it is Christ. Death, then, will bring more."

What is the sum and substance of all this? The secret of living is the same as the secret of joy: Both revolve around the centrality of Jesus Christ. In other words, the pursuit of happiness is the cultivation of a Christ-centered, Christ-controlled life.

Three Things to Remember

When Christ becomes our central focus—our reason for existence—contentment replaces our anxiety as well as our fears and insecurities. This cannot help but impact three of the most prevalent joy stealers in all of life.

1. He broadens the dimensions of our circumstances. This gives us new confidence. Chains that once bound and irritated us no longer seem so irksome. Our limitations become a challenge rather than a chore.

2. He delivers us from preoccupation with others. This causes our contentment level to rise. Other people's opinions, motives, and criticisms no longer seem all that important. What a wonderful deliverance!

3. He calms our fears regarding ourselves and our future. This provides a burst of fresh hope on a daily basis. Once fear is removed, it is remarkable how quickly peace fills the vacuum. And when we get those three ducks in a row, it isn't long before we begin to laugh again. What a way to live! Let me urge you not to let anything keep you from it.

Since it is your unalienable right to pursue happiness, I suggest that you *get with it* right away. For some, it is like breaking the spell you have been under for half your life, maybe longer. Won't that take a little extra energy? Probably. You're too tired to exert yourself . . . too tired to pursue *anything* more? Maybe this anonymous piece will help change your mind.

I'm Tired

Yes, I'm tired. For several years I've been blaming it on middle-age, iron poor blood, lack of vitamins, air pollution, water pollution, saccharin, obesity, dieting, underarm odor, yellow wax build-up, and a dozen other maladies that make you wonder if life is really worth living.

But now I find out, tain't that.
I'm tired because I'm overworked.

The population of this country is 200 million. Eighty-four million are retired. That leaves 116 million to do the work. There are 75 million in school, which leaves 41 million to do the work. Of this total, there are 22 million employed by the government.

That leaves 19 million to do the work. Four million are in the armed forces, which leaves 15 million to do the work. Take from that total the 14,800,000 people who work for the state and city governments and that leaves 200,000 to do the work. There are 188,000 in hospitals, so that leaves 12,000 to do the work. Now, there are 11,998 people in prisons. That leaves just 2 people to do the work. You and me. And you're standing there reading this. No wonder I'm tired.[4]

To you I say, *let go.* Let go of your habit of always looking at the negative. Let go of your need to fix everybody else's unhappiness. Let go of your drive to compete or compare. Let go of your adult children, especially your attempts to straighten out their lives. (I read recently that parents are never happier than their least-happy child. What a joy stealer!) Let go of all your excuses. And may I add one more? Let go of so many needless inhibitions that keep you from celebrating life. Quit being so protective . . . so predictable . . . so proper.

Far too many adults I know are as serious as a heart attack. They live with their fists tightened, and they die with deep frowns. They cannot remember when they last took a chance or risked trying something new. The last time they tried something really wild they were nine years old. I ask you, where's the fun? Let's face it, you and I are getting older—it's high time we stop acting like it!

Sooner than we realize, all of us will be looking out that window at a blank wall.

4

Laughing Through Life's Dilemmas

LIFE GETS COMPLICATED.

I can't speak for you, but for me dilemmas are a regular occurrence. Some folks—at least from all outward appearances—seem to deal with life on a black-and-white basis. Stuff they encounter is either right or wrong. Not for me. Somehow I wind up in the gray area more often than not. Perhaps that's been your experience too.

If so, folks like us can appreciate the frustrations Charlie Brown frequently has, as portrayed in Charles Schulz's famous "Peanuts" cartoons. Like the one where Lucy is philosophizing and Charlie is listening. As usual, Lucy has the floor, delivering one of her dogmatic lectures.

"Charlie Brown," she begins, "life is a lot like a deck chair. Some place it so they can see where they're going. Others place it to see where they've been. And some so they can see where they are at the present."

Charlie sighs, "I can't even get mine unfolded!"

More than a few of us identify with Charlie. Life's dilemmas leave us unsettled and unsure. We find ourselves, like the old saying, between a rock and a hard place.

Familiar Dilemmas

Dilemmas have the potential of being some of life's most demanding joy stealers. Being stuck between two possibilities where a case could be made for going either way . . . ah, that's a tough call. We've all been there. I think they fall into at least three categories.

Volitional Dilemmas

A volitional dilemma occurs when we want to do two different things at the same time.

Young couples who have been married for two or three years, sometimes less, are often trying to finish their schooling, yet they are anxious to start a family. Which should they do? To start having children means extra financial pressure and an even greater struggle with time and energy drain. Yet to wait several years means that they may be in their thirties, and they would much rather begin parenting earlier than that. Which do they do?

Another volitional dilemma occurs when we find ourselves unhappy in our church. The problem is exacerbated by the fact that we have been members for many years and have our closest friends there. Do we stick it out and try to help bring about needed changes, which may not be too promising and could create ill feelings, or do we graciously declare our disagreement and leave?

Emotional Dilemmas

Emotional dilemmas are even more intense. They occur when we entertain contrary feelings about the same event.

Not too many months ago our younger son, Chuck, discovered that his longtime pet had a dreadful skin disease. Sasha, a beautiful white Samoyed, had been his dog for many years. To say they were close is to understate the inseparable bond between them. No matter what Chuck tried—and believe me, he tried everything—nothing helped. The dog became increasingly miserable. You have already guessed the dilemma. To provide Sasha relief meant putting her to sleep . . . an option so painful to Chuck he could scarcely discuss it.

If you think that one is difficult, how about dealing with a rebellious adult son or daughter? He or she has moved out of the home but is living a lifestyle that is both personally destructive and disappointing to you. It's obvious that some financial assistance could be put to good use. In fact, a request is made. Do you help or do you resist? Seems so objective, so simple on paper, but few dilemmas are more heartrending.

Geographical Dilemmas

Geographical dilemmas occur when we desire to be in two places at the same time. We love living where we have been for years, but moving would bring an encouraging financial advancement, not to mention the opportunity to cultivate new friendships and enjoy some much-needed changes. To leave, however, would be difficult because of the ages of the kids (two are older teenagers) and the longstanding relationships we have enjoyed at our church, in our neighborhood, and especially with our friends. We weigh both sides. Neither is ideal, yet both have their benefits—a classic geographical dilemma.

I am aware that there are some crossovers within these three categories, but by separating them we are able to see that each pulls at us and introduces numerous and deep feelings of strain, which can quickly drain our reservoir of joy. I might also add that being older and wiser does not mean we are immune to the problem. As Charlie Brown admitted, even seasoned veterans of life can find it difficult to get their deck chairs unfolded.

Paul's Personal Dilemma

All this brings us back to the man we have been getting to know better, Paul, a prisoner of Rome in his own house. We have watched him react positively to his circumstances, and we have cheered him on as he wrote words of encouragement to his friends in Philippi. Now we find ourselves identifying with his own personal dilemma to which he admits in the familiar words:

> For to me, to live is Christ, and to die is gain. But if I am to live on in the flesh, this will mean fruitful labor for me; and I do not know which to choose. But I am hard-pressed from both directions, having the desire to depart and be with Christ, for that is very much better; yet to remain on in the flesh is more necessary for your sake.
>
> *Philippians 1:21–24*

There can be no doubt: Paul's dearest friend, in fact his most intimate relationship on earth, was Christ. No one else meant more to him; therefore, the thought of being with Him brought Paul great joy.

His feelings could be those so beautifully summed up in an old gospel song:

> Jesus is all the world to me,
> My life, my joy, my all;
> He is my strength from day to day,
> Without Him I would fall. . . .

Jesus is all the world to me,
I want no better friend;
I trust Him now, I'll trust Him when
Life's fleeting days shall end.

Beautiful life with such a Friend;
Beautiful life that has no end;
Eternal life, eternal joy,
He's my Friend.[1]

When someone who is eternal and lives in heaven means that much to you, an inescapable dilemma is created: You want to be with Him! Now!! That explains why Paul did not hesitate to write "to die is *gain.*" However, his work on earth was unfinished. God had more He wanted to do through His servant who was then under house arrest in Rome. Paul knew that, which was what caused the dilemma. He was between a rock and a hard place, or as he put it, "hard-pressed from both directions." And what were they?

1. "Having the desire to depart and be with Christ" (which he called "very much better"), and
2. "To remain on in the flesh . . . for your sake" (which he admitted, "is more necessary").

Let me spell all that out in even greater detail. To do so we need to analyze the benefits and the liabilities on both sides.

To Depart

The benefits? He would be with Christ instantly. He would be free of all earth's hassles and limitations, pain and frustrations. He would immediately experience uninterrupted peace and the joy of unending pleasure in the most perfect of all places.

The liabilities? He would be absent from those who needed him, which would seriously affect their spiritual growth. He would no longer be a witness to the Roman guards assigned to watch him or an encouragement to those who came to visit him. In addition, his missionary outreach to those who had not heard of Christ would instantly cease. Furthermore, all those whose cause he championed would be without a voice of authority and affirmation. As relieving as death may have seemed, it was not without its liabilities.

My mind rushes back to 1865 when our country was torn asunder by the Civil War. Abraham Lincoln stood in the gap as a source of strength when many grieving families were doubting and when helpless slaves were despairing. We can only imagine the pressure of that awful position. The photographs taken of the man before the war and during the conflict tell their silent story of a battle-weary warrior who must have longed for relief. Suddenly a shot was fired in Ford's Theater and everything changed. Our sixteenth president finally knew peace as he had never known it before. Were there benefits? Yes! For him they were immediate and eternal. But the liabilities cannot be ignored: political chaos and rivalry among those in authority, heartbreaking sorrow added to an already grieving nation, and the voice of the African-American's most eloquent and powerful advocate forever silenced.

To Remain

If the apostle Paul remained on and continued his ministry, the benefits were obvious. He would have a hand in the spiritual growth of many, his role as mentor to the Philippians (and many others) would be sustained, and his vision for reaching a world without Christ would continue to rekindle the fires of evangelism everywhere he went. And we cannot forget the man's writing ministry. By remaining, his inspired pen would go on flowing.

The liabilities? He would remain absent from his heavenly home. The bonds of his imprisonment would not be broken, his pain would only increase, and his threatened future would intensify. And after all he had been through, who needed more? Bring on the relief!

You and I might think that the man was mature enough to hammer out this decision without too much of a struggle. After all, he was a strong and faithful soldier of the Christian faith, a wise counselor, and a spiritually minded man of God. Surely he could decide on his own. Yet, according to his own testimony, he admitted, "I do not know which to choose" (v. 22). Both made logical sense. Neither would be wrong . . . a real tossup. The Lord must lead, no question.

Horatius Bonar put his finger on the best solution to such a dilemma when he wrote:

> Thy way, not mine, O Lord,
> However dark it be!
> Lead me by Thine own hand,
> Choose out the path for me.

Smooth let it be or rough,
  It will be still the best;
Winding or straight, it leads
  Right onward to Thy rest.

I dare not choose my lot;
  I would not, if I might;
Choose Thou for me, my God;
  So shall I walk aright.

The kingdom that I seek
  Is Thine; so let the way
That leads to it be Thine;
  Else I must surely stray.

Take Thou my cup, and it
  With joy or sorrow fill,
As best to Thee may seem;
  Choose Thou my good and ill;

Choose Thou for me my friends,
  My sickness or my health;
Choose Thou my cares for me,
  My poverty or wealth.

Not mine, not mine the choice,
  In things or great or small;
Be Thou my guide my strength,
  My wisdom, and my all![2]

This is a timely moment for me to return to the greater theme of this book—joy. When we arrive at such dilemmas in life and are unable to decipher the right direction to go, if we hope to maintain our joy in the process, we must (repeat *must*) allow the Lord to be our Guide, our Strength, our Wisdom—our all! It is easy to read those words, but so tough to carry through on them. When we do, however, it is nothing short of remarkable how peaceful and happy we can remain. The pressure is on His shoulders, the responsibility is on Him, the ball is in His court, and an unexplainable joy envelops us. As viewed by others, it may even be considered outrageous joy.

To be sure, such an unusual method of dealing with dilemmas is rare—there aren't many folks willing to turn the reins over to God—and calls for humility, another rare trait among capable people. But it works!

The Lord is a Master at taking our turmoil and revealing the best possible solution to us.

As Peter once wrote:

> Humble yourselves, therefore, under the mighty hand of God, that He may exalt you at the proper time, casting all your anxiety upon Him because He cares for you.
>
> *1 Peter 5:6–7*

When we do that, He trades us His joy for our anxiety. *Such a deal!* As He then works things out and makes it clear to us which step to take next, we can relax, release the tension, and laugh again.

This is extremely hard for Type A personalities. If you happen to be more intelligent than the average person, it's even more difficult. And if you are the super-responsible, I-can-handle-it individual who tends to be intense and impatient, letting go and letting God take charge will be one of life's most incredible challenges. But I urge you, do it! Force yourself to trust Another who is far more capable and intelligent and responsible than you (or a thousand like you) ever could be. And in the meantime, enjoy!

Because I used to be much more driven and demanding (especially of myself), I would often search for things to read that would help me cool my jets. One excellent piece, written by a friar in a Nebraska monastery, has contributed more to my less-intense lifestyle than the author will ever know. I hope it will bring similar benefits your way.

> If I had my life to live over again, I'd try to make more mistakes next time.
> I would relax, I would limber up, I would be sillier than I have been this trip.
> I know of very few things I would take seriously.
> I would take more trips. I would be crazier.
> I would climb more mountains, swim more rivers, and watch more sunsets.
> I would do more walking and looking.
> I would eat more ice cream and less beans.
> I would have more actual troubles, and fewer imaginary ones.
> You see, I'm one of those people who lives life prophylactically and sensibly hour after hour, day

after day. Oh, I've had my moments, and if I had to do it over again I'd have more of them.
In fact, I'd try to have nothing else, just moments, one after another, instead of living so many years ahead each day. I've been one of those people who never go anywhere without a thermometer, a hot-water bottle, a gargle, a raincoat, aspirin, and a parachute.
If I had to do it over again I would go places, do things, and travel lighter than I have.
If I had my life to live over I would start barefooted earlier in the spring and stay that way later in the fall.
I would play hookey more.
I wouldn't make such good grades, except by accident.
I would ride on more merry-go-rounds.
I'd pick more daisies.[3]

I know, I know. Just tolerating the idea of making mistakes and playing hookey and taking the time to pick daisies is tough for a lot of us. And admittedly some have gone too far in this direction. It's one thing to err, but when you wear out the eraser before the pencil, you're overdoing it.

Nevertheless, many need the reminder that life is more than hard work and serious decisions and ultra-intense issues. I have often been comforted with the thought that "He gives to His beloved even in his sleep" (Ps. 127:2). How easy to forget that "God is for us" (Rom. 8:31) and "richly supplies us with all things to enjoy" (1 Tim. 6:17). Some of us need to read those statements every day until we really begin to believe them.

Well, did Paul experience God's leading? Was he ever removed from the horns of his dilemma? Did he get his deck chair unfolded? You bet. Read it for yourself.

> And convinced of this, I know that I shall remain and continue with you all for your progress and joy in the faith, so that your proud confidence in me may abound in Christ Jesus through my coming to you again.
>
> *Philippians 1:25–26*

Somehow the Lord made it clear to Paul that His plan was to have him remain and continue doing what he was doing. Though departing would have brought the man instant relief and rewards for a job well done, he accepted God's decision and unselfishly pressed on.

A Spiritual Challenge

The closing words of Paul's opening chapter to his friends in Philippi are words of challenge—to them and to us.

> Only conduct yourselves in a manner worthy of the gospel of Christ; so that whether I come and see you or remain absent, I may hear of you that you are standing firm in one spirit, with one mind striving together for the faith of the gospel; in no way alarmed by your opponents—which is a sign of destruction for them, but of salvation for you, and that too, from God. For to you it has been granted for Christ's sake, not only to believe in Him, but also to suffer for His sake, experiencing the same conflict which you saw in me, and now hear to be in me.
>
> *Philippians 1:27–30*

What stands out to me is Paul's initial reminder that others are not responsible for our happiness. We are. "Whether I come and see you or remain absent," he expects to hear that they are together. What an important reminder!

So many live their lives too dependent on others. Such clinging vines draw most, if not all, of their energy from another. Not only is this unhealthy for the clinger, but it also drains too much energy from the clingee!

Paul would have none of that, and neither should we. Maturity is accelerated when we learn to stand firm on our own. There may be occasions when others play helpful roles during needy episodes of our lives, but those should be the exception rather than the rule. Codependent people are not joyful people.

Does this discount the need for close and harmonious relationships? Hardly. In fact, after encouraging a healthy independence, Paul turns the coin to the other side and suggests a need for balance: "with one mind striving together." Why? Because life includes tests, and some of those tests involve "opponents" who are not to alarm us. By striving together, we keep from being intimidated and frightened.

Great comfort comes when we realize that our striving is not an isolated series of battles fought one-on-one, but that we are fighting together against a common foe. There is a sense of camaraderie and support when we realize we are in the ranks of the faithful, a "mighty army" of those set apart by Christ, a force to reckon with.

After speaking at a church recently, I noticed an interesting sign as we were leaving the parking lot. It read:

YOU ARE NOW ENTERING
THE MISSION FIELD

Nice reminder. And even more encouraging, we enter it together. So we need to remember:

1. We are not alone.
2. We are promised the victory.
3. We are called (among other things) to suffer.
4. We are in good company when conflicts arise.

Paul reminds his friends at Philippi that their conflicts are the same as his conflicts. The Greek word translated *conflicts* here is the term from which we get our word *agony.* We agonize together just as we stand and strive for the gospel together. I gain strength from the thought that our sufferings and conflicts are on a par with Paul's. Agony is agony, pure and simple. It makes mature believers out of all of us. It also develops our spiritual muscles and gives us fresh courage to face whatever foe we may encounter. And let us never forget . . . our side ultimately wins!

In the early days of Christianity, a scoffer once inquired, "What is your Carpenter doing now?" And the answer of the unperturbed Christian was bold: "Making a coffin for your Emperor!"[4]

Never, ever forget that our role is twofold: not only "to believe in Him" (that's the delightful part), but also "to suffer for His sake" (the difficult part). That poses yet another dilemma, which would perhaps fall under a fourth category—the *practical* dilemma. We who love the Lord and faithfully serve Him, doing our best to live for His glory, occasionally find ourselves suffering for the cause rather than being rewarded for our walk. The dilemma: Do we run toward it or run from it?

Most in our day would consider anyone a fool who pursued anything but comfort and ease. But since when did the majority ever vote in favor of Christ? If this happens to be your current way of life, if suffering and difficulty have come your way because of your walk with Him, take heart. You are in good company. And some glorious day in the not-too-distant future, God will reward you for your faithfulness. You will have forgotten the pain of pressing on. And, like never before, you will laugh again.

Our Personal Response

Two final principles emerge from the things we have been thinking about in this chapter.

- Making right decisions amidst dilemmas forces us to rethink our priorities.

There is nothing quite like a dilemma to bring us back to the bedrock of what we consider essential. Happy is the one who sets aside selfish ambition and personal preference for God's will and way.

- Choosing right priorities forces us to reconsider the importance of Christ in our lives.

There are many voices these days. Some are loud, many are persuasive, and a few are downright convincing. It can be confusing. If you listen long enough you will be tempted to throw your faith to the winds, look out for number one, let your glands be your guide, and choose what is best for you. Initially you will get a rush of pleasure and satisfaction, no question. But ultimately you will wind up disappointed and disillusioned.

Malcolm Muggeridge died in the fall of 1990. He had been a foreign correspondent, newspaper editor, editor of *Punch* magazine, and a well-known television personality in Great Britain. As an adult, he finally turned to Christ and wrote of his own dilemmas as a journalist-turned-believer. Among his works are *Jesus Rediscovered, Christ and the Media, Something Beautiful for God,* and his multivolume autobiography, *Chronicles of Wasted Time.* He frequently spoke and wrote of "feeling like a stranger" in the world.

In an interview a few years before his death, Muggeridge was asked if he would be willing to explain that feeling. His answer is worth repeating.

> I'd very gladly do so, because I've thought about it often. In the war, when I was in North Africa, I heard some lieutenant colonel first use the phrase "displaced person." That phrase was very poignant to me. But it's also a very good definition of a person who's come to see that life is not about carnal things, or success, but is about eternity rather than time. . . . I don't really belong here, I'm simply staying here.[5]

Since I am committed to what is best for you, I am not going to suggest, "Oh, well, do whatever." I am going to challenge you to keep an eternal perspective, even though you are in the minority, even though you are surrounded by a host of success-oriented individuals who are urging you to ignore your conscience and grab all you can now. You want joy? You really want what is best? Simply consider yourself a displaced person and go God's way. His is the most reliable route to follow when life gets complicated. It will have its tough moments, but you will never regret it.

Some glorious day, trust me, you will look back on the dilemma that now has you so stressed out . . . and you will finally get your deck chair unfolded. You will then sit down on it and laugh out loud.

5

The Hidden Secret of a Happy Life

I HAVE BEEN WRITING A LOT about choosing joy and about cultivating a good sense of humor. On several occasions I have mentioned the value of one's attitude, which is the secret behind learning how to laugh again. Cultivating the right attitude, in my opinion, is absolutely crucial. Now let's take a deeper look at the subject of our attitude.

The dictionary on my desk defines attitude as "a manner of acting, feeling, or thinking that shows one's disposition . . . opinion, mental set." That means that how we think determines how we respond to others. As a matter of fact, I have found that my view of others is a direct reflection of my own "mental set."

> Our attitude toward the world around us depends upon what we are ourselves. If we are selfish, we will be suspicious of others. If we are of a generous nature, we will be likely to be more trustful. If we are quite honest with ourselves, we won't always be anticipating deceit in others. If we are inclined to be fair, we won't feel that we are being cheated. In a sense, looking at the people around you is like looking in a mirror. You see a reflection of yourself.[1]

Since I am a minister of the gospel, much of my time is spent studying the Bible and then sharing the things I have discovered. Lately my study has led me into the Gospel written by an ancient physician named Luke. As he began to do his research on the most incredible individual who ever lived on our planet, Dr. Luke was led to portray Jesus as a man. This portrayal provides fascinating information for anyone interested in Jesus' interpersonal relationships.

As I have pored over Luke's descriptions and observations, looking for insights into the Savior's life, I have been intrigued by His responses to others. How could any man be as patient as He was? How could He keep His cool under constant fire? How could He demonstrate so much grace, so much compassion, and at the same time so much determination? And when faced with the Pharisees' continued badgering and baiting, how could He restrain Himself from punching their lights out? As a man, He had all the emotions we have as human beings. What was it that gave Him the edge we so often lack? *It was His attitude.* To return to Webster's words, He acted and felt as He did because of His "disposition," His "mental set."

All this brings up a question: What is the most Christlike attitude on earth? Think before you answer too quickly. I am certain many would answer *love.* That is understandable, for He did indeed love to the uttermost. Others might say *patience.* Again, not a bad choice. I find no evidence of impatience or anxious irritability as I study His life. *Grace* would also be a possibility. No man or woman ever modeled or exhibited the grace that He demonstrated right up to the moment He breathed His last.

As important as those traits may be, however, they are not the ones Jesus Himself referred to when He described Himself for the only time in Scripture. I am thinking of those familiar words:

> Come to Me, all who are weary and heavy-laden, and I will give you rest. Take My yoke upon you, and learn from Me, for I am gentle and humble in heart; and you shall find rest for your souls. For My yoke is easy, and My load is light.
>
> *Matthew 11:28–30*

Did you catch the key words? "I am gentle and humble in heart," which might best be summed up in the one word *unselfish.* According to Jesus' testimony, that is the most Christlike attitude we can demonstrate. Because He was so humble—so unselfish—the last person He thought of was Himself.

ANALYZING UNSELFISHNESS

To be "humble in heart" is to be submissive to the core. It involves being more interested in serving the needs of others than in having one's own needs met.

Someone who is truly unselfish is generous with his or her time and possessions, energy and money. As that works its way out, it is demonstrated in various ways, such as thoughtfulness and gentleness, an unpretentious spirit, and servant-hearted leadership.

- When a husband is unselfish, he subjugates his own wants and desires to the needs of his wife and family.
- When a mother is unselfish, she isn't irked by having to give up her agenda or plans for the sake of her children.
- When an athlete is unselfish, it is the team that matters, not winning the top honors personally.
- When a Christian is unselfish, others mean more than self. Pride is given no place to operate.

As Isaac Watts wrote early in the eighteenth century:

> When I survey the wondrous cross
> On which the Prince of glory died,
> My richest gain I count but loss,
> And pour contempt on all my pride.[2]

What strange-sounding words! Not because they are archaic but because everyone today is so selfish—and we are never told by our peers to be otherwise. Ours is a day of self-promotion, defending our own rights, taking care of ourselves first, winning by intimidation, pushing for first place, and a dozen other self-serving agendas. That one attitude does more to squelch our joy than any other. So busy defending and protecting and manipulating, we set ourselves up for a grim, intense existence—and it is not a modern problem.

Greece said, "Be wise, know yourself."

Rome said, "Be strong, discipline yourself."

Religion says, "Be good, conform yourself."

Epicureanism says, "Be sensuous, satisfy yourself."

Education says, "Be resourceful, expand yourself."

Psychology says, "Be confident, assert yourself."

Materialism says, "Be possessive, please yourself."

Ascetism say, "Be lowly, suppress yourself."

Humanism says, "Be capable, believe in yourself."

Pride says, "Be superior, promote yourself."

Christ says, "Be unselfish, humble yourself."

When I write that last line, I find myself shaking my head and smiling. In our selfish, grab-all-you-can-get society, the concept of cultivating an unselfish, servant-hearted attitude is almost a joke to the majority. But, happily, there are a few (I hope you are one of them) who genuinely desire to develop such an attitude. I can assure you, if you carry out that desire, you will begin to laugh again—and I mean really laugh. It is the hidden secret of a happy life.

At our church in Fullerton, California, we are always looking for better ways to communicate with one another. It is easy for those of us in leadership to think everyone in the congregation is in the know when, in fact, they may be in the dark. We who stand up front and do the teaching and preaching can think everything we say is clear when it may not be. One method that has helped the congregation respond is the use of a tear-off section on our Sunday bulletins. Frequently folks will ask questions on these stubs or make a statement that helps them get a more realistic or complete view of something I have said from the pulpit.

Several Sundays ago someone wrote: "Chuck, I understand what you said today. I appreciate your commitment, and I believe every word of it. My problem is knowing how to do it!" I call that an extremely honest and humble response.

You may feel the same way about the things I have been saying regarding the value of maintaining an unselfish attitude. Perhaps you would even agree that unselfishness is the stuff of which Christlikeness is made . . . but how do we pull it off? You need to have it spelled out in more explicit, practical ways? Fair enough.

EXAMINING CHRISTLIKENESS

Let's go back to the little letter Paul wrote to his friends in Philippi. I think what he says regarding the attitude of unselfishness will help lift the fog of indefiniteness and enable us to get down to the nubbies of how to make it happen.

He begins this section with a plea:

> If therefore there is any encouragement in Christ, if there is any consolation of love, if there is any fellowship of the Spirit, if any affection and compassion, make my joy complete by being of the same mind, maintaining the same love, united in spirit, intent on one purpose. Do nothing from selfishness or empty conceit, but with humility of mind let each of you regard one another as more important than himself; do not merely look out for your own personal interests, but also for the interests of others.
>
> *Philippians 2:1–4*

These opening lines conclude with the theme of what is on his mind—"others." As we read Paul's initial plea, it is obvious that his major concern is that there not be disunity or conflict among his friends. It is as if he is pleading: Whatever else may happen, my friends, don't let a selfish attitude sneak in like a thief and steal your joy or interrupt your closeness.

What Is Needed?

Most of all, harmony is needed . . . a like-minded spirit with one another. I like the way The Living Bible renders the opening lines of this paragraph:

> Is there any such thing as Christians cheering each other up? Do you love me enough to want to help me? Does it mean anything to you that we are brothers in the Lord, sharing the same Spirit? Are your hearts tender and sympathetic at all? Then make me truly happy by loving each other and agreeing wholeheartedly with each other, working together with one heart and mind and purpose.
>
> *Philippians 2:1–2* TLB

What a wonderful way to live one's life! That "one heart and mind and purpose" suggests unity, a genuine Spirit-filled unselfishness that breeds strength and spreads cheer.

Is this suggesting uniformity? Does it mean we always have to agree on everything? Is that what harmony is all about? No. There is a difference between unity and uniformity. Uniformity is gained by pressure from without. The English word *uniformity* has within it the word *uniform.* We dress alike, look alike, sound alike, think alike, act alike. But that is neither healthy nor biblical. Unity comes from deep within. It is the inner desire to conduct oneself in a cooperative manner . . . to be on the same team, to go for the same objectives, for the benefit of one another.

As Harry A. Ironside said,

> It is very evident that Christians will never see eye to eye on all points. We are so largely influenced by habits, by environment, by education, by the measure of intellectual and spiritual apprehension to which we have attained, that it is an impossibility to find any number of people who look at everything from the same standpoint. How then can such be of one mind? The apostle himself explains it elsewhere when he says, "I think also that I have the mind of Christ." The "mind of Christ" is the lowly mind. And, if we are all of *this* mind, we shall walk together in love, considering one another, and seeking rather to be helpers of one another's faith, than challenging each other's convictions.[3]

Interestingly, Paul admits that their maintaining such a spirit of harmony would "make my joy complete." Harmony promotes happiness. If you question that, you've not worked at a place where disharmony reigns or lived in a home fractured by disunity. Joy cannot survive such settings. If we hope to laugh again, harmony needs to be restored.

How Is It Accomplished?

The question, I repeat, is how? How is it possible to pull off such an unselfish attitude when we find ourselves surrounded by quite the opposite? Let's look a little closer at what Paul wrote:

> Do nothing from selfishness or empty conceit, but with humility of mind let each of you regard one another as more important than himself; do not merely look out for your own personal interests, but also for the interests of others.
>
> *Philippians 2:3–4*

As I consider his counsel, three practical ideas emerge that may help us cultivate an unselfish attitude.

First, never let selfishness or conceit be your motive. That's right, *never*. That is Paul's advice, isn't it? "Do *nothing* from selfishness or empty conceit" (emphasis mine).

Second, always regard others as more important than yourself. Though this is not a natural trait, it can become a habit—and what an important one!

Third, don't limit your attention to your own personal interests—include others. I think it was Andrew Murray who said: "The humble person is not one who thinks meanly of himself; he simply does not think of himself at all."

Some may try to dissuade you from what may appear to be an unbalanced, extremist position. They may tell you that anyone who adopts this sort of attitude is getting dangerously near self-flagellation and a loss of healthy self-esteem. Nonsense! The goal is that we become so interested in others and in helping them reach their highest good that we become self-forgetful in the process.

Go back momentarily to Paul's choice of words, "humility of mind." As we pursue this attitude (exalting Christ) and get involved in the same objective (being of help and encouragement to others), we set aside our differences (harmony) and lose interest in pleasing ourselves (unselfishness). Perhaps the closest we come to that is when we are forced to mutually endure hard times.

Martyn Lloyd-Jones, writing in England shortly after World War II, recalled the terror of the blitzkrieg bombing attacks of Hitler's Luftwaffe:

> How often during that last war were we told of the extraordinary scenes in air-raid shelters; how different people belonging to different classes, there, in the common need to shelter from the bombs and death, forgot all the differences between them and became one. This was because in the common interest they forgot the divisions and the distinctions. That is why you always tend to have a coalition government during a war; in periods of crises and common need all distinctions are forgotten and we suddenly become united.[4]

I have seen similar scenes out here in California in the midst of an awful fire that sweeps across thousands of acres, until finally those flaming fingers reach into a residential section. What happens? Immediately people pull together. They pay no attention to who makes what salary, which kind of car a person drives, or how much they might receive from their neighbor by helping out. Totally disregarding any benefit they personally might derive from their acts of heroism (usually nothing) and with no thought of personal danger, they "regard one another as more important" than their own possessions or safety. When we are forced to focus only on the help we can be to others in a time of crisis, we begin to demonstrate this Christlike attitude.

To be truthful about it, it does not always require a crisis. I have found that just having a large family—say, four or five kids—is enough to teach us how selfishness fouls up the works. I recall when Cynthia and I began to have children, I thought two would be perfect. "Alpha and Omega" . . . *ideal!* Along came our third . . . and not too many years later a fourth.

Now, you need to understand the kind of guy I am. I like my shoes spit-shined rather than stepped on and scuffed up. And I like my clothes hanging in the closet in an orderly and neat manner rather than drooled on and wrinkled up. And I really like milk in a glass on the table and not on the floor. I especially like a clean car with no fingerprints on the windows and no leftover school assignments spread across the floorboards.

So what does the Lord do to help broaden my horizons and assist me in seeing how selfish I am? Very simple: He gives me four busy kids who step on shoes, wrinkle clothes, spill milk, lick car windows, and drop sticky candy on the carpet. You haven't lived until you've walked barefoot across the floor in the middle of the night and stomped down full force on a jack . . . or a couple of those little Lego landmines. I'll tell you, you learn real quick about your own level of selfishness.

You see, this is not some deep, ethereal, or theological subject we're thinking about. Being unselfish in attitude strikes at the very core of our being. It means we are willing to forego our own comfort, our own preferences, our own schedule, our own desires for another's benefit. And that brings us back to Christ. Perhaps you never realized that it was His attitude of unselfishness that launched Him from the splendor of heaven to a humble manger in Bethlehem . . . and later to the cross at Calvary. How did He accept all that? Willingly.

CHRIST'S LIFE . . . BEFORE AND AFTER

A significant transitional statement appears at this juncture in Paul's words to the Philippians.

> Have this attitude in yourselves which was also in Christ Jesus. . . .
>
> *Philippians 2:5*

Christ Jesus, what a perfect example of an unselfish attitude! What Paul has been pleading for among his friends at Philippi, he illustrates in the person of Jesus Christ. In effect, he is saying, "You want to know what I'm getting at? You would like a 'for instance' to help you better understand what I mean by 'looking out for . . . the interest of others'? I call before you the perfect example: Christ Jesus."

Take a look at how He modeled this attitude:

> Have this attitude in yourselves which was also in Christ Jesus, who, although He existed in the form of God, did not regard equality with God a thing to be grasped, but emptied Himself, taking the form of a bond-servant, and being made in the likeness of men. And being found in appearance as a man, He humbled Himself by becoming obedient to the point of death, even death on a cross.
>
> *Philippians 2:5–8*

Everything that was involved in Jesus' becoming human began with an attitude of submission . . . a willingness to cooperate with God's plan for salvation. Rather than lobbying for His right to remain in heaven and continuing to enjoy all the benefits of that exalted role as the second member of the Godhead and Lord of the created world, He willingly said yes. He agreed to cooperate with a plan that would require His releasing ecstasy and accepting agony. In a state of absolute perfection and undiminished deity, He willingly came to earth. Leaving the angelic hosts who flooded His presence with adoring praise, He unselfishly accepted a role that would require His being misunderstood, abused, cursed, and crucified. He unhesitatingly surrendered the fellowship and protection of the Father's glory for the lonely path of obedience and torturous death.

Don't miss the steps downward:

1. He emptied Himself.
2. He took the form of a servant.
3. He was made in the likeness of humanity.
4. He humbled Himself by becoming obedient unto death.
5. He accepted the most painful and humiliating way to die—crucifixion.

Did He realize all this ahead of time? Of course. Was He aware that it would require such an extensive sacrifice? Without question. Did He do it all with a grim face and tight lips? Not at all. How do we know? You will find the answer to that tucked away in Hebrews 12:2,

> Fixing our eyes on Jesus, the author and perfecter of faith, who for the joy set before Him endured the cross, despising the shame, and has sat down at the right hand of the throne of God.
>
> *Hebrews 12:2*

Look at that! He saw those of us who would benefit from His sacrifice as "the joy set before Him." We're back to our theme—joy! He did not come to us grudgingly or nursing a bitter spirit. He came free of all that. While it was certainly not a pleasurable experience, He accepted His coming among us and His dying for us willingly and unselfishly.

And what ultimately happened? Read and rejoice!

> Therefore also God highly exalted Him, and bestowed on Him the name which is above every name, that at the name of Jesus every knee should bow, of those who are in heaven, and on earth, and under the earth, and that every tongue should confess that Jesus Christ is Lord, to the glory of God the Father.
>
> *Philippians 2:9–11*

Paul seems especially fond of compound superlatives. "God supremely exalted Him!" He was welcomed back with open arms. Heaven's applause was the supreme reward for His earthly sacrifice. Once again submission paid a rich dividend. We are told that two things occurred after the price for sin was paid:

1. God highly exalted Jesus Christ to the pinnacle of authority.
2. God bestowed on Him a name of highest significance: *Kurios Iesous Christos* . . . "Jesus Christ—Lord!"

No one else deserves that title. Only one is LORD. All knees will ultimately bow before Him. Above the earth? All angels will bow . . .

and all who have gone on before us. On the earth? Every living human being . . . those who love and worship Him and, yes, even those who deny and despise Him. One day in the future, all on earth will bow. Under the earth? The devil and his demonic forces along with those who have died without faith, unbelieving and lost.

> The lost will never be reconciled. Heaven and earth will eventually be filled with happy beings who have been redeemed to God by the precious blood of Christ. . . .
>
> But "under the earth" will be those who "have their part" in the outer darkness, the lake of fire. They flaunted Christ's authority on earth. They will have to own it in hell! They refused to heed the call of grace and be reconciled to God in the day when they might have been saved.[5]

A Concluding Encouragement and Example

My emphasis in this chapter has been on the attitude that releases joy and launches it from our lips, the hidden secret of a happy life on earth—an attitude of unselfishness. My encouragement to you is that you not put it off until it is a little more convenient. Many will tell you that you will be taken advantage of if you begin to live for others or if you don't defend your rights and "get even." I offer the opposite counsel: God will honor your decision to demonstrate an attitude of humility. You will find that feelings of hate will be replaced with a relieving flood of peace and happiness. As Solomon has written, "When a man's ways are pleasing to the Lord, He makes even his enemies to be at peace with him" (Prov. 16:7).

Actually, it all begins with your knowing Jesus Christ in a personal way . . . and your allowing Him to take the blows of life for you. If you willingly do His will, you will find He gives you joy that even the angels of heaven cannot experience. Someday our voices will join the angelic host and together we will make great music! But our joy will outdo theirs.

There is an old gospel song I seldom hear anymore. Its chorus states what I'm trying to communicate:

> Holy, holy, is what the angels sing,
> And I expect to help them make the courts of heaven
> ring;

> But when I sing redemption's story, they will fold their
> wings,
> For angels never felt the joys that our salvation
> brings.[6]

When we acknowledge that Jesus Christ is Lord and begin to release our cares, our disappointments, and our heartaches to Him, we not only keep our equilibrium, we also keep our sense of humor. Joys multiply when we have Someone to bear our burdens.

I mentioned earlier that I serve on the board of my alma mater. That assignment carries with it many serious responsibilities but also several joyous benefits. One of those has been the privilege of getting better acquainted with a fine group of Christian gentlemen who serve as colleagues on the same leadership team. One of them is a man I have admired from a distance for many years—Tom Landry. As head coach of the Dallas Cowboys for twenty-nine years and a member of the National Football League Hall of Fame, his record speaks for itself. But what I find even more admirable are his character, his integrity, and his humility. Now that I have gotten to know the man "up close and personal," my appreciation for him has only increased.

Most of us were surprised and disappointed at the way a new owner of the Cowboys released Coach Landry from his position. I had the privilege of watching and listening to him during that time . . . even having a few personal conversations without microphones or television cameras or news reporters nearby. He had ample opportunities to blast the new management by criticizing their methods and defending himself. Not once—not a single time—following his forced resignation did I hear an ugly remark or a blaming comment cross Tom Landry's lips. The only response was something like, "You know, Chuck, a fellow in my position has to realize it's going to be taken from him whether or not he is ready for it to happen. It's just a matter of being willing to accept that." Those are the unselfish words of a man who was told rather hurriedly to clean out his desk and be on his way . . . after giving almost three decades of his life to something he loved. Most others in his place would have held a news conference within hours and blasted the new management unmercifully.

I have been with Coach Landry on numerous occasions since then. We have had him at our church to speak to a gymnasium full of men with their sons and friends. It has been delightful to observe a total absence of bitterness in the man and, at the same time, the continued presence of a sense of humor and the joy of Christ. Personally, I am convinced his current attitude is a greater message to those to whom he speaks than all those years of success and championship seasons. It is reassuring to know that joy can endure hardship as long as that Christlike attitude of unselfishness is in place.

6

While Laughing, Keep Your Balance!

DIED, AGE THIRTY. BURIED, AGE SIXTY.

That's an appropriate epitaph for too many Americans. Mummification sets in on a host of young men and women at an age when they should be tearing up the track. All of us have so much more to offer for so much longer than we realize; it would boggle our minds if we could envision our full potential.

I came across an article way back in 1967 that I still return to on occasion. Entitled "Advice to a (Bored) Young Man," it communicates how much one person can contribute, if only—

> Many people reading this page are doing so with the aid of bifocals. Inventor? *B. Franklin*, age 79.
>
> The presses that printed this page were powered by electricity. One of the first harnessers? *B. Franklin*, age 40.
>
> Some are reading this on the campus of one of the Ivy League universities. Founder? *B. Franklin*, age 45.
>
> Some got their copy through the U.S. Mail. Its father? *B. Franklin*, age 31.
>
> Now, think fire. Who started the first fire department, invented the lightning rod, designed a heating stove still in use today? *B. Franklin*, ages 31, 43, 36.
>
> Wit. Conversationalist. Economist. Philosopher. Diplomat. Printer. Publisher. Linguist (spoke and wrote five languages). Advocate of paratroopers (from balloons) a century before the airplane was invented. All this until age 84.
>
> And he had exactly two years of formal schooling. It's a good bet that you already have more sheer knowledge than Franklin had when he was your age.

> Perhaps you think there's no use trying to think of anything new, that everything's been done. Wrong. The simple, agrarian America of Franklin's day didn't begin to need the answers we need today.
>
> Go do something about it.[1]

After digesting a list like that, my immediate response is *Wow!* Who wouldn't be impressed? Examples like Benjamin Franklin are nothing short of fantastic. But they can also be frustrating.

I'm trying to put myself into the house slippers of a mother of four or five young children who does well to get dressed by eleven o'clock in the morning . . . or the recently unemployed forty-five-year-old husband and father who is spending his day on a job search, caught somewhere between pressure and panic. Furthermore, a lot of us do well just finding time to read about such inventions, to say nothing of spending the time it takes to discover them.

To keep things in balance it is helpful to remember the words of humorist Mark Twain: "Few things are harder to put up with than the annoyance of a good example."[2]

Admiration for a great person may inspire us, but it cannot enable us. Great potential notwithstanding, it is easy to feel overwhelmed.

WRONG RESPONSES TO RIGHT EXAMPLES

So what are the options frustrated folks take when exposed to great examples? To be sure, some *fake it.* Just polish the image and make a good appearance. Many make a career of doing that and never get caught. Others try to once and it backfires in spades. Back in 1990 a scandal hit the music industry. Milli Vanilli, who had won a Grammy Award for the album "Girl You Know It's True," finally had to confess it wasn't. They had lip-synced the entire recording, which resulted in the disgrace of having to return the Grammy.

To all that, Jimmy Bowen, president of Capitol Records, replied:

> Ya have to remember that music is a mirror of the times. And when the mirror is close to what's happening, that's what sells. The times we live in are very plastic. There are a lot of phony things happening in people's daily lives. So Milli Vanilli is just playing the game.[3]

Another spokesperson in the same newspaper article added,

> As technology allows music producers to use increasingly sophisticated electronic trickery to make albums and videos, the Milli Vanilli scandal will only repeat itself—unless audiences stop valuing image more than content.[4]

Another common technique when facing a great example is to *hurry the process.* I find that our generation, more than any in the past, wants more, *quicker.* "Don't slow me down by making me pay a price or go through some long and painful process. I don't want to wait until I'm in my fifties, sixties, or seventies. I want it now."

Regardless of your opinion of him, you have to agree that Liberace was one of the most popular entertainers of the latter half of the twentieth century. Recently I was interested to discover these comments on his style from the late pianist himself:

> "My whole trick," he says, "is to keep the tune well out in front. If I play Tschaikovsky, I play his melodies and skip his spiritual struggles. Naturally, I condense. I have to know just how many notes my audience will stand for. If there's time left over, I fill in with a lot of runs up and down the keyboard."[5]

There is another option, quite common in Christian circles. When faced with an example to whom we feel we cannot measure up, we *strive harder.* The old familiar song states this philosophy: "Striving to please Him in all that I do."

I ask you, is that the Christian life? If the answer is not faking it and if it is not hurrying things, is it striving hard for it? You want to live the rest of your life striving to please Him in all that you do? Some who are painfully honest will admit, "I'm doing my best. I'm trying. But I'm exhausted." Surely that's not God's plan.

Christ, Our Example

What may be true of other examples is not true of Jesus. Whether they be president or statesman, inventor or novelist, athlete or artist, all other great examples may inspire, but they cannot enable. They may motivate us, but they have no power to change us. There is nothing of Ben Franklin left over that can make you or me the inventor he was. But when it comes to Christ, things are different. He says, in effect, "You want to live My life? Here is My power." Lo and behold, He strengthens us within. "You want to please My heavenly Father? Here's My enablement." And He enables us by His Spirit.

Having failed far more than I have succeeded at many of my dreams, I find that very encouraging. And perhaps you would have to say the same thing. Having been swamped by sin all our lives, struggling to find our way to the top of the water to breathe, we can find great hope in the ability He gives us not only to breathe but to swim freely. You see, Christ not only lived an exemplary life, He also makes it possible for us to do the same. He gives us His pattern to follow *without* while at the same time providing the needed power *within.* And guess what that makes us able to do? Laugh again!

I mean it in the right sense when I say that for years Jesus has made me laugh. Because we have His example to follow and His power to pull it off, you and I no longer have to fake it or hurry it or strive for it. Once He gets control of our minds, the right attitudes bring about the right actions.

LIFE, OUR CHALLENGE

Having established the preeminent role Christ plays in our minds, we need to see how all that works its way out in our lives. Which brings us back to the little letter Paul wrote his friends in Philippi. In this choice missive promoting outrageous joy, he spells out the importance of keeping ourselves balanced as we take on the challenges of life. In doing this he specifies three of the most significant areas we must deal with:

- Balancing purpose and power (2:12–13)
- Balancing attitude and action (2:14–16)
- Balancing seriousness and joy (2:17–18)

Let's take them in that order.

Balancing Purpose and Power

> So then, my beloved, just as you have always obeyed, not as in my presence only, but now much more in my absence, work out your salvation with fear and trembling; for it is God who is at work in you, both to will and to work for His good pleasure.
>
> *Philippians 2:12–13*

We need to keep in mind that Paul is writing to Christians ("my beloved"), so obviously these words have nothing to do with his readers' becoming Christians—they already are. Therefore, the idea of working out one's salvation must be referring to living out one's faith—carrying it out correctly. In other words, we, as God's people, are charged with the importance of obedience. Just as Christ, our example, was "obedient to the point of death" (2:8), so we are to carry out our purpose with equal diligence.

Interestingly, the word translated "work out" was the same Greek term popularly used for "working a mine" or "working a field." In each case there were benefits that followed such diligence. The mine would yield valuable elements or ore . . . the field would yield crops. Paul's point is clear: By working out our salvation, we bring the whole purpose to completion . . . we carry out our reason for existence. So let's not stop short!

When a musician has a fine composition placed before her, that music is not the musician's masterpiece; it is the composer's gift to the musician. But it then becomes the task of the musician to work it out, to give it sound and expression and beauty as she applies her skills to the composition. When she does, the composition reaches its completed purpose and thrills the hearts of her listeners.

When we become ill, we go to a physician. He diagnoses our ailment and prescribes the proper treatment. He hands us a small slip of paper upon which he has written the correct prescription, and we take it to the pharmacist who fills that prescription and gives us the medication. So far, everything has been done for us—diagnosis, prescription, medication. It now becomes our responsibility to follow the doctor's orders exactly as stated. By working out the process we enjoy the benefits of the physician's and pharmacist's contributions to our health. We recover.

Spiritually speaking, the ultimate goal or purpose of our lives is "His good pleasure." Our lives are to be lived for God's greater glory—not our own selfish desires.

Are we left to do so all alone? Is it our task to gut it out, grit our teeth, and do His will? Not at all. Here's the balance: *God is at work in us!* He is the one who gives us strength and empowers our diligence. As He pours His power into us, we do the things that bring Him pleasure. Take special note that His pleasure (not ours), His will (not ours), His glory (not ours) are what make life meaningful. And therein lies a potential conflict, since most of us prefer to have things go our way. All this brings us back to that famous A-word—attitude.

Balancing Attitude and Action

> Do all things without grumbling or disputing; that you may prove yourselves to be blameless and innocent, children of God above reproach in the midst of a crooked and perverse generation, among whom you appear as lights in the world, holding fast the word of life, so that in the day of Christ I may have cause to glory because I did not run in vain nor toil in vain.
>
> *Philippians 2:14–16*

The first part of Paul's counsel here represents the negative side and the last part, the positive. The two provide another needed balance.

Negatively, watch your attitude! A bad attitude reveals itself from two sides: something we do alone—"grumbling"—and something we do when we are with others—"disputing." Both of these joy stealers need to be exposed.

What exactly is grumbling? It is not loud, boisterous grousing but rather low-toned, discontented muttering. It is negative, muted comments, complaining and whining. Disputing, however, is vocal, ill-natured argumentation . . . verbal expressions of disagreement that stir up suspicion and distrust, doubt and other disturbing feelings in others.

Some folks, like the British novelist J. B. Priestly (by his own admission), spread negative germs by their bad attitudes and acrid tongues. He once declared:

> I have always been a grumbler. I am designed for the part—sagging face, weighty underlip, rumbling, resonant voice. Money couldn't buy a better grumbling outfit.[6]

Ever been around a sourpuss like that? We all have. And even when we try to resist being influenced by such negativism, we find some of it rubbing off. How unfair to pass around the poison of pessimism! But it happens every day, and it steals our joy. It creates an atmosphere of wholesale negativism where nothing but the bad side of everything is emphasized. It is enough to make you scream!

I couldn't help but smile when I read Barry Siegel's satirical article "World May End with a Splash" in the *Los Angeles Times.* In a lighthearted way it shows how ridiculous it is to let negativism take charge:

> Alarmists, worrying about such matters as nuclear holocaust and pesticide poisoning, may be overlooking much more dire catastrophes. Consider what some scientists predict: If everyone keeps stacking *National Geographics* in garages and attics instead of throwing them away, the magazine's weight will sink the continent 100 feet some time soon and we will all be inundated by the oceans.
>
> If the number of microscope specimen slides submitted to one St. Louis Hospital laboratory continues to increase at its current rate, that metropolis will be buried under 3 feet of glass by the year 2024. If beachgoers keep returning home with as much sand clinging to them as they do now, 80 percent of the country's coastline will disappear in 10 years. . . .
>
> [It has also been reported] that pickles cause cancer, communism, airline tragedies, auto accidents and crime waves. About 99.9% of cancer victims had eaten pickles some time in their lives. . . . So have 100% of all soldiers, 96.8% of Communist sympathizers and 99.7% of those involved in car and air accidents. Moreover those born in 1839 who ate pickles have suffered 100% mortality rate and rats force-fed 20 pounds of pickles a day for a month ended up with bulging abdomens and loss of appetite.[7]

Crazy stuff, but isn't that the way it is when grumbling and complaining are allowed to run wild? Those who hope to laugh again—those who genuinely wish to get beyond the doomsday mentality that pervades so much of today's newscasts, shop talk, and run-of-the-mill conversations among Christians and non-Christians alike—must learn to "do all things without grumbling or disputing." Verbal pollution takes a heavy toll on everyone. Furthermore, who gave anyone the right to pollute the air with such pessimism? I agree with the person who said:

> We have no more right to put our discordant states of mind into the lives of those around us and rob them of their sunshine and brightness than we have to enter their houses and steal their silverware.[8]

I would love to hurry on past this subject, but I'd be less than honest if I left the impression that this is never my problem. I must confess that I, too, occasionally battle with negativism. When I do, it is usually my wife Cynthia who suffers the brunt of it. She has been pretty patient to endure it for more than thirty-seven years. I'm not as bad as I used to be, but every once in a while it surfaces.

Some of my readers know the ongoing debate that Cynthia and I have about bougainvillea. Years ago she really wanted us to plant several containers of bright red bougainvillea. It is a wonderful plant if you look at just the blossoms. But hidden within the plant are thorns . . . I mean those suckers are wicked! When Cynthia looks at bougainvillea, she sees only blossoms. When I look at the plant, I see only thorns. Unfortunately, there is a house not far from our home with a spectacular blooming bougainvillea climbing off the roof out front. Whenever we pass that house, Cynthia likes to drive a little slower and enjoy the blossoms. At certain times of the year she will point out, "Look how beautifully that bougainvillea is blooming." I will usually respond, without looking, "Do you realize the size of its thorns? I mean they are big . . . and they grow all over that plant. You may not see them, but if you walk close enough, you may never get free. It could catch you and hold you for half a morning."

Cynthia isn't convinced. She even said to me on one occasion, "Do you realize, honey, that every time—I mean *every time*—I mention bougainvillea, you grouse about the thorns?" (I might add that that conversation led to a dispute between us.)

In a lighthearted moment several years ago, I revealed our ongoing disagreement from the pulpit of our church, and much to my chagrin some anonymous soul sent us ten five-gallon containers of bougainvillea. I never told my wife, however, and we still have not planted bougainvillea. It is not God's will that we have bougainvillea. Too many thorns. Cynthia says she is confident that heaven will be full of bougainvillea. Since heaven is a perfect place, I maintain they would have to be a thornless species.

Positively, *prove that you are different!*

> . . . prove yourselves to be blameless and innocent, children of God above reproach in the midst of a crooked and perverse generation, among whom you appear as lights in the world, holding fast the word of life, so that in the day of Christ I may have cause to glory because I did not run in vain nor toil in vain.
>
> *Philippians 2:15–16*

Ours is a world of crooks and perverts, says my friend Ray Stedman, when he teaches this passage of Scripture. He is right. And since that is true, we need to model lives that are not like the majority. A positive attitude makes a major statement in our "crooked and perverse generation." We don't need to shout it out or make a superpious appearance; just don't grumble or dispute.

Paul goes further as he identifies four startling differences between those who know Christ and those who don't. These four descriptive words make all the difference in the world. Unlike our unbelieving friends, we are to be:

1. *Blameless.* This suggests a purity of life that is both undeniable and unhypocritical . . . free of defect.
2. *Innocent.* This means unmixed and unadulterated . . . inexperienced in evil . . . untainted in motive . . . possessing integrity.
3. *Above reproach.* This description is used of sacrificial lambs offered on altars and means free of blemish.
4. *Lights.* Actually the term used here means "luminaries," meaning we are to shine like stars surrounded by darkness.

In fact, Paul goes on to say that as we shine like stars, we are "holding fast the word of life."

Where did we pick up the mistaken idea of "This little light of mine, I'm gonna let it shine"? We are never called "little lights" in the Bible . . . we are *stars.* Bold, blazing, light-giving stars! This aching, hurting, confused world of lost humanity exists in dark rooms without light. Let it shine, fellow star! Why? Jesus answers that question in the sermon He delivered on the mountain:

> Let your light shine before men in such a way that they may see your good works, and glorify your Father who is in heaven.
>
> *Matthew 5:16*

No need to shout, scream, or make a scene. Just shine. Just live a life free of grumbling and disputing. The difference will jolt them awake. Furthermore, we will not live our lives "in vain." And speaking of that, Paul declares that he "did not run in vain nor toil in vain." What a claim to make as one begins to get up in years: No wasted effort!

My good friend David Roper, a pastor in Boise, Idaho, was, for a number of years, associate pastor alongside Ray Stedman at Peninsula Bible Church. You may know and appreciate Dave's ministry and writings, as I certainly do. Many years ago while Dave was ministering in Palo Alto on the campus of Stanford University, he arrived early one morning before the Bible study group had gathered. He was standing near an open courtyard and noticed an overgrown area where some kind of stonework was buried beneath vines and overgrowth. Dave's curiosity led him to go over and pull the vines away and tear back some of the overgrowth. When he did, he uncovered an ornate, hand-sculptured, stone birdbath. Though beautiful and unique, it was no longer being used. All the work the sculptor had put into that birdbath was wasted. When he saw this, Dave said he was moved to pray, "Lord, keep me from wasted effort. Don't let me build birdbaths with my life."

You and I can "run in vain and toil in vain" so easily. And afterward, looking back on that life, we will have to live with those vivid memories and feelings, "in vain . . . all wasted effort." We may not be in the category of a Ben Franklin, but we have the power of Jesus Christ working within us to give us all that is needed to make whatever impact He would have us make.

Balancing Seriousness and Joy

Not allowing our lives to become useless birdbaths—that is an extremely serious thought. But Paul gets even more serious:

> But even if I am being poured out as a drink offering upon the sacrifice and service of your faith, I rejoice and share my joy with you all. And you too, I urge you, rejoice in the same way and share your joy with me.
>
> *Philippians 2:17–18*

I find another word picture worth analyzing here. Paul speaks of the possibility of his "being poured out as a drink offering." This picture is drawn from a practice the pagans had of pouring out a chalice of wine before or after their meals in honor of the gods they worshiped. It was called a libation and was poured out either to gain the favor of or soften the anger of their gods.

Paul's thought is a serious analogy: I may never get out of this situation alive. It may be God's will that my life be poured out as a libation.

Even if that is so, even if it means the end of my life, this pouring out of my days on your behalf is worth every moment. Even if this imprisonment is my last, I rejoice!

I want to underscore something about Paul here: *There lived a balanced man.* While imagining that he might be living his final days, the single most serious thought a person could have, he was still able to rejoice. He refused to focus only on the dark side. He refused to let even the possibility of immediate and sure death steal his joy. In fact, he urged his friends to "rejoice in the same way."

Amazing! We cannot get through any major section of this letter without returning to Paul's themes of joy, rejoicing, and laughter. What a balanced man! A seasoned and scarred veteran missionary, yet all the while possessing a keen sense of humor. I have known a few men and women like that in my lifetime, and they never fail to bring refreshment and new hope. To remain superserious all the time and fill one's mind with only the harsh and painful realities of life keeps the radius of our perspective too tight and the tunnel of our hope too long. Paul refused to do that, and he wanted to make sure his Philippian friends followed suit.

Virtually every day I can find at least one thing to laugh about. There may be a few exceptions, but those days are rare indeed. Even though pain or difficult circumstances (Paul had both on a daily basis) may be our faithful companions, we encounter something each day that can prompt a chuckle or, for that matter, a hearty burst of laughter. And besides, it's healthy!

Experts tell us that laughter not only makes our serious lives lighter, but laughter also helps control pain in at least four ways: (1) by distracting our attention, (2) by reducing the tension we are living with, (3) by changing our expectations, and (4) by increasing the production of endorphins, the body's natural painkillers.[9] Laughter, strange as it may seem, turns our minds from our seriousness and pain and actually creates a degree of anesthesia. By diverting our attention from our situation, laughter enables us to take a brief excursion away from the pain.

Sometimes it is not literal pain but a too-serious mind-set. When our world begins to get too serious, we need momentary interruptions of just plain fun. A surprising day off, a long walk in the woods, a movie, an enjoyable evening relaxing with a friend over a bowl of popcorn, a game of racquetball or golf—these diversions can make all the difference in our ability to cope with life's crushing demands. We need to give ourselves permission to enjoy various moments in life even though all of life is not in perfect order. This takes practice, but it's worth the effort. It helps break guilt's stranglehold on us.

> Some saints can't enjoy a meal because the world is starving. They can't joyfully thank God for their clothing and shelter because the world is naked and homeless. They are afraid to smile because of the world's sadness. They're afraid to enjoy salvation because of the world's lost ones. They can't enjoy an evening at home with their families because they feel they ought to be out 'saving souls'. They can't spend an hour with an unforgiven one without feeling guilty if they haven't preached a sermon or manifested a 'sober Christian spirit'. They know nothing of balance. And they're miserable because of it. They have no inner incentive to bring people into a relationship with Christ which would make them feel as miserable as they themselves feel. They think the Gospel is 'good news' until you obey it and then it becomes an endless guilt-trip.
>
> There are leisure centres, sports centres, sewing centres, diet centres, entertainment centres and guilt centres. This last group is usually called 'Churches'. The endless harping on the string of guilt is part of the reason for all this gloom and uncertainty.[10]

Self, Our Battle

I want to close this chapter on balance with a warning. Old habits are terribly hard to break. Down inside of you is a voice that continues to nag you as you read these pages. It is saying, "No, no, no, No, NO!" As soon as you attempt to bring some necessary balance into your life, you are going to have a fight on your hands. After all, self has had its way for years. Giving you the freedom to laugh again and bring some needed joy into your life is not on self's agenda.

No matter. This invisible master needs to be brought back under the authority of Christ if you ever hope to laugh again. A life lived under the dominion of self is both unsatisfying and unproductive.

Here are a couple of suggestions for getting started:

1. Control self's urges to take the credit. When self reigns supreme, it lives for moments of personal gratification. Wean it away. Once you are able to see how out of balance you have become, you will have fresh strength to control its urges. Self needs to be bucked off its high horse.

John Wooden, former coach of the UCLA Bruins basketball team for so many national championship seasons, gives this helpful advice:

Talent is God-given, be humble;
Fame is man-given, be thankful;
Conceit is self-given, be careful.[11]

2. Conquer self's tendency to take charge. The longer you live the more you will realize the value of having Christ call the shots in your life. Not self, Christ. But that age-old battle will continue. Self wants to gain the mastery and convince you that it is a reusable source of energy. It is not. Self cannot be trusted. Any day you forget that and turn the controls over to self will be another day you will operate on strictly human energy, and you will lack the Spirit's power.

Back in the fall of 1990, I had an opportunity to minister to the military servicemen and women in Mannheim, Germany, along with two colleagues, Paul Sailhamer and Howie Stevenson. Since that area of Europe is Martin Luther Country, during our off-hours we visited the reformer's old haunts, the places he lived and wrote and served his Lord. There is something deeply invigorating about looking at a historic wall black with age or walking through a stone courtyard or standing in an ancient cathedral where a great man or woman once made history. It is as if that voice still speaks from the woodwork or that inimitable shadow still darkens the wall.

We stood where Luther stood at Worms when he defended himself before the Roman Church, a history-making moment known today as the Diet of Worms. There the most significant officials of the church had gathered to hear the German monk's declaration of the doctrine of salvation by grace alone—*Sola Fide.* In that emotion-charged moment he stood alone, unintimidated and resolute.

Just before Luther's audience with the pope, the prelates, the cardinals, and the emperor, a friend moved alongside the maverick monk and asked, "Brother Martin, are you afraid?" Luther responded with a marvelous answer: "Greater than the pope and all his cardinals, I fear most that great pope, self."[12]

And so should we. But if we hope to bring things back into balance—if we hope to change our habits of negative thinking, which leads to grumbling and a too-serious mentality—we'll have to dethrone this master and give the right Master His rightful place over our lives. Not until we do, I remind you, will we begin to laugh again.

7

Friends Make Life More Fun

IF I HAVE LEARNED ANYTHING during my journey on Planet Earth, it is that people need one another. The presence of other people is essential—caring people, helpful people, interesting people, friendly people, thoughtful people. These folks take the grind out of life. About the time we are tempted to think we can handle things all alone—boom! We run into some obstacle and need assistance. We discover all over again that we are not nearly as self-sufficient as we thought.

In spite of our high-tech world and efficient procedures, people remain the essential ingredient of life. When we forget that, a strange thing happens: We start treating people like inconveniences instead of assets.

This is precisely what humorist Robert Henry, a professional speaker, encountered one evening when he went to a large discount department store in search of a pair of binoculars.

> As he walked up to the appropriate counter he noticed that he was the only customer in the store. Behind the counter were two salespersons. One was so preoccupied talking to "Mama" on the telephone that she refused to acknowledge that Robert was there. At the other end of the counter, a second salesperson was unloading inventory from a box onto the shelves. Growing impatient, Robert walked down to her end of the counter and just stood there. Finally, she looked up at Robert and said, "You got a number?"
>
> "I got a what?" asked Robert, trying to control his astonishment at such an absurdity.
>
> "You got a number? You gotta have a number."
>
> Robert replied, "Lady, I'm the only customer in the store! I don't need a number. Can't you see how ridiculous this is?" But she failed to see the absurdity and insisted that Robert take a number before agreeing to

wait on him. By now, it was obvious to Robert that she was more interested in following procedures than helping the customer. So, he went to the take-a-number machine, pulled number 37 and walked back to the salesperson. With that, she promptly went to her number counter, which revealed that the last customer waited on had been holding number 34. So she screamed out, "35! . . . 35! . . . 36! . . . 36! . . . 37!"

"I'm number 37," said Robert.

"May I help you?" she asked, without cracking a smile.

"No," replied Robert, and he turned around and walked out.[1]

Now, there's a lady who's lost sight of the objective. I might question whether something like that ever happened if I had not experienced similar incidents in my own life. How easily some get caught up in procedures and lose sight of the major reason those procedures were established in the first place. Without people there would be no need for a store. Without people, who cares how efficient a particular airline may be? Without people a school serves no purpose, a row of houses no longer represents a neighborhood, a stadium is a cold concrete structure, and even a church building is an empty shell. I say again: We need each other.

A while back I came across the following piece that addresses this very subject with remarkable insight:

How Important Are You?

More than
you think.
A rooster
minus a hen
equals
no baby chicks.
Kellogg minus
a farmer
equals
no corn flakes.
If the nail
factory closes,
what good is the
hammer factory?
Paderewski's
genius wouldn't have
amounted to much
if the

piano tuner
hadn't shown up.
A cracker maker
will do better
if there's a
cheesemaker.
The most skillful
surgeon needs
the ambulance driver
who delivers the
patient.
Just as Rodgers
needed Hammerstein
you need someone
and someone
needs you.[2]

Since none of us is a whole, independent, self-sufficient, super-capable, all-powerful hotshot, let's quit acting like we are. Life's lonely enough without our playing that silly role.

The game's over. Let's link up.

People are important to each other. Above all, people are important to God. Which does not diminish His authority and self-sufficiency at all. The creation of humanity on the sixth day was the crowning accomplishment of the Lord's Creation handiwork. Furthermore, He put into mankind His very image, which He did not do for plant life or animals, birds, or fish. It was for the salvation of humanity, not brute beasts, that Christ came and died, and it will be for us that He will someday return. The major reason I am involved in a writing ministry and a broadcasting ministry and a church ministry is that people need to be reached and nurtured in the faith. This could be said of anyone serving the Lord Christ.

Couldn't God do it all? Of course, He is God—all-powerful and all-knowing and all-sufficient. That makes it all the more significant that He prefers to use us in His work. Even though He could operate completely alone on this earth, He seldom does. Almost without exception, He uses people in the process. His favorite plan is a combined effort: God plus people equals accomplishment.

I often recall the story of the preacher who saved up enough money to buy a few inexpensive acres of land. A little run-down, weather-beaten farmhouse sat on the acreage, a sad picture of years of neglect. The land had not been kept up either, so there were old tree stumps, rusted pieces of machinery, and all sorts of debris strewn here and there, not to mention a fence greatly in need of repair. The whole scene was a mess.

During his spare time and his vacations, the preacher rolled up his sleeves and got to work. He hauled off the junk, repaired the fence, pulled away the stumps, and replanted new trees. Then he refurbished the old house into a quaint cottage with a new roof, new windows, new stone walkway, new paint job, and finally a few colorful flower boxes. It took several years to accomplish all this, but finally, when the last job had been completed and he was washing up after applying a fresh coat of paint to the mailbox, his neighbor (who had watched all this from a distance) walked over and said, "Well, preacher—looks like you and the Lord have done a pretty fine job on your place here."

Wiping the sweat from his face, the minister replied, "Yeah, I suppose so . . . but you should have seen it when the Lord had it all to Himself."

God has not only created each one of us as distinct individuals, He also uses us in significant ways. Just stop and think: Chances are you are where you are today because of the words or the writings or the personal influence of certain people. I love to ask people how they became who they are. When I do, they invariably speak of the influence or the encouragement of key people in their past.

I would be the first to affirm that fact. When I look back across the landscape of my life, I am able to connect specific individuals to each crossroad and every milestone. Some of them are people the world will never know, for they are relatively unknown to the general public. But to me personally? Absolutely vital. And a few of them have remained my friends to this very day. Each one has helped me clear a hurdle or handle a struggle, accomplish an objective or endure a trial—and ultimately laugh again. I cannot even imagine where I would be today were it not for that handful of friends who have given me a heart full of joy. Let's face it, friends make life a lot more fun.

SPECIAL FRIENDS IN PAUL'S LIFE

It is easy to forget that the late, great apostle Paul needed friends too. Being ill on occasion, he needed Dr. Luke. Being limited in strength and unable to handle the rigors of extensive travel alone, he needed Barnabas and Silas. Being restricted in freedom, he needed other hands to carry his letters to their prescribed destinations. And on several occasions he needed someone to actually write out his letters. But isn't it interesting that though we know quite a bit about Paul, we know very little about his circle of friends? Yet in reality, they were part of the reason he was able to move through life as well as he did.

Returning to the letter he wrote to the Philippians, we come upon the mention of two names—a man Paul calls "my son" in another of his writings and a man he calls here "my brother." Since these two men played such significant roles in Paul's life that they deserved honorable mention, let's spend the balance of this chapter getting better acquainted with both. They were friends who made Paul's life richer and more enjoyable.

A "Son" Named Timothy

Being held under Roman guard in his house arrest, Paul found himself unable to travel back to Philippi, so he decided to send his young friend Timothy. More than any other individual, Timothy is mentioned by Paul in his writings. We saw his name earlier, in fact, in the opening line of this very letter: "Paul and Timothy, bond-servants of Christ Jesus."

Who was Timothy?

- He was a native of either Lystra or Derbe, cities in southern Asia Minor . . . today called Turkey.
- He was the child of a mixed marriage: Jewish mother (Eunice) and Greek father (never named).
- Since he remained uncircumcised until he was a young adult, Timothy's childhood upbringing was obviously more strongly influenced by the Greek than the Jewish parentage.
- However, his spiritual interest came from the maternal side of his family. Both Eunice and her mother Lois reared him to be tender toward the things of the Lord. We learn this from two comments Paul makes later in life in his second letter to his young friend.

> For I am mindful of the sincere faith within you, which first dwelt in your grandmother Lois, and your mother Eunice, and I am sure that it is in you as well.
>
> *2 Timothy 1:5*

You, however, continue in the things you have learned and become convinced of, knowing from whom you have learned them; and that from childhood you have known the sacred writings which are able to give you the wisdom that leads to salvation through faith which is in Christ Jesus.

2 Timothy 3:14–15

- Paul, no doubt, led Timothy into a personal relationship with the Lord Jesus Christ. This explains why the older referred to the younger as "my beloved and faithful child in the Lord" (1 Cor. 4:17).
- Once Timothy joined Paul (and Luke) as a traveling companion, the two remained close for the rest of Paul's life. We read of the beginning of their friendship in the early part of Acts 16.

> And he [Paul] came also to Derbe and to Lystra. And behold, a certain disciple was there, named Timothy, the son of a Jewish woman who was a believer, but his father was a Greek, and he was well spoken of by the brethren who were in Lystra and Iconium. Paul wanted this man to go with him; and he took him and circumcised him because of the Jews who were in those parts, for they all knew that his father was a Greek.
>
> *Acts 16:1–3*

So much for a quick survey of Timothy's background. What is of interest to us is how Paul wrote of him to the people of Philippi.

But I hope in the Lord Jesus to send Timothy to you shortly, so that I also may be encouraged when I learn of your condition. For I have no one else of kindred spirit who will genuinely be concerned for your welfare. For they all seek after their own interests, not those of Christ Jesus. But you know of his proven worth that he served with me in the furtherance of the gospel like a child serving his father. Therefore I hope to send him immediately, as soon as I see how things go with me; and I trust in the Lord that I myself also shall be coming shortly.

Philippians 2:19–24

As I ponder those words, three things jump out at me. All three have to do with how Paul viewed his friend.

First, *Timothy had a unique "kindred spirit" with Paul.* The single Greek term Paul used for "kindred spirit" is a combination of two words, actually: "same souled." This is the only time in all of the New Testament the term is used. We might say Paul and Timothy possessed an "equal spirit," or that they were "like-minded." Mathematically speaking, their triangles were congruent. Just think of the implications of the comment Paul makes: "I have no one else of kindred spirit."

They thought alike. Their perspectives were in line with each other. Timothy would interpret situations much like Paul, had the latter been there. In today's slang, they hit it off. When the older sent the younger on a fact-finding mission, he could rely on the report as being similar to one he himself would have brought back. Being of kindred spirit in no way suggests they had the same temperament or even that they always agreed. What it does mean, however, is that being alongside each other, neither had to work hard at the relationship; things flowed smoothly between them. I would imagine that it was not unlike the closeness David enjoyed with Jonathan, about which we read "the soul of Jonathan was knit to the soul of David, and Jonathan loved him as himself." And a little later, "he loved him as he loved his own life" (1 Sam. 18:1; 20:17).

Coming across a person with a kindred spirit is a rare find. We may have numerous casual acquaintances and several good friends in life, but finding someone who is like-souled is a most unusual (and delightful) discovery. And when it happens, both parties sense it. Neither has to convince the other that there is a oneness of spirit. It is like being with someone who lives in your own head—and vice versa—someone who reads your motives and understands your needs without either having to be stated. No need for explanations, excuses, or defenses. Paul enjoyed all these relational delights with Timothy, along with a spiritual dimension as well.

Second, *Timothy had a genuine concern for others.* That statement opens a window for us into the young man's makeup. When Timothy was with others, his heart was touched over their needs. Compassionate individuals are hard to find these days, but they were hard to find back in those days too. Remember what Paul wrote?

> For they all seek after their own interests, not those of Christ Jesus.
>
> *Philippians 2:21*

Not Timothy. Timothy modeled what Paul wrote earlier concerning an unselfish attitude.

> Do nothing from selfishness or empty conceit, but with humility of mind let each of you regard one another as more important than himself; do not merely look out for your own personal interests, but also for the interests of others.
>
> *Philippians 2:3–4*

That was Timothy. No wonder Paul felt so close to him. Friends like that remind us of the importance of helping others without saying a word. One man writes with understanding:

> A few years ago I stood on the banks of a river in South America and watched a young man in western clothes climb out of a primitive canoe. The veteran missionary with whom I was traveling beamed at the young man and whispered to me, "The first time I saw him he was a naked Indian kid standing right on this bank, and he pulled in my canoe for me. God gave me a real concern for him, and eventually he came to Christ, committed himself to the Lord's work and is just returning home after graduating from seminary in Costa Rica." I could understand the beam on the missionary's face, and I think Paul beamed when he talked of his men. And he had good cause to be thrilled with them.[3]

Third, *Timothy had a servant's heart.* Paul also mentioned Timothy's "proven worth," meaning "caliber"; he was that caliber of man. And what was that? He served like a child serving his father.

Question: How can one grown man serve on behalf of another grown man "like a child serving his father"?

Answer in one word: Servanthood.

In the world of leadership we are overrun with hard-charging, tough-minded, power-loving people who equate position with power. But people can wield power in any position, just as long as they maintain control over something others want.

Which reminds me of a homey little story that illustrates positional power. A new factory owner went to a nearby restaurant for a quick lunch. The menu featured a blue plate special and made it clear—absolutely no substitutions or additions. The meal was tasty, but the man needed more butter. When he asked for a second pat of butter, the waitress refused. He was so irritated he called for the manager . . . who also refused him and walked away (much to the waitress's delight). "Do you people know who I am?" he asked indignantly. "I am the owner of that factory across the street!" The waitress smiled sarcastically and whined, "Do you know who *I* am, sweetie? I'm the one who decides whether you get a second pat of butter."

Not all power moves are that blatant. Some leaders dangle others under their authority. I read a classic example of this in Leighton Ford's excellent book, *Transforming Leadership.*

> Eli Black, an entrepreneurial businessman, was well-known for two things. The high point of his life was when he engineered the takeover of the United Fruit Company. The end came when he jumped from the forty-second floor of the Pan American Building in New York.
>
> One of his executives, Thomas McCann, wrote about Black in his book *An American Company.* He describes a luncheon meeting with Black and two other managers.
>
> As they sat down, Black smiled and asked if they were hungry. McCann replied that he was starving. Moments later a waiter came with a plate of cheese and crackers. Black reached out and took it, but instead of passing it around he placed it before him and clasped his hands in front of it.
>
> "Now," he asked, "what's on the agenda?"
>
> For several minutes they talked about a building they were going to put up in Costa Rica. McCann, who had not had breakfast, kept his eyes on the cheese and crackers. The only way he could get to them would be to reach across his boss's arm, and Black's body language made it clear that that would be a violation of his territory.
>
> At a brief pause in the discussions, McCann said, "How about some cheese and crackers?" Black never even glanced at McCann, so he rephrased it. "You're not planning on eating those crackers and cheese all by yourself are you, Eli?" Again, no answer. The conversation continued, and McCann leaned back in his chair, giving up all hope of a snack.
>
> Moments later Black made it clear that there was nothing wrong with his hearing. He continued to question and make comments.
>
> Then, says McCann:
>
>> He unclasped his hands and picked up the knife. . . . I watched the knife dig down into the bowl of cheese; the other hand reached out and selected a Ritz cracker from the plate and Black poised the cracker on his fingertips as he carefully stroked a rounded, tantalizing mound of cheese across its face.
>>
>> The cracker remained balanced on the fingertips of Black's left hand for at least the next five minutes. He asked questions about the

height of the building from the street and its height above sea level . . . the color and materials . . . the size of the lobby. . . . My eyes never left the cracker. . . .

I leaned back again, this time accepting my defeat.

It was then that Black reached across the table and placed the cracker on my butter plate. He put the knife down where he had found it, and he refolded his hands before him, keeping the food within their embrace for himself alone to dispense or to keep. Black didn't say a word, but his expression made it clear that he felt he had made his point.

Eli Black symbolized perfectly one use of power. Next to truth, the power question is the most important issue for the leader. And it is precisely in relation to power that the leadership of Jesus stands in the greatest contrast to popular understandings of leadership.[4]

Unlike that entrepreneur, Timothy conformed to the Jesus model. He didn't strut his stuff. Like Paul, he served. By sending Timothy to the people of Philippi, Paul felt he was sending *himself.* No fear of offense. No anxiety over how the young man might handle some knotty problem he might encounter. Not even a passing thought that he might throw his weight around, saying, "As Paul's right-hand man. . . ." The aging apostle could rest easy. Timothy was the man for the job. Paul must have smiled when he finally waved good-bye. Friends like Timothy relieve life's pressure and enable us to smile.

A "Brother" Named Epaphroditus

Because the two men were closer, Paul wrote of who Timothy was. But when he mentions this second gentleman, Epaphroditus, he puts his finger on what he did. Another contrast: Timothy would be going to Philippi sometime in the future, but Epaphroditus would be sent immediately, probably carrying this letter Paul was writing.

Epaphroditus had been sent to Rome to minister to Paul, but shortly after arriving the man became terribly ill. Ultimately he recovered, but not before a long struggle where he lingered at death's door. News of his illness might have traveled back to Philippi, and the man was concerned that his friends back home would be worried about him. Furthermore, when he returned earlier than expected, some might think he returned as a quitter, so Paul was careful to write strong words in his defense.

> But I thought it necessary to send to you Epaphroditus, my brother and fellow worker and fellow soldier, who is also your messenger and minister to my need; because he was longing for you all and was distressed because you had heard that he was sick. For indeed he was sick to the point of death, but God had mercy on him, and not on him only but also on me, lest I should have sorrow upon sorrow. Therefore I have sent him all the more eagerly in order that when you see him again you may rejoice and I may be less concerned about you. Therefore receive him in the Lord with all joy, and hold men like him in high regard; because he came close to death for the work of Christ, risking his life to complete what was deficient in your service to me.
>
> *Philippians 2:25–30*

And toward the end of the same letter . . .

> But I have received everything in full, and have an abundance; I am amply supplied, having received from Epaphroditus what you have sent, a fragrant aroma, an acceptable sacrifice, well-pleasing to God.
>
> *Philippians 4:18*

When Epaphroditus first arrived, he brought a gift of money from the Philippians. This tells us the people back home trusted him completely. When he gave the gift to Paul, he brought enormous encouragement to the apostle . . . but shortly thereafter, Epaphroditus fell ill. So the apostle writes with deep affection, referring to him as, "brother . . . fellow worker . . . fellow soldier . . . messenger . . . minister to my need." I'd call those admirable qualities in a friend. Bishop Lightfoot says that Epaphroditus was one in "common sympathy, common work, and common danger and toil and suffering"[5] with the great apostle. When you've got someone near you with credentials like that, life doesn't seem nearly as heavy.

- Why did Paul send Epaphroditus back? To put the people at ease and to cause them to rejoice (there's that word again) upon hearing from Paul by letter.
- What was to be their response back home? Extend a joyful welcome and hold Epaphroditus in high regard.
- Why did he deserve their respect? Because he had risked his life in coming to minister to Paul . . . he had exposed

> himself to danger. We would say he had flirted with death to be near his friend.

In those days when people visited prisoners who were held captive under Roman authority, they were often prejudged as criminal types as well. Therefore, a visitor exposed himself to danger just by being near those who were considered dangerous. The Greek term Paul uses here for "risking"—*paraboleuomai*—is one that meant "to hazard with one's life . . . to gamble." Epaproditus did just that.

> In the early church there were societies of men and women who called themselves *the parabolani,* that is, *the riskers or gamblers.* They ministered to the sick and imprisoned, and they saw to it that, if at all possible, martyrs and sometimes even enemies would receive an honorable burial. Thus in the city of Carthage during the great pestilence of A.D. 252 Cyprian, the bishop, showed remarkable courage. In self-sacrificing fidelity to his flock, and love even for his enemies, he took upon himself the care of the sick, and bade his congregation nurse them and bury the dead. What a contrast with the practice of the heathen who were throwing the corpses out of the plague-stricken city and were running away in terror![6]

A special joy binds two friends who are not reluctant to risk danger on each other's behalf. If a true friend finds you're in need, he or she will find a way to help. Nor will a friend ever ask, "How great is the risk?" The question is always, "When do you need me?" Not even the threat of death holds back a friend.

This reminds me of the six-year-old girl who became deathly ill with a dread disease. To survive, she needed a blood transfusion from someone who had previously conquered the same illness. The situation was complicated by her rare blood type. Her nine-year-old brother qualified as a donor, but everyone was hesitant to ask him since he was just a lad. Finally they agreed to have the doctor pose the question.

The attending physician tactfully asked the boy if he was willing to be brave and donate blood for his sister. Though he didn't understand much about such things, the boy agreed without hesitation: "Sure, I'll give my blood for my sister."

He lay down beside his sister and smiled at her as they pricked his arm with the needle. Then he closed his eyes and lay silently on the bed as the pint of blood was taken.

Soon thereafter the physician came in to thank the little fellow. The boy, with quivering lips and tears running down his cheeks, asked, "Doctor, when do I die?" At that moment the doctor realized that the naive little boy thought that by giving his blood, he was giving up his life. Quickly he reassured the lad that he was not going to die, but amazed at his courage, the doctor asked, "Why were you willing to risk your life for her?"

"Because she is my sister . . . and I love her," was the boy's simple but significant reply.

So it was between Epaphroditus and his brother in Rome . . . and so it is to this day. Danger and risk don't threaten true friendship; they strengthen it. Such friends are modern-day members of *the parabolani,* that reckless band of friends—riskers and gamblers, all—who love their brothers and sisters to the uttermost. Each one deserves our respect. When we need them, they are there. I have a few in that category. Hopefully, you do too.

Three People Who Deserve a Response

As I think about how all this ties in with our lives today, I am reminded of three categories of special people and how we are to respond to them.

First, there are still a few Timothys left on earth, thank goodness. *When God sends a Timothy into our lives, He expects us to relate to him.* It is often the beginning of an intimate friendship, rarely experienced in our day of superficial companionship. With a Timothy, you won't have to force a friendship; it will flow. Nor will you find yourself dreading the relationship; it will be rewarding. When a Timothy comes along, don't hesitate . . . *relate.*

Second, there may be a modern-day Epaphroditus who comes to your assistance or your rescue. *When God sends an Epaphroditus to minister to us, He expects us to respect him.* This is the type of person who reaches out when he has nothing to gain and perhaps much to lose . . . who gambles on your behalf for no other reason than love. His or her action is an act of grace. Don't question it or try to repay it or make attempts to bargain for it. Just accept it. Grace extended in love is to be accepted with gratitude. The best response to an Epaphroditus? *Respect.*

And there is a third person I haven't said much about in a personal way. But since we are approximately halfway through Paul's letter, as well as this book, it is time I introduced you to this third friend. His name is Jesus Christ. *Since God sent Christ to take away our sins and bring us to heaven, He expects us to receive Him.* If you think a Timothy can mean a lot to you or an Epaphroditus could prove invaluable, let me assure you that neither can compare as a substitute for Jesus. With nail-scarred hands He reaches out to you and waits for you to reach back in faith. I tell you without a moment's hesitation, there is no one you will ever meet, no friend you will ever make, who can do for you what Jesus can do. No one else can change your inner heart. No one else can turn your entire life around. No one else can remove not only your sins but the guilt and shame that are part of that whole ugly package. And now that the two of you have been introduced, only one response is appropriate. Only one. *Receive.*

I began this chapter by stating that people need other people. You need me. I need you. Both of us need a few kindred spirits, people who understand us and encourage us. Both of us need friends who are willing to risk to help us and, yes, at times, to rescue us. Friends like that make life more fun. But all of us—you, me, Timothy-people, Epaphroditus-people, *all of us*—need a Savior. He awaits your response. The everlasting relief He brings is enough to make us not only laugh again, but laugh forever.

8

Happy Hopes for High Achievers

LAST NIGHT I MET A MAN who told me he needed to work harder at being happier.

He said he had been reared in an ultraserious home. "We didn't talk about our feelings . . . *we worked.* My father, my mother, most of my sisters and brothers bought into that way of life," he sighed. "Somehow we all had the idea that you could achieve whatever you wanted in life if you just worked hard enough and long enough." And then he came to the crux of his concern: "Funny thing . . . in my sixty-plus years I have achieved about everything I dreamed of doing and I have been awarded for it. My problem is that I don't know how to have fun and enjoy all these things hard work has brought me. I cannot remember the last time I laughed—I mean *really* laughed."

As he turned to walk away, I thought this throwaway line was the most revealing thing he said: "I suppose I now need to work harder at being happier."

I reached over, took him by the arm, and pulled him back close enough to put my arms around him for a solid, manly hug. "You've worked hard for everything else in your life," I said quietly. "Why not try a new approach for joy? Trust me on this one—a happy heart is not achieved by hard work and long hours. If it were, the happiest people on earth would be the workaholics . . . and I have never met a workaholic whose sense of humor balanced out his intensity." We talked a few more minutes, but I'm not sure I made a dent in his thinking. Most likely, at this very moment that high achiever is up and at it (it's early Monday morning) pursuing a game plan to earn happiness. *It ain't gonna happen.*

The problem is that human achievement results in earthly rewards, which fuels the fire for more achievement leading to greater rewards.

"Problem . . . what problem?" you and the man I met last night may ask. This: None of that results in deep-down satisfaction, an inner peace, a soul-level contentment, or lasting joy. In the process of achieving more and earning more, few if any learn to laugh more. This is especially true if you're the classic Type A. Hear me out.

Something within all of us warms up to human strokes. We are motivated to do more when our efforts are noticed and rewarded. That is why they make things like impressive trophies and silver platters and bronze plaques and gold medals. Most folks love putting those things on display. Whether it is an athletic letter on a sweater in high school or a Salesperson-of-the-Month plaque on the wall, we like the recognition. What does it do? It drives us on to do more, to gain greater recognition, to achieve more valuable rewards, better pay, or higher promotions.

Virtually every major field of endeavor has its particular award for outstanding achievement. Universities award scholarships; companies give bonuses; the film industry offers the Oscar; the television industry, the Emmy; the music industry, the Grammy; and the writing industry, the Pulitzer Prize. The athletic world has an entire spectrum of honors. Whether garnering individual awards for exceptional achievement or team trophies for championship play, winning players are applauded and record-setting coaches are affirmed (and envied). Furthermore, most folks are awed simply by being around celebrities. Recently I read a funny story that perfectly illustrates this fact:

> A tourist was standing in line to buy an ice cream cone at a Thrifty Drug store in Beverly Hills. To her utter shock and amazement, who should walk in and stand right behind her but Paul Newman! Well the lady, even though she was rattled, determined to maintain her composure. She purchased her ice cream cone and turned confidently and exited the store.
>
> However, to her horror, she realized that she had left the counter without her ice cream cone! She waited a few minutes till she felt all was clear, and then went back into the store to claim her cone. As she approached the counter, the cone was not in the little circular receptacle, and for a moment she stood there pondering what might have happened to it. The she felt a polite tap on her shoulder, and turning was confronted by—you guessed it—Paul Newman. The famous actor then told the lady that if she was looking for her ice cream cone, she had put it into her purse![1]

While I was sitting in the Great Western Forum the other evening watching the Los Angeles Lakers, I looked up toward the ceiling and saw all those NBA championship banners hanging high. I glanced toward one wall bright with spotlights and read the names on jerseys that have been retired: Baylor, Chamberlain, West, Abdul-Jabbar, and, most recently, Johnson. What an honor to have one's name placed on public display for all the world to see! It is society's way of saying, "You are great!"

There is nothing wrong with that as long as we remember it is an earthly system exalting earthly people who are rewarded for earthly accomplishments. But how easy it is to forget that not one of those accomplishments gives a person what he or she may lack deep within—that's why they can't bring lasting satisfaction. And much more importantly, none of them earns God's favor.

The Great Temptation among High Achievers

All this leads me to a terribly important subject I have been wanting to address. Having had that conversation with Mr. High Achiever last evening, I'm unable to restrain myself any longer . . . and I especially have in mind those of you who can't stand coming in second because you face a great temptation.

What is it? It is the temptation to believe that earthly honors will automatically result in heavenly rewards. This kind of thinking is at the root of a humanistic philosophy of life that says: "By working hard and accomplishing more than most, I will earn God's favor and receive His nod of approval." I don't know of a more subtle, albeit heretical, philosophy than that, yet it is universally accepted as true. And so, the tragedy is, enough is never enough. Life is reduced to work, tasks, effort, an endless list of shoulds and musts . . . minus the necessary fun and laughter that keeps everything in perspective.

Why does it happen? What is it that drives us on so relentlessly? Are you ready? Take a deep breath and allow yourself to tolerate the one-word answer: PRIDE. We work and push and strive so we can prove we are worthy . . . we are the best . . . we deserve top honors. And the hidden message: I can gain righteousness all on my own, by my own effort, ingenuity, and energy. And because I can, I must! And why is this heretical? Because ultimately this philosophy says: (1) I really won't need divine righteousness (after all, God helps those who help themselves, right?), and (2) I will find lasting joy in my own achievement. This will bring me ultimate satisfaction. Both are dead-end roads found on Fantasy Island.

A longtime friend of mine openly confessed:

> Work had always been highly esteemed in our family, and hard work was seen as the primary tool for success. I figured if it were good to work ten hours, it would be even better to work fourteen.
>
> In college, I seemed to have the energy to withstand the pressure. I remember times at Stanford when I wouldn't even go home at night. Instead, I would push a table up near the door of the cafeteria at 3 a.m. and sleep on it, using my books as a pillow. And then in the morning, when I had to be at work, the first person to open the door would knock me off the table, and I'd wake up and start the day. I convinced myself that I was sleeping "faster" than anyone else. . . .
>
> During the years when I was a coach and an area director for Young Life, I would work twelve, fourteen, even fifteen hours a day, six or seven days a week. And I would come home feeling that I hadn't worked enough. So I tried to cram even more into my schedule. I spent more time promoting living than I did living. . . . My life wasn't abundant; it was a frantic sprint from one hour to the next.
>
> I can remember times when fatigue left me feeling isolated and alienated—feelings that previously had been foreigners to me. Unprepared for such parasites on my energy, I became frustrated, and laughter, which had always been my most treasured companion, had silently slipped away. . . .
>
> I was dominated by "shoulds," and "ought to's," and "musts." I would awaken unrefreshed in the morning, with a tired kind of resentment, and hurry through the day trying to uncover and meet the demands of others. Days were not lived but endured. I was exhausted trying to be a hope constantly rekindled for others, straining to live up to their images of me. I had worked hard to develop a reputation as one who was concerned, available, and involved—now I was being tyrannized by it. Often I was more at peace in the eyes of others than in my own.
>
> The Western mind and culture leave little time for leisure, prayer, play, and contemplation. Hurry needs answers; answers need categories; categories need labeling and dissecting. The pace I was trying to maintain had no time for rhythm and awe, for mystery and wonder. I barely had time to care adequately for friends or for myself. In order to keep up my incessant activity, God was simply reduced to fit into my schedule. I suffered, because he didn't fit.[2]

Pride not only expresses itself in high-achieving hard work, but also keeps us from asking for help. We love to leave the impression that no matter what, we can handle it—no help wanted!

I remember when my family and I lived in New England. We weren't accustomed to snow in the winter. It threw us a real nasty curve. We found ourselves somewhat confused when we faced our first wintry blast. For example, I couldn't figure out why people didn't park on the street. I thought, *That's the best place in the world . . . nobody parks there. In fact, there are no "No Parking" signs anywhere.* So I parked on the street. I remember being sort of proud of my original idea when I locked the car for the night. That was about the time the snow began to fall. In fact, it snowed all night. It never even dawned on me that snowplows worked the street all night long, pushing back the fallen snow.

The next morning when I crawled out of our warm bed, I discovered why nobody parked on the street. I looked out front and thought somebody had stolen my car! Stunned to find huge mounds of crusted snow and ice on both sides of the street, I took my pick and shovel and began to do archaeological work in hopes of finding a blue four-door sedan. After digging like mad for at least twenty minutes, I finally got to something hard. When I saw blue I thought, *That's my color . . . must be my car.* About that time a friend drove by. He stopped, smiled, rolled down his window, and asked, "Hey, Chuck, can I help you?" I immediately responded, "No, thanks—I'm doing fine." He shrugged and drove on. About half an hour later I wondered why I hadn't said yes. The simple answer: I was proud. I could dig out my own car, thank you. Stupid pride!

You know what else I did? When I finally got down to my ice-covered car and saw all the ice on the windows, my first thought was, *It's dumb to stand here and scrape off all that ice.* So I went inside and got a bucket of steaming hot water and dumped it over the front window. Trust me, not only did the ice come off, so did my windshield. I was stunned as it shattered with a loud bang and fell into the front seat. I thought, *So that's why everybody scrapes the ice off windshields.* Let me tell you, when I drove the car to the glass shop, I had clear vision! It was ten degrees in the car, but I had clear vision.

Do you know the first thing I did when I broke my front window? I looked around to see if anybody was watching. Why? Pride, plain and simple. I didn't want anyone to know what a foolish thing I had done. Pride encourages us to hide our stupidity rather than admit it. And I remember that throughout the entire episode I did not have much fun. I don't recall laughing either at myself or at my circumstance.

There is always that one telltale sign when pride takes charge: the fun leaves. A driven high achiever may smile on occasion, but it is a surface grin, not a strong, quiet sense of satisfaction. Deep within, he or she is really thinking, *Life is much too busy, much too serious to waste it on silly things like relaxation and laughter.* Staying wound up that tight can cause the mind to snap. G. K. Chesterton was never more correct than when he wrote, "Madmen are always serious; they go mad from lack of humour."[3]

THE HONEST TESTIMONY OF A HIGH-ACHIEVING PHARISEE

All this brings us back to a little letter written to a small band of believers living in ancient Philippi. Because the writer, Paul, felt so close to them, he wasn't afraid to be honest and allow them to see the dark side of his past. But before doing so he underscores the underlying theme of his letter by reminding them to find the joy in living.

> Finally, my brethren, rejoice in the Lord. To write the same things again is no trouble to me, and it is a safeguard for you.
>
> *Philippians 3:1*

The Living Bible says:

> Whatever happens, dear friends, be glad in the Lord. I never get tired of telling you this and it is good for you to hear it again and again.

Paul is about to launch into his past—those intense years of his own existence when he worked so hard to impress God. But before he does that, he wants to make sure that they hear yet again the importance of being people of outrageous joy. He calls that "a safeguard." How true. Not only were the pressures of life enough to steal their joy, there were also the ever-present legalists—ancient grace killers—on the loose. And nobody can rob people of joy quicker than a few narrow-minded legalists. Paul's great concern was that his Philippian friends continue to enjoy their freedom in Christ and not allow *anything* or *anyone* to get the best of them. He never got tired of telling them that.

A Warning to His Close Friends

I am not dreaming up the idea that legalists were on the loose. Neither have I been too strong in my comments. Paul himself calls them "dogs . . . evil workers." See for yourself:

> Beware of the dogs, beware of the evil workers, beware of the false circumcision.
>
> *Philippians 3:2*

Strong words! When he refers to them as dogs, Paul doesn't have in mind the little lap dogs we enjoy as pets or those obedient, loyal creatures we pamper and nourish. No, the dogs of his day were dirty, disease-carrying scavengers who ran in packs through the streets and narrow alleys of a city. Unable to be controlled and potentially dangerous, they posed a menacing threat to anyone who got in their way. With that word picture in mind, Paul warns, "Watch out . . . beware! These people will assault you and you will lose your joy."

He goes further: "Beware of evil workers." These legalists taught that people were saved by works—by keeping the Law (an impossibility). Such folks live on to this day, spreading their heresy. Their message is full of exhortations to do more, to work harder, to witness longer, to pray with greater intensity, because enough is never enough. Such folks are "evil workers" who will take away what little bit of joy you may be able to muster. I would also add that when you never know how much is enough to satisfy God, you are left in a continual state of shame and obligation. Your mind never rests. The message of the legalists always finds you lacking. It never brings relief. We need to beware of such messengers. They are, according to Scripture, evil workers.

By calling them "false circumcision" people, Paul meant they believed in mutilation, not merely circumcision, for salvation. They taught, if circumcision was good, castration was even better! One *must* (there's that word again) work exceptionally hard to be acceptable to God—give up, take on, put away, add to, try harder, contribute more—before there could be assurance of divine acceptance. The result of all that? Confidence in the flesh! You worked hard . . . you sacrificed . . . you labored intensely . . . you received it. And in the process you had every reason to be proud of it. I say again . . . heresy!

With quiet and firm reassurance, Paul communicates the simple truth to his friends:

> For we are the true circumcision, who worship in the Spirit of God and glory in Christ Jesus and put no confidence in the flesh.
>
> *Philippians 3:3*

Those last six words—"put no confidence in the flesh"—what a helpful relief! God's grace has again come to our rescue. And in the process He gets the glory. All the credit goes to Him, as certainly it should. When it comes to our vertical and eternal relationship with God, unlike the humanist's message, we put no confidence in the flesh. Salvation through human works? No way. Human pride? No reason. The gift that brings back the laughter—God's gift of eternal life with Him—is based on what He has done for us and not what we have done for Him. Maybe you need to read that sentence again. It explains why we put no confidence in the flesh. Those who do have missed the whole point of grace.

A Revealing of His Proud Record

These words about "confidence in the flesh" triggered a lot of emotion in Paul. While writing them he must have experienced a flashback to the way he was for so many years—in fact, all of his adult life. Before his conversion, he was the personification of a proud Pharisee. Nobody's trophy case was larger. Had they given an award for high achievement in the field of religion, Paul would have won top honors in his nation year after year after year. His wall could have been covered with plaques, diplomas, framed letters from influential individuals, and numerous artifacts—all impressive.

> . . . If anyone else has a mind to put confidence in the flesh, I far more.
>
> *Philippians 3:4*

When he writes those words, Paul is not padding the report or trying to appear important. As we are about to read, he had earned the respect of every law-keeping Judaizer in the known world. When he said, "I far more," he had the record to prove it. For example:

> Circumcised the eighth day, of the nation of Israel, of the tribe of Benjamin, a Hebrew of Hebrews; as to the Law, a Pharisee; as to zeal, a persecutor of the church; as to the righteousness which is in the Law, found blameless.
>
> *Philippians 3:5–6*

That pedigree and brief list of achievements may not seem impressive to you today, especially if you are not Jewish, but do not discount their significance. Paul was the ultimate high achiever of his day. As one New Testament scholar explains:

> If ever there was a Jew who was steeped in Judaism, that Jew was Paul. Let us . . . look again at the claims he had to be the Jew *par excellence*. . . . He was circumcised on the eighth day; that is to say, he bore in the body the badge and the mark that he was one of the chosen people, marked out by God as His own. He was of the race of Israel; that is to say, he was a member of the nation who stood in a covenant relationship with God, a relationship in which no other people stood. He was of the tribe of Benjamin. This is a claim which Paul reiterates in *Romans* 11:1. What is the point of this claim? The tribe of Benjamin had a unique place in the history of Israel. It was from Benjamin that the first king of Israel had come, for Saul was a Benjamite . . . . Benjamin was the only one of the patriarchs who had actually been born in the land of promise. When Israel went into battle, it was the tribe of Benjamin which held the post of honour. The battle-cry of Israel was: "After thee, O Benjamin". . . .
>
> In lineage Paul was not only an Israelite; he was of the aristocracy of Israel. He was a Hebrew of the Hebrews; that is to say, Paul was not one of these Jews of the Dispersion who, in a foreign land, had forgotten their own tongue; he was a Jew who still remembered and knew the language of his fathers.
>
> He was a Pharisee; that is to say, he was not only a devout Jew; he was more—he was one of "The Separated Ones" who had foresworn all normal activities in order to dedicate life to the keeping of the Law, and he had kept it with such meticulous care that in the keeping of it he was blameless.
>
> . . . Paul knew Judaism at its best and at its highest; he knew it from the inside; he had gone through all the experiences, both of height and of depth, that it could bring to any man.[4]

Did you observe how Paul categorized his achievements? On an accelerated scale:

- "As to the Law"
- "As to zeal"
- "As to righteousness"

It is the last one that stands out—the ultimate! "When I added up all those things in my mind, I had arrived. When compared to all others, I qualified as *righteous.*" Paul outstripped all his contemporaries, eclipsed all other lights. As A. T. Robertson summed up so eloquently, Paul had—

> A marvellous record, scoring a hundred in Judaism. . . . He was the star of hope for Gamaliel and the Sanhedrin.[5]

In today's terms, that proud Pharisee known as Saul of Tarsus won all the marbles—the Pulitzer, the Medal of Honor, the Most Valuable Player, the Heisman, the Gold Medal . . . the Nobel of Ancient Jewry. Had they had newspapers or magazines in his day, his picture would have been on the front page, and the headlines would have read, RELIGIOUS ZEALOT OF THE DECADE. His was the name dropped by everybody who was anybody. Any search for a model to follow would have led to the scholar from Tarsus, but you would have to move fast to stay up. He wasn't nearly finished with his plan to rid the world of Christians. The last entry in his Daytimer read, "Next stop: Damascus." On that fateful trip, everything changed.

A Change in His Entire Life

While riding the crest of that wave of international fame, Saul of Tarsus met his match in the person of Jesus Christ. While still on the outskirts of the city of Damascus, he was suddenly struck blind by a blazing light from heaven and silenced by a voice that must have sounded like the roar of a dozen Niagaras: "Saul . . . Saul . . . why are you persecuting Me?" Though blinded by the light, at that moment the Pharisee got his first glimpse of perfect righteousness. And for the first time in his life he was humbled. His robes of self-righteousness were nothing more than filthy rags. All his trophies and plaques and impressive earthly honors were as worthless as wood, hay, and stubble. One glimpse of true, heaven-sent righteousness was enough to convince him forever that he had spent his entire life on the wrong road traveling at breakneck speed toward the wrong destination for all the wrong reasons.

Now we can appreciate the importance of that little word "but" in the midst of Paul's listing of all his achievements:

> But whatever things were gain to me, those things I have counted as loss for the sake of Christ. More than that, I count all things to be loss in view of the surpassing value of knowing Christ Jesus my Lord, for whom I have suffered the loss of all things, and count them but rubbish in order that I may gain Christ, and may be found in Him, not having a righteousness of my own derived from the Law, but that which is through faith in Christ, the righteousness which comes from God on the basis of faith.
>
> *Philippians 3:7–9*

But! God called an abrupt and absolute halt to Saul's maddening pace. His entire frame of reference was altered. His whole perspective changed. His way of thinking and, of course, his way of life were radically transformed from that day forward. He saw, for the first time, how utterly and completely misguided he had been. As this newfound, divine perspective replaced the old hunger for earthly applause and the old drive for human righteousness, he felt himself bankrupt, reduced to ground zero. And all those honors he had worked for and relished for so long? He counted them as "loss" and "rubbish." Having clothed himself in the pride of self-achievement, he now stood stark naked and spiritually bankrupt. Having once set records when evaluated by other men and women, he now realized what a total failure he had been when appraised by his Master and Lord. And at that epochal moment divine righteousness was credited to his empty account, and he saw himself reclothed in the imputed righteousness of Christ. That changed everything within him and about him.

A Statement of His Consuming Passion

Did all of life stop there? Was that all there was to it? Hardly. That was when Paul really started to live. It was at that point the man began to laugh again! With a transformed heart he testified that his desire regarding Christ was that he might—

> . . . know Him, and the power of His resurrection and the fellowship of

> His sufferings, being conformed to His death; in order that I may attain to the resurrection from the dead.
>
> *Philippians 3:10–11*

It is difficult to believe that a man as hard-charging and determined as Saul of Tarsus could pen such tender words. Look at them again. Perhaps we could call them Paul's credo. Rather than being driven by confidence in the flesh, his consuming passion was to spend the balance of his years on earth knowing Christ more intimately, drawing upon His resurrection power more increasingly, entering into His sufferings more personally, and being conformed to His image more completely. His dreams of making it all on his own were forever dashed on the solid rock of Jesus Christ.

THE PLAIN TRUTH TO ALL WHO RESPOND

If you are among the high achievers I've been writing to in this chapter, I commend you for reading this far. These are not the kinds of things you normally think about, I realize. Your world doesn't leave much room for personal weakness, does it? You don't rely on help from anything (or anyone) but your own reservoir of resourcefulness, do you? All your life you've been coming on strong, fighting and pushing for top honors and hopefully getting your own sweet way, haven't you? The things you are most proud of are your achievements, naturally, for that's really all you've got to show for all your hard work. In many ways, you've arrived, at least in the opinion of others. Yours is an enviable list of accomplishments. Let me name a few:

- Your respected position with a nice-sounding title
- Your salary with some enviable perks
- Your growing popularity among your peers
- Those awards you've hung on your walls
- That fine automobile sitting in your parking space (and that parking space!)
- A wardrobe full of elegant and stylish clothes
- A nice place to go home to . . . maybe more than a summer home . . . a winter home

- The probability of accomplishing and earning more
- A sense of power in knowing you can buy whatever you want any time you want it
- The feeling of accomplishment—you did it!

Granted, those are the kinds of things most folks you know spend their entire lives hoping to achieve. And now you find yourself a member of that elite club: High Achievers Anonymous (except by then they're not usually anonymous). Maybe we could say they are members of the MITTT Club—*Made It to the Top.*

But let's look deeper. Let's look at another list:

- How is your personal life? I'm referring to the real you that's there when nobody's looking . . . like when you're all alone in your car or boat or plane. Are you personally contented and at peace?
- And what about your marriage? And your relationship with your children? Everything okay there?
- While you are allowing me to get this close, may we take a look at your inner person? Are you secure or still rather afraid? Any habits out of control? Any addictions you can't seem to conquer?
- Let me ask a few what ifs: What if you became ill? What if you lost your earning power? What if you lost your title? What if your next physical exam led to the discovery of a lump . . . and that lump proved malignant? What if you had a stroke? Are you ready to die?
- Are there some secrets that haunt you? Are there some terrorizing worries that won't go away . . . that money won't erase?
- Finally, has life become more fun for you? Do you laugh—I mean really laugh—now that you have "arrived"? Or are you still too driven to relax?

If you've answered those questions honestly—or even taken the time to read them—then you're ready to hear the rest.

First, spending your life trusting in your own achievements brings you the glory now but leaves you spiritually bankrupt forever. Read that again, please. And as you do, think of that first-century man we've been reading about, Saul of Tarsus. Think of what his life would have been if he had never responded positively to the claims of Christ.

Second, stopping today and trusting in Christ's accomplishment on the cross will give Him the glory now and provide you with perfect righteousness forever.

You're intelligent, so let me ask you: *Which option makes better sense?* And just in case you think high achievers can't change, remember that man from Tarsus. He didn't merely exchange one religion for another . . . he didn't swap off one system of rites and ceremonies for another system of rules and regulations. The popular opinion these days is that folks need to change their religion or start going to a different church. That is nonsense. Saul didn't get a new religion or merely change churches after his Damascus Road experience. He was thoroughly and radically converted, like the man who wrote these words:

> I had walked life's path with an easy tread,
> Had followed where comfort and pleasure led;
> And then by chance in a quiet place—
> I met my Master face to face.
>
> With station and rank and wealth for goal,
> Much thought for body but none for soul,
> I had entered to win this life's mad race—
> When I met my Master face to face.
>
> I had built my castles, reared them high,
> Till their towers had pierced the blue of the sky;
> I had sworn to rule with an iron mace—
> When I met my Master face to face.
>
> I met Him and knew Him, and blushed to see
> That His eyes full of sorrow were fixed on me;
> And I faltered, and fell at His feet that day
> While my castles vanished and melted away.
>
> Melted and vanished; and in their place
> I saw naught else but my Master's face;
> And I cried aloud: "Oh, make me meet
> To follow the marks of Thy wounded feet."

My thought is now for the souls of men;
I have lost my life to find it again
Ever since alone in that holy place
My master and I stood face to face.[6]

9

Hanging Tough Together . . . and Loving It

ONE DAY EVERY YEAR LITTLE BOYS all across America dream big dreams. They may not say so, but inside their heads are mental images of themselves being viewed by millions of people all around the world. In their imaginations they will one day wear the uniform and be a part of some championship team battling for the ultimate prize, a sparkling silver trophy in the shape of a football. We call that day of dreams "Super Bowl Sunday." Amazingly, a few of those little boys who dream big dreams do wind up playing in the big game.

Over twenty-five years ago when the first Super Bowl game was played, a ten-year-old boy sat beside his father in the stands of the Los Angeles Coliseum. As he watched players like Bart Starr, Paul Hornung, Boyd Dowler, Fuzzy Thurston, Carrol Dale, and other outstanding athletes on Vince Lombardi's great Green Bay Packers team dominate their opponents, he daydreamed of one day being down on that gridiron. And that is exactly what happened as James Lofton, a wide receiver for the Buffalo Bills (and the oldest man on the team), finally made it to the top and had his dream come true. Through strong and weak seasons, team changes, and several injuries as a professional football player, Lofton persevered—and his determination paid off. The Bills haven't won a Super Bowl, but James Lofton played in two of them.[1]

I cannot tell you what makes football fans out of other people, but I can tell you why I follow the game with such interest. Far beyond the smashing and the pounding, the aches and pains of the game, I see an analogy between football and life. Those who hang tough, refusing to give up no matter how difficult or demanding or disappointing the challenges may be, are the ones who stand the best chance of winning. They are also the ones who find the greatest satisfaction and delight in their years on earth. Henry David Thoreau said it best:

> If one advances confidently in the direction of his dreams, and endeavors to live the life which he has imagined, he will meet with a success unexpected in common hours.[2]

That may sound like the ending to a fairy tale, almost as if some Disney character were telling us to wish upon a star while standing near the castle in Fantasyland, but it is not that at all. I see in Thoreau's statement a long and untiring determination in the same direction. Not a get-rich-quick scheme or some overnight success plan, but a confident advancement in the right direction over the long haul. Dreams are important, no question; yet they must be mixed with the patient discipline of staying at the tough tasks, regardless.

A BRIEF STOP AT TODAY'S BOOKSHELVES

This is not the popular message we hear today. I was struck by this realization recently while browsing through a new bookstore not far from my home. As I wandered through the section on management and motivation, the titles made a bold statement about how society feels regarding patience and long-term diligence:

- *Passport to Prosperity*
- *Winning Moves*
- *True Greed*
- *Leadership Secrets of Attila the Hun*
- *Winning Through Intimidation*
- *Cashing In on the American Dream (How to Retire at 35)*
- *The Art of Selfishness*
- *Techniques That Take You to the Top*
- *How to Get What You Really Want*
- *Secrets to Quick Success*

Who's kidding whom? In spite of all those eye-catching, cleverly worded titles, the so-called secret to quick *anything* beneficial is light-years removed from the truth. In the final analysis, the race is won by right objectives relentlessly pursued. Whether it is an athlete reaching the Super Bowl, parents rearing a houseful of kids, a young woman earning her Ph.D., or a gifted musician perfecting his skill on an instrument, hanging tough over the long haul is still the investment that pays the richest dividends. And, I might add, it brings the greatest joy.

A Lingering Look at Paul's Prescription

In the previous chapter we looked at the former life of the apostle Paul. As a young scholar he had won bragging rights over all his peers. His heritage, his schooling, his accomplishments, his zeal, his position, his passion were all part of his being groomed for a seat on the Supreme Court of the Jews, the Sanhedrin. That all-powerful name recognition gave him the edge . . . until he was intercepted by the resurrected, sovereign Christ . . . stunned and crushed by the revelation of the Son of God.

John Pollock, in a work entitled *The Man Who Shook the World,* describes it well.

> Paul could not believe what he heard and saw. All his convictions, intellect and training, his reputation, his self-respect, demanded that Jesus should not be alive again. He played for time and replied, "Who are you, Lord?" He used a mode of address which might mean no more than "Your honor."
>
> "I am Jesus, whom you are persecuting. It is hard for you, this kicking against the goad."
>
> Then he knew. In a second that seemed an eternity Paul saw the wounds in Jesus' hands and feet, saw the face and knew that he had seen the Lord, that he was alive, as Stephen and the others had said, and that he loved not only those whom Paul persecuted but Paul: "It is hard for *you* to kick against the goad." Not one word of reproach.
>
> Paul had never admitted to himself that he had felt pricks of a goad as he raged against Stephen and his disciples. But now, instantaneously, he was shatteringly aware that he had been fighting Jesus. And fighting himself, his conscience, his powerlessness, the darkness and chaos in his soul. God hovered over this chaos and brought him to the moment of new creation. It wanted only his "Yes."
>
> Paul broke.
>
> He was trembling and in no state to weigh the pros and cons of changing sides. He only knew that he had heard a voice and had seen the Lord, and that nothing mattered but to find and obey his will.
>
> "What shall I do, Lord?"[3]

I was sitting in chapel back in 1959 at Dallas Theological Seminary, listening to Dr. Alan Redpath, then pastor of the famed Moody Memorial Church. I was taking notes, as I often did while listening to chapel speakers, and suddenly I stopped writing. Dr. Redpath had made a statement that burned its way deeply into the creases of my brain: "When God wants to do an impossible task, He takes an impossible man and crushes him." In the intervening years I have learned how right Dr. Redpath was. That is often the plan God uses when dealing with strong-willed, stubborn people.

Paul was both, so we should not be surprised that he was crushed. "Shattered," says Pollack. That is why verse 7 of Philippians 3 begins with "but." In effect, Paul admits, "I had achieved all those honors, I had won all the awards, I had gotten all the applause, I had impressed all my contemporaries . . . *but* God pulled every one of them off the wall. He put all that into correct perspective as He crushed my pride, won my heart, and came to live within me."

> But whatever things were gain to me, those things I have counted as loss for the sake of Christ. More than that, I count all things to be loss in view of the surpassing value of knowing Christ Jesus my Lord, for whom I have suffered the loss of all things, and count them but rubbish in order that I may gain Christ, and may be found in Him, not having a righteousness of my own derived from the Law, but that which is through faith in Christ, the righteousness which comes from God on the basis of faith.
>
> *Philippians 3:7–9*

I have been justified! God's love has invaded! Christ's presence has taken up residence! He has changed me! The load of sin is lifted . . . the source of righteousness has shifted! My relationship with God now rests on faith, not works. What a relief!

Paul was clearly a changed man. To his own amazement he began to laugh again.

But what now? Had he arrived? Was there nothing more to do but sit around and dream, dream, dream? No. In his own words, "I press on . . . I press on."

> Not that I have already obtained it, or have already become perfect, but I press on in order that I may lay hold of that for which also I was laid

> hold of by Christ Jesus. Brethren, I do not regard myself as having laid hold of it yet; but one thing I do: forgetting what lies behind and reaching forward to what lies ahead, I press on toward the goal for the prize of the upward call of God in Christ Jesus. Let us therefore, as many as are perfect, have this attitude; and if in anything you have a different attitude, God will reveal that also to you; however, let us keep living by that same standard to which we have attained.
>
> *Philippians 3:12–16*

I find his opening lines not a little relieving. With a background like his it would be easy to think he had life by the tail. I've met a few superpious men and women who held a rather inflated opinion of themselves, almost to the point where you wonder if they have started to believe all their own press releases. (I confess, when I come across people like that, I have this strong urge to visit with their married partners and ask them what it is like living with someone who has "arrived." Mates are good at setting the record straight.)

As I read over Paul's comments, which sort of summarize his philosophy of life, five ideas emerge.

1. The plan is progress, not perfection. Twice, right out of the chute, he states that he is far from perfect: "Not that I have obtained it . . . become perfect . . . I do not regard myself as having laid hold of it yet. . . ."

What is "it"? Christlikeness. True and complete godliness in final form, with no room for improvement. Nobody on earth qualifies for this one.

Part of the reason hanging tough is tough is the imperfection that continues to mark our lives. Frequent reminders of our humanity still rear their ugly heads. That is true of ourselves, and it is true of others. We, ourselves, are imperfect, living in an imperfect world, surrounded by imperfect people, who continue to model imperfections on a daily basis. Happy is the person who keeps that in mind. You will find that life is not nearly as galling if you remember that the goal is to press on in spite of the lack of perfection.

Perfectionists have a whale of a battle with this. They want life to be lived flawlessly by everyone. That is why I have said for years that perfectionists are people who take pains—and give them to others.

If a man as capable as Paul freely admitted he had not arrived, we should have little difficulty saying the same. Nevertheless, progress is the main agenda of life. If you can see changes in your own life as compared to, say, a year ago or more, take heart! You are on the right road.

2. The past is over . . . forget it! The original word Paul used when he wrote, "forgetting what lies behind," was a Greek term that meant fully forgetting, *completely* forgetting. Actually, it was an ancient athletic term used of a runner who outran another in the same race: Once he got into the lead, he would never turn and look back; he would forget about the other runner. The one in the lead focuses on the tape before him rather than the other runners behind him.

Some of the unhappiest people I have ever known are living their lives looking over their shoulder. What a waste! Nothing back there can be changed.

What's in the past? Only two things: great attainments and accomplishments that could either make us proud by reliving them or indifferent by resting on them . . . or failures and defeats that cannot help but arouse feelings of guilt and shame. Why in the world would anyone want to return to that quagmire? I have never been able to figure that one out. By recalling those inglorious, ineffective events of yesterday, our energy is sapped for facing the demands of today. Rehearsing those wrongs, now forgiven in grace, derails and demoralizes us. There are few joy stealers more insidious than past memories that haunt our minds. Paul says to forget the past! Good advice to all who hope to hang tough.

3. The future holds out hope . . . reach for it! I am not the first to point out that Paul may have had in mind the chariot races so popular in the Olympic Games as he wrote of "reaching forward to what lies ahead." He could have been thinking of the chariot racer standing in that small, two-wheeled cart with long, leather reins in his hands, leaning forward to keep his balance. Can you picture it?

The analogy is clear. In this race called life, we are to face forward, anticipating what lies ahead, ever stretching and reaching, making life a passionate, adventurous quest. Life was never meant to be a passive coexistence with enemy forces as we await our heavenly home. But it's easy to do that, especially when we arrive at a certain age (from our mid-fifties on), to sort of shift into neutral and take whatever comes our way.

Let me pause here in midstream and ask you three direct questions:

- Have you left the past—I mean fully moved on beyond it?
- Are you making progress—some kind of deliberate progress with your life?
- Do you passionately pursue some dream—some specific goal?

Robert Ballard suddenly flashes into my mind. Does that name mean anything to you?

Robert Ballard was a man with a quest. He wanted to find the *Titanic.* And on September 1, 1985, he discovered the sunken ship in the North Atlantic, more than 350 miles off the coast of Newfoundland. I get chills when I read his description of the first time he sent down that bright probe light and saw that sight more than two miles below the surface of those cold waters:

> My first direct view of *Titanic* lasted less than two minutes, but the stark sight of her immense black hull towering above the ocean floor will remain forever ingrained in my memory. My lifelong dream was to find this great ship and during the past 13 years the quest for her has dominated my life.[4]

What is your particular quest? For what are you leaning forward? There is something wonderfully exciting about reaching into the future with excited anticipation, and those who pursue new adventures through life stay younger, think better, and laugh louder! I just spoke with a middle-aged man who told me he hopes to teach himself Mandarin, one of the Chinese dialects, so that when he takes an early retirement in a few years he can go to China and teach English as a second language. He was smiling from ear to ear as he shared his plans, and I encouraged him to keep reaching forward for what lies before.

Cynthia and I recently had lunch with a wonderful couple in their thirties who are seriously considering a mid-career change. He will go to seminary and she will go to work to put him through. They have been thinking about it for years. Both are so excited, so motivated. They said we were the first ones to sound enthusiastic; all the others they had mentioned this to were quick to point out all the possible things that could go wrong. All the sacrifices they would have to endure. Why focus on that? I told them to keep reaching forward . . . to pursue their dream. And do I need to mention it? Both were laughing again as they walked away.

- The plan is progress, not perfection.
- The past is over, forget it.
- The future holds out hope, reach for it.

4. The secret is a determined attitude . . . maintain it! Paul specifically mentions having the right attitude. I wrote about this earlier in the book, but perhaps this is a good time to return to it since attitude is such a vital ingredient in the life of anyone who plans to hang tough. Here, the right attitude is important for those who are on the road to maturity . . . who are growing and are ready for the next lesson to be learned.

By the way, I like the gracious way Paul allows others the liberty to grow at their own pace: "If anyone has a different attitude, God will reveal that to him." But as far as the apostle was concerned, hanging tough and maintaining a determined attitude belonged together.

This reminds me of something similar written elsewhere in the New Testament:

> Consider it all joy, my brethren, when you encounter various trials, knowing that the testing of your faith produces endurance. And let endurance have its perfect result, that you may be perfect and complete, lacking in nothing.
>
> *James 1:2–4*

He does not mean that we reach perfection—we have already established that that is not the goal. He has maturity in mind. James says the same thing:

> Dear brothers, is your life full of difficulties and temptations? Then be happy, for when the way is rough, your patience has a chance to grow. So let it grow, and don't try to squirm out of your problems. For when your patience is finally in full bloom, then you will be ready for anything, strong in character, full and complete.
>
> *James 1:2–4 TLB*

I think of the process as a domino effect. Trials and tests come that impact our patience and give it a chance to grow (do they ever!).

As patience begins to develop, strong character is cultivated, moving us ever onward toward maturity. There is no shortcut! But by refusing to squirm out of your problems, you find yourself becoming the man or woman you have always wanted to be. And did you notice that little tidbit of advice? "Then be happy [there's that reminder again!] . . . for when the way is rough . . . you will be ready for anything. . . ." No major change will shock you.

For years all the members of our family lived under the same roof. Even as one after another of our adult children married and moved into their own homes, they still lived nearby. Our lives remained intertwined, and we maintained a close harmony. And then, almost overnight, we were separated. It was as if a bomb exploded and blew us all around the country.

Our older son, Curt, and his wife, Debbie, plus their three children remained nearby. Happily, they were not involved in the wholesale reshuffling of the Swindoll deck. But our older daughter, Charissa, and her husband, Byron, with their two children moved to Atlanta as Byron changed jobs and joined the Ronald Blue Company. Our younger daughter, Colleen, moved to the Chicago area with her husband, Mark, as he began studying for the ministry at Trinity Evangelical Divinity School. And our younger son, Chuck, moved to Orlando to begin his training as a sound engineer at Full Sail Center for the Recording Arts.

All three of those moves happened suddenly within a period of three months . . . boom, boom, boom! As Cynthia and I sat all alone on our sun porch one morning following the sudden scattering of the Swindoll tribe, our heads still swimming in the backwash of it all, we sort of caught our breath and decided that we would neither fight it nor whine about it. We deliberately chose to maintain a good attitude, which meant accepting what had occurred and adjusting to the new challenge of keeping close ties as best we could between Southern California, Chicago, Atlanta, and Orlando.

Since God is sovereign and is in the midst of everything that happens to us, the sudden trial of being so far removed from one another was something we could all endure. And we have. Our long distance phone bill and our travel expenses tell their own tale, I can assure you. But behind it all—on everyone's part—the secret to hanging tough together . . . and loving it has been everyone's attitude. Who knows? We may live to see the day when we're all back in the same geographical region and our home is, once again, filled with wall-to-wall children—*and grandchildren*—and we will long for the peace and quiet we had finally gotten used to! No, just kidding.

It occurred to Cynthia and me recently that we had reared our children to keep a close watch over their attitudes. All through their growing-up years we preached and tried hard to model positive attitudes, cooperative attitudes, willing and happy attitudes. Laughter has always been heard in our home, so why not apply all that now? It has worked wonders! Because of that, I have been particularly grateful for the piece Bob Benson wrote several years ago.

Laughter in the Walls

I pass a lot of houses on my way home—
some pretty,
some expensive,
some inviting—
but my heart always skips a beat
when I turn down the road
and see my house nestled against the hill.
I guess I'm especially proud
of the house and the way it looks because
I drew the plans myself.
It started out large enough for us—
I even had a study—
two teenaged boys now reside in there.
And it had a guest room—
my girl and nine dolls are permanent guests.
It had a small room Peg
had hoped would be her sewing room—
two boys swinging on the dutch door
have claimed this room as their own.
So it really doesn't look right now
as if I'm much of an architect.
But it will get larger again—
one by one they will go away
to work,
to college,
to service,
to their own houses,
and then there will be room—
a guest room,

a study,
and a sewing room
for just the two of us.
But it won't be empty—
every corner
every room
every nick
in the coffee table
will be crowded with memories.
Memories of picnics,
parties, Christmases,
bedside vigils, summers,
fires, winters, going barefoot,
leaving for vacation, cats,
conversations, black eyes,
graduations, first dates,
ball games, arguments,
washing dishes, bicycles,
dogs, boat rides,
getting home from vacation,
meals, rabbits, and
a thousand other things
that fill the lives
of those who would raise five.
And Peg and I will sit
quietly by the fire
and listen to the
laughter in the walls.[5]

5. *The need is keeping a high standard . . . together.* Those who hang tough do better when doing so with others. That is especially true in times of severe crisis. As Benjamin Franklin said at the signing of the Declaration of Independence: "We must all hang together, or assuredly we shall all hang separately."[6] And while pulling together we need to keep a high standard. As the apostle wrote to his Philippian friends, "Let us keep living by that same standard."

Agreeing on the same basics while encouraging each other to hang in there day after day is one of the many benefits of locking arms in close friendship with a small group of Christians. The group not only holds us accountable, but also reminds us we are not alone. I have found that I don't get as weary when I pull up close alongside a few like-minded brothers and take the time to cultivate a meaningful relationship. It is practical *and* biblical:

> And let us not lose heart in doing good, for in due time we shall reap if we do not grow weary.
>
> *Galatians 6:9*

> Therefore, my beloved brethren, be steadfast, immovable, always abounding in the work of the Lord, knowing that your toil is not in vain in the Lord.
>
> *1 Corinthians 15:58*

A WORKABLE PLAN FOR EVERYDAY LIVING

Let me see if I can wrap up this chapter in a single statement. Progress is maintained by:

Forgetting yesterday's glory and grind
and by
Focusing on tomorrow's challenging opportunities
while we
Keep the right attitude and remember
we are in it together.

In all honesty, I am convinced that that is a winning game plan for hanging tough . . . and loving it. In fact, I suggest you duplicate that formula on a small sheet of paper or a three-by-five card and tape it to your bathroom mirror or clip it to the sun visor of your car. Repeat it until it gets transferred to your memory and becomes your motto for the month. I have begun doing that, and do you know what? You guessed it—I've started to laugh again . . . even though half the family is still spread across the country.

Let's lock arms and "press on toward the goal for the prize of the upward call of God in Christ Jesus." Is it a deal?

I can still remember sitting as a small boy in a little church in my hometown, El Campo, Texas, listening to those gospel songs sung by some of the simplest and best folks on earth. They were my mom's and dad's Christian friends and family members—people of my simple roots. One song stands out in my memory above all the rest, a refrain seldom heard in most churches today. It is more than a song. It's a prayer that declares our commitment to enduring the long haul and maintaining a high standard.

> I'm pressing on the upward way,
> New heights I'm gaining every day;
> Still praying as I onward bound,
> Lord, plant my feet on higher ground.
>
> Lord, lift me up and let me stand,
> By faith, on heaven's table-land,
> A higher plane than I have found;
> Lord, plant my feet on higher ground.[7]

10

It's a Mad, Bad, Sad World, But . . .

RIGHT ABOUT NOW A FEW OF YOU have had it up to here with being told you need to laugh more. All this stuff about being positive and maintaining a good attitude may be starting to wear thin. You might have started to wonder if the two of us—you and I—are living on the same planet. Maybe you are wondering if Swindoll is really in touch with the raw and wicked side of life. If so, let me reassure you—I am.

I live in the Greater Los Angeles area, remember, which is not anyone's idea of a quaint and quiet village filled with caring people living in lovely harmony. Some of the people I am around and some of the sights I see are enough to make me want to get in my car and drive in the other direction. Hopefully, I wouldn't get shot on the freeway trying to get out of town! Acts of violence and the grossest form of criminal behavior are so prevalent that our local television news reporters could easily fill their hour every evening with nothing but that kind of news. Our area is the breeding ground for the full spectrum of human depravity. Sadly, it is here that many cults originate. It is here that one can find every form of pornography, abuse, addiction, and demonic activity, not to mention the ever-present homeless people I see every day. And then there are the tragic emotional breakdowns and marital breakups I hear about on a regular basis. This place is b-a-a-a-a-d!

Do I live on an idyllic island removed from reality where love is abundant and the soft winds of joy blow through the palm trees? Is this the sort of place a person would choose to raise a family who is hoping to escape the harsh realities of a world gone mad? You know better. There are days I would love to pack up and find a nice protected space away from all the noise and nonsense . . . all the fast-lane greed and filthy air . . . all the conflicts and pressures an overcrowded city like ours includes. But then God gets my attention and reminds me that He hasn't called me to Shady Brook Lane where folks sit on the front porch and swing till dark, snapping peas and watching lightning bugs. My world—my mission, my calling—is the city where life gets ugly and people get hostile and kids are exposed to too much too soon. In this area where depravity is relentlessly on display, only the fit survive.

And that is exactly why I've decided to write a book like this. In a world this bad, laughter is the last thing anyone would expect to hear. Trust me, when you laugh in the midst of *this* cesspool environment, people want to know why. "Laughter is hope's last weapon," as I read recently, and I think it is time we put that weapon to use. Out here, only those who are firm in their faith can laugh in the face of tragedy. As Flannery O'Connor wrote:

> Where there is no belief in the soul, there is very little drama. . . . Either one is serious about salvation or one is not. And it is well to realize that the maximum amount of seriousness admits the maximum amount of comedy. Only if we are secure in our beliefs can we see the comical side of the universe.[1]

The Christian is a weird sort, let's face it. We are earthlings, yet the Bible says we are citizens of heaven. This world may not be our home, but it is our residence. Furthermore, we are to live in the world, but we are not to be of the world. And since joy is one of our distinctives, laughter is appropriate even though we are surrounded by all manner of wrong and wickedness. It can get a little confusing, as A. W. Tozer pointed out rather graphically:

> A real Christian is an odd number anyway. He feels supreme love for One whom he has never seen, talks familiarly every day to Someone he cannot see, expects to go to heaven on the virtue of Another, empties himself in order to be full, admits he is wrong so he can be declared right, goes down in order to get up, is strongest when he is weakest, richest when he is poorest, and happiest when he feels worst. He dies so he can live, forsakes in order to have, gives away so he can keep, sees the invisible, hears the inaudible, and knows that which passeth knowledge.[2]

OUR LORD'S STRANGE STRATEGY

In light of all that, doesn't it seem odd of God not to provide an immediate escape route to heaven as soon as we are converted? Why would He leave us in the midst of such an insane, godless setting? I ask you, why? What kind of strange strategy could He have in mind, leaving heaven-bound people riveted to this hell-bound earth?

The answer is worth pursuing, and I don't know of a more qualified source for that answer than Jesus Christ Himself. As I examine His words to His disciples prior to His crucifixion, I find at least three definitive statements that explain what we can expect as we are left on earth.

1. We can have inner peace in the midst of outer pressure and pain. Read Jesus' words slowly and carefully:

> These things I have spoken to you, that you may be kept from stumbling. They will make you outcasts from the synagogue; but an hour is coming for everyone who kills you to think that he is offering service to God.
>
> *John 16:1–2*

> But when He, the Spirit of truth, comes, He will guide you into all the truth; for He will not speak on His own initiative, but whatever He hears, He will speak; and He will disclose to you what is to come.
>
> *John 16:13*

> These things I have spoken to you, that in Me you may have peace. In the world you have tribulation, but take courage; I have overcome the world.
>
> *John 16:33*

If those words mean anything, they provide straight talk about life minus a cushy comfort zone. We won't be sheltered from life's blows. Settle it in your mind once for all: Christians are not supernaturally protected from the blasts, the horrors, the aches, or the pains of living on this globe. Christians can be unfairly treated, assaulted, robbed, raped, and murdered. We can suffer financial reversals, we can be taken advantage of, abused, neglected, and divorced by uncaring mates. Then how can we expect to be joyful, unlike those around us? Because He promises that deep within He will give us peace . . . an unexplainable, illogical inner peace.

2. We are insulated by divine power, yet we are not to live an isolated existence. Again, pay close attention to Jesus' counsel:

> These things Jesus spoke; and lifting up His eyes to heaven, He said, "Father, the hour has come; glorify Thy Son, that the Son may glorify Thee, even as Thou gavest Him authority over all mankind, that to all whom Thou hast given Him, He may give eternal life. And this is eternal life, that they may know Thee, the only true God, and Jesus Christ whom Thou hast sent."
>
> *John 17:1–3*

> And I am no more in the world; and yet they themselves are in the world, and I come to Thee. Holy Father, keep them in Thy name, the name which Thou hast given Me, that they may be one, even as We are. While I was with them, I was keeping them in Thy name which Thou hast given Me; and I guarded them, and not one of them perished but the son of perdition, that the Scripture might be fulfilled. But now I come to Thee; and these things I speak in the world, that they may have My joy made full in themselves. I have given them Thy word; and the world has hated them, because they are not of the world, even as I am not of the world. I do not ask Thee to take them out of the world, but to keep them from the evil one.
>
> *John 17:11–15*

Take another glance at that last statement. Jesus is praying, deliberately asking the Father *not* to remove us from all the earthly garbage, all the daily debris that gathers around this old sin-cursed planet. Then how can any of us ever laugh again? He insulates us! The fires of unrestrained passion may blaze all around us, but He gives us the power of His protective shield to steer us clear of contamination. And don't think the person of the world doesn't notice.

3. We may be unique, but we must be unified. God is pleased with our differences. No two of us are exactly alike, so each person is able to reach out to his or her own sphere of influence. However, our strength comes from our unity.

> They are not of the world, even as I am not of the world. Sanctify them in the truth; Thy word is truth. . . . that they may all be one; even as Thou, Father, art in Me, and I in Thee, that they also may be in Us; that the world may believe that Thou didst send Me. . . . I in them, and Thou in Me, that they may be perfected in unity, that the world may know that Thou didst send Me, and didst love them, even as Thou didst love Me.
>
> *John 17:16–17, 21, 23*

The idea is this: That they (Christians left on earth) may be brought together into a unit—one powerful force for good—in a society weakened by independence and isolation. As people of the world who have no sense of eternal purpose see this unified front, they will realize their own emptiness and seek to find out what makes the difference. What a strategy! All the more reason for Christ's forever family to remain joyfully unified under the authority of His Majesty, King Jesus.

Our world may be a mad, bad, sad place . . . totally out to lunch, spiritually speaking. But impossible to reach and win? Not on your life. Christ's strange strategy is effective because it defies being ignored.

- peace in pressure and pain
- insulated not isolated
- unique but unified

Stop and think. Is it easy to overlook a person who is at peace when you are gripped by panic? And if you are weak within, does someone who seems strangely insulated make you curious? Furthermore, why would anybody laugh in a cesspool society like ours? I repeat, it is an ingenious strategy.

The Christian's Marching Orders

All that brings us back to Paul's letter written to his friends in Philippi. He is writing to Christians—peaceful, joyful, strong, insulated people—who live in the real world. He wants them to know how to get a big job done. And so, he tells them, living for Christ means marching in step with His drumbeat.

> Brethren, join in following my example, and observe those who walk according to the pattern you have in us. For many walk, of whom I often told you, and now tell you even weeping, that they are enemies of the cross of Christ, whose end is destruction, whose god is their appetite, and whose glory is in their shame, who set their minds on earthly things. For our citizenship is in heaven, from which also we eagerly wait for a Savior, the Lord Jesus Christ; who will transform the body of our humble state into conformity with the body of His glory, by the exertion of the power that He has even to subject all things to Himself.

> Therefore, my beloved brethren whom I long to see, my joy and crown, so stand firm in the Lord, my beloved.
>
> *Philippians 3:17—4:1*

Here I find several helpful tips on how to make our lives count . . . how to do more than sit around, waiting for Christ's return. Four specifics come to my mind as I read Paul's wise counsel.

First, *we need examples to follow.*

> Brethren, join in following my example, and observe those who walk according to the pattern you have in us.
>
> *Philippians 3:17*

The bad news is: Ours is an arduous, long, and sometimes tedious journey through Cesspool Cosmos. And, observe, it is a walk, not a sprint. The good news is: We are not alone on this demanding pilgrimage, which means that some folks we are traveling with make awfully good models to follow. So, follow them!

I like it that while Paul invited believers to follow him, he also acknowledged that others were worth being followed as well. This is a good place to be reminded that no one person on earth is to be our single source of instruction or our only object of admiration. When that happens we can easily get tunnel vision and draw dangerously close to idolizing an individual. We are told to follow others' example but not to focus fully on one person, no matter how godly or gifted he or she may be. Happy and balanced are those in God's army who have several mentors and respect many heroes.

What is it we look for when searching for examples to follow? I like the things Paul listed for Timothy:

> But you [Timothy] followed my teaching, conduct, purpose, faith, patience, love, perseverance, persecutions, and sufferings, such as happened to me at Antioch, at Iconium and at Lystra; what persecutions I endured, and out of them all the Lord delivered me! And indeed, all who desire to live godly in Christ Jesus will be persecuted.
>
> *2 Timothy 3:10–12*

And never forget that those we follow are to be diligent followers of Christ Himself. He remains the Master Mentor.

Be imitators of me, just as I also am of Christ.

1 Corinthians 11:1

Before I leave this subject, let me point out a few practical suggestions for determining your role models:

- Choose your mentors slowly.
- Study their private lives carefully.
- Spend time with them regularly.

Some who make a good public impression may lack solid character qualities behind the scenes. If you ignore that, you can easily be deceived and disillusioned.

I know from personal experience the downside of following such a model. Without getting into details, there was a time when I was young in the faith and terribly vulnerable. A strong leader with a great deal of charisma sort of swept me off my feet. He became my sole source of teaching, and for several years his was the only voice of authority I took seriously. My respect for the man bordered dangerously near idolatry, though I would have denied it at the time. If he was teaching, I was there to drink in every word. His interpretations became my convictions. Even his mannerisms and terminology rubbed off so much that I lost my own sense of confidence and identity; both were bound up in him. Looking back, I also realize I became extremely serious—fanatically serious—about everything. Thankfully, through a chain of events only the Lord could have orchestrated, all that slowly changed. Several subtle things came to the surface, causing me to question the man's private life. And when I challenged some of the things he was teaching, he made it abundantly clear that no one was *ever* to question him. That did it. My respect for the man quickly eroded. More importantly, I realized that I had been looking up to someone who was not the one I should be following, certainly not exclusively. Hard lesson learned, but a good one.

Interestingly, when I broke that fixation, God began to show me many other things I had been blinded to, and His Word brought fresh insights. With my spiritual equilibrium restored, a new sense of perspective returned, along with a sense of humor that had lain dormant too long. In short, it cleared the way for me to become myself rather than a shadow of someone else. Graciously, in the years that followed, God brought me several wonderful mentors, who did indeed follow Christ. Each one has contributed immeasurably to my spiritual growth.

So, learn from my mistake. We need examples (plural!) to follow. As we integrate their godly characteristics into our lives, we become better people.

Second, *we live among many who are enemies of the cross.* This fact keeps us from following every strong personality we meet. "Many," says Paul, "are enemies."

> For many walk, of whom I often told you, and now tell you even weeping, that they are enemies of the cross of Christ, whose end is destruction, whose god is their appetite, and whose glory is in their shame, who set their minds on earthly things.
>
> *Philippians 3:18–19*

Paul is firm, but he is not judgmental. He is committed to the truth, which sometimes hurts. But is he proud of the contrast between himself and those he calls enemies? No. He states that what he is saying makes him weep.

If you and I are ever going to get involved in sharing the joys of knowing and walking with Christ, we must come to terms with the fact that people without Christ in their lives are lost—absolutely and undeniably L-O-S-T.

In fact, Paul gives us one of the clearest and most pointed descriptions of the person who is lost. He or she is:

- *Destined for eternal hopelessness.* That is their future. The reality of hell should be enough to prompt *anyone* to turn to Christ.
- *Driven by sensual appetites.* Anyone who is exposed to the world of the unbeliever soon finds out how up-to-date the counsel of Paul really is. The timeworn motto, "Eat, drink, and be merry" is still very much in vogue. Sensuality is the fuel that lights their fire.
- *Dedicated to material things.* Virtually *everything* draws the lost person toward possessions . . . things that have price tags, things that are tangible, things that can be owned and must be maintained. In the words of Paul, they "set their minds on earthly things."

When all this is added up, is it surprising that the sound of laughter has been drowned out? As you read over the list, you realize anew the emptiness, the boredom of such an existence. No laughter here.

Now the point of this analysis of the lost is not to judge or to condemn or to leave the impression that Christians are better than non-Christians. It is to remind us that God has placed us among them. They are, in fact, in the majority! Our mission is not to argue with them or put them down or make them feel ashamed; it is to reach out to them! To *win* them. To help them realize there is much more to life than they have ever known. To model a different lifestyle that is so convincing, so appealing, that their curiosity will be tweaked, so they might discover what they are missing. The non-Christian world may be lost and running on empty, but they are not stupid or unaware of their surroundings. When they come across an individual who is at peace, free of fear and worry, fulfilled, and genuinely happy, no one has to tell them that something is missing from their lives. Ours may be a mad, bad, sad world, but it is not *blind.* And it is certainly not unreachable. Interesting them in something meaningful and different is not an impossibility. Who doesn't want relief? Freedom from addictions? A purpose for living? A reason to laugh again?

I mentioned earlier that I am engaged in a radio ministry, Insight for Living. Frequently listeners will call and/or write to communicate the changes that have happened in their lives as a result of listening to the broadcasts. We have file drawers full of such letters, each one telling how a person was attracted to the program, often because of what was missing in his or her own life.

I shall never forget one such letter from a young woman who had reached the absolute end of her rope. She had checked into a motel, planning to take her life. Throughout the night she sat on the side of the bed and mentally rehearsed her miserable existence. She had endured numerous failed relationships with men and had had several abortions. She was empty, angry, and could see no reason to go on. Finally, just before dawn, she reached in her purse and pulled out a loaded pistol. Trembling, she stuck it in her mouth and closed her eyes. Suddenly the clock radio snapped on. Apparently the previous occupant had set the radio to come on at that precise time on that precise station . . . and the musical theme of "Insight for Living" filled the room. The uplifting sounds startled her. She tried to ignore it, but couldn't. She heard my voice and found herself strangely attracted to the message of new hope and authentic joy that she had never heard in her entire life. Before the thirty-minute broadcast ended, she gave her life to Jesus Christ. When she contacted us to tell us what had happened, she said she could still taste the cold steel from the gun barrel she had pulled from her mouth.

Not all stories are that dramatic. Some call or write, requesting help to get past the horrible scars of years gone by. Some are victims of abuse. Others write of another kind of emptiness—affluent boredom and materialistic greed, where enough was never enough—but they have nothing else to fill the void. Businessmen and women on a maddening pace to get to the top contact us about their lack of happiness and contentment, their dreadful feelings of distance from their mates and children, and their disillusionment with "the system." Many mention extramarital affairs they are not able to stop or addictions they cannot control: alcoholism, drugs, food, sex.

In each case, it seems, they realize that Christ is able to provide what is missing, and they want to or have entrusted their lives to Him. Most mention their feelings of hopelessness and their inability to help themselves. They long to be free . . . free to live rather than merely exist in a revolving door of repeated defeats . . . free enough to laugh again. It is *that* ingredient we notice in virtually all the letters of transformed lives . . . joy—*outrageous* joy.

Third, *we belong to those who are bound for heaven.*

> For our citizenship is in heaven, from which also we eagerly wait for a Savior, the Lord Jesus Christ; who will transform the body of our humble state into conformity with the body of His glory, by the exertion of the power that He has even to subject all things to Himself.
>
> *Philippians 3:20–21*

Isn't that a great thought? "Our citizenship is in heaven." But let's never forget that our involvements are on earth. That may create a little tension now and then, but what a challenging opportunity! Only heaven-bound people are objective enough to make a major difference on earth. While we "eagerly wait for a Savior," we are able to introduce earth-bound people to a whole new way of life. Can you imagine the curiosity that a bunch of us could arouse just by living lives of relaxed laughter, enjoying delightful fun together? Bystanders would stare in wonder and amazement. They couldn't stand it, being left out. They would *have* to know what they were missing and why we are able to have so much fun, and it would be our joy to tell them. *I love it!* Ours may be a mad, bad, sad old world, but impossible to impact? Get serious! No, on second thought, *get happy!*

I have never been able to figure out why heaven-bound citizens of glory have become so grim. In only a matter of time we shall be transformed from our present condition and conformed into Christ's image—what a change! And in light of that, why is a little temporary period of tough times on earth so all-fired important? It's time we looked different and sounded different. It is time we began to laugh again.

Solomon was absolutely right:

> A joyful heart is good medicine,
> But a broken spirit dries up the bones.
>
> *Proverbs 17:22*

Did you know that laughter actually does work like a medicine in our systems? It exercises our lungs and stimulates our circulation. It takes our minds off our troubles and massages our emotions. Laughter decreases tension. When we laugh, a sort of temporary anesthesia is released within us that blocks the pain as our attention is diverted. As I mentioned earlier, laughter is one of the healthiest exercises we can enjoy. It literally brings healing.

Who hasn't heard about Norman Cousins' remarkable experience? In his excellent book, *Anatomy of an Illness as Perceived by the Patient,* he tells about his battle with an "incurable" disease and the pain he endured as his body's collagen was deteriorating. That, by the way, is the fibrous material that holds the body's cells together. In Cousins' own words, he was "becoming unstuck."

He decided to take matters into his own hands and treat himself (with his doctor's approval) by (1) taking vitamins, (2) eating only healthy food, and—are you ready for this?—(3) undergoing "laugh therapy" by watching old, funny Marx Brothers movies, clips from "Candid Camera," and cartoons . . . and anything else that would make him laugh. He found that if he laughed hard for ten minutes straight, he could enjoy about two hours of relief from pain. To his doctor's amazement, Cousins eventually recovered.[3] The man lived many years beyond anyone's expectations . . . anyone's but his! Norman Cousins' remarkable story reminds me of another of Solomon's proverbs, "The cheerful heart has a continual feast" (Prov. 15:15 NIV).

Think of the impact we could have as earth-free citizens of heaven living hilariously enjoyable, responsible, yet wonderfully carefree lives among people who cannot find anything funny in their shattered world of madness, badness, and sadness. If Laurel and Hardy, the Three Stooges, and the Marx Brothers could help Norman Cousins recover, just think of the healing power that could come from the joy of Jesus Christ. No comparison. But we can't forget the key: You and I . . . we must be the ones who model the message if we ever hope to help our world laugh again. It was G. K. Chesterton who wrote:

> I am all in favor of Laughing. Laughter has something in it in common with the ancient winds of faith and inspiration; it unfreezes pride and unwinds secrecy; it makes men forget themselves in the presence of something greater than themselves; something (as the common phrase goes about a joke) that they cannot resist.[4]

Fourth, *we must stand firm, but not stand still.*

> Therefore, my beloved brethren whom I long to see, my joy and crown, so stand firm in the Lord, my beloved.
>
> *Philippians 4:1*

Earlier Paul admonished us to "be confident in the Lord" (1:6). Later, to "have the Lord's attitude" (2:5). Next, to "rejoice in the Lord" (3:1). And now he is saying we are to "stand firm in the Lord" (4:1). All the way through the letter to the Philippians the focus has been not on our circumstances or on others or on ourselves, but on the Lord, our source of life and love, confidence and joy.

Here we are being told to "stand firm." But let's not confuse this with standing still. In a world like ours, it is easy to get caught up in the system and lose our stability, hence the command, "Stand firm." In other words, keep your equilibrium . . . don't let the highs and lows sway you . . . get a firm grip on that eternal relationship you have with the Lord and don't let go. He will give you the strength to go on, and He will continue bringing to your attention the thoughts that will keep you positive, affirming, and winsome.

In the final lines of this chapter, I want to encourage you to be all you can be in this world that long ago lost its way. You may not know it and you may not feel like it, but to someone else you are the only source of light and laughter. They may be mad or they may be bad or they may be sad, but, I repeat, they are not unreachable. The real question is this: Are you willing to do the reaching?

It may be a long reach. And sometimes we get our hands slapped . . . our feelings hurt. That's okay. Hurting people often hurt people. But we have God on our side.

So come on out of your shell and reach. Even though the reachable may sometimes act unreachable, keep on reaching. And remember, a good mixture of compassion and realism is essential.

I like the wry comment Barbara Johnson makes in her book, *Splashes of Joy in the Cesspools of Life:*

> The rain falls on the just and also on the unjust, but
> chiefly on the just,
> Because the unjust steals the just's umbrella.[5]

No problem . . . like I've been saying, it's a mad, bad, sad world. Even if you get wet doing it, keep reaching, and, for sure, keep laughing.

11

Defusing Disharmony

IN A PARABLE SHE ENTITLES "A Brawling Bride," Karen Mains paints a vivid scene, describing a suspenseful moment in a wedding ceremony. Down front stands the groom in a spotless tuxedo—handsome, smiling, full of anticipation, shoes shined, every hair in place, anxiously awaiting the presence of his bride. All attendants are in place, looking joyful and attractive. The magical moment finally arrives as the pipe organ reaches full crescendo and the stately wedding march begins.

Everyone rises and looks toward the door for their first glimpse of the bride. Suddenly there is a horrified gasp. The wedding party is shocked. The groom stares in embarrassed disbelief. Instead of a lovely woman dressed in elegant white, smiling behind a lace veil, the bride is limping down the aisle. Her dress is soiled and torn. Her leg seems twisted. Ugly cuts and bruises cover her bare arms. Her nose is bleeding, one eye is purple and swollen, and her hair is disheveled.

"Does not this handsome groom deserve better than this?" asks the author. And then the clincher: "Alas, His bride, THE CHURCH, has been fighting again!"[1]

Calling them (and us) "the church," the apostle Paul writes to the Ephesians:

> Christ . . . loved the church and gave Himself up for her . . . to make her holy and clean . . . so that He could give her to Himself as a glorious church without a single spot or wrinkle or any other blemish, being holy and without a single fault.
>
> *Ephesians 5:25–27* NASB/TLB

Wonderful plan . . . but hardly a realistic portrayal. I mean, can you imagine what the wedding pictures would look like if Christ claimed

His bride, the church, *today?* Try to picture Him standing next to His brawling bride. It is one thing for us to survive the blows of a world that is hostile to the things of Christ, but to be in disharmony with one another, fighting and arguing among ourselves—unthinkable.

Puritan Thomas Brookes once penned these words: "For wolves to worry lambs is no wonder, but for lambs to worry one another, this is unnatural and monstrous."[2]

Unthinkable and unnatural though it may seem, the bride has been brawling for centuries. We get along for a little while and then we are back at each others' throats. After a bit we make up, walk in wonderful harmony for a few days, then we turn on one another. We can switch from friend to fiend in a matter of moments.

In a "Peanuts" cartoon, Lucy says to Snoopy: "There are times when you really bug me, but I must admit there are also times when I feel like giving you a big hug."

Snoopy replies: "That's the way I am . . . huggable and buggable."

And so it is with us and our relationships within the ranks of God's family. I'm not referring to the variety of our personalities, gifts, tastes, and preferences—that's healthy. The Master made us like that. It's our mistreatment of each other, the infighting, the angry assaults, the verbal misrepresentations, the choosing of sides, the stubborn wills, the childish squabbles. An objective onlooker who watches us from a distance could wonder how and why some of us call ourselves Christians. "Well," you ask, "must we always agree?" No, absolutely not. But my question is this: Why can't we be *agreeable?* What is it that makes us so ornery and nitpicking in our attitudes? Why so many petty fights and ugly quarrels? Why so little acceptance and tolerance? Aren't we given the direct command to "keep the unity of the Spirit in the bond of peace"? What makes Christ's bride forget those words and have so many verbal brawls?

ANALYZING CONFLICT'S CAUSE AND EXTENT

James asked similar questions back in the first century—which tells us that disharmony is not solely a twentieth-century malady. Even back in the days when life was simple and everyone's pace was slower, there were squabbles.

> What is the source of quarrels and conflicts among you? Is not the

source your pleasures that wage war in your members? You lust and do not have; so you commit murder. And you are envious and cannot obtain; so you fight and quarrel. You do not have because you do not ask. You ask and do not receive, because you ask with wrong motives, so that you may spend it on your pleasures.

James 4:1–3

James never was the type to beat around the bush. With penetrating honesty he asks and answers the critical question. The terms he uses are extremely descriptive: "quarrels and conflicts." The first term is from the Greek word for "war." It conveys a scene of broad and bloody hostility between opposing parties. The second represents smaller skirmishes, local and limited battles, even a chronic state of disharmony. During World War II there were two massive "theaters" of warfare, vast territories on opposite sides of our country: the European theater of war and the Pacific theater of war. Within both numerous skirmishes and individual battles took place. That is the idea here.

The same can be seen to this day within the ranks of religion. England and Ireland have sustained their territorial and denominational "quarrel" for centuries. People on both sides are still being killed and crippled by real bombs and real bullets. Less bloody perhaps, but no less real are the denominational quarrels in our own land—fights and splits within the ranks. Seminaries quarrel as one theological position takes up arms against another. The disputes appear civil and sophisticated as each side publishes its position in journals and books, but behind the veil of intellectualism is a great deal of hostility.

And then there are those "conflicts" between local churches as well as among members of the same church. Small, petty battles . . . arguments, power struggles, envyings, catty comments, silent standoffs, and even lawsuits between members of the body of Christ. These may not be on the national news, but they can get ugly.

A pastor from another state recently told me that some of the members of his board of elders had not spoken to one another for over a year. A concerned board member from a different church in another state said he had recently resigned because he had gotten exhausted from doing nothing but "putting out fires" and "trying to keep church members happy." His particular church had been through two major splits in the past seven years over reasons that would make you smile and shake your head in disbelief. Such are the "conflicts among us."

Why We Have Them

James points to "the source" as he addresses the issue. His answer may seem strange: "Is not the source your pleasures that wage war in your members?"

"Pleasures" doesn't sound very hostile, does it? Maybe not in our English language, but the Greek word is the one from which we get "hedonism." It means the strong desire to get what one does not have, which includes the idea of satisfying oneself . . . the passion to get what one wants, regardless. Such an intense craving drives us to shameful and selfish actions. As James puts it, such pleasures lead us to "wage war"—*strateuo*—from which we get "strategy." Our desire to get what we want prompts us to strategize: to put a plan in motion that will result in *my* getting *my* way.

Is this a determined effort? Look again at what James writes:

> You lust and do not have; so you commit murder. And you are envious and cannot obtain; so you fight and quarrel. You do not have because you do not ask.
>
> *James 4:2*

I'd call that determined! If it calls for a fight, *fight!* If it means an argument, *argue!* If it will require getting other people to back me up, *enlist!* If stronger words will help me reach my objective and get what I want, *murder!*

I realize we don't carry weapons to church—not literally. That is not necessary, since the muscle behind our teeth is always ready to launch its killing missiles. We may not bring blood from another's body, but we certainly know how to make them squirm and hopefully surrender. And we never admit it is because we are selfish or because we crave our own way—there's always a principle at stake or a cause worth fighting for that's bigger than personalities. Sure, sure.

I realize that on a few occasions conflicts will arise. There *are* those times when it is essential to stand one's ground and refuse to compromise biblical principles. But more often than not the nasty infighting among us is embarrassingly petty. And, unfortunately, the world has a field day watching us fight and quarrel for the silliest of reasons.

Ways We Express Our Disharmony

Rationalizing our wrong attitudes and actions, we Christians will go to amazing lengths to get our way. The history of the church is strewn with the litter of battle. I repeat, some of those fights were unselfish and necessary. To have backed away would have meant compromising convictions clearly set forth in the Scriptures. But more often than not the "quarrels and conflicts" have expressed themselves in personal power plays, political maneuvering, strong-minded and selfish parishioners determined to get their own way, stubborn pastors who intimidate and bully others, unbending and tightfisted board members who refuse to listen to reason, and, yes, those who seem to delight in stirring up others through rumor and gossip. It's just a mess! Sometimes I wonder how the Shepherd puts up with us. We can be such wayward, stubborn sheep! And to think He sees it all—each and every cutting word or ugly act—yet loves us still. Only because of His grace are we able to continue on.

Marshall Shelley, in his book *Well-Intentioned Dragons,* talks about disharmony in the church from another perspective. Sometimes it is from folks who don't necessarily mean to be difficult, but they are.

> Dragons, of course, are fictional beasts—monstrous reptiles with lion's claws, a serpent's tail, bat wings, and scaly skin. They exist only in the imagination.
>
> But there are dragons of a different sort, decidedly real. In most cases, though not always, they do not intend to be sinister; in fact, they're usually quite friendly. But their charm belies their power to destroy.
>
> Within the church, they are often sincere, well-meaning saints, but they leave ulcers, strained relationships, and hard feelings in their wake. They don't consider themselves difficult people. They don't sit up nights thinking of ways to be nasty. Often they are pillars of the community—talented, strong personalities, deservingly respected—but for some reason, they undermine the ministry of the church. They are not naturally rebellious or pathological; they are loyal church members, convinced they're serving God, but they wind up doing more harm than good.
>
> They can drive pastors crazy . . . or out of the church.
>
> Some dragons are openly critical. They are the ones who accuse you of being (pick one) too spiritual, not spiritual enough, too dominant, too laid back, too narrow, too loose, too structured, too disorganized, or ulterior in your motives.

These criticisms are painful because they are largely unanswerable. How can you defend yourself and maintain a spirit of peace? How can you possibly prove the purity of your motives? Dragons make it hard to disagree without being disagreeable.

Relationships are both the professional and personal priority for pastors—getting along with people is an essential element of any ministry—and when relationships are vandalized by critical dragons, many pastors feel like failures. Politicians are satisfied with 51 percent of the constituency behind them; pastors, however, feel the pain when one vocal member becomes an opponent.

Sightings of these dragons are all too common. As one veteran pastor says, "Anyone who's been in ministry more than an hour and a half knows the wrath of a dragon." Or, as Harry Ironside described it, "Wherever there's light, there's bugs."[3]

LOOKING THROUGH THE KEYHOLE OF A FIRST-CENTURY CHURCH

I would be a lot more discouraged about the problem of disharmony among believers if I didn't remember that it has been around since the church began. Those early churches were anything but pockets of perfection. Christians in places like Corinth and Galatia, Rome and Thessalonica had their troubles just like those living in towns and cities all around our world today. Even Philippi—as fine a group of Jesus People as they were—had their own skirmishes, one of which Paul pinpointed in his letter to them.

> Therefore, my beloved brethren whom I long to see, my joy and crown, so stand firm in the Lord, my beloved.
>
> I urge Euodia and I urge Syntyche to live in harmony in the Lord. Indeed, true comrade, I ask you also to help these women who have shared my struggle in the cause of the gospel, together with Clement also, and the rest of my fellow workers, whose names are in the book of life.
>
> *Philippians 4:1–3*

In his typical fashion, Paul starts with a general principle before he addresses a specific concern; then he wraps things up as he makes a request. Behind it all is his unspoken desire that the Philippians defuse the disharmony and begin to laugh again. When disharmony persists, the first thing to go is the sweetest sound that can be heard in a church—

laughter. Perhaps it had been too long since the Philippians had enjoyed the presence of one another. Paul's hope is that once this difficulty is cleared up, their joy might return.

A Primary Principle

Solving problems that grow out of disharmony among believers calls for a return to standing firm in the things of the Lord, not satisfying self.

> Therefore, my beloved brethren whom I long to see, my joy and crown, so stand firm in the Lord, my beloved.
>
> *Philippians 4:1*

Earlier in the letter Paul had written:

> Only conduct yourselves in a manner worthy of the gospel of Christ; so that whether I come and see you or remain absent, I may hear of you that you are standing firm in one spirit, with one mind striving together for the faith of the gospel.
>
> *Philippians 1:27*

Actually, the idea of standing firm is one of the apostle's favorite topics. For example:

> "Stand firm in the faith" (1 Cor. 16:13).
> "Keep standing firm" (Gal. 5:1).
> "Now we really live, if you stand firm in the Lord" (1 Thess. 3:8).
> "So then, brethren, stand firm" (2 Thess. 2:15).

Why place such an emphasis on standing firm in the Lord? What's the big deal? Let me suggest to you that it is one of the most foundational principles of maintaining harmony:

STANDING FIRM IN THE LORD
PRECEDES
RELATING WELL IN THE FAMILY

What would standing firm include? Following Christ's teachings. Respecting His Word. Modeling His priorities. Loving His people.

Seeking and carrying out His will. It has been my observation that those who are committed to these things have little difficulty relating well to other members of God's family. Not surprisingly the very next issue Paul brings up has to do with two in the church at Philippi who needed to "live in harmony" with one another. But before I go into that, this might be a good time for you to ask yourself, "Am I one who stands firm *in the Lord?*" Other options create havoc: Standing firm *for what I want* . . . or, standing firm *in honor of tradition* . . . or, standing firm *with a couple of my friends.*" Unquestionably, those three positions represent the antithesis of "standing firm in the Lord."

A Relational Need

Having stated the principle, Paul puts his finger on the specific conflict at Philippi. He even names names.

> I urge Euodia and I urge Syntyche to live in harmony in the Lord.
>
> *Philippians 4:2*

Let me mention several observations:

1. These are two women in the church at Philippi (feminine names).
2. They are mentioned nowhere else in the Scriptures.
3. The specific details of their dispute are not explained.
4. Paul's counsel is to urge them toward harmony: "I urge . . . I urge" (he neither rebukes them nor pontificates).
5. He appeals to their conscience . . . their hearts (intrinsic motivation).

I am just as impressed with what Paul does not do.

He does not spell out a step-by-step process; that was for the two women to work out on their own. Equally impressive, he does not pull rank by adding a warning or a threat, like, "I'll give you two weeks to clear this up," or "If you don't straighten up, I will. . . ."

Paul handled the matter with dignity and grace. While he was deeply concerned ("I urge . . . I urge"), he did not attempt to take charge of the situation from a distance. If anyone is tempted to think Paul was too passive or should have said more, a quick reading of other renderings may help:

- "I plead with . . . I plead with . . ." (NIV).
- "Please, please, with the Lord's help, quarrel no more—be friends again." (TLB).
- "Euodias and Syntyche, I beg you by name to make up your differences as Christians should!" (PHILLIPS).

By repeating the verb ("I urge . . . I urge"), Paul leaves the impression that there was fault on both sides. In fact, the Vulgate, the Latin version of Scripture, uses different verbs in the appeal, which seems to emphasize mutual wrong.

I have seldom seen an exception to this: When disharmony arises between two people or two groups, there is some measure of fault on both sides. The road leading to a breakdown in harmony is never a one-way street. Both parties must be encouraged to see each other's fault, each other's failure . . . and meet on common ground with a mutual willingness to listen and to change.

And what is that common ground? The statement Paul makes includes the answer: "live in harmony in the Lord." Just as we are to "stand firm" in Him, so are we to find agreement in Him. Both sides need to make Him their focus if a solution is ever going to be found. It is as if the Apostle of Grace is saying, "It is important that both release their grudge and state their forgiveness and adopt the same attitude as their Lord when He unselfishly came from heaven to earth to be our Savior. Only then will there be renewed harmony."

One more thought before moving on. Everything we know of these two women is: They quarreled. Down through the centuries the only answer that could be given to the question: "Who were Euodia and Syntyche?" has been "They were two women from Philippi who lived in disharmony." That prompts me to ask you: If *your* life were to be summed up in a single statement, what would that statement be?

An Affirming Request

Occasionally a dispute is so deep and longstanding that it calls for a third party—an objective, unprejudiced arbitrator—to come between those in conflict to help bring restoration. That is Paul's request here:

> Indeed, true comrade, I ask you also to help these women who have shared my struggle in the cause of the gospel, together with Clement also, and the rest of my fellow workers, whose names are in the book of life.
>
> *Philippians 4:3*

All sorts of suggestions have been made as to the identity of the one called "true comrade." One scholar suggested Barnabas. If so, why didn't Paul call him by name? Another said it could have been Epaphroditus. But, again, one wonders why he would have been called by name earlier yet referred to as "true comrade" here. A curious suggestion has been a person named Sunzugos, which is the Greek transliteration of "comrade." One fanciful idea is that the person was one of their husbands (I doubt that either husband would have relished that role) . . . another, that it was Paul's wife!

The name of the mediator is not nearly as important as the help that he or she could bring ("help these women"). Why did this mean so much to Paul that he included it in his letter? Because these women were important. They had "shared in the struggle" with Paul, and they belonged to the same spiritual family. Their clash was hurting the fellowship among the Christians at Philippi, so it needed resolution . . . soon. The bride needed to stop brawling!

Someone has said that Christians trying to live in close harmony is the next thing to impossible. The scene is not unlike the old forest folktale where two porcupines were huddled close together on a cold, cold night up in northern Canada. The closer they got to stay warm, the more their quills pricked each other, making it virtually impossible for them to remain side by side. Silently, they scooted apart. Before long, they were shivering in the wintry gale, so they came back together. Soon both were poking and jabbing each other . . . so they separated again. Same story . . . same result. Their action was like a slow-moving, monotonous dance—back and forth, back and forth.

Those two women in Philippi were like the Canadian porcupines; they needed each other, but they kept needling each other. Unfortunately, the disruptive dance of disharmony did not stop in that first-century church.

May I speak to you heart-to-heart, as friend-to-friend, before ending this chapter? In all honesty, have my words opened an old wound that has never healed? Did the imaginary scene of a brawling bride bring back a few ugly memories of an unresolved conflict in your past . . . or maybe several of them? Is there someone you continue to blame for the hurt you had to endure, bringing pain that never got reconciled? If so, do you have any idea how much emotional energy you are burning up nursing that wound? And while I'm asking questions: Are you aware of the joy-stealing effect an unforgiving spirit is having on your life? If your bitterness is deep enough, you've virtually stopped living. It is no wonder you have also stopped laughing!

Please listen to me. *It is not worth it.* You need to come to terms with this lingering, nagging issue *now.* The peace and contentment and joy that could be yours are draining away, like water down the drain of an unplugged bathtub. It is time for you to call a halt to the dispute; the disharmony must be defused. But it won't happen automatically. You are an essential part of the healing equation. You must do something about it.

Start by telling God how much it hurts and that you need Him to help you to forgive the offense. If you have a friend who is close enough to you to help you work your way through the process, reach out and say so. Get rid of all the poison of built-up anger and pour out all the acid of long-term resentment. Your objective is clear: Fully forgive the offender. Once that is done, you will discover that you no longer rehearse the ugly scenes in your mind. The revengeful desire to get back and get even will wane, and in its now-empty space will come such an outpouring of relief and a new spirit of joy that you won't feel like the same person. That deep frown on your brow and those long lines on your face will slowly disappear. And before too long you will get reacquainted with a sound you haven't made for months, maybe years. It is called laughter.

A resentful, unforgiving spirit and a carefree, happy heart never existed in the same body. Until you take care of the former you won't be able to enjoy the latter.

Considering the Lessons This Teaches Us . . .

I can think of at least four practical lessons we have learned from the things we have been considering.

1. Clashes will continue to occur. I wish I could promise you otherwise, but as long as depravity pollutes humanity, we can forget about a

conflict-free environment. So, don't be surprised when another skirmish breaks out.

2. Not all conflicts are wrong. Not all disagreements require reconciliation. As I recall, it was Jesus who said that He brings "a sword" into certain relationships. Occasionally it is right to be defiant and to fight. When critical biblical lines are drawn and the issues at stake have nothing to do with personal preferences or individual personalities, surrendering to a cause that would lead to wrong is wrong.

3. If the disagreement *should* be resolved and *could* be resolved but is not, then stubbornness and selfishness are at the core. We may be adults in age and height, but we can be awfully childish in attitude. Come on, give in. To persist in this lack of harmony brings hurts far greater than the small radius of your relationship.

4. Should you be the "comrade" needed to assist in the reconciliation, remember the threefold objective:

- The ultimate goal: Restoration (not discipline)
- The overall attitude: Grace (not force)
- The common ground: Christ (not logic or the church or tradition or your will)

There is something magnanimous about the name of Jesus that softens our attitude and defuses disharmony. Somehow the insertion of His name makes it inappropriate to maintain a fighting spirit.

The truth of that was underscored when I read of something that happened over one hundred years ago.

Charles H. Spurgeon, Baptist minister of London, England, had a pastor-friend, Dr. Newman Hall, who wrote a book entitled, *Come to Jesus.* Another preacher published an article in which he ridiculed Hall, who bore it patiently for a little while. But when the article gained popularity, Hall sat down and wrote a letter of protest. His answer was full of retaliatory invectives that outdid anything in the article which attacked him. Before mailing the letter, Hall took it to Spurgeon for his opinion.

Spurgeon read it carefully then, handing it back, asserted it was excellent and that the writer of the article deserved it all. "But," he added, "it just lacks one thing." After a pause Spurgeon continued,

"Underneath your signature you ought to write the words, 'Author of *Come to Jesus.*' "

The two godly men looked at each other for a few minutes. Then Hall tore the letter to shreds.[4]

12

Freeing Yourself Up to Laugh Again

CYNTHIA AND I ARE INTO Harley-Davidson motorcycles.

I know, I know . . . it doesn't fit our image. Who really cares? We stopped worrying about our image years ago. We should be ashamed of ourselves? We aren't. We're having a mutual mid-life crisis? We hope so. We should be better examples to the youth? They love it! Actually, it's only a few crotchety adults who don't. What are we going to say to our grandkids? "Hey, kids, wanna ride?" And how are we supposed to explain it to "the board?" They don't care either. This is *California*, remember?

We are having more fun than anybody can imagine (except fellow Harley riders). One of the best things about the whole deal is that those guys and gals down at the bike shop don't have a clue as to who we are. We have *finally* found a place in our area where we can be out in public and remain absolutely anonymous. If anybody down there happens to ask our names, we'll just tell 'em we're Jim and Shirley Dobson. Those Harley hogs don't know them either.

You should have been in the showroom when I first sat on one of those big bikes. Cynthia stood a few feet away and just stared. She didn't know whether to laugh out loud or witness to me. She compromised and hopped on behind after I winked at her. She couldn't resist. As soon as she leaned forward and whispered in my ear, "Honey, I could get used to this," I knew it wouldn't be long before we'd be truckin' down the asphalt without a worry in the world.

We sat there and giggled like a couple of high school sweethearts sipping a soda through two straws. She liked the feel of sitting close to me (she couldn't resist, naturally), and I liked the feel of her behind me and that giant engine underneath us. And that inimitable Harley *roar.* Man, it was great!

Suddenly, sitting on that shiny black Heritage Softail Classic with thick leather saddlebags, we were on the back streets of Houston in 1953 all over again, roaring our way to a Milby High School football game. She was wearing my letterman's sweater and red-and-white saddle oxfords, and I had a flattop with a ducktail and a black leather jacket with fringe and chrome studs!

When we came back to our senses, we realized that somehow we were sorta misfits. I mean, a responsible senior pastor and radio preacher in a suit and tie with a classy, well-dressed woman who is executive vice president of Insight for Living perched on a Harley-Davidson in a motorcycle showroom. Everybody else was wearing t-shirts, torn jeans, boots, black leather stuff, and sported tattoos. I saw one guy who had a tattoo on each arm . . . one was of a snarling bulldog with a spiked collar and the other was the Marine insignia—the eagle, globe, and anchor of the Corps! A few folks were glancing in our direction as if to say, "Get serious!" And Cynthia leaned up again and whispered, "Do you think we ought to be in here?"

"Of course, honey, who cares? After all, *I'm a Marine!* What I need is a pair of black jeans and leather chaps and all you need is a tattoo, and we'll blend right in." The jeans and chaps for me, probably someday. But Cynthia with a tattoo? I rather doubt it. Somehow I don't think it would go over very big at formal church dinners and the National Religious Broadcasters banquets.

We have had one hilarious time with this in our family. Especially since I raised all four of our kids with only one unchangeable Swindoll rule: "You will not *ever* ride on or own a motorcycle!" Now the old man and his babe are roaring all around town. And it's our now-grown kids who are trying to figure out what's happened to their parents and what to say to *their* kids when they see their grandparents tooling down the freeway like a couple of gray-haired teenagers. Actually, we're getting concerned lately that our children may be a little too strict with *their* kids. "Ya gotta lighten up, guys," as they say down at the Harley hangout. The only one of the bunch who fully understands is our youngest, Chuck—but that makes sense. He rides a Harley too.

What's happening? What would ever possess me to start messing around with a motorcycle, cruising some of the picturesque roads down by the ocean, or taking off with my son for a relaxed, easygoing two or three hours together? What's this all about?

It's about forgetting all the nonsense that every single moment in life is serious. It's about breaking the thick and rigid mold of predictability. It's about enjoying a completely different slice of life where I don't have to concern myself with living up to anyone else's expectations or worry about who thinks what. It's about being with one of our kids in a world that is totally on his turf (for a change), not mine, in a setting that is just plain fun, not work. It's about being me, nobody else.

It's about breaking the bondage of tunnel vision. It's about refusing to live my life playing one note on one instrument in one room and finding pleasure in a symphony of sounds and sights and smells. It's about widening the radius of a restrictive and demanding schedule where breathing fresh air is sometimes difficult and thinking creative thoughts is occasionally the next thing to impossible.

Bottom line, it's about freedom. That's it, plain and simple. It's about being free.

It's about entering into a tension-free, worry-free world where I don't have to say something profound or fix anyone or do anything other than feel the wind and smell the flowers and hug my wife and laugh till we're hoarse. That's it in a nutshell . . . it's about freeing ourselves up to laugh again.

In Jesus' day He took His twelve disciples across a lake to enjoy some R&R alone on a mountainside. Who knows what they did for fun? Maybe they climbed rocks or swam in a cool lake or sat around a campfire and told a few jokes. Whatever, you can count on this—they laughed. Today, Cynthia and I prefer to hop on the old Harley. If Jesus lived on earth today, He might ride with us. But something in me says He probably wouldn't get a tattoo. Then again, who knows? He did a lot of other stuff that made the legalists squirm. He knew the truth . . . and the truth had really set Him free.

Getting Serious About Being Set Free

Americans did not invent the idea of freedom. Even though we have fought wars for it and built monuments to it, it is not original with us. It began with God, way back in the Garden of Eden when He made Adam and Eve. God made them—and He has made you and me—to enjoy the pleasures and the responsibilities of freedom. How?

- God made us with a mind . . . that we might think freely.
- God made us with a heart . . . that we might love freely.
- God made us with a will . . . that we might obey freely.

Let me analyze those three factors from a strictly human viewpoint. By making us in His image, God gave us capacities not given to other forms of life. Ideally, He made us to know Him, to love Him, and to obey Him. He did not put rings in our noses that He might pull us around like oxen, nor did He create us with strings permanently attached to our hands and feet like human marionettes to control and manipulate our every move. What pleasure would He have in the love of a puppet or the obedience of a dumb animal?

No, He gave us freedom to make choices. By His grace we are equipped to understand His plan because we have a mind with which we can know Him. We are also free to love and adore Him because we have emotions. He takes pleasure in our affection and devotion. We can obey His instructions, but we are not pawns on a global chessboard. It is in the voluntary spontaneity of our response that He finds divine pleasure. When His people *freely* respond in worship and praise, obedience and adoration, God is glorified to the maximum.

There is a downside to all this, however. Because we are free to do these things, we are also free *not* to do them. We are free to make wrong choices—how well we know! In fact, we can continue to make them for so long we can wind up in our own self-made prison of consequences. That prison of our own choosing can hold us in such bondage that we are unable to escape. When that occurs, we experience the ultimate in earthly misery. It is called *addiction.* If you have ever been in such bondage or worked with someone who is, you know firsthand how horrible an existence it can be. Strange as it may seem, an addiction is the tragic consequence of freedom . . . freedom out of control . . . freedom gone to seed.

What God Has Promised

It is at this point that God is ultragracious. He takes no cruel delight in seeing us squirm, trapped in a dungeon of our own making. In fact, that is a large part of the reason He sent His Son to this earth. He sent Him on a mission of mercy to set the captives free. One of the earliest declarations of Christ's Great Commission (His mission statement) is found in Isaiah's ancient prophecy. Though written seven centuries before His birth, this was the coming Messiah's "job description":

> The Spirit of the Lord GOD is upon me,
> Because the LORD has anointed me
> To bring good news to the afflicted;
> He has sent me to bind up the brokenhearted,
> To proclaim liberty to captives,
> And freedom to prisoners;
> To proclaim the favorable year of the LORD,
> And the day of vengeance of our God;
> To comfort all who mourn,
> To grant those who mourn in Zion,
> Giving them a garland instead of ashes,
> The oil of gladness instead of mourning,
> The mantle of praise instead of a spirit of fainting.
> So they will be called oaks of righteousness,
> The planting of the LORD, that He may be glorified.
>
> *Isaiah 61:1–3*

Don't miss those words, "To proclaim liberty to captives and freedom to prisoners."

Lest you think the prophet was writing of himself, notice what Jesus did and said more than seven hundred years later when He was beginning His ministry in Nazareth. Read these words carefully as you imagine the scene:

> And He came to Nazareth, where He had been brought up; and as was His custom, He entered the synagogue on the Sabbath, and stood up to read. And the book of the prophet Isaiah was handed to Him. And He opened the book, and found the place where it was written,
>
> "THE SPIRIT OF THE LORD IS UPON ME,
> BECAUSE HE ANOINTED ME TO PREACH THE GOSPEL TO THE POOR.
> HE HAS SENT ME TO PROCLAIM RELEASE TO THE CAPTIVES,
> AND RECOVERY OF SIGHT TO THE BLIND,
> TO SET FREE THOSE WHO ARE DOWNTRODDEN,
> TO PROCLAIM THE FAVORABLE YEAR OF THE LORD."

> And He closed the book, and gave it back to the attendant, and sat down; and the eyes of all in the synagogue were fixed upon Him. And He began to say to them, "Today this Scripture has been fulfilled in your hearing."
>
> *Luke 4:16–21*

Isn't that interesting? Of all the Scriptures He could have read, Jesus selected that section from Isaiah. He not only stated that "release to the captives" and "setting free those who are downtrodden" were on His earthly agenda, but that He was beginning to fulfill Isaiah's prophecy that very day.

Hundreds of years before the Messiah came, God promised that He would set the captives free. Obviously He wasn't referring to opening all prison doors and breaking the bars on every jail. The captives He had in mind were those in bondage to sin. And He also stated that He would provide sight for the blind, physically and spiritually. What grand promises!

Let's glance briefly at one more New Testament scene.

> Jesus therefore was saying to those Jews who had believed Him, "If you abide in My word, then you are truly disciples of Mine; and you shall know the truth, and the truth shall make you free." They answered Him, "We are Abraham's offspring, and have never yet been enslaved to anyone; how is it that You say, 'You shall become free'?" Jesus answered them, "Truly, truly, I say to you, everyone who commits sin is the slave of sin. And the slave does not remain in the house forever; the son does remain forever. If therefore the Son shall make you free, you shall be free indeed."
>
> *John 8:31–36*

What I find significant is the promise from Jesus' lips; namely, that a knowledge of the truth is freeing . . . and once freed, we "shall be free indeed." This refers to a deeply personal freedom, an inner emancipation from what has bound you long enough. What a marvelous thought!

How We Have Responded

If the truth could be known, we have only halfheartedly believed God's promise to us. Even though He has made us to be free and to be released from whatever binds us, many have chosen to live enslaved. By opting for bad choices, they have given all sorts of addictions opportunity to take control. And instead of enjoying the benefits of freedom, many live in its backwash as helpless, hopeless captives.

Jean Jacques Rousseau, the eighteenth-century French philosopher, was never more correct than when he said, "Man was born free, and everywhere he is in chains."[1]

The Most Universal of All Addictions

It is time to get specific. So far I have dealt in generalities and not once zeroed in on any one addiction, so you probably feel safe. No longer. Lest you and I start to feel a little smug, thinking we are safe because we don't have a habit so captivating that we are held in bondage, I might as well go to the one addiction that tops all others—worry. Anxiety addicts abound!

The trouble with worry is that it doesn't seem all that harmful. It is a little like the first few snorts of cocaine. A person may know down inside it is not good, but surely it can't be as bad as some have made it out to be. Foolish thinking.

When it comes to worry, we blithely excuse it. For example, one evening we say to a friend, "Hey, don't worry," Our friend responds, "Well, maybe I shouldn't, but you know me. I'm just the worrying type." We answer back, "Yeah, well, I sure understand. I myself am a worrier. Can't blame somebody for feeling a little concerned tonight."

What if we changed that conversation to refer to drinking too much alcohol. Imagine this: "Hey, things will work out." Our friend responds, "Well, maybe I shouldn't, but you know me. I'm just the liquor-drinking type." Answering back, we say, "Yeah, well, I sure understand. I myself drink too much. Can't blame somebody for drinking a couple extras tonight." Suddenly, worry takes on a new significance.

Analyzing the Problem

Of all the joy stealers that can plague our lives, none is more nagging, more agitating, or more prevalent than worry.

We get our English word *worry* from the German word *wurgen,* which means "to strangle, to choke." Our Lord mentioned that very word picture when He addressed the subject on one occasion.

> The sower sows the word. And these are the ones who are beside the road where the word is sown; and when they hear, immediately Satan comes and takes away the word which has been sown in them. And in a similar way these are the ones on whom seed was sown on the rocky places, who, when they hear the word, immediately receive it with joy; and they have no firm root in themselves, but are only temporary; then, when affliction or persecution arises because of the word, immediately they fall away. And others are the ones on whom seed was sown among the thorns; these are the ones who have heard the word, and the worries of the world, and the deceitfulness of riches, and the desires for other things enter in and choke the word, and it becomes unfruitful.
>
> *Mark 4:14–19*

In other words, when worry throttles our thinking, choking out the truth, we are unable to bear fruit. Along with becoming mentally harassed and emotionally strung out, we find ourselves spiritually strangled. Worry cuts off our motivation and lifeline of joy.

In spite of all these consequences, more people are addicted to worry than all other addictions combined. Are you one of them? If you are, you might as well put on hold all the things I have been saying in this book about being more joyful and carefree with an optimistic attitude. You will need to come to terms with your anxiety addiction before you find yourself freed up enough to laugh again.

I know what I'm writing about, believe me. There was a time in my own life when worry controlled me and the tentacles of tension choked much of the fun out of my life. I cared too much about what people thought and said, so I ran a little scared on a daily basis. And then I wasn't sure about my future either. So I worried about that. The churning intensified after I joined the Marines. Cynthia and I had not been married very long. Where would we be stationed? What if I got sent overseas? How would Cynthia do without me . . . and vice versa? The worry list grew once I got my orders—*Okinawa!* Why would God allow this to happen? I mean, the recruiting office promised me that would *never* happen (you're smiling, right?). One by one, day after day, my worries intensified as my joy faded. Prayer was only a formality.

It was while Cynthia and I were separated by the Pacific Ocean for well over a year that I was forced to come to terms with my anxiety addiction. I finally determined to stop that nonsense. I began taking God and His Word much *more* seriously and myself a lot *less* seriously (we usually get those two reversed). I found that prayer was never meant to be a ritual but an actual calling out to God for help . . . and each time I did, He came through. I also discovered that He was in control of life's circumstances as well as the details of my life and my wife. In fact, she was in better care under His sheltering wings than she ever could have been under my roof. She and I both did just fine; matter of fact, *incredibly well.* I kept a journal and I also wrote her letters, sometimes four or five a week. Looking back, I realize it was in the midst of that lonely, involuntary separation that I began to cultivate an interest in writing. (Who would have ever guessed what that letter writing in a little Quonset hut at Camp Courtney, not far from Naha, Okinawa, would lead to?) As I gave my anxieties to God, He took them and solved every one of the things I placed in His care. As I relaxed the tension, He moved in with sovereign grace. It was *wonderful.*

The major turning point occurred when I did an in-depth study of Philippians 4:4–9, which I can still vividly remember. It was then I began . . .

Understanding God's Therapy

Do you realize that God has a sure-cure solution to worry? Has anyone ever told you that if you perfect the process you will be able to live a worry-free existence? Yes, you read that correctly. And if you know me fairly well, you know that I seldom make statements anywhere near that dogmatic. But in this one I am confident. If you will follow God's stated procedure, you will free yourself to laugh again.

First, let's let the Scriptures speak for themselves:

> Rejoice in the Lord always; again I will say, rejoice! Let your forbearing spirit be known to all men. The Lord is near. Be anxious for nothing, but in everything by prayer and supplication with thanksgiving let your requests be made known to God. And the peace of God, which surpasses all comprehension, shall guard your hearts and your minds in Christ Jesus.
>
> *Philippians 4:4–7*

Next, let's get six words clearly fixed in our minds. These six words form the foundation of God's therapeutic process for all worrywarts.

WORRY ABOUT NOTHING,
PRAY ABOUT EVERYTHING

Say that over and over until you can say it without looking. Say the six words aloud. Close the book. Close your eyes. Picture the words in your mind. Spend a minute or more turning them over in your head. What qualifies as a worry? Anything that drains your tank of joy—something you cannot change, something you are not responsible for, something you are unable to control, something (or someone) that frightens and torments you, agitates you, keeps you awake when you should be asleep. All of that now needs to be switched from your worry list to your prayer list. Give each worry—one by one—to God. Do that at this very moment. Tell the Lord you will no longer keep your anxiety to yourself.

Now then, once you buy into this all-important plan God has provided for those who wish to be free, you will begin to have time left in your day . . . lots of extra time and energy. Why? Because you used to spend that time worrying. Your addiction, like all addictions, held you captive. It took your time, it required your attention, it forced you to focus on stuff you had no business trying to deal with or solve.

So what now? How do you spend the time you used to waste worrying? Go back to the words from Paul to the Philippians. As I read them over, I find three key words emerging:

. . . **rejoice** (v. 4)

. . . **relax** (v. 5)

. . . **rest** (v. 7)

They look pretty easy, but for someone who has worried as long as *you* have, they are not. You haven't done much of any of these three lately, have you?

To begin with, REJOICE! Worry about nothing . . . pray about everything, and *REJOICE!*

> Rejoice in the Lord always; again I will say, rejoice!
>
> *Philippians 4:4*

Because we have repeated the term and several synonyms throughout the book so often, the whole idea could begin to lose its edge. Don't let it. Rejoicing is clearly a scriptural command. To ignore it, I need to remind you, is disobedience. In place of worry, start spending time enjoying the release of your humor. Find the bright side, the sunny side of life. Deliberately look for things that are funny during your day.

Loosen up and laugh freely. Laugh more often. Consciously stay aware of the importance of a cheerful countenance. Live lightheartedly! Stop reading only the grim sections of the newspaper. Watch less television and start reading more books that bring a smile instead of a frown. That's exactly why you picked up this one! We put a cover on it that would attract your attention (I think my publisher did a bang-up job, don't you?), and as you thumbed through it you probably thought something like, *I need to quit being so serious—maybe this book will help.* Don't stop with this book. Choose others like it. Feed your mind more uplifting "thought food."

Locate a few acquaintances who will help you laugh more at life. Ideally, find Christian friends who see life through Christ's eyes, which is in itself more encouraging. Have fun together. Share funny stories with each other. Affirm one another.

> Shared laughter creates a bond of friendship. When people laugh together, they cease to be young and old, master and pupils, worker and driver. They have become a single group of human beings, enjoying their existence.[2]

Fred Allen, one of my favorite humorists of yesteryear, used to say that it was bad to suppress your laughter because when you do, he said, it goes down and spreads your hips.[3] Maybe that explains those extra pounds.

Solomon writes that "a cheerful heart has a continual feast" (Prov. 15:15), and he is right. I find that a spirit of cheer spreads rapidly. Before you know it, others have joined you at the table. Choose joy! There are very few days in my life during which I find nothing to laugh at. Laughter is the most familiar sound in the hallway where my staff and I work alongside each other. And what a contagious thing is outrageous joy . . . everybody wants to be around it. So, rejoice!

Next, RELAX! Worry about nothing . . . pray about everything, and *RELAX!*

> Let your forbearing spirit be known to all men. The Lord is near.
>
> *Philippians 4:5*

Where do I find "relax" in Paul's statement? See that unusual expression, "forbearing spirit"? It means "gentleness," or "easy." We would say "easygoing." It is "sweet reasonableness" . . . the idea of a relaxed, easygoing lifestyle. A worry-filled world can increase your tension to a dangerous level. Physically, it can take a serious toll on your health.

Lighten up! So much of what we get nervous about and jumpy over never happens anyway. Let me get downright specific. Relax more with your children. Take it easy, especially if they are junior highers (whom my friend, Kenny Poure, calls "pre-people"). If your son or daughter is struggling through a stage in the stormy adolescent years, have a heart. Back off. Loosen the strings. You will realize later that God was there all along—in control—taking care of business, His business. Oh, if only I had applied more of this when our children were younger. Every once in a while, during one of my unrelaxed, high-tension, tightwire acts, one of our kids would say, "Just take a deep breath, Dad." Ouch! When I took their advice, my "forbearing spirit" resurfaced.

My dear friend, Ruth Harms Calkin, describes our dilemma with this insightful reminder:

Spiritual Retreat

This was my calculated plan:
I would set aside my usual schedule—
The menial tasks that wedge in routinely.
In the peace and quiet of my living room
I would relax in Your glorious presence.
How joyfully I envisioned the hours—
My personal spiritual retreat!
With Bible and notebook beside me
I would study and meditate—
I would intercede for the needy world.

But how differently it happened, Lord:
Never has the phone rung so persistently.
Sudden emergencies kept pouring in
Like summer cloudbursts.
My husband came home ill.
There were appointments to cancel
Plans to rearrange.
The mailman brought two disturbing letters
A cousin whose name I couldn't remember
Stopped by on her way through town.
My morning elation became drooping deflation.

And yet, dear Lord
You were with me in it all!
I sense Your vital presence—
Your sure and steady guidance.
Not once did You leave me stranded.
Perhaps, in Your great wisdom
You longed to teach me a practical truth:
When *You* are my Spiritual Retreat
I need not be a spiritual recluse.[4]

And then, REST! Worry about nothing . . . pray about everything, and *REST!*

> Be anxious for nothing, but in everything by prayer and supplication with thanksgiving let your requests be made known to God. And the peace of God, which surpasses all comprehension, shall guard your hearts and your minds in Christ Jesus.
>
> *Philippians 4:6–7*

I know of few Scriptures that have helped me more than the words you just read. Go back and read them once again, this time slower. Maybe seeing them in The Living Bible will help. That's where I picked up the idea of resting.

> Don't worry about anything; instead, pray about everything; tell God your needs and don't forget to thank him for his answers. If you do this you will experience God's peace, which is far more wonderful than the human mind can understand. His peace will keep your thoughts and your hearts quiet and at rest as you trust in Christ Jesus.
>
> *Philippians 4:6–7 TLB*

Paul writes of God's peace which "shall guard your hearts and your minds." When he mentions peace as a "guard," he uses a military term for "marching sentry duty" around something valuable and/or strategic. As we rest our case, as we transfer our troubles to God, "Corporal Peace" is appointed the duty of marching as a silent sentry around our minds and our emotions, calming us within. How obvious will it be to others? Go back and check—it will "surpass all comprehension." People simply will not be able to comprehend the restful peace we will model. In place of anxiety—that thief of joy—we pray. We push the worrisome, clawing, monster of pressure off our shoulders and hand it over to God in prayer. I am not exaggerating; I must do that hundreds of times every year. And I cannot recall a time when it didn't provide relief. In its place, always, comes a quietness of spirit, a calming of the mind. With a relieved mind, rest returns.

Rejoice. Relax. Rest. The three substitutes for worry. And impatience. And turmoil.

Correcting Our Perspective

Three simple exercises will help you stay worry free.

1. Feed your mind positive thoughts.

> Finally, brethren, whatever is true, whatever is honorable, whatever is right, whatever is pure, whatever is lovely, whatever is of good repute, if there is any excellence and if anything worthy of praise, let your mind dwell on these things.
>
> *Philippians 4:8*

No matter what you're dealing with or how bad things seem to be or why God may be permitting them, deliberately letting your mind dwell on positive, uplifting thoughts will enable you to survive. Literally. I frequently quote those words from Philippians 4:8 to myself. I say things like, "Okay, Chuck, it's time to let your mind dwell on better things." And then I go over the list and deliberately replace a worry with something far more honorable or pure or lovely, something worthy of praise. It never fails; the pressure I was feeling begins to fade and the peace I was missing begins to emerge.

2. Focus your attention on encouraging models.

> The things you have learned and received and heard and seen in me, practice these things.
>
> *Philippians 4:9a*

In the Philippians' case, Paul was their model. From his example, there were things to be learned and received and heard and seen. What a demonstration of encouragement he provided!

In your case and mine, it will help to focus our attention on someone we know and/or admire. That life, that encouraging model will give us a boost, a quick charge when our battery starts getting low.

3. Find "the God of Peace" in every circumstance.

> . . . and the God of peace shall be with you.
>
> *Philippians 4:9b*

This is the crowning achievement of recovering from anxiety addiction. Instead of living in the grip of fear, held captive by the chains of tension and dread, when we release our preoccupation with worry, we find God's hand at work on our behalf. He, our "God of peace," comes to our aid, changing people, relieving tension, altering difficult circumstances. The more you practice giving your mental burdens to the Lord, the more exciting it gets to see how God will handle the things that are impossible for you to do anything about. And as a result—you guessed it—you will begin to laugh again.

A Principle . . . A Parrot

What is it, in the final analysis, that makes worry such an enemy of joy? Why does anxiety addiction take such a devastating toll on us? I have been thinking about that for months, and I believe I have the answer, which we might call a principle. At first it may seem simplistic, but this *is* the crux of the problem. This is exactly why anxiety holds us in such bondage.

WORRY FORCES US TO FOCUS
ON THE WRONG THINGS

Instead of essentials, we worry about nonessentials. Rather than looking at the known blessings that God provides today—so abundantly, so consistently—we worry about the unknown and uncertain events of tomorrow. Invariably, when we focus on the wrong things, we miss the main thing that life is all about.

That fact is vividly illustrated by one of my favorite stories. After more than forty years of marriage, this woman's husband suddenly died. For several months she sat alone in her house with the shades pulled and the door locked. Finally she decided she needed to do something about her situation. The loneliness was killing her.

She remembered that her husband had a friend who owned a nice pet store—a pet might be good company. So she dropped in one afternoon to look over the selection. She looked at dogs, cats, goldfish—even snakes! Nothing seemed quite right. She told the store owner she wanted a pet that could be a real companion—"almost like another human being in the house."

Suddenly he thought of one of his prized parrots. He showed her the colorful bird.

"Does it talk?"

"Absolutely . . . a real chatterbox. Everybody who comes in the store is astounded by this parrot's friendly disposition and wide vocabulary. That's why it's so expensive."

"Sold!" She bought the expensive parrot and hauled it home in a large, elegant cage. At last she had a companion she could talk to, who could answer back. Perfect!

But there was a problem. A full week passed without the bird's saying one word. Beginning to worry, she dropped by the pet shop.

"How's the parrot doing? Quite a talker, huh?"

"Not one word. I haven't been able to get a sound out of that bird. I'm worried!"

"Well, did you buy a *mirror* when you got the parrot and the cage last week?"

"Mirror? No. There's no mirror in the cage."

"That's your problem. A parrot needs a mirror. It's funny, but while looking at itself, a parrot starts to feel comfortable. In no time it will begin to talk." So she bought the mirror and put it into the cage.

Time passed, still nothing. Each day the woman talked to the bird, but not a peep came out of its beak. For hours on end she would talk as the parrot stared in silence. Another week passed without a word. By now she was really getting worried.

"The parrot isn't talking," she told the pet store owner. "I'm worried. All that money, the mirror—and still nothing."

"Say, did you buy a *ladder* when you got the cage?"

"A ladder? No. I didn't know it needed a ladder. Will that make it talk?"

"Works like a charm. The parrot will look in the mirror and get a little exercise, climbing up and down this ladder several times. Before long you won't believe what you hear. Trust me, you need the ladder."

She bought the ladder and put it into the cage next to the mirror . . . and waited. And waited. Another seven, eight days, still nothing. By now her worry was approaching the panic stage. "Why doesn't it talk?" That was all she could think about. She returned to the store in tears . . . with the same complaint.

"Did you buy a *swing*? "

"A swing! No. I have the cage, a mirror, and a ladder—I thought I had everything. I had no idea I needed a swing."

"Ya gotta have a swing. A parrot needs to feel completely at home. It glances in the mirror, takes a stroll up and down the ladder, and before long it's on the swing enjoying itself—and bingo! I've found that parrots usually talk when they are perched on a swing."

The woman bought the swing. She attached it to the top of the cage near the ladder and coaxed the parrot up the ladder and onto the swing. Still, absolute silence. For another ten days not one sound came from the cage.

Suddenly she came bursting into the pet store, really steaming. The owner met her at the counter.

"Hey, how's the parrot? I'll bet—"

"It died! My expensive bird is dead in the bottom of the cage."

"Well, I can't believe that. I'm just shocked. Did it ever say anything at all?"

"Yes, as a matter of fact, it did. As it lay there taking its last few breaths, it said very faintly, 'Don't they have any *food* down at that store?' "

There is no greater waste of our time and no greater deterrent to our joy than worry. By turning our attention to the wrong things, worry leads us to live our lives for the wrong reasons . . . and God is grieved. As I mentioned earlier in the book, God gives to His beloved even in our sleep. As we rejoice, relax, and rest, He relieves, renews, and restores.

A weary Christian lay awake one night trying to hold the world together by his worrying. Then he heard the Lord gently say to him, "Now you go to sleep, Jim; I'll sit up."[5]

13

Don't Forget to Have Fun As You Grow Up

I LIKE THE QUESTION ONCE ASKED by Satchel Paige, that venerable alumnus of baseball: "How old would you be if you didn't know how old you were?" An honest answer to that question depends on an honest admission of one's attitude. It has nothing to do with one's age. As someone young at heart has written:

> Remember, old folks are worth a fortune—silver in their hair, gold in their teeth, stones in their kidneys, lead in their feet, and gas in their stomachs.
>
> I have become a little older since I saw you last, and a few changes have come into my life since then. Frankly, I have become quite a frivolous old gal. I am seeing five gentlemen every day.
>
> As soon as I wake up, Will Power helps me get out of bed. Then I go to see John. Then Charlie Horse comes along, and when he is here he takes a lot of my time and attention. When he leaves Arthur Ritis shows up and stays the rest of the day. He doesn't like to stay in one place very long, so he takes me from joint to joint. After such a busy day I'm really tired and glad to go to bed with Ben Gay. What a life!
>
> P.S. The preacher came to call the other day. He said at my age I should be thinking about the hereafter. I told him, "Oh, I do all the time. No matter where I am—in the parlor, upstairs, in the kitchen, or down in the basement—I ask myself what am I here after?"[1]

The longer I live the more I become convinced that our major battle in life is not with age but with maturity. All of us are involuntary victims of the former. There is no choice involved in growing older. Our challenge is the choice of whether or not to grow up. It was Jesus who asked, "Who of you by worrying can add one inch to your height. . . or subtract one day from your age?" (Matt. 6:25–31). In other words, don't waste your time worrying about how old you are getting. Age is a matter of fact. Maturity, on the other hand, is a matter of choice.

You may be thinking, *Well, Chuck, that is all well and good, but you can't teach an old dog new tricks.* To which I respond with two reminders:

1. I am not writing to "old dogs." You are a person who has the capacity to think and to decide. Furthermore, if you are a Christian, you have the power of Christ within you, which means sufficient inner dynamic to effect incredible changes. If you are not a Christian, there is no time like the present to take care of that.

2. I am not teaching "tricks." The things you are reading are attainable and meaningful techniques that, when applied, can help you break old habits and form new ones. Admittedly the process of change may not come easy, but many have done it and you can too. The real question is not, "Am I able?" but, "Am I willing?"

Our becoming more mature is toward the top of the list on God's agenda for us. Repeatedly He mentions it in His Book:

> As a result, we are no longer to be children, tossed here and there by waves, and carried about by every wind of doctrine, by the trickery of men, by craftiness in deceitful scheming; but speaking the truth in love, we are to grow up in all aspects into Him, who is the head, even Christ.
>
> *Ephesians 4:14–15*

> Therefore, putting aside all malice and all guile and hypocrisy and envy and all slander, like newborn babes, long for the pure milk of the word, that by it you may grow in respect to salvation.
>
> *1 Peter 2:1–2*

> But solid food is for the mature, who because of practice have their senses trained to discern good and evil. Therefore leaving the elementary teaching about the Christ, let us press on to maturity, not laying again a foundation of repentance from dead works and of faith toward God.
>
> *Hebrews 5:14—6:1*

You and I are growing older. That's automatic. But that does not necessarily mean we are growing up. How important it is that we do so! And it will not happen unless we get control of our attitude, which turns us in the right direction. Let me urge you not to feed your mind with thoughts like: *I'm too far gone to change;* or, *Having been through all the things I've been through, there is no way I can alter my attitude.* Wrong! It is childish to play in the traffic of fear or let the hobgoblins of habit impede our progress. No one can win a race by continually looking back at where he or she has been. That will only demoralize, immobilize, and ultimately paralyze. God is for us. God's goal is that we move toward maturity, all our past failures and faults and hangups notwithstanding. I have seen many adults who thought they couldn't change begin to change. So I'm no longer willing to sit back and let anyone stay riveted to yesterday, thinking, *Woe is me.* Some of the most sweeping changes in my own life have occurred in my adult years. If it can happen in me, there is an enormous amount of hope for you. Attitudes can soar even if our circumstances lag and our past record sags.

God's specialty is bringing renewal to our strength, not reminders of our weakness. Take it by faith, He is well aware of your weaknesses; He just sovereignly chooses not to stop there. They become the platform upon which He does His best work. Cheer up! There is great hope. You won't be the first He helped from puberty to maturity.

That Elusive Quality Called Maturity

If maturity is all that important, we need to understand it better. The clearer it is in our minds, the easier it will be to get a focus on the target.

Exactly What Is It?

To be mature is to be fully developed, complete, and "grown up." Becoming mature is a process of consistently moving toward emotional and spiritual adulthood. In that process we leave childish and adolescent habits and adopt a lifestyle where we are fully responsible for our own decisions, motives, actions, and consequences. I heard someone say recently that maturity is developed and discerning competence as to how to live appropriately and to change rightly. In a word, it is *stability.* We never "arrive." We are always in the process of moving toward that objective. I have also observed that when maturity is taking place, balance replaces extremes and a seasoned confidence replaces uneasy feelings of insecurity. Good choices replace wrong ones.

How Is It Expressed?

Several things come to mind when I think of how all this works its way out. Marks of maturity are emerging—

- When our concern for others outweighs our concern for ourselves
- When we detect the presence of evil or danger before it is obvious
- When we have wisdom and understanding as well as knowledge
- When we have more than high ideals but also the discipline to carry them out
- When our emotions are tempered by responsibility and thoroughness
- When our awareness of needs is matched by our compassion and involvement
- When we not only understand a task but also have the fortitude to stay at it until it is done
- When we have a willingness to change, once we are convinced that correction is in order
- When we have the ability to grow spiritually by an independent intake of God's Word

One person summarized it in these words:

> Maturity is the ability to do a job whether you are supervised or not; finish a job once it's started; carry money without spending it. And last, but not least, the ability to bear an injustice without wanting to get even.[2]

TWO SIDES OF THE SAME QUALITY

Most folks I know would agree that those things describe where we would like to be personally. When we think of growing up, that is what we have in mind. Once we are there, who wouldn't have reason to rejoice? But the fact is, if we maintain the right attitude we are able to rejoice while in the process of getting there. That is what is so exciting about Paul's words to his friends in Philippi. Throughout the letter he has continued to emphasize and encourage outrageous joy in spite of difficult circumstances, because of Christ. In fact, that is exactly where this next section begins.

> But I rejoiced in the Lord greatly, that now at last you have revived your concern for me; indeed, you were concerned before, but you lacked opportunity.
>
> *Philippians 4:10*

Who is saying this? Some young turk who has just turned the deal on his first million? A superstar who recently signed an unbelievable contract? Some guy in his twenties about to set sail on a magnificent adventure? Not on your life. Would you believe, a sixty-plus-year-old Jew chained to a Roman guard under house arrest, not knowing if tomorrow he will be killed, brought to court, or set free? Though getting up in years, he is rejoicing. Though without the comforts of home and the privileges of privacy, he is happy. Though he doesn't have a clue regarding his future, he is smiling at life. Though he is set aside, forced to stay in one place, completely removed from the excitement of a broader minisry, he is still rejoicing, still laughing. No matter what happened to him, Paul refused to be caught in the grip of pessimism.

Maturity of Paul

We are able to get a pretty good glimpse here of the man who truly practiced what he preached. I find in this section of his letter at least four characteristics of maturity in Paul's life.

1. He is affirming.

> But I rejoiced in the Lord greatly, that now at last you have revived your concern for me; indeed, you were concerned before, but you lacked opportunity.
>
> *Philippians 4:10*

The words could sound mysterious if you didn't understand that behind them is the financial support of the Philippians. When he writes that they had revived their concern for him, Paul means that they had sent another contribution to help him press on. Don't miss a little detail here. When he says, "You were concerned before, but you lacked opportunity," he means they had wanted to send an offering to him earlier, but they either didn't know where he was or they had no way to get it to him. Normally it is the other way around! We have an opportunity to send our support, but we lack concern.

I am impressed with Paul's affirmation of his friends. This is a thank-you letter . . . a "receipt letter," if you will. The implication is so thoughtful: Even when I didn't hear from you, you were concerned for me. Paul thought better of others, not less. He upheld their intentions. Even when he didn't hear from his friends, he did not doubt that they cared.

We appreciate what people do. We affirm who they are. When we say thank you to someone who completes a task, we are expressing our appreciation. But when we acknowledge and express our gratitude for what others are—in character, in motive, in heart—we are affirming them personally. A mark of maturity is the ability to affirm, not just appreciate. How easy to see people (especially family members and fellow workers at our place of employment) as doers of tasks, but a task-oriented mentality is incomplete. And as important as appreciation for a job well done may be, it too is incomplete. People are not human tools appointed to accomplish a set of tasks, but human beings with souls, with feelings. How essential it is to recognize and affirm the unseen, hidden qualities that make an individual a person of worth and dignity. The best leaders (like Paul) appreciate and affirm.

Max DePree is chairman and chief executive officer of Herman Miller, Inc., the furniture maker that was named one of *Fortune* magazine's ten best managed and most innovative companies. It was also chosen as one of the hundred best companies to work for in America. In his book, *Leadership Is an Art,* DePree touches on the importance of understanding and acknowledging the diversity of people's inner gifts and unseen talents. What he describes has to do with affirmation.

> My father is ninety-six years old. He is the founder of Herman Miller, and much of the value system and impounded energy of the company, a legacy still drawn on today, is a part of his contribution. In the furniture industry of the 1920s the machines of most factories were not run by electric motors, but by pulleys from a central drive shaft. The central drive shaft was run by the steam engine. The steam engine got its steam from the boiler. The boiler, in our case, got its fuel from the sawdust and other waste coming out of the machine room—a beautiful cycle.
>
> The millwright was the person who oversaw that cycle and on whom the entire activity of the operation depended. He was a key person.
>
> One day the millwright died.

My father, being a young manager at the time, did not particularly know what he should do when a key person died, but thought he ought to go visit the family. He went to the house and was invited to join the family in the living room. There was some awkward conversation—the kind with which many of us are familiar.

The widow asked my father if it would be all right if she read aloud some poetry. Naturally, he agreed. She went into another room, came back with a bound book, and for many minutes read selected pieces of beautiful poetry. When she finished, my father commented on how beautiful the poetry was and asked who wrote it. She replied that her husband, the millwright, was the poet.

It is now nearly sixty years since the millwright died, and my father and many of us at Herman Miller continue to wonder: Was he a poet who did millwright's work, or was he a millwright who wrote poetry?

In our effort to understand corporate life, what is it we should learn from this story? In addition to all of the ratios and goals and parameters and bottom lines, it is fundamental that leaders endorse a concept of persons. This begins with an understanding of the diversity of people's gifts and talents and skills.[3]

2. He is contented.

Not that I speak from want; for I have learned to be content in whatever circumstances I am.

Philippians 4:11

As valuable as affirmation may be, maturity is never more obvious than when an individual evidences contentment. And no one was a better model than Paul, who "learned to be content," regardless of his situation. To him it made no difference whether he was freed or bound to a soldier . . . whether the day was hot and humid or bleak and frigid . . . whether the Philippians sent a gift or failed to make contact. How wonderfully refreshing. How incredibly mature!

Some people are thermometers. They merely *register* what is around them. If the situation is tight and pressurized, they register tension and irritability. If it's stormy, they register worry and fear. If it's calm, quiet, and comfortable, they register relaxation and peacefulness.

Others, however, are thermostats. They *regulate* the atmosphere. They are the mature change-agents who never let the situation dictate to them.

You are probably thinking, *I wish I had that "contentment gift."* Wait. It isn't a gift. It is a learned trait. Paul admits that he has developed the ability to accept and to adapt. Remember? He wrote, "I have *learned* to be content."

That reminds me of the comment we heard from several men who had been prisoners of war during the Vietnam War and survived the horrors of Hanoi. A number of those brave men said the same thing: "We learned after a few hours what it took to survive, and we just adapted to that." They didn't whine and complain because they had been captured. They didn't eat their hearts out because the conditions were miserable and the food was terrible. They chose to adapt.

Interestingly, the Greek term translated "content" does not mean, "I don't care what happens—I'll remain indifferent, numb." No, this unusual term suggests "self-sufficient," and in the context of this letter it means being at peace in Christ's sufficiency. How could Paul adapt and endure? What was it that relieved the tension and allowed him to be so relaxed within? He was convinced that Christ was in the midst of his every day, pouring His power into him. When we believe that, *anything* is bearable. *Nothing* is out of control. When we genuinely have that attitude, laughter comes easily, naturally.

3. He is flexible.

> I know how to get along with humble means, and I also know how to live in prosperity; in any and every circumstance I have learned the secret of being filled and going hungry, both of having abundance and suffering need.
>
> *Philippians 4:12*

What an enviable list. Three strong contrasts illustrate the man's ability to adapt.

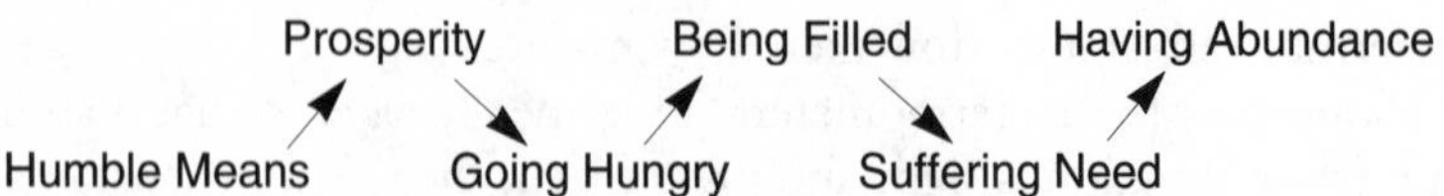

In the yo-yo of life, it is essential to flex. Paul wasn't ticked off because he was on the street, sleeping under a bridge with a growling stomach. Neither was he uneasy in the penthouse, enjoying delicious meals in abundance. When without, he didn't grumble. And when blessed he didn't act unworthy and ashamed. Mature men and women can handle both without disturbing their spiritual or emotional equilibrium.

For some strange reason, most Christians I know struggle more with having an abundance than with suffering great need. Maybe that explains the tendency among Christians to judge and criticize other believers who have wealth and lovely possessions, even though they earned it honestly and hold it all loosely. What graceless immaturity! For some weird reason we would rather brag about how little we have than thankfully relax in a context of God-given prosperity. Am I promoting some kind of "prosperity" gospel? In no way; I think such teaching is heresy. But my concern here is that we be just as willing "to rejoice with those who rejoice" as we are "to weep with those who weep" (Rom. 12:15). When I meet those who cannot do both with equal passion and support, I realize that the problem is immaturity. What concerns me the most is the lack of interest in learning to change in that area.

4. He is confident.

> I can do all things through Him who strengthens me.
>
> *Philippians 4:13*

I mentioned earlier that Paul demonstrated self-sufficiency in his contentment. Here is the statement I referred to when I said that he was sufficient in Christ's sufficiency. The Living Bible puts it this way:

> For I can do everything God asks me to with the help of Christ who gives me the strength and power.

No statement in Scripture speaks more clearly of the indwelling Christ. Our Savior not only *lives* within each of His people, He also *pours His power* into us. And that alone is enough to make us confident.

Consider again Paul's statement. Whatever we may substitute for "Christ" fails to fit the statement. Let's try several.

"I can do all things through *drugs.*" No.

"I can do all things through *education.*" No.

"I can do all things through *money.*" No.

"I can do all things through *success.*" No.

"I can do all things through *friends.*" No.

"I can do all things through *positive thinking.*" No.

"I can do all things through *political office.*" No.

Nothing else fits . . . only Christ. Why? Because nothing and no one else is able to empower us and provide the strength we need. Because the Christian has the Lord Himself dwelling within, the potential for inner strength (i.e., confidence) is unlimited. This explains why those who gave their lives for whatever righteous cause down through the ages did so with such courage. Often they were physically weak individuals, small in stature, but they refused to back down. Only the indwelling, empowering Christ can give someone that much confidence. It is almost as if He gives us a feeling of victorious invincibility. That kind of mature confidence enables us to laugh in the face of resistance.

Maturity of the Philippians

We found four qualities of maturity in Paul.

- Affirming others
- Contented, regardless
- Flexible, whatever the situation
- Confident through Christ

I find it interesting that his Christian friends in Philippi, according to what he wrote of them, also demonstrated maturity. I find at least three characteristics in their lives.

1. Personal compassion.

> Nevertheless, you have done well to share with me in my affliction. And you yourselves also know, Philippians, that at the first preaching of the gospel, after I departed from Macedonia, no church shared with me in the matter of giving and receiving but you alone.
>
> *Philippians 4:14–15*

Paul had numerous needs as he traveled on his missionary journeys. He endured hardship and disappointments, heartaches and afflictions.

Through it all, the Philippians lent their support. In fact, no other church demonstrated such personal compassion—a mark of maturity. They never second-guessed the apostle in his decision to move on; they supported him. They neither judged him when things went well nor complained when times were hard and he had no fruit to show for his labor; they supported him. They felt pain when he hurt, they prayed for him when he was unable to stay in touch, and they sent friends to comfort him when he was in prison. What a church! No wonder he felt such affection for them.

2. Financial generosity.

> For even in Thessalonica you sent a gift more than once for my needs. Not that I seek the gift itself, but I seek for the profit which increases to your account.
>
> *Philippians 4:16–17*

There is perhaps no finer evidence of maturity than financial generosity. When people graciously and liberally release their treasure to the cause of Christ, it is a sign that they are growing up. The people of Philippi were models of this—"even in Thessalonica." That was a wealthier city than Philippi. Yet even when Paul was there, the Philippians kept right on giving.

By the way, don't rush over that second sentence ("Not that I seek . . .") too quickly. Paul wasn't interested in getting their money; rather, he was seeking their best interest. Am I saying he didn't need their financial contributions? On the contrary. He probably could not have survived without them.

We need a whole new mentality when it comes to thinking clearly about money. The greed of this era has caused the subject of money to be tainted and misunderstood. Money, however, is not evil. It is immature to think it is. While it can be abused and can become the cause for all sorts of evil (1 Tim. 6:10), how one handles this medium of exchange is often a good barometer of one's spiritual and emotional growth. Very few things get accomplished in the realm of ministry without the presence of generous financial support from God's choice servants. Let's face it, money and ministry often flow together. There is nothing unspiritual about admitting the need for money in our lives. To quote the great Sophie Tucker:

From birth to eighteen, a girl needs good parents.
From eighteen to thirty-five, she needs good looks.
From thirty-five to fifty-five, she needs a good personality.
From fifty-five on, she needs cash.[4]

Paul's need was for cash, no question about it. Because his friends were mature, they responded generously.

3. Sacrificial Commitment.

> But I have received everything in full, and have an abundance; I am amply supplied, having received from Epaphroditus what you have sent, a fragrant aroma, an acceptable sacrifice, well-pleasing to God.
>
> *Philippians 4:18*

As Paul took stock of his situation, he realized he couldn't have been better taken care of. As he put it, he was "amply supplied." He had more than enough. Thanks to the sacrificial commitment of the Philippians, his needs were wonderfully met. And isn't that the way it is supposed to be? As the gift is given, prompted by the Spirit of God, it comes as "a fragrant aroma," giving God great delight.

It is as if Paul's heart suddenly bursts forth with gratitude as he writes this splendid promise to his friends:

> And my God shall supply all your needs according to His riches in glory in Christ Jesus.
>
> *Philippians 4:19*

When God is in our hearts of compassion, prompting us to get involved in helping others . . . when He is in our acts of generosity, honoring our support of those engaged in ministry . . . and when He is in our strong commitment, using our sacrifices to bless other lives, He does not forget us in our need. It is all so beautiful, so simple, so right. It is enough to make every one of us *laugh out loud!*

But there is a flip side to all this where something meant to be simple and beautiful can become slick and ugly. The whole subject of finances and fund raising and remaining pure, humble, and grateful in the handling of money is a heavy weight hanging on the thin wires of integrity and accountability. Because a few ministries, rare negative examples, have made the news over the misuse of funds, some would discredit all ministries who need the support of God's people. That is both unfortunate and unfair. All physicians are not viewed with suspicion because a few have been guilty of malpractice. God honors the sacrificial commitment of His people and promises His blessing on those who give that His work might go on.

It is as if Paul is summing up his thoughts with the final verse:

My God . . .

your needs . . .

His riches. . . .

When those three ingredients blend together under the control of the Holy Spirit, it is *something* to behold!

Before we bring this chapter to a close, I want to address the importance of earning the respect of those who continue to support a ministry. As Paul maintained a life of trust and faith and quiet confidence in God, the people in Philippi did not hesitate to stand with him financially. Though he occasionally enjoyed times of abundance and prosperity, Paul never became enamored by his success. He assumed nothing and continued to walk humbly with his God. He refused to believe his own press clippings or lose sight of God's hand in it all.

When the PTL scandal grabbed the attention of the national media, so many in the church, including myself, watched in embarrassed disbelief. As one disgraceful act after another became public knowledge, our disbelief turned to shock and shame. All of us wondered how such things could have happened in a ministry. Some of the answers were provided in an interview *Christianity Today* did with Richard Dortch, who was on staff as PTL grew in popularity. Of special interest to me was his description of how the managers of that organization came to define success:

> It is all tied to how many stations we have on our network or how big our building is. It is so easy to lose control, to compromise without recognizing it. At PTL, there was not time taken for prayer or family because the show had to go on. We were so caught up in God's work that we forgot about God.[5]

With unusual candor, Mr. Dortch also mentioned the incredible impact of television on the one up-front under the bright lights, always before an applauding audience:

> A television camera can change a preacher quicker than anything else. Those who sit on the sidelines can notice the changes in people once they get in front of a camera. It turns a good man into a potentate. It is so easy to get swept away by popularity: Everybody loves you, cars are waiting for you, and you go to the head of the line. That is the devastation of the camera. It has made us less than what God has wanted us to become.[6]

Mr. Dortch's words sound forth another grim reminder that maturity, integrity, and accountability must remain present if we hope to know the blessing of God. People's support is a sacred trust, never to be taken lightly.

MAKING MATURITY A PERSONAL MATTER

How can these truths get lifted from the printed page and transferred to our lives? What's necessary if we hope to break the selfish syndrome and accelerate our growth toward maturity? Let me leave you three bones to chew on:

1. Look within . . . and release. What is it down inside you that is stunting your growth? When you probe around and find something you are hanging onto too tightly, deliberately let go. Yes, you can. You just read it from Paul's pen. You "can do all things through Christ." Let Him help you pry your fingers loose. Inner joy begins when you have "no other gods before you."

2. Look around . . . and respond. Don't wait for someone else. Act on your own, spontaneously. The Philippians saw Paul in his need and they responded . . . again and again. Even though other churches did not follow their example, those folks from Philippi saw the need and responded. Is there some need you can help meet? Risk responding.

3. Look up . . . and rejoice. You are the recipient of His riches—enjoy them! Realize anew all He has done for you; then rejoice in the pleasure of getting involved with others. Among the happiest people are those who voluntarily serve others to the glory of God. Some of the saddest are people who have ceased all contact with those in need.

A comment from Jeanne Hendricks' fine volume, *Afternoon,* has helped me remember this:

> Living is not a spectator sport. No one, at any price, is privileged to sit in the stands and watch the action from a distance. Being born means

> being a participant in the arena of life, where opposition is fierce and winning comes only to those who exert every ounce of energy.[7]

Laughter is definitely connected to staying involved with people. Stay involved! You will never regret it. Furthermore, it will help you grow up as you find yourself growing old. And the more involved you remain, the less concern you will have for how old you are.

By the way, how old *would* you be if you didn't know how old you were?

14

A Joyful, Grace-Filled Good-bye

THIS HAS BEEN THE MOST ENJOYABLE BOOK I have written. The chapters have flowed together (an author's dream!), and the theme of outrageous joy and laughter has lifted my own spirits immensely. I am convinced the Lord knew I needed a dose of my own medicine. With all the heaviness and "bad-news blues" I have had to wade through lately, I was ready for a lighthearted shot in the arm. It worked. I hope it has for you too.

All that prompts a confession: I get weary of believers who live their entire lives with such long faces and nothing but woe-is-me words pouring from their mouths. I realize that life isn't one continually blooming rose garden (mine certainly isn't), but surely it is more than Lamentations Lane. I look at some who claim to be "happy within," and I wonder if maybe they were baptized in freshly squeezed lemon juice. When did we buy into that nonsense? Each time I look up and see Dr. Dryasdust and his wife Grimly making their way toward me, I find myself wanting to run and hide or, better, be raptured out!

Reminds me of a cartoon every mother of small children will appreciate. A little freckled-faced boy, five or six years old, is standing in his pajamas outside his parents' bedroom door—which is shut *and locked.* He looks like the type who would keep six or seven healthy adults jumping. The bottom of his pajamas is unsnapped, his diaper is bagging and soaked, his teddy bear has had its nose torn off and one button-eye is dangling, the other missing. He is staring at a sign, hanging from the doorknob, on which his mom has scribbled

CLOSED FOR BUSINESS!
MOTHERHOOD OUT OF ORDER

There are days I'm tempted to do the same on my study door. Only my sign would read something like:

I'VE HEARD ENOUGH!
MINISTER OUT OT ORDER
GONE RIDIN' ON MY HARLEY
BE BACK IN TWO DAYS—MAYBE

There are days a guy like me (and perhaps you can identify) starts running out of ideas on how to help folks fix their messed-up lives. Sometimes the more I try, the worse the mess. Ever had that happen? Then you understand. But maybe not as well as a fellow named R. D. Jones. "Dear Abby" mentioned him in one of her newspaper columns several months ago. It had to do with a typographical error in the classified section of a small-town newspaper and the subsequent disastrous attempts to correct it. Things went from bad to worse to *horrible.*

Monday: FOR SALE—R. D. Jones has one sewing machine for sale. Phone 948–0707 after 7 p.m. and ask for Mrs. Kelly who lives with him cheap.

Tuesday: NOTICE—We regret having erred in R. D. Jones' ad yesterday. It should have read: One sewing machine for sale. Cheap. Phone 948–0707 and ask for Mrs. Kelly who lives with him after 7 p.m.

Wednesday: NOTICE—R. D. Jones has informed us that he has received several annoying telephone calls because of the error we made in his classified ad yesterday. His ad stands corrected as follows: FOR SALE—R. D. Jones has one sewing machine for sale. Cheap. Phone 948–0707 p.m. and ask for Mrs. Kelly who loves with him.

Thursday: NOTICE—I, R. D. Jones, have NO sewing machine for sale. I SMASHED IT. Don't call 948–0707, as the telephone has been disconnected. I have not been carrying on with Mrs. Kelly. Until yesterday she was my housekeeper, but she quit.[1]

I suggest that R. D. Jones pick up a copy of my book on Friday and start reading right away. And Mrs. Kelly should spend the whole weekend in it, nonstop.

At times like that we need to find relief from life's blistering winds of disappointment and discouragement. For me, nothing works better than a break in the schedule where hearty laughter and a whole change of pace takes my mind off the demands and deadlines. And of all the books in the Bible that help bring a fresh perspective, Philippians tops the list. Again and again it reminds us that we can choose joy regardless of our circumstances, our financial status, our occupation, our past failures, or our current distresses. Thank goodness, things don't have to be perfect or nearly perfect in order for us to focus on the bright side of life.

Where Have We Been?

Since we have come to the last few words Paul wrote his friends at Philippi, this is a good time to do a little review of where we have been. Threaded through the fabric of this delightful letter has been an overriding theme of joy and rejoicing.

- In chapter 1 of the letter we found *joy in living*. Can you remember? It was there the Apostle of Grace communicated, "For me to live is Christ" (1:21). As long as Christ is central in my life, nothing can steal that joy He brings.
- In chapter 2 of Philippians we discovered there is *joy in serving*. And from whom do we learn this? Again, Christ is the model. With an attitude of submission and acceptance, He left the splendor of heaven in order to come and serve others on earth.
- In chapter 3 *joy in submitting* was the prominent message. Christ, according to that chapter, is our goal. Paul lists all his accomplishments and human effort then admits that, compared to Christ, those things he "counted as loss." Zero. Compared to Christ's righteousness, human effort is nothing more than cotton candy.
- In chapter 4 we learned there is *joy in resting*. Why? Because Jesus Christ is our cause for contentment. We can rest in Him, and as we do, He pours His power into us. When He does that our confidence is re-ignited and restored.

This little letter, the most upbeat of all those Paul wrote, never fails to silence the naysayers and lift our spirits. Surrounded by so many who are down in the mouth, convinced we are headed for doom (with statistics to prove it), we need the reminder that Christ is still triumphant. Our circumstances may be challenging, but God is not wringing His hands, wondering how He is going to work things out. That kind of negative reasoning deserves one of my favorite Greek words in response: *Hogwash.*

I love the way G. Campbell Morgan addresses all this:

> I have no sympathy with people who tell us today that these are the darkest days the world has ever seen. The days in which we live are appalling, but they do not compare with conditions in the world when Jesus came into it. Historians talk of the *Pax Romana* and make much of the fact that there was peace everywhere, the Roman peace. Do not forget that the Roman peace was the result of the fact that the world had been bludgeoned brutally into submission to one central power. . . .
>
> Notwithstanding the prevailing conditions, the dominant note of these Letters, revealing the experience of the Church, is a note of triumph. The dire and dread facts and conditions are never lost sight of—indeed, they are there all the way through. The people are seen going out and facing these facts—and suffering because of these facts—but we never see them depressed and cast down, we never see them suffering from pessimistic fever. They are always triumphant. That is the glory of Christianity. If ever I am tempted to think that religion is almost dead today, it is when I listen to the wailing of some Christian people: "Everything is wrong," or "Everything is going wrong." Oh, be quiet! Think again, look again, judge not by the circumstances of the passing hour but by the infinite things of our Gospel and our God. And that is exactly what these people did.[2]

I love his spunk when encountering the grumblers and doomsayers: "Oh, be quiet!"

HOW DO WE PROCEED?

Let's take a look at Paul's closing comments. Read his words slowly, deliberately pausing at the important terms he uses:

> And my God shall supply all your needs according to His riches in glory in Christ Jesus. Now to our God and Father be the glory forever and ever. Amen.

> Greet every saint in Christ Jesus. The brethren who are with me greet you. All the saints greet you, especially those of Caesar's household.
>
> The grace of the Lord Jesus Christ be with your spirit.
>
> *Philippians 4:19–23*

Unlike the fanfares of a grand symphonic cadence, Paul says farewell in an understated manner. I find about four staccatolike statements.

First, *he writes of the glory of the Lord's plan.* Hidden in the throne room of God's celestial existence are "riches in glory." He blesses us and He provides for us according to those riches. He draws upon that infinite supply base as He meets our every need. And when He does, He gets the corresponding glory . . . forever. Look how Paul puts it:

> And it is he who will supply all your needs from his riches in glory, because of what Christ Jesus has done for us. Now unto God our Father be glory forever and ever. Amen.
>
> *Philippians 4:19–20* TLB

God gives from His "riches in glory," and, in turn, He receives the glory. We would say He gets the credit. Need a few examples?

- When your boss walks in and congratulates you—you are being promoted—God gets the glory. Of course you feel good about it and you worked hard for it, but the credit is God's.
- An illness has plagued you for weeks, perhaps months. While you prayed and sought qualified medical attention during that time, little changed. To your own amazement, God steps in and solves the dilemma. Who can ever explain the healing that He miraculously performed? We cannot explain it, but we *can* give Him the glory. And because we can, we *must.*
- One of your children has been a special challenge. Virtually since birth, he (or she) has been difficult. About the time you are ready to throw up your hands and say, "I've had it!" the Lord steps in and "supplies all your need according to His riches in glory," and your almost-grown challenge suddenly changes and begins to model manners, responsibility,

> and courtesy. As a result, God gets the glory . . . as you begin to laugh again.

How happy are those to whom God demonstrates His glory.

Second, *he mentions the greeting of the saints.*

> Greet every saint in Christ Jesus. The brethren who are with me greet you. All the saints greet you, especially those of Caesar's household.
>
> *Philippians 4:21–22*

As you can imagine, those words have spurred imaginations for centuries. The intriguing part is Paul's reference to "Caesar's household." Could he have in mind the emperor's wife and children? Would it be broader than that and encompass the in-laws and distant relatives? Does Paul mean the *literal* household?

The most reliable scholarship suggests that it is a reference to an incredibly large body of people in Italy and the surrounding provinces, slaves and free citizens alike . . . members of the elite Imperial Guard that waited on Caesar, doing his special work. And we should not forget the network of executives and administrators, secretaries and courtiers in and about Caesar's royal palace.

If you find this fascinating, as I certainly do, the following quotations will tweak your interest further.

J. B. Lightfoot writes:

> It has been assumed that this phrase must designate persons of high rank and position, powerful minions of the court, great officers of state, or even blood relations to the Emperor himself. . . . The 'domus' or 'familia Caesaris' . . . includes the whole of the imperial household, the meanest [lowest] slaves as well as the most powerful courtiers. . . . In Rome itself . . . the 'domus Augusta' must have formed no inconsiderable fraction of the whole population; but it comprised likewise all persons in the emperor's service, whether slaves or freemen, in Italy and even in the provinces.[3]

William Ramsey, in his fascinating classic, *St. Paul, the Traveller and the Roman Citizen,* adds this:

> The new movement made marked progress in the vast Imperial household. . . . The Imperial household was at the centre of affairs and

> in most intimate relations with all parts of the Empire. . . . There can be no doubt that . . . Christianity effected an entrance into Caesar's household before Paul entered Rome; in all probability he is right also in thinking that all the slaves of Aristobulus (son of Herod the Great) and of Narcissus (Claudius's favourite freedman) had passed into the Imperial household, and that members of these two *familiae* are saluted as Christians by Paul (Rom. 16:10–16).[4]

One other, from Alfred Plummer of Trinity College at Oxford:

> There were many Jews among the lower officials in Nero's household, and it was perhaps among them that the Gospel made its first converts.[5]

Legend has it that while Nero was out of town, his wife listened to the Christian message and turned her life over to Christ. When Nero returned and discovered she had been converted to Christ, his anger knew no bounds! Perhaps it was that which led to his rash decision to behead Paul.

The point I am making is that the remarkable spread of the gospel is enough to make all of us laugh out loud! Christ had invaded and infiltrated the very citadel of unbelief. Isn't that a great thought? In the very rooms where His name had been an unmentionable, Christ as Lord was now being openly discussed. And all of that was happening right under Nero's nose—yet he couldn't stop it!

Our minister of music at the church I serve, Howie Stevenson, and his wife, Marilyn, along with several friends from our church and many others from the United States, had the privilege of taking their talents to Moscow during the Russian Orthodox Easter in 1991. It was a vast gathering of Christians and non-Christians alike. The actual place of ministry was the Palace of Congress where the Supreme Soviet had met for years. You've seen the massive room on television, with the enormous oversize picture of Lenin hung before all in attendance. Except, in this case, Lenin's portrait was covered. And instead of communism's propaganda being proclaimed, Bill Bright, of Campus Crusade for Christ, preached the gospel. Howie, accompanied by his wife and two of my favorite musical artists, Stephen Nielson and Ovid Young, on dual pianos, led a large choir who presented the praises of Jesus Christ in the very stronghold of atheism.

The halls were filled with the majestic music of the Messiah, Jesus Christ, whose message of forgiveness and grace was announced by television to millions of viewers in the land of Russia . . . the very place where a few years ago you would be immediately arrested for merely mentioning the name of Jesus Christ.

On Sunday afternoon the group went into Red Square and distributed more than a hundred thousand pamphlets that conveyed the message of Christ, including Testaments and Bibles in the language of the people. (Actually they were warned against doing that too aggressively because they might be mobbed by people starving for more information about Christ.)

Isn't that great! They announced in music and spoken word that Jesus Christ is the Savior, the Lord, the risen Supreme One. We could say that Christ was proclaimed "even in Lenin's household." I must confess, when Howie reported on the marvelous success of their trip and everyone in our church applauded vigorously, I thought, *In your face, Lenin! Our God reigns.*

As I write this I am smiling. The thought of that triumphant message being publicly proclaimed in a once-forbidden region of our world is enough to make me laugh out loud. I cannot help but wonder if Paul, chained to that uniformed and armed guard in his little house in Rome, didn't smile with delight as he pictured the irresistible, life-changing movement of Christianity pushing its way into the least likely areas of Nero's domain. Yes, *our God reigns!*

Third, *Paul reaffirms the grace of the Savior.* We would expect this from him, wouldn't we? Grace had become the very theme of his life by now. Law had come by Moses, but grace came through Jesus Christ. It was grace that reached Paul en route to Damascus. It was grace that saved him as he realized all those accomplishments of his past were deeds done in the flesh. It became obvious to him that grace would be his message as he was used by God to minister to Gentiles and offer them the hope of sins forgiven and a home in heaven. And it was grace that assured him of his own eternal destiny. Any man whose life had been transformed so radically, so completely, because of God's matchless grace would naturally shout it from the housetop for the rest of his life.

As John Newton wrote with equal passion centuries later:

> Through many dangers, toils, and snares,
> I have already come;
> 'Tis grace hath brought me safe thus far,
> And grace will lead me home.[6]

I never sing that grand old hymn without thanking God anew that in spite of all those things He could have held against me, He accepted me, forgave me, included me in His family, and will some day receive me into glory. If that isn't enough to make us laugh again, I don't know what is.

What a magnificent letter Paul wrote from Rome to his friends far away in Philippi. I can imagine the gray-haired apostle reaching his manacled arm over to Epaphroditus, taking the stylus from his hand . . . and forming these closing words with his own fingers:

> **To our God and Father be the glory forever and ever. Greet every saint in Christ Jesus. . . . All the saints greet you, especially those of Caesar's household. . . . Grace . . . be with your spirit. Amen.**
>
> **Paulos**

And with that Paul rolled up the scroll, embraced his friend with a smile, and sent him on his way with letter in hand, having prayed for journey mercies. I can see Paul smiling as he waved a joyful, grace-filled good-bye to a man he would never see again on earth.

A Treasured Legacy

When I completed my own study of the letter to the Philippians, I experienced a nostalgic serendipity. As I was putting away my research materials along with pen and paper, an old book by F. B. Meyer, one of my favorite authors, caught my attention. It happened to be his work on Philippians, but I had not consulted it throughout my months of study.

Thinking there might be something in it to augment my study, I decided to pull it from the shelf and leaf through it before I went home for the day. I turned off the overhead light in my study, and, with only the light from my desk lamp, I leaned back in my old leather desk chair and opened Meyer's book.

To my unexpected delight, it was not the words of F. B. Meyer that spoke to me that evening, but the words of my mother. For as I began looking through it, I realized this book was one of the many volumes which had found their way from her library into mine after her death back in 1971. Little did she know when she wrote in it years before that her words would become a part of her legacy to me, her youngest. I sat very still as I took in the wonder.

In her own inimitable handwriting, my mother had made notes in the text and along the margins throughout the book. When I got to the end, I noticed she had penned these words on the inside of the back cover, "Finished reading this May 8, 1958."

I looked up in my dimly lit study and pondered, *1958.* My mind took me back to a tiny island in the South Pacific where I had spent many lonely months as a Marine. I recalled that it was *in May of 1958* that I had reached a crossroad in my own pilgrimage. In fact, I had entered the following words in my journal: "The Lord has convinced me that I am to be in His service. I will begin to make plans to prepare for a lifetime of ministry." Amazingly, it was in the same month of that very year that my mother had finished reading Meyer's book. As I looked back over the pages, I found one reference after another to her prayers for me as I was away . . . her concern for my spiritual welfare . . . her desire for God's best in my life. And occasionally she had inserted a clever quip or humorous comment.

Turning back to the front of the book, I found another interesting entry, also with a date. It read, "Chart of Philippians mailed to me by Charles when he was ministering in Massachusetts, 1966." As I glanced over the chart, another memory swept over me. I recalled putting that chart together and sending it to her during my years in New England. Once again I looked up and momentarily relived those years between 1958 and 1966. What a significant passage! All through that time, I now realize my mother had prayed for me and loved me and sought God's best for me.

Across the room in my study hangs an original oil painting with a light above it, shedding a golden glow down over the colorful canvas. The painting was my mother's gift to me some years after I entered the ministry. She had painted it. It is of a shepherd surrounded by a handful of sheep on a green hillside.

I had looked at this painting countless times before, but this time was unique. In the bottom right corner I looked at her name and the date . . . only days before she passed into the Lord's presence. Caught in that nostalgic time warp, I turned off my desk lamp and stared at the lighted painting. There I sat, twenty years after she had laid the brush aside, thanking God anew for my mother's prayers, my pilgrimage, and especially His presence. Faithfully, graciously, quietly He had led me and helped me and blessed me. I bowed my head and thanked Him for His sustaining grace . . . and I wept with gratitude.

Suddenly the shrill sound of the telephone broke the silence. My younger son, Chuck, was on the line wanting to tell me something funny that had happened. I quickly switched gears and enjoyed one of those delightful, lighthearted father-son moments. As we laughed loudly together, he urged me to hurry home.

Following his call I placed the F. B. Meyer book back on the shelf. As I was leaving my study, I paused beside the painting and thought of the significant role my parents had played in those formative years of my life . . . and how the torch had been passed on from them to Cynthia and me to do the same with our sons and daughters . . . and they, in turn, with theirs.

As I switched off the light above the painting, I smiled and said, "Good-bye, Mother." In the darkness of that room I could almost hear her voice answering me, "Good-bye, Charles. I love you, Son. I'm still praying for you. Keep walking with God . . . and don't forget to have some fun with your family tonight."

What a treasured legacy: devoted prayers, lasting love, hearty laughter. That's the way it ought to be.

Conclusion

God's sense of humor has intrigued me for years. What amazes me, however, is the number of people who don't think He has one. For the life of me, I can't figure out why they can't see it. He made you and me, didn't He? And what about all those funny-looking creatures that keep drawing us back to the zoo? If they aren't proof of our Creator's sense of humor, I don't know what is. Have you taken a close look at a wombat or a two-toed sloth, a giant anteater or a warthog lately? They're hilarious! Every time I look at a camel I chuckle, recalling the words of some wag who said it reminded him of a horse put together by a committee. I honestly wonder if God didn't laugh Himself as He dropped some of those creatures on our planet eons ago.

God's humor, unfortunately, does not occupy any significant place in serious works of theology. I know; I've been checking them for years and been disappointed. In my four intensive years of study in an excellent graduate school of theology, I don't recall one time that any prof addressed the subject of God's sense of humor. And in all my reading since then—thirty years of searching—seldom have I found anything more than a lighthearted throwaway line on the subject.

That's too bad. Because the impression we are left with is that our Lord is an all-too-serious Sovereign who has no room in His character for at least a few moments of fun. At best this frowning, uptight caricature suggests He is a heavenly representation of some venerable, earthly theologian—only older and wiser. Please!

Surely it is not blasphemous to think that laughter breaks out in heaven on special occasions. Why shouldn't it? There is every reason to believe that would happen in His infinite, holy presence, where all is well and no evil abides. After all, God sees everything that transpires in this human comedy of errors . . . He understands it all.

He must have smiled, for example, when Elijah mocked the false prophets on Mount Carmel, asking whether their gods had gone on a journey or fallen asleep or were *indisposed* (1 Kings 18:27)! And what about that fellow named Eutychus who listened to Paul preach and fell out of a third-story window (Acts 20:9)? Don't worry, he recovered . . . but are you going to sit there and tell me God didn't find humor in that scenario?

Think of how many times preachers have gotten their tongues twisted and blurted out stupid stuff. Once while I was explaining that many of the people in Christ's day expected Him to come and break the yoke of Rome, out came "roke of Yome." But that wasn't nearly as bad as the time I was describing the unusual strategy Joshua and his warriors employed to bring down the walls of Jericho. Instead of saying they were to march around the wall, I chose to say that they circumscribed the wall, but inadvertently it came out, "circumcised the wall" . . . which brought the house down. You're telling me God didn't laugh?

One of my mentors tells me that he was once introduced by a country preacher as "the professor of the Suppository Preaching Department." I asked him what he did after he got up to preach. He smiled and said, "Well, Chuck, I just stood up and supposited the Word, like I always do." Surely the God we serve finds those moments as funny as we do.

And what about those embarrassing typos and misworded announcements that appear in church bulletins, like:

- This afternoon there will be a meeting in the north and south ends of the church. Children will be baptized at both ends.
- The choir will be participating in the local community sing, which is open to everyone. They will be sinning at 6:00 p.m. this Sunday.
- There will be a sin-in at the Johnsons' home this evening, immediately following the pastor's message, "Intimate Fellowship."
- Affirmation of Faith No. 738: "The Apostles' Greed"
- Solo: "There Is a Bomb in Gilead"
- Order of Service: Silent Prayer and Medication

- This was printed after a church potluck: "Ladies, if you have missing bowels, you will find them in the church kitchen."
- Pastor Brown will marry his son next Sunday morning.

Such stories abound! And you will never convince me that God doesn't get a kick out of such things and laugh with some of us in our well-meant seriousness.

I believe He fully understands us in our imperfect humanity. He understands little children who pick their noses in church because they are bored stiff. It's no big deal to Him. He must smile at some of the notes children send their pastor, too, like this one I read recently:

Dear Pastor,

I know God loves everybody, but He never met my sister.

Yours sincerely,
Arnold

A friend of mine told me about another one that read:

Dear Paster,

My father couldn't give more **$$money$$** to the chrch. HE is a good chrischen but has a *cheap* boss.

Ronald

Surely God smiles with understanding when he hears prayers like the one Erma Bombeck says she has prayed for years: "Lord, if you can't make me thin, then make my friends look fat."

Isn't God the One who urges us to "Make a joyful noise unto the Lord"? Why do we always think that means singing? Seems to me the most obvious joyful noise on earth is laughter. We say we believe in laughing and having a happy countenance. I'm not sure. I've seen folks quote verses like "Rejoice in the Lord always" while their faces look like they just buried a rich uncle who willed everything to his pregnant guinea pig. Something is missing.

We all *look* so much better and *feel* so much better when we laugh. I don't know of a more contagious sound. And yet there are so many who never weary of telling us, "Life is no laughing matter." It may not be for them, but I must tell you, it often is for me. Knowing that God is causing "all things to work together for good," and remembering that we, His people, are on our way to an eternal home in the heavens without fears or tears, takes the sting out of this temporary parenthesis of time called earthly life.

The returning prodigal was absolutely amazed by his father's immediate acceptance, reckless forgiveness, and unconditional love. Having been so distant, so desperate, so utterly alone, he knew no way to turn but homeward. Then, at the end of his rope, he found himself suddenly safe in his dad's embrace, smothered with kisses, and surrounded by extravagant grace. The fatted calf . . . a soft, warm robe, comfortable new sandals, and the costliest ring were all his . . . no strings attached . . . no probation required. Not surprisingly, that home was soon filled with "music and dancing." As Jesus told the story, He was careful to add, "And they began to be merry."

Then why shouldn't we?

Throughout these pages I have been urging you to lighten up. I could not have done so without knowing that Someone, like the prodigal's father, is diligently searching for you. Every day He scans the horizon and waits patiently for you to appear. He has spared no expense. A blood-smeared cross on which His Son died is now a painful memory, but it was essential to solve the sin problem.

Every day He says to our world, "All is forgiven . . . come on home." His arms are open, and there is a wide, wide smile on His face. The band is tuning up. The banquet is ready to be served. All that is needed is you.

Come on home. You will be so glad you did. In fact, before you know it, you'll begin to laugh again.

Notes

Introduction

1. James S. Huett, ed., *Illustrations Unlimited* (Wheaton, Ill.: Tyndale, 1988), 101.

Chapter 1 / Your Smile Increases Your Face Value

1. G. K. Chesterton, *Orthodoxy* (New York: Dodd, Mead and Co., 1954), 298.

2. Adapted from "The Chair Recognizes Mr. Buckley," quoted in *Tabletalk* 17, no. 1 (March 1992): 9.

3. Jane Canfield, in *Quote/Unquote,* comp. Lloyd Cory (Wheaton, Ill.: Victor Books, 1977), 144.

4. Helen Mallicoat, "I Am," in Tim Hansel, *Holy Sweat* (Waco, Tex.: Word Books, 1987), 136. Used by permission.

5. Hansel, *Holy Sweat,* 58–59.

Chapter 2 / Set Your Sails for Joy

1. Ella Wheeler Wilcox, "The Wind of Fate," in *The Best Loved Poems of the American People,* comp. Hazel Felleman (Garden City, N.Y.: Garden City Books, 1936), 364.

2. Kenneth S. Wuest, *Philippians in the Greek New Testament* (Grand Rapids, Mich.: William B. Eerdmans Publishing Co., 1942), 26–27.

3. William Griffin, "On Making Saints," *Publishers Weekly,* 5 October 1990, 34.

4. Anonymous.

5. John Powell, *Why Am I Afraid to Tell You Who I Am?* (Chicago, Ill.: Argus Communications Co., 1969), 54–55.

6. Ibid., 56.

7. Ibid., 56–57.

8. Ibid., 57–58.

9. Ibid., 61–62.

10. Howard Taylor and Mary G. Taylor, *Hudson Taylor's Spiritual Secret* (Chicago: Moody Press, 1932), 152.

11. Wilcox, "The Wind of Fate," 364.

Chapter 3 / What a Way to Live!

1. G. W. Target, "The Window," from *The Window and Other Essays* (Boise, Idaho: Pacific Press Publishing Association, 1973), 5–7.

2. Stuart Briscoe, *Bound for Joy: Philippians—Paul's Letter from Prison* (Glendale, Calif.: Regal Books, 1975), 25.

3. Samuel Johnson to Lord Chesterfield, 19 September 1777, cited in John Bartlett, *Familiar Quotations,* ed. Emily Morison Beck (Boston, Mass.: Little, Brown and Co., 1980), 355.

4. Anonymous.

Chapter 4 / Laughing Through Life's Dilemmas

1. From "Jesus Is All the World to Me," Will L. Thompson [1847–1909].

2. Horatius Bonar, "Thy Way, Not Mine," *Baker's Pocket Treasury of Religious Verse,* ed. Donald T. Kauffmann (Grand Rapids, Mich.: Baker Book House, 1962), 219. Used by permission.

3. Anonymous.

4. Quoted by J. Foster, *Then and Now* (London, 1945), 83, cited in Ralph P. Martin, *The Epistle of Paul to the Philippians* (Grand Rapids, Mich.: William B. Eerdmans Publishing Co., 1959), 88.

5. "God's Gargoyle: An Interview with Malcolm Muggeridge," *Radix/Right On* (May 1975): 3.

Chapter 5 / The Hidden Secret of a Happy Life

1. Canfield, *Quote/Unquote,* 23.

2. From "When I Survey the Wondrous Cross," Isaac Watts [1674–1748].

3. Harry A. Ironside, *Notes on the Epistle to the Philippians* (Neptune, N.J.: Loizeaux Brothers, 1922), 38–39.

4. D. Martyn Lloyd-Jones, *The Life of Joy: An Exposition of Philippians 1 and 2* (Grand Rapids, Mich.: Baker Book House, 1989), 142–43.

5. Ironside, *Notes on the Epistle to the Philippians,* 47.

6. From "Holy, Holy, Is What the Angels Sing," Rev. Johnson Oatman, Jr.

Chapter 6 / While Laughing, Keep Your Balance!

1. "Advice to a (Bored) Young Man," cited in Ted W. Engstrom, *Motivation to Last a Lifetime* (Grand Rapids, Mich.: Zondervan, 1984), 23–24.

2. Mark Twain, *Pudd'nhead Wilson* [1894], "Pudd'nhead Wilson's Calendar," cited in Bartlett, *Familiar Quotations,* 624.

3. Jimmy Bowen, cited in Sharon Bernstein, "When Entertainment LipSyncs Modern Life," *Los Angeles Times,* 29 November 1990, F1.

4. Ibid.

5. Eugene H. Peterson, *Five Smooth Stones for Pastoral Work* (Atlanta, Ga.: John Knox Press, 1980), 47.

6. J. B. Priestly in *Macmillan Dictionary of Quotations* (Norwalk, Conn.: Easton Press, 1989), 120.

7. "World May End with a Splash," *Los Angeles Times,* 9 October 1982.

8. Julia Seton, *Quote/Unquote,* 67.

9. Laurence Peter and Bill Dana, *The Laughter Prescription* (New York: Ballantine Books, 1987), 8.

10. Jim McGuiggan, *The Irish Papers* (Fort Worth, Tex.: Star Bible Publications, 1992), 42.

11. John Wooden, *They Call Me Coach* (Waco, Tex.: Word Books, 1972), 184.

12. Source unknown.

Chapter 7 / Friends Make Life More Fun

1. Michael LeBoeuf, *How to Win Customers and Keep Them for Life* (New York: Berkley Books, 1987), 84–85.

2. "How Important Are You," © United Technologies Corporation, 1983. Used by permission.

3. Briscoe, *Bound for Joy,* 92–93.

4. Leighton Ford, *Transforming Leadership* (Downers Grove, Ill.: InterVarsity Press, 1991), 139–41.

5. J. B. Lightfoot, *St Paul's Epistle to the Philippians* (London: Macmillan and Co., 1908), 123.

6. William Hendriksen, *New Testament Commentary* (Grand Rapids, Mich.: Baker Book House, 1962), 144–45.

Chapter 8 / Happy Hopes for High Achievers

1. Joe Lomusio, *If I Should Die Before I Live* (Fullerton, Calif.: R. C. Law & Co., 1989), 144–45.

2. Tim Hansel, *When I Relax I Feel Guilty* (Elgin, Ill.: David C. Cook Publishing Co., 1979), 20–22.

3. G. K. Chesterton, *The Napoleon of Notting Hill* (New York: Paulist Press, 1978), 37.

4. William Barclay, *The Mind of St Paul* (New York: Harper and Brothers Publishers, 1958), 17–19.

5. Archibald T. Robertson, *Word Pictures in the New Testament,* vol. 4 (Nashville, Tenn.: Broadman Press, 1931), 453.

6. "I Met My Master," *Poems That Preach,* ed. John R. Rice (Wheaton, Ill.: Sword of the Lord Publishers, 1952), 18. Used by permission.

Chapter 9 / Hanging Tough Together . . . and Loving It

1. *Los Angeles Times,* 27 January 1991.

2. Henry David Thoreau, cited in Bartlett, *Familiar Quotations,* 590.

3. John Pollock, *The Man Who Shook the World* (Wheaton, Ill.: Victor Books, 1972), 18.

4. Robert Ballard, "A Long Last Look at Titanic," *National Geographic* 170, no. 6 (December 1986): 698–705.

5. Bob Benson, *Laughter in the Walls* (Nashville, Tenn.: Impact Books, 1969), 16–17. Used by permission.

6. Benjamin Franklin, at the signing of the Declaration of Independence [4 July 1776], cited in Bartlett, *Familiar Quotations,* 348.

7. From "Higher Ground," Johnson Oatman, Jr. [1856–1926].

Chapter 10 / It's a Mad, Bad, Sad World, But . . .

1. Flannery O'Connor, *Mystery and Manners* (New York: Farrar, Straus and Giroux, 1969), 167.

2. A. W. Tozer, *The Root of Righteousness* (Harrisburg, Pa.: Christian Publications, 1955), 156.

3. Norman Cousins, *Anatomy of an Illness as Perceived by the Patient* (New York: Norton, 1979), 25–43.

4 G. K. Chesterton, *The Common Man* (New York: Sheed and Ward, 1950), 157–58.

5. Barbara Johnson, *Splashes of Joy in the Cesspools of Life* (Dallas, Tex.: Word Publishing, 1992), 65.

Chapter 11 / Defusing Disharmony

1. Karen Mains, *The Key to a Loving Heart* (Elgin, Ill: David C. Cook, 1979), 143–44.

2. Thomas Brookes, *The Golden Treasure of Puritan Quotations,* ed. I. D. E. Thomas (Chicago, Ill.: Moody Press, 1975), 304.

3. Marshall Shelley, *Well-Intentioned Dragons* (Waco, Tex.: Word Books/CTi, 1985), 11–12.

4. Leslie B. Flynn, *You Don't Have to Go It Alone* (Denver, Colo.: Accent Books, 1981), 117.

Chapter 12 / Freeing Yourself Up to Laugh Again

1. Jean Jacques Rousseau, *Du Contrat Social* [1762], bk. 1, chap. 1, cited in Bartlett, *Familiar Quotations,* 358.

2. W. Grant Lee, in Bartlett, *Familiar Quotations,* 174.

3. Fred Allen, in *Quote/Unquote,* 174.

4. Ruth Harms Calkin, "Spiritual Retreat," *Lord, You Love to Say Yes* (Elgin, Ill.: David C. Cook, 1976), 16–17. Used by permission.

5. Quoted by Ruth Bell Graham, *Prodigals and Those Who Love Them* (Colorado Springs, Colo.: Focus on the Family Publishing, 1991), 44.

Chapter 13 / Don't Forget to Have Fun As You Grow Up

1. Anonymous.

2. Fred Cook, in *Quote/Unquote,* 200.

3. Max DePree, *Leadership Is an Art* (New York: Dell Publishing, 1987), 7–10. Used by permission of Doubleday, a division of Bantam Doubleday Dell Publishing Group, Inc.

4. Sophie Tucker, quoted in Rosalind Russell and Chris Chase, *Life Is a Banquet* (New York: Random House, 1977), 2.

5. Quoted in "I Made Mistakes," interview with Richard Dortch, *Christianity Today,* 18 March 1988, 46–47.

6. Ibid.

7. Jeanne Hendricks, *Afternoon* (Nashville, Tenn.: Thomas Nelson Publishers, 1979), 103.

Chapter 14 / A Joyful, Grace-Filled Good-bye

1. From the California Newspaper Association.

2. G. Campbell Morgan, *The Unfolding Message of the Bible* (Westwood, N.J.: Fleming H. Revell Co., 1961), 367.

3. J. B. Lightfoot, *Notes on the Epistle to the Philippians,* 171.

4. W. M. Ramsay, *St Paul, the Traveller and the Roman Citizen* (London: Hodder and Stoughton, 1895), 352–53.

5. Alfred Plummer, *A Commentary on St Paul's Epistle to the Philippians* (London: Robert Scott Roxburghe House, 1919), 107.

6. From "Amazing Grace," John Newton [1725–1807].

Flying Closer to the Flame

Publications by Charles R. Swindoll

Books

Come Before Winter
Compassion: Showing We Care in a Careless World
Dropping Your Guard
Encourage Me
For Those Who Hurt
The Grace Awakening
Growing Deep in the Christian Life
Growing Strong in the Seasons of Life
Growing Wise in Family Life
Hand Me Another Brick
Improving Your Serve
Killing Giants, Pulling Thorns
Laugh Again
Leadership: Influence That Inspires
Living Above the Level of Mediocrity
Living Beyond the Daily Grind, Books 1 and 2
Living on the Ragged Edge
Make Up Your Mind
The Quest for Character
Recovery: When Healing Takes Time
Rise and Shine
Sanctity of Life
Simple Faith
Standing Out
Starting Over
Strengthening Your Grip
Stress Fractures
Strike the Original Match
The Strong Family
Three Steps Forward, Two Steps Back
Victory: A Winning Game Plan for Life
You and Your Child

Minibooks

Abraham: A Model of Pioneer Faith
David: A Model of Pioneer Courage
Esther: A Model of Pioneer Independence
Moses: A Model of Pioneer Vision
Nehemiah: A Model of Pioneer Determination

Booklets

Anger
Attitudes
Commitment
Dealing with Defiance
Demonism
Destiny
Divorce
Eternal Security
Fun Is Contagious
God's Will
Hope
Impossibilities
Integrity
Leisure
The Lonely Whine of the Top Dog
Moral Purity
Our Mediator
Peace . . . in Spite of Panic
Prayer
Sensuality
Stress
Tongues
When Your Comfort Zone Gets the Squeeze
Woman

CHARLES R. SWINDOLL

FLYING CLOSER to the FLAME

W PUBLISHING GROUP™

www.wpublishinggroup.com

A Division of Thomas Nelson, Inc.
www.ThomasNelson.com

Library of Congress Cataloging-in-Publication Data

Swindoll, Charles R.
Flying closer to the flame : a passion for the Holy Spirit / Charles R. Swindoll.
p. cm.
Includes bibliographical references.
ISBN 0-8499-1001-3
1. Holy Spirit. 2. Spiritual life—Christianity. I. Title.
BT121.2.S955 1993
231'.3—dc20 93-5950
CIP

3 4 5 6 9 RRD 9 8 7 6 5 4 3 2 1

Printed in the United States of America.

It is with great admiration that I dedicate this book to my esteemed teacher, mentor, and, best of all, friend since 1959,

Dr. Donald K. Campbell

For forty years he has faithfully served his Lord on the faculty and in the administration of my alma mater, Dallas Theological Seminary, and since 1986 has served as the distinguished president of the school.

I thank my God upon every remembrance of this biblical scholar, outstanding theologian, and Christian gentleman, who, for as long as I have known him, has been flying close to the flame.

Contents

Acknowledgments

Books are like people. Each has its own personality. Furthermore, some require a great deal of assistance and support from a team of individuals, while others do not make such demands.

This volume falls into the latter category. Quietly and lovingly it was conceived in my mind. The thoughts and ideas that grew into pages and chapters emerged slowly, sometimes with great difficulty. I have been amazed at the things the Lord has brought into my life during the process of putting my thoughts into print. I have been through it! But this is not to say that the book was accomplished without anyone else's encouragement or assistance.

My closest friends at Word Publishing became aware of and mentioned the need for a book on the Holy Spirit about the time I began doing my research on the subject. We were all more than mildly concerned about much of what has been published and purchased on this subject over the past few years. As I read many of those works, I found myself disheartened to think that an ever-increasing number of people were reading (and believing!) things that lacked not only biblical support, but plain old common sense.

Through the urging of Byron Williamson at Word, I decided to turn my research into a volume that would provide trustworthy information and at the same time stretch the thinking of many superconservative Evangelicals without sounding like I had the final answer for the world. I also determined to remain positive and affirming wherever possible, rather than throw mud or point fingers at those with whom I disagree. I'm especially grateful that Byron, Kip Jordon, and David Moberg have been supportive as I have tried to walk the fine line of accuracy without sounding arrogant or angry. Doing that has taken time—a lot of time—which makes me indebted to all three for their patience.

As usual, Helen Peters, my extremely competent, longtime, ever-faithful executive assistant, has taken my rough draft of handwritten tablet pages and with ease and efficiency turned them into a manuscript any publisher would be envious to receive. Even as I was finishing this book, Helen decided to take early retirement, leaving her office at the church where we have worked together for more than twenty wonderful years. She will still assist me in my publishing ministry, but not having her on site on a daily basis has brought a huge feeling of loss to me personally. Since I began publishing back in the mid-1970s, Helen has been there to work her wonders and add her words of support. To say that I am thankful for her assistance is to state the obvious. If you find these pages helpful, much of the credit goes to her . . . as well as my editor, Judith Markham. They worked together, turning my original and primitive lines into meaningful and well-connected thoughts.

The congregation of the First Evangelical Free Church of Fullerton, California, also deserves my acknowledgments. As I hammered out my ideas in the study, the most natural place to communicate them was to this flock I have pastored since 1971. How encouraging they have been! Sunday after Sunday, as I would declare the fruit of my study, various ones would invariably challenge something I said, or ask for clarification, or simply thank me for going beyond the bounds of safety and taking the risk of originality while not altogether ignoring traditional boundaries.

Flying closer to the flame often required my leaving the comfort zone and being willing to be misunderstood. I am thankful that they never clipped my wings. It is because of their enthusiastic response that I felt the freedom to dare drawing closer and to declare the truth as I discovered and understood it.

So, here it is—a fresh and somewhat surprising series of thoughts on Him whom our Savior sent to be among us, to live within us, to work His will through us, to manifest His glory for us, and to reveal the truth to us. If this volume proves to be as helpful to you as the original thoughts and applications have been to me, we can both give our praise to Christ, who did not leave us "as orphans" but gave us "another Helper" to be with us forever (John 14:16, 18).

Introduction

This is a book about some of the intimate workings of the Holy Spirit. Unlike most books on the subject, you will find it personal, practical, and positive.

It is not primarily a theological workbook designed to analyze and criticize. There are enough of those. Neither is it a two-fisted, negative warning against all the errors floating around and among the ranks of Christians. Again, others have already done that. I have no interest in entering the arena of a debate that was going on long before I was born and will continue long after I'm gone.

My great hope in these pages is to step away from the heat of theological battle and move quietly and closely to the One who has been sent alongside to help. He longs to empower us with His dynamic presence, change our attitudes, warm our hearts, show us how and where to walk, comfort us in our struggles and our sorrows, strengthen us in the weak and fragile places of our lives, and literally revolutionize our pilgrimage from this planet to paradise.

Candidly, this is a book for the heart much more than for the head. I'm not saying you won't need to think or approach these subjects intelligently, but this is not an exhaustive theological treatment of the person and work of the Holy Spirit. Please keep that in mind. My goal, however, is to have you travel beyond the cognitive level and enter into the journey on a personal level.

Since the Spirit of God was sent not only to be studied but ultimately to be experienced, it seems to me we have stopped short of God's intended purpose if we merely discuss and debate His presence instead of exulting in Him on an intimate basis. Long enough have non-charismatic, evangelical Christians (I am both) stood at a distance, frowning and throwing scriptural stones at those in God's family who do not dot every *i* or cross each *t* exactly the same as we. At the same time, long enough has the "lunatic fringe" of a few extremists been allowed to speak for all Christendom, leaving the impression that they are the standard and representative of the majority (they are neither).

What we need is a balanced, experiential view of the Spirit. It should be biblical, of course. Without that we are awash. But it cannot stop at sterile, heady truth on the printed page. It also must be personal, deeply and intimately personal. Without that we miss the whole purpose for which He was sent. In addition, we become defensive in attitude, resistant in spirit, and even arrogant in knowledge—ironically, all the things that grieve the Spirit and keep Him at a distance.

While I can understand the zeal and desire that prompt such things, I am saddened by the outcome: fractured bones and painful bruises in the body of Christ. As our love and respect for one another diminish, the unity we are commanded to keep breaks down and the walls between us get thicker.

Let's face it, most of us are intrigued by the Holy Spirit. Like moths we are attracted to the warmth and the light of His flame. Our desire is to come closer . . . to draw nearer, to know Him more fully and intimately, to enter into new and stimulating dimensions of His workings . . . without getting burned. I know that is true of me, and I suspect you often feel the same.

During my growing-up years, including my years in seminary, I kept a safe distance. I was taught to be careful, to study Him from a doctrinal distance but not to enter into any of the realms of His supernatural workings or to tolerate the possibility of such. Explaining the Spirit was acceptable and encouraged; experiencing Him was neither. Today, I regret that. I have lived long enough and ministered broadly enough to realize that flying closer to the flame is not only possible, it is precisely what God wants.

He is interested in transforming us from the inside out. Flying closer to the flame sets that in motion. He is at work in dozens of different ways, some of them supernatural. Flying closer to the flame makes us acutely aware of that. He is interested in showing us the Father's will and providing us with the dynamics necessary for experiencing satisfaction, joy, peace, and contentment *in spite of our circumstances.* Flying closer to the flame gives us the correct perspective for entering into those (and so many other) experiences. Isn't it time we did?

If you are totally fulfilled in your Christian experience, seldom frustrated, and rarely dissatisfied with yourself, this is not a book for you. Furthermore, if you do not long for a more intimate and uninterrupted relationship with the living God, where you and He are "in sync" and where you regularly sense His presence and power, you don't need to read the pages that follow.

But if you wonder whether you may be missing out on something spiritually . . . or if you desire to move from merely an intellectual faith to an intimate relationship with God . . . or if you would love to explore new regions and realms of His Word that you are intrigued by but have tended to shy away from lest you get burned by "becoming too emotional" or "falling into error," this is the book for you. Fly with me, won't you?

If you are one of the vast number of people who have never known the joy, the sheer ecstasy of walking more intimately with God, yet have known there was more . . . so much more . . . I pray that these pages will draw you in, calm your fears, encourage you to come closer and know the warmth of His eternal flame. I understand what you have been going through . . . and I welcome you as a fellow pilgrim who is weary of a sterile, unproductive, predictable existence. Jesus' promise of an "abundant life" surely includes more than that!

I am absolutely convinced that there are phenomenal and thrilling things hidden in the Scriptures, awaiting discovery and application. I am equally confident that such discoveries and applications will open new vistas of the walk of faith that many have never given themselves permission to view or enjoy. No need to be shy or afraid. As Jesus promised, "the Spirit of truth . . . will guide you into all the truth." As He uses these pages to do just that, we can anticipate unspeakable joy with incredible results.

So come along and journey with me as we, together, fly closer to the flame.

Chuck Swindoll
Fullerton, California
Fall 1993

1

Let's Get Reacquainted with the Spirit

MISS THOMPSON HAD A TOUGH TASK. Her Sunday school lesson plan called for teaching her primary class about the Trinity. It was difficult enough holding their attention with stories and creative object lessons, but when it came to keeping them interested in the identity, attributes, and purpose of the Father, Son, and Spirit . . . well, that was next to impossible.

While thinking through her lesson, she had a creative thought: She would use a big, thick pretzel, with its three holes in the middle. Perfect!

When Sunday morning came she stood before her class, holding the pretzel high in the air, explaining how it was made up of one strand of dough but was so intricately interwoven that there were three distinct holes, each one having its own special shape.

She pointed first to the hole at the top. "Children, this is like God the Father. Think of this first hole as your heavenly Father." She then pointed to the second, explaining slowly and carefully, "This is like God the Son. Think of the hole here on the right as Jesus, your Savior." The class of fresh little faces seemed to be following her with keen interest, so she continued, "And this third hole is God the Holy Ghost. Just as this is one pretzel made up of three separate holes, so the Trinity is one unit made up of three distinct Persons: Father, Son, and Holy Ghost."

Miss Thompson had the children repeat those names aloud: "Father . . . Son . . . and Holy Ghost." Again and again she had the class say the names.

Hoping to cement this concept in their minds, she singled out little Johnny, sitting close to the front, and asked him if he could repeat the names of the "holey" members of the Trinity for the rest of the class. Though reluctant, he slowly stood to his feet and took the pretzel she held out to him.

"This here is God . . . God the Father," he said, pointing to the first hole." (Miss Thompson smiled with delight.) "And this one is Jesus." (Again she beamed over his excellent memory.) "And this third one is . . . uh . . . the *Holy Smoke*."

Such stories make us smile, often recalling with amusement our own childish "bloopers." But if the truth were told, many adults could not even come that close. To most folks, the person, work, and ministry of the Holy Spirit are a mystery. He is not only invisible but also confusing and even a little bit eerie . . . especially when, for years, He was referred to as "It" and formally addressed as "the Holy *Ghost*."

All of us have had earthly fathers, so trying to understand the concept of a heavenly Father is not all that difficult. In traditional homes, the father is the one who is in charge, making the big decisions and being ultimately responsible for the family's overall direction, leadership, and stability. There are exceptions and room for discussion, but in the final analysis, it is Dad who casts the final vote.

The Son of God is not difficult to identify either. He was born as a human being and grew up alongside His mother, much like we did. Because He was a flesh-and-blood person, there is little mystery surrounding our mental image of Christ, and His role as the Son of God is fairly clear to us. Our familiarity with His suffering and death causes us to feel close to Him and grateful for Him. He is the One who has implemented the Father's plan.

But the Holy *Ghost?* Not even changing His title to "Spirit" helps that much. Certainly to the uninitiated the name still sounds borderline weird. If His name is vague, it is no surprise that most find His work and ministry the same. And since those who attempt to explain His workings are usually theologians, who are often notoriously deep and unclear themselves, it is no wonder the general public doesn't have a clue to understanding what He is about—to say nothing of feeling intimately related to Him. To many, He is still the divine "It."

Candidly, I am just as culpable as those complex-thinking theologians who have attempted to "explain" the inscrutable Spirit of God. Way back in the 1960s I taught a course on the third member of the Trinity. When I picked up my pen to write this book, I thought it might be helpful to glance over those old notes. My immediate problem was locating them! Had I filed them under *H* for "Holy Spirit"? No. How about *S* for "Spirit"? Nope. Maybe they were tucked away in my subject file under the letter *G* as in "Holy Ghost"? Wrong again. Or *T* for "Trinity"? Not a chance. I stayed at it until I unearthed them . . . filed under *P* for *Pneumatology.* That ought to tell you a lot about how I approached the subject three decades ago: strictly theoretical and theological and not at all relational.

Don't get me wrong. There is nothing—absolutely nothing—wrong with theology. Sound doctrine gives us strong roots. Those who lack such stability can easily fall into extremism and error. However, to track a subject this intimate strictly from an impersonal distance, keeping everything safely theoretical and coolly analytical, won't cut it. There has been too much of that already! What we need is a much more personal investigation of the intimate workings of the Spirit without losing our anchor on theological truth.

Admittedly, some of the Spirit's workings are more theoretical than experiential. For example:

- He is God—co-equal, co-existent, and co-eternal with the Father and the Son.
- He possesses all the attributes of Deity.
- He regenerates the believing sinner.
- He baptizes us into the universal body of Christ.
- He indwells all who have been converted.
- He seals us, keeping every believer securely in the family of God.

And there are a dozen or more equally significant characteristics and workings I could name. These things are all true, but there is *so much more* we've hardly acknowledged, to say nothing of experienced. And though true, they make virtually *no difference* in our conscious existence!

- Why should it thrill anyone to be able to explain the difference between grieving the Spirit and quenching the Spirit? So what if the day-to-day evidences of His power are absent?
- How does it help anyone all that much to know that the Greek term, translated "Helper" or "Comforter" in the New Testament, is *Parakletos*? Does that do anything for us? Are we able to relate to God better because we know that fact?
- Who cares if you and I can define the presence and work of the Holy Spirit prior to and after Pentecost? At the risk of being tarred and feathered, I no longer get excited about such distinctions, especially since many who love to debate those distinctions seem so out of touch with the intimacies of the Spirit's presence on a personal level.
- And what's the big deal about whether He does this or that before, during, or after the Great Tribulation? Those subjects may excite a handful of heady intellectuals tucked away in the cloistered classrooms of a seminary, but, believe me, they mean next to nothing to someone who is running out of hope and needs God's touch desperately.

Get real! We don't need another theological encyclopedia on pneumatology nearly as much as we need an easy-to-understand volume on the practical difference the Spirit can make in our lives on a personal and lasting level. And that's what this book is all about: not "Holy Smoke," but real-to-life reasons we need the

Spirit . . . and the incredible difference He can make in the way we live on a personal basis.

Where Are We Going in This Book?

I have decided to go after the real issues and the practical side of the Holy Spirit—mainly the seldom-mentioned dimensions of His work with us individually and His ministry among us collectively. Why? Because these are the things that give us an edge on living in a sin-cursed world, surrounded by people who have lost their verve for life. It is when these things come alive in us that we become unique instruments in God's hands. I believe that's what you really want, and, I can assure you, I do too!

Let's get specific. Here are some examples of things we are going to be looking into as the succeeding chapters unfold—a random sampling with accompanying Scriptures.

1. The "testifying" work of the Spirit. Have you ever wondered what Paul meant when he told his friends from Ephesus:

> "And now, behold, bound in spirit, I am on my way to Jerusalem, not knowing what will happen to me there, except that the Holy Spirit solemnly testifies to me in every city, saying that bonds and afflictions await me."
>
> Acts 20:22–23

2. The Spirit's "groanings" as well as His "interceding" on our behalf:

> For we know that the whole creation groans and suffers the pains of childbirth together until now. And not only this, but also we ourselves, having the first fruits of the Spirit, even we ourselves groan within ourselves, waiting eagerly for our adoption as sons, the redemption of our body. . . .
>
> And in the same way the Spirit also helps our weakness; for we do not know how to pray as we should, but the Spirit Himself intercedes for us with groanings too deep for words;

and He who searches the hearts knows what the mind of the Spirit is, because He intercedes for the saints according to the will of God.

Romans 8:22–23, 26–27

3. Another curious work of the Holy Spirit about which very little has been written has to do with His "searching all things," including "even the depths of God." And what about His revealing those things to us? Talk about intriguing!

But just as it is written,

"THINGS WHICH EYE HAS NOT SEEN AND
EAR HAS NOT HEARD,
AND WHICH HAVE NOT ENTERED THE
HEART OF MAN,
ALL THAT GOD HAS PREPARED FOR THOSE
WHO LOVE HIM."

For to us God revealed them through the Spirit; for the Spirit searches all things, even the depths of God. For who among men knows the thoughts of a man except the spirit of the man, which is in him? Even so the thoughts of God no one knows except the Spirit of God. Now we have received, not the spirit of the world, but the Spirit who is from God, that we might know the things freely given to us by God, which things we also speak, not in words taught by human wisdom, but in those taught by the Spirit, combining spiritual thoughts with spiritual words.

1 Corinthians 2:9–13

All my adult life I have heard about, as well as affirmed, the ministry of the *Word.* I still believe in it—now more than ever. But there is more. There is also the ministry of *God!* As His Spirit probes the Father's "depths" and searches those mysterious, unfathomable labyrinths of His will and His truth, He teaches them to us by "combining spiritual thoughts with spiritual words." We shall dig deeply into what that means.

4. Another "unmentionable" would be the "anointing" of

the Spirit, referred to in earlier versions of the English Bible as the "unction" of the Spirit.

> Children, it is the last hour; and just as you heard that antichrist is coming, even now many antichrists have arisen; from this we know that it is the last hour. They went out from us, but they were not really of us; for if they had been of us, they would have remained with us; but they went out, in order that it might be shown that they all are not of us. But you have an anointing from the Holy One, and you all know.
>
> 1 John 2:18–20

5. Periodically, someone will suggest that we should "test the spirits." In some unusual manner such "testing" helps us "know the Spirit of God," according to the apostle John. Perhaps you have wondered about these words for years, as I have:

> Beloved, do not believe every spirit, but test the spirits to see whether they are from God; because many false prophets have gone out into the world. By this you know the Spirit of God: every spirit that confesses that Jesus Christ has come in the flesh is from God; and every spirit that does not confess Jesus is not from God; and this is the spirit of the antichrist, of which you have heard that it is coming, and now it is already in the world.
>
> 1 John 4:1–3

6. John also writes about the "witness" of the Spirit, another curious comment very few ever bother to examine.

> And who is the one who overcomes the world, but he who believes that Jesus is the Son of God? This is the one who came by water and blood, Jesus Christ; not with the water only, but with the water and with the blood. And it is the Spirit who bears witness, because the Spirit is the truth. For there are three that bear witness, the Spirit and the water and the blood; and the three are in agreement. If we receive the witness of men, the witness of God is greater; for the

witness of God is this, that He has borne witness concerning His Son.

1 John 5:5–9

I think you're getting the drift of where we are going. In the process, I want to address certain terms that have been linked with the Spirit of God: terms like *power* and *presence, revelation* and *visions, miracles* and *healings*, even *intuition, guidance*, and *God's voice.* How seldom we feel comfortable addressing these subjects, but we need to have a better understanding of them if we hope to fly closer to the flame.

Even though we are not one full chapter into the book, some of you are probably getting uneasy . . . almost as if you feel guilty or afraid. Perhaps you're starting to wonder about me. *Maybe Chuck's getting a little weird with all that wind blowing on him on the Harley . . . and from hanging around those strange-looking motorcycle riders. Yep, that must be it!*

Wrong.

I've been turning these things over in my mind for more than two decades. In fact, I can remember sitting in a seminary classroom wondering why certain verses weren't mentioned or why the professor seemed uptight and defensive when some young man pressed him a little strongly on verses he had chosen to bypass.

Or perhaps you are feeling a little nervous about the direction I might take on some of these controversial issues.

Relax! We have everything to gain and nothing to lose by allowing the truth to emerge. It's the truth, remember, that sets us free. So let's not rush to judgment or try to find some popular label or theological category in which to dump these things. Nor should we ever be afraid of the flame!

The inescapable fact is this: Most (yes, most) Christians you and I know have very little dynamic or joy in their lives. Just ask them. They long for depth, for passion, for a satisfying peace and stability instead of a superficial relationship with God made up of words without feelings and struggles without healings. Surely there is more to the life of faith than church meetings, Bible study, religious jargon, and periodic prayers. Surely the awesome Spirit of God wishes to do more within us than what is presently going on! There are scars He wants to remove. There are fractured feelings He wants to heal. There are insights He longs to reveal. There are profound dimensions of life He would dearly love to open up. But none of the above will happen automatically—not as long as He remains a sterile, untouchable blip on our theological PC.

He is the comforting Helper, remember? He is the Truth-Teacher, the will-of-the-Father Revealer, the Gift-Giver, the Hurt-Healer. He is the inextinguishable flame of God, my friend. *HE IS GOD.* To remain at a distance from Him is worse than wrong; it is downright *tragic.* Flying closer to the flame, therefore, is better than good; it is absolutely *magnificent.*

Discovering the Spirit's Significance

Maybe all this emphasis on the Holy Spirit seems overdrawn to you. Could it be that you have never been shown from the Scriptures just how significant a role the Lord intended Him to play in your life? Before bringing this chapter to a close, let me help you see three contributions He makes, without which life is reduced to dull and gray.

First, His Permanent Presence Within Us

Jesus sat alone with His twelve disciples in a small, second-story room the night before He was crucified. They had a meal together, followed by the Last Supper. Judas was dismissed. Earlier, Jesus had washed His disciples' feet. A brief discussion about that arose. Then, almost without interruption, He "delivered His soul." By that I mean He communicated the most intimate and the most important information and instruction they could hear. His words are found in chapters 14–16 of the Gospel by John, a section that has come to be known as "The Upper Room Discourse." He began:

"Let not your heart be troubled; believe in God, believe also in Me. In My Father's house are many dwelling places; if it were not so, I would have told you; for I go to prepare a place for you. And if I go and prepare a place for you, I will come again, and receive you to Myself; that where I am, there you may be also. And you know the way where I am going." Thomas said to Him, "Lord, we do not know where You are going, how do we know the way?" Jesus said to him, "I am the way, and the truth, and the life; no one comes to the Father, but through Me. . . . I will not leave you as orphans; I will come to you."

John 14:1–6, 18

We sit calmly as we read those words and as we try to imagine the disciples hearing them. But they were *anything* but calm! Jesus was announcing His departure, and they were struggling with feelings of abandonment. Their stomachs must have churned when He used the word "orphans," for that is *exactly* how they felt. For more than three years they had been inseparable. He was there when they awoke. He was with them through virtually every situation they faced. When they called for help, He was usually nearby and able to step in. When they said "Good night," He was there to respond. Suddenly, all that would change. He was leaving them—permanently. And though they were adults, the sting of His departure left them feeling orphaned.

I recall having that feeling when my dad died back in 1980. My mother had passed on nine years earlier; now I was without both parents. I was more than forty-five years old, had a family of my own, and was neck deep in ministry. Nevertheless, his departure marked a passage in my life after which things would never be quite the same. No more visits. No more phone calls. No opportunity to sit and talk through something I was facing . . . to have him listen and respond. In a strange way I felt orphaned, and to this day I still have occasions when I miss being able to see my father, to hear his voice, to watch him respond.

That was how the disciples felt. No more meals together. No more discussions beside the sea. No more quiet talks around the fire at night. No more shared laughter . . . or tears . . . or watching Him handle some thorny situation. Orphaned.

And yet He promised not to leave them as orphans. "Plan B" was already in motion.

> "And I will ask the Father, and He will give you another Helper, that He may be with you forever; that is the Spirit of truth, whom the world cannot receive, because it does not behold Him or know Him, but you know Him because He abides with you, and will be in you."
>
> John 14:16–17

Aha! Jesus promised them that His replacement would be "another Helper," namely, the Holy Spirit. And, unlike Jesus, who had only been with them, He (the Spirit) would be *in* them. Quite a difference! Not too many days hence, when the Spirit would arrive, He would slip inside them and live within them forever. No more temporary companionship; the Spirit's presence would be (and still is) a permanent presence. It had never been like that before. Not even in the lives of those Old Testament greats. But from now on . . . yes!

Jesus' departure was essential in order for the Spirit to begin His permanent indwelling. Jesus said so.

> "But I tell you the truth, it is to your advantage that I go away; for if I do not go away, the Helper shall not come to you; but if I go, I will send Him to you."
>
> John 16:7

So then, we need to turn next to the place in Scripture where Jesus' departure is recorded—Acts 1—to see what He said about the Spirit's coming, for it is there we find the next significant contribution of the Spirit.

Second, His Unparalleled Dynamic Among Us

> And gathering them together, He commanded them not to leave Jerusalem, but to wait for what the Father had prom-

> ised, "Which," He said, "you heard of from Me; for John baptized with water, but you shall be baptized with the Holy Spirit not many days from now."
>
> And so when they had come together, they were asking Him, saying, "Lord, is it at this time You are restoring the kingdom to Israel?" He said to them, "It is not for you to know times or epochs which the Father has fixed by His own authority; but you shall receive power when the Holy Spirit has come upon you; and you shall be My witnesses both in Jerusalem, and in all Judea and Samaria, and even to the remotest part of the earth."
>
> Acts 1:4–8

Our Lord's ascension was only moments away. Naturally, He wanted to bid farewell to His closest companions. As they stood alongside, He reassured them: "you shall receive power when the Holy Spirit has come upon you" (v. 8). Not *if* the Spirit comes, but *when*. And upon His arrival, *power* would be received.

Now, Jesus was not saying that power would begin to exist at that point, for power had always been one of God's characteristics. Power was present at Creation. Power opened the Red Sea. Power brought water from the rock and fire from heaven. In fact, it was that same magnificent power that had brought Christ back from beyond at His resurrection. But those kinds of supernatural manifestations were not what He was promising. The disciples would not be creating worlds or parting seas or taking the place of God.

What Christ promised them was enabling power. Another kind of power, as A. T. Robertson correctly observed:

> Not the "power" about which they were concerned (political organization and equipment for the empire on the order of Rome) . . . this new "power" (*dunamin*), to enable them (from *dunamai*, to be able), to grapple with the spread of the gospel in the world.[1]

Jesus was saying, in effect, "You will receive a new enablement, a new dynamic, altogether different from what you have ever experienced before." I would suggest that this promised "power" also included an inner confidence, almost to the point of invincibility, regardless of the odds they were sure to face.

F. F. Bruce, in his splendid volume on the Book of Acts, states that:

> they would be clothed with heavenly power—that power by which, in the event, their mighty works were accomplished and their preaching made effective. As Jesus Himself had been anointed at His baptism with the Holy Spirit and power, so His followers were now to be similarly anointed and enabled to carry on His work.[2]

The power (I prefer to use the term *dynamic*) that Jesus promised the disciples, directly—and us indirectly—was the Spirit's unparalleled help and enablement, which would immeasurably surpass their own human ability.

Think of it! It's the very same dynamic that is resident within every Christian today. But where has it gone? Why is it so seldom evident among us? What can be done to get it in motion as it once was? Those are some of the questions that prompted me to dig deeply into this study.

Third, His Affirming Will for Us

In His statement prior to His departure, Jesus included an additional promise to His disciples. "You shall be My witnesses," He said. The Spirit would free their lips so that they would *witness* consistently of Him. First, in Jerusalem, where they would be located when the Spirit came. Next, in Judea and Samaria, the surrounding regions beyond the city. Ultimately, "even to the remotest part of the earth." The Spirit's presence would spur them on, enabling them to speak openly and boldly of their Savior. He is still longing to do that within and through us today, affirming God's will for us.

A quick glance at the fourth chapter of Acts reveals the results of this Spirit-filled dynamic: *perseverance*. Peter and John had been preaching in the streets of Jerusalem, where they were later arrested, confronted, and threatened by the officials. Undaunted by the threats, the disciples stood toe-to-toe with the officials. Their calm perseverance did not go unnoticed.

> Now as they observed the confidence of Peter and John, and understood that they were uneducated and untrained men, they were marveling, and began to recognize them as having been with Jesus.
>
> Acts 4:13

Why? Why would the religious officials marvel at untrained and unlearned men? Because they were impressed by their firm resolve. Their thoughts might have been: *These are a different kind of men. They are not like the soldiers we deal with or the politicians or our fellow officials.* As a result, they began to recognize that these were Jesus people . . . these were men who had once been with Jesus. How would they know that? *The dynamic!*

Not long afterward, the disciples were called back before the Jewish Supreme Court and told in no uncertain terms to knock it off!

> "We gave you strict orders not to continue teaching in this name, and behold, you have filled Jerusalem with your teaching, and intend to bring this man's blood upon us." But Peter and the apostles answered and said, "We must obey God rather than men."
>
> Acts 5:28–29

Friend, that is persistent, invincible dynamic! Normally folks are intimidated in the official setting of a courtroom. Not those men!

Remember Acts 1:8? "You shall receive power." You'll be witnesses. You'll have perseverance to stand firm, regardless.

A few moments later these same Spirit-enabled men set the record straight:

> "The God of our fathers raised up Jesus, whom you had put to death by hanging Him on a cross. He is the one whom God exalted to His right hand as a Prince and a Savior, to grant repentance to Israel, and forgiveness of sins. And we are witnesses of these things; and so is the Holy Spirit, whom God has given to those who obey Him."
>
> Acts 5:30–32

And what happened? Did they lick their wounds and curl up in some cave until the situation cooled down? Were they frightened and disillusioned? On the contrary. Even after they were threatened and brutally beaten,

> . . . they went on their way from the presence of the Council, rejoicing that they had been considered worthy to suffer shame for His name. And every day, in the temple and from house to house, they kept right on teaching and preaching Jesus as the Christ.
>
> Acts 5:41–42

The Spirit's enablement . . . that's heaven-sent "power"! And the good news is that the same Spirit who filled believers in the first century can fill us in the twentieth. And the same dynamic can be ours . . . the same boldness and determination, invincibility and perseverance in the midst of danger.

Removing the Resistance Between Us and Him

Doesn't all of this sound appealing? Haven't you longed for such fortitude, such confident faith? These traits were never meant to be restricted to century-one saints. Nowhere in the Scriptures do I find a statement that limits the Spirit's presence or dynamic to some bygone era. The same One who promised a handful of frightened followers new dimensions of divine enablement is anxious to fulfill that in us today.

Frankly, I'm ready for it, aren't you? We need it, and it is ours to claim . . . so *let's claim it!*

To do so, at least three forces of resistance must be removed. Until we remove them, our hope for that first-century kind of life-changing, supernatural power will remain just that—a hope, a theoretical dream, something we can read about in ancient history but never know firsthand. And what are these forces of resistance?

1. The barrier of the fearful unknown.
2. The wall of traditional limitations.
3. The obstacle course of personal excuses.

Read that list again, only this time pause after each one and think about the presence of that particular resistance in your own life.

I want to close this first chapter with a brief but honest confession: I am not, by nature, a person who changes easily. I was raised by a very stable, consistent mother and father who provided a solid home where my brother, sister, and I grew up securely. We were taught to love God, believe in Christ, trust and obey the Bible, and be faithful in church attendance. Much of my theology was hammered out on the anvil of those early years at home.

As I grew up, my roots were strengthened in the fundamentals of the Christian faith. My training in seminary drove those roots even deeper. By the time I graduated, I had many convictions and few questions, especially in the realm of the Holy Spirit. But during thirty-plus years of ministry both in the United States and abroad, I have come to realize that there are dimensions of the Spirit's ministry I have never tapped. There is also a dynamic power in His presence I have witnessed that I long to know more of firsthand. I now have questions and a strong interest in many of the things of the Spirit I once felt were settled.

I do not fear digging into these intimate and mysterious realms, for He is "the Spirit of truth" and Jesus, my Lord, promised that He would "guide you [us] into all the truth" (John 16:13). I invite you to come with me on this exciting and creative journey. I encourage you not to be afraid as we, together, fly closer to the flame.

As we get reacquainted with the One who lives within us, who knows? We may make some discoveries that will necessitate our shifting here and there in our longstanding theology. No problem. I've seen enough people who have stopped thinking and changing to know that that's not for me. I have the feeling it's not for you either . . . otherwise, you would have already laid this book aside before finishing this first chapter.

If you are still willing to risk, read on. The next chapter moves even closer to the flame.

2

The Main Agenda of God's Spirit: Transformation

IN 1983 JOHN SCULLEY QUIT his post at Pepsico to become the president of Apple Computer. He took a big risk leaving his prestigious position with a well-established firm to join ranks with an unproven little outfit that offered no guarantees, only the excitement of one man's transforming vision. Sculley says he made the risky move after Apple cofounder Steve Jobs goaded him with the question, "Do you want to spend the rest of your life selling sugared water or do you want a chance to change the world?"

The original disciples were a handful of unlikely misfits, nothing more than a "rather ragged aggregation of souls," as Robert Coleman puts it in his *Master Plan of Evangelism*.[1] But the remarkable fact is that they were the same ones who later "turned the world upside down," according to the testimony of people in the first century. How can anyone explain the transformation? Was it some crash course they took, some upbeat seminar on leadership? No. Then maybe it was really the work of angels, but the disciples were given credit for it? No, the biblical record clearly states that it was the same group of once-timid men Jesus had trained. Perhaps some high-powered "heavenly drug," some miracle-inducing chemical, was inserted into their bodies that changed the men overnight? *Enough!*

There is only one intelligent answer: It was the arrival and the empowerment of the Holy Spirit. He alone transformed those frightened, awkward, reluctant men into strong-hearted, unintimidated, invincible prophets of God. Instead of feeling abandoned and orphaned, instead of spending the rest of their lives with "sugared water," they became directly involved in changing the world. Once the Spirit took up residence with them, once He was given complete control of their lives, He put His agenda into full operation, and they were never the same. They embodied His dynamic. They no longer held back or stood in the shadows or looked for excuses not to be engaged in obeying their Lord's mandate to "go and make disciples of all nations." Once "another Helper" came, transformation occurred . . . immediate transformation.

A Brief Glance at the "Orphaned" Disciples

To appreciate this transformation as fully as we should, we need a before-and-after portrait of the men who walked with Christ. Let's start with the scene we glanced at earlier in chapter 1—the Last Supper.

Judas had left. The meal had been eaten. The taste of bread and wine were still on their tongues as their Lord began to unveil the reality of His departure. Their stomachs churned with the thought of going on without Him. They were troubled, even though He urged them, "Let not your heart be troubled . . ." (John 14:1). They were confused, as Thomas's question reveals, "Lord, we do not know where You are going, how do we know the way?" (John 14:5). Another in the group was bothered about the change in plans as he asked, "Lord, what then has happened that You are going to disclose Yourself to us, and not to the world?" (John 14:22).

Later, Peter denied Him . . . and He was the leader of the group (Mark 14:53–72)! Ultimately, when push came to shove, "all the disciples left Him and fled" (Matt. 26:56). Every last one of them deserted their Master.

At His resurrection they were surprised at the thought of His body not being in the tomb. And that same evening, after knowing of His resurrection, the disciples were hiding out together behind closed doors. Why? They were hiding "for fear of the

Jews" (John 20:19). If that were not enough, even after He came among some of them, Thomas firmly resisted, declaring he had to witness everything firsthand or (in his own words) "I will not believe" (John 20:25).

Troubled, confused, bothered, disloyal, fearful, doubting . . . these men were anything but valiant warriors for Christ. Prior to the Spirit's transforming work, they were wimps! To them, when the original game plan was aborted, the mission was considered *unaccomplished*.

I often return to Coleman's realistic description of the disciples. It is anything but flattering.

> What is more revealing about these men is that at first they do not impress us as being key men. None of them occupied prominent places in the Synagogue, nor did any of them belong to the Levitical priesthood. For the most part they were common laboring men, probably having no professional training beyond the rudiments of knowledge necessary for their vocation. Perhaps a few of them came from families of some considerable means, such as the sons of Zebedee, but none of them could have been considered wealthy. They had no academic degrees in the arts and philosophies of their day. Like their Master, their formal education likely consisted only of the Synagogue schools. Most of them were raised in the poor section of the country around Galilee. Apparently the only one of the twelve who came from the more refined region of Judea was Judas Iscariot. By any standard of sophisticated culture then and now they would surely be considered as a rather ragged aggregation of souls. One might wonder how Jesus could ever use them. They were impulsive, temperamental, easily offended, and had all the prejudices of their environment. In short, these men selected by the Lord to be His assistants represented an average cross section of the lot of society in their day. Not the kind of group one would expect to win the world for Christ.[2]

You may not appreciate such a forthright portrayal of the disciples, but from what I read of them in the Gospel accounts, it is accurate. Prior to the coming of the Spirit and His transforming presence in their lives, they bore all the marks of men least likely to survive, to say nothing of succeed.

An Enlightening Discovery of Personal Transformation

Jesus knew His men much better than they knew themselves. He knew Judas was deceptive and Peter was rash. He knew Thomas struggled with doubt and that John was a dreamer. He knew how petty and competitive they were . . . how selfish and fragile. He knew the final Eleven thought of themselves as fiercely loyal, but when the chips were down, they would slink into the shadows. He knew that a new dynamic was imperative if His mission for the establishment of the church and the evangelization of the world had any hope of being accomplished. Therefore, when He promised "another Helper," He meant One who would transform them from the inside out. He knew that the only way they would ultimately do "greater works" than He had accomplished would be through the Spirit's presence and power.

Little did the disciples realize how much they lacked. Most of them (perhaps all of them) thought they had more going for them than was the case. Peter, remember, assured his Lord, "I will lay down my life for You," and "Even though all may fall away, yet I will not" (John 13:37; Mark 14:29). What a comedown when they later realized that they were not nearly as resilient or loyal or courageous as they had assured Him they would be.

We've all been there, haven't we? About the time we get out on a limb thinking we're pretty capable, we get sawed off by a sudden and embarrassing discovery. At that point we realize we aren't nearly as effective or competent as we had convinced ourselves we were.

I read a classic example of this recently in Max DePree's splendid volume, *Leadership Jazz*.

> The story goes that a German machine tool company once developed a very fine bit for drilling holes in steel. The tiny bit

> could bore a hole about the size of a human hair. This seemed like a tremendously valuable innovation. The Germans sent samples off to Russia, the United States, and Japan, suggesting that this bit was the ultimate in machining technology.
>
> From the Russians, they heard nothing. From the Americans came a quick response inquiring as to the price of the bits, available discounts, and the possibility of a licensing arrangement.
>
> After some delay, there was the predictable, polite response from the Japanese, complimenting the Germans on their achievement, but with a postscript noting that the Germans' bit was enclosed with a slight alteration. Excitedly, the German engineers opened the package, carefully examined their bit, and to their amazement discovered that the Japanese had bored a neat hole through it.[3]

When the Spirit of God bored His way into the lives of those awaiting His arrival in that upstairs room somewhere in Jerusalem, His transforming presence was immediately evident. As I read what transpired in the early part of the Book of Acts, I am able to identify at least four transforming changes among those who received the Spirit.

First, ***their human frailties were transformed into supernatural gifts and abilities.***

From the moment the Holy Spirit arrived, nothing about the disciples remained the same. When His power, His dynamic (the Greek term is *dunamis*) fell upon them, they even spoke in another language.

> And when the day of Pentecost had come, they were all together in one place. And suddenly there came from heaven a noise like a violent, rushing wind, and it filled the whole house where they were sitting. And there appeared to them tongues as of fire distributing themselves, and they rested on each one of them. And they were all filled with the Holy Spirit and began to speak with other tongues, as the Spirit was giving them utterance.
>
> Acts 2:1–4

Try to imagine those phenomena occurring back to back.

- A noise, an incredibly loud roar (the Greek term is the word from which we get our English word *echo*), not unlike the sound of a violent hurricane unleashing its earsplitting fury on some coastal village.
- A large "ball" of fire, spontaneously separating into smaller flames, each in the shape of a tongue that came to rest upon each person in the room.
- As this occurred, each of the individuals was simultaneously "filled with the Holy Spirit." From their lips flowed words they had never spoken before in languages they had never learned.

This experience completely revolutionized their lives. Those who had been troubled and fearful no longer struggled with those feelings. The once frightened, unsure, confused, timid men never again evidenced such inadequacies. From that time on they were bold in faith and confident in their God. They were *transformed*.

Suddenly they were able to speak in languages not their own. So clear and accurate were those languages that those who heard them were shocked.

> And when this sound occurred, the multitude came together, and were bewildered, because they were each one hearing them speak in his own language. And they were amazed and marveled, saying, "Why, are not all these who are speaking Galileans? And how is it that we each hear them in our own language to which we were born? Parthians and Medes and Elamites, and residents of Mesopotamia, Judea and Cappadocia, Pontus and Asia, Phrygia and Pamphylia, Egypt and the districts of Libya around Cyrene, and visitors from Rome, both Jews and proselytes, Cretans and Arabs—we hear them in our own tongues speaking of the mighty deeds of God."
>
> Acts 2:6–11

It is noteworthy that the original term used for "language" in verses 6 and 8 is the Greek word *dialektos,* from which we get "dialect." Remarkable! Those untrained, monolingual Galileans were suddenly able to communicate in the native dialects of individuals from regions far removed from Palestine.

And if that were not enough, some in the group were given the supernatural ability to touch another life and restore physical health.

> Now Peter and John were going up to the temple at the ninth hour, the hour of prayer. And a certain man who had been lame from his mother's womb was being carried along, whom they used to set down every day at the gate of the temple which is called Beautiful, in order to beg alms of those who were entering the temple. And when he saw Peter and John about to go into the temple, he began asking to receive alms. And Peter, along with John, fixed his gaze upon him and said, "Look at us!" And he began to give them his attention, expecting to receive something from them. But Peter said, "I do not possess silver and gold, but what I do have I give to you: In the name of Jesus Christ the Nazarene—walk!" And seizing him by the right hand, he raised him up; and immediately his feet and his ankles were strengthened. And with a leap, he stood upright and began to walk; and he entered the temple with them, walking and leaping and praising God.
>
> Acts 3:1–8

Before we get the idea that these men suddenly "glowed" with some kind of aura or in some other way appeared different, however, let's hear the testimony of Peter:

> And while he was clinging to Peter and John, all the people ran together to them at the so-called portico of Solomon, full of amazement. But when Peter saw this, he replied to the people, "Men of Israel, why do you marvel at this, or why do you gaze at us, as if by our own power or piety we had made him walk?"
>
> Acts 3:11–12

Clearly, Peter and John were still "just plain Peter and John." They didn't promote themselves as miracle workers or divine healers. They seemed to be as amazed over this as those who witnessed what had happened. Having been transformed by the Helper whom Jesus had sent, the disciples did not turn the scene into a man-glorifying sideshow.

Second, *their fearful reluctance was transformed into bold confidence.*

Remember an earlier scene when these same men, afraid of being found out by the Jews, hid silently behind closed doors? The last thing they wanted was to be pointed out as followers of Jesus. They were frozen in fear.

No longer. According to this narrative, they poured into the public streets of Jerusalem preaching Christ and urging total strangers to repent and to believe in the name of Jesus.

> And with many other words he [Peter] solemnly testified and kept on exhorting them, saying, "Be saved from this perverse generation!"
>
> Acts 2:40

Later, when Peter and John had been arrested and were being interrogated, their quiet confidence did not go unnoticed:

> Now as they observed the confidence of Peter and John, and understood that they were uneducated and untrained men, they were marveling, and began to recognize them as having been with Jesus.
>
> Acts 4:13

The followers of Jesus didn't look any different physically. They didn't suddenly become learned men. Nor were they abruptly made cultured and sophisticated. No, they remained rawboned fishermen and a couple of "good ol' boys." But deep within their beings, down inside, they were nothing like they had been. They were *transformed.*

Third, *their fears and intimidation were transformed into a sense of invincibility.*

Webster states that intimidation is timidity, being afraid, overawed, deterred with threats. These men, having been invaded by God's Spirit, were none of the above.

- Instead of running from the public, they ran toward them.
- Instead of hoping not to be seen, they exhorted total strangers to repent.
- Instead of being frightened by insults, warnings, and threats, they stood face-to-face with their accusers and did not blink. When told to keep it quiet, they answered unflinchingly, "We must obey God rather than men" (Acts 5:29).

Even when called before the Council, the supreme ruling body of the Jews, this handful of "uneducated and untrained men" stood like steers in a blizzard. They weren't about to back down, even if they were forced to stand before some of the same prejudiced and cruel judges who had unjustly manipulated the trials against Jesus of Nazareth. They refused to be overawed. Such invincible courage!

Where does one get such boldness today? From studying at Oxford or Yale or Harvard? Hardly. How about from reading the biographies of great men and women? That may stimulate our minds, but it cannot transform our lives. Then perhaps the secret of such boldness is a mentor, someone whose walk with God is admirable and consistent. Again, as helpful as heroes and models may be, their influence cannot suddenly infuse us with invincible courage. The Spirit of God alone is able to make that happen.

It was not until He came and filled those frail and frightened men with His supernatural "dynamic" that they were genuinely (and permanently) changed deep within—*transformed.*

Fourth, *their lonely, grim feelings of abandonment were transformed into joyful perseverance.*

On the heels of their second arrest, Peter and John let out all the stops! Refusing to tell their frowning accusers what they wanted to hear, they looked them squarely in the eye and pulled no punches.

> And when they had brought them, they stood them before the Council. And the high priest questioned them, saying, "We gave you strict orders not to continue teaching in this name, and behold, you have filled Jerusalem with your teaching, and intend to bring this man's blood upon us." But Peter and the apostles answered and said, "We must obey God rather than men. The God of our fathers raised up Jesus, whom you had put to death by hanging Him on a cross. He is the one whom God exalted to His right hand as a Prince and a Savior, to grant repentance to Israel, and forgiveness of sins. And we are witnesses of these things; and so is the Holy Spirit, whom God has given to those who obey Him."
>
> Acts 5:27–32

I find it absolutely amazing that those men, once so petty and competitive and self-centered, are now so strong-hearted, so incredibly confident. So did the officials.

> But when they heard this, they were cut to the quick and were intending to slay them. But a certain Pharisee named Gamaliel, a teacher of the Law, respected by all the people, stood up in the Council and gave orders to put the men outside for a short time. And he said to them, "Men of Israel, take care what you propose to do with these men. For sometime ago Theudas rose up, claiming to be somebody; and a group of about four hundred men joined up with him. And he was slain; and all who followed him were dispersed and came to nothing. After this man Judas of Galilee rose up in the days of the census, and drew away some people after him, he too perished, and all those who followed him were scattered. And so in the present case, I say to you, stay away from these men and let them alone, for if this plan or action should be of men, it will be overthrown; but if it is of God, you will not be able to overthrow them; or else you may even be found fighting against God." And they took his advice;

> and after calling the apostles in, they flogged them and ordered them to speak no more in the name of Jesus, and then released them.
>
> Acts 5:33–40

The Jewish leaders must have thought, "That ought to do it. A firm warning, a bloody flogging, and this strong threat ought to shut them up for good!"

It didn't. As we saw earlier,

> So they went on their way from the presence of the Council, rejoicing that they had been considered worthy to suffer shame for His name. And every day, in the temple and from house to house, they kept right on teaching and preaching Jesus as the Christ.
>
> Acts 5:41–42

The Amplified Bible says they were "dignified by the indignity."

The flogging, the warning, and the threat merely fueled the fire of their determination. In fact (did you catch it?), they left "rejoicing." And upon their return to the company of their friends, joy filled everyone's hearts, not sadness . . . not disillusionment. The wimps had become warriors!

The Spirit of God may have reminded them of the words of their now-departed Lord: "In the world you have tribulation, but take courage; I have overcome the world" (John 16:33). In fact, Peter himself would later write:

> Beloved, do not be surprised at the fiery ordeal among you, which comes upon you for your testing, as though some strange thing were happening to you; but to the degree that you share the sufferings of Christ, keep on rejoicing; so that also at the revelation of His glory, you may rejoice with exultation.
>
> 1 Peter 4:12–13

Quite likely he was recalling that day when he and John had been dragged before the Council and unfairly beaten. Instead of wondering, "Why did the Lord leave us alone?" or "Where is He when we need Him?" their joyful perseverance won the day. No resentment. No feelings of abandonment. No pity party for PLOM members only (Poor Little Ol' Me).

Why? Because the disciples had been radically changed. Not merely motivated or momentarily mesmerized—they were *transformed*.

A Straightforward Analysis of How It Happened

But how? What did it? How could these same men who had earlier run for cover now stand tall, refusing to be backed down or even whipped down?

One possible explanation that comes to mind is *positive thinking*. Maybe one or two in the little band of disciples looked around and said, "Now that Christ has left, it is time for us to look at the bright side of things and be responsible."

Very, very doubtful. Positive thinking doesn't go very far when folks are getting the skin beaten off their backs—and it certainly doesn't keep them rejoicing in the midst of it. Nor does positive thinking suddenly change a person who is naturally and normally intimidated into one who is invincible. Having a positive attitude is a wonderful thing, but it is unable to bring about wholesale transformation.

Another possibility is a *better environment*. Maybe things lightened up. Perhaps the public had a change of heart and became more open and willing to accept responsibility for crucifying Christ. Caesar himself may have decided that followers of Christ were not really that much of a concern to the mighty Roman Empire.

You're smiling. You know that things got increasingly more hostile, more intense.

Well, perhaps someone *taught a seminar* on "How to Endure Suffering: Twelve Steps Toward a Successful Life."

No, you know better.

If you ever go to Rome, spend some time in the catacombs. Walk slowly through the narrow, labyrinthine paths that lead deep into the bowels of that subterranean world and you will see sights you'll never forget. You will feel like groaning as you stare at slender little berths where broken bodies were placed. You may even see the writings or touch the sign of the fish or a cross, a crown, or some other equally eloquent, albeit mute, reminder of pain. As you brush along those ancient graves in silence, much of the superficial stuff you read today about being happy through suffering will seem terribly shallow. At the same time, the few signs that pulsate with true triumph in Christ will take on new meaning. What you will witness firsthand will be the evidence of transformed lives.

The Best (and Only) Conclusion

No course was taught. No cheerleader led the disciples in mind-bending chants that gave them a positive attitude. No change in environment brought about their transformation. It was the Spirit of God and nothing else. It was the life-changing, attitude-altering, dynamic power of the living Lord that swept over them and became permanently resident within them.

Remember Jesus' promises? Let me quickly review several of them:

> "Truly, truly, I say to you, he who believes in Me, the works that I do shall he do also; and greater works than these shall he do; because I go to the Father."
>
> John 14:12

> "And I will ask the Father, and He will give you another Helper, that He may be with you forever; that is the Spirit of truth, whom the world cannot receive, because it does not behold Him or know Him, but you know Him because He abides with you, and will be in you. I will not leave you as orphans; I will come to you."
>
> John 14:16–18

> "But the Helper, the Holy Spirit, whom the Father will send in My name, He will teach you all things, and bring to your remembrance all that I said to you."
>
> John 14:26

> "But you shall receive power when the Holy Spirit has come upon you; and you shall be My witnesses both in Jerusalem, and in all Judea and Samaria, and even to the remotest part of the earth."
>
> Acts 1:8

God kept His word. And the disciples were never the same.

A Probing Question Only You Can Answer

Is the Spirit of God being allowed to transform *your* life? In case you think that's an irrelevant question, read the opening words of Romans 12:

> I urge you therefore, brethren, by the mercies of God, to present your bodies a living and holy sacrifice, acceptable to God, which is your spiritual service of worship. And do not be conformed to this world, but be transformed by the renewing of your mind, that you may prove what the will of God is, that which is good and acceptable and perfect.
>
> Romans 12:1–2

Don't miss the twofold command: "Do not be *conformed* . . . but be *transformed*" (italics mine).

Are you honest enough with yourself to answer my question? Is the Holy Spirit being allowed to transform your life?

There are only two possible answers: yes or no. If your answer is no, there are two possible reasons. Either you do not have the Spirit within you (i.e., you're not a Christian), or He is there but you prefer to live life on your own. I'll address that in more detail in the pages that follow. For now . . . let me urge you to do some soul-searching.

Speaking in tongues or healing the lame or explaining the supernatural phenomena recorded in the early section of the Book of Acts are intriguing subjects and, of course, important. But they can so easily become theological smoke screens, points of debate, and safe places in which to hide from the hard, probing question regarding you and your personal life.

My main concern is the Spirit's main agenda: Are *you* allowing *Him* to transform *your life?* If not, why not?

Flying closer to the flame may seem risky . . . but it is the best place to be. In fact, it is the only way to live.

3

My Sin . . . and "The Things of the Spirit"

I WAS MINISTERING AT A CONFERENCE with my long-time musical colleague, Dr. Howard Stevenson. He was leading the conferees in the singing of several wonderful choruses of worship, as only Howie can do it, and decided to teach everyone some very meaningful and tender motions to the old chorus "Spirit of the Living God." One of the motions involved our holding our hands up as we sang "Fill me . . . use me." It was handled so tastefully and graciously by Howie that I was confident everyone would participate. Wrong. Later, a few mentioned that they didn't know Howie and I were "charismatics" (the way they said it, the label sounded almost like a term of profanity).

What a ridiculous, rigid, and narrow response! Since when is there anything wrong with lifting our hands to God in praise and worship? It is biblical, you know. And since when does a certain posture deserve a label? It wasn't uncommon for folks in biblical days to fall prostrate before God in humiliation and prayer. Wonder what we would be called if we started doing that?

We need to take God out of our man-made box.

To make that happen, we need to relax a little. No, relax *a lot!* We need to be less defensive, less intense, and allow the truth of God to speak for itself. If that means changing here or there, so be it. Never forget, it is truth that sets us free. If you are missing out on all He wants to do in you and through you, then, in the words of the late British writer J. B. Phillips, your God is too small.[1]

Yet, at the same time, we must treat Him with the awesome honor He deserves. Flying closer to the flame does not suggest a disrespectful or casual familiarity with a holy God, but rather a more spontaneous, intimate, and dynamic relationship with Him who delights in our calling Him "Abba, Father." The key to such intimacy is the Holy Spirit. For too long we have kept our distance instead of pulling up closer and giving ourselves permission to worship and walk with Him in fresh and creative ways.

We need to maintain a healthy balance between being careful and being open. Being careful should not make us resistant to truth any more than being open should lead us into error.

Martin Lloyd-Jones, that superb expositor who served London's Westminster Chapel for more than twenty years, expressed it well:

> We must be very careful in these matters. What do we know of the realm of the Spirit? What do we know of the Spirit falling on people? What do we know about these great manifestations of the Holy Spirit? We need to be very careful "lest we be found fighting against God," lest we be guilty of "quenching the Spirit of God."[2]

So far everything has been kept at a nice, safe distance. The Spirit's flame has been burning, but we have not flown so close that we've felt too much heat, right? Oh, we've talked about the Spirit transforming our lives, but mainly we've focused on Jesus and His disciples, an upstairs room in Jerusalem, and the folks who formed the early church. The "tongues of fire" touched them (not us) and the supernatural manifestations were what they experienced (not us). So everything's been cool.

Until now.

In this chapter, I want to bring *us* into the picture. We're going to be flying a little closer to the flame. But don't worry . . . you're safe.

The Spirit . . . My Sin

In his letter to the Romans, Paul does a masterful job of preparing the reader for his first mention of the Holy Spirit. For almost half the letter, the subject is sin. Sin, sin, and more sin for five consecutive chapters.

When he introduces sin (in the first three chapters), the scene is foul; all hope seems lost. Mankind is wicked to the core, totally depraved, morally adrift, humanly hopeless. Anyone who reads Romans 1–3 and doesn't come to that conclusion has missed the message by a mile.

In Romans 4 and 5, Christ is introduced. Since He has redeemed us from sin's domination, a bright light of hope appears on the horizon. His death at Calvary brought the promise of relief, restored peace with God, and made it possible for God to declare us righteous on the basis of Christ's redeeming work on our behalf. This is known as "justification."

Sin's power was at last diffused, and the bondage was broken—at least theoretically. Sin was not eradicated, but its permanent hold on us was once-for-all released. When the sinner believes in the Lord Jesus Christ, a new Master enters the picture . . . and the old master (the devil) hates it! He called the shots so long, he thinks he is still king of the mountain.

Knowing this to be true, Paul then does major surgery on the subject in the next three chapters. Let me summarize:

• *Romans 6:* Sin no longer has power over us. We have been emancipated. The freedom is ours to claim. Enjoy your liberty, but don't take advantage of it. Since you're free from your old master, don't let sin reign over you any longer. The liberating message of Romans 6 is pretty well capsulized in these two verses:

> Therefore do not let sin reign in your mortal body that you should obey its lusts, and do not go on presenting the members of your body to sin as instruments of unrighteousness; but present yourselves to God as those alive from the dead, and your members as instruments of righteousness to God.
>
> Romans 6:12–13

• *Romans 7:* But sin is still present within me; I sometimes struggle over who is going to be in charge. I may have been emancipated, but the old master is very much alive . . . and there are times he gives me fits.

Every Christian I know can identify with Paul's honest admission:

> For we know that the Law is spiritual; but I am of flesh, sold into bondage to sin. For that which I am doing, I do not understand; for I am not practicing what I would like to do, but I am doing the very thing I hate.
>
> Romans 7:14–15

You and I may have a new Master, but sin is still there within us, still crouching near the door, ready to pounce! The battle is so relentless, so ruthless, it sometimes gets depressing . . . which may have been the very reason Paul finally let it all out:

> Wretched man that I am! Who will set me free from the body of this death?
>
> Romans 7:24

Great question! Who indeed is able to give me the victory over my old master . . . who indeed will "set me free" from the clawing, clutching, clinging presence of sin?

And we're back to the same magnificent solution: the Transformer Himself—THE HOLY SPIRIT! Which becomes the subject of—

• *Romans 8:* The Spirit provides a new dimension of living. The depressing syndrome set forth in Romans 7 is overcome in Romans 8. The "law of sin and of death" that habitually condemned us in our lost estate has been conquered by "the Spirit of life in Christ Jesus." That is why "There is therefore now no condemnation for those who are in Christ Jesus" (8:1).

Paul deliberately paces himself in the writing of Romans. Chapter after chapter, he deals with sin, sin, and more sin . . . with not one word of relief from the dark side. And then, as the curtain seems to be closing and the reader reaches rock bottom with no way through and no way out . . . Eureka! Enter "the Spirit of life." The curtain quickly reopens, the stage is flooded with light, and the Transformer is introduced. What great writing!

Read this grand section of Romans 8 slowly, thoughtfully.

> There is therefore now no condemnation for those who are in Christ Jesus. For the law of the Spirit of life in Christ Jesus has set you free from the law of sin and of death. For what the Law could not do, weak as it was through the flesh, God did: sending His own Son in the likeness of sinful flesh and as an offering for sin, He condemned sin in the flesh, in order that the requirement of the Law might be fulfilled in us, who do not walk according to the flesh, but according to the Spirit. For those who are according to the flesh set their minds on the things of the flesh, but those who are according to the Spirit, the things of the Spirit. For the mind set on the flesh is death, but the mind set on the Spirit is life and peace, because the mind set on the flesh is hostile toward God; for it does not subject itself to the law of God, for it is not even able to do so; and those who are in the flesh cannot please God. However, you are not in the flesh but in the Spirit, if indeed the Spirit of God dwells in you. But if anyone does not have the Spirit of Christ, he does not belong to Him. And if Christ is in you, though the body is dead because of sin, yet the spirit is alive because of righteousness. But if the Spirit of Him who raised Jesus from the dead dwells in you, He who raised Christ Jesus from the dead will also give life to your mortal bodies through His Spirit who indwells you.
>
> So then, brethren, we are under obligation, not to the flesh, to live according to the flesh—for if you are living according to the flesh, you must die; but if by the Spirit you are putting to death the deeds of the body, you will live. For all who are being led by the Spirit of God, these are sons of God.
>
> Romans 8:1–14

Why is the Spirit suddenly introduced in this manner? Because there is no way you or I could curtail and control the fleshly side of our lives apart from Him. But the good news is this: Because He is in us, we can. And because we can . . . we *must!*

My Flesh . . . His Spirit

Since both the Spirit and the flesh are resident within each believer, invariably there is a struggle going on beneath the surface of our lives. Every day we live it is there, simmering on the back burner of our minds. It is like a war in the soul . . . a bloodless battle that won't go away.

This does not mean we're carnal; it means we're human. There is no sin in admitting to the struggle. In fact, if you don't believe such a struggle exists, you haven't been honest with yourself nor have you spent sufficient time in the latter half of Galatians 5.

> But I say, walk by the Spirit, and you will not carry out the desire of the flesh. For the flesh sets its desire against the Spirit, and the Spirit against the flesh; for these are in opposition to one another, so that you may not do the things that you please.
>
> Galatians 5:16–17

To make it even clearer than that, let's look at a paraphrase of verse 17 from The Living Bible:

> For we naturally love to do evil things that are just the opposite from the things that the Holy Spirit tells us to do; and the good things we want to do when the Spirit has His way with us are just the opposite of our natural desires. These two forces within us are constantly fighting each other to win control over us and our wishes are never free from their pressures.

The Amplified Bible renders the central part of that verse, "these are antagonistic to each other—continually withstanding and in conflict with each other."

Isn't that the truth? Deep within the recesses of our minds there is this invisible, albeit hostile, battleground. On one side are my fleshly desires; on the other, the blessed Spirit of God. One is dark; the other light. One is evil; the other righteous. One is full of lethal drives and desires; the other is nothing but wholesome and healthy.

Because that conflict is carried out in the invisible realm, we seldom think of it in such objective terms, but the contrasts could not be more antithetical. If it were not for the restraining presence of the Spirit, you and I would be the personification of wickedness. No sin would be too extreme. No act of disobedience too rebellious. The darkness of our souls would be blacker than a thousand caverns at midnight. Unrestrained, the flesh knows no bounds within the dark sphere of iniquity.

When the Flesh Is Dominant

Perhaps that may seem exaggerated. Could I have overstated our potential for evil? You decide:

> Now the deeds of the flesh are evident, which are: immorality, impurity, sensuality, idolatry, sorcery, enmities, strife, jealousy, outbursts of anger, disputes, dissensions, factions, envyings, drunkenness, carousings, and things like these, of which I forewarn you just as I have forewarned you that those who practice such things shall not inherit the kingdom of God.
>
> Galatians 5:19–21

Quite a list, isn't it? Looks terribly bleak to me. In fact, it's the same list of sins that could be applied to those outside of Christ. And that's just the point! When God's people traffic in these things, the world cannot tell the difference between *us* and *them.*

Before we go further, perhaps I should clarify the meaning of the phrase, "those who practice such things shall not inherit the kingdom of God."

Paul selects words very carefully. For example, "practice." The tense of the original verb suggests "habitually practices." In other words, it refers to one whose entire life is consumed by such evil. Clearly that is a description of the lifestyle of depraved sinners who have no escape in themselves.

But before we cluck our tongues at those who "habitually practice" such things, let's keep in mind that our old nature remains just as dark and depraved as theirs, even though the Spirit resides within us. Were it not for the presence of God's Spirit, our wickedness would know no bounds.

But He is there . . . He lives within . . . He prompts us to live above the dregs of depravity. Were that not true, we would be hopelessly awash in the activities of the flesh.

When the Spirit Takes Control

The good news is: We don't have to serve the old master any longer! Now that we have our Lord's divine, dynamic presence perpetually living within us, we can live above all that . . . and we can do so on a consistent basis. By the Spirit's filling, evidences of our new nature emerge.

So what occurs? What, for example, is produced when the Spirit is in full control? Paul answers that question directly.

> But the fruit of the Spirit is love, joy, peace, patience, kindness, goodness, faithfulness, gentleness, self-control; against such things there is no law.
>
> Galatians 5:22–23

And that is just a brief sampling of what He produces within us. Magnificent thought! By turning the controls of our life over to Him who lives within, we begin to model the life Christ modeled when He lived and walked on earth. When that happens, the transformation process kicks in.

The choice is ours. Remember Romans 8:5?

> For those who are according to the flesh set their minds on the things of the flesh, but those who are according to the Spirit, the things of the Spirit.

For years I wondered what "the things of the Spirit" were. Now I know!

We can produce "the things of the flesh" by setting our mind on such . . . or we can produce "the things of the Spirit" by giving Him control of our life. It's that simple. We become the followers of whichever master we choose to obey. That is precisely what Paul wrote to the first-century Christians in Rome:

> Do you not know that when you present yourselves to someone as slaves for obedience, you are slaves of the one whom you obey, either of sin resulting in death, or of obedience resulting in righteousness?
>
> Romans 6:16

Living under the control of our flesh is a deathlike existence. We are miserable, feel guilty and ashamed, and the emptiness within is worse than bad. But when we are operating under the dominating influence of the Spirit, "the things of the Spirit" are reproduced in us and through us.

And what are some of them? Romans 8 leaves us with quite a list.

* *Life and peace.*

> For the mind set on the flesh is death, but the mind set on the Spirit is life and peace.
>
> Romans 8:6

* *Absence of fear and closeness to God.*

> For you have not received a spirit of slavery leading to fear again, but you have received a spirit of adoption as sons by which we cry out, "Abba! Father!"
>
> Romans 8:15

* *Inner assurance . . . doubts gone!*

> The Spirit Himself bears witness with our spirit that we are children of God, and if children, heirs also, heirs of God and fellow-heirs with Christ, if indeed we suffer with Him in order that we may also be glorified with Him
>
> Romans 8:16–17

> And in the same way the Spirit also helps our weakness; for we do not know how to pray as we should, but the Spirit Himself intercedes for us with groanings too deep for words; and He who searches the hearts knows what the mind of the Spirit is, because He intercedes for the saints according to the will of God.
>
> Romans 8:26–27

* *Inner awareness that "all things" are working together for good and God's glory.*

> And we know that God causes all things to work together for good to those who love God, to those who are called according to His purpose.
>
> Romans 8:28

Leaving Room for Mystery

When Jesus and Nicodemus met one night to discuss spiritual things, the Lord gave the inquiring Pharisee—and us—a lot to think about, including statements about the flesh and the Spirit. At one point He said:

> "The wind blows where it wishes and you hear the sound of it, but do not know where it comes from and where it is going; so is every one who is born of the Spirit."
>
> John 3:8

Normally we apply that statement to salvation, meaning that the Spirit moves silently, mysteriously, and unexpectedly, prompting various individuals to turn to Christ and be born again. That is true, but I suggest that Jesus' words also indicate that the Spirit continues to move like the wind that blows. How silently and how mysteriously He works within us! In unexpected and spontaneous ways, He works out God's perfect and profound will.

> How unsearchable are His judgments and unfathomable His ways!
>
> Romans 11:33

We are unwise to restrict the workings of the Spirit to one simplistic system we feel we can analyze and explain. Let's not do that! Let's not try to box Him in.

Remember . . . He is like the wind . . . mysteriously on the move . . . blowing here, changing there, altering plans, creating stretching situations, stimulating wholesome desires, prompting decisions. These are all included in "the things of the Spirit," and only those who fly closer to the flame are sensitive enough to realize that.

So? Move closer. Don't be afraid. Be open and willing to let fresh wonder in. Leave plenty of room for the Spirit to work . . . to move . . . to reveal . . . to bring new dimensions of freedom. Paul experienced this, as he admits to his friends in Corinth:

> But just as it is written,
>
> "THINGS WHICH EYE HAS NOT SEEN AND
> EAR HAS NOT HEARD,
> AND WHICH HAVE NOT ENTERED THE
> HEART OF MAN,
> ALL THAT GOD HAS PREPARED FOR THOSE
> WHO LOVE HIM."
>
> For to us God revealed them through the Spirit; for the Spirit searches all things, even the depths of God. For who among men knows the thoughts of a man except the spirit of the man, which is in him? Even so the thoughts of God no one knows except the Spirit of God. Now we have received, not the spirit of the world, but the Spirit who is from God, that we might know the things freely given to us by God, which things we also speak, not in words taught by human wisdom, but in those taught by the Spirit, combining spiritual thoughts with spiritual words.
>
> 1 Corinthians 2:9–13

Of special interest to me here is that unusual comment he makes regarding how "the Spirit searches all things, even the depths of God." As we plumb those "depths" by means of the Spirit, we discover many of "the things freely given to us by God."

Such "things" do not enter our conscious minds so long as sin dominates. But when we are filled with the Spirit (we'll look at that in detail in the next chapter), our minds and hearts are open to spiritual dimensions we never knew existed and we begin to be truly transformed.

Three Absolutely Thrilling Thoughts

Let me leave you with three thoughts God gave me as I wrote this chapter. After reading each one, close your eyes and allow the words to sink into your mind.

- There are realms of earthly experience we have never traveled. (As we fly closer to the flame, the Spirit can open them up to us.)

  Pause and think it over . . .
- There are depths of God's will we have never tapped. (As we fly closer to the flame, the Spirit can reveal them to us.)

  Pause and think it over . . .
- There are dimensions of supernatural power we have never touched. (As we fly closer to the flame, the Spirit will allow that to happen.)

  Pause and think it over . . .

4

Is the Spirit's Filling That Big a Deal?

HAVE YOU EVER SENSED the need for an acute awareness of the Spirit of God? I have, as I'm sure you have. For most of us those times come wrapped in various packages:

- We face some awful trial from which we cannot escape.
- A physician tells us he is concerned about the x-rays.
- The telephone rings in the middle of the night, leaving us reeling over news of some tragedy.
- We need to know God's will in an important matter, which could lead to life-changing results.
- We are the target of an attack that becomes complicated and ugly.

On such occasions worry kicks in, our stomach churns, our head spins. We get the jitters. We feel the beginning stages of panic. We need help . . . and not the kind someone else can provide.

We need God. We need Him to step in, calm our fears, and take charge. More than all that, we need the confidence that He is there at that very moment. It's not that we expect an audible voice from heaven or a moving-picture vision of the future in Technicolor. Not that. What we need most is that inner reassurance that He is there, that He cares, that He is in full control.

Some years ago my phone rang in the middle of the day on a Friday. It was someone from our older daughter's school telling me that Charissa had been in an accident. She had been practicing a pyramid formation with her cheerleading squad when someone at the bottom slipped, causing the whole human pyramid to collapse. Charissa had been at the top and, consequently, fell the farthest, hitting the back of her head with a sharp jolt. Her legs and arms had gone numb, and she was unable to move even her fingers. After notifying the paramedics, the school official had called me.

My wife, Cynthia, was away at the time, so I raced to the school alone, not knowing what I'd find or how serious our daughter had been injured. En route, I prayed aloud. I called out to the Lord like a child trapped in an empty well. I told Him I would need Him for several things: to touch my daughter, to give me strength, to provide skill and wisdom to the paramedics. Tears were near the surface, so I asked Him to calm me, to restrain the growing sense of panic within me.

As I drove and prayed, I sensed the most incredible realization of God's presence. It was almost eerie. The pulse that had been thumping in my throat returned to normal. When I reached the school parking lot, even the swirling red and blue lights atop the emergency vehicle didn't faze my sense of calm.

I ran to where the crowd had gathered. By that time the paramedics had Charissa wrapped tightly on a stretcher, her neck in a brace. I knelt beside her, kissed her on the forehead, and heard her say, "I can't feel anything below my shoulders. Something snapped in my back, just below my neck." She was blinking through tears.

Normally, I would have been borderline out of control. I wasn't. Normally, I would have been shouting for the crowd to back away or for the ambulance driver to get her to the hospital immediately! I didn't. With remarkable ease, I stroked the hair away from her eyes and whispered, "I'm here with you, sweetheart. So is our Lord. No matter what happens, we'll make it through this together. I love you, Charissa." Tears ran down the side of her face as she closed her eyes.

Calmly, I stood and spoke with the emergency medical personnel. We agreed on which hospital she should go to and what route we would take. I followed in my car, again sensing the

Spirit's profound and sovereign presence. Cynthia joined me at the hospital, where we waited for the x-rays and the radiologist's report. We prayed, and I told her of my encounter with the Spirit's wonderful presence.

In a few hours we learned that a vertebrae in Charissa's back had been fractured. The doctors did not know how much damage had been done to the nerves as a result of the fall and fracture. Neither did they know how long it would take for the numbness to subside or if, in fact, it would. The physicians were careful with their words, and I can still remember how grim both of them seemed. We had nothing tangible to rely on, nothing medical to count on, and nothing emotional to lean on . . . except the Spirit of God, who had stayed with us through the entire ordeal.

Sunday was just around the corner (it always is). I was exhausted by Saturday night, but again God's Spirit remained my stability. In human weakness and with enormous dependence, I preached on Sunday morning. The Lord gave me the words, and He proved His strength in my weakness. (I am told by our audio tape department that that particular message remains one of the most requested sermons on tape of all the messages I've delivered since I first became pastor of the church back in 1971.)

Amazing! God the Holy Spirit filled me, took full control, gave great grace, calmed fears, and ultimately brought wonderful healing to Charissa's back. Today she is a healthy, happy wife and mother of two, and the only time her upper back hurts is when she sneezes! When that happens and I'm with her, I usually look at her and ask, "Did that hurt?" Invariably, she nods and says, "Yeah, it did." I smile, she smiles back, and for a moment we mentally return to that original scene where she and I felt a very real awareness of the Spirit's presence.

The Christian life is a life lived on a spiritual plane—a realm that includes dimensions foreign to those who are non-Christians. To them, such scenes as I have just described are unreal and borderline unacceptable. A better word is foolish. That's understandable, since they haven't the Spirit within them. Remember what Paul wrote the Corinthians?

> But a natural man does not accept the things of the Spirit of God; for they are foolishness to him, and he cannot understand them, because they are spiritually appraised.
>
> 1 Corinthians 2:14

The Greek term translated "foolishness" is *moros,* from which we get "moronic." That fits. To the skeptical unbeliever, "the things of the Spirit" are totally stupid, absolutely ridiculous. A waste of time. But to us who understand how to operate in a world where things are "spiritually appraised," it is remarkable how much goes on in that dimension. In fact, let's return to some spiritual "basics."

Christianity 101

To enter the Christian life, a person must begin at the right place: conversion. That means we must be rightly related to the Lord Jesus Christ. No matter what our background may be, regardless of name, sex, status, language, color, or culture, everyone begins the Christian life the same way: by coming to Christ in faith, accepting His sacrifice on the cross as sufficient payment for sin.

> Jesus said to him, "I am the way, and the truth, and the life; no one comes to the Father, but through Me.
>
> John 14:6

> For by grace you have been saved through faith; and that not of yourselves, it is the gift of God; not as a result of works, that no one should boast.
>
> Ephesians 2:8-9

> And the witness is this, that God has given us eternal life, and this life is in His Son. He who has the Son has the life; he who does not have the Son of God does not have the life.
>
> 1 John 5:11-12

Then, to live the Christian life, a person must continue under the control of the right power—the power of the Holy Spirit.

To enter these new dimensions of the spiritual life, we must be rightly related to the Holy Spirit.

> As you therefore have received Christ Jesus the Lord, so walk in Him.
>
> Colossians 2:6

We become Christians because we "received Christ Jesus the Lord." We become empowered and filled with the Spirit as we "walk in Him."

Both are essential if we hope to enjoy all the benefits of the Christian life, for it is possible to be converted and yet not live on a spiritual plane. It is one thing to become a Christian. It is another thing entirely to become a Spirit-filled Christian. The tragedy is that so many are converted and so few Spirit-filled. When this happens, a person misses the best God has to offer us on earth.

What fuel is to a car, the Holy Spirit is to the believer. He energizes us to stay the course. He motivates us in spite of the obstacles. He keeps us going when the road gets rough. It is the Spirit who comforts us in our distress, who calms us in times of calamity, who becomes our companion in loneliness and grief, who spurs our "intuition" into action, who fills our minds with discernment when we are uneasy about a certain decision. In short, He is our spiritual fuel. When we attempt to operate without Him or to use some substitute fuel, all systems grind to a halt.

A Necessary Reminder of Who—and Whose—We Are

While the fuel and the car may help illustrate salvation and spirituality, it breaks down (no pun intended) at one important point. We own our car; we don't own ourselves. We have been purchased by another, and the price was Jesus' death on the cross. Jesus' blood was payment in full for our sins.

> Or do you not know that your body is a temple of the Holy Spirit who is in you, whom you have from God, and that you

> are not your own? For you have been bought with a price: therefore glorify God in your body.
>
> 1 Corinthians 6:19-20

We do not belong to ourselves, nor should we operate independently of the Spirit of God. Now that we have been converted, we are the Lord's, and as our Master, He has every right to use us in whatever way He chooses. In living out the Christian life, we have one major objective: to "glorify God in [our] body."

Since the believer's body is considered the "temple of the Holy Spirit," it stands to reason that He should be glorified in it and through it. He owns it! This completely rearranges our reason for existence. When you operate your life from this perspective, it changes everything. That explains why it is so important to view every day—sunup to sundown—from the spiritual dimension. When we do, nothing is accidental, coincidental, meaningless, or superficial. Things that happen to us are under our Lord's supervision because we are His, and we are to glorify Him, regardless. Since we belong to Him and His Spirit lives in us, we are in good hands. We occupy, in fact, the best possible situation on earth.

This means that words like "accidents" or "coincidences" should be removed from our vocabulary. Seriously! When events transpire that we cannot understand or explain, we are reminded that we are not our own. Rather than being upset, frustrated, or confused, we need to allow His Spirit to fill us with the divine fuel we need to serve Him and honor Him in those events—to glorify Him.

Let me remind you that as a Christian, you have the Holy Spirit. You don't need to pray for Him to come into your life; He's already there. He came to reside within you when you were converted, even though you may not have known it. Remember how Paul put it in the verses we just considered?

> Or do you not know that your body is a temple of the Holy Spirit who is in you, *whom you have from God 7"* (italics mine).
>
> 1 Corinthians 6:19

A little later on in the same letter, we are told that we have been "baptized" by the Spirit into the universal "body" of Christ. Read these words slowly and carefully:

> For by one Spirit we were all baptized into one body, whether Jews or Greeks, whether slaves or free, and we were all made to drink of one Spirit.
>
> 1 Corinthians 12:13

Every child of God has been "identified" with and made a part of the body. Never question that again! Romans 8:9 says the same thing in different words:

> But if anyone does not have the Spirit of Christ, he does not belong to Him.

Establish this dual truth once and for all: If you are a Christian, you have the Spirit living within you at all times; if you are not a Christian, you do not have the Spirit.

The wonderful part of all this is that by having the Spirit, you and I have all the "fuel" we need. Since He indwells us, He is there, ready to energize us and empower us at any time.

When I got that phone call about my daughter, I didn't ask God to "send Your Holy Spirit . . . I need Him with me to strengthen and stabilize me." No, I acknowledged that He was already there, and I consciously engaged the gears that gave Him full control. Why? Because I wanted to "glorify God" in the midst of the events that were transpiring. So I asked Him to fill me with fresh and dynamic power . . . which He did.

An Essential Revelation of What We Have

Even though every believer has the Holy Spirit, it is possible to operate our lives apart from His control. But when that happens—which it does with many Christians every day—what is missed is nothing short of tragic. When we operate under His control, the potential for peace and joy, calm and comfort, guidance and insight, confidence and courage know no bounds. That is not an exaggeration; it is fact. This is why an understanding of the filling of the Spirit is absolutely crucial.

How Are We Filled with the Spirit?

To return to my analogy, our tank is full. We need no more fuel, nor should we attempt to use a substitute fuel. We, as believers, have all the fuel that is needed for all the power, insight, comfort, guidance, courage, and dynamic we will ever need. The question is, How do we get the fuel flowing so we can operate our lives as God intended? Or, to use the scriptural terms, How are we filled with the Spirit? Is there a certain technique?

Let's examine the primary biblical reference on the filling of the Holy Spirit, Ephesians 5, which begins:

> Therefore be imitators of God, as beloved children; and walk in love, just as Christ also loved you, and gave Himself up for us, an offering and a sacrifice to God as a fragrant aroma . . . for you were formerly darkness, but now you are light in the Lord; walk as children of light.
>
> Ephesians 5:1-2, 8

Ephesians 5 begins with three strong commands:

- "be imitators of God"
- "walk in love"
- "walk as children of light."

Clearly, the Christian life is a life that honors God and demonstrates Christlikeness. Those who "imitate God" do both as they walk in love and walk in light. No wonder we are warned:

> Therefore be careful how you walk, not as unwise men, but as wise.... So then do not be foolish, but understand what the will of the Lord is.
>
> Ephesians 5:15, 17

What is that "will of God"? We are told clearly and succinctly in the next verse:

> And do not get drunk with wine, for that is dissipation, but be filled with the Spirit.
>
> Ephesians 5:18

Interestingly, in the Scriptures we are never commanded to "Be baptized in the Spirit!" or "Be indwelt by the Spirit!" or "Be gifted!" or "Be sealed!" But here in a context of various commands, we are clearly commanded to "Be filled with the Spirit!" Therefore, it is something we are to obey. In fact, there are two commands. The first is *negative:* "do not get drunk with wine"; and the second is *positive:* "but be filled with the Spirit."

I have heard it taught that these two ought to be combined in some way. For example, some say that the fullness of the Spirit is like spiritual inebriation . . . Like a "divine intoxication." It's as if the believer is virtually out of control under the influence of the Spirit. When "drunk with wine," a person is physically filled with alcohol; when "drunk in the Spirit," one is spiritually allied with Him.

I question this interpretation, given the context. This verse is not comparing the two; it is offering them as contrasts to one another. This is emphasized by Paul's adding that drunkenness "is dissipation," which means debauchery, excess, existing hopelessly out of control. But the Spirit-filled Christian is never "out of control." On the contrary, you may recall that among the list of the fruit of the Spirit is *self-control* (Galatians 5:23). Rather than likening these two, I suggest it is better to contrast them. As John R W. Stott correctly observes:

> We can indeed agree that in both drunkenness and the fullness of the Spirit two strong influences are at work within us, alcohol in the bloodstream and the Holy Spirit in our hearts. But, whereas excessive alcohol leads to unrestrained and irrational licence, transforming the drunkard into an animal,

> the fullness of the Spirit leads to restrained and rational moral behaviour, transforming the Christian into the image of Christ. Thus, the results of being under the influence of spirits on the one hand and of the Holy Spirit of God on the other are totally and utterly different. One makes us like beasts, the other like Christ.[1]

Since the climax of Paul's argument is reached in his command regarding the filling of the Spirit, let's probe deeper. Stay with me . . . and you will soon see what good sense this makes.

I am indebted to Dr. Stott for four very helpful observations regarding this crucial verse of Scripture:[2]

First, *the command is in the imperative mood: "You* BE FILLED with the Spirit!" This is no casual, polite, calm suggestion, but a firm, straightforward command. We have no more freedom to ignore this duty than we do to overlook the ethical commands that surround it, such as "work hard," "speak the truth," "be kind," "forgive." You see, "be filled with the Spirit" is like all those other commands. So, Christian, let me admonish you to obey God's strong command. The imperative mood demands obedience!

Second, *the verb "be filled" is in the plural form.* The apostle Paul is not directing this to one special group of people or one superspiritual saint in the church at Ephesus or, for that matter, to the church in general. He is saying to all of us—individually and collectively—that we, as a universal body of Christians, must be filled with the Spirit of God.

Third, *it is in the passive voice.* Did you notice that? "Be filled" is the command, not "Fill yourself up with the Spirit." Or, as The New English Bible renders it: "Let the Holy Spirit fill you." But don't make too much of that. Just as a person gets drunk by drinking alcohol, so an individual is filled with the Spirit by involving himself or herself in the process that leads to it.

For example, I cannot be filled with the Spirit while I have known and unconfessed sin present within me. I cannot be filled with the Spirit while at the same time conducting my life in the energy of the flesh. I cannot be filled with the Spirit while I am walking against God's will and depending upon myself. I need to be sure that I have taken care of the sins that have emerged in my life, that I have not ignored the wrong that I have done before God and to others. I need to walk in dependence on the Lord on a daily basis. Jesus emphasizes the same thought in John 15, where He commands us to abide in the vine. Why? Because "apart from Me you can do nothing" (15:5). And when Jesus says nothing, He means ***nothing***.

Many a morning I begin my day by sitting on the side of the bed and saying:

> This is Your day, Lord. I want to be at Your disposal. I have no idea what these next twenty-four hours will contain. But before I begin, before I sip my first cup of coffee, and even before I get dressed, I want You to know that from this moment on throughout this day, I'm Yours, Lord. Help me to be a branch that abides in the vine, to lean on You, to draw strength from You, and to have You fill my mind and my thoughts. Take control of my senses so that I am literally filled with Your presence and power and dynamic. I want to be Your tool, Your vessel today. I can't make it happen. Without You I can accomplish nothing. And so I'm saying, Lord, fill me with Your Spirit today.

Since it works for me, I suggest you give it a try.

Fourth, *the command to "be filled" is in the present tense.* It is a continuous appropriation, not some great high-and-mighty, once-in-a-lifetime moment where you experience the fullness of the Spirit and from then on you are on an all-time high that never wanes. Instead, we are regularly to pray, "Fill me, Lord, for this moment . . . fill me in this hour . . . fill me as I'm facing this challenge."

It's like we are saying, "Lord, I want to be filled. I want to be used. I want to be available. I deliberately and consciously make myself dependent upon You."

The Spirit's filling is like walking. When we are little, every tiny step is a conscious effort and a magnificent achievement. Soon, we learn to link two or three steps together before we fall. And then before you know it, by the time we've reached four or five, we're walking and not even thinking about it. Walking has simply become a part of life.

Over time, as we experience His filling, it becomes a constant part of our consciousness and our life. But we begin deliberately, slowly, and carefully. As the sun tips its hat in the early morning, we say to the Lord: "Lord this is Your day. As these hours unfold, I want to walk with You, allowing Your Spirit full control. Since I belong to You and no day is a waste, help me live it under Your empowering authority."

Now, please be careful. I know as I write this that I have engineer-types reading my words. And engineer-types love techniques. They love a step-by-step, logical process. They love details. Like, "Okay, every step, Lord, this is for You (step 1). And, Lord, may I be filled with the Spirit. And, Lord, this is Your day (step 2). So, Lord, help me with . . . (step 3)."

But the walk of faith by the Spirit's filling isn't mechanical. Instead, it's as if we're saying:

> I am in the process, Lord, of fulfilling Your will. I want to glorify Your name. I belong to You. I pledge my allegiance to You today. Enable me in my walk to have the discernment to walk in obedience and not in disobedience, to sense wrong when I encounter it and to stay away from it. Keep me strong when temptations come. Guard my tongue from saying the wrong thing or saying too much or speaking too quickly. Enable me to restrain profanity and resist outbursts of anger. Lord, help me in my walk. Fill me with Your Spirit. Take my eyes, take my tongue, take my emotions, take my will, and use me, Lord, because I want to be under Your control on a continuing basis.

This is called the Christian walk.

What Happens When We Are Filled with the Spirit?

So now we're ready for the next crucial question: What happens when I am filled with the Spirit? In Ephesians 5, after the command to "be filled with the Spirit," we are told of four results in the Christian's life.

> . . . be filled with the Spirit, speaking to one another in psalms and hymns and spiritual songs, singing and making melody with your heart to the Lord; always giving thanks for all things in the name of our Lord Jesus Christ to God, even the Father; and be subject to one another in the fear of Christ.
>
> Ephesians 5:18-21

First, *His filling affects our speaking.* To begin with, we are "speaking to one another." This is a vital part of what is called Christian fellowship. Or, as Paul puts it in his letter to the Colossians:

> Let the word of Christ richly dwell within you, with all wisdom teaching and admonishing one another with psalms and hymns and spiritual songs, singing with thankfulness in your hearts to God. And whatever you do in word or deed, do all in the name of the Lord Jesus, giving thanks through Him to God the Father.
>
> Colossians 3:16-17

When we are filled with the Spirit, we begin to relate to others in the family of God. We want to hear what they have to say. We want to learn from one another. And we also want to contribute to each other's welfare. If we see our brothers and sisters in a dangerous or perilous situation, we want to warn them.

Second, *His filling leads us to melodious hearts.* We not only speak to one another; we live in harmony with one another.

> . . . in psalms and hymns and spiritual songs, singing and making melody with your heart to God.
>
> Ephesians 5:19

Life takes on a special lilt. Joy comes again.

As he leads our worship and serves as music pastor at our church, Howie Stevenson frequently exhorts us to do what we do "heartily." It's one of his favorite expressions. And it's an appropriate biblical word, for the Spirit's filling opens our hearts and moves us into an enthusiastic overflow of worship.

One of the characteristics of Spirit-filled believers is that they don't wait until Sunday to worship. They have a daily worship occurring in their lives. We may be singers. We may not be singers. (Or at least we don't sing in public!) But all of us can have an inner melody that bubbles up spontaneously out of our lives. And I have observed that when I am walking in the Spirit there is usually a song on the tip of my tongue because there is a melody flowing through my heart. There is, even in a broader sense, a desire to live in harmony with my brothers and sisters.

Third, *His filling makes us thankful people.*

> . . . always giving thanks for all things in the name of our Lord Jesus Christ to God, even the Father.
>
> Ephesians 5:20

One of the telltale signs of the Spirit-filled life is gratitude. Show me a grumbler, and I'll show you a person who has distanced herself or himself from the Spirit of God. When we are filled with the Spirit, there is an overwhelming sense of thankfulness. We are not hard to please. We are happy to have whatever God provides. We're not spoiled or "choosy."

Fourth, *His filling leads us to submit to each other.*

> . . . and be subject to one another in the fear of Christ.
>
> Ephesians 5:21

When we are filled with the Spirit, we become more submissive to those in our lives.

If we are in leadership, a servant-hearted style replaces a demanding, dogmatic style. A God-directed humility emerges.

If we are married, our Spirit-filled heart prompts us to want to serve our mates, not control them. Difficult though it may be for some dominant male types to accept, in marriage there is to be a mutual submission to one another, a teachability, an openness. Not only for the wife toward her husband, but for the husband toward his wife.

> Husbands, love your wives, just as Christ also loved the church and gave Himself up for her.
>
> Ephesians 5:25

Just as Christ loved the church, the Spirit-filled husband loves his wife. Submission is not a one-way street.

Recently I heard Jack Hayford tell about a married couple who had attended a seminar taught by one of those male demagogues determined to show that Scripture teaches that the man is IN CHARGE at home. It was the kind of terrible teaching on submission that turns women into lowly doormats. Well, the husband just loved it! He had never heard anything like it in his life, and he drank it all in. His wife, however, sat there fuming as she listened to hour after hour of this stuff.

When they left the meeting that night, the husband felt drunk with fresh power as he climbed into the car. While driving home, he said rather pompously, "Well, what did you think about that?" His wife didn't utter a word . . . so he continued, "I think it was great!"

When they arrived home, she got out and followed him silently into the house. Once inside, he slammed the door and said, "Wait right there . . . just stand right there." She stood, tight-lipped, and stared at him. "I've been thinking about what that fellow said tonight, and I want you to know that from now on *that's* the way it's gonna be around here. You got it? *That's* the way things are gonna run in this house!"

And having said that, he didn't see her for two weeks. After two weeks, *he could start to see her just a little bit out of one eye.*

I have discovered over the years that there is something really twisted in the mind of a man who thinks that submission is limited to the woman. I have also discovered that there is seldom a problem with submission in the home when a husband has a heart that is genuinely submissive to God. The reason is clear: With a heart submissive to God, the Spirit-filled man truly loves his wife as Christ loved the church . . . there's no one else on earth he loves quite like her. And he demonstrates it by listening when she speaks . . . by respecting her opinion . . . by caring for her . . . by releasing many of his own rights. Part of love is sharing. When a wife knows that she is enveloped in that kind of respectful affection, she has no trouble at all yielding to her husband.

The Spirit-filled walk will not only change a life; in the process it absolutely transforms a home.

A Practical Response to How We Live

Let me conclude by reminding you once again that we do not need to plead for God's presence. We have it. We don't need to spend our days wondering why some people have an edge on the power. We have it too. We don't need to toss and turn through sleepless nights, struggling over our inability to claim the same superdynamic power that some televangelist seems to have and we don't. Let me repeat, as a Christian you have the Spirit of God.

But even though this is true, several probing questions are in order:

- Are you engaging the gears?
- Are you keeping short accounts on those things that break fellowship with God?
- Are you walking in conscious dependence on the Lord?
- Are you saying to Him at the beginning of—and frequently throughout—the day, "Lord, my life is Yours"?

Finally, I want to close with three important reminders to believers regarding the Spirit-filled life.

First, *abnormal experiences are not necessary to Christian maturity.*

Some groups in the evangelical community place a great deal of emphasis on phenomenal, exceptional manifestations of the Spirit. Others find themselves uncomfortable with this type of expression; they may even feel that it can't be defended from the Scriptures. Let me encourage you, whatever your frame of reference, to be gracious, be tolerant.

As a matter of fact, I would pass on to you the advice of Gamaliel, who gave this counsel to his friends as they were wondering what to do with the apostles who were turning the world upside down:

> "And so in the present case, I say to you, stay away from these men and let them alone, for if this plan or action should be of men, it will be overthrown; but if it is of God, you will not be able to overthrow them; or else you may even be found fighting against God."
>
> Acts 5:38-39

So my plea to those whose particular persuasion does not happen to fit a particular expression of the fullness of the Spirit (I'm trying to stay away from all the labels), be tolerant of those for whom it is.

When I was fresh out of seminary, I felt it necessary to correct all the things that I didn't agree with. I felt it necessary to be the self-appointed crusader and to address all those expressions of the faith that did not coincide with my convictions. But over the years I have found that that is a great way to waste a lot of energy. God did not call me to clean up the entire world (which, being interpreted, means to straighten others out so they would get in step with my convictions), I have learned over the years to be a lot more tolerant and a little wiser.

Second, *the fullness of the Spirit is for all of us, as believers, to enjoy, but how it works its way out in each person's life is another matter.*

So for those who plate a great deal of emphasis on the supernatural, remember: Rejoice in the comfort He has brought you in your walk, but don't try to force your experience upon everyone else. Don't feel you must be a zealous proselyte for your convictions, and don't stereotype all Christian experiences. You will blend a lot more easily into the body of Christ and you will find a great deal more satisfaction in your walk with the Lord if you will simply accept that as your own personal experience. But please don't look down your nose as though you have something that others don't have which makes you especially spiritual.

Let's live comfortably with each other and with our experiential differences . . . even different expressions of the fullness of the Spirit.

Third, *let us seek to enjoy our vast common ground, rather than establish and defend our own theological turf.*

I have said for years that there are more things that draw us together than there are things that separate us. We should be enjoying the vast common ground of our faith rather than defending some particular area of theological or experiential persuasion. Relax. You take care of your responsibilities before the Lord and let your brothers and sisters take care of theirs. Let's allow God to be God and understand that we are all in His family.

Shortly after his conversion in 1929, C. S. Lewis wrote this note to a friend: "When all is said (and truly said) about divisions of Christendom, there remains, by God's mercy, an enormous common ground."[3]

Since the common ground is so enormous, I suggest that we ask the Spirit of God to give us "enormous tolerance" with one another, which includes great joy in His presence, so that we do not feel the need to get everybody to walk in lockstep with us.

There was a time in my Christian life when if I heard a person say some of the things I've been suggesting, I would probably have labeled him or her a quasi-heretic—you know, soft, not really a person of conviction. But I don't feel that now. I've come to realize that God not only uses a whole lot of people, He uses some I don't even particularly like. And to the surprise of those who don't really like me that much, I, too, am being used. While we may be small-minded, our Father is not. He delights in blessing the full spectrum of His people in innumerable ways.

Aren't you glad that we are not God? Aren't you glad that our loving Father, who is the source of our fuel and our reason for existence, is still on the throne and is still committed to using each one of us for His glory?

May our "enormous common ground" be the foundation that supports us, rather than a battlefield that separates. The secret for making that happen? The filling of the Spirit . . . nothing more, nothing less, nothing else.

Spirit of the living God, fall afresh on me!
Be honored in my submissive spirit.
Be seen and heard in my melodious heart.
Be observed in my thankfulness.
Be glorified in the fellowship and worship that I have with others in Your family.

5

The Spirit Who Surprises

I HAVE JUST EXPERIENCED ONE of the greatest surprises of my life. Certainly, it is *the* greatest surprise in more than twenty years of my life. Looking back on the whole thing, I now realize it was the Spirit of God who orchestrated every one of the events. My head is still swimming. I'm certain that my pulse won't return to normal for several more days.

I have accepted the invitation from my alma mater, Dallas Theological Seminary, to become its next president. In all candor, I am still trying to believe it, especially since I was so firmly convinced thirteen months ago that I should *not* say yes. In fact, when asked to reconsider my decision six months later, I was even more convinced I was not the one for the job. So, after giving myself more time to think it through, I said no again, only this time with greater assurance than before. I even requested that the presidential search committee accept my no as absolutely final. I was convinced beyond all doubt.

And then the Spirit took over.

I'll not attempt to spell out all the details of what transpired, who was involved, or how my thinking was changed. But I can assure you that there was one surprise after another: an unexpected conversation that proved to be what I would call an attention-grabber . . . an unpredictable suggestion at just the right time, which made it impossible to ignore . . . an individual who challenged me to look at the picture in a completely different way . . . and then one person after another (plus one significant group of people after another) who affirmed the idea and encouraged me to accept the position.

And so here I sit, only hours removed from a whirlwind of activities connected with my accepting the school's offer. It will be an unusual arrangement (another of the Spirit's many surprises), whereby I will remain a pastor of a local church, yet still be free to provide the vision, direction, and motivation for the seminary. My plan is to be on hand as much as possible through the year to touch and influence the lives of those in training for a lifetime of ministry. And because of the gifts, diligence, willingness, and competence of a man who will come aboard with me as the provost of the school—Dr. John Sailhamer—I will not have to concern myself with all the time-consuming and energy-draining details that normally sap the strength and blur the vision of a school's president.

Only time will tell how well all this will work, but today I am still shaking my head in amazement. When I realize how full of surprises our God really is, a fresh burst of excitement rushes through me. He has many such things in mind for all of us. If you do not believe that, you are in for a massive surprise! The geography and the details of His plan will be different for each one of us, of course, but the Spirit's sovereign working is far beyond what the human mind can ever imagine. That is precisely what the prophet meant when he wrote:

> "For My thoughts are not your thoughts,
> Neither are your ways My ways," declares the Lord.
> "For as the heavens are higher than the earth,
> So are My ways higher than your ways,
> And My thoughts than your thoughts."
>
> Isaiah 55:8–9

The problem with most of us is not that our theology is heretical, but that it has become predictable, which, to me, is a synonym for dull and boring. It was never meant to be. The One whom our Lord Jesus sent is the life-giving, always-energizing Spirit, who wants to work in us in phenomenal ways so that we are able to tap the unfathomable depths of God. But the tragedy is that far too many of God's people would rather leave such thoughts safely etched on the pages of Scripture than experience them in practical ways in everyday life.

A Reminder of What Jesus Promised

We have already looked at Jesus' promise to send the Spirit, but maybe it would help to review those words once again:

> "And I will ask the Father, and He will give you another Helper, that He may be with you forever; that is the Spirit of truth, whom the world cannot receive, because it does not behold Him or know Him, but you know Him because He abides with you, and will be in you. . . .
>
> "These things I have spoken to you, while abiding with you. But the Helper, the Holy Spirit, whom the Father will send in My name, He will teach you all things, and bring to your remembrance all that I said to you."
>
> John 14:16–17, 25–26

Twice the term *Helper* is used by our Lord in this section. That word is translated into English from a combination of two Greek terms, *para* (alongside) and *kaleo* (to call). The One whom our Lord will "call alongside" for the purpose of giving us assistance will specifically carry out dual functions. Did you observe them as you read Jesus' promise?

1. He will teach "all things."
2. He will "bring to your remembrance" what Jesus has said.

In other words, it is the Lord's desire to disclose truth rather than hide it and to have us remember rather than forget. Think of it this way: God wants us to know His will so we can walk in it and experience the full manifestations of His power, His blessings. He isn't running away and hiding the pearls of His promises or the gems of His wisdom. No, He has given us His Spirit to reveal those things to us . . . to remind us again and again that Jesus' words are both reliable and true. As we grasp the reality of those things, we are often surprised, since they are so different from what we expect.

An Often-Overlooked Ministry of the Spirit

Shortly before He was arrested and crucified, Jesus made this important prediction and promise. Read it very carefully.

> "But I tell you the truth, it is to your advantage that I go away; for if I do not go away, the Helper shall not come to you; but if I go, I will send Him to you. And He, when He comes, will convict the world concerning sin, and righteousness, and judgment; concerning sin, because they do not believe in Me; and concerning righteousness, because I go to the Father, and you no longer behold Me; and concerning judgment, because the ruler of this world has been judged. "I have many more things to say to you, but you cannot bear them now. But when He, the Spirit of truth, comes, He will guide you into all the truth; for He will not speak on His own initiative, but whatever He hears, He will speak; and He will disclose to you what is to come.
>
> John 16:7–13

Exactly what is it Jesus predicts? He assures us the Spirit will do for us what we cannot do for ourselves. But of special interest to me is His concluding comment. After telling us what the Spirit of God will do regarding sin, righteousness, and judgment, He makes a sweeping prediction most of us have never accepted at face value; namely, "He will guide you into all the truth." Imagine!

For years I embraced a limited view of that statement, even though Jesus specifically used the word "all." I felt He was referring only to the truth of Scripture. That certainly would be included in the category of "the truth," but is it limited to that? Think before you answer. In fact, look down at verse 15:

> "All things that the Father has are Mine; therefore I said, that He takes of Mine, and will disclose it to you."
>
> John 16:15

If one of the Spirit's tasks is to guide us into and disclose the truth, who says that means only the truth of Scripture? Why couldn't it include the truth of His will? Or the truth about another person? Or the truth regarding both sides of a tough decision? Why couldn't those things be a part of "what is to come," which He promised "to disclose" to you and me?

I am devoting chapter 7 to the inner promptings of the Spirit, so there is no need for me to take a lot of time now to develop these thoughts. But it may be helpful to spend a few minutes pondering the questions I just asked.

Think about times in your own past when the Spirit guided you or disclosed something to you. It might have occurred when you were stuck in a passage of Scripture. You needed to understand what it meant, but nothing came clear. And then, to your surprise, in a relatively brief period of time everything opened up. I cannot number the times that has happened to me.

And haven't you struggled with a decision? The more you wrestled, the greater the struggle. In the beginning you felt as if you were standing in a thick, dark cloud. Then, gradually, the fog lifted and you could see your way through. I am suggesting that such can be traced to the Spirit's work of revealing.

Interestingly, Jesus said, "He will not speak on His own initiative, but whatever He hears, He will speak." I find that a curious remark. Not "whatever He reads," as if He were looking over our shoulder into the pages of the Bible, but "whatever He hears." From whom does He "hear" the things He reveals? I believe the ultimate source must be God the Father. After all, it is His plan that is being worked out.

I can think of several surprising moments when I have been the recipient of the Spirit's disclosures.

- Biblical insights I would otherwise have missed.
- A sudden awareness of God's will or the presence of danger or a sense of peace in the midst of chaos.
- A surge of bold confidence in a setting where there would otherwise have been fear and hesitation.
- A quiet, calm awareness that I was not alone, even though no one else was actually with me.
- The undeniable, surrounding awareness of evil . . . even the dark sinister presence of demonic forces.

In each case I was made aware of "the truth," which the Spirit disclosed to me. It was either there at the moment or it soon (sometimes later) was revealed to me.

While I was counseling with a troubled individual recently, the person became exceedingly anxious. Tears flowed. Feelings of panic seized him and he shook uncontrollably. It was an extremely emotional moment for him as his wife sat near him, feeling so helpless. Then, seemingly out of nowhere, I got a flash of insight, sparked by something she said. It tied in beautifully with a scriptural principle I had spoken on several days earlier. The wife's comment, coupled with the biblical principle, plus a thought that came to me as the three of us sat together, led me to say a sentence or two, nothing more. The result was a total surprise.

The man suddenly paused and stared into my eyes. He blinked several times without saying a word. I could tell he was processing the information. He wiped the tears from his face, shook his head a time or two, and said, "That's it. That is exactly what I needed to hear, but I couldn't—I needed to figure it out." He stood up, gave me a firm handshake, and left with his arm around his smiling wife.

What happened? I am convinced the Spirit who surprises guided us into that moment of truth and with surgical precision revealed the statement that needed to be said and heard.

Some Examples of the Spirit's Inner Workings

What Jesus taught before He went to the cross and ultimately left the earth, the apostle Paul addresses in a little more detail in his letter to the Corinthians. That explains why we have some examples in 1 Corinthians 2 of the Spirit's inner workings.

The more I look into these things, the more fascinated I am by them. The more I dig below the surface, the more I am beginning to see how much I have missed before in my study of the Scriptures. So much of what He does is so surprising that we usually think of it only as coincidence. Because we cannot see the Spirit of God, we tend to overlook His presence in our midst in general and in our individual lives in particular.

Demonstrating God's Unique Power

In his letter to the Corinthians, the apostle Paul looks back on his early days in Corinth when he was just founding the church, and he calls to mind his ministry when he was among them. I find it significant that the very first thing he puts his finger on is the demonstration of God's unique power as he gives his own testimony about the Corinthian ministry.

> And when I came to you, brethren, I did not come with superiority of speech or of wisdom, proclaiming to you the testimony of God.
>
> 1 Corinthians 2:1

He states first what he did *not* do. He did not come strutting a self-serving, fleshly motivated superiority of speech or displaying his wisdom.

Was he a brilliant man? You know he was brilliant. He had studied under Gamaliel and other exceptional mentors. And famous? Saul of Tarsus was surely a household name among century-one Jews. He was the up-and-coming Sanhedrinist. He was a Pharisee of Pharisees. He was the arch persecutor of the church.

He was a man with advanced degrees and relentless passion. It is not an overstatement to say he was second to none.

And then—*surprise!* The Spirit of God entered his life at his conversion, and the apostle Paul went through a transformation that changed his whole direction in life. His entire approach, his entire philosophy of life, was altered. So transforming was the change that when he came to this "ancient entertainment center," Corinth of Greece, to serve the Lord among people who looked for impressive eloquence and fleshly demonstrations of human wisdom, he deliberately refused to perform for their satisfaction. Paul had no interest in being a "showstopper."

Well, what *did* he do?

> For I determined to know nothing among you except Jesus Christ, and Him crucified. And I was with you in weakness and in fear and in much trembling.
>
> 1 Corinthians 2:2–3

Go back and ponder his self-description: "weakness . . . fear . . . trembling." Now, if I were to ask you to describe Paul, I doubt that you would use any one of those three words. Because when we think of Paul, we think of a man of enormous strength and capability, a man who had the ability to speak on any subject with hardly a misplaced word. In fact, Apollos was the eloquent one, not Paul, who came with apparent weakness, in a spirit of fear and also much trembling.

By the way, Paul's honesty is a good reminder for you and me when we find ourselves in places where we are intimidated, where we feel fearful and very weak. Surprisingly, that is when the Spirit of God does His best work. For when you and I are weak, God shows His strength.

Paul learned that, as he writes in 2 Corinthians 12. The Lord showed him that when he was weak and unable, incapable and inadequate, God took up the slack. The ministry of the Spirit of God came in like a flood and made those occasions the most powerful and profound of his life and ministry in Corinth.

How could he have been strong in his weakness, powerful in his fears, and effective in his trembling? The answer is in verses 4 and 5.

> And my message and my preaching were not in persuasive words of wisdom, but in demonstration of the Spirit and of power, that your faith should not rest on the wisdom of men, but on the power of God.
>
> 1 Corinthians 2:4–5

There's that word again—*power,* from the Greek term ***dunamis.*** It keeps resurfacing in our study of the Spirit—a dynamic invariably linked to the Holy Spirit.

When the Corinthian believers left the meetings where they had come to be ministered to by Paul, they left talking about the Lord, not the one who had ministered. And that pleased Paul immensely. Why? Because he had received ***dunamis*** from the Helper! The Helper empowered the man's message, ignited his leadership, and shaped his inimitable style. As a result, the awesome presence of God was felt.

Don't be afraid either of those words or of that reality. Don't resist it because it seems "too emotional." There are occasions where the presence of God is so obvious that it is like electricity upon the gathering. I have been in certain meetings when everyone in attendance was able to sense the dynamic power of the Spirit of God.

The most recent experience I had like this occurred while I was ministering earlier this year in Brisbane, Australia. Several of our leadership team from my radio ministry, "Insight for Living," had been invited to a church on the east coast of "the land down under." We weren't in the meeting ten minutes before we realized how obviously present the Spirit of God was. The music was full of joyful, meaningful praise. There were spontaneous occasions that added to the refreshing delight of the evening. I sensed unusual freedom as I spoke and as people listened and responded. I did not know the folks who were there, and they had never seen me before. Prior to that occasion I had only been to Australia once, so culturally I was a novice. But the bond that formed between us was instant and genuine. I loved it!

As our leadership team left, we agreed: This was clearly the work of the Spirit. Later, as we tried to describe to others the significance of that time, we could not do it. Furthermore, I have discovered that such Spirit-empowered occasions cannot be duplicated. It isn't like a stage play, where one outstanding performance after another can be repeated. The work of God's Spirit is absolutely unique.

Paul's experience among the Corinthians, by his own testimony, was clearly a demonstration of the work of the Spirit. Not unlike our Brisbane meeting, God was in it from start to finish.

Searching God's Hidden Wisdom

Having introduced the "demonstration of the Spirit," Paul digs even deeper as he writes about His "searching" work. Read the following words slowly and carefully:

> Yet we do speak wisdom among those who are mature; a wisdom, however, not of this age, nor of the rulers of this age, who are passing away; but we speak God's wisdom in a mystery, the hidden wisdom, which God predestined before the ages to our glory; the wisdom which none of the rulers of this age has understood; for if they had understood it, they would not have crucified the Lord of glory; but just as it is written,
>
> "THINGS WHICH EYE HAS NOT SEEN AND
> EAR HAS NOT HEARD,
> AND WHICH HAVE NOT ENTERED THE
> HEART OF MAN,
> ALL THAT GOD HAS PREPARED FOR THOSE
> WHO LOVE HIM."
>
> 1 Corinthians 2:6–9

The apostle returns to Isaiah's words and paraphrases them, probably drawing from the Septuagint, which was the Bible of Paul's day.

We are unable, he says, in and of ourselves, to sit down and figure out the "wisdom of God"—regardless of how much intelligence one may have or how many advanced degrees one has earned. God's wisdom is not discovered from such human sources. The human mind, all on its own, cannot plumb the depths of God's truths. You and I are dependent upon Another to know them. Those truths must come from the Godhead. And the One appointed to that specific task? The Holy Spirit, who lives within every child of God. He resides within us, not to be dormant and passive, but actively engaged in revealing God's hidden wisdom. Neither can we glean such wisdom from one another. Deep, divine wisdom must come from God as we allow ourselves to fly closer to the flame.

Let's go further:

> For to us God revealed them through the Spirit; for the Spirit searches all things, even the depths of God.
>
> 1 Corinthians 2:10

Another surprise! The Spirit of God is the One who gleans truth from within the Godhead and then reveals this wisdom to individuals like you and me. Thanks to the Holy Spirit, such deep truths are deposited into our minds. Without the Helper's supernatural assistance, we're sunk! He must reveal, or we don't receive.

I sometimes think of the Holy Spirit as a deep-sea diver who goes to the depths searching for treasures. The diver drops off the side of the boat. As the bubbles rise to the water's surface, he drops deeper, deeper, deeper . . . probing through all the mysteries of the deep that the human eye cannot see from above. Finally he surfaces again, bringing with him treasures from some sunken vessel. Sometimes the treasures are so precious they are priceless. Without the diver, however, they would remain hidden forever.

The Spirit of God, in the same manner, searches the deepest realms of the wisdom of God to lift out truths we need to know and understand. He not only digs them up, He is able to bring them to our attention. What a magnificently important work!

> Oh, the depth of the riches both of the wisdom and knowledge of God! How unsearchable are His judgments and unfathomable His ways! FOR WHO HAS KNOWN THE MIND OF THE LORD, OR WHO BECAME HIS COUNSELOR? OR WHO HAS FIRST GIVEN TO HIM THAT IT MIGHT BE PAID BACK TO HIM AGAIN? For from Him and through Him and to Him are all things. To Him be the glory forever. Amen.
>
> Romans 11:33–36

Theology has been called "the queen of the sciences." Before it, all other earthly truths must bow. Only those who have a grasp of the wisdom and the magnificent, profound, unfathomable plan of God can fit truth into its proper place in whatever era they may live. A true education occurs when theology is given its proper priority. Our forefathers knew that. That is why, when the earliest universities were founded, it was for the purpose of establishing a literate and learned ministry, so that the people might continue to keep the wisdom of God in focus with the needs of human beings.

Revealing God's Deep Thoughts

In the Corinthian letter, Paul refers to the same "depth of God" that he mentioned in Romans 11.

> For who among men knows the thoughts of a man except the spirit of the man, which is in him? Even so the thoughts of God no one knows except the Spirit of God.
>
> 1 Corinthians 2:11

If I could look deeply into your eyes and study you for several hours, I would still be unable to know what was going on in your mind. I would also be unable to tell what was in your spirit. Yet you and I are aware of what is going on in our own minds, aren't we?

Within the mind of God there is this vast, unfathomable treasure house of truth called "wisdom." Obviously it is all known by the living God. And the Spirit of God, being deity Himself, knows all of that mysterious, hidden, magnificent wisdom. It comprises a body of truth that is essential for living; in fact, sometimes it is essential for surviving the times in which we live. Now the "clincher" is—

> Now we have received, not the spirit of the world, but the Spirit who is from God, that we might know the things freely given to us by God.
>
> 1 Corinthians 2:12

Is that marvelous or what? At the moment of salvation, you and I were given the Spirit of God. We were identified with the body of Christ. We were made a part of the family. Included in that "original package" was the profound workings of the Holy Spirit within our being. As He came to live within us, He was fully equipped to reveal God's wisdom, having searched the deep things of God. And what a vital body of truth it is!

When we are facing an impasse, the Spirit of God is there to assist us through it. When we are experiencing grief and loss, the Spirit of God is there to give wisdom and insight in the crucible of our pain. When we encounter the unknown, the Spirit of God is there to keep us from being intimidated. He lives within us to reveal, to teach, to direct. And how often those things that come from Him are total surprises—far beyond human thoughts. As Isaiah wrote, the thoughts that come from God are "high above the earth" and totally different from mere human knowledge.

Let me go one step further and say that this may very well explain how you and I can have inner confidence and assurance regarding certain matters when others don't. Haven't you had that happen? You have pored over something in prayer, waited on God, searched His truths in the Scriptures, and then come to a settled conviction: "This is what I ought to do." Or perhaps, "This is what I ought not to do." Others don't agree with you. Others around you cannot see the logic of it. Yet it is as though you are "bound in the Spirit" to carry out your conviction because you know it is what God would have you do. It may seem surprising to some and stupid to others, but you know it's what you must do. The longer I live, the more I believe that that kind of wisdom, conviction, and knowledge is the work of the Spirit.

I want to show you an example. A scene very similar to the one I just described actually happened among the leaders in Ephesus as Paul was saying good-bye. They were about to put their arms around each other and bid farewell for the last time. But just before they did, Paul told them:

> "And now, behold, bound in spirit, I am on my way to Jerusalem, not knowing what will happen to me there, except that the Holy Spirit solemnly testifies to me in every city, saying that bonds and afflictions await me. But I do not consider my life of any account as dear to myself, in order that I may finish my course, and the ministry which I received from the Lord Jesus, to testify solemnly of the gospel of the grace of God."
>
> Acts 20:22–24

Look at that! The Holy Spirit is literally *testifying* to Paul. And what is He saying? He is saying that "in every city bonds and afflictions" will occur. We shall look at this scene in much greater detail later, but for now try to imagine Paul's confidence, which grew out of the Spirit's "inner voice."

The Spirit does not always lead us into places of comfort. Sometimes it is God's surprising plan to lead us into a difficult place to serve as His representative. Paul's experience was just that. He was saying, in effect, "I'm going to Jerusalem, and I know before I get there that trouble awaits." And that is exactly what happened. If you study the rest of the story, you will see a man dependent on God for survival.

The Spirit revealed much of what awaited Paul, testifying that "bonds and afflictions" were on the horizon of his future. Well, if he knew this ahead of time, some may ask, why would he go on such a threatening mission? Because he was God's servant. Obedience out of self-sacrificial trust was his only option.

> "But I do not consider my life of any account as dear to myself, in order that I may finish my course, and the ministry which I received from the Lord Jesus, to testify solemnly of the gospel of the grace of God."
>
> Acts 20:24

That is what I call having the long view of life. If we were only looking at today, we would be very cautious, very protective of ourselves. But we must look at life in light of eternity. We are a part of the plan. Like Paul, our desire must be to finish the course, strong in faith.

Paul could say: "I'm on my way to Jerusalem. And I know that difficulties await me, because through the Spirit, I have been given this insight. God made it clear to me." Some today would be tempted to call this a premonition. I would not use that word to describe the Spirit's work within us. Rather, this is the preliminary prompting of the Holy Spirit within us. I freely confess that it is difficult to pin it down. It's hard to describe it in exact terms. It is like nailing a poached egg to a tree. You can't get everything to stick. Certainly, in this case, it was the surprising work of the Spirit in Paul's life.

Teaching God's Profound Insights

And so it is the Spirit of God who takes the things of God and communicates them to His own. How? Read Paul's comment very carefully:

> . . . which things we also speak, not in words taught by human wisdom, but in those taught by the Spirit, combining spiritual thoughts with spiritual words.
>
> 1 Corinthians 2:13

By the Spirit's "combining spiritual thoughts with spiritual words," we are led into new and unexpected territory. We have a growing confidence in His providing all the strength we'll need to face whatever lies ahead. Because . . .

- We have a "Helper" who has been "called alongside."
- In place of weakness, He brings power.
- In place of ignorance, He brings knowledge.
- In place of human knowledge, He brings divine wisdom and profound insights from the depths of God's plan.
- As we grasp these depths, combining spiritual thoughts and words, we gain confidence in His will.
- And even though it may be surprising, when God is in it, there is only one option: *obedience.*

Which brings us back to where this chapter started: my surprising awareness that I should stop resisting and respond in the affirmative to the call to become the next president of Dallas Theological Seminary.

Somehow, in His perfect plan, this is His will for me. And because that is true, I have only one option. It is obedience.

But I am *still* surprised.

6

Draw Me Nearer . . . Nearer

ARE YOU PLEASED WITH your Christian walk? By that I mean, are you absolutely, unequivocally, and unconditionally satisfied with the level of your relationship with Christ . . . with the power of God's presence in your life? Or do you, in unguarded moments, entertain thoughts like:

I wonder if there may be more?

I wonder if my prayer life could be more passionate, more dynamic, more confident?

Is the Lord really first in my thinking?

When I get sick, why do I first think of calling my doctor instead of calling on my God?

Why, when I have a serious financial need, do I first think of some bank I could go to for a loan rather than the courts of heaven for divine assistance?

Well, if those sorts of thoughts trouble you, you are not alone.

Let me read you a few excerpts from a letter I received from a friend of mine whom I greatly respect. He is a Christian businessman, works for a Christian organization, has a fine Christian wife and family. He is an Evangelical, a conservative, but he is not what some would call a "charismatic" Christian. I say all that not to typecast him, but to help you understand where he is coming from.

In the section of his letter he calls "scatter-shooting," he writes:

There's a yearning in the evangelical world for a greater sense of intimacy with God. I believe we have had too much head and not enough heart.

People are intrigued now with the Holy Spirit. Like the proverbial moth and flame, they don't know how close they can fly without burning their wings. They are attracted to the flame for some unexplainable reason; still, they are frightened by the Holy Spirit.

There is a fear among us Evangelicals that we have missed out on something spiritually. The abundant life we've sought is not altogether fulfilling. There is a craving for spiritual intimacy with God that is seldom, if ever, satisfied. Could it be that what is really missing—the thing that would give us an appetite for daily prayer and Bible study and personal dynamic—is the empowering of a more profound measure of the Holy Spirit? Don't we need to let the Holy Spirit out of the closet?

Evangelicals may have believed the spiritual world is flat; that if they sail too close to the edge of the Christian experience, they'll fall off the edge into emotional oblivion. So we've run away from all but the most intellectualized expressions of the Spirit, as though He were some kind of sea monster.

Evangelicals are "reasoned believers," almost too logical, yet we've always suspected that too much emotion has been let out of our Christian experience. Many of us yearn for spiritual passion, which has become only a flicker of light, to be turned up several notches. Somebody with evangelical credibility needs to tell us that it's okay to get closer to the flame. [He then challenges me to do that.]

Maybe God still works miracles—at least in some measure. If not, then why do we pray for God's help when we are sick or diseased? Are our prayers for God's intervention merely psychological games we play on ourselves, knowing that God no longer acts decisively (much less miraculously) in our world today? Evangelicals are secretly concerned that we have become "deists" who think God's last acts were a few miracles after the Resurrection. Since about A.D. 70, has God

> gone off into the back room, leaving blind spiritual and physical laws in control? Isn't there an option besides deism and Oral Roberts? Can we free God to work pro-actively in His world?
>
> Let's face it, Chuck, the Charismatics scare us. We are secretly relieved when fringe nuts like [he names several well-known extremists] have their sordid laundry aired out in the press. The truth is that mainstream Charismatics are also embarrassed by such extremists. Let's don't throw the baby out with the bath water.
>
> How would a new, unintimidated theology of the Holy Spirit change our experiences in worship, in prayer, in witness, in spiritual confidence? Some of us need a revolution, Chuck.
>
> Isn't it about time Evangelicals revisited the doctrine of the Holy Spirit without concern that it will sound too charismatic? Shouldn't we leave God more room to work directly in our lives today? E.T. has had a deeper, more positive personal impact on the lives of some people than the Holy Spirit.
>
> After you've had a chance to review this letter, I'd love to visit with you by phone. I may be so far off-base that it scares you to death. If so, I'll understand.[1]

I love that man. I love his courage. I love his probing mind, his honesty, his creativity. I am especially impressed that he isn't afraid to put his finger on a nerve and push a little harder. Even if it makes some of us uncomfortable and uneasy, at least it makes us think!

The tragedy is that some have stopped thinking altogether. For many in the conservative evangelical ranks the quest is over. There is nothing more to discover, no new territory to examine, nothing else to experience. As the old saying goes, they are "saved, sanctified, galvanized, and petrified." That troubles me most of all.

Now on behalf of many of us, let me make an open and unguarded confession: There are times you and I desire more fulfilling expressions of faith. There are times we wish for more evidences of the dynamic of the Spirit of God in our lives. But fear restrains us! Fear of being misunderstood by our brothers and sisters in the faith . . . fear of being mislabeled . . . fear of going off the emotional deep end and getting weird . . . fear of getting away from Scripture and slipping into error. We are afraid of wading too far out into the doctrinal waters, getting way over our heads, then not being able to swim back to shore.

Now I can just hear some of you saying, "Swindoll is losing it. Next he'll be going to Tibet to meditate on top of some mountain." Don't bet on it.

Please, be assured, I have never in my life been more committed to the Scriptures. I was born in 1934, so I'm no spring chicken . . . yet at this age, I can honestly say that I love Christ more deeply and believe His Word more firmly than ever in my life. Virtually every day of my life I am digging into the treasures of the Word of God. So let me put your mind at ease. I am probably more theologically orthodox than I've ever been in my life. But that does not mean I have stopped learning. I am still thinking, and I am still dissatisfied with the status quo.

The fact of the matter is, I simply am not convinced that our understanding and appropriation of the Holy Spirit is all it can be or all it should be. While I don't think we need "more of God" (an impossibility, since we have all of Him!), I do think we need to act upon all that we have. I don't believe we need to pray for some new thing to come upon us, but I do believe we need to appropriate in much greater measure what is already within us.

It's like the brain. During our entire lives, we use maybe one-tenth or less of it—one tiny portion of it—and the rest of it just lies there like a gray glob, learning nothing new, just marking time. I cannot believe that is God's desire for His people when it comes to the spiritual resources He has given us.

As I have already written, I think the Spirit of God, who resides inside every believer, is ready to take charge and instill within us not only a dynamic but also a quiet confidence in life. Yet most sort of stumble along from day to day virtually unaware of or unconcerned about the vast provisions that are ours to claim.

My prayer is that we remain open and teachable—like my friend—and that our God may lead us and reveal fresh truths from His Word, including blowing some of the dust off old truths and bringing them back to life. I hope the pages of this book will clear the debris from some great truths that await our appropriation.

I want to spend the rest of my years challenging people to go to the very edge of their faith . . . to risk new thoughts . . . ponder new ideas . . . enter into new experiences without fear. The truth is, we have pulled too far back from some of the best things the Lord has for us.

A Closer Examination That Enlightens Us

If we are going to fly a lot closer to the sacred flame, we need to relearn and hopefully rediscover by closer examination what He has said in His Book. For example, let's return to Ephesians 5. Here we find a list of don'ts.

- Ephesians 5:3. *Don't be immoral, impure, or greedy.*

  > But do not let immorality or any impurity or greed even be named among you, as is proper among saints.

- Ephesians 5:4. *Don't lose control of your tongue.*

  > . . . and there must be no filthiness and silly talk, or coarse jesting, which are not fitting, but rather giving of thanks.

- Ephesians 5:6. *Don't be deceived.*

  > Let no one deceive you with empty words, for because of these things the wrath of God comes upon the sons of disobedience.

- Ephesians 5:11. *Don't participate in evil deeds . . . deeds of darkness.*

  > And do not participate in the unfruitful deeds of darkness, but instead even expose them.

- Ephesians 5:15. *Don't be unwise.*

  > Therefore be careful how you walk, not as unwise men, but as wise.

- Ephesians 5:17. *Don't be foolish.*

  So then do not be foolish, but understand what the will of the Lord is.

- Ephesians 5:18. *Don't get drunk.*

  And do not get drunk with wine, for that is dissipation, but be filled with the Spirit.

All these don'ts tell me that God cares more about the details of our personal lives than most folks would ever believe. He names these things, calling them to our attention, because they will hurt us if we tolerate and/or traffic in them.

He then brings everything to a climax as He offers one grand, positive command. After "Don't, don't, don't, don't, don't, don't, don't," He says, "Do" (at least that's the implied directive).

- Ephesians 5:18 ". . . *but be filled with the Spirit.*"

In place of all these things that the world will try to tell you are emotionally and physically stimulating, come back to the person of the intimate Spirit and let Him fill your life.

When the Lord delivered your salvation, His Spirit came within you as part of the package deal, remember? The Spirit was in the initial "gift package." Without your even knowing it, the Spirit of God took up permanent residence within you. And when He entered your life, He brought with Him—for you—the full capacity of His power. Without Christ, you and I were like a vast, empty reservoir awaiting the coming of a downpour. As salvation became a reality, this emptiness became full to the point of running over. The Spirit of God has filled our internal capacity with power and dynamic.

Now in light of that, allow Him to take full control! That is the command. Instead of being filled with alcohol, instead of being filled with drugs, instead of being filled with filthy talk, instead of being filled with immorality, be filled with the dynamic Spirit of God. Like the wind that fills the sails, allow His power to propel your life.

Is He filling you like that? Have you responded to God's strong command?

Can you think of a time in your life when you really could say, "I remember being so filled with the thoughts of God and the power of God that I felt invincible in the midst of my trials"? That is what can happen. More importantly, that's what God wants for us. We can truly and actually be "filled" with His dynamic power.

A wonderful example of this is recorded in Acts 6, where it tells how the apostles were engaged in leading the early church. And wouldn't you know it? A complaint arose because some of the people in the church didn't have enough food. The problem was exacerbated by the fact that some were being helped while others were being overlooked. At the heart of the problem was preferential treatment. While the local Jews were being cared for, the Hellenistic Jews were being ignored.

> Now at this time while the disciples were increasing in number, a complaint arose on the part of the Hellenistic Jews against the native Hebrews, because their widows were being overlooked in the daily serving of food. And the twelve summoned the congregation of the disciples and said, "It is not desirable for us to neglect the word of God in order to serve tables."
>
> Acts 6:1–2

Perhaps we could call this one of the earliest church business meetings! There may have been hundreds present, maybe thousands. After everyone had gathered, the apostles told them that something had to be done. Somebody needed to help in the daily serving of food to the needy.

> "But select from among you, brethren, seven men of good reputation, full of the Spirit and of wisdom, whom we may put in charge of this task. But we will devote ourselves to prayer, and to the ministry of the word."
>
> Acts 6:3–4

Isn't that an interesting list of qualifications for service? From among them (implying that not everyone would meet the qualifications), they were to choose seven men of "good reputation," full of "wisdom," and "full of the Spirit." Here in the early church, the leaders—the apostles—were saying they wanted Spirit-filled men to carry out this role of service.

And the others agreed with their assessment, for "the statement found approval with the whole congregation" (6:5).

As a result, "they chose Stephen," who is identified as "a man full of faith and of the Holy Spirit." Stephen was a man in whom the intimate Spirit was carrying out His dynamic work. His sail was full of the blessed wind of the Spirit. The flame of God had set his spirit ablaze. He was moving through life with the hand of God upon him. He was walking in the light, abiding in the vine.

Shortly after being selected, Stephen was cornered by:

> . . . some men from what was called the Synagogue of the Freedmen, including both Cyrenians and Alexandrians, and some from Cilicia and Asia.
>
> Acts 6:9

These men "rose up and argued with Stephen." Could Stephen hold his own before a threatening crowd like that? You better believe it! We read that his antagonists:

> were unable to cope with the wisdom and the Spirit with which he was speaking.
>
> Acts 6:10

His critics lacked sufficient strength to take a stand against him. Literally, they were unable to *withstand*. With Stephen's inner being filled to capacity with the igniting presence of the Spirit, they didn't stand a chance. Stephen must have been wired!

A. T. Robertson suggests that, "Stephen was like a battery charged and in action."[2] That doesn't mean he ran roughshod over people. It means that under the dominant control of the Spirit, he was unintimidated by and invincible before his critics.

Bold as a lion, confident in God, under the full control of the Spirit of God, he moved through the waters of resistance without getting off course. They were unable to hold him back. The Spirit's filling was obvious to all.

Make no mistake, they hated him because of that. The opposition party grew increasingly more hostile, until their anger and their hatred turned to murder.

> Then they secretly induced men to say, "We have heard him speak blasphemous words against Moses and against God." And they stirred up the people, the elders and the scribes, and they came upon him and dragged him away, and brought him before the Council. And they put forward false witnesses who said, "This man incessantly speaks against this holy place, and the Law; for we have heard him say that this Nazarene, Jesus, will destroy this place and alter the customs which Moses handed down to us." And fixing their gaze on him, all who were sitting in the Council saw his face like the face of an angel.
>
> Acts 6:11–15

What does that mean? Well, having never seen an angel, it is difficult to say. I would suspect Stephen glowed. Almost without exception, where there are evidences of the presence of heaven upon earth there is an aura—like a glowing, shining light. In this case, I believe it was visible, which explains why they said he had the "face of an angel."

In spite of the mounting pressure Stephen was facing, he delivered a sermon, among the best I have ever read. Standing before the angry group of people—their arms folded, their frowns deep, their jaws set, and their minds fixed on stoning the preacher—Stephen preached. (Sounds like some church situations today!)

Ever spoken to a hostile crowd? Probably never this hostile. I remember preaching Christ from free-speech platforms in the 1960s. Talk about exciting! Places like the University of Oklahoma in Norman . . . the University of California at Berkeley.

What stretching, exciting experiences! You had to be Spirit-filled or you could never have withstood their verbal attacks. Some even threw things at us. But that was like saying "Sic 'em" to a hungry Rottweiler. Churchill's words had new meaning: "Few things in life are more exhilarating than being shot at without result."

In times like that, God's Spirit gives unintimidated confidence. That's precisely what Stephen had. Remember, the man was filled with God's Spirit. He was the personification of cool, calm courage.

What happened? Hold on tight. The scene gets ugly.

> Now when they heard this, they were cut to the quick, and they began gnashing their teeth at him.
>
> Acts 7:54

They were livid!

> But being full of the Holy Spirit, he gazed intently into heaven and saw the glory of God, and Jesus standing at the right hand of God.
>
> Acts 7:55

"But being full of the Holy Spirit . . . "—why would the writer suddenly insert that comment? Because that was the unseen source of Stephen's strength. That was the reason behind his invincibility and perseverance. I am confident that his voice didn't even tremble.

Incredible. With death's hot breath blowing against the back of his neck, Stephen literally saw that ageless, penetrating light of God's glory pouring out of heaven. Full of the Spirit, he saw what no other eyes could see. He testified,

> "Behold, I see the heavens opened up and the Son of Man standing at the right hand of God."
>
> Acts 7:56

Not only did he see the glory of God, he saw Jesus standing at the right hand of God. (By the way, remember when Christ ascended? The Scriptures state that at that time our Lord was *seated* at the right hand of the throne of God. But Stephen saw Jesus standing up. I wonder . . . maybe He stands up for certain individuals when they die. Perhaps, with nail-scarred hands outstretched, He was saying, "Come on home, sweet Stephen. Come on home, dear servant of Mine. Enough of that.")

On the basis of this account, I wonder if those filled with the Spirit at certain moments of desperate crisis in their lives are enabled to witness things no one else can see?

Just wondering . . .

> But they cried out with a loud voice, and covered their ears, and they rushed upon him with one impulse. And when they had driven him out of the city, they began stoning him, and the witnesses laid aside their robes at the feet of a young man named Saul. And they went on stoning Stephen as he called upon the Lord and said, "Lord Jesus, receive my spirit!" And falling on his knees, he cried out with a loud voice, "Lord, do not hold this sin against them!" And having said this, he fell asleep.
>
> Acts 7:57–60

Somehow God gave Stephen the supernatural ability to deliver a message in the mist of insuperable odds. Even at that incredible moment, he offers words of praise to God and words of forgiveness to his murderers. Is that kind of "overcoming" part of the filling of the Spirit? It was for Stephen. Why shouldn't it be for us?

Is that the kind of walk with Christ you have? Is that the dynamic that is characterizing your life these days? If so, you are rare, I can assure you. If not, why not? If that is possible, then why aren't there similar manifestations in our circles today?

Just asking . . .

Questions and Observations That Intrigue Us

It was almost as if his being filled with the Spirit provided Stephen with some kind of special readiness for battle. Could this have been some kind of "anointing"?

Again, I'm just asking . . .

Let's begin our probe into the "anointing" of the Spirit by reviewing a couple of things we learned earlier. Do you recall why we have received the Spirit? First Corinthians 2 explains:

> Now we have received, not the spirit of the world, but the Spirit who is from God, that we might know the things freely given to us from God, which things we also speak, not in words taught by human wisdom, but in those taught by the Spirit, combining spiritual *thoughts* with spiritual *words.*
>
> 2 Corinthians 2:12–13

First, we received "the Spirit who is from God" that we might "speak" the thoughts given to us by God ("combining spiritual *thoughts* with spiritual *words*").

> But a natural man does not accept the things of the Spirit of God; for they are foolishness to him, and he cannot understand them, because they are spiritually appraised. But he who is spiritual appraises all things, yet he himself is appraised by no man.
>
> 2 Corinthians 2:14–15

And second, we received the Spirit that we might "appraise all things."

Appraise means "to sift, to discern." Is that part of the filling? No doubt. By being filled with the Spirit, we are given a discernment that filters incidentals from essentials, truth from error. In other words, Christians are provided with an inner filtering system.

Now we are ready for 1 John 2, which speaks of the "anointing" from God. This is a letter clearly written to believers, whom John affectionately calls "little children."

> But you have an anointing from the Holy One, and you all know.
>
> 1 John 2:20

Some translations of the Bible put the "all" at the end of the sentence: "And you know all," which makes it sound like when you have an anointing, you have all knowledge. I think, rather, that the original text suggests that "all" is the subject—"you all know." So? So it's for everyone. "Little children, you have an anointing, and all of you, therefore, have a knowledge." There is something from God that links anointing with knowing.

> And as for you, the anointing which you received from Him abides in you, and you have no need for any one to teach you; but as His anointing teaches you about all things, and is true and is not a lie, and just as it has taught you, you abide in Him.
>
> 1 John 2:27

This particular usage of *anointing* is found only three times in the New Testament, and all three are in this chapter of 1 John. The term comes from the Greek word *chrisma*. In ancient days, chrisma was an ointment, like a thick oil. Kings were anointed with chrisma, as were priests when they were inducted into the sacred office.

On the basis of that, I suggest that this "anointing" happens once, which explains John's comment, "You have an anointing." Also, John says that it "abides in you." So it is permanent; this "anointing" won't leave. Each believer has it. It happens once. It is permanent. And it "teaches you about all things."

The original word here is *oida,* which means knowledge, but not *experiential* knowledge.

Electricity is in all our homes; we're aware of it. That's *oida* knowledge. We know it theoretically, intellectually. If I get a paper clip and go to an electrical outlet in my home and stick that little piece of metal in the slot, suddenly I *experience* electricity! That's *ginosko* knowledge.

My point here is that John uses *oida,* not *ginosko.* Which tells us that there is something about the Holy Spirit's presence that provides you and me with an innate knowledge, an inner awareness. Such knowledge is included in the anointing.

In other words, you and I have a sixth sense. It is something that the worldling does not have, because he doesn't have the Spirit. When you have Christ, you have the Spirit. And when you have the Spirit, you have the anointing. You know something that cannot be taught and cannot be learned. You have a discernment, a built-in awareness, an inner compass, if you will.

Would this anointing explain what we commonly call intuition? I don't know, but I do think it's in that family. Are we giving credit to intuition that really belongs to the Holy Spirit? I cannot say for sure, but perhaps we are.

Here's another intriguing question: If we are full of the Spirit, can we envision things others cannot? Again, I'm not affirming it, I'm only asking. Since Stephen was able to do so, can any believer? Since the Spirit searches all things, could He give us insight and on-the-spot discernment that transcend human ability, academic learning, and personal training? He's God; why couldn't He?

And if that is true, wouldn't those who oppose us find themselves unable to stand against us . . . unable to "withstand"? I lean toward saying yes. It's what we might call a "supernatural sense of invincibility." And at times I have experienced it, that underlying sense of absolute confidence. Perhaps you have as well. In those moments of unusual courage—without any credit to myself—I am not afraid to stand absolutely alone.

Could that inner confidence be part of the anointing?

A Few Words of Warning

I hope all this won't get kicked sideways in your mind and twist up some awfully good theology. To keep that from happening, let me caution you with a few words of warning.

Balance is always preferred to extremes. So as I previously reminded you: *Keep your balance in all things.* A scriptural word for it is *moderation.* Stay reasonable, Christian friend. Don't go home and start praying for some middle-of-the-night visions; that's not biblical. Keep a level head. Don't get weird.

Don't start looking for the face of Jesus in an enchilada. Or try to convince me that some cloud formation represents the Last Supper. Don't start setting dates for Jesus' return. Don't play with snakes and scorpions. Don't sacrifice your solid biblical roots and orthodox theology on the altar of bizarre experiences. Don't start attending meetings where legs are lengthened and teeth are filled. That kind of sideshow stuff may draw a crowd, but it is not the anointing.

The anointing is a knowledge. You know something. You discern something. It is an inner awareness. It is a surge of strengthening assurance. And never forget it always exalts the Lord and gives all glory to God.

Let me also add: *Stay with the Scriptures.* While our individual experiences may vary somewhat as the Lord uses each of us in unique ways, we must never—and I mean never—get too far from the revealed and reliable Word of God. If you do, you will begin to use your experience as a basis for your beliefs, and the Scriptures will diminish in importance as you make more and more room for more strange experiences.

I have pastor friends who have done just that. And today when I talk with them, I find that they no longer believe that the Bible is God's *final* Word. They are now convinced that He is still revealing inspired truth. My reaction? Whoa! If that's true, then how do I know where His Word starts and their vivid imagination stops . . . and how much of it can I trust? No matter how persuasive the preacher, you and I need God's inspired Word, not additional revelations of "truth." When *that* happens, we are hopelessly awash.

One theologian has sounded a very wise warning:

> The issue of Biblical inspiration and authority lies close to the heart of Christian theology. It is a continental divide

> running through the center of its landscape. Where we stand on the divine integrity of Scripture will determine the nature and content of the gospel we proclaim to the world. . . .
>
> The distinctive mark of theology in our day is its dreadful ambiguity. Something needs to be done to check the pretended autonomy of this unbiblical thought. The chaos of American theology today can be traced back to its roots in the rejection of Biblical infallibility. For Christian theology rests upon the truth claim implicit in the doctrine of inspiration. Scripture is the principium of theology. Only because the Bible embodies objectively true communication about the nature of God, the condition of man, and the provision of His salvation, is it possible to begin the theological task. The question of inspiration is then not the plaything of the theological specialist; it is the eminently practical foundation on which the gospel rests. . . . Preaching is not the act of unfolding our personal convictions. It is the duty of informing men of all that God has spoken. To move off from the pages of Scripture is to enter into the wastelands of our own subjectivity.[3]

A Final Suggestion That Frees Us

There is much more to the Spirit's work within us than you and I have ever known or ever allowed ourselves to experience, but *do not be deceived.* Stay with God's Book of truth. Bounce everything off the written Word of God.

But as long as you keep the plumb line true, just remember that you may have a great deal of space between where you are and where the Spirit wants you to be.

Come nearer . . . don't be afraid to fly closer to the flame. It can revolutionize your prayer life, your daily witness, your own struggling, timid self-image, and for sure your confidence in God. It can give you strength and tranquility in the midst of sickness, even Stephen-like assurance in the face of death.

Ever since I started this book many months ago, an old hymn has been in my mind and on my lips:

I am thine, O Lord, I have heard Thy voice
And it told Thy love to me;
But I long to rise in the arms of faith,
And be closer drawn to Thee.

Consecrate me now to Thy service, Lord,
By the pow'r of grace divine;
Let my soul look up with a steadfast hope,
And my will be lost in Thine.

There are depths of love that I cannot know
Till I cross the narrow sea;
There are heights of joy that I may not reach
Till I rest in peace with Thee.

Draw me nearer, nearer, nearer, blessed Lord,
To the cross where Thou hast died;
Draw me nearer, nearer, nearer, blessed Lord,
To Thy precious, bleeding side.[4]

As I sang that grand old hymn in the shower last night, the thought crossed my mind: Must I wait until I get to "that narrow sea" before those intimate moments with God can be experienced? Must I wait until I "rest in peace with Thee" before I am able to reach such "heights of joy"? I used to think so. I don't anymore.

Lord, how grateful we are for this will of Yours, for this Word of Yours. Help us in the midst of the search to be kept from error. And while doing that, Lord, protect us as we fly closer to the flame. Take away the fear. Give us a holy boldness in faith. Stop us when we tend to run afraid of such new truths as this, but enable us to come closer and to listen better. And may we discover in the process a sweetness of relationship and a depth of intimacy with You such as we have never known before, all for Your glory. We "long to rise in the arms of faith" and be transformed by the power of your Spirit. So, draw us nearer, blessed Lord . . . nearer to You. In the Savior's dear name. Amen.

7

Those Unidentified Inner Promptings

HAVE YOU EVER ATTENDED a UFO convention? I did once. Well, I didn't actually attend it, though I felt as if I had.

What happened was I was staying at the same hotel where some kind of UFO convention was being held. Every elevator was full of UFO devotees. Every line waiting for a cab, every meeting room, every restaurant table, even the lobby was choked with these folks. And let me tell you, some of those people are scary!

What took place during the day was wild enough, but after sunset things really got crazy. At all hours of the night you could see men and women in a nearby public park or standing near their windows or perched on hotel ledges—most of them with binoculars—scanning the stellar spaces and mumbling to each other. While one stared into the sky, looking for unidentified flying objects, another took notes, drawing diagrams and charts of whatever was being observed. Everywhere you looked there were little pockets of people pointing here and there, all excited about the things they were seeing in the night sky.

Funny, I never saw anything. Maybe I was too skeptical or too ignorant to know what to look for, but when I looked up, all I ever saw was your basic blue-black sky, moon, stars, and, every once in a while, clouds floating by.

I remember the first night in particular, when two people staying in the room next to mine on the ninth floor were so elated over what they saw they couldn't restrain their excitement. It was about half past two, maybe three o'clock in the morning when all the noise started. Finally, I crawled out of bed and went to my window. My lights were off, so I could get a better view. By the time I had sufficiently awakened and was able to stumble over to the window, they had gathered four or five other friends in their room and everybody was looking out the window, discussing how obviously visible something was in the distance. I peered out to where they were pointing. At first I thought there was something there and my pulse rate jumped a few notches, but then I realized it was only the light from the hotel hallway shining under the door and reflecting in my windowpane. I rubbed my eyes, squinted, and again scanned the sky very carefully. Honest . . . there was nothing there. Absolutely nothing.

That kind of stuff continued night after night all week long, and here I am, still waiting to spot my first UFO. Several months ago I really thought I saw one in the sky, toward the south of where I live here in Fullerton . . . but then it dawned on me that what I was getting excited over were the last few skyrockets from the nearby Disneyland fireworks finale. I'm still waiting to spot my first UFO.

Some well-meaning Christians remind me of those UFO people. They are always seeing what others can't see. They get all excited over stuff they experience . . . and when you don't, they make it sound like it's your fault! Because they are so sure they are right—and because so many like-minded, equally sincere folks are standing by nodding yes, yes, yes—very few have the courage to look them in the eye and say, "I don't see it!" Most of us just shrug our shoulders, roll our eyes, and let it pass.

Well, that may be okay when it comes to UFOs, but when it has to do with the things of the Spirit, it can't be shrugged off. Who really cares that much if a bunch of people claim to see spinning discs in the sky or futuristic wheels with bright lights flashing and weird-looking people with antennae sticking out of their heads climbing up and down ladders that glow in the dark? Most of that is so harmless it is humorous. But when strange sideshow tactics are carried out in the name of the living God . . . when multiple thousands (millions?) are being led astray from the truth, duped into investing their time and pouring their money into so-called ministries that promise "miracles" on a daily basis and extrabiblical supernatural "revelations" that keep the crowd coming, it's neither harmless nor humorous.

And so if you think I'm leaning in that direction by urging people to fly closer to the flame, I need to set the record straight. I am not. God's work is not done in a circus atmosphere. God's Spirit does not do stunts. And while I'm at it, God's true messengers don't offer supernatural directives that come from visions or trances. And their so-called prophecies aren't that at all. They are neither inspired nor reliable. Count on it—if it isn't between Genesis and Revelation, it is not divinely inspired, supernaturally infallible, or absolutely inerrant.

Quite frankly, you and I don't need more revelations from God; what we need is to observe and obey the truth that He has already revealed in His Book. God's Word is inerrant, absolute, and final.

My purpose for writing this volume, then, is not to suggest that we need new and fresh revelations from the Lord, but that we need to explore His Word and *expand our understanding of what He has already revealed* . . . which brings me to the subject of this chapter: Not UFOs but UIPs. What about all those "unidentified inner promptings" we tend either to ignore or misinterpret? Could they be connected in some way with the Spirit's working within us? Five come immediately to mind:

- You are experiencing an uneasy churning in the pit of your stomach. It is related to a decision you need to make, and you can't seem to figure it out. There is no specific biblical answer; either way you choose could be supported in the Scriptures. Interestingly, as you imagine going down one side of the fork in the road, the churning intensifies . . . but when you track the other side, it diminishes. You "sense" within yourself that that is what you should do, so you do it and it proves to be the right choice. We commonly call that "intuition" or more generally "finding God's will" . . . but is that unidentified inner prompting a part of the Spirit's working?

• You are spending time in God's Word. You are trying to discern what it means . . . what it is saying regarding a situation you are facing. The truth seems veiled, hidden from you. You are stumped. You begin to pray for enlightenment, for a much clearer understanding of His mind on this subject. You read the passage again and again. Suddenly, the whole picture develops clearly in your mind. You "see" it . . . you nod excitedly, knowing that you have unlocked the vault. You are able to grasp the meaning of what earlier seemed vague, perhaps even confusing. We call that "insight." In reality, why couldn't that be the supernatural inner prompting of the Spirit as He illuminates your understanding of God's Word and will? It isn't mere human insight, is it?

• You are going through a severe time of testing. Your heart is heavy . . . your mind preoccupied. The pain doesn't go away. Instead, you lose your appetite, you suffer from insomnia, you become increasingly more isolated, pensive, maybe a bit irritable. The heaviness hangs like an anchor. Often, tears come unexpectedly. And then, almost overnight, the ninety-five-pound weight is lifted off your chest. Amazingly, your turmoil subsides and a wonderful tranquility comes in its place. We commonly call that "relief," but is that all it is? Why couldn't this UIP be the direct result of the Spirit of God bringing supernatural comfort, inner healing, and a divine surge of peace?

• There is a growing sense of unrest and/or conflict between you and another person close to you. It could be with someone who works for you or with you. It might be a friend, a family member, or your partner in marriage. You wish things would change on their own, but they are only getting worse. Then, at just the right moment, using carefully chosen words, you address the issue(s) head-on. Good things happen as a result of the meeting; changes occur. We call it an "intervention," a time of serious confrontation. Yet couldn't this be the empowering of the Spirit? Might it not be His inner prompting, infusing you with the necessary courage to stand toe-to-toe with the person and talk straight about the problem?

• You are in a relationship with an individual who is becoming increasingly more difficult to deal with. Pressure mounts with each week that passes. It seems as though you won't be able to escape a showdown, though you doubt how beneficial such a verbal encounter would be. You pray fervently. Just when the situation reaches the unbearable stage, a turn of events occurs that completely removes the person from your life. You could not have orchestrated a more perfect arrangement of events, but the fact is you didn't actually do anything to put the scenario into motion. It just happened. We call that a "coincidence," but is that really what it was? Who's to say it wasn't another of those UIPs where God's sovereign Spirit stepped in and choreographed the whole thing, leaving you wonderfully affirmed and at ease?

We Are Fearfully and Wonderfully Made

When God created humanity, He put something of Himself in each of us. Unlike the beasts of the field or the birds of the sky or the blooming plants in the dirt, He placed within us His "image."

> And God created man in His own image, in the image of God He created him; male and female He created them.
>
> Genesis 1:27

That "image" sets human beings apart from all other living things on earth. With body, soul, and spirit, we are able to get in touch not only with our feelings, but with Him, our Creator. And, equally important, He is able to communicate with us. Unlike other creatures who operate their lives out of instinct, we are equipped with sufficient "internal machinery" to connect with the living God.

In fact, when we become children of God through faith in His Son, that connection with Him takes on a whole new dimension. As Paul wrote so clearly,

> For all who are being led by the Spirit of God, these are sons of God. For you have not received a spirit of slavery leading

> to fear again, but you have received a spirit of adoption as sons by which we cry out, "Abba! Father!" The Spirit Himself bears witness with our spirit that we are children of God.
>
> Romans 8:14–16

Look closely at that concluding comment. God's Spirit literally communicates with—bears witness with—our inner being, called here "our spirit." In other words, an entire system of inner communication is established at the time of salvation, making it possible for us to receive whatever it is the Spirit wishes to communicate!

The psalmist used another expression in describing our uniqueness as human beings. In the magnificent Psalm 139 we are told that the link between us and God's Spirit is not only a reality, it is inescapable:

> Where can I go from Thy Spirit?
> Or where can I flee from Thy presence?
> If I ascend to heaven, Thou art there;
> If I make my bed in Sheol, behold, Thou art there.
> If I take the wings of the dawn,
> If I dwell in the remotest part of the sea,
> Even there Thy hand will lead me,
> And Thy right hand will lay hold of me.
>
> Psalm 139:7–10

Wonderful, comforting thought: We and He are supernaturally interwoven and inseparable. Wherever you or I go, He goes. Whatever we think, He knows. In fact, He oversaw our conception and He gave us our personality as well as our physical makeup. The same psalm verifies this:

> For Thou didst form my inward parts;
> Thou didst weave me in my mother's womb.
> I will give thanks to Thee, for I am fearfully and
> wonderfully made;
> Wonderful are Thy works.

> And my soul knows it very well.
> My frame was not hidden from Thee,
> When I was made in secret,
> And skillfully wrought in the depths of the earth.
> Thine eyes have seen my unformed substance;
> And in Thy book they were all written,
> The days that were ordained for me,
> When as yet there was not one of them.
>
> Psalm 139:13–16

Don't miss that special line: "I am fearfully and wonderfully made." One Jewish commentator states, "Reflection upon the marvels of the human body, even with his elementary anatomical knowledge, inspired the Psalmist with awe and wonder."[1]

It's true. Caught up in the wonder of it all, the ancient writer exclaims how uniquely created we are. I suggest that uniqueness includes secret inner chambers and hidden capacities other created beings lack. I also would suggest that such an inner system provides for the reception of divine information and the understanding of biblical truths, unknown to the animal kingdom. By being "fearfully and wonderfully made," we are equipped to grasp the Spirit's messages as well as sense His compelling, awesome presence. That explains why we can hear His "still small voice" and decipher messages of peace or warning, conviction or guidance. God created us with that capacity.

In fact, a very familiar verse of Scripture points out how God's message can penetrate deep within us.

> For the word of God is living and active and sharper than any two-edged sword, and piercing as far as the division of soul and spirit, of both joints and marrow, and able to judge the thoughts and intentions of the heart.
>
> Hebrews 4:12

Don't hurry past those words just because you may be familiar with the verse. God's truths are able to enter into our "soul and spirit," exposing to us "the thoughts and intentions of the heart."

Amazing! As the Spirit ignites the fuel of God's written revelation, the flame bursts upon us and engulfs us with an inner awareness. No surgeon can operate on the soul or the inner spirit. That is the invisible realm where God's Spirit does His work. No matter how brilliant the neurologist may be, with all his knowledge of the brain and nervous system, he cannot touch the spirit within us. That is God's special abode. Medical men and women are able to understand gross anatomy—and the study of it is fascinating—but how little they know (and how little we know) of the soul and spirit . . . the inner realm where the Spirit of God dwells. That explains why you can be in the midst of recovery from major surgery and still experience no anxiety . . . because the Spirit of God is at work within you, bringing about that otherwise unidentified inner prompting of peace.

I hesitate to use this term, but this is all very *mysterious.* It is one of those examples of divine truth we cannot nail down and dissect with precision; however, we also cannot deny it. Every one of us in God's family has experienced at one time or another some inner prompting of the Spirit. We call them other things. We call them hunches or intuition. We call them premonitions. We call them flashes of insight. Or we may call them simply a sense of peace. In reality, however, all these things we identify in human terms are part of His working. Yet we so seldom connect these inner promptings with Him, and we somehow feel strange when we try to identify them. We shouldn't.

Inner Promptings Then and Now

Let's look at four biblical examples of the work of the Spirit . . . four occasions when the Spirit did a unique work in someone's life. And remember, if He did it then, He can do it today.

1. *In times of loneliness and desperation, the Spirit prompts hope and encouragement.*

The life of the prophet Elijah, a man intimately acquainted with the presence of God, provides strong evidence that "truth is stranger than fiction." The man stood alone before evil King Ahab and pronounced a drought. It didn't rain for three and a half years. During the time of that drought, God sent ravens to feed Elijah; every morning and evening they brought him bread and meat. When Elijah commanded the fire of God to fall on the altar that was flooded with water, the fire fell, to the amazement of the prophets of Baal, who were thereafter slain. Finally, on the heels of these and other great occasions of victory, when the prophet was most vulnerable, Jezebel, the wicked wife of King Ahab, threatened his life. The weary prophet couldn't handle it. He caved in.

> Now Ahab told Jezebel all that Elijah had done, and how he had killed all the prophets with the sword. Then Jezebel sent a messenger to Elijah, saying, "So may the gods do to me and even more, if I do not make your life as the life of one of them by tomorrow about this time." And he was afraid and arose and ran for his life and came to Beersheba, which belongs to Judah, and left his servant there. But he himself went a day's journey into the wilderness, and came and sat down under a juniper tree; and he requested for himself that he might die, and said, "It is enough; now, O LORD, take my life, for I am not better than my fathers."
>
> 1 Kings 19:1–4

Now ideally the prophet Elijah should have said, "Lord, I ask You to come down and be my protector, my very present help in this time of need. Calm my fears. Be my shield and my defender." But he didn't do that. Instead, he ran for his life and then slumped into a deep depression.

Deep in the woods, in an unusual moment of desperation, loneliness, and despair, Elijah sat down under a tree and asked the Lord to take his life. (Apparently the thought of suicide did not enter his mind.) Emotionally, physically, spiritually, he was at the bottom.

A more pathetic picture of heartbreaking loneliness can hardly be found in the Scriptures. There he sat, full of self-pity and disillusionment.

And what did God do? Our gracious God neither shamed him nor rebuked him; instead, with compassion and gentleness, He ministered to His servant.

> So He said, "Go forth, and stand on the mountain before the LORD." And behold, the LORD was passing by! And a great and strong wind was rending the mountains and breaking in pieces the rocks before the LORD; but the LORD was not in the wind. And after the wind an earthquake, but the LORD was not in the earthquake. And after the earthquake a fire, but the LORD was not in the fire; and after the fire a sound of a gentle blowing.
>
> 1 Kings 19:11–12

Let's pause right here. The old King James Version says that "after the fire" there was "a still, small voice." The New King James Bible renders it in a similar manner, but gives this footnote, "a delicate, whispering voice." The New International Version states that "after the fire came a gentle whisper." Can you picture the scene? Elijah, wrapped in his desolation, loneliness, and despair, is standing there in the howling wind, looking at the fire, feeling the earthquake. But the Lord was in none of it. And all of a sudden those phenomena subside and there is this "delicate whispering voice." Somehow, deep within the prophet's heart he hears something from God.

One reliable commentator states:

> It was not in the tempest that Jehovah was; . . . it was not in the earthquake that Jehovah was; . . . it was not in the fire that Jehovah was. . . . It was in a soft, gentle rustling that He revealed Himself to him [Elijah].[2]

I am unable to explain how Elijah sensed God's voice or exactly what the Spirit said, but clearly He connected with the prophet.

And what did Elijah do? Soon after that encounter with God, he wrapped himself in his mantle, and he moved toward the mouth of the cave. He didn't run from God; he moved toward Him.

I must admit, there have been times in my life when the Lord's promptings have been just as real to me as Elijah's experience was to him. No, I didn't hear an audible voice . . . I didn't see a vision . . . but His presence was so real I felt I could touch Him. Quite honestly, *it was magnificent.* Rather than being boisterous and bold, it was gentle and quiet . . . almost as if He were saying, "I have everything under control. Trust me. Depend on Me. Wait patiently for Me to work."

Now it is important to remember that some of the most profound ministries of the Spirit of God are not public or loud or large. Sometimes His most meaningful touch on our lives comes when we are all alone.

I urge you to include in your schedule time to be alone with God. I am fortunate to live within ninety minutes of the mountains . . . and less than forty-five minutes from the beach. Those are great places to commune with God. You do have places where you can get away for a long walk, don't you? I hope it's in a wooded area. The gentle breeze blowing through the forest is therapeutic. Sometimes just being alone out in God's marvelous creation is all that's needed for the scales to be removed from your eyes and for you to silence the harassment and the noise of your day and begin to hear from God. On those occasions the Lord ministers to us in a gentle whispering.

I took a walk in a forest some six thousand feet high a few weeks ago. There, all alone in the cold, surrounded by snow about a foot deep, I stood and leaned against a tree and poured out my heart to God. I must have done this for fifteen or twenty minutes . . . then I just listened. It was wonderful. Several things I had been concerned about fell into place there in His presence.

Scripture says, "Be still, and know that I am God." Elijah was still, and that was all he needed to find encouragement from the living God. Take time. Be still. Unload the weight of your soul. Listen.

2. *In times of threatening fears, the Spirit prompts calm determination and courage.*

Something Paul experienced in this regard during his third missionary journey is worth a second look.

> "And now, behold, bound in spirit, I am on my way to Jerusalem, not knowing what will happen to me there, except that the Holy Spirit solemnly testifies to me in every city, saying that bonds and afflictions await me. But I do not consider my life of any account as dear to myself, in order that I may finish my course, and the ministry which I received from the Lord Jesus, to testify solemnly of the gospel of the grace of God."
>
> Acts 20:22–24

This is a deeply emotional and moving account because the apostle is saying good-bye to his longtime friends from Ephesus. Adding to the emotion was the realization that he probably would not see them again.

Initially what I find interesting and intriguing is that Paul says he is "bound in the Spirit." I think he means that he is "bound by the Holy Spirit" rather than being tied up in knots within his own spirit. In other words, he was captured in thoughts of, surrounded by the presence of, unable to get away from the reminders of God's heaven-sent Helper. In some supernatural manner, the Spirit communicated with Paul's spirit as he "solemnly testified," saying, in effect, "You're in for trouble, Paul. No matter what city you enter, you are going to encounter intensified trouble." (That is exactly what happened.) A threatening fear could have seized him and sidetracked him. But it didn't. Why? Because Paul was not all that important to Paul. Remember what he wrote on another occasion?

> For to me, to live is Christ, and to die is gain. But if I am to live on in the flesh, this will mean fruitful labor for me; and I do not know which to chose.
>
> Philippians 1:21–22

Strictly from the human viewpoint, when you and I know that trouble and afflictions await us, we are frightened. That does not occur when the Spirit of God brings a sense of reassurance.

Could this not explain the relentless courage and determination of the martyrs and the missionaries of years gone by? If you're like me, when you read about their lives, you shake your head and think, "I cannot imagine how they endured such trials! How did they continue in such threatening times? How could they have not dreaded each dawn?" How? It was the Spirit of God! They were "bound in the Spirit" in the midst of those threatening fears.

Could this not explain the courage and determination of the Reformers? You read their stories and you realize how shallowly and superficially many of us live our lives. Though they lost reputation, occupation, status, and in some cases were burned at the stake, they stood resolute and confident. How could they do that? They were "bound in the Spirit."

When we fly closer to the flame, an unidentified inner prompting often says to our spirits, "I am here. I am aware of what you are going through. I know of the threats. I will take you through them." Perhaps the hymn writer knew of such divine promptings when he wrote those immortal lyrics:

> When through fiery trials thy pathway shall lie,
> My grace all-sufficient shall be thy supply;
> The flame shall not hurt thee; I only design
> Thy dross to consume, and thy gold to refine.[3]

A warning is appropriate here. This does not mean we presume on God, or are foolish and needlessly daring, or flirt with danger in the energy of the flesh. That is not the kind of courage we're talking about. What I am referring to is the remarkable way fear flees when the Spirit communicates His presence and gives us an "inner transfusion" of His incredible power.

3. *In times of potential danger and disaster, the Spirit prompts inner reassurance.*

One of the most exciting and adventuresome accounts in the New Testament is recorded in Acts 27. If you enjoy sailing, life on the open sea, the power of the wind and the waves, and the physical challenge of surviving a storm in the deep, you will love this chapter. It includes all that and more, as danger intensifies with each new scene.

> And when it was decided that we should sail for Italy, they proceeded to deliver Paul and some other prisoners to a centurion of the Augustan cohort named Julius. And embarking in an Adramyttian ship, which was about to sail to the regions along the coast of Asia, we put out to sea, accompanied by Aristarchus, a Macedonian of Thessalonica. And the next day we put in at Sidon; and Julius treated Paul with consideration and allowed him to go to his friends and receive care. And from there we put out to sea and sailed under the shelter of Cyprus because the winds were contrary. And when we had sailed through the sea along the coast of Cilicia and Pamphylia, we landed at Myra in Lycia. And there the centurion found an Alexandrian ship sailing for Italy, and he put us aboard it. And when we had sailed slowly for a good many days, and with difficulty had arrived off Cnidus, since the wind did not permit us to go farther, we sailed under the shelter of Crete, off Salmone; and with difficulty sailing past it we came to a certain place called Fair Havens, near which was the city of Lasea.
>
> And when considerable time had passed and the voyage was now dangerous. . . .
>
> Acts 27:1–9

Are you getting the picture? The seas are getting rougher. Dark storm clouds are gathering. The wind is whipping the sails. The currents are getting stronger. The old ship is groaning and creaking as it pitches and rolls in the angry Mediterranean. It's in the midst of this that Paul addresses those on the ship:

"Men, I perceive that the voyage will certainly be attended with damage and great loss, not only of the cargo and the ship, but also of our lives." But the centurion was more persuaded by the pilot and the captain of the ship, than by what was being said by Paul. And because the harbor was not suitable for wintering, the majority reached a decision to put out to sea from there, if somehow they could reach Phoenix, a harbor of Crete, facing southwest and northwest, and spend the winter there. And when a moderate south wind came up, supposing that they had gained their purpose, they weighed anchor and began sailing along Crete, close inshore. But before very long there rushed down from the land a violent wind, called Euraquilo; and when the ship was caught in it, and could not face the wind, we gave way to it, and let ourselves be driven along. And running under the shelter of a small island called Clauda, we were scarcely able to get the ship's boat under control. And after they had hoisted it up, they used supporting cables in undergirding the ship; and fearing that they might run aground on the shallows of Syrtis, they let down the sea anchor, and so let themselves be driven along. The next day as we were being violently storm-tossed, they began to jettison the cargo; and on the third day they threw the ship's tackle overboard with their own hands. And since neither sun nor stars appeared for many days, and no small storm was assailing us, from then on all hope of our being saved was gradually abandoned.

Acts 27:10–20

Have you ever been in a situation like that? Perhaps a howling blizzard or a tornado?

My brother Orville and his family endured Hurricane Andrew in South Florida. They listened as 150-mile-an-hour winds ripped off timbers and flung them through the house like spears. Doors were torn from their hinges and windows exploded. Both their cars were severely damaged. But in the midst of all this, Orville, his wife, and several others were crouched in the bedroom, praying. Incredibly, that room was the only room that suffered no damage. Anyone who lived through Hurricane Andrew can testify to its power, its danger, and to the disaster left in its wake.

It's a similar scene of danger here in Acts 27, and on top of everything else, those enduring it are at sea! They have already lost control, and now they begin losing their cargo. What most people fear in such situations, of course, is losing their life. And so, in the midst of this scene of panic, Paul addresses his shipmates and speaks with confidence, saying:

> "Men, you ought to have followed my advice and not to have set sail from Crete, and incurred this damage and loss. And yet now I urge you to keep up your courage, for there shall be no loss of life among you, but only of the ship.
>
> Acts 27:21–22

Question: How could he say that? Did he have some kind of premonition? The world may say so, but that's not the correct explanation. It is the work of the Spirit of God that gives this kind of courage. It doesn't come naturally. In the same way, how could my brother not panic in the midst of that hurricane with his precious family huddled around him? It was because the Spirit of God protected him and preserved him and gave him a sense of inner reassurance.

Paul verifies that his confidence came from the Lord. In fact, he says that he had been visited by an angel!

> "For this very night an angel of the God to whom I belong and whom I serve stood before me, saying, 'Do not be afraid, Paul; you must stand before Caesar; and behold, God has granted you all those who are sailing with you.' Therefore, keep up your courage, men, for I believe God, that it will turn out exactly as I have been told. But we must run aground on a certain island."
>
> Acts 27:23–26

His message was reassuring, but it was not unrealistic. Right up front he warned them that they would run aground. But not to worry . . . everyone would make it safely to shore. Read the closing scene and allow your imagination to run free:

> But when the fourteenth night had come, as we were being driven about in the Adriatic Sea, about midnight the sailors began to surmise that they were approaching some land. And they took soundings, and found it to be twenty fathoms; and a little farther on they took another sounding and found it to be fifteen fathoms. And fearing that we might run aground somewhere on the rocks, they cast four anchors from the stern and wished for daybreak. And as the sailors were trying to escape from the ship, and had let down the ship's boat into the sea, on the pretense of intending to lay out anchors from the bow, Paul said to the centurion and to the soldiers, "Unless these men remain in the ship, you yourselves cannot be saved." Then the soldiers cut away the ropes of the ship's boat, and let it fall away. And until the day was about to dawn, Paul was encouraging them all to take some food, saying, "Today is the fourteenth day that you have been constantly watching and going without eating, having taken nothing. Therefore I encourage you to take some food, for this is for your preservation; for not a hair from the head of any of you shall perish." And having said this, he took bread and gave thanks to God in the presence of all; and he broke it and began to eat. And all of them were encouraged, and they themselves also took food. And all of us in the ship were two hundred and seventy-six persons. And when they had eaten enough, they began to lighten the ship by throwing out the wheat into the sea. And when day came, they could not recognize the land; but they did observe a certain bay with a beach, and they resolved to drive the ship onto it if they could. And casting off the anchors, they left them in the sea while at the same time they were loosening the ropes of the rudders, and hoisting the foresail to the wind, they were heading for the beach. But striking a reef where two seas met, they ran the vessel aground; and the prow stuck fast and remained immovable, but the stern began to be broken up by the force of the waves. And the soldiers' plan was to kill the

> prisoners, that none of them should swim away and escape; but the centurion, wanting to bring Paul safely through, kept them from their intention, and commanded that those who could swim should jump overboard first and get to land, and the rest should follow, some on planks, and others on various things from the ship. And thus it happened that they all were brought safely to land.
>
> Acts 27:27–44

Note that all were ultimately present and accounted for. They were soaked, but safe . . . exactly as God had said.

How could Paul remain so encouraged? Because the Spirit of God, using an angelic messenger, prompted him to be confident in danger and to stand firm on that promise. Such events may indeed be rare—perhaps only once or twice in a lifetime. But my point is this: Paul wasn't merely a brave man who loved challenges. He was prompted by God to be of good courage, even though his circumstances were frightening. If you doubt that, it's been too long since you were at sea in a raging storm.

4. *In times of great sorrow and pain, the Spirit ministers grace to us.*

Tucked away in the first few verses of 2 Corinthians 12 is a classic example of God's ministry in the midst of human misery.

> And because of the surpassing greatness of the revelations, for this reason, to keep me from exalting myself, there was given me a thorn in the flesh, a messenger of Satan to buffet me—to keep me from exalting myself! Concerning this I entreated the Lord three times that it might depart from me.
>
> 2 Corinthians 12:7–8

The writer is Paul, who admits to having a thorn in the flesh—probably some physical ailment that brought excruciating, unrelenting pain. And so, naturally, he asked the Lord to bring relief . . . but relief didn't come. On three separate occasions he prayed that God would take away the pain. All three times the answer was the same. "No." But then God communicated something to Paul's inner spirit that brought him an enormous sense of relief. I call this message another of the Spirit's "inner promptings." And what was it God made known to Paul in his pain?

> And He has said to me, "My grace is sufficient for you, for power is perfected in weakness."
>
> 2 Corinthians 12:9

Grace. The God of all grace ministered grace to His hurting servant. Grace to endure. Grace to handle the pain. Grace to face the future. Grace to accept God's no. What a profound impact that had on the man!

> Most gladly, therefore, I will rather boast about my weaknesses, that the power of Christ may dwell in me. Therefore I am well content with weaknesses, with insults, with distresses, with persecutions, with difficulties, for Christ's sake; for when I am weak, then I am strong.
>
> 2 Corinthians 12:9b–10

I write from firsthand experience in this matter. I can't tell you the number of times God's power has been perfected and revealed in my own weakness. Some messages that I have received from God's Word and delivered in times of enormous weakness and inadequacy in my own life have been messages most blessed of God. I struggled through them, didn't feel like anybody would even want to listen, and couldn't wait to get out of the places where I was teaching or preaching because of my own disappointment or struggle at the time. But later I heard response after response telling how God had used those words in the lives of listeners.

When the Spirit of the Lord ministers grace, He prompts within us an unusual measure of divine strength. Somehow, in the mystery of His plan, He turns our pain into a platform upon which He does some of His best work.

Two Practical Suggestions

From UFOs to Mediterranean shipwrecks, we have covered a lot of ground in this chapter. So let me just add a couple of suggestions to help us keep our balance through all this.

First, *when you are not sure that something is from the Spirit, tread softly.* Back off. Use the Scriptures as your guide. If they are of the Lord, those unidentified inner promptings won't contradict anything biblically. Peace will remain your companion. The Lord doesn't lead against His own revealed Word. So don't get on a hobbyhorse over something that is questionable or clearly unbiblical.

Second, *when you are confident that it's of God, stand firm, even against other people's doubts.* Be strong and resolute. That's a part of walking by faith. There are times when other people will say, "There is no way in the world God could be in this"; yet you know absolutely in your heart that He is. At times like that, simply stand firm. You won't be able to convince them, but that's all right. God is still doing unusual things. BUT don't get weird. You can be confident in God without becoming spooky or seeing lots of things no one else can see.

Which reminds me, if I ever run into you at a UFO convention, you and I are going to have a talk.

8

The Spirit and Our Emotions

"DON'T SLAM THE DOOR."

"Eat everything on your plate."

"Say ma'am and sir."

"Don't run inside the house."

"Keep your shoes shined."

"Don't talk with your mouth full."

"Work first, play later."

Sound familiar? Those are some of the rules by which I was raised. You can probably identify with one or two. Most families have them . . . you know, mottoes to live by.

Another that stands out in my mind was one of my mother's favorites: "You can't trust your feelings." To this day I can clearly recall her words as she warned us kids against relying on our emotions: "What you really want, son, are the facts. Facts are your friends . . . feelings will change on you."

As I grew up and became a Christian, this attitude was affirmed again and again. In the churches I attended, the pastors warned against "getting too emotional." Teachers in Sunday school agreed. If you're looking for something to give substance to your faith, they said, stay with the facts, not your feelings. Later, as I got under way in seminary, the same axiom was drilled into my head. Start with the facts. Make them the building blocks of your theology. Then, on the basis of those facts, live by faith. Your feelings will fall in line. Often, feelings were treated as if they either didn't exist or, if they did, were not important, sort of like second-class citizens. Just ignore your feelings; they'll fall in line . . . they'll catch up.

I am not alone in this experience. One writer puts it this way:

> In my youth as a Christian I was greatly helped by the story about Faith, Feelings, and Facts, companions together along a tricky pathway. The first two followed Facts who was in the lead. The story taught me that objective truth (Facts) was what mattered, and that my eyes of faith should be pinned on the facts, rather than on my emotions.
>
> Mr. Faith, you may remember, was often bothered when Mr. Feelings got into difficulties. However, when he took his eyes off Facts and turned to help Mr. Feelings, he himself invariably got into difficulties until he remembered that his job was to follow Facts, not to worry about Feelings. And according to the story, sooner or later Feelings would catch up.
>
> The story teaches both a truth and a lie. The truth is that our faith is based on facts, not on feelings. The lie was that feelings always caught up.[1]

How true! Our faith is based on facts—rock-solid, reliable, essential facts—not feelings.

It is not true, however, that our feelings always catch up.

Something else bothers me about this, too, and that is all the things I have been taught against feelings . . . almost as if emotions are spurious, never reliable, hardly worth mentioning. And even worse, it is as if emotions are never prompted by the Spirit of God . . . that they are far removed from anything connected with true spirituality.

Where did we get such an idea? Since when is the Spirit's work limited to our minds and our wills but not our hearts? Why is it that so many of us Evangelicals are so afraid of feelings? What has happened to us? Why must our theology and the expression of our faith be devoid of emotion? After all, God made us whole people; He created us with minds, wills, and hearts. And if He created us with the capacity to feel, shouldn't we be free to talk about our feelings, to express them, and to value them in ourselves and in others?

Rather than their being unimportant, I have found that my feelings often represent some of the most sensitive areas in my life touched by the Spirit of God. Not infrequently do my emotions play a vital role in how and where the Spirit is guiding me, giving me reasons to make significant decisions, cautioning me to back off, and reproving me for something in my life that needs immediate attention.

How else but through feelings do we experience that "peace that passes understanding"? Peace is, in the final analysis, an emotion.

How else but through feelings can we sense the presence of evil and the dangers of subtle temptations? Uneasy warning signals within us are actually emotional reactions, aren't they?

How else but through feelings are we prompted to "rejoice with those who rejoice, and weep with those who weep" (Rom. 12:15)?

And when we give God our praise, is it not from the depths of our emotions?

Don't feelings play a prominent role in our acts of righteous indignation, as well as in maintaining a positive attitude toward suffering, rejoicing in the Lord, loving others, and giving thanks in everything?

All these are things the Lord commands us to do; yet we could not obey apart from the release of our emotions. Strangely, however, many believers are still hesitant to let them out; they still "don't trust their feelings."

We are strange creatures: proud of our brains, stubborn in our wills, but ashamed of our emotions—though we deny all three! One of the many benefits of flying closer to the flame is that it allows us to warm up to our emotions, which is nothing more than allowing ourselves the freedom to be real, to be whole.

I have seen some incredible things in my adult life that illustrate the absence of this. Like a friend of mine who lost his wife after a long and bitter bout with cancer. He watched her in the downward-spiraling process survive several major surgeries, endure the humiliating experiences connected with chemotherapy, and literally become a living skeleton. Even though the whole tragedy was agony for her and heartbreaking for him, he never once broke—even when death finally came as a long-awaited relief. He never admitted to me his own emotional exhaustion, feelings of grief over losing his lovely wife, anger at the disease, or questions that surely haunted him in the middle of those nights.

Instead, he always maintained a calm, quiet acceptance, quoted several verses of Scripture, and even smiled with gratitude over others' concern for his wife's welfare. As I would press him for how he must be feeling—the loneliness, the awful struggle, the helplessness of watching his beloved slipping from his arms—there was never a tear, never a crack in his countenance. Even at the memorial service in her honor he was busy comforting others instead of being crushed by his own grief. While I heard a few admirable comments about how strong he was through it all—"like the rock of Gibraltar," someone whispered—I found myself increasingly more concerned over his lack of emotion . . . his inability to admit his grief and genuinely mourn her death. I still wonder if he thought that his reaction was "the proper Christian response" so he dared not let those real feelings show.

Becoming a Christian is not synonymous with becoming superhuman. Expressing one's emotions is not a mark of immaturity or carnality. The loss of a loved one is just as much a loss for the believer as it is for the nonbeliever. A killer disease like cancer—especially in its final stages—arouses the same feelings in the Christian's heart as in the heart without Christ. Pain is pain. Loss is loss. Death is death. At such times tears are not only acceptable, they are appropriate and expected. It is part of being real, being human. Nothing is gained by denial or proven by remaining stoic.

The apostle Paul did not write that Christians are not to grieve, but that we do not grieve as if we "have no hope" (1 Thess. 4:13). There should be a lot of room in our theology for feelings of loss and tears, just as there is room for lighthearted, joyous feelings and great laughter. The Spirit of God prompts both. I have been concerned for years that too many so-called mature evangelical Christians have little room in their lives for either . . . which reminds me of another "rule" repeated in too many Christian homes: "Do not cry . . . it's a sign of weakness." Will somebody please point out to me where that is found in the Scriptures?

God Has Made Us "Whole People"

Speaking of the Scriptures, let's take a look at when and how God created humanity. And in doing so, let's pay close attention to how man and woman differ from planets and plants, fish and fowl. This search takes us all the way back to Creation, recorded in Genesis 1 and 2.

Genesis 1 is a general survey of the great Creation, beginning with the opening words of the Bible:

> In the beginning God created the heavens and the earth. And the earth was formless and void, and darkness was over the surface of the deep; and the Spirit of God was moving over the surface of the waters.
>
> Genesis 1:1–2

God was directly engaged in the whole creative activity and, interestingly, the Spirit of God was equally active, hovering over (literally) the process. As we read through this chapter we discover the divine plan being worked out miraculously and meticulously. From one *day* to the next, from one *category* to the next, life is being created and established—vegetation, birds, fish, animals, reptiles—it's all there, unfolding from God's fiat word and creative power.

Finally, the time arrives for the creation of humans. The Godhead—Father, Son, Spirit—agrees that this category will be unique:

> Then God said, "Let Us make man in Our image, according to Our likeness . . ."
>
> Genesis 1:26

Intriguing words, "Our image . . . Our likeness." The following verse verifies precisely what transpired:

> And God created man in His own image, in the image of God He created him; male and female He created them.
>
> Genesis 1:27

Twice the inspired record states that, unlike all other created life, mankind bears the "image" of the Creator. Plant life does not have this "image," nor do the birds of the air, the fish of the sea, or the beasts of the field. Only mankind.

And what is that "image"? Volumes have been written by theologians attempting to answer that question. Rather than getting involved in such a detailed analysis, let me summarize my answer by using the words *personality* and *nature*. God gave humanity a personality, or nature, like His own.

God has a "mind"—intellect. When He created Adam and Eve, God gave them the same. He gave them an intelligence that was higher than other created life. This is illustrated not only in the command to "rule over the fish . . . the birds . . . the cattle and over all the earth" (Gen. 1:26), but also in Adam's naming all the creatures God had created (Gen. 2:19). The first man and woman were able to communicate with each other verbally, to make observations about one another, and to understand their Creator's instructions—all characteristics of intelligence. Ultimately, they were given this kind of mind that they might know their God.

God has a "heart"—emotions. When He created Adam and Eve, God gave them the same. Their emotional makeup and capacity were unique. Combined with their intellect, they could feel what no other created life could feel. The full spectrum of emotions was there for them to experience . . . from intense affection and exuberant joy to intense anger; they could feel disappointment, sadness, comfort, refreshment, excitement, and ecstasy. All this and so much more were theirs at creation. Adam's delight in seeing Eve for the first time (Gen. 2:23) is a good example of his emotions. A literal reading of that verse suggests that he burst forth with strong feelings of excitement when God brought her to him for the first time: "Now—at last!" And their intimate joy in marital love offers yet another example of their capacity to feel deeply (Gen. 2:25). Ultimately, Adam and Eve were given emotions that they might love their God.

God has a "will"—volition. When He created the first couple, God gave them the same. Nothing else in creation had this ability. Mixed with their intellectual and emotional capacities, this volitional ability enabled Adam and Eve to understand and reason things through, feel the emotions of the issues, then make decisions and act upon them. God appealed to Adam's will when He gave him commands, like:

> "From any tree of the garden you may eat freely; but from the tree of the knowledge of good and evil you shall not eat, for in the day that you eat from it you shall surely die."
>
> Genesis 2:16–17

God gave Adam and Eve a will that they might obey their God.

The Significant Presence of Our Feelings

Let's spend a few minutes on some of the salient emotions that are a part of our God-given personality. Though it may come as a surprise to some Christians who have never felt the freedom to acknowledge and to affirm their emotions, the New Testament is full of comments regarding the presence of feelings. Two verses from the Corinthian letters come to mind:

> But just as it is written,
>
> "THINGS WHICH EYE HAS NOT SEEN AND
> EAR HAS NOT HEARD,
> AND WHICH HAVE NOT ENTERED THE
> HEART OF MAN,
> ALL THAT GOD HAS PREPARED FOR THOSE
> WHO LOVE HIM."
>
> 1 Corinthians 2:9

> For God, who said, "Light shall shine out of darkness," is the One who has shone in our hearts to give the light of the knowledge of the glory of God in the face of Christ.
>
> 2 Corinthians 4:6

God's work in salvation is directed to the heart, not just the mind. When the Lord begins His saving work in the life of the sinner, He goes right to the heart!

Interesting, isn't it? Entering into the heart, targeting the emotions of the sinner, the Lord begins His persuasive convincing. When a person chooses to reject the things of God, it means that those things have not entered into his or her *heart.* The mind of that unredeemed one is blinded, yes, but the heart is also untouched . . . unconvinced . . . unmoved.

This helps explain why so much is said in Scripture regarding a hard heart, a dull heart, a calloused heart. The Pharaoh in Moses' day comes to mind. In spite of all that happened, all the misery of the plagues and all the evidence he witnessed, his heart remained unmoved. The stubborn Egyptian leader remained hard of heart. The Spirit of God never invaded and took His rightful place on the seat of his emotions.

If you are saved, part of the reason God got your attention and came into your life is that He reached your heart and He softened your feelings toward Him.

Paul testifies that his own heart's passion was for the salvation of his fellow Jews.

> Brethren, my heart's desire and my prayer to God for them is for their salvation.
>
> Romans 10:1

He later writes that genuine salvation occurs not simply because we say so, but because we have a heartfelt belief.

> That if you confess with your mouth Jesus as Lord, and believe in your heart that God raised Him from the dead, you shall be saved; for with the heart man believes, resulting in righteousness, and with the mouth he confesses, resulting in salvation.
>
> Romans 10:9–10

Obviously this use of the word *heart* is broader than just a reference to the emotions, but it would certainly include such.

I would challenge you to do a study of your own on the emotions mentioned in the New Testament. If you do, you will be amazed at the number of feelings—human, everyday feelings—God underscores. In some cases He prompts them; in others, He works through them or He speaks to them. They are interwoven through the entire fabric of truth. Let me mention several examples:

Joy and Cheer

> Now this I say, he who sows sparingly shall also reap sparingly; and he who sows bountifully shall also reap bountifully.
>
> 2 Corinthians 9:6

Using a vivid illustration from the world of agriculture, Paul writes that a light sowing will result in a light harvest, while a generous sowing will yield a generous harvest. He then applies this to the contributing of one's money to God's eternal work on earth:

> Let each one do just as he has purposed in his heart; not grudgingly or under compulsion; for God loves a cheerful giver.
>
> 2 Corinthians 9:7

I find it interesting that we purpose to give in our heart—another example of volition teaming up with emotions. When we give as we should, for all the right reasons, we are "cheerful." In fact, the Greek term so translated is the word from which we get "hilarious."

Love

Look next at 2 Timothy 1:7:

> For God has not given us a spirit of timidity, but of power and love and discipline.

Two opposite emotions are mentioned here: One is not prompted by God (timidity, or cowardice), and the other one is (love). If there is one word that could easily be the theme of the New Testament, it would be *love* (*agape*). This particular term is a uniquely Christian word, indicating an active pursuit in seeking the highest good of another. *Agape* appears frequently in John's writings, especially the letter of 1 John, where we find the verse that is a favorite of many:

> We love, because He first loved us.
>
> 1 John 4:19

Fear

I mentioned this emotion earlier, but it would be helpful to underscore it by going back into the Old Testament and seeing it clearly in the ancient book of wisdom, the Proverbs:

> The fear of the Lord is the beginning of knowledge.
>
> Proverbs 1:7

God honors such feelings of "fear," a term that suggests an awesome respect for our Lord with an accompanying hatred for sin. This does not mean that we are frightened by God, but that we have a holy respect for Him . . . so great that sin is allowed no place in our conscious life.

Praise

At least eleven of the psalms, including the last five, begin with the same words: "Praise the Lord!" This is not simply an intellectual response based on facts. It is an emotional act of worship, praising and extolling the living God. Praise includes deep feelings of adoration and heartfelt affection, and God honors those spontaneous "bursts" of our adoration.

Other Feelings

Joy . . . love . . . fear . . . praise . . . those are basic and very powerful emotions. Yet they are only a few of the many emotions referred to in Scripture as an integral part of our spiritual lives. For example, in the section of Scripture that follows—just one section—note how many of these commands involve feelings generated within our hearts:

> Let love be without hypocrisy. Abhor what is evil; cling to what is good. Be devoted to one another in brotherly love; give preference to one another in honor; not lagging behind in diligence, fervent in spirit, serving the Lord; rejoicing in hope, persevering in tribulation, devoted to prayer, contributing to the needs of the saints, practicing hospitality. Bless those who persecute you; bless and curse not. Rejoice with those who rejoice, and weep with those who weep. Be of the same mind toward one another; do not be haughty in mind, but associate with the lowly. Do not be wise in your own estimation. Never pay back evil for evil to anyone. Respect what is right in the sight of all men. If possible, so far as it depends on you, be at peace with all men.
>
> Romans 12:9–18

Thinking of strong emotions, I am particularly drawn to those lines that state that when our brothers and sisters hurt, we hurt . . . we "weep with those who weep." Those are deep feelings that come from the Spirit of God, who is Himself moved over our sorrow.

While my wife and I were traveling abroad, we got word through a fax that two of her longtime, closest friends were seriously ill. One was in the final stage of her battle with cancer (she has recently died), and the other had had a massive stroke. I stood near and watched my wife as she read this message. Before she could even finish reading the words on that sheet, she broke into tears. A piece of paper communicated information from across the ocean, giving only a brief account of two good friends, but that was sufficient to cause her to sob. I took her into my arms and held her close as the Spirit of God "hovered over" her emotions while her heart was breaking. Miles separated her from these two friends she loved deeply. She was unable to be there, to touch them, to talk to them, to stroke their hair, or to embrace them. But she was able to cry her heart out as she felt the pain of loss, helplessness, and grief. The deep feeling she expressed came from the Spirit of God.

Unusual Feelings

Have you ever been annoyed with someone else? Yes, I'm sure everyone has. Let me show you how even that can come from God's Spirit. I'm thinking of an account in Acts 17 that records an incident that occurred during Paul's second missionary journey. The apostle had been engaged in evangelism up in Macedonia, and when he came down into Greece, he waited for his friends Silas and Timothy at Athens. And . . .

> while Paul was waiting for them at Athens, his spirit was being provoked within him as he was beholding the city full of idols.
>
> Acts 17:16

It has been said that in those days there were more idols in Athens than there were people. Imagine that. Such an overwhelming presence of idolatry "provoked" Paul, and that emotion became the spark that lit the fire in his belly. Deep within his soul he was burdened about the condition of that city. God gave him those feelings. The result?

> So he was reasoning in the synagogue with the Jews and the God-fearing Gentiles, and in the market place every day with those who happened to be present.
>
> Acts 17:17

Another unusual account appears in Acts 19, during the evangelization of Ephesus, a city of prominence in the first century. It was, however, a city given over to superstition and idolatry. So we shouldn't be surprised to read:

> And God was performing extraordinary miracles by the hands of Paul, so that handkerchiefs or aprons were even carried from his body to the sick, and the diseases left them and the evil spirits went out. But also some of the Jewish exorcists, who went from place to place, attempted to name over those who had the evil spirits the name of the Lord Jesus, saying, "I adjure you by Jesus whom Paul preaches." And seven sons of one Sceva, a Jewish chief priest, were doing this. And the evil spirit answered and said to them, "I recognize Jesus, and I know about Paul, but who are you?" And the man, in whom was the evil spirit, leaped on them and subdued all of them and overpowered them, so that they fled out of that house naked and wounded. And this became known to all, both Jews and Greeks, who lived in Ephesus; and fear fell upon them all and the name of the Lord Jesus was being magnified. Many also of those who had believed kept coming, confessing and disclosing their practices. And many of those who practiced magic brought their books together and began burning them in the sight of all; and they counted up the price of them and found it fifty thousand pieces of silver.

So the word of the Lord was growing mightily and prevailing.
Acts 19:11–20

What an incredible account! But so it goes when God's work is taking place and the enemy is being confronted. Isn't it interesting that the people were led to confess their secret lives and disclose their private practices of evil?

Have you ever been in a revival like that? I have seen it happen. I have witnessed occasions when the Spirit of God does such an effective work of cleansing that people can no longer contain their secret sins. When the Spirit works on the emotions of a person, hearts that were once calloused and hardened are softened, breeding a respect for God and a hatred of sin.

You may have known people who used to express their emotions and were colorful, enthusiastic types, stimulating to be around; then, because of an accident or a disease or a stroke, those same people became emotionally "deadened." The contrast is remarkable! I am thinking of a young man who was in a terrible auto accident. The lack of oxygen to his brain during his recovery precipitated damage that robbed him of his emotions. Prior to that tragic series of events, he was a quick, exciting, fun-loving, and responsive fellow everyone enjoyed being around. Today, his "emotionless" condition is heartbreaking to behold. When his father died several months ago, he communicated the fact to me—the day after it happened—with no more feeling than if he were mentioning the time of day or the weather that afternoon.

Though it may seem a quantum leap of comparison, I have witnessed a similar loss of emotion among those who enter seminary! Many enter those classrooms of theological learning full of zeal for the lost, a warm-hearted hunger for God, and a teachable, humble spirit. But unhappily, years later, many leave with an altogether different attitude and spirit. Something strange occurs during those years in the cloistered halls and under piles of books in the library. Instead of falling more deeply in love with Christ and others in the body, many seem to fall in love with learning and slowly slip out of touch with reality. Theological discussions and debates become more stimulating than being with real-world people and ministering to real-world needs. Instead of those seminary years heightening their enthusiasm, it kills it; instead of their growing knowledge of God humbling them further and making them aware of their own ignorance, it puffs them up, making them aloof, heady, dull, and dry. (If you think I'm exaggerating, ask their wives . . . visit with their children!)

This need not be, and it certainly is not the fault of learning theology, as some would suggest. And, I am exceedingly delighted to add, for some this emotional erosion never occurs. They remain warm, in touch, and gracious men and women of God. The problem rests with the learner, who substitutes theory for reality . . . and discounts the value of remaining balanced in mind and heart.

Some Necessary Warnings We Need to Heed

This is a good time for me to pause and mention three basic warnings so that our flying closer to the flame will take place without fear of getting our wings singed.

Intellectualism

Intellectualism is what we have just been talking about, but it is not reserved for seminary students. It can occur whenever we refuse to allow our emotions to serve their proper function. By holding them in constant check, by restraining the natural flow of our feelings, we can begin to rely strictly on the intellect for our walk with Christ. As Paul states so clearly, "knowledge makes arrogant" (1 Cor. 8:1).

In schools or churches where the Bible becomes a textbook for learning facts to the exclusion of having one's heart warmed and one's life changed, intellectualism crouches at the door, ready to seize its victims. It reminds me of the oft-heard warning: "Be careful that going to Bible school or seminary doesn't damage your faith!" It would probably be discouraging to know how many do lose their faith in the midst of a sterile, intellectual climate.

If we hope to counteract intellectualism, there must always be Spirit-filled warmth and a climate of devotion to the person of Christ. Staying real helps.

Emotionalism

This occurs when we go to the other extreme, making emotions the heart and center of life. Emotionalism results when one builds one's faith on the sands of experience rather than on the solid, reliable rock of faith based on facts. A life of solid faith starts with a clear understanding of biblical doctrine. Balance calls for both mind and heart . . . in that order. They need to be woven together carefully, slowly, and correctly like a God-given tapestry.

Fanaticism

Fanaticism occurs in a context of excessive and intense devotion to information that lacks balance, discernment, and wisdom. Fanatics become so enthralled with a teaching that the mind focuses solely on that while the emotions take control and one's actions become bizarre and unhealthy.

A classic example would be falling into the bondage of one of the cults. In these instances, a single authority figure requires blind loyalty. That person is not accountable or open to criticism or correction, and this exclusive spirit is often accompanied by paranoid reactions. There is an unwholesome lack of balance—including the absence of a healthy sense of humor—and the inability to enter into a broad spectrum of interests and activities.

This, of course, is not limited to the cults. Any one of us is able to fall into extremes and become fanatical, losing ourself in certain intense pursuits.

Convinced that that interest is the *only interest* worth pursuing, we can then become impatient with others because they are not as charged up as they should be about *our* single-minded concern. At that point our emotions get out of control, fuel the fire of zeal, and shout, "Full speed ahead!" This explains why fanatics become offensive without knowing it and how they can ignore basic responsibilities of life without concern. The subjects can be (and usually are) religious or doctrinal in nature, such as prophecy, the gifts of the Spirit, witnessing, prayer, legalism, freedom, knowledge (as an end in itself), some social concern, and a hundred other possibilities.

Be warned! When the Spirit of God is not in full control, there is the tendency in all of us—*and that includes you*—to go haywire emotionally. Wise are those who keep their balance . . . even when flying closer to the flame. Correction: *especially* when flying closer to the flame.

Some Traditional Sayings We Need to Clarify

I want to close this chapter by clarifying some traditional sayings. Since we started this chapter by mentioning a very common one, let me return to it first.

Never trust your feelings. As I said earlier, many of us were raised on that statement. But I think it needs to be tempered. It is the word *never* that I stumble over. Since peace, which is an emotion, is a part of the inner affirmation that God gives us when we are in the nucleus of His will, you and I *better* trust it! If you aren't comfortable with the word *trust,* then how about *being open* to it? We are instructed to "let the peace of Christ rule in your hearts" (Col. 3:15), so we certainly must give peace its due.

Another feeling we hear little about in Christian circles is intuition. This is the ability to perceive or know something without conscious reasoning. It is a very private emotion. Something inside of you churns, saying, "No, I wouldn't do that." Or it smiles and says, "Yes, this is good. This is what you ought to do—or at least *consider* doing."

One man tells me that he has learned over the years that the best way to lead his business is by intuitive leading. "I just know in my spirit when something is right or something is wrong," he says. And in case you are wondering, his business is doing exceedingly well.

To be sure, there needs to be seasoned wisdom along with keen discernment if we hope to operate intuitively. But even though it is a feeling, trusting is not all bad. There are times we *better* trust our feelings.

Experience proves nothing is another traditional saying. In fact, I used to say that myself, but I'm not nearly as dogmatic as I used to be. I have lived long enough to know that there are times when experience is extremely valuable and can certainly prove something. Something I experienced years ago comes to mind.

I have the dubious record of holding one of the shortest pastorates in the history of the church: I was the pastor of a church for less than twelve hours! Let me explain.

I was serving in one church when another church in a nearby city began pursuing me. I wasn't looking to change pastorates at that time, but they were interested in me. So Cynthia and I prayed and discussed the possibility, and I decided to look deeper into the situation. I had dinner with the chairman of the board, I got counsel from a few friends, and I thought carefully through the process. Finally, after I had spent some time with their board, I candidated. When we came to the night for the congregational vote, they voted yes. Everyone seemed delighted, including Cynthia and me.

As I recall, it was a unanimous vote. That's the way it ought to be, I thought, as Cynthia and I drove home late that evening. Yet I felt I should be more excited than I was, and I didn't say much to Cynthia in the car. She started talking about how we would need to sell our home and find another place to live. I said less and less. Once we got home I told her I was exhausted and dropped into bed . . . but sleep didn't come. My mind was whirling. I was miserable. Finally, shortly after dawn, I telephoned the chairman of the board.

"Bill?"

"Yes."

"Hey, I'm not coming."

"You're not what? You told us last night—"

"I know . . . I know. I have been your pastor for less than twelve hours. I'm no longer the pastor. The answer is no."

"Why?"

"I just don't feel right about it, Bill."

"Well, maybe we ought to talk about it."

And I knew we could talk about it until kingdom come, but I would not be changing my mind because I knew I should not go. I can't explain that. You know what it was? Primarily, my response was based on a series of feelings. I experienced a growing uneasiness, and I learned how valuable such an emotion can be. It was right! And I am so glad I finally submitted to my feelings.

That entire (somewhat embarrassing) experience proved something to me: that I can think at the moment something is right and later realize it is wrong.

Many years ago I had a woman say to me, "I remember saying to my father as I was walking down the aisle with him at my wedding, 'Daddy, I should not be here doing this.' And my daddy said, 'Keep walking, honey. Keep walking.'"

I am sure her father meant well, but that was the wrong answer. The marriage didn't last. Her feelings were right.

Now I know that feelings of panic often surface when one thinks about taking that final step toward marriage. But this young woman felt a deep inner reluctance . . . something was telling her that she should not be walking down that aisle, she should not be getting married to that man. Great guy. Fine gal. But not good for each other.

I understand uneasy feelings connected with weddings. I have had grooms almost vomit thinking about walking down the aisle. So we talk about it. Around 99 percent of the time, he's just nervous. But if a bride or groom is *really* sure it ought not to happen . . . cancel! Pay attention to feelings like that.

Such experiences can prove many things!

When it comes to experience, tradition also says: *Experience is the best teacher*. Let me add a word to that, and I'll accept the statement. *Guided* experience is the best teacher.

Experience alone is not the best teacher, but when we have been guided by someone who is reliable, it is the best teacher. If you don't agree with that, try laying a brick wall. I can always tell when I am standing next to a first-experience, homemade wall. The guy is always proud of it, but it looks horrible. If we want experience to teach its best lessons, having a guide helps.

Finally, tradition says: *Let your conscience be your guide*. Well, it all depends on the condition of your conscience! Sometimes one's conscience is reliable, sometimes not.

Conscience is like a compass. If a compass is faulty, you'll quickly get off course. A conscience gets its signals from the heart, which can be dulled, hardened, or calloused. Furthermore, a conscience can be overly sensitive or can even drive one mad.

Someone who has been reared by legalistic parents who used guilt and shame to manipulate their children often has a conscience that is overly sensitive. Some have consciences so twisted and confused, they need extensive help before they can start thinking correctly. Sometimes it takes the help of a good Christian therapist . . . someone who can help an individual with a shame-based conscience to understand how things got all fouled up. Sometimes a long-term friendship helps give grace to a conscience that has known only legalism. A conscience that is legalistic is not a good guide. A libertine conscience is not a good guide either, nor is a calloused conscience.

In order for one's conscience to be a good guide, one the Spirit can direct, it needs to be healthy, sensitive, and capable of getting God's message and truth.

This is a good time to add that the message of Christ is not devoid of emotions. When one realizes the true condition of the heart without God and ponders the impact of his or her sinfulness, there is an emotional reaction—greater in some than in others.

But there is an emotional reaction. *I have offended. I have grieved the heart of God. I have driven nails into Christ's hands with my sins.* That does something to my emotions when I, as a sinner, realize that. When the truth of forgiveness and grace and God's overwhelming love pour over me, there is an emotional reaction. And I must admit that. When I realize that God has reserved a home in heaven for me—a reprobate sinner who was running in the other direction when He stopped me, turned me around in grace, and brought me to Himself—that brings an emotional response. Don't deny those emotions!

And there are emotions on the journey from earth to heaven. When we come to the deathbed of a loved one, for example, feelings stream out as we think of that person's earthly departure . . . feelings of our loss on this earth . . . feelings of joy for them in heaven. Again, don't deny those feelings!

The music of the gospel is rich with emotion. Without those feelings, such music becomes little more than a professional performance. The message of the gospel is to be delivered with emotion, not just intellect. Otherwise, it becomes little more than a lecture. Church gatherings that restrain Spirit-led emotions can become dull and routine, perfunctory, lacking excitement, encouragement, and enlightenment.

God gave you a mind. Use it to know Him better. Study the doctrines that put steel into the cement of your faith. Exercise your mind!

God gave you a will. Use it to obey Him. Make decisions that honor Him and please Him. Exercise your will!

And God gave you emotions. Don't be afraid of them. Let them out. Allow your heart to show through. Exercise your emotions!

If we refuse to open up, to allow the full prism of His love and truth to shine through our lives, we will miss much of the color life has to offer.

> "I can't see, I can't see,"
> says the man who won't look.

Are there colors in the rainbow?
   Are the meadows still green?
Are flowers still blooming,
   and butterflies seen?

"I can't hear, I can't hear,"
   says the man who won't listen.
Have birds stopped their singing?
   The brooks lost their song?
Has music stopped playing,
   the symphonies gone?

"I don't feel, I don't feel,"
   says the man who won't care.
Aren't feelings but knowing
   of good things and bad?
Of caring for others
   of gladness and sad?

"There's no life, there's no life,"
   says the man who won't live.
Life is naught but what is sought;
   yes, life is simply living.
And life is not collecting things,
   life is really giving.

"I'm not loved, I'm not loved,"
   says the man filled with rage.
Isn't love just reflections
   of what you first give
For all of the others,
   with whom you must live?

"There's no God, there's no God,"
   says the man with no faith.
See God's hand in the stars
   in the skies.
In the prayers of a child,
   in your silent sighs.

—Anonymous

9

Thinking Theologically About Sickness and Healing

OURS IS A WORLD OF enormous pain and hurt.

Every one of us knows someone who is enduring an intensely difficult time of physical or emotional trauma—or both.

We know sincere people of faith who have prayed for healing in their lives . . . and still they suffer.

We are also aware that there are those today who claim to have been healed instantaneously. They tell remarkable stories of miracles; they attended a meeting where an individual with certain "powers" touched them or simply spoke to them and . . . *whoosh!* . . . the Spirit healed them of their affliction.

Why are some healed, while many—*in fact, most*—are not? Why can some look back and claim a miracle while others must endure excruciating years of exhausting pain?

Some would prefer to overlook this, shrugging it off simply as "some have faith, others don't." Many of us cannot do that, however. We believe in the living God just as much as those who claim healing. We certainly want to serve His Son and uphold the work of the Spirit with equal sincerity and with passion. Yet we wonder how some could be relieved of an affliction almost overnight, while others must live with pain through lingering years of their lives. I know people right now in the church where I serve who wait for God to touch their lives and bring them back to a place of health they once knew. I also know people who were so sick they were rapping on death's door, yet only months later experienced healing and relief. All of this creates a dilemma within us. Needing to find answers to things that don't make sense, we are driven to do serious study on this subject as set forth in Scripture.

Because this dichotomy between sudden miraculous healings and an absence of miracles is such an important subject, and because of the high level of interest in healing and miracles today, I want to spend the next three chapters addressing this matter head-on in hopes of determining how all this relates—or does not relate—to the Spirit.

Dr. John White, in a book entitled *When the Spirit Comes with Power,* begins by describing several different and unusual events. One occurs in Malaysia, another one in Ohio, and yet another in Argentina. He describes these events rather carefully. Each falls into the category of phenomena—things that occurred which could not be explained in keeping with human logic. The question is: Were those things of the Spirit or were they not? Dr. White summarizes the stories with these words:

> Asia. North America. South America. These are three stories that I know about personally. I could also recount episodes from Africa and Europe. And there appear to be hundreds, if not thousands, of similar occurrences around the globe. What does it all mean? What are these reports of extreme emotional reactions and unusual behavior currently observed around the world among Christians of various theological persuasions—reports of great weeping or laughter, shaking, extreme terror, visions, falling (or what is sometimes called "being slain in the Spirit"), being "drunk with the Spirit" and other revival experiences? Something is certainly going on, and that something seems potent. Is it revival? Is it from God?
>
> We must be cautious in evaluating new religious movements. Many new movements are mediocre and a few, extremely dangerous. False fire burns fiercely, an angel of light still spreads his wings, and the elect continue to be deceived.
>
> Too often, however, we rely on rumor to determine what is going on. Sometimes our fear causes us to condemn

> too quickly, especially concerning something new and spectacular. But is there a baby in the bath water? God himself has been known to act spectacularly so that there is always a danger of missing him in our skepticism. He is still at work in the world.[1]

We have already covered several intriguing subjects in this book on the Holy Spirit. I willingly and freely admit that I have not taken the "safe route." I have taken this risk because I, too, am unable to pass off many of these things with a shrug . . . or to simply claim that all the supernatural things I cannot explain are of the devil. Neither do I feel comfortable merely ignoring them. I have to think about them, and more often than not, I have to give answers that deal with that tough question: Why?

When issues like this arise, I must dig deeply into the Book of Truth to find reliable answers. And even then some of it remains vague, sometimes mysterious. Even one as gifted as Jonathan Edwards, the eighteenth-century intellectual and scholar who graduated from Yale (at age seventeen!) and became one of America's greatest philosophers and theologians, admitted this:

> And it has been very observable, that persons of the greatest understanding, and who had studied most about things of this nature, have been more confounded than others. Some such persons declare, that all their former wisdom is brought to nought, and that they appear to have been babes, who knew nothing.[2]

I confess to you, there are times I feel exactly like that! I will also freely admit that there are realms of this subject I do not know and probably never will know. And even after lengthy study, there are some things I simply can never explain with absolute certainty. But as we look at this together, hopefully some things regarding this matter of healing and miracles will become clearer. Yet I can assure you, some things will remain a mystery.

Before we begin, however, let me tell you why we must proceed with caution and why I want to be careful about what I write.

Second Corinthians 11 is a chapter written with passion by the apostle Paul to people he loved dearly and deeply. We can feel his passion simply by reading his words:

> For I am jealous for you with a godly jealousy; for I betrothed you to one husband, that to Christ I might present you as a pure virgin. But I am afraid, lest as the serpent deceived Eve by his craftiness, your minds should be led astray from the simplicity and purity of devotion to Christ.
>
> 2 Corinthians 11:2–3

Paul writes with the heart of a pastor, and I can certainly identify with that. Like Paul, I am intensely jealous for those whom I serve in ministry, for all those within the scope of our influence. Furthermore, his hope is my hope—to "present you as a pure virgin." I have had the privilege of leading some in our flock to Christ, introducing them to the joy of knowing God and walking with Him, and my heart is linked with them in their spiritual growth. But I agree with Paul: *I am afraid for many of them.* The thought of their being led astray greatly concerns me. I don't know of a pastor worth his salt who doesn't struggle with that same fear; namely, that his parishioners' "minds should be led astray from the simplicity and purity of devotion to Christ." Though I am not normally a worrier, I am more than slightly concerned over what people do with their pain, their brokenness, and especially their need for relief. Why? Because there are so many unbiblical and erroneous answers being offered which will only deceive, disillusion, disturb . . . and bring greater confusion.

Unfortunately, I have known individuals who have become so caught up in a pursuit of miracles that their devotion to Christ waned. My great hope is that this section of the book will keep that from happening in many lives.

Possible Sources of "Phenomenal Events"

I believe that miracles and healings—what we refer to as "phenomenal manifestations"—have four possible sources.[3]

First, *the manifestation could be self-induced.* This is another way of saying that the "miracle" or the "healing" could have a psychological explanation, in that it was either consciously or unconsciously self-induced.

For example, many people suffer from psychosomatic illnesses stemming from mental or emotional disturbances. When the mind or the emotions are healed, however, there is often a remarkable healing of the related physical ailment. Bodily pain or illnesses are erased simply by the removal of that which was troubling the individual.

Second, *the source of the manifestation could be highly charged, emotional meetings.* We could also call this category "mass hysteria" or "mass hypnosis." It is no secret that gifted speakers (especially preachers) can be extremely persuasive and accomplish amazing things with suggestible audiences. I have been in such meetings and watched it happen. In those situations the alleged "healing of the Spirit" is the result of brainwashing, mind-bending techniques employed by those who know how to move an audience.

Third: *The source could be satanic.* As we just read in 2 Corinthians 11, "the serpent deceived Eve." Paul's concern was that his friends in Corinth could have their minds led astray by the adversary's deceptive powers. Demonic forces love to ape the work of God. We must never forget that when Satan and his evil forces are involved in something, it is more often in the realm of light than in the realm of darkness!

Lucifer originally revealed himself as the angel of light, not the angel of darkness. He is not an ugly, grotesque creature with a red epidermis. On the surface he is an appealing, brilliant, persuasive, incredibly impressive being, as are his demons. He woos and wins people with logic and persuasive arguments and reasonable approaches. It looks right. It sounds good. It seems plausible. Yet it is still, at the core, satanic.

Even though the enemy of our souls may not prompt most phenomenal manifestations, no one can deny he is actively engaged in some.

Fourth, *the source could, in fact, be God.* Who could ever doubt God's power to heal? To deny that is to deny the Scriptures! He who creates life can certainly bring healing to it. Most evangelical Christians I know would not hesitate to say that the Lord heals. We have seen Him bring healing to fractured marriages, broken lives, and scarred emotions. Who of us would doubt then that He could heal physical and mental diseases? Why else do we pray for Him to intervene when we or someone we love gets sick?

I have a wonderful mental list of individuals whom I have known, prayed for, and stood with through times of great and threatening sicknesses. Today they are strong specimens of health. In many cases the attending physicians virtually gave up on them. I am convinced—and I assure you *they* are convinced—the Lord healed them. And so please do not close this book, toss it aside, and say with a sigh, "Swindoll does not believe that God heals." I do. I do with all my heart.

What I do not believe is that God has placed His healing powers in a few "anointed individuals" who claim to do divine healings. Nor do I believe that God is the source of all the proliferation of so-called healings today.

I realize that there are thousands of folks who sincerely believe it was the Lord who touched their lives and relieved their pain. My response is a cautious "perhaps He did . . . but maybe it wasn't God at all."

Foundational Facts Regarding Sin and Sickness

While I strongly advocate flying closer to the flame, I believe we must do so intelligently, cautiously, and wisely. Otherwise we can get burned. I know what I'm talking about having met and talked with many a "burn victim" in my years of pastoral ministry. It has been my observation that solid doses of sound theology could have prevented most of them from being consumed by error.

Those who search for reliable spiritual understanding must discipline themselves to think theologically. In the case of divine healing, we need to understand how God has put us together and how sin and sickness are interrelated. And as I examine the issues regarding sickness and healing, six facts seem essential to lay a solid theological foundation.

First: *Primarily, there are two types of sin—original and personal.*

Original sin is traced all the way back to the Garden of Eden, where Adam and Eve yielded to the temptation of the devil, fell into sin, and thereby lost their innocence. In their fall into sin, they introduced corruption—a spiritual pollution—that has permanently damaged humanity. This is called *Adamic sin*—or original sin—and it lies at the very core of our sin nature.

Ever since the Fall, it has been impossible to be born into this world without sin. We get it from our parents, who got it from theirs, who got it from theirs . . . all the way back to everyone's original parents, Adam and Eve. When Adam sinned, his act of disobedience polluted the stream of humanity, not unlike sewage waste pollutes a river.

> Therefore, just as through one man sin entered into the world, and death through sin, and so death spread to all men, because all sinned.
>
> Romans 5:12

Those words do not paint a very pretty picture, but the portrait is real nonetheless. The old hypothetical question: "If Adam and Eve had never sinned, would they have lived forever?" is answered easily: *Of course.* God's plan for them was a plan of innocence and perfection. His desire was that His created beings would walk with Him throughout their lives. His command, therefore, was that they not yield to the temptation to eat of the knowledge of the tree of good and evil.

> And the LORD God commanded the man, saying, "From any tree of the garden you may eat freely; but from the tree of the knowledge of good and evil you shall not eat, for in the day that you eat from it you shall surely die."
>
> Genesis 2:16–17

Adam and Eve disobeyed, and the consequences were tragic. Suffering, sickness, and death were introduced into the human race, all stemming from sin. Had there never been sin, there would never have been suffering or sickness or death. Remember the words?

> . . . and so death spread to all . . . because all sinned.
>
> Romans 5:12b

Because all humans have this Adamic nature within, we commit personal sins. Instead of obeying, we disobey. Instead of choosing to walk with God, we resist Him, we run from Him, we fight against Him. For,

> all have sinned and fall short of the glory of God.
>
> Romans 3:23

We are sinners by birth (original sin), and therefore we become sinners by choice (personal sin). In acting disobediently, we bear the fruit of our Adamic root. Because deceit rests in our nature, you and I deceive. Because disobedience rests in our nature, we rebel. Because lawlessness is at our inner core, we act it out in life.

I am not proud to admit it, but sometimes when a red light stays red longer than I think it should, I impatiently run it. I am not justifying my actions. On the contrary, I know in my mind I should not run it. It is dangerous—and it is against the law. But every once in a while I run a red light. Why? Because I am a rebel by nature. And before you start feeling a little smug, let me remind you, *so are you!* Your rebellion may just take another form.

There is original sin and there are personal sins. Both result in serious consequences.

Second: *Original sin introduced sickness, suffering, and death to the human race.*

> "The soul who sins will die."
>
> Ezekiel 18:4
>
> For since by a man came death, by a man also came the resurrection of the dead. For as in Adam all die, so also in Christ all shall be made alive.
>
> 1 Corinthians 15:21–22
>
> "Man, who is born of woman,
> Is short-lived and full of turmoil."
>
> Job 14:1

No one is immune from sin and its consequences. As beautiful and lovely as your little girl, boy, or grandchild may be, that child was born with a sin nature. And that nature not only prompts disobedience, it is the source of sickness, suffering, and ultimately death. Those things are a part of the "fallout" of the Adamic nature. They are interwoven in all of humanity.

Third: *Often there exists a direct relationship between personal sins and physical sickness.*

At times, disobedience and rebellious acts are directly linked to some illness in the body.

Numerous examples of this are found in the Scriptures. Among the most notorious would be King David after his affair with Bathsheba.

As a result of his sinful behavior, David suffered grave physical and emotional consequences. The struggle he went through while hiding his adultery (including the murder of Bathsheba's husband) and living as a hypocrite and rebel led to such a crescendo of inner turmoil that David became physically ill. After Nathan confronted David and the king came to terms with his sin, he wrote a song of remembrance . . . his own painful testimony of those months of misery:

> When I kept silent about my sin, my body wasted
> away
> Through my groaning all day long.
> For day and night Thy hand was heavy upon me;
> My vitality was drained away as with the fever-heat of
> summer.
>
> Psalm 32:3–4

David suffered intensely because he disobeyed God and then refused to face his sin. Guilt began eating away at him until it became so unbearable that he literally sighed and groaned as he was physically wasting away. He lost his appetite. He suffered from insomnia. He could not think clearly. He lost his energy. He suffered from a fever that wouldn't go away.

Imagine that kind of life. If you have ever been there, you don't need me to describe it. And while they may not have reached these proportions, most of us have known painful periods in our lives when we left our personal sins unaddressed and unconfessed. And the misery didn't leave until we dealt with our sin and disobedience. That is what happened to David:

> I acknowledged my sin to Thee,
> And my iniquity I did not hide;
> I said, "I will confess my transgressions to the LORD";
> And Thou didst forgive the guilt of my sin.
>
> Psalm 32:5

What was it that made him sick? Guilt. What drained his energy? Guilt. What took away his happiness, his smile, his ability to think, his leadership skills? Guilt. There was a direct relationship between David's personal sins and the physical and emotional sickness that impacted his life.

Another example would be something Paul refers to in one of his letters to the Corinthians when he instructs them about their inappropriate behavior at the Lord's Table. Some, if you can believe it, used this as an occasion for gluttony and drunkenness. The apostle's words of reproof are powerful:

> For this reason many among you are weak and sick, and a number sleep.
>
> 1 Corinthians 11:30

In other words, their sin had resulted in weakness and sickness . . . and even in death!

Now remember, in such cases, the confession of sin begins the process of healing. The recovery may not be instantaneous (it usually isn't), but I have seen occasions when it has been. More often than not, however, the suffering begins to fade in intensity as the person experiences relief from guilt.

Fourth: *Sometimes there is no relationship between personal sins and human afflictions.*

This is a good time for me to caution you about being the messenger of God to every person who is ill, telling them, "There must be something wrong in your life." Occasionally you may be the appointed Nathan in some David's life. You may be the appointed one to say, "You are the man," or "You are the woman." But seldom do we have a right to say that. Because in many cases suffering or illness is not the result of personal sin.

A classic example of this would be the man who was born blind (referred to in John's Gospel). His congenital blindness had nothing to do with personal sins, either his own or his parents'.

> And as He passed by, He saw a man blind from birth. And His disciples asked Him, saying, "Rabbi, who sinned, this man or his parents, that he should be born blind?" Jesus answered, "It was neither that this man sinned, nor his parents; but it was in order that the works of God might be displayed in him.
>
> John 9:1–3

Jesus Himself states clearly that the man's physical affliction had nothing to do with personal sins.

Hebrews 4:14–15 also comes to mind.

> Since then we have a great high priest who has passed through the heavens, Jesus the Son of God, let us hold fast our confession. For we do not have a high priest who cannot sympathize with our weaknesses, but one who has been tempted in all things as we are, yet without sin.

If our weaknesses were always the result of sin, the writer would issue the command: "Confess your sins and you will be healed." But he says here, in effect, "Seeing us struggling with weaknesses, our Lord is moved over our affliction. He is touched with our struggles." He *doesn't* say, "Therefore, deal with the sin in your life and you will recover." On the contrary, His heart is moved over your pain. He grieves with you over the length of your depression. He sits alongside you in the hospital room as you live with the consequences of this dread malignancy . . . He is with you as you go through chemotherapy. He is touched with feelings of sympathy for you in your weaknesses.

Why? Because on these occasions there is no direct relationship between personal sins and sicknesses. Therefore, it is not a matter of confessing sins and claiming instant healing.

I have known people who have been gravely ill and have searched their heart to find whatever sin may have brought on their affliction. They confess and confess and confess. But their illness doesn't leave. Slowly, painfully, they waste away, wondering what they could have done that caused their sickness . . . when, in fact, their condition was not related to personal sin at all.

Fifth: *Sometimes it is not God's will that we be healed.*

Paul had the supernatural gift of healing that God gave the apostles. Yet he admits, "Trophimus I left sick at Miletus" (2 Tim. 4:20). Why was he "left sick"? Paul doesn't say, but if it were God's will that all be healed, that would not have occurred.

Then, in Philippians, we learn of a man named Epaphroditus who received God's mercy, even as his illness remained.

> Because he was longing for you all and was distressed because you had heard that he was sick. For indeed he was sick to the point of death, but God had mercy on him, and not on him only but also on me, lest I should have sorrow upon sorrow.
>
> Philippians 2:26–27

Here is a man who was sick—in fact, sick to the point of death—yet Paul, who had the gift of healing, was helpless to turn things around. Ultimately, God did have "mercy on him," but there was no instant turnaround in his condition.

Finally, consider Paul himself.

> And because of the surpassing greatness of the revelations, for this reason, to keep me from exalting myself, there was given me a thorn in the flesh.
>
> 2 Corinthians 12:7

The apostle suffered from a severe affliction—"a thorn in the flesh." The Greek term translated "thorn" means a sharp stake. Whatever it was, it brought piercing pain. Paul calls it a messenger of Satan (obviously allowed by God) to keep him genuinely humble.

Pain does that. You don't meet many arrogant people who are living with lingering pain. Pain buffets us. It breaks and humbles us.

And Paul says, "Concerning this." Concerning what? The thorn! The thorn!

> Concerning this I entreated the Lord three times that it might depart from me.
>
> 2 Corinthians 12:8

Time after time he pleaded for relief. When the pain reached the unbearable stage, this devoted servant of God begged God to take it away. Three times he made the same request: Heal me. Heal me. Heal me. Each time God's answer remained firm. No. No. No.

I repeat . . . sometimes it is not God's will that we be healed. Therefore, be very careful what you promise a person who is sick. If it were God's will for all people to be well, then there would be no sick people in the world. Or if it were the Lord's will to heal all those in His family, not one Christian would be ill.

Think biblically. Think theologically. If passages like this (and others) make a point clear, accept the truth, seek to understand it, and then apply it! God is there. Just because He chooses not to bring healing does not mean He has forsaken us. He is with us through the hardest time. His grace is still sufficient.

Sixth: *On some occasions it is God's will that we be healed.*

Since I plan to spend the next chapter dealing with this point, for now let's just take a quick glance at several verses in James 5.

> Is anyone among you suffering? Let him pray. Is anyone cheerful? Let him sing praises. Is anyone among you sick? Let him call for the elders of the church, and let them pray over him, anointing him with oil in the name of the Lord; and the prayer offered in faith will restore the one who is sick, and the Lord will raise him up, and if he has committed sins, they will be forgiven him.
>
> James 5:13–15

Yes, there are times when our Lord sovereignly chooses to "restore the one who is sick." This is His prerogative. As we shall see, when He miraculously intervenes, the healing is immediate, thorough, and permanent. And when that happens, He alone deserves the praise—never some human instrument.

I have heard it said that education is going from an unconscious to conscious awareness of one's ignorance. That statement applies to the Scriptures just as much as it does to life in general. Education in the Word of God awakens me to the vast realm of my ignorance. And I tend to back away and become less dogmatic about a lot of things once I become aware of this magnificent God whom I love and serve.

Flying closer to the flame does not remove all the mysteries contained in His will.

10

A Biblical Case for Healing

SOMETHING OCCURRED IN FEBRUARY 1975 that I will never forget. Cynthia and I, along with a number of alumni from Dallas Theological Seminary, were returning from the school's fiftieth anniversary celebration.

Back in those days they flew 747s between Dallas and the West Coast, and on this particular flight there were a number of empty seats in the large coach section. Our group was having a delightful time, reminiscing and laughing, telling stories from our student days. Perhaps it was our own high spirits that first made us notice the sad-looking couple several rows behind us. The woman was sitting near the aisle, but her husband was lying down, stretched out across four or five of the seats in the center section.

As we walked back and forth during the flight—getting something to drink or going to the bathroom—we made conversation with several passengers, including this couple. Both were friendly but extremely serious, and he did not look well. When the woman discovered that the people in our group were former classmates at a seminary and were now involved in various kinds of ministry, her interest in us heightened. And that's when she told us their story.

They were from Louisiana, she said, and her husband was deathly ill with cancer. They had been in touch with a famous "faith healer" on the West Coast (whom you would know if I named the person), and they had been promised that if they would come to Los Angeles and bring money, the so-called healer could guarantee her husband's relief from pain. When they returned to Louisiana, he would no longer have the cancer.

They were not "church people," as she put it, but they had watched this religious person on television. They had seen all the "wonders" and "healings" and "miracles" on television. By now, they were down to very few options. Together, they had agreed that this was what they should do.

The two of them were stacking all their hopes on that single promise, and to make certain they would have enough money, they sold everything they owned, including their home. They also had depleted their entire retirement savings. In fact, she showed me the bag of cash in her purse. (She mentioned that the contacts in the healing ministry had requested she bring cash.)

Through tears, she sighed, "I am willing to give up everything we own in order that my husband might be healed." Then she looked into my eyes, obviously longing for reassurance, and asked, "What do you think of such things?"

I'm sure you can appreciate the delicate and awkward silence that passed between us. My answer required tact mixed with honesty. Silently I prayed for just the right words. Then I opened my Bible and shared with her the things I believed. The woman listened carefully. Her husband tried to enter into our conversation, but he was obviously so ill that he was almost fading in and out of consciousness.

I mentioned my reservations and especially my concern regarding the depletion of all their savings. I restrained from unloading my strong convictions against paying someone for "doing a miracle." I did, however, try to explain my interpretation of what the Scriptures teach regarding healing versus healers.

She sighed and said, "I don't mean this the wrong way, but I hope you are wrong, because we have tried everything else. We believe God has led us to do this."

As we concluded our conversation, I said, "I'll tell you what: Here is my name, the address of the church I pastor in Fullerton, and my phone number." I also scribbled my home phone number on the little card I gave her. "Will you promise me that if your husband is healed, you will call me?"

With a smile she said, "Absolutely. I will call you, and you and I can celebrate."

I assured her, "I will truly celebrate with you," and then I prayed with the two of them shortly before our plane landed.

That was almost twenty years ago. I'm still waiting for her call.

Do I believe God can heal? With my whole heart! Do I believe God does heal? Absolutely. Have I seen cases where God has healed? Yes, I have, and I will mention a couple of them in this chapter.

Now the critical question: Do I believe God has placed His healing powers in a few "anointed individuals" who claim to do divine healings? I say, unequivocally, I do not. In fact, I don't think I have ever ministered to any more disillusioned souls than those who had been promised healing by an alleged "healer" and then were not healed.

In this day of the resurgence of so-called divine healers, my convictions may not represent a popular position. I realize that. In no way does this mean, however, that I do not believe God has the power to heal . . . and, on unique occasions, He does do so. I believe that with all my heart. The problem comes when attention is focused on a person who claims healing powers, or on the series of emotionally overpowering events that surround a so-called healing service. If those "divine healers" are authentic and "anointed" miracle workers of God, why aren't they out going floor-to-floor in hospitals and emergency wards? Why don't they prove the truth of their ministry there . . . humbly . . . unobtrusively . . . free of charge? Then I would have reason to believe they are servants of the living God in whose lives the Spirit is consistently pouring out His power to heal.

The all-powerful, living God certainly has the power to heal. However, in His inscrutable plan He has not removed all suffering, sickness, disease, and death from this world. I do not pretend to know why He sovereignly chooses to heal this one and not that one . . . a few and not all. But that is His choice; that is His right. I must minister to both. And ultimately, of course, even those who are healed at some point in their life must face the death of their earthly body. As someone has remarked, "We're all terminal!"

There are times when it is God's will that someone be healed, and when that is true, He does so miraculously and immediately. Be sure that you remember those two words, for they go together. When God is involved in the healing, it is both *immediate* and it is *miraculous.* Furthermore, it is free . . . as free as the gift of eternal life.

Remember when Peter and John happened upon the man crippled from birth who sat beside the temple begging? The man was hoping for a few shekels, but Peter said to him:

> "I do not possess silver and gold, but what I do have I give to you: In the name of Jesus Christ the Nazarene—walk!"
>
> Acts 3:6

And the man stood up and walked. Immediately! Miraculously! Freely! No one in that community had ever seen him walk before . . . yet he walked. And there is every reason to believe he remained permanently healed, for God's miraculous work in a person's life is *permanent.*

Back in the late 1950s I became close friends with a man who had been a fellow marine. Our friendship deepened as time passed, even though miles separated us. I was ministering in the state of Massachusetts, and he lived in Texas. Then one day I received a call from him.

"I need your prayers as I've never needed them before," he said in a rather grim voice. My immediate response was: "What is it?"

He said, "I have been diagnosed as having cancer of the tongue." Though he didn't cry easily, his voice broke as he continued. "I have been to the best medical specialists I can find here in the city of Dallas. They are all convinced it is cancer." He had also gotten a second opinion. And a third. They suggested he go to the Mayo Clinic in Rochester, Minnesota, so he and his wife were making the trip, carrying his x-rays with them. They were hoping, with the help of the doctors at the Mayo Clinic, he could at least come out of the surgery with a portion of his tongue.

"I'm asking you and about four other close friends to pray," he said. "Would you and Cynthia pray fervently for me?" He added, "I'm not announcing the need. I know that God can bring healing if it is His will, so let's pray for that. *Let's ask the Spirit of God to heal me!*" He assured me he had nothing sinful in his life that could have caused this to occur. "All I know is that the doctor says I have this malignant tumor. It is clearly evident in the x-rays. I just want you to pray that God, if it is His perfect will, will do a miracle." I assured him we would certainly pray with and for him.

As soon as I hung up the phone, I walked down the stairs to a little place in our basement where I would often go for quietness and prayer. Cynthia prayed with me for a while, then left to care for our children who were still small. I stayed for almost an hour, and as I prayed, God's "unidentified inner prompting" gave me an unusual sense of reassurance. I did not hear any voice. I did not see any vision. But I had an unusual feeling of confidence and a sense of peace about my friend's situation. I read several Scriptures, prayed for perhaps forty-five minutes, then I left it with God.

Two or three days later my phone rang again. I heard the voice of my friend on the other end of the line. By then he was in Minnesota, calling me from the Mayo Clinic.

"I have great news," he said.

I smiled to myself. "Well, what is it?"

"I have seen several specialists, and my wife and I have just met with our attending physician. He is baffled, Chuck. He tells us there is no cancer."

"Hey, this is great!" I replied. "Tell me what they said."

"Well," he responded, "actually they put me through all the tests again and took more x-rays. They don't believe I brought the correct x-rays with me, because the x-rays they took disagree so much with the ones I brought. I now have before me two sets of x-rays. One shows the cancer in the tongue as it was in Dallas. The other x-rays, taken here in Minnesota, are clear—no cancer." And with a touch of humor he continued, "So we had a remarkable flight from Dallas to Minnesota. Somehow, in some miraculous manner, the malignant tumor is nowhere to be found."

It was not only miraculous, it was also instantaneous, and it remained permanent. He never again had a problem with the pain or the growth in his tongue. My friend was a middle-aged man and had many wonderful years in front of him, which he lived to the fullest. His subsequent death—many years later—was brought on by an unrelated disease.

I can't explain what happened. He couldn't either. I have no powers within me that produce healing in anyone else. The God I know is the same God you know, and I simply trusted Him and prayed for His will to be done. The Spirit of God healed my friend sovereignly and silently. And best of all, God got all the glory.

Following the Steps Prescribed in Scripture

I find it curious that most folks take their cues from televangelists and other religious public figures rather than the Bible when it comes to seeking divine healing. I find it even more curious in light of the sideshow tactics of these performers. I remember seeing—on one of the rare occasions when I've tuned in—one rather popular individual sling his suit coat against the sick and the crippled and blow his breath on them. While his audience screamed and applauded, I flinched and grieved, thinking, *What kind of a show is this?* As I watched one person after another suddenly keel over, I wondered, *Who originated the strange idea that that's what it means to be "slain in the Spirit"?*

But what I really wonder is why folks don't follow the prescribed steps spelled out in the Scriptures instead of joining in the theatrics of the media circus? Without meaning to sound harsh, who canceled out the inspired guidelines and substituted the current script and style? I'm serious. Why do so many evangelical Christians adopt all the fleshly pizazz and ignore the simple one-two-three process described in the New Testament? Could it be they just don't know? Perhaps.

I'm referring to the instructions set forth in James 5:13–16. If you have never given serious thought to these words, and if you sincerely wish to pursue the Spirit's healing work in your life, please read the rest of this chapter slowly and carefully. Set aside all the other stuff you have heard and witnessed on television . . . and focus your full attention on God's inspired instructions.

> Is anyone among you suffering? Let him pray. Is anyone cheerful? Let him sing praises. Is anyone among you sick? Let him call for the elders of the church, and let them pray over him, anointing him with oil in the name of the Lord; and the prayer offered in faith will restore the one who is sick, and the Lord will raise him up, and if he has committed sins, they will be forgiven him. Therefore, confess your sins to one another, and pray for one another, so that you may be healed. The effective prayer of a righteous man can accomplish much.
>
> James 5:13–16

Those Who Are "Suffering"

Clearly, James sets forth three categories of people in the church. First, there are those whom he identifies simply as suffering—"Is anyone among you suffering?" There is nothing more said to the "suffering" than, "Let him pray."

Intrigued by the term *suffering,* I did a quick search on the Greek term *kakopatheia* and discovered it is used in this form only here in the New Testament. Actually it is used in one other form only three times, and on those occasions it is found in 2 Timothy, Paul's last letter. Each of the three times Paul uses it, it is translated "suffer hardship." I found that the word means "to be the brunt of mistreatment, to be suffering from persecution, from misunderstanding, to be suffering from hard times or difficult times." The original word does not refer to a physical disease.

Our friends who lost their homes in the terrible rains and fires and earthquakes out here in California went through ***kakopatheia*** . . . hard times. Individuals who are experiencing persecution at work because of their faith are enduring ***kakopatheia***. They are going through hardship. Those going through such times are instructed to pray. That's it. They are not promised anything special—not even assured that the pain will pass or that the suffering will stop. But in the praying, new strength comes to the petitioner, strength to endure, the ability to withstand hardship. So when such external difficulties occur, the very best answer is to pray . . . tap into the source of invincible power!

Those Who Are "Cheerful"

The second category is the antithesis of suffering: "Is anyone cheerful?" Happily, there are always a few who are cheerful. What are they to do? "Let him sing praises!" We are instructed not to hold back our praise.

I get so weary of somber Christians who look like they have been baptized in lemon juice—like it's borderline carnal to laugh and have a great time, to sing heartily and enjoy the overflowing blessings of God.

I have spent some time with Christians who have been blessed with prosperity. When we are together they are cheerful and full of praise. But they often say that they haven't the freedom to express their joy openly. "We don't dare let anybody know that it has been a marvelous year for us. We don't let the word out that our business is doing great." Such prosperity is considered taboo in many Christian circles. Nonsense! When the Lord blesses someone else abundantly, we should rejoice with him or her without feeling that He must bless us in the same way before we can do so. May the Lord give us such maturity and grace.

Being cheerful is not limited to those who are prosperous. I have known cheerful Christians in every walk and circumstance of life. To all who are cheerful, regardless of anything external, James says, "Let him sing praises." Let the joyful times roll!

Those Who Are "Sick"

This third category is the one we will focus on for the balance of this chapter: "Is anyone among you sick?" The term translated "sick" is the Greek word *astheneo,* which means "to be weak, to be without strength." It suggests even "to be disabled, to be incapacitated." This is talking about a serious illness, not merely a headache or chronic backache or twenty-four-hour flu.

The man we met on the airplane back in 1975 would qualify. He was so sick they had to transport him off the plane in a wheelchair. He was *astheneo.*

Now let's walk, step-by-step, through the procedure described here in James 5. Remember, this is based on inspired instructions from the Spirit of God as He moved upon James to write these things.

First, *the sick person takes the initiative.*

> Is anyone among you sick? Let him [let the sick one] call for the elders of the church . . .
>
> James 5:13

Often the elders and other church leaders are the last to know when someone is sick. Sometimes parishioners who are ill feel neglected and even think that pastors and elders really don't care when, in fact, they have never been told!

Let me make it very clear: There is no massive crystal ball in a pastor's study. There is no all-knowing computer that reads out all the names of the congregation on a daily basis and puts those who are feeling bad in flashing lights. I don't mean to make light of this. My point is that the only way for pastors or elders to know anyone is seriously ill is for someone to communicate that need.

Second, *when the elders arrive, they carry out two functions.* Before describing those dual functions, let me point out a particular construction in the original Greek sentence that will help clarify this part of the healing procedure. It is found in verse 14, which reads, *literally:*

> Is anyone among you sick? Let him call for the elders of the church, and let them pray over him, *having anointed him with oil* in the name of the Lord [emphasis mine].

Yes, the instructions are to be followed in the correct order: "let them pray over him, having anointed him with oil." The anointing with oil, therefore, would *precede* the time spent in prayer. Stay with me. As you see the passage unfold, you will understand the significance of this.

There are two Greek words for "anoint." One always has a religious and ceremonial connotation; the other, a practical one. David's head was anointed with oil before he came to the throne of Israel . . . a ceremonial anointing, acknowledging that he was the king-elect. However, you would never tell someone that you "anointed" your bike with oil because it was squeaking . . . or that you "anointed" your sewing machine with oil. Such a procedure is practical. It has no religious connotation at all. Now, of the two words, it is the latter that is used here, the practical one. "Anointing," therefore, is not really a good rendering of the original term. "Rubbing" would be a better translation.

When the Good Samaritan stopped and took care of the man who had been beaten along the road to Jericho, he poured oil and wine into the man's wounds. He "rubbed" those ingredients into the man's wounds. The same term appears in ancient Greek medical treatises where oil was prescribed for the purpose of medication. All of this may seem like needless and tedious detail, but in fact these things are basic to an accurate understanding of God's inspired instructions.

"Anoint" here refers to the practical application of proper medicine, or, in today's terms, to the appropriate professional help as well as prescribed medication. In other words, "See your doctor and follow his instructions." That comes first. *Then,* after appropriate medical attention, there is to be prayer.

I'll tell you how strongly I believe in following this process. I find it very hard to pray for someone who refuses to consult a doctor and follow his or her orders . . . or who refuses to take the medication that is prescribed . . . or who refuses the therapy recommended. Unlike the so-called divine healers, I believe it is biblical for those who are seriously ill not only to seek medical attention, but to do that *first.*

Those seeking miracles, first and foremost, often consider the consulting of a physician as an unwillingness to trust God. Such an extremist position is not only unwise, it is unbiblical. Back in ancient days, because there were so few medical doctors, it fell upon the elders to apply appropriate medication, such as oil applied to the body, or whatever may have been necessary. Medical assistance is not an enemy of the healing process.

A man I have admired from a distance is Dr. C. Everett Koop, the former United States surgeon general. In a book entitled *The Agony of Deceit,* Dr. Koop writes the chapter, "Faith-Healing and the Sovereignty of God." He begins by declaring:

> I don't know how many operations I actually performed in my surgical career. I know I performed 17,000 of one particular type, 7,000 of another. I practiced surgery for thirty-nine years, so perhaps I performed at least 50,000 operations.[1]

That gives you some idea of his enormous experience in the disciplines of medicine. He continues:

> A surprising number of Christians are convinced God will not be believed unless He makes tumors disappear, causes asthma to go away, and pops eyes into empty sockets. But the gospel is accepted by God-given faith, not by the guarantee that you will never be sick, or, if you are, that you

> will be miraculously healed. God is the Lord of healing, of growing, of weather, of transportation, and of every other process. Yet people don't expect vegetables without plowing. They don't expect levitation instead of getting in a car and turning a key—even for extraordinarily good and exceptional reasons.
>
> Although God *could* do all of this, Christian airline pilots do not fly straight into a thunderstorm after asking God for a safe corridor, although He could give them such safety. We do not have public services and ask God to remove all criminals, prostitutes, and pornographers from our midst, although He *could* do that too. God could eliminate AIDS from our planet. While we pray for a speedy discovery of successful treatment, I must do all I can to employ medical science in its task, as all health care professionals must do.[2]

In my opinion, not enough is said from evangelical pulpits regarding those who serve the sick in the field of medicine—physicians, nurses, therapists, you name it. What a fine and necessary body of caring people. But they are not miracle workers. They do not pretend to be. But they have received careful training and therefore have wisdom and understanding needed by those who are sick. And many of them who are Christians have a quiet, sincere appreciation for the presence of God in the midst of their profession. While there may be a few who are unqualified and uncaring, they do not represent the majority in the medical field. If our Lord cared enough about medication to mention it in a passage such as this, it certainly should be honored and applied in our age of advanced technology.

In the process of finding relief from sickness, medical assistant and proper medication play an important role. Remember, however, following the oil, they were to pray. Being men of faith, genuinely committed to God's will being carried out, the elders would have prayed fervently, believingly, offering up strong, confident, and yet humble prayers of intercession.

Third: *Specific results are left in the Lord's hands.* His will was sought, not the empty promises of some earthly individual.

> . . . let them pray over him, anointing him with oil *in the name of the Lord* [emphasis mine].

Don't overlook those last few words. Doing something "in the name of the Lord" was a colloquialism in that day for "the will of God." Today we might say, "Have them apply the oil, then pray for the will of God." And the result?

> . . . and the prayer offered in faith will restore the one who is sick.

Be careful not to yank that statement out of its context and quote it alone. Verses 14 and 15 are inseparably woven together in the same piece of biblical tapestry. The elders are praying over this person in the name of the Lord—that is, invoking God's will, asking God's presence, God's blessing—and the result? Actually, it's in God's hands. When it is His sovereign will to bring healing, it will occur. And in that case, "the prayer offered in faith will restore the one."

The Greek word here translated "restore" is *sozo.* It means "to save." So the prayer offered in faith will literally save the sick person's life. Why? Because in that case it is God's will for healing to occur.

> . . . and the Lord will raise him up, and if he has committed sins, they will be forgiven him.

There is another important term here: "The Lord *will raise* him up." This looks miraculous to me . . . a case of instantaneous healing. And don't overlook the additional comment: "if he has committed sins, they will be forgiven him."

Perhaps the person's past was marked by sins—extended, serious sins. If this is the root of the problem, there will be an admission of it in the process of the healing. Remember the third "foundational fact" in the previous chapter? There is often a direct relationship between personal sins and physical sickness.

This reminds me of an experience I had many years ago when I was ministering at a church in another city. The person who was seriously ill was a believer who happened to be the wife of a medical doctor. She suffered from terrible, almost unbearable pain all across her back. Physicians could not find the cause. Several competent orthopedic specialists worked together on her case, all to no avail. Then they wondered, could the pain be the result of some psychological struggle? A psychiatrist was consulted; still no relief. She sought neurological counsel as well. Perhaps the problem was centered in the spine, the nervous system. Again they were unable to find the answer.

Her incredible pain had led the physicians to begin intense medication that could become habit forming, and her husband was very concerned about that, naturally, as was she. Finally, they hospitalized the woman.

Because we were longtime friends, she contacted me and asked, "I wonder, Chuck, if you could get together a group of the elders from the church and if several of you could come and pray?" I responded, "Certainly we'll come." And we went, about six or seven of us.

We walked into her hospital room on a Sunday night following the evening service. She was in such pain she could hardly talk. "I don't know what I'm going to do," she said. "I'm getting desperate." Her husband was on call that night, so he was not there when we arrived; he came in later as we were praying. I talked with her briefly about the medication and the assistance she was getting. She had no complaints. She felt everyone was doing all they could do. She asked, "What can *we* do? What can we *do?*" I replied, "We can do what God instructed us to do . . . *pray*. We will pray that if it is His sovereign will, He will save you, restore you, raise you up!"

We closed the door, turned the lights down, and several of us dropped to our knees and began to pray. I finished my prayer by pleading with God to bring relief and, if it were His will, to bring full restoration. As another man began to pray, the woman reached down and touched me on the shoulder. She was pushing on me, as if she wanted to say something. I reached over to the man who was praying and took him by the knee and held tightly, as if to say, "Wait a minute." He stopped. Spontaneously, she said, "Excuse me for interrupting, but the pain is all gone." And she began to weep. Several of us wept as well. We were so grateful to God at that moment.

"I must tell all of you something," the woman said, and she sat up in bed—something she had not been able to do for days. Actually I think she could have gotten up and walked out of the hospital, stepped into her car, and driven home that night. The pain was completely gone. She said, "I need to tell you something about my life." Quietly, yet without hesitation, she began to unfold a story of sin that had been a part of her lifestyle. It is not necessary that I go into the details . . . only to say that she had been living a life of deception before us as well as before her family. But there had been something compelling about our prayer and the sincerity of our faith gathered around her that brought her to such a burning awareness of her sin she couldn't even let us finish. God heard her prayer of confession and desire for repentance.

Let's not miss verse 16:

> Therefore, confess your sins to one another, and pray for one another, so that you may be healed. The effective prayer of a righteous man can accomplish much.

This does not refer to a general public acknowledgment before the whole church of every dirty, lustful thought you have had in the last week. That is not the context. The verse refers to a person who is ill and who knows that he or she is living a lifestyle that is wrong and therefore needs to bring that out into the open, to confess it to those who are spiritually concerned and praying for him or her. The result? Cleansing within . . . healing without.

My friend was released from the hospital the next day; she never returned. In less than a week, she was jogging, enjoying full, pain-free health. And to my knowledge she never had the pain again. She wrote me on two occasions to thank me again and again, though I deserved no thanks. All I did—along with a group of like-minded men—was do what God's Word instructed and counted on God to do His will. And in that case, it was to raise her up . . . miraculously and instantaneously.

As a small group of individuals who had no "healing gifts" prayed and asked God to intervene, He did. It was God who did the healing. When we discovered that the proper "oil" had been applied, there was nothing left to do but get as close to the flame as possible . . . and *pray.*

Four Practical Principles to Claim

As we carefully work our way through these instructive verses, several timeless principles emerge, all of which are worth claiming today.

1. *Confession of sin is healthy—employ it.* When you find that you are wrong, say it. When you have done something offensive to another person, admit it. Confess it to God and then find the person you have hurt and confess it to that person. Full confession can lead to full restoration.

2. *Praying for one another is essential—practice it.* When someone says, "Will you pray for me?" take the request to heart. Don't just glibly respond, "Oh, yeah, sure," then promptly forget about it. Ask for some details. Write down the specific requests. I have a little notepad on my desk in my study, and when someone requests prayer, I write down the person's name and needs. I won't remember if I don't write it down. Later on, I like to follow up and ask if God has answered prayer.

3. *Medical assistance is imperative—obey it.* Regardless of the ailment, the nature of the illness, or the excuses you may be tempted to use to cut that corner, seeking medical assistance is

both wise and helpful. And when the physician prescribes or suggests—obey!

4. *When healing comes from God—claim it.* Praise Him for it. Don't give credit for your healing to some person on this earth. God alone is responsible for your relief. Healing doesn't come because you pay someone for it or stand in line for it or appear before some individual who claims he or she is able to do it. Healing comes because God sovereignly and mysteriously chooses to say yes to you. It falls under the heading of undeserved favor—GRACE.

I close by quoting Dr. Everett Koop once again:

> The faith healer may say that faith makes God act. If you follow that line of reasoning, God is in His heaven, but Bosworth rules the world! In Matthew 8:2–3, where Jesus heals a leper, we read:
>
> > Behold, a leper came and worshiped Him, saying, "Lord, if You are willing, You can make me clean." Then Jesus put out His hand and touched him, saying, "I am willing; be cleansed." And the leper departed. *And slowly, over the course of the next several weeks, his symptoms began to disappear.*
>
> I am sure you realize that this is not what the Bible says. I put it in those terms because that conforms to a lot of "miraculous healings" today. The healing takes place next month. But what the Word of God says is this: "'I am willing; be cleansed.' And *immediately* his leprosy was cleansed" (NKJV, italics added).
>
> Now I know that all healing comes from God, but if we are to pursue this matter of faith healing so that I do not have any questions, this is what I want to see: I want to see a person with one leg suddenly ("immediately") have two. In fact, I want to see a person cold, flat-out dead, get up and walk. Now it is not that I want to see these miracles take place just to satisfy my own curiosity. I want to see them happen in such a way that there is no praise attributed to the faith healer. And I want to see it done in a situation that is not a

> carnival. Now if all of those conditions were in place, I suspect that a healing service would occur very much in private. . . .
>
> Giving that great Reformed theologian from Princeton, B. B. Warfield, credit for his contribution to my thinking on this subject, let me summarize in the following way. There is no promise anywhere in the Scriptures of miraculous healing for those who will claim it. Anywhere. No facts exist that compel us to believe that such miraculous healing should be expected. Such *miraculous* healing is unnecessary, because God is perfectly capable of healing people by natural means. The employment of such a method is contrary to the way God works in other modes of dealing with us. Miraculous healings of the type I have been describing would be contrary to the very purpose of "miracle." If miracles were commonplace, they would soon lose their significance.[3]

Yes, God does heal. And when He does, it is miraculous . . . immediate . . . permanent . . . and free. It's all in His hands. But don't look for healings around every corner. God's not in the sideshow business. After all, "if miracles were commonplace, they would soon lose their significance."

11

When the Spirit Brings a Slow Recovery

HIPPOCRATES WAS A GREEK physician considered by many to be "the Father of Medicine." It was he who wrote the Hippocratic Oath taken by all those entering the practice of medicine. He lived about 450 to 375 B.C., which made him a contemporary of such philosophers as Socrates, Dionysius, Plato, and Aristotle. Hippocrates wrote much more than the famous oath that bears his name, and most of his writings, as we might expect, have to do with human anatomy, medicine, and healing.

In a piece entitled *Aphorisms,* for example, he wrote: "Extreme remedies are very appropriate for extreme diseases." In *Precepts,* these words appear in the first chapter: "Healing is a matter of time." While reading those pieces of human wisdom recently, it occurred to me that one might connect them in a paraphrase that would have a rather significant and relevant ring to it: "Recovering from extreme difficulties usually requires an extreme amount of time."

In our world of "instant" everything, that may not sound very encouraging. Yet it is, more often than not, true. The deeper the wound, the more extensive the damage, the greater amount of time is needed for recovery. Wise counsel, Hippocrates! We tend to forget your insightful advice.

Where would the old Greek get such wisdom? His *Aphorisms* and *Precepts* sound almost like the Proverbs of Solomon. As a matter of fact, his writings sound a bit like Solomon.

While entertaining that thought the other day, I pondered an idea I had never considered before. Hippocrates lived sometime between Solomon the king and Paul the apostle—what is known in biblical history as the between-the-Testaments era, that four-hundred-year span when no Scripture was being written, although the Old Testament books were being compiled. So could it be that the Greek physician-philosopher, in his research, came across some of Solomon's writings and rephrased a line or two? For example, isn't it possible that something from Solomon's journal (Ecclesiastes, by name) could have found its way into Hippocrates' writings? Consider the first few lines from Ecclesiastes 3:

> There is an appointed time for everything. And there is a time for every event under heaven—
>
> A time to give birth, and a time to die;
> A time to plant, and a time to uproot what is planted.
> A time to kill, and a time to heal;
> A time to tear down, and a time to build up.
>
> Ecclesiastes 3:1–3

Tucked away in that third verse is the phrase that intrigues me, "a time to heal." Perhaps I am only imagining all this, but I cannot help but wonder if Hippocrates' words, "Healing is a matter of time," might have found their origin in Solomon's statement. In any event, the statement remains sound, both medically and biblically. Except in cases of God's miraculous intervention, healing takes time. And, I repeat, the greater the disease or damage, the longer it takes to heal.

I have been concerned about this issue for a long, long time. Throughout my years in ministry I have had a great deal of contact with people who hurt. In every church I've pastored, in every community in which I've lived, anguish and affliction have abounded. And the pain has come from every conceivable source.

Those who have seemed most disillusioned, however, have been the ones who prayed for but did not experience a quick recovery. Many of them were promised such by people who held out the hope of a miracle. When the anticipated divine intervention did not transpire, their anguish reached the breaking point. I have looked into their faces and heard their cries. I have witnessed their response—everything from quiet disappointment to bitter, cursing cynicism . . . from tearful sadness to violent acts of suicide. And most have been sincere, intelligent, Christian people.

Even though I would love to perform instant miracles for those who need healing (or at least promise recovery "within a week or two"), I am not able to do so. Maybe that is the reason I am so intrigued with the combined thoughts of Hippocrates and Solomon. Since I deal constantly with people in pain, I am left to search for answers that make sense, even though they will never make headlines.

This chapter is about the answers I have found. I have no cure-all solutions to offer, no secret formula that will have you on your feet, smiling, in twenty-four hours. I wish I did, but I don't. I do have some things to say, however, that may give you fresh hope and renewed perspective in the recovery process.

Everything I have to say finds it origin in Scripture, God's unfailing, ever-reliable Book of Truth. If you are weary of the sensational, if the get-well-quick answers haven't worked for you, if it seems that the miracles of overnight relief are for someone else, then perhaps this chapter is especially for you. If your healing is taking a long time, I hope you will find comfort in these pages. And the plain fact is this: For most folks, healing is a slow, arduous process. It takes time.

Time to Heal

I have seen a lot of bumper stickers that read: I'D RATHER BE SAILING. But I have never seen one that read: I'D RATHER BE SHIPWRECKED! I doubt I ever will. Sailing across the water is an exhilarating experience, but sinking under the water is nothing short of terrifying, especially if the sea is rough and the winds are stormy.

Having spent over a month on the ocean during my days in the Marine Corps, I have had my share of high waves and maddening windstorms. On one occasion the swells were somewhere between thirty and forty feet high, and no one—not even the skipper (we found out later!)—thought we would ever see land again. Talk about feeling helpless! Going through such life-threatening situations gives one an absolutely realistic perspective on and respect for the sea. I never see a large ocean-going vessel without having a flashback to my days on the Pacific. How different from what I expected! Instead of an uninterrupted calm, relaxed voyage in the buoyant waters of the deep, my whole world was turned topsy-turvy. Every time I hear some novice speak glibly about how much fun it would be to sail a little boat across the seas, I shudder inside. What we expect is seldom what we experience.

This came home to me in a fresh way some time ago when I read about the twenty-year reunion of most of those who were involved in the formation of the old American Football League. The seasoned sports veterans and owners swapped stories and enjoyed an evening of laugher and reflections together. Among those present was Al Davis, currently the owner of the Los Angeles Raiders, who remembered that all those sitting at his table had stared with envy at Nicky Hilton, who was to speak on that eventful evening in 1959 when they first met to form the league. Everyone's feelings of expectation were only heightened when the man was introduced as having recently made $100,000 in the baseball business in the city of Los Angeles.

Mr. Hilton stood to his feet as the place broke into thunderous applause. Then he stepped to the microphone and said he needed to correct what had been said. It was not he who had had that experience; it was his brother Baron. And it wasn't in Los Angeles, but San Diego. And it wasn't baseball, it was football. And it wasn't $100,000, it was $1 million . . . and he didn't make it, he *lost* it!

Realism always takes the wind out of idealism's sails!

Historical Interruption

That's exactly what happened to Paul, who lived during the first century. For years he had one great dream: to go to Rome, the capital of the empire. The driving force of his life was to have an audience with the Caesar (Nero) and, eyeball-to-eyeball, present to him the claims of Jesus Christ.

A Dream Becomes a Nightmare

Not a bad idea! Sounds like a worthy objective . . . and when you consider that getting there called for a lengthy trip aboard ship from Palestine to Italy, you could almost envision a Mediterranean cruise to boot. But it wasn't a cruise (as we saw in chapter 7); it was a disaster. The ship didn't sail; it sank. And he didn't arrive immediately in Italy; he landed fifty miles out of Sicily. And it wasn't the splendid metropolis of Rome; it was the rugged island named Malta.

That's the bad news! The good news is that "they all were brought safely to land" (Acts 27:44).

All 276 swam, gagged, gasped, struggled, and finally sloshed ashore, soaked and exhausted . . . but safe. It was an unexpected, tumultuous, distant detour.

That's how it is when you find yourself dumped on an island named Malta when all along you had Italy in your sights and the dream of Rome in your heart.

The Beginning of Recovery

Allow me, however, to add a practical dimension to this story that is easily overlooked. Sometimes we sailors on the sea of life need what places like Malta can provide. It may seem to be a barren, lonely, desperate spot, but its solitude is therapeutic, and in its quiet, gentle breezes are renewal, refreshment, and healing. In a word, I'm referring to full recovery from some longstanding struggle, which, I remind you, takes time.

May I go deeper? God plans our Maltas. These transitional islands may seem forlorn and fearsome, especially if you arrive there on the ship of despair, suffering from a neurotic drive to accomplish more, more, more. Those who opt for burning out en route to Rome fear rusting out at Malta, but that doesn't occur. On the contrary, it takes Malta to show us how to stop just existing and start living again. What appears as nothing more than the death of a dream is, in actuality, the first step in the process of healing.

As any student of the New Testament would tell you, Paul's life over the previous twelve to fifteen months had been anything but serene. He had appeared before several frowning judges in one courtroom scene after another. He had experienced mob violence, physical abuse, demonic and satanic oppression, imprisonment, the pain of misunderstanding by friend and foe alike, and more than one threat on his life. Most of those things he endured alone . . . so toss in the loneliness factor. The storm at sea was a fitting and climactic analogy for those long months prior to the voyage to Rome. Forgive me if I sound uncaring, but it took a shipwreck to jolt Paul's perspective back into focus. The disaster at sea followed by the forced change of pace on Malta was precisely what he needed for the process of recuperation and repair to begin.

Sir Winston Churchill, prime minister of England during the 1940s and 1950s, was a leader I have admired for many years. Through intense years of political pressure, heightened by his country's devastating war with Nazi Germany, Churchill maintained a remarkable sense of balance. His wisdom and wit remained intact, and panic never seemed to drain his inner reservoir of confident hope. He once wrote a brief essay entitled "Painting As a Pastime" in which he unveiled his secret of sustaining such a peaceful mind-set.

> Many remedies are suggested for the avoidance of worry and mental overstrain by persons who, over prolonged periods, have to bear exceptional responsibilities and discharge

> duties upon a very large scale. Some advise exercise, and others, repose. Some counsel travel, and others retreat. Some praise solitude, and others, gaiety. No doubt all these may play their part according to the individual temperament. But the element which is constant and common in all of them is Change.
>
> Change is the master key. A man can wear out a particular part of his mind by continually using it and tiring it, just in the same way as he can wear out the elbows of his coat. There is, however, this difference between the living cells of the brain and inanimate articles: one cannot mend the frayed elbows of a coat by rubbing the sleeves or shoulders; but the tired parts of the mind can be rested and strengthened, not merely by rest, but by using other parts. It is not enough merely to switch off the lights which play upon the main and ordinary field of interest; a new field of interest must be illuminated. It is no use saying to the tired mental muscles—if one may coin such an expression—"I will give you a good rest." "I will go for a long walk," or "I will lie down and think of nothing." The mind keeps busy just the same. If it has been weighing and measuring, it goes on worrying. It is only when new cells are called into activity, when new stars become the lords of the ascendant, that relief, repose, refreshment are afforded.
>
> A gifted American psychologist has said, "Worry is a spasm of the emotion; the mind catches hold of something and will not let it go." It is useless to argue with the mind in this condition. The stronger the will, the more futile the task. One can only gently insinuate something else into its convulsive grasp. And if this something else is rightly chosen, if it is really attended by the illumination of another field of interest, gradually, and often quite swiftly, the old undue grip relaxes and the process of recuperation and repair begins.[1]

Lest you think that "doing nothing" is all that is involved in one's stopover at Malta, Churchill's counsel has been mentioned here. Paul does not merely walk along the beach and finger a few seashells . . . nor does he spend weeks staring at sunsets, wiggling his toes in the sand. For him to heal, change was needed, not simply stoic silence.

Personal Treatment

Dr. Luke, the writer of the Acts narrative, mentions a couple of the incidents that transpired between Paul and the island natives. The New English Bible refers to these people as "rough islanders," implying that they had limited education and were driven by superstitious beliefs, which is seen in the account we're about to examine.

Extraordinary Kindness

Initially, the shipwreck victims were greeted with extraordinary kindness. An early-winter rainstorm drenched the island and left everyone shivering because of the cold. Unusually hospitable, the islanders built a large fire and treated the visitors with a marked degree of kindness.

Suddenly, however, the scene changes.

> And the natives showed us extraordinary kindness; for because of the rain that had set in and because of the cold, they kindled a fire and received us all. But when Paul had gathered a bundle of sticks and laid them on the fire, a viper came out because of the heat, and fastened on his hand. And when the natives saw the creature hanging from his hand, they began saying to one another, "Undoubtedly this man is a murderer, and though he has been saved from the sea, justice has not allowed him to live."
>
> Acts 28:2–4

Unjust Criticism

Aroused and angered by the fire, a viper crawled out of the stack of timber and attached itself to Paul's hand. The snake's bite was so deep and penetrating that Paul was unable to shake his hand free. When the natives witnessed this, they jumped to a conclusion that was both cruel and inaccurate: They were suddenly convinced that Paul's calamity was proof that he was guilty of some crime.

Interestingly, even though these barbarians (the actual Greek term here that is translated "natives") lacked education and refined culture, they had an inner standard of justice. Their opinion, however incorrect, was an instantaneous one: "Undoubtedly this man is a murderer." To them the snakebite represented justice having her due.

There is something amazingly relevant about this episode. A "punishment" mind-set is not limited to rough islanders in the Mediterranean. Heathen tribespeople aren't the only ones who jump to the erroneous conclusion that those who suffer are simply "getting what they deserve." Justified punishment—"calamity is proof of guilt." Abominable theology!

I wish there were some way for sufferers to be delivered from such unjust and unfair criticism. It is painful enough to endure the severe blows of life . . . but when words of condemnation coming from superstition and prejudice bite into us, causing the venom of guilt to spread and poison our minds, it is almost more than we can bear.

Inappropriate Exaltation

Quickly, however, Paul shook off the viper. As it fell into the fire, leaving him free from any ill effects, the natives' eyes grew large with amazement. They waited and waited for Paul to drop dead. When he didn't, when they witnessed his resilience, "they changed their minds and began to say that he was a god."

I cannot help but smile when I read this abrupt change of opinion. First, the man is a murderer; now he's a god. When calamity struck, he was getting his due—punishment by death. But once he recovered, he was suddenly catapulted to the superhuman realm, and they were ready to worship him.

A. T. Robertson, a New Testament scholar of yesteryear, points out Paul's similar experience in reverse many years before this encounter on Malta. That one occurred in Lystra, where Paul was first elevated to the place of a god, Mercury, only to be stoned shortly thereafter by the very same people who had earlier deified him. With seasoned wisdom, Dr. Robertson adds this biting comment, "So fickle is popular favor."[2]

It is quite possible that your situation today has been intensified by a similar reversal of opinion. You once knew success. You had the respect of others. You were in demand: a competent, admired, highly honored individual who drank daily from the well of fresh praise . . . right? How things have changed! You now find yourself "shelved" and virtually passed by, perhaps even hated by a few. Your world has suffered a head-on collision, and you're bloody from having gone through the windshield of reversed reputation. Those who once quoted you now criticize you. "So fickle is popular favor."

If that is the case, let me remind you . . . full recovery calls for a *healing that will take time.* And it cannot occur, unfortunately, without some scars remaining. The two scars you will have to deal with the most are disillusionment, which comes from sudden deflation, and bitterness, the result of prolonged blame. As you fly closer to the flame, the Spirit will help you come to terms with both.

Relational Concern

Now back to our story on Malta. The writer includes a couple of vignettes from the island that speak with relevance to us today.

> Now in the neighborhood of that place were lands belonging to the leading man of the island, named Publius, who welcomed us and entertained us courteously three days. And it came about that the father of Publius was lying in bed afflicted with recurrent fever and dysentery; and Paul went in to see him and after he had prayed, he laid his hands on him and healed him. And after this had happened, the rest of the people on the island who had diseases were coming to him

> and getting cured. And they also honored us with many marks of respect; and when we were setting sail, they supplied us with all we needed.
>
> Acts 28:7–10

Take a moment to notice the repeated pronouns "us" and "we." The writer of the narrative is obviously including himself. Who is he? Luke. And what is his profession? Physician. My point is this: Here is a physician, an educated, well-trained medical doctor whose expertise is the diagnosis of disease—in this case, "recurrent fever and dysentery," which caused Publius's father to be bedridden. Dr. Luke could diagnose the ailment, but he was at a loss to bring about a cure. Paul, however, as an apostle, possessed the supernatural, God-given ability to do what Luke could not do.

Instant Healing

Initially, Dr. Luke stood back as God worked through His servant Paul who, after praying for the afflicted man, "laid his hands on him and healed him." The word originally used by the physician-writer is *iaomai,* a Greek term that refers, more often than not, to instantaneous healing. Paul, please understand, was not the source of such power, only the vehicle . . . the human instrument through whom God supernaturally worked.

I am as impressed with Dr. Luke's lack of envy as I am with the apostle Paul's spiritual gift. The physician stepped aside. Although we may be certain his medical training left no room for divine miracles, his theology did! Without a moment's hesitation the professional was willing to stand back and watch God do the unusual.

And that last word is worth repeating for emphasis—an on-the-spot miracle is *unusual,* an exception to the general rule. As we have stated in the two previous chapters, there are times when God does indeed heal . . . instantly, miraculously, unexplainably. But, I repeat, such miracles are rare—unusual exceptions to the rule.

For too long people have been led to believe that in virtually every case they can "expect a miracle." And to make matters worse, when the miracle doesn't occur, they are told that something is wrong with them: they are harboring sin . . . they are not strong enough in their faith . . . and on and on. I shall restrain myself from grinding an ax at this point, but I must state that there are few areas in which there is greater confusion than this concept of instant healing. Sufferers are being promised miracles by many alleged authorities—some are sincere, some naive, some professional con artists—and when the miracle does not come, the damage done is always tragic and occasionally irreparable.

Prolonged Recovery

Look again at the last part of this account:

> And after this had happened, the rest of the people on the island who had diseases were coming to him and getting cured. And they also honored us with many marks of respect; and when we were setting sail, they supplied us with all we needed.
>
> Acts 28:9–10

As the word of that miracle traveled across the island, others with ailments came for healing. A cursory reading of what occurred could leave us with the impression that everyone who came received a similar instantaneous miracle. Not so. The original term used by Dr. Luke to describe the people's being "cured" is altogether different from the one he used for Publius's father. This word is *therapeuo,* from which we get our English word, "therapy." One reputable commentator writes that:

> *Healed* . . . might better be translated . . . *were treated.* It suggests not miraculous healings but medical treatment,

> probably at the hands of Luke the physician. Verses 10 and 11 suggest that this medical ministry lasted through the three months stay at Malta.[3]

In other words, these people went through a process, a prolonged period of recovery, which lasted for three months—maybe longer.

Sometimes healing is instantaneous—*iaomai* recovery. More often than not, though, healing takes time—*therapeuo* recovery, under the care and watchful eyes of a competent physician. It is important to remember that the Holy Spirit is involved in both kinds of healings, not just the miraculous ones. Remember that! It is easy to overlook during the long and often anguishing months (sometimes years) of recovery.

Practical Lessons

We seldom think in terms of the lessons to be learned from, or the benefits connected to, prolonged recovery. As I mentioned earlier, we like quick turnarounds, instant changes from sickness to health. We much prefer hearing accounts of miracles as opposed to long, nonsensational stories of slow recoveries. In fact, we tend to be impatient with those who can't seem to take our advice and "snap out of it" or "get well soon," like the greeting card urges them to do. But like it or not, the wise words of Hippocrates are true: "Healing is a matter of time."

Respect . . . Rather Than Resentment

The one who needs time to heal, the individual who requires several months—perhaps, several years—to recover, is often the recipient of resentment. This works against the healing process. Instead of being affirmed and encouraged to press on through the pain, the sufferer encounters resentment, impatience, and uninvited advice that lacks understanding and reveals disrespect. The result is predictable.

This is especially true of those who must climb out of a background of emotional trauma. It took years for the damage to be done, yet many expect overnight recovery. For some there is the added stigma of attempted suicide or time spent in a psychiatric ward or mental hospital. For some their past has been strewn with the litter of a prison experience, a divorce, a rape, child abuse, molestation, or some other ego-shattering blow to their self-esteem. No one on the face of the earth would love to be healed quickly and get back in the mainstream of life more than these strugglers, but for them the therapy—the healing—is a prolonged and painful process, not an instant miracle.

Some, I realize, may go to extremes, play on our sympathy, and take advantage of our compassion. But more often than not, those who are recovering want nothing more than to be well, whole, responsible, functioning adults who carry their share of the load. Just as it is possible to hurry the very young through childhood, not giving them the benefit of growing up slowly and securely, so it is possible to hurry the very ill through recovery, robbing them of the benefits of healing slowly and permanently.

May I ask a favor? Please read that last sentence again, this time with feeling.

Wisdom . . . Not Just Knowledge

Now, let me speak directly to the sufferer for a moment. A major benefit of taking time to heal occurs within you where the Spirit is doing some of His best work. Almost imperceptibly, you are becoming a person with keener sensitivity, a broader base of understanding, and a longer fuse! Patience is a by-product of pain. So is tolerance with others and obedience before God. It is difficult to know how to classify these characteristics, but for lack of a better title, let's call the whole package *Spirit-given wisdom.*

For too many years in your life you may have operated strictly on the basis of knowledge . . . the human absorption of facts and natural reaction to others. But affliction has now entered your life, and even though you would much prefer to have it over with, it has not ended. The pain you are forced to endure is reshaping and remaking you deep within.

It is as David, the psalmist, once wrote:

> Before I was afflicted I went astray,
> But now I keep Thy word. . . .
> It is good for me that I was afflicted,
> That I may learn Thy statutes. . . .
> I know, O LORD, that Thy judgments are righteous,
> And that in faithfulness Thou hast afflicted me.
>
> Psalm 119:67, 71, 75

David admits that a much greater desire to obey (v. 67), a much more teachable spirit (v. 71), and a much less arrogant attitude (v. 75) were now his to claim, thanks to prolonged affliction.

Human knowledge comes naturally. It is enhanced by schooling and enlarged by travel. But with it there often comes carnal pride, a sense of self-sufficiency, and tough independence. This kind of knowledge can cause us to become increasingly less interested in the spiritual dimension of life. As our reservoir of horizontal knowledge grows, our skin gets thicker and often our inner being (called "the heart" in Scripture) becomes harder.

Then comes pain. Some physical ailment levels us to mere mortality. Or an emotional collapse. A domestic conflict explodes, and we are reduced to a cut above zero. The affliction (whatever it may be) paralyzes our productivity, and we are cast adrift in a sea of private turmoil and possibly public embarrassment. And to make matters worse, we are convinced we will never, ever recover.

At just such a dead-end street, divine wisdom waits to be embraced, bringing with it a beautiful blend of insight—the kind we never had with all our knowledge—genuine humility, a perception of others, and an incredible sensitivity toward God. During the time it is taking us to heal, wisdom is replacing knowledge. The vertical dimension is coming into clearer focus.

Balance . . . Freedom from Extremes

Finally, we cannot ignore the value of balance. I have already mentioned this concept several times in regard to other matters of the Spirit, but it plays an equally important role when it comes to healing. It has been my own experience, as well as my observation of others, that a lengthy recovery time rivets into our heads the importance of bringing our lives back from the fringes of the extreme. And I especially have in mind either the extreme of too much work (where our world is too structured, too product-oriented, too intense and responsible—to the point of neurosis) or too little work (where irresponsibility, inactivity, and indifference mark our paths). During the recovery stage, it is amazing how God enables us to see the foolish extremes of our former lives.

Eugene Peterson, in a work entitled *A Long Obedience in the Same Direction,* expresses well what I am trying to describe as he compares Western and Eastern cultures:

> The Christian has to find a better way to avoid the sin of Babel than by imitating the lilies of the field, who "neither toil nor spin." The pretentious work which became Babel and its pious opposite which developed at Thessalonica are displayed today on the broad canvasses of Western and Eastern cultures respectively.
>
> Western culture takes up where Babel left off and deifies human effort as such. The machine is the symbol of this way of life that attempts to control and manage. Technology promises to give us control over the earth and over other people. But the promise is not fulfilled: lethal automobiles, ugly buildings, and ponderous bureaucracies ravage the earth and empty lives of meaning. Structures become more important than the people who live in them. Machines become more important than the people who use them. We care more for our possessions with which we hope to make our way in the world than for our thoughts and dreams which tell us who we are in the world.

> Eastern culture, on the other hand, is a variation on the Thessalonican view. There is a deep-rooted pessimism regarding human effort. Since all work is tainted with selfishness and pride, the solution is to withdraw from all activity into pure being. The symbol of such an attitude is the Buddha—an enormous fat person sitting cross-legged, looking at his own navel. Motionless, inert, quiet. All trouble comes from doing too much; therefore, do nothing. Step out of the rat race. The world of motion is evil, so quit doing everything. Say as little as possible; do as little as possible; finally, at the point of perfection, you will say nothing and do nothing. The goal is to withdraw absolutely and finally from action, from thought, from passion.
>
> The two cultures are in collision today and many think that we must choose between them.[4]

As a result of this tendency toward extremes, many people break, and the inner destruction leaves them in shambles. It takes time to reorder and balance out our personal lives. Little wonder, then, that the Spirit does not always choose to work in a hurry.

There are many who teach that there is "healing in the atonement." By this they mean that the one who believes in Jesus Christ's atoning death for sin not only receives deliverance from sin but also deliverance from sin's by-products—sickness and disease. They base this teaching on Isaiah 53:5, a verse of Scripture that appears in a passage predicting the Messiah's death. Allow me to state the verse in its surrounding context.

> Surely our griefs He Himself bore,
> And our sorrows He carried;
> Yet we ourselves esteemed Him stricken,
> Smitten of God, and afflicted.
> But He was pierced through for our transgressions,
> He was crushed for our iniquities;
> The chastening for our well-being fell upon Him,
> And by His scourging we are healed.

> All of us like sheep have gone astray,
> Each of us has turned to his own way;
> But the LORD has caused the iniquity of us all
> To fall on Him.
>
> He was oppressed and He was afflicted,
> Yet He did not open His mouth;
> Like a lamb that is led to slaughter,
> And like a sheep that is silent before its shearers,
> So He did not open His mouth.
>
> Isaiah 53:4–7

A close and careful look at the prophet's words will reveal that the context is one of great physical pain that the Messiah would endure on the cross. But the point is this—His suffering is for our spiritual benefit. The subject being dealt with is the sinner's "transgressions," our "iniquities." The death of the Messiah provides the solution to our spiritual deadness. Our sins are forgiven because He once for all cleansed us when He was crucified. Hence, by His physical death, we are granted spiritual healing.

I agree that there is healing in the atonement . . . spiritual healing from the sins that kept us from God, healing from the overcoming power and influence of our adversary, healing from the grave that once frightened us, and healing from death that would otherwise conquer us.

And, of course, God promises to heal all of us of all illness and affliction once we pass from this life into glory. Such instant healing is part of the eternal package we receive when these bodies "put on immortality" (1 Cor. 15:53).

Our Response

There are several possible responses you may have to what I have written on the subjects of miracles, healings, and recovery.

First, it is possible that you honestly disagree with what I have presented. You are convinced that God works in a different way than I have described and that miracles are the rule, not the exception. I appreciate your open-minded attention, and I respect your right to disagree. My prayer is that God will comfort and encourage you as you trust Him to intervene. If He does, I will rejoice with you. If He does not, I hope you will not become disillusioned, confused, and bitter, as have so many I have dealt with who approached their situation from that perspective.

Second, you may find yourself encouraged and relieved because these things make sense. You agree that miracles can occur, healings do happen, but, more often than not, recovery takes time. And you are affirmed in the recovery process. Perhaps you were getting anxious and jumping to some false conclusions, misreading God's silence. You have decided to rest rather than strive. I am sincerely grateful that you have decided to "hang tough." Your renewed determination to learn and to grow through these stretching days will be *abundantly* rewarded. The roots grow deep when the winds are strong. Working through is always—always—more painful than walking out. But in the end, ah, what confident honesty, what calm assurance, what character depth!

Third, you may still be making up your mind. Some of this sounds reasonable. You identify and agree with several of the issues I have raised, but in the final analysis you are not ready to come down with both feet and say, "Yes, that's where I stand." You may be pleased (and surprised) to know that I consider this an intelligent response. The subject of pain is a profound one. The process involved in working through some of these issues is difficult, sometimes terribly complex. I may be able to address them in these few pages, but, believe me, in no way have I mastered the message I proclaim. How all these things fit together into God's perfect plans, I am not anywhere near prepared to say. Why human evil and its consequences are allowed such green lights by a holy God is another baffling paradox.

So my counsel to all, no matter how you respond to these last three chapters, is that you join me in continuing to search for answers. Let's listen to the wisdom of the Scriptures. Let's pay close attention to the "still small voice" of God who whispers to us in our pleasure and shouts to us in our pain. And most of all, let's not allow a few technical definitions or theological differences to push us apart. We still need each other.

It is difficult enough to handle life when we stand together. But doing battle with one another in addition to struggling through our shipwrecks, our Maltas, our storms, and our thorns can be almost unbearable. We need all the support we can get during recovery. As we take time to heal, let's also take time to hear . . . to care . . . to accept . . . to affirm one another.

12

Power, Power . . . We've Got the Power!

ANY BOOK ON THE HOLY SPIRIT must give some space to the subject of power, since our Lord promised His disciples this one thing when the Spirit came upon them. Remember His words?

> "But you shall receive power when the Holy Spirit has come upon you; and you shall be My witnesses both in Jerusalem, and in all Judea and Samaria, and even to the remotest part of the earth."
>
> Acts 1:8

To those men, in that era, that heaven-sent, undeniable power from the One whom Jesus dispatched following His ascension manifested itself in dozens of different ways, many of them visible and supernatural. They were empowered to stand and preach before the public, unashamed and unafraid. They experienced such dynamic internal changes that they had the ability to speak in languages and dialects unknown to them. Some of them performed miraculous feats, others healed diseases instantly and permanently, discerned error, confronted evil, raised the dead, and endured the most torturous of deaths without flinching.

Something transformed those timid, awkward, fearful disciples into bold, devoted, inspiring men of God . . . and that something was *power.*

To be sure, that transitional interlude as the infant church was born and began to grow was a unique time. A time when miracles authenticated God's presence in human lives and God's message through human lips. Without the completed Scriptures, how would people know who were the anointed of God? Furthermore, in spreading the gospel rapidly across vast unevangelized regions, the ability to speak in many tongues was invaluable. Clearly, it took enormous power to launch the good ship *Ecclesia.*

But what about the power of the Spirit today? Can we—should we—expect "a miracle a day"? Should "supernatural power" be the watchword of every believer, whereby every one of us can expect "signs and wonders" on a regular basis? Is something wrong with us if we don't consistently witness or experience the Spirit of God's phenomenal presence and mighty workings? What are the evidences of Spirit-filled power today?

Let me set the record straight right away. In spite of what is being communicated these days, God's Word does not toss around the word *power* loosely; nor are we personally promised supernatural manifestations on a day-to-day basis. (As a friend of mine once said, "If miracles occurred every day, they wouldn't be called 'miracles' . . . they'd be called 'regulars.'") I have examined the Scriptures carefully and thoroughly for years, and nowhere do I find phenomenal demonstrations occurring on a daily basis in the lives of believers in biblical times. Neither then nor now could people expect to "name it and claim it." It is not only frustrating to people, it is erroneous to hold out such unrealistic expectations of incredible "power."

Today, however, power is in. There is "power evangelism" . . . "power prayer" . . . "power preaching" . . . "power healing" . . . "power encounters" and "power ministry" of every shape and size . . . even "power ties" available in various colors that "power ministers" can wear on "power Sundays." Talk about an overused, abused word! And the not-so-subtle message all this leaves is obvious: "If I'm not operating within the 'power' realm, something is missing from my life. I need to plug into this incredible 'power' source, so I, too, can tell amazing stories of mind-boggling miracles."

While I am just as interested in being a Spirit-filled minister of the gospel as anyone in God's family, I would caution all of the Lord's people against such unrealistic and unbiblical expectations. Power is promised us, yes, and in the person of the Holy Spirit we do have the source of that power within us—all of us do! But in no way does this mean that with the snap of our fingers we can expect to invoke some supernatural manifestation. It doesn't work like that . . . it never did!

Understanding First Things First

Let's return to basics . . . two foundational issues we touched on earlier. One has to do with salvation, the other with being Spirit-filled.

How would you complete these two sentences?

- I am a Christian because ____________________.
- I am filled with the Spirit when ____________________.

What does it mean to be a Christian? How can a person say with assurance that he or she is a member of God's forever family? Let's allow God's Word to answer that for us.

> But as many as received Him, to them He gave the right to become children of God, even to those who believe in His name.
>
> John 1:12

A little later, John's Gospel records Jesus' conversation with a man who had questions about how he could have eternal life with God.

> Jesus answered and said to him, "Truly, truly, I say to you, unless one is born again, he cannot see the kingdom of God. . . . That which is born of the flesh is flesh, and that which is born of the Spirit is spirit. Do not marvel that I said

> to you, 'You must be born again.' The wind blows where it wishes and you hear the sound of it, but do not know where it comes from and where it is going; so is everyone who is born of the Spirit."
>
> John 3:3, 6–8

> "He who believes in the Son has eternal life; but he who does not obey the Son shall not see life, but the wrath of God abides on him."
>
> John 3:36

Is it that narrow? Is becoming a Christian limited solely to knowing Christ? Again, let's let Jesus answer that for us.

> Jesus said to him, "I am the way, and the truth, and the life; no one comes to the Father, but through Me."
>
> John 14:6

That is an exclusive statement, no question about it. But the truth is as narrow as Christ has declared it, and it is truth because He said it. The first sentence I asked you to complete could read as follows: I am a Christian because *I am rightly related to the Son of God*. Later in the New Testament we read similar words as those we just looked at in the Gospel by John.

> For there is one God, and one mediator also between God and men, the man Christ Jesus.
>
> 1 Timothy 2:5

> And the witness is this, that God has given us eternal life, and this life is in His Son. He who has the Son has the life; he who does not have the Son of God does not have the life.
>
> 1 John 5:11–12

Very simple. Very clear. People are not born right with God. That is why everyone who hopes to spend eternity with Him must be born from above, born anew spiritually. Furthermore, people do not become Christians because they go to church or because they have been christened as babies or because they have been dedicated as children or because they have been baptized or because they are sincere and mean well and pay their bills. Becoming a Christian has nothing to do with what we do or with how hard we work. No, it's a matter of grace, not works.

> For by grace you have been saved through faith; and that not of yourselves, it is the gift of God; not as a result of works, that no one should boast.
>
> Ephesians 2:8–9

Let me illustrate. I have a book in my hand. If I were to hand it to you and say, "It's yours; I'd like you to have it," and you were to take it, I would be giving you a gift. When you take the gift, you become the possessor of what was once mine. Because you took it, it's yours.

Likewise, salvation is a gift. God reached out to you and me at the cross, where His Son paid the penalty of sin by dying in our place, and He gave us eternal life in His Son. All He asks is that we reach out in faith and take His gift.

And so . . . how does one become a Christian? By being rightly related to Jesus Christ, the Son of God. This is Salvation 101. It's as basic as you can get.

What must I do then to get the source of God's power into my life? This may surprise you, but the answer is *nothing*. He comes to live within you when you believe in Christ. You don't make a single contribution to your standing before God by doing this or promising that or giving up certain things. The transaction is based on grace—God's matchless, unmerited favor. When you and I receive the gift of eternal life, wrapped inside that gift is the Holy Spirit. He comes as part of the "initial salvation package." We are never commanded to pray for the Holy Spirit or to be baptized by the Holy Spirit or to be regenerated by the Holy Spirit or to be sealed by the Holy Spirit. Why? Because all of those things occur at the moment we are born anew.

So you have in your hands the book I gave you as a gift. Now, what if you were to say to me, "I would really, really love to have every chapter of this book." I would answer, "You have all the chapters. They are all there and they are all yours to read and enjoy. You have the book; therefore you have everything in it." So it is with Christ. Upon receiving Him, we have everything that comes with the gift of salvation . . . and that certainly includes the person of the Holy Spirit.

> For even as the body is one and yet has many members, and all the members of the body, though they are many, are one body, so also is Christ. For by one Spirit we were all baptized into one body, whether Jews or Greeks, whether slaves or free, and we were all made to drink of one Spirit.
>
> 1 Corinthians 12:12–13

And because we have the Spirit, the source of power is within us.

This brings me to the second sentence I asked you to complete, which could read: I am filled with the Spirit when *I am rightly related to the Spirit of God.*

When we are, the "power" within us is unleashed and we become His vessels of honor, ready and available for whatever service He wishes us to perform. When filled, the "power" that raised Christ from the dead becomes the motivating force behind our lives. Think of it! It was this very power Paul referred to when he wrote of his deep desire to fly closer to the flame:

> [For my determined purpose is] that I may know Him—that I may progressively become more deeply and intimately acquainted with Him, perceiving and recognizing and understanding [the wonders of His Person] more strongly and more clearly. And that I may in that same way come to know the power outflowing from His resurrection [which it exerts over believers]; and that I may so share His sufferings as to be continually transformed [in spirit into His likeness even] to His death.
>
> Philippians 3:10 AMP

The filling of the Spirit not only means that our lives are totally available to God, but it also includes such things as keeping short accounts, being sensitive to whatever may have come between us and Him . . . and walking in complete dependence upon Him.

When we do, He is able to work through us, speak through us, use us, direct us without restraint, and empower our gifts and our efforts in ways we could never accomplish on our own. It isn't that we need more of the Spirit (an impossibility); it is that we need His power, His working, His cleansing, His freeing. And as He fills us, all that and so much more take place.

To return to the P word: The Christian life is not some kind of ecstatic "power life" with hour-by-hour, day-after-day phenomenal experiences. The blessed Spirit of God does not provide "power surges" of incredible proportions.

Am I saying He never causes phenomenal, even miraculous things to occur? No. But what I am saying is that when He does, it is the exception rather than the rule. Our Lord is not in competition with Fantasyland.

My concern is that we have as realistic and relevant a view of this as the Scriptures allow—and nothing more. But make no mistake about it, when it comes to power, power . . . we've got the power!

Understanding the Continual, Normal Evidences of the Spirit's Empowering

So, then, you may ask, "What is this realistic and relevant view of the Christian life? What can I expect to see as continual and normal evidences of Christ in my life?" Numerous things come to mind.

Because I am a Christian and therefore rightly related to the Son of God:

- I am in Christ.
- I live in Him and He lives in me.

- I know the relief of being cleansed from personal sins.
- I am able to live above sin's dominating control.
- I have immediate access to the Father through prayer.
- I can understand the Scriptures.
- I am able to forgive—and should forgive—whoever wrongs me.
- I have the capacity to bear fruit, daily, continually, routinely.
- I possess at least one (sometimes more than one) spiritual gift.
- I worship with joy and with purpose.
- I find the church vital, not routine or boring.
- I have a faith to share with others.
- I love and need other people.
- I look forward to having close fellowship with fellow Christians.
- I am able to obey the teaching of the Word of God.
- I continue to learn and grow toward maturity.
- I can endure suffering and hardship without losing heart.
- I depend and trust in my Lord for daily strength and provisions.
- I can know God's will.
- I live in anticipation of Christ's return.
- I have the assurance of heaven after I die.

This list could continue for pages, but perhaps this sampling will alert you to the fact that these are the kinds of unique possessions, experiences, and blessings that are ours by God's grace to enjoy simply because we have been accepted into His family. They are ours to claim every day. And when we add them all together, they represent an impressive list of incredible realities.

While none of the above would be considered miraculous—at least in the usual sense of the term—they are certainly remarkable. And when we remind ourselves that these are normal and continually ours to enjoy, the Christian life becomes the most enviable lifestyle one can imagine.

This may not be "power Christianity," but it is certainly the "abundant life" Christ promised. Get that straight . . . or you will live your life disappointed and frustrated, always looking for something more ecstatic or supernatural in nature.

Several years ago a pilot told me that flying an airplane consists of hours and hours of sheer boredom, interrupted periodically with split seconds of sheer panic.

I would never use the word *boredom* to describe the Christian life, but you get the point. God can (and sometimes does) step into our world in supernatural ways and manifest His power. It is remarkable how on occasion He interrupts the routine (if we could call the things I listed routine) with something phenomenal that only He could have done. We acknowledge that and praise Him for it . . . but, I repeat, we should not expect that day after day.

In some ways, the normal Christian life is not unlike the normal married life. The normal married life is not soft music, Saran-Wrap negligees, and night-after-night in a bubbly hot tub. The normal married life is not soft-footed waiters serving you tea in the afternoon at the Ritz-Carlton Hotel while you watch the surf break on Maui. It's not letters in the mail several times a month announcing that you and your mate have won $50 million in the lottery jackpot. It's not a husband coming home with flowers every afternoon. It's not $500 gift certificates to Nordstroms each Saturday morning. It's not happy, carefree teenagers anxious to help with the dishes and thrilled to keep their rooms clean. It's not a mother-in-law with a face like Michelle Pfeiffer and a heart like Mother Teresa.

If you are a bride- or groom-to-be anticipating that, I've got only three words for you. *Get a life!* Visit with any married couple for a day or two (especially those with small children), and you will come back to reality real fast.

In the same way, some Fantasyland concept of Christianity frustrates much more than it thrills. The wide-eyed, smiling televangelist won't tell you this, but I'm giving you the straight scoop.

So much for a quick summary of the Christian life. Now how about the Spirit-filled life? Let me suggest another list for you to ponder. These are things you and I can claim when the Spirit is in full control.

When we are Spirit-filled and therefore rightly related to the Spirit of God:

- We are surrounded by the Spirit's omnipotent shield of protection, continually and routinely.
- We have an inner dynamic to handle life's pressures.
- We are able to be joyful . . . regardless.
- We have the capacity to grasp the deep things of God that He discloses to us in His Book.
- We have little difficulty maintaining a positive attitude of unselfishness, servanthood, and humility.
- We have a keen sense of intuition and discernment; we sense evil.
- We are able to love and be loved in return.
- We can be vulnerable and open.
- We can rely on the Spirit to intercede for us when we don't even know how to pray as we should.
- We need never fear evil or demonic and satanic assault.
- We are enabled to stand alone with confidence.
- We experience inner assurance regarding decisions as well as right and wrong.
- We have an "internal filtering system."
- We can actually live worry-free.
- We are able to minister to others through our spiritual gift(s).

- We have an intimate, abiding "Abba relationship" with the living God.

When I buried my dad, who outlived my mother by nine years, for the first time I found myself feeling alone, even though I was an adult and a father of four. While feeling strangely and suddenly "orphaned," the thought dawned on me that I have the Spirit of God to be my constant companion and counselor for the rest of my life. How wonderful! He lives as a permanent resident. His earthly address is my body!

Again, none of the things on the list above could be called phenomenal . . . they are neither miraculous in nature nor supernatural manifestations . . . but they are ours to claim simply because the powerful Spirit of God is filling us. This is not "power filling," but the normal, albeit wonderful, Spirit-filled life.

And frankly, these evidences are the kinds of things we need and can count on far more than those exceptional moments of sheer ecstasy. These are the things we can count on because we are rightly related to the Son of God and to the Spirit of God. We do not need continual, highly charged "power visions" or "power encounters" nearly as much as we need to be filled with the sustaining, all-powerful Spirit of God.

I say again, power, power . . . we've got the power! Who does? Every child of God who walks in the power of the Holy Spirit. When we do, we are "freed up" to enjoy incredible release from the things that would otherwise hold us in bondage. What great liberty!

> Now the Lord is the Spirit; and where the Spirit of the Lord is, there is liberty.
>
> 2 Corinthians 3:17

Just look at that promise.

Liberty is another word for freedom. Freedom from what? Freedom from constraint and from fear. Freedom from tedious perfectionism. Freedom from a confining, boring, predictable life. Freedom from bondage. Freedom from addictions. Freedom to be, to do, to become. And such freedom comes from simply having the Spirit and allowing Him to fill us. Again, it is not "power freedom." It is a quiet, gentle release from all that binds us so that we can be whole, completely authentic. When in grief, we are free to cry. When experiencing joy, we are free to laugh.

Admitting Occasional Exceptional Experiences

Am I saying that we never experience the miraculous? I am not. Or that we should consider all supernatural manifestations today as coming from the devil? No. I am suggesting, however, that we be discerning. He is God. He can do anything, anytime, anywhere. That is His prerogative.

Many times people come to me and say, "Would you pray for so-and-so?" and they will name a wife, a husband, a mother, a dad, a child, or a friend who's dying. Doctors have given up hope and encouraged them not to expect anything but death. So they ask, "Would you just pray for that person?" My answer invariably is, "Yes, of course." And I do. But beyond that I really have no right to promise those people that their loved ones will be healed and live. Not being God and not knowing God's specific will, I pray for God's glory to be manifested. I pray that if it is His will He might bring about a miraculous healing. And I pray that He will give strength to those who wait and minister to the dying. But I have no right to make a "power promise." *Neither does anyone else!*

Let me remind you that when we talk about the Spirit of God, we are not talking about a small part of the whole. The Spirit of God is, in fact, God. And as a member of the Godhead, He is incomprehensible and infinite in nature. His work can seem mysterious, and at times His presence, terribly obscure. Humanly speaking, I sometimes feel His plan is a bit confusing and illogical. (But that's my problem, not His.) Because I cannot unravel His divine tapestry or explain in detail the work of His hands, it does not mean that there is something wrong with His plan.

Zophar the Naamathite said to Job in utter despair, "Can we by searching find out God?" The implication is no.

And since this is true, let's let God be God. Let's not feel that we must explain every part of Him or defend His plan or describe His will to the nth degree. We would do well to employ three words on a regular basis: "I don't know."

With these things in mind, I conclude this chapter with three final thoughts:

First, *God is the God of the miraculous.* Please do not misquote or misrepresent me by saying that Swindoll does not believe in the miraculous. God is God; therefore, miracles fall from His hands. They do occur. But let's be true to the Scriptures and correctly state that those miracles are the exceptions, not the norm. They aren't "regulars." Nor do they occur on command. They occur when God, in His marvelous, mysterious, inscrutable plan, causes them to happen.

Second, *God is the God of the supernatural.* Again, Scripture suggests that supernatural phenomena are occasional, not routine. But be careful what you tag "miraculous" or "phenomenal." Don't toss those words around loosely. It's like the word "awesome." Everything today is awesome. Ballplayers are awesome! Toyotas are awesome! Nonsense. Only God is awesome. And if He is pleased to carry out some phenomenal manifestation, I stand back and applaud it and would not even attempt to explain it . . . and certainly not act as though I caused it.

Third, *God is the God of the mysterious.* Because He is God, He can—and does—cause things to occur that we cannot explain. However, I remind you again, such mysteries are occasional and exceptional. To quote A. W. Tozer:

> Left to ourselves we tend immediately to reduce God to manageable terms. We want to get Him where we can use Him, or at least know where He is when we need Him. We want a God we can in some measure control. We need the feeling of security that comes from knowing what God is like, and what He is like is of course a composite of all the

religious pictures we have seen, all the best people we have known or heard about, and all the sublime ideas we have entertained.

If all this sounds strange to modern ears, it is only because we have for a full half century taken God for granted. The glory of God has not been revealed to this generation of men. The God of contemporary Christianity is only slightly superior to the gods of Greece and Rome, if indeed He is not actually inferior to them, in that He is weak and helpless while they at least had power.

If what we conceive God to be He is not, how then shall we think of Him? If He is indeed incomprehensible, as the Creed declares Him to be, and unapproachable, as Paul says He is, how can we Christians satisfy our longing after Him? The hopeful words, "Acquaint now thyself with him, and be at peace," still stand after the passing of the centuries; but how shall we acquaint ourselves with One who eludes all the straining efforts of mind and heart? And how shall we be held accountable to know what cannot be known? . . .

The answer of the Bible is simply "through Jesus Christ our Lord." In Christ and by Christ, God effects complete self-disclosure, although He shows Himself not to reason but to faith and love. Faith is an organ of knowledge, and love an organ of experience. God came to us in the incarnation; in atonement He reconciled us to Himself, and by faith and love we enter and lay hold on Him.

"Verily God is of infinite greatness," says Christ's enraptured troubadour, Richard Rolle; "more than we can think; . . . unknowable by created things; and can never be comprehended by us as He is in Himself. But even here and now, whenever the heart begins to burn with a desire for God, she is made able to receive the uncreated light and, inspired and fulfilled by the gifts of the Holy Ghost, she tastes the joys of heaven.[1]

I have a very good friend whose son has been through an incredibly difficult period of illness. I have ached with him and his wife, and Cynthia and I have prayed for them frequently in the last few months. For a while nothing was going right. Things that were bad only got worse. They faced a wall of impossibilities they could not scale. And then—a breakthrough occurred. They were put in touch with a specialist, a gifted, insightful physician who, through a particular technique, introduced them to the source of the problem. And this little fellow who had been laid aside for months is now well on his way to full recovery, for which we praise our sovereign God and His empowering Spirit.

It would be the tendency of some to cry, "Miraculous!" No, it was no miracle. It was, in fact, a delicate, scientific, carefully honed procedure of diagnosis and treatment that worked on the boy. Was God in it? Absolutely. Doctors diagnose and treat; God alone can heal. God, in powerful grace, led in the finding of the physician. God prompted another person to provide all the finances since the couple had meager resources. And God used the procedure to heal the boy's life.

His power was evident from start to finish . . . but it was no "power healing." What happened? Several of us joined our hearts with our friends and decided to fly closer to the flame as together we trusted Him who has all the power to do whatever is best. It happened quietly, slowly, thoroughly . . . and powerfully.

13

Is That All There Is to the Spirit's Ministry?

IN MY ALMOST SIXTY YEARS on this old earth, I have discovered that one of the best ways to arrive at the right answers is to start with the right questions. And so I have come to this vast subject of the Holy Spirit with more searching questions than hard-and-fast answers. Maybe that is what first attracted me to a disarming little book titled *Dear God: Children's Letters to God.*

A little girl named Lucy asks God: "Dear God, are You really invisible or is that just a trick?"

Norma asks: "Dear God, did You mean for a giraffe to look like that or was that an accident?"

One of my favorites was asked by Nan: "Dear God, who draws the lines around all the countries?"

And Neil writes: "Dear God, I went to this wedding and they kissed right in church. Is that okay?"

Lois asks, "Dear God, I like the Lord's prayer best of all. Did You have to write it a lot or did You get it right the first time?"

From Joanne, "I would like to know why all the things You said are in red."

Darla asks, "Did You really mean *Do unto others as they do unto you?* Because if You did, then I'm going to fix my brother."

Peter requests, "Will You please send Dennis Clark to a different camp this year?"

And Anita asks, "Is it true my father won't get in heaven if he uses his bowling words in the house?"[1]

Hilarious, charming, innocent . . . and oh, so perceptive! Don't you wrestle at times with questions that flip through your mind and snag in one of those creases up there? I certainly do! And let's be painfully candid and honest about it, most of us have many more questions than we do absolute answers . . . just like these children.

Most folks don't make me nervous, but those who do are the ones who have convinced themselves that they have pretty well buttoned up all the theological hatches. They see themselves as answer-givers rather than question-askers. You have a problem? Just ask; they'll unload the truck on you. And especially important to them is that you be impressed with their storehouse of knowledge. What bothers me most, though, is their lack of childlike curiosity . . . for "children" of God, that's pretty arrogant. Most of the answer-givers have stopped asking the hard questions. Their arrogance has not only stopped their ears, it has closed their minds.

That's not the case with Seymour. I've saved his question for last: "Dear God, How come You did all those miracles in the old days and You don't do any now?"[2]

Anyone who studies the lives of Moses or Elijah or Jesus is haunted by that question. Recorded in the pages of the Great Book are back-to-back phenomenal events and miraculous moments during the lifetimes of those three. But how rarely they occur today. "Dear God, have those things ended? Is that all there is to the Spirit's ministry? If things have changed so, have we reached the end of His powerful presence and workings?"

Evidences of His Presence

Remember early on in the book when we looked at Jesus' words to His faithful few just before He was grabbed by a mob, rushed through a series of trials, and hammered to a cross? We heard Him promise that even though He was leaving, He would not leave them as orphans.

> "And I will ask the Father, and He will give you another Helper, that He may be with you forever."
>
> John 14:16

He had been their Helper all along their three-plus years together. When they needed anything, all they had to do was say, "Jesus," and He would be there to help. "Lord, we weren't able to cast out demons." So He said, "Stand back. Let me show how this is done." Or "Lord, we reached this impasse and we weren't able to—" "Let Me help you with that." He had been their Helper . . . but no longer.

Now He promises "Another Helper," for which John uses the term that meant "Another of the same kind." And so when we ask, "Is that all there is?" the answer is no, we haven't reached the end of the Spirit's era. Jesus promised His disciples directly . . . and us indirectly: "He will be there forever." And who is this next Helper?

> "That is the Spirit of truth, whom the world cannot receive, because it does not behold Him or know Him, but you know Him because He abides with you, and will be in you."
>
> John 14:17

Jesus was suggesting a new, much more intimate relationship. In effect, He was saying, "You've been engaged to Him during My earthly ministry, but when I leave you're going to be married to Him. So far it's been like dating. When I leave and He comes, it will be like marriage. It won't be a distant, formal relationship where the two of you go home separately every night to different places. No, there will be a permanent intimacy, a oneness. In fact, He will live in you forever."

A few minutes later He assured them:

> "But I tell you the truth, it is to your advantage that I go away; for if I do not go away, the Helper shall not come to you; but if I go, I will send Him to you."
>
> John 16:7

And then He added:

> "But when He, the Spirit of truth, comes, He will guide you into all the truth; for He will not speak on His own initiative,

> but whatever He hears, He will speak; and He will disclose to you what is to come."
>
> John 16:13

They would need help to get through the tough spots, and He, the Spirit, would be there to provide that assistance.

When I was in the marines, in January 1958 our troopship sailed into Yokohama harbor. Though years had passed since the end of World War II, that harbor was still a place of danger because of underwater mines that had not yet been removed. At the mouth of the harbor, our ship stopped and took aboard a Japanese harbor pilot to lead us through the treacherous waters. Slowly and cautiously he steered us through those dark, uncharted waters. As we stood on deck, we could see nothing but the surface below us and the harbor ahead of us. But the harbor pilot steered the ship with confidence, knowing every turn to take to bring us safely to the pier.

In the same way, our Lord promised that the Helper would guide us into all the truth, steering us through life, pointing out the shoals and the reefs and the mines ahead. While we see only the surface, He sees into the depths and beyond the horizon.

As we have discovered in earlier chapters, the Spirit of God works deeply and intimately to transform our lives. He passionately desires to direct our steps, cleanse our thoughts, heal our wounds, take over our worries, reveal God's will, and protect us from evil. All this and so much more is ours through the dynamic presence of the One whom Jesus sent to be our Helper.

Have we reached the end . . . is that all there is to the Spirit's ministry? The answer is a resounding No! Absolutely not! Within us and around us every day we see evidences of His dynamic power.

We see the Spirit at work in our lives. We can know the Spirit's presence by witnessing it in our own lives. His work is continually going on. Paul states very clearly that our bodies represent the Spirit's temple:

> Or do you not know that your body is a temple of the Holy Spirit who is in you, whom you have from God, and that you are not your own? For you have been bought with a price: therefore glorify God in your body.
>
> 1 Corinthians 6:19–20

> The Spirit Himself bears witness with our spirit that we are children of God, and if children, heirs also, heirs of God and fellow heirs with Christ, if indeed we suffer with Him in order that we may also be glorified with Him.
>
> Romans 8:16–17

When we are with other Christians, the witness of the Spirit verifies our spiritual connection, even though we may speak different languages and come from differing cultures. It's a wonderful connection. I can sit down with a body of believers in Russia and feel an immediate sense of accord . . . a family identification . . . and yet I don't speak a word of Russian. That is the Spirit's work.

Furthermore, when we encounter enemy attacks, the Spirit's work is evident because there is a sense of confidence and security in our faith.

> You are from God, little children, and have overcome them; because greater is He who is in you than he who is in the world.
>
> 1 John 4:4

We see the Spirit empowering gifted Christians for ministry. Those gifts and ministries differ and vary, but the same Holy Spirit is at work.

> Now there are varieties of gifts, but the same Spirit. And there are varieties of ministries, and the same Lord. And there are varieties of effects, but the same God who works all things in all persons. But to each one is given the manifestation of the Spirit for the common good.
>
> 1 Corinthians 12:4–7

When I hear a gifted teacher expound the Scriptures, I am benefiting from the Spirit's work in that person's life. When I hear of or see people gifted in evangelism winning people to Christ, I know the work of the Spirit is involved. When I see people showing mercy and encouragement, demonstrating hospitality, and helping others, I am witnessing the work of the Spirit.

We see the Spirit restraining lawlessness.

> For the mystery of lawlessness is already at work; only he who now restrains will do so until he is taken out of the way. And then that lawless one will be revealed whom the Lord will slay with the breath of His mouth and bring to an end by the appearance of His coming.
>
> 2 Thessalonians 2:7–8

Now, I can hear your immediate reaction. "What? Restraining lawlessness? Have you looked at the headlines lately?" And granted, the world does seem chaotic and out of control. Lawlessness appears to be at an all-time high. But think about it . . . What would this world be like if the controlling influence of the Spirit of God were lifted from this earth? Think about what it would be like if all the believers, empowered with the Spirit of God, suddenly disappeared. When the restrainer (the controlling power of the Spirit) is removed, there will be expressions and outbreaks of evil like we have never witnessed.

We may think, *It can't get any worse.* But it will. When the restrainer is lifted from this earth, it will indeed! But for now we know His work is evident because He continues to restrain lawlessness.

Finally, *we see the Spirit regenerating the lost.* He is still expanding the ranks of the church. Remember Jesus' words?

> "Truly, truly, I say to you, unless one is born again, he cannot see the kingdom of God. . . . That which is born of the flesh is flesh, and that which is born of the Spirit is spirit. Do not marvel that I said to you, 'You must be born again.'"
>
> John 3:3, 6–8

The Spirit is still at work, leading people to Christ . . . still building His church.

Recently I got a letter I was tempted to frame! It is from a young physician. And as you read these excerpts, remember . . . you are reading about the work of the Spirit on one person's life. Imagine the thousands of stories that could be written every day!

> Not too long ago I finished a rotation at the Loma Linda Veterans Hospital and one of my patients was in the Navy during World War II. He served in the Battle of Midway and was on the USS *Lexington* which was sunk in that battle. The individual I met was literally just a skeleton of the man who fought for our country. He now was on the losing end of a battle against a certain type of lung cancer that is well known as being the most deadly and the most rapidly fatal type of lung cancer. The malignancy is usually located near the mainstem bronchus which is the main "tube" that brings air into each lung, so as the tumor grows it will progressively suffocate the patient. In addition to slowly suffocating, the patient will also suffer indescribable bone pain secondary to the cancer's propensity to spread to bones throughout the body. . . .
>
> [This disease] is brought on by hard living and excessive smoking, which was exactly the history of this patient. Because you too were once a "military man," you will know what I am describing when I say that this patient used to be as tough as nails, feared nothing, and lived life with incredible reckless abandon. However, forty years of hard living had caught up and had beaten him. He now weighed less than ninety pounds (in his prime he weighed close to two hundred pounds), he was unable to sit up in bed secondary to severe weakness and pain, he had lost all of his hair secondary to chemotherapy. He was only able to speak a few words at a time, otherwise he would get too short of breath.
>
> I knew after my first talk with him that he would not live another week. I am not the type of medical student who usually shares Christianity to patients, but this man was an

> exception. After taking time to build a relationship with him, I asked him if he were afraid of dying. He stated that he had absolutely no fear of death. I was shocked by his confidence because at this point I only knew of his military days, and I figured that he was just giving me a "tough guy" image (but I should have known that people on their deathbed usually cease seeing the need to be false). But he continued and told me the events of his life, and because he had to take many pauses to catch his breath, this took quite a while.
>
> He rehashed to me his wild Navy days during the war up until the point two years ago when he was in the depths of depression and feelings of hopelessness. He was living back east at the time, he had been divorced several times, and did not know where his children were living, and he was now living all alone. He was at the point of considering suicide when on the radio came a program he had never heard before. He stated that the show was entitled "Insight for Living." He said that right then and there, after listening to only this one show, he accepted Christ into his life as his personal Savior. He later moved out to Orange County, California, but he never did attend the First Evangelical Free Church of Fullerton because he was too embarrassed of his past life to go to the church that Chuck Swindoll spoke at. At this point I took the liberty of telling him that you too used to be in the military, and I told him that Chuck Swindoll would have been proud to meet him because he was a genuine Christian. . . . At this statement, he smiled the biggest smile possible.
>
> Our conversation came to a close at this point and I told him that I would see him the next morning. However, during the night, he fell into a coma and died two days later, never regaining consciousness.[3]

The Spirit of God did all that! Just think . . . one voice from the middle of nowhere, one statement, and a man's whole life is regenerated.

Yes, the Spirit is still at work transforming lives. He is still touching people. Still using folks like you and me. The Spirit of

God is very much alive and well on Planet Earth. His ministry is far from over!

Few people could express my closing thoughts on the Holy Spirit better than the late, great Charles Haddon Spurgeon:

> Common, too common is the sin of forgetting the Holy Spirit. This is folly and ingratitude. . . . As God, He is good essentially. . . . He is good benevolently, tenderly bearing with our waywardness, striving with our rebellious wills; quickening us from our death in sin, and then training us for the skies as a loving nurse fosters her child. . . . He is good operatively. All His works are good in the most eminent degree: He suggests good thoughts, prompts good actions, reveals good truths, applies good promises, assists in good attainments, and leads to good results. There is no spiritual good in all the world of which He is not the author and sustainer. . . . They who yield to His influence become good; they who obey His impulses do good, they who live under His power receive good. . . . Let us revere His person, and adore Him as God over all, blessed for ever; let us own His power, and our need of Him by waiting upon Him in all our holy enterprises; let us hourly seek His aid, and never grieve Him; and let us speak to His praise whenever occasions occur. The church will never prosper until more reverently it believes in the Holy Ghost.[4]

May these chapters not only help you understand the work and enter into the power of the Holy Spirit, but, more than that, may they lead you to the most exciting and fulfilling experience in life . . . flying closer to the flame.

Epilogue

Throughout this book, I have encouraged you to stay open and teachable, and I appreciate your willingness to do so. But I have also warned you of the need to guard yourself against error, that you not be swept up into movements and groups and extremes that will hurt you and disillusion you rather than help, encourage, and strengthen you. So as we look forward to flying closer to the flame as the Spirit of God controls and transforms our lives, we need to keep a few practical and helpful checkpoints in mind.

Checkpoint 1: *Always let your Bible be your guide.* Whenever you are in doubt or confusion, always go back to the Bible. Anytime you are not sure . . . or feel uneasy. . . or wonder if something may not be quite right—it's the Bible you need to consult.

Checkpoint 2: *Be discerning.* It pays to be a little suspicious, even a tad skeptical. To keep asking questions. To check out the character of the one doing the teaching. Don't be gullible. Keep thinking clearly. Be discerning.

Checkpoint 3: *Stay balanced.* In other words, guard against extremism. If you find things getting a little fanatical, put on the brakes. Christ builds His body with stable, contagious Christians. Fanatics are not contagious, they are frightening. If you are alienating those who are strong in their walk with Christ, something is wrong. If you have been following someone's teaching and things are starting to get a little weird, pay attention to that "unidentified inner prompting."

One other little tip on staying balanced: If you are becoming more and more exclusive, you are probably moving toward error.

When God's in it, He blends the flow of truth into the whole body of Christ. If you are beginning to think you have a corner on what's right, something's wrong. You are losing your balance.

Checkpoint 4: *Seek the counsel of men and women you admire.* If you are beginning to wonder about what's being taught, spend some time with those who are not caught up in the things you have been hearing and following. You need a calm, objective, wise perspective. Seek it out.

Checkpoint 5: *Keep the unity.* Keeping the unity of the Spirit is not simply a nice option, it is a biblical command to keep the body strong. It is an essential part of our walk. Don't allow yourself to be deliberately divisive. There are a few occasions when one must stand alone and walk away, but those times are exceptions, not the rule.

Notes

Chapter 1
Let's Get Acquainted with the Spirit

1. Archibald Thomas Robertson, *The Acts of the Apostles,* vol. 3. of *Word Pictures in the New Testament* (Nashville, Tenn.: Broadman Press, 1930), 10.
2. F. F. Bruce, *Commentary on the Book of Acts* (Grand Rapids, Mich.: Eerdmans, 1954), 38–39.

Chapter 2
The Main Agenda of God's Spirit: Transformation

1. Robert E. Coleman, *The Master Plan of Evangelism* (Old Tappan, N.J.: Revell, 1964), 23.
2. Ibid., 22–23.
3. Max DePress, *Leadership Jazz* (New York: Doubleday, 1992), 14–15.

Chapter 3
My Sin . . . and "The Things of the Spirit"

1. J. B. Phillips, *Your God Is Too Small* (New York: Macmillan, 1987).
2. Martin Lloyd-Jones, as quoted in and reprinted from John White, *When the Spirit Comes with Power* (Downers Grove, Ill.: InterVarsity Press, 1988), 13. Used by permission of InterVarsity Press, P.O. Box 1400, Downers Grove, Ill. 60515

Chapter 4
Is the Spirit's Filling That Big a Deal?

1. John R. W. Stott, *Baptism and Fullness: The Work of the Holy Spirit Today* (Downers Grove, Ill.: InterVarsity Press, 19__), 57.

2. Ibid.
3. C. S. Lewis, *Christian Reflections,* ed. Walter Hooper (Grand Rapids, Mich.: Eerdmans, 1974), preface.

Chapter 6
Draw Me Nearer . . . Nearer

1. A personal letter. Used by permission.
2. Archibald Thomas Robertson, *The Acts of the Apostles,* vol. 3. of *Word Pictures in the New Testament* (Nashville, Tenn.: Broadman Press, 1930), 76.
3. Clark H. Pinnock, "Our Source of Authority: The Bible," *Bibliotheca Sacra,* vol. 124, no. 494 (April-June 1967): 150, 151.
4. Fanny J. Crosby, 1875.

Chapter 7
Those Unidentified Inner Promptings

1. A. Cohen, *The Psalms* (London: Soncino Press, 1958), 453.
2. C. F. Keil and F. Delitzsch, *The Books of the Kings,* in *Biblical Commentary on the Old Testament,* trans. James Martin (Grand Rapids, Mich.: Eerdmans, n.d.), 258.
3. "How Firm a Foundation," *Rippons Selection of Hymns,* 1787.

Chapter 8
The Spirit and Our Emotions

1. John White, *When the Spirit Comes with Power: Signs and Wonders Among God's People* (Downers Grove, Ill.: InterVarsity Press, 1988), 48, 49. Used by permission of InterVarsity Press, P.O. Box 1400, Downers Grove, Ill. 60515

Chapter 9
Thinking Theologically About Sickness and Healing

1. John White, *When the Spirit Comes with Power: Signs and Wonders Among God's People* (Downers Grove, Ill.: InterVarsity Press, 1988),

17–18. Used by permission of InterVarsity Press, P.O. Box 1400, Downers Grove, Ill. 60515
2. Jonathan Edwards, "A Faithful Narrative of a Surprising Work of God," in *The Works of Jonathan Edwards,* vol. 1 (Edinburgh: Banner of Turth, 1974), 354.
3. I am indebted to Dr. John White for these ideas. See John White, *When the Spirit Comes,* 60–61.

Chapter 10
A Biblical Case for Healing

1. C. Everett Koop, "Faith-Healing and the Sovereignty of God," in *The Agony of Deceit,* ed. Michael Horton (Chicago: Moody Press, 1990), 169. Copyright 1990, Moody Bible Institute of Chicago. Used by permission.
2. Ibid., 173–74.
3. Ibid., 176–77.

Chapter 11
When the Spirit Brings a Slow Recovery

1. Winston S. Churchill, "Painting as a Pastime," reprinted with the permission of Charles Scribner's Sons, an imprint of Macmillan Publishing Company from AMID THESE STORMS by Winston Churchill.Copyright 1932 Charles Scribner's Sons; copyright renewed © 1960 Winston S. Churchill.
2. Archibald Thomas Robertson, *The Acts of the Apostles,* vol. 3. of *Word Pictures in the New Testament* (Nashville, Tenn.: Broadman Press, 1930), 480.
3. Charles F. Pfeiffer and Everett F. Harrison, eds., *The Wycliffe Bible Commentary* (Chicago: Moody Press, 1962), 1176.
4. Taken from Eugene H. Peterson, *A Long Obedience in the Same Direction* (Downers Grove, Ill.: InterVarsity Press, 1980), 102, 103. Used by permission of InterVarsity Press, P.O. Box 1400, Downers Grove, Ill. 60515
5. C. S. Lewis, *The Problem of Pain* (New York: Macmillan, 1962), 93.

Chapter 12
Power, Power . . . We've Got the Power!

1. A. W. Tozer, *The Knowledge of the Holy* (New York: Harper & Brothers, 1961), 16–17.

Chapter 13
Is That All There Is to the Spirit's Ministry?

1. Taken from Stuart Hample and Eric Marshall, comps., *Children's Letters to God* (New York: Workman Publishing, 1991), 6, 7, 9, 11, 14, 17, 21, 26, 44.
2. Ibid., 49.
3. A personal letter. Used by permission.
4. Charles Haddon Spurgeon, *Spurgeon's Morning and Evening* (Grand Rapids, Mich.: Zondervan, 1965), 95.

The Mystery of God's Will

Publications by Charles R. Swindoll

BOOKS

Active Spirituality
The Bride
Come Before Winter
Compassion: Showing We Care in a Careless World
David: A Man of Passion and Destiny
Dear Graduate
Dropping Your Guard
Encourage Me
Esther: A Woman of Strength and Dignity
The Finishing Touch
Flying Closer to the Flame
For Those Who Hurt
The Grace Awakening
Growing Deep in the Christian Life
Growing Strong in the Seasons of Life
Growing Wise in Family Life
Hand Me Another Brick
Home: Where Life Makes Up Its Mind
Hope Again
Improving Your Serve
Intimacy with the Almighty
Joseph: A Man of Integrity and Forgiveness
Killing Giants, Pulling Thorns
Laugh Again
Leadership: Influence That Inspires
Living Above the Level of Mediocrity
Living Beyond the Daily Grind, Books I and II
The Living Insights Study Bible—General Editor
Living on the Ragged Edge
Make Up Your Mind
Man to Man
Moses: A Man of Selfless Dedication
The Quest for Character
Recovery: When Healing Takes Time
The Road to Armageddon
Sanctity of Life
Simple Faith
Starting Over
Start Where You Are
Strengthening Your Grip
Stress Fractures
Strike the Original Match
The Strong Family
Suddenly One Morning
Tale of the Tardy Oxcart
Three Steps Forward, Two Steps Back
Victory: A Winning Game Plan for Life
You and Your Child

MINIBOOKS

Abraham: A Model of Pioneer Faith
David: A Model of Pioneer Courage
Esther: A Model of Pioneer Independence
Moses: A Model of Pioneer Vision
Nehemiah: A Model of Pioneer Determination

BOOKLETS

Anger
Attitudes
Commitment
Dealing with Defiance
Demonism
Destiny
Divorce
Eternal Security
Forgiving and Forgetting
Fun Is Contagious!
God's Will
Hope
Impossibilities
Integrity
Intimacy with the Almighty
Leisure
The Lonely Whine of the Top Dog
Make Your Dream Come True
Making the Weak Family Strong
Moral Purity
Our Mediator
Peace . . . in Spite of Panic
Portrait of a Faithful Father
The Power of a Promise
Prayer
Reflections from the Heart—A Prayer Journal
Seeking the Shepherd's Heart—A Prayer Journal
Sensuality
Stress
This is No Time for Wimps
Tongues
When Your Comfort Zone Gets the Squeeze
Woman

CHARLES R. SWINDOLL

The MYSTERY of GOD'S WILL

What Does He Want For Me?

W PUBLISHING GROUP

www.wpublishinggroup.com

A Division of Thomas Nelson, Inc.
www.ThomasNelson.com

THE MYSTERY OF GOD'S WILL
by Charles R. Swindoll

Published by W Publishing Group, a Division of Thomas Nelson Inc.,
P. O. Box 141000, Nashville, Tennessee 37214.

Library of Congress Cataloging-in-Publication Data

Swindoll, Charles R.
The mystery of God's will / by Charles R. Swindoll.
p. cm.
Includes bibliographical references.
ISBN 0-8499-1133-8 (HARDCOVER)
ISBN 0-8499-4329-4 (TRADEPAPER)
1. God—Will. 2. Christian life. I. Title.
BV4509.5.S96 1999
248.421—DC21
99-043573
CIP

Printed in the United States of America

99 00 01 02 03 04 05 06 BVG 9 8 7 6 5 4 3 2 1

Dedication

These recent years have been marked by
times of uncertainty and mystery
for my wife and me.

God has seemed a paradox in many ways
as we have continued to seek His will
and walk in obedience to His Word.

He has sometimes been so close
we could almost feel the flapping of angels' wings
as they hovered around His throne . . .
but at other times, He has seemed so distant
we felt strangely confused, even abandoned.

Those are not easy waters for a Christian couple to navigate,
especially when you feel you are journeying
without answers and lacking reassurance.

Two couples have meant the most to us
during these turbulent, soul-searching months:

DAVID AND WENDY CHAVANNE

and

JOHNNY AND CASEY KOONS

Because of the love they have demonstrated to us
through their loyal friendship, encouraging words,
compassionate acts of mercy, and intercessory support,
I gratefully and affectionately dedicate this book to them.

Contents

Introduction

All deep earnest thinking is but the intrepid effort of the soul
to keep the open independence of her sea, while
the wildest winds of Heaven and earth conspire to
cast her on the treacherous, slavish shore.

—Herman Melville, *Moby Dick*

So much of the confusion we encounter in life goes back to our not understanding God and how He does His inscrutable work in our lives. In recent years, I have struggled with many of what I am calling "mysteries" in my own life. As a result, I have come to a new understanding of God's will. In the past, I often viewed the Christian life, or even just life in general, as a matter of getting from here to there . . . from point A to point B. I now believe that God's will for us in this life is not some black-and-white objective equation designed to take us to an appointed destination here on earth as much as it is about the journey itself. It is not so much about our own well-thought-through "mission" for our lives as it is about what matters to Him in our lives.

Our human tendency is to focus solely on our calling—on where we should go, how we should get there, and what exactly we should do about it. God's concern is the process that He is taking us through to mature us and ready us, making us more like His Son. In other words, all of us—including *you*—are works in process.

Think of the men and women in Scripture who were made aware of their calling from the Lord, but who soon discovered that carrying out that call or arriving at that place of service was extremely convoluted, often surprising, and occasionally downright painful. In fact, sometimes they didn't get "there" at all, at least not where they had expected to go.

Abraham was told to sacrifice his son Isaac. That was to be his mission, clearly stated and plainly communicated by the Lord. But in the final analysis, God was testing him, all the time having other plans in mind. Surprising to Abraham? Yes. Mysterious? Absolutely.

David was anointed to become king of Israel. That was the stated goal. Samuel said so. But within a short time, David became the object of King Saul's jealousy and wrath. And for a dozen or more years, the pressure he endured mounted to such an extent that David must have wondered if he would ever even live to see his day on the throne. Unexpected by David? Certainly.

And what about poor Hosea? What a scandal his life was. Yet it was the Lord's will that Hosea marry the adulterous Gomer, taking her back after her continued unfaithfulness. Another mystery . . . from our point of view.

Then there was Joseph, maligned, mistreated, and falsely accused. How could that possibly be God's will for one of His chosen vessels, seemingly called by God to be a great leader? Well, it was.

Or consider John the Baptizer, who was beheaded at the whim of Herod's stepdaughter. Talk about mysterious! How in the world could that be the will of God for one He loved much and had used so mightily?

And Paul. After being so clearly called by God as the apostle to the Gentiles, he spent the balance of his life jumping from one frying pan into another fire. How did God's will work in his reaching that goal? Painful. Full of obstacles. Interrupted. Mysterious!

The list would go on endlessly if we were to recount all the mysterious ways of God's will and work in the lives of His people down through the centuries.

It is these mysterious, surprising, and, yes, often distressing aspects of God's will that I intend to address in the following pages. For some reason, I don't find much written on the subject. Far more often I read of how clearly and calmly the Lord takes His people from here to there, with little struggle and almost no doubt. It's quick, simple, and easy . . . or so I'm told.

Because that has not been my experience, and because I rarely find it modeled in the Scriptures or in people's lives today, it seemed appropriate that the mysterious, vague, and disturbing side of obedience be acknowledged. There is no harm in not being able to explain why or in admitting that followers of Christ are frequently at a loss to find human logic in the path He designs for us to walk. If nothing else, I hope this book will give you permission to confess, "This is beyond my ability to understand. It's a mystery."

As is true in the writing of all books, this has not been strictly a solo work. I have three people, especially, to thank for their behind-the-scenes assistance.

First, my very diligent and determined friend, Judith Markham, whose editorial assistance proved, once again, invaluable.

Second, Mary Hollingsworth, who helped me put the finishing touches on the final manuscript . . . before my deadline!

And third, Julie Meredith, who traced all my quotations, verified their accuracy and secured the permissions in an efficient and timely manner.

My appreciation for these capable ladies knows no bounds. In many ways, you hold this book in your hands because they did their work so well.

Of course, as always, I have my wife, Cynthia, to thank for her encouragement and affirmation. It was our own mysterious (and often *painful)* journey together during recent years that prompted my writing on this subject. Thankfully, she hung in there with me when we had great confusion, few answers, and little strength.

—Chuck Swindoll
Dallas, Texas

Part I

The Buffetings of God's Will

God will not look you over for medals,
degrees, or diplomas, but for scars.

—Elbert Hubbard, *The Note Book*

By trying we can easily learn to endure adversity.
Another man's, I mean.

—Mark Twain, *Following the Equator*

1

A Process and a Puzzle

The best is perhaps what we understand the least.

—C.S. Lewis, *A Grief Observed*

'Tis very puzzling on the brink of what is called eternity
to stare and know no more of what is *here* than *there.*

—Byron, *Don Juan*

People wish to be settled:
only as far as they are unsettled
is there any hope for them.

—Emerson, *Essays: First Series*

Chapter One

A Process and a Puzzle

THE FLAG OF SORROW flew at half mast over many an American heart in mid-July, 1999. Another tragedy. Another in a long line of familiar names from the famous Kennedy clan tasted death much earlier than anyone would have predicted . . . and in a way most would never have guessed.

Ironically, this one happened seven short miles off the same shore of the same sleepy resort island where young John played as a lad. Will the sadness never end for this grief-stricken, shock-stunned family? The list is a litany of tragedies and surprises that reads like a modern-day book of lamentations. Horrible assassinations, sudden deaths, carnal scandals, tragic and life-threatening illnesses, and now a desperate search at sea for the remains of three lives that ended as strangely as any of us could have imagined. There are some who have suggested it is some sort of "curse" that haunts them. To be sure, unanwered questions swarm all over the Kennedys.

Regardless of where you and I may stand politically, ethically, and morally—in spite of whether we agree or disagree with their lives and lifestyles—every one of us turns the same three-letter word over and over in our heads: *Why?* We find ourselves wondering how much longer the plague, if that's what it is, will remain and who of their number will be next. It's a mystery.

Even as Christians, who firmly believe in a God of order and compassion, One who "tenderly cares for His own," we cannot deny the reality that much of what He does and most of why He does it falls into that category . . . at least from our vantage point. And it isn't just one family's mystery—we all live with mysteries, not just the rich and famous. They surround all of us through all of life. The healthy and hearty as well as the sick, the handicapped, and the dying. The young and the old. The godly and the godless.

It's time to say it: More often than not we face life in a quandary. Searching, disturbing questions far outnumber absolute, air-tight answers. Even though we love the Lord and are committed to His plan. Even though we obey His Word and seek His will. If we're honest enough to admit it, there are days—no, there are even months—when we simply cannot figure out what God is up to.

The longer I live, the more I believe that one of the most profound subjects in the Christian life is the will of God. The deeper we dig into it, the more we realize how little we know. When we stop and think deeply about the way He leads us along, we must conclude that it is one of the most mysterious subjects in the spiritual life. Yet I've observed that we use words like "It's the will of God" or "We hope God will have His will and way in this" rather glibly.

Someone has said that getting an education is going from an unconscious to a conscious awareness of our own ignorance. When we do a serious study of the will of God, we go from an unconscious to a conscious awareness of how mysteriously He leads us along. Perhaps this explains why our walk with our Lord is often inconsistent and why it is sometimes more of a struggle than a relief. Let's face it: Much of His plan simply doesn't make sense . . . not to us.

So much of understanding this is a matter of the will—not God's will, but our will. I certainly know that in my own heart I do not always really want to do His will.

We say we do, of course. If we were asked to respond with yes or no to the question, all of us would say, "Yes, I want to know His will." But *doing* God's will is another matter entirely, because almost without exception it requires risk and adjustment and change. We don't like that. Even using those words makes us squirm. Experiencing the reality of them is even worse. We love the familiar. We love the comfortable. We love something we can control—something we can get our arms around. Yet the closer we walk with the Lord, the less control we have over our own lives, and the more we must abandon to Him. To give Him our wills and to align our wills to His will requires the abandonment of what we prefer, what we want or what we would choose.

So as we approach this "archaeological study" of the will of God, let's recognize that we dig into it knowing that everything within us will at times resist doing what He wants us to do.

A PUZZLE WE WILL NEVER SOLVE

What is God's will and what is not God's will? How can we know God's will? Is it common to miss God's will or is that even possible? How did God reveal His will in biblical days? Is it the same way He reveals His will today? Are there prerequisites for knowing God's will? Can I really know that I am doing God's will? That I am in His will? If so, how? And if I'm not doing God's will, how do I know that? Can anyone else help me discern God's will? If I do His will does He always reward me?

All these and more are common questions every thoughtful believer grapples with at one time or another in life.

I jokingly say to people at times, "It's easier for me to know God's will for my *wife* than it is for me to know God's will for my *life."* The reality is, of course, that we often operate on that principle. We believe we know what our spouse ought to do, or what our child ought to do, or what our neighbor ought to do, or what our friend ought to do. But the tough thing is knowing what I ought to be doing.

Who can help us discern that? Who can we lean on, rely on? Are there any examples of those who have walked in His will? Or, what about the opposite? Are there any examples of those who have strayed from His will? Is God's will ever a surprise? And if so, why would He choose to surprise us? Is that fair?

In the following pages, I want to grapple with many of these questions in one form or other. But before we begin, I need to make an admission, which will in some ways be a disclaimer. I admit: *This subject is inscrutable.* Please read those four words again. During my years in seminary, one of my mentors used to say, "One of your problems as young theologians is trying to unscrew the inscrutable." So there are times I will say, without reservation or hesitation, "I do not know the answer." It is a profound, unfathomable subject. Although we have been given so much direction and clarification in the Word of God, there is far more that is beyond our human understanding. So determine right now not to let that trouble you—even you perfectionist types who want to sweep every corner clean and get every part of the subject covered and clearly understood. You will never, ever be able to do that with this subject. Benjamin Disraeli put it well: "To be conscious that you are ignorant is a great step to knowledge."

But don't take my word for it. Let's learn from Scripture. Look at Job 9, where Job is answering Bildad, who, along with Eliphaz and Zophar, has come to bring a bit of comfort to his suffering friend, Job. I write that with tongue in cheek, of course, because these guys really came to accuse Job. As Job himself says later on, "Sorry comforters are you all. What a sorry lot of counselors you have been!"

If you take the time to read Job 8, you'll see how Bildad unloads a major guilt trip on Job. Then in 9:1–12 Job responds. You can almost picture him as he throws his arms in the air and cries,

> In truth I know that this is so, but how can a man be in the right before God?
>
> If one wished to dispute with Him [God], he could not answer Him once in a thousand times.
>
> Wise in heart and mighty in strength, who has defied Him without harm?
>
> It is God who removes the mountains, they know not how, when

He overturns them in His anger;

Who shakes the earth out of its place, and its pillars tremble; who commands the sun not to shine, and sets a seal upon the stars;

Who alone stretches out the heavens, and tramples down the waves of the sea;

Who makes the Bear, Orion, and the Pleiades, and the chambers of the south;

Who does great things, unfathomable,
And wondrous works without number.

Job is awed by the Creator who "shakes the earth out of its place." Californians know that feeling well—that uneasy, insecure feeling of the earth shaking beneath them. He speaks of the One who "commands the sun not to shine, and sets a seal on the stars." We can set our watches by these heavenly lights God put in motion from the beginning. He does "great things," says Job, things that are "unfathomable." When it comes to God's workings and plans, we will never be able to say, "Finally, I've got it! I've figured it all out!"—not until we get to heaven, when we will know as we are known.

"The first sound we will hear from every throat when we get to heaven is 'Ahhhh,'" says my good friend Jay Kesler. "Now I see it! Now I realize why. Now it all makes sense before my eyes, this great once-mysterious panorama of events."

My mentor, the late Ray Stedman, had a helpful description of this. I can still remember his talking about moving from earth to heaven: "We move from the very restricted and limited realm to this massive panorama of the whole scene. And it will be good." It all will have worked together for good, including the tragedies and the calamities and the heartaches, the illnesses and diseases and what we call premature deaths, the terrible deformities and birth defects and congenital illnesses. All will unfold, and we will see that God's plan was right. But not until then. That is Job's point:

[He] does great things, unfathomable, and wondrous works without number.

> Were He to pass by me, I would not see Him; were He to move past me, I would not perceive Him.
>
> Were He to snatch away, who could restrain Him? Who could say to Him, "What art Thou doing?"
>
> (Job 9:10–12)

Who hasn't been tempted to shake a fist at God and cry, "What are You doing?" A child is kidnapped and brutally murdered. "God, what are You doing to us?" A husband drives to the hardware store on Saturday morning and is hit head-on and killed by a drunk driver. Just that quickly he is taken from his wife and family. "What in the world is God up to?" A young mother has routine surgery, develops unforeseen complications, and dies. "God, what are You doing?" It is unfathomable.

So many things that happen in this life are past searching out. I can't explain His plan. I can only unfold from the Scriptures how unfathomable it really is.

The psalmist gives voice to this eloquently in Psalm 139:1–2:

> O Lord, Thou hast searched me and known me.
> Thou dost know when I sit down and when I rise up;
> Thou dost understand my thought from afar.
> Thou dost scrutinize my path and my lying down,
> And art intimately acquainted with all my ways.

Before I ever have a thought, You know it's on its way. You know when it strikes my brain and what's going to come as a result of it. You know it long before I have the thought. Yet we still have the freedom to think that thought and follow through on that action. This is part of the unfathomable nature of our God. "You know it from afar. You scrutinize my path."

For Christmas one year we bought our children what was called "Ant City." This consisted of clear plastic plates on either side, filled with sand and ants. From our vantage point outside and above, we could see what these busy little creatures were doing underground. We watched as they tunneled their way around, leaving a maze of trails.

In a similar fashion, God scrutinizes our paths. From where we are, tunneling along, all we see is the sand immediately ahead, behind, and beside us. But from His vantage point, He can see exactly where we've been and precisely where we're going. "He is intimately acquainted with all my ways."

I know my wife, Cynthia, very well, but I am not intimately acquainted with *all* her ways, even though we have been married almost forty-five years. As well as I may know my wife or my children or a friend, I will never be "intimately acquainted" with *all* of their ways. My finite nature hinders such knowledge.

God, however, knows each one of us individually. He numbers the very hairs of our head (which is a bigger challenge for some than for others). The hopes, the wayward thoughts, the directions, the decisions, the indecision, the motives, the words we think but don't say . . . He knows all of those.

> Even before there is a word on my tongue,
> Behold O Lord, Thou dost know it all.
> You have enclosed me behind and before,
> You have laid Your hand upon me.
> Such knowledge is too wonderful for me;
> It is too high, I cannot attain to it. (Psalm 139:4–6)

"I may be Your son," David was saying, "and I may write Your music, Lord, and I may be the king of Your people, but, Lord, Your ways are still beyond me. They remain unfathomable to me. I can't understand or explain what You're doing. Such knowledge is too great for me. I can't reach it. I can't attain to it."

Why is it that in the same family one child will go one direction and one another? "It is too high, I cannot attain to it." All of us are sinners. So why does one couple break up in six months and another stay together for sixty years? Why are some individuals called to serve in small, obscure, and difficult places while others serve in comfort in a large arena, surrounded by support. Why, why, why? "It is too high, I cannot attain to it."

So let's settle this point right at the outset. All of these things and so many more we will never understand in this life. Despite all of our searching and all of our study of the Scriptures, we'll never be able to see everything clearly, to fully grasp and understand and answer all the questions. They are beyond our comprehension—a puzzle, a mystery.

In *Keep a Quiet Heart,* Elisabeth Elliott says, "Today is mine. Tomorrow is none of my business. If I peer anxiously into the fog of the future, I will strain my spiritual eyes so that I will not see clearly what is required of me now." [1]

Much of what happens in life we simply have to take by faith. Answers will not be forthcoming. These are the tensions of reality, and if we get marooned on the tensions, we will not be able to travel further. That is as our heavenly Father planned it.

Who can ever explain the events that occurred at Columbine High school in April, 1999, in Littleton, Colorado? The tragedy is beyond our comprehension—fourteen teenagers and one teacher dead, most of them Christians. How could that be? Why would a loving, caring, gracious God—who does all things well—*even permit* such an event? In our minds, none of the above squares with our understanding of goodness and grace. How could it?

Was all that a part of His plan? Could it be that, in this strange unfolding of His will, we have failed to leave sufficient room for His permission of evil? Job asked his wife what I now ask you, "Shall we indeed accept good from God and not accept adversity" (Job 2:10)? *It's a mystery* . . . based on how we see things and how we evaluate fairness and how we gauge goodness.

God is the Potter; we are the clay. He's the Shepherd; we are the sheep. He's the Master; we are the servant. No matter how educated we are, no matter how much power and influence we may think we have, no matter how long we have walked with Him, no matter how significant we may imagine ourselves to be in His plans (if any of us could even claim significance), none of that qualifies us to grasp the first particle of why He does what He does when He does it and how He chooses to do it.

> "For My thoughts are not your thoughts,
> Neither are your ways My ways," declares the LORD.
> "For as the heavens are higher than the earth,
> So are My ways higher than your ways,
> And My thoughts than your thoughts."
> (Isaiah 55:8–9)

> Oh, the depth of the riches both of the wisdom and knowledge of God! How unsearchable are His judgments and unfathomable His ways! "For who has known the mind of the Lord, or who became His counselor?" (Romans 11:33–34).

In an old work by Origen, *On First Principles,* the great church father underscores what the apostle of grace meant when he wrote that statement:

> Paul did not say that God's judgments were hard to search out but that they could not be searched out at all. He did not say that God's ways were hard to find out but that they were impossible to find out. For however far one may advance in the search and make progress through an increasing earnest study, even when aided and enlightened in the mind by God's grace, he will never be able to reach the final goal of his inquiries.[2]

As I think about God's unfathomable ways and the theme of this book, I am reminded of the six-year-old boy who had been given an assignment to draw anything he wanted to draw. But when everyone else in the class had finished drawing, he was still sitting there working on his picture. Finally the teacher walked back and looked over his shoulder.

"What are you drawing?" she asked.

"I'm drawing a picture of God," said the boy.

"You need to remember, Johnny, no one has ever seen God. Nobody knows what He looks like."

"Well . . . they will when I'm through," said Johnny.

That's what I would love to think about this book: that when I have finished writing and the printer has finished printing and all my readers have finished reading, that people will at least know what the will of God looks like. But even though I think we will all have learned some things together, in all humility and reality, I know that you won't find it all, or see it all in these pages. So, don't get your hopes up!

What I hope we will do is learn how to turn to God and rely on Him to work out His will in our lives. Hopefully we will realize the enormity of our own ignorance and our need to trust Him and then let it be. Just let it be. If His plan for you is a surprise or, perhaps, a disappointment, let it be. I urge you to come to terms with the disappointment and accept the surprise. Go ahead . . . call it a mystery. Let Him have His way with your life, for nothing is worse than resisting and resenting the One who is at work in you.

The amazing thing is that even in the midst of disappointment, surprise, and mystery you will discover how very reliable and trustworthy God is—and how secure you are in His hands. And oh, how we need that in this day of relativism and vacillation, filled with empty talk and hidden behind a lot of semantic footwork. In the midst of "spin city," it is the Lord who talks straight. It is the Lord who has preserved Truth in black and white in His Word. And it is the Lord who has the right to do as He wishes around us, to us, and in us. He's the Potter, remember. Puzzling as the process may be to us, He stays with His plan. There is no need for us to know all the reasons, and He certainly doesn't need to explain Himself. Potters work with the clay, they don't fret over it . . . or ask permission to remake the clay into whatever they wish.

And if we're going to let God be God, then we're forced to say He has the right to take us through whatever process He chooses. The journey may be painful as well as puzzling . . . including a tragedy at sea seven miles off Martha's Vineyard and a massacre in a school in Littleton, Colorado.

2

God Decrees . . . God Permits

The way of God is complex, He is hard for us to predict.
He moves the pieces and they come somehow into a
kind of order.

—EURIPIDES, *Helen*

There is something fundamentally flawed about a purely academic interest in God. God is not an appropriate object for cool, critical, detached, scientific observation and evaluation. No, the true knowledge of God will always lead us to worship. . . . Our place is on our faces before Him in adoration.

—John R. W. Stott, *Romans: God's Great News for the World*

Chapter Two

God Decrees . . . God Permits

THINKING THEOLOGICALLY is a tough thing to do. It works against our human and horizontal perspective on life. Thinking vertically is a discipline few have mastered. We much prefer to live in the here-and-now realm, seeing life as others see it, dealing with realities we can touch, analyze, prove, and explain. We are much more comfortable with the tactile, the familiar, the logic shaped by our culture and lived out in our times.

But God offers a better way to live—one that requires faith, as it lifts us above the drag and grind of our immediate little world, opens new dimensions of thought, and introduces a perspective without human limitations. In order to enter this better way, we must train ourselves to think theologically. Once we've made the switch, our focus turns away from ourselves, removing us from a self-centered realm of existence and opening the door of our minds to a God-centered frame of reference, where all things begin and end with Him.

A prophet named Jeremiah was called by God to minister on His behalf. Jeremiah was afraid to accept the assignment because, from his perspective, he was too young, too inexperienced . . . simply too inadequate. The Lord silenced such horizontal thinking by telling Jeremiah that He knew him even before he was conceived and had set him apart even before he was born. God also promised to protect him and to deliver him and to use him mightily. That started Jeremiah thinking theologically. God had decreed certain things. Jeremiah needed to obey without fear or hesitation. Hard times would surely come—all of which God would permit to happen. But Jeremiah could take great comfort in knowing that God would have His way in spite of the hardships ahead. God had called him and would protect him. And even the opposition Jeremiah would encounter (which God permitted to occur) would not stop or alter God's plan (which He had decreed would occur).

For the rest of this chapter I urge you to think theologically. It will help. By doing so, you will grasp the importance of both the decreed will of God and the permitted will of God.

GOD'S DECRETIVE WILL

The first facet of God's will is what we shall call His decretive will: His sovereign, determined, immutable will. Our friend Job spoke of this when he said,

> Man, who is born of woman,
> Is short-lived and full of turmoil. . . .
> Since his days are determined,
> The number of his months is with Thee,
> And his limits Thou hast set so that he cannot pass.
> (Job 14:1, 5)

Job's words tell us that the decreed will of God is running its course precisely as arranged by our great God. This aspect of the will of God is not something that we can anticipate ahead of time; we can only know it after it has happened.

There are occasions when we are surprised by His decreed will . . . like when we get the results back from our physical exam and the MRI reveals a tumor we had no idea was there. Or when a thirty-seven-year-old wife smiles across the supper table and informs her forty-five-year-old husband, "We're going to have another baby." And their youngest is in high school! Or when the stock market plunges in one day to a ten-year, record-setting low.

It may seem to many that the One who made us is too far removed to concern himself with such tiny details of life on this old globe. But that is not the case. His mysterious plan is running its course right on schedule, exactly as He decreed it.

This world is not out of control, spinning wildly through space. Nor are earth's inhabitants at the mercy of some blind, random fate. When God created the world and set the stars in space, He also established the course of this world and His plan for humanity.

Not all believe this, obviously. To some, this teaching is disturbing and distasteful. And so they go searching for other gods.

Some months ago when I was on a flight to Southern California, my seatmate pulled out a well-worn, thick paperback called *All the Religions of the World.* As he read, I thought to myself, I wish I could take him by the hand and introduce him to the one God who is the Lord of all and over all—the One who satisfies as none of the religions of the world will ever do. I tried, unsuccessfully.

The apostle Paul addressed this very issue when he preached in Athens. The city was filled with idols, for the ancient Athenians had a cast of multiple-thousands when it came to gods and goddesses. They had even erected a monument "To an Unknown God." Then, in a masterful stroke of homiletic genius, Paul said, in effect, "Allow me to introduce you to Him, this God you have missed." (See Acts 17:16–34.)

There is only one God, and He is responsible for the sovereignly decreed plan over this earth.

> I am the LORD, and there is no other;
> Besides Me there is no God.
> I will gird you, though you have not known Me;
> That men may know from the rising to the setting of the sun

That there is no one besides Me.
I am the LORD, and there is no other;
The One forming light and creating darkness,
Causing well-being and creating calamity;
I am the LORD who does all these.
(Isaiah 45:5–7)

Through Isaiah's pen the Lord declares that He is the one who forms light and creates darkness, causes well-being and creates calamity. This is another of those "unexplainables." I don't know why a tornado destroys one neighborhood and not another. I just know that even in this calamity God's plan is not frustrated or altered. Either that, or He isn't God. He is not sitting on the edge of heaven, wondering what will happen next. That's not the God of the Scriptures. So while we cannot fathom the "Why?" of this age-old question, we do know that Scripture states that God is not surprised by calamity. Somehow or other, it's all part of His mysterious will.

Now that is a tough concept to justify. So my advice is quite simple: Quit trying. While this is not the verse you send in a note of comfort to somebody who has just gone through a great tragedy, it is a verse you need to comfort yourself with when you are going through your own calamity. Remember, nothing is a surprise to God, not even our slightest trials. His plan may seem unfair, humanly illogical, and lacking compassion, but that's because we dwell in the here and now. We lack the vertical view. In fact, we sometimes quarrel with God, as the prophet Isaiah testifies:

"Woe to the one who quarrels with his Maker—
An earthenware vessel among the vessels of earth!
Will the clay say to the potter, 'What are you doing?'
Or the thing you are making say, 'He has no hands'? . . .
"It is I who made the earth, and created man upon it.
I stretched out the heavens with My hands,
And I ordained all their host.

> "I have aroused him in righteousness,
> And I will make all his ways smooth;
> He will build My city, and will let My exiles go free,
> Without any payment or reward," says the Lord of hosts.
> (Isaiah 45: 9, 12–13)

At one time in my life statements like that made me cringe and become resentful. Not until I released my grip on my horizontal perspective did I find any comfort in God's sovereignty. Little by little, it began to settle in my mind, bringing relief instead of fear. God is in charge, not us! I address this in detail in chapter 5.

This determined, decreed dimension of God's will has four qualities: (1) It is absolute. (2) It is immutable, which means "unchangeable." (3) It is unconditional. (4) It is always in complete harmony with His plan and His nature. In other words, the decreed will of God will be holy, it will be just, it will be good, it will be righteous; therefore, it will be best. And it will all work toward those ends.

The subject of God's will is woven throughout the tapestry of God's truth as revealed in Scripture. We have seen it in Isaiah. Now let's observe it in Romans:

> We know that God causes all things to work together for good to those who love God, to those who are called according to His purpose.
>
> For whom He foreknew, He also predestined to become conformed to the image of His Son, that He might be the first-born among many brethren;
>
> and whom He predestined, these He also called; and whom He called, these He justified; and whom He justified, these He also glorified. (Romans 8:28–29)

Mark in the margin of your Bible beside these verses: "Decreed will of God." His decreed will is at work in your life. He's chipping away in your life, causing you to take on the character of His Son, Jesus Christ.

A sculptor was asked how he could carve a lion's head out of a large block of marble. "I just chip away everything that doesn't look like a lion's head," was his reply. God works away in our being and chips away everything that doesn't look like Christ—the impatience, the short temper, the pride, the emotional drives that lead us away from our Father. He's shaping us into His image. That's His predetermined plan. And He's committed to it. Nothing we can do will dissuade Him from that plan. He stays at it. He is relentless. And He never runs out of creative ideas.

That's why He sends one person to the mission field in China and another to the bank building in downtown Seattle. That's part of His sovereign plan to shape individuals into the image of Christ. It doesn't mean that the person who goes to China is holier or more in the will of God than the person who goes into banking. You're wrong only if you don't go where He is leading you. How do you know it was part of His decreed will? Because it has happened. Just glance back over your past. You will be able to identify your own personal list of God's decretive will in your life. Grant Howard in *Knowing God's Will—and Doing It* writes,

> Can I know the determined will of God for my life? Yes—after it has occurred! You now know that God's determined will for your life was that you be born of certain parents, in a certain location, under certain conditions, and that you be male or female. You now know that God determined for you to have certain features, certain experiences, certain teachers, certain interests, certain friends, a certain kind of education, and certain brothers or sisters, or perhaps to be an only child. In other words, everything that has happened in your life to this moment has been part of God's determined will for your life. It has happened because He has determined it to be so.[1]

"Wait a minute, wait a minute," I hear you saying. "I've got a question." We all have questions about this. I told you it was profound. I told you we couldn't understand it. We want to be in charge.

We want to say, "No, this is up to me. I choose my own friends. I choose my own interests. I decided where I wanted to go to college."

Now it's *my* turn to say, "Wait a minute." Who sent out the proclamation that you are now in charge? It's not up to you. You're the clay; He's the Potter. Remember? You're the branch; He's the Vine. You're the servant; He's the Master. It's all in His hands. What a wonderful way to live!

What may seem at the time like a series of mysterious, illogical events is, in fact, God at work in ways too deep to explain, too profound for you to grasp . . . right now. Grant Howard continues,

> What about the future? Can I know any part of God's determined will for my life in the future? Your spiritual position and your eternal destiny are the only two things you can know with certainty. If you are in Christ now, you can know for certain you will remain in Christ at every moment in the future. The remainder of your future is hidden from you until it happens. Your career, your marriage partner, your home location, your grades in school, your sicknesses, accidents, honors, travels, income, retirement are all part of God's determined will but are not revealed ahead of time. Apart from your spiritual position and eternal destiny, all that will happen in your life cannot be predicted with absolute certainty.[2]

Stop and think. Who would have guessed five years ago that you'd be doing what you're doing right now, or that you would have experienced over those five years what you've experienced? Not one of us. And I have news for you. You have no idea what the next five years will bring. The future is just as uncertain and exciting and full of risk and wonder as the past five years you have lived. But whatever that future brings is also absolute, immutable, unconditional, and in complete harmony with God's nature and plan.

"Our God is in the heavens; He does whatever He pleases" (Psalm 115:3). This is the verse Lila Trotman quoted when she heard that her husband, Dawson Trotman, founder of The Navigators, had drowned at Scroon Lake, New York. Dawson plunged into the water to rescue two girls who had been thrown out of a speedboat, and then he himself drowned. The friend who was with him ran down the shoreline and found Lila. "Lila, Dawson's gone," he screamed. "He's gone!" That's when Lila calmly quoted Psalm 115:3. She took comfort in God's determined will. What seemed to many as a premature and untimely death, later was seen as God's perfect plan for the fine organization Daws had founded and launched.

More than once through the years that verse has helped me think theologically, saving me from sleepless nights . . . from hours of agonizing over, *Why?*

Even the death of our Savior was part of the determined will of God:

> Men of Israel, listen to these words: Jesus the Nazarene, a man attested to you by God with miracles and wonders and signs which God performed through Him in your midst, just as you yourselves know—this Man, delivered up *by the predetermined plan and foreknowledge of God,* you nailed to a cross by the hands of godless men and put Him to death. (Acts 2:22–23, italics mine)

Though unbelieving men nailed Jesus to His cross, it occurred, "by the predetermined plan and foreknowledge of God." It was exactly at the time and in the place and by the means God had determined. And what looked to the eleven confused disciples as mysterious, as well as unfair and unjust (humanly speaking, it was all of the above and more), God looked at it and said, "That is what I've planned. That's the mission that My Son came to accomplish."

That's why Jesus' final words from the cross before He died were "It is finished." God's redemption plan had been completed—Jesus' payment for our sin. And then He slumped in death.

> And God raised Him up again, putting an end to the agony of death, since it was impossible for Him to be held in its power. (Acts 2:24)

That's exactly what will happen beyond our death. He will raise us up by His grace, putting an end forever to the agony of death, since we will not be held by its power. God has *decreed* it so. That is a wonderful thought to claim at a graveside, isn't it?

This means, however, that there are some things God cannot and will not do because they do not conform to His nature. For example, God cannot and will not lie (Numbers 23:19; Hebrews 6:18). God cannot and does not tempt anyone to sin (James 1:13–15). Those actions would be against His nature and, therefore, against His will.

"Let no one say when he is tempted, 'I am tempted by God,'" writes James, and he uses an interesting syntax when he writes this. In the original language James used a more subtle expression, meaning, "Let no one say when he is tempted, 'I've been tempted indirectly by God.'"

That's a familiar angle, isn't it? Remember the first couple, Adam and Eve? "The woman You gave me, she caused me to sin." (Indirectly, "Lord, You're the one who made me sin.") And we've been doing that ever since. "Lord, if You hadn't given me this nature, I wouldn't have checked into the Internet, and I wouldn't have gone to that chat room, and I wouldn't have gotten involved with that woman, which led to the affair. I mean, if You hadn't given me the time to do this . . ." Not only is that nonsense, it's terrible theology. God cannot, does not, and will not tempt us. He never solicits us to do evil.

Also, God will never contradict His own nature to make a point. "If we are faithless, He remains faithful; for He cannot deny Himself," Paul writes in 2 Timothy 2:13. God is eternally consistent.

Of course we haven't even scratched the surface of this subject of the decretive will of God, but this at least gives us a place to start.

Just remember: No one ultimately is able to frustrate God's plan . . . no one. No one who lets us down surprises God. No one who walks away from his or her responsibilities causes God to wonder why.

In the final analysis, God will have His way. What He has determined will transpire.

But what about evil? What is God's role regarding earthly matters that do not reflect His holy character?

GOD'S PERMISSIVE WILL

The other realm of the will of God is His permissive will, which represents what God allows. For example, God allowed Job to go through suffering. God didn't cause the suffering. He permitted it.

Satan came to God and accused Job of being one of those individuals whom the Lord had carefully protected. "Who wouldn't trust a God who protects His servant from harm? But you touch Job, you touch his life, you touch his family, you touch his health, and he'll curse You."

"All right," said the Lord. "I will allow you to do all that."

I don't know why God did that. How could He call that fair or merciful? From my perspective, it wasn't. It's part of His mysterious will. But I'm not God. I'm merely the clay; He's the Potter. Admittedly, when we read the whole story, we see what wonderful things Job learned about God through this ordeal.

> Then Job answered the Lord, and said,
> "I know that Thou canst do all things,
> And that no purpose of Thine can be thwarted. . . .
> Therefore I have declared that which I did not understand,
> Things too wonderful for me, which I did not know."
> (Job 42:1–3)

As a result, for succeeding generations, Job's name has been synonymous with patience.

Another example and element of the permissive will of God is found in 2 Peter 3:9:

> The Lord is not slow about His promise, as some count slowness, but is patient toward you, not wishing for any to perish but for all to come to repentance. (2 Peter 3:9)

There's the very top of God's "wish list." He wishes that all would come to Him and repent—that none would perish. But all will not repent; some never will. The apostle Paul said, in effect, "I've done all of these things that I might by all means save some (1 Cor. 9:19–22)." He knew that all would not be saved.

Every time I stand up to preach, I pray, "Lord, bring everyone in this place who is without Christ to Yourself." But I'm a realist. And I know that some will choose not to accept Christ. That's part of His plan. From God's perspective, they are not among the elect. This is a tension—another of those unfathomables, those imponderables. If He's not wishing for any to perish, then why doesn't He save everyone? Because it's not part of His sovereign plan. He predetermined the plan of salvation, knowing that many would refuse it. The plan is set. Fixed. Unchanged and unchanging. But some prefer darkness to light, so they willfully refuse to turn to Christ for salvation.

You see, this is where the whole matter of evil comes into play. And this is one of the irreconcilable difficulties in our theology: the tension between the determined will of God and the responsibility of humanity. We need to make Christ known to the whole world, knowing all the while that not everyone in the world will believe.

Charles Spurgeon, one of the great sovereign grace Baptists of yesteryear, put it well when he said, "If God had put a white stripe down the back of every one of the elect, I'd spend my days in London going up and down the streets lifting up shirttails. But because He said, 'Whosoever will may come,' I preach to them all."

God does not wish for anyone to perish but for all to come to repentance. He does not cause sin, but He does permit it. He is not pleased when His creation yields to temptation, but He uses even that to accomplish His purposes.

Pause right now and read Acts 4:27–31.

> "For truly in this city there were gathered together against the holy servant Jesus, whom Thou didst anoint, both Herod and Pontius Pilate, along with the Gentiles and the peoples of Israel, to do whatever Thy hand and Thy purpose predestined to occur.

> "And now, Lord, take note of their threats, and grant that Thy bond-servants may speak Thy word with all confidence, while Thou dost extend Thy hand to heal, and signs and wonders take place through the name of Thy holy servant Jesus."
>
> And when they had prayed, the place where they had gathered together was shaken, and they were all filled with the Holy Spirit, and began to speak the word of God with boldness.

You will find the disciples preaching out in the open, telling both Jews and Gentiles about the death and resurrection of Jesus. They are dodging verbal bullets right and left. Then they retreat a bit and regroup, encourage each other, and go back out to witness to God's offer of salvation to all people. They are scourged and whipped and threatened, only to return again . . . they're back out preaching. They are tortured and imprisoned, and they're still witnessing. It reminds me of one of those big plastic punching dolls: you keep knocking it down and it keeps bouncing right back up. This is one of those bouncing-back-up moments.

In His permissive will, God used godless Gentiles like Pontius Pilate and Herod to carry out His purposes and plans. No matter what our station or status in life, we're all servants—one way or the other—of the sovereign Lord of the universe. He can do whatever He wills with any of us.

DO WE KNOW ANYTHING FOR SURE?

God's Word clearly declares that certain things are not the will of God and never will be the will of God in the Christian life. It also clearly teaches that certain things are the will of God for the believer. We don't have to pray to "find leading" on this. We only have to dig through the Scriptures to mine it for ourselves. Once unearthed, these truths sparkle like the richest ore or brightest gemstone.

This is solid, immutable, unchangeable, biblical, God-given truth. The unsaved will never understand it, nor should we try to make them live up to it. This is strictly the will of God for the child of God. For example, sexual immorality is never the will of God.

> For this is the will of God, your sanctification; that is, that you abstain from sexual immorality. (1 Thessalonians 4:3)

I'm reminded of the Ten Commandments here—a full and complete list of divine prohibitions (read Exodus 20:3–17). Another clearly stated set of actions God hates is conveyed in Proverbs 6:16–19.

Now that we've looked at a few of the negatives, let's consider some of the things that Scripture explicitly tells us are the will of God for our lives.

> Rejoice always; pray without ceasing; in everything give thanks; for this is God's will for you in Christ Jesus. (1 Thessalonians 5:16–18)

"Should I give thanks? Is that the will of God for my life?" You don't have to pray about that. He says it here loud and clear: Rejoice. Pray without ceasing. Give thanks in everything. Give thanks when you are being tested, stretched, and forced to wait. Yes, give thanks. Give thanks for the patience you are learning. Give thanks for the way God is working in your life through this trial. Give thanks.

Peter, one of Jesus' closest friends, reminds us of two more responses that are always the will of God. The first has to do with submission. The second relates to an obedient walk in a wayward world.

> Submit yourselves for the Lord's sake to every human institution, whether to a king as the one in authority, or to governors as sent by him for the punishment of evildoers and the praise of those who do right.
>
> For such is the will of God that by doing right you may silence the ignorance of foolish men. (1 Peter 2:13–15)

While we may not know what the will of God is for the future, He has given us a whole list of requirements that are in His will for every believer:

- Obey your parents (Ephesians 6:1)
- Marry a Christian (1 Corinthians 6:15)
- Work at an occupation (1 Thessalonians 4:11–12)
- Support your family (1 Timothy 5:8)
- Give to the Lord's work and to the poor (2 Corinthians 8—9; Galatians 2:10)
- Rear your children by God's standards (Ephesians 6:4)
- Meditate on the Scriptures (Psalm 1:2)
- Pray (1 Thessalonians 5:17)
- Have a joyful attitude (1 Thessalonians 5:16)
- Assemble for worship (Hebrews 10:25)
- Proclaim Christ (Acts 1:8)
- Set proper values (Colossians 3:2)
- Have a spirit of gratitude (Philippians 4:6)
- Display love (1 Corinthians 13)
- Accept people without prejudice (James 2:1–10)

And the list goes on and on.

This is the will of God for your life as a child of God, no matter who you are or where you live. Nothing mysterious here!

The better you get to know the Word of God, the less confusing is the will of God. Those who struggle the least with the will of God are those who know the Word of God best.

We see the importance of the Scriptures clearly when we consider another of those often-asked questions: How did God reveal His will in biblical times? And does He do the same today?

LOOKING FOR GUIDANCE

"God's guidance in the Old Testament reached down into the details of daily life while His guidance in the New Testament is expressed in more general commands and principles," says Garry Friesen in his book *Decision Making and the Will of God.*[3]

In biblical times, God revealed His will in a number of ways, but most of them fall into three categories that are clearly verified in Scripture.

First, God used miraculous events to reveal His will.

Before there was Genesis through Revelation, before there was a completed, written revelation of the mind of God, He occasionally used miracles to reveal His will. Examples? The burning bush (Exodus 3:1–10). How did Moses know it was God telling him to return to Egypt and deliver the Israelites? The burning bush. The fact that a bush burned in the wilderness wasn't a miracle. That happens to this day. Lightning strikes, and poof, foliage catches fire and burns. But this brush fire wouldn't go out. Miraculously, it burned and burned. And that's what caused Moses to stop and listen and hear God's will.

Or what about the Red Sea? How did Moses know he should cross the Red Sea? The sea miraculously opened up, making a dry pathway for Moses and the Israelites (Exodus 14:21–29). Pretty sure indication that it was God's will for him to walk across, right?

In the time of the Judges, Gideon wanted to know God's will. He left a lamb fleece out overnight, and God indicated His will by leaving dew on the fleece one time, and another time, no dew (Judges 6).

In the days of the early church, how did Peter know that it was God's will for him to leave prison? God opened the doors and brought him out miraculously (Acts 12:1–16).

Today, God rarely reveals His will through miraculous events. People may think they see a miracle—like a parking place at the mall during Christmas season or the face of Jesus in an enchilada—but that's not the way God works today. As my friend Gary Richmond says, "If miracles happened that often, they'd be called regulars."

Not that God no longer does miracles. He does. But miracles, by their very definition, are extremely rare. In my lifetime, I probably could name three I've been aware of, and they were so obviously miracles of God that no other explanation would work. But God's standard method of revealing His will is not through miracles. So, please, don't get caught in that trap. Guard against anticipating or searching for miracles to find God's will. You don't need them.

God used miracles in ancient times because that was the way He spoke to His people prior to His Word being written. Today, He speaks to us through His Word.

Second, God spoke through visions and dreams.

Abraham saw visions, and Joseph dreamed dreams (Genesis 15:1; 40:8; 41:25). God spoke to Abraham through visions, just as He spoke to Joseph through dreams. He even used an Egyptian Pharaoh's dreams and Joseph's interpretation of those dreams to preserve Egypt from the ravages of a terrible drought and famine. God worked His will for both the Israelites and the Egyptians through visions and dreams.

In New Testament times, Peter saw a sheet coming down from heaven with all kinds of food on it—including what would have been the equivalent of a ham sandwich to a Jew. He saw food that God had forbidden the Jews to eat. Now, however, God said, "Eat." Peter said, "I can't eat." And God said, "Eat." Through this vision of the sheet and the miraculous provision of this food, Peter discovered that it was God's will for him to take the gospel message to the Gentiles (Acts 10:10–23).

Third, God revealed His will through direct revelation.

God spoke His will to His prophets, who in turn delivered the message to the people. "Amos, do this." "Isaiah, say that." "Jeremiah, go over there." The prophets spoke as oracles of God. "For no prophecy was ever made by an act of human will, but men, moved by the Holy Spirit spoke from God" (2 Peter 1:21).

The Greek word here is *pherô,* and it literally means to be "moved along apart from one's own power." It's a nautical term used for a ship without a rudder or a sail, carried along at the mercy of the waves and the wind and the current. Here the word is used for the prophets, moved not by their own power, but by the power of God as He spoke through them and revealed His will.

God no longer speaks through prophets. I don't care what they tell you on television. Or, to quote John Stott:

> The Christian preacher is not a prophet. That is, he does not derive his message from God as a direct and original revelation. Of course, the word "prophet" is used loosely by some people today. It is not uncommon to hear a man who preaches with passion described as possessing prophetic fire; and a preacher who can discern the signs of the times, who sees the hand of God in the history of the day and seeks to interpret the significance of political and social trends, is sometimes said to be a prophet and to have prophetic insight. But I suggest this kind of use of the title "prophet" is an improper one.[4]

What, then, is a prophet? The Old Testament regarded him as the immediate mouthpiece of God. . . . the prophet was God's "mouth," through whom God spoke His words to man. The prophet spoke neither his own words nor in his own name. . . . The Christian preacher, therefore, is not a prophet. No original revelation is given to him; his task is to expound the revelation which has been given once for all. (Jude 3). The last occurrence in the Bible of the formula "the word of God came unto" refers to John the Baptist (Luke 3:2). He was a true prophet.

> Now that the written word of God is available to us all, the word of God in prophetic utterance is no longer needed. The word of God does not come to men today. It has come once and for all; men must now come to it.

Gaining a clear understanding of this concept will save you days of heartache and months of confusion. How many times have you heard someone say, "The Lord told me to do so and so"? I confess to you, in my unguarded moments I want to ask, "Was His voice a baritone or a bass? You're telling me you heard His voice?" Of course when people say they have actually heard God's voice, I get even more spooked!

Have you exhausted His Word so completely that you now must

have a literal voice to guide you? Never! We have an inexhaustible source of truth in God's Word. Go there. It will never contradict God's plan or work against God's nature. You can rely on it. It has come down to us through the centuries. As we derive precepts and principles from the Scriptures, based on a careful, intelligent interpretation of His truth, we're able to apply it in numerous ways to our circumstances today. God's Word and God's will are inseparably connected. His Word is God's final revelation, until He sends His Son and takes us home to be with Him. Yes . . . *final.*

> God, after He spoke long ago to the fathers in the prophets in many portions and in many ways, in these last days has spoken to us in His Son, whom He appointed heir of all things, through whom also He made the world. (Hebrews 1:1–2)

Tell me you have determined God's will from the Scriptures, careully studied within the context in which it was given, and you've got my attention and my respect. Don't regale me with tales of a night vision or some "word of knowledge" in a dream. Don't talk to me about a voice, especially one you heard in the middle of the night while standing in your kitchen. (It was probably just a bad case of indigestion.) I don't mean to be flippant about serious spiritual matters, but this kind of extra-biblical revelation is not only spurious, it's downright dangerous. It invariably leads you astray, away from the truth of God. Your curiosity and your fascination will take over, eclipsing the authority of the Scriptures.

Those who have a high view of biblical revelation, I find, have a very low view of any kind of extra-biblical revelation. Can God do it? Certainly. He is God, and He is able to do whatever He pleases. Does God do it? In all my years of ministry, I've never found a reliable incident of such revelation. On the other hand, I've seen sincere people get into a lot of trouble and confusion because they relied on extra-biblical truth rather than on the Word of God.

Several years ago I witnessed this in the lives of a fine pastor and his wife. Originally in his ministry, this gifted young man was committed to the clear and practical exposition of the Word. The church he was pastoring grew, not only in numbers but also in harmony as they related to one another in love. It was a strong, healthy body.

Then, through an intriguing chain of events, the pastor and his wife began to rely more on dreams and visions for direction and less on the truth of the Scriptures. The congregation became divided as some in the flock began to seek God's will through various extrabiblical phenomena while others resisted such teaching. Ultimately, the rift fractured the fellowship. The pastor left and began another church a few miles away as his loyal followers joined him, while others stayed to pick up the pieces. Hard feelings and broken relationships now remain. Confusion has replaced harmony. The final authority of that pastor is no longer based on the written Word of God but, more and more, on dreams, visions, strange interpretations of the Bible, and erroneous teaching that highlights experience.

God's Word provides all the light we will ever need on our journey through this life. It's "a lamp to our feet and a light to our path (Psalms 119:105)." It brings light to our darkened minds. It helps us think theologically. Strange and mysterious though His leading may seem, when we derive our understanding from a serious investigation of the written Word of God, we will not be led astray. And we will continue to stand on the solid rock of God's Word of truth.

All other ground is sinking sand.

3

Moving from Theory to Reality

Moving from failure to failure
without any loss of enthusiasm.

—Winston Churchill's definition of success

Confusion is a word we have invented
for an order which is not understood.

—Henry Miller, *Tropic of Capricorn*

Chapter Three

Moving From Theory to Reality

I'M TOTALLY CONFUSED . . . How in the world do I find the will of God for my life?" I cannot number how many times through the years I have heard that question. It's a dilemma that has caused people to devise some very strange methods to reach some even stranger conclusions.

Years ago, I read about a man who was driving through Washington, D.C., when his car stalled in front of the Philippine Embassy. He took that to mean that he should be a missionary to the Philippines.

Then there was the woman who wasn't sure she ought to go on a trip to Israel. One night she was reading through the travel brochures and tour information and noticed that the flight was to be on a 747. She woke up the next morning, saw 7:47 on her digital clock, and took that as a sign she should go to Israel.

This sort of nonsense is what I call "voodoo theology." It is nothing more than superstition. We must guard ourselves from being lured into this kind of thinking.

God has spelled out many of His directives very clearly in Scripture, as we saw in the previous chapter, but many of the things we grapple with are not specifically dealt with in His Word. I'll give you some examples.

You've got a son who excels in a particular sport and several fine universities have offered him scholarships. Which school do you choose? Well, that can be a tough choice, but you'll never find the specific answer in a verse of Scripture. If you do, you're reading something into it.

You're single and dating, praying for God to lead you to the right mate for life. But there's nothing in the Bible that states, "Marry John" or "Don't marry Shirley" or "You should date Frank." God gives general principles in His Word—for example, "Do not be unequally yoked together with unbelievers"—but we have to apply them.

You have a good job in Southern California, but you're tired of the smog and the traffic-clogged commute. A company in Colorado offers you a similar position at the same income level. Should you move or stay where you are? A number of factors will enter into your decision, but you will not find the answer directly stated in the Scriptures. If you think you do, you're getting weird.

We sincerely want these specific decisions in our lives to be in accordance with God's will. Deep within, we wish His specific directives would be spelled out in the Scriptures. We'd love to have Him lead us by the hand . . . how reassuring that would be! One of our great old hymns puts it this way: "Guide me, O Thou great Jehovah, / Pilgrim through this barren land; / I am weak, but Thou art mighty; / Hold me with Thy powerful hand." Wouldn't it be a relief to take God by His powerful hand and let Him lead you where He wants you to go?

We don't want to miss God's best for our lives. We want to be held on a steady course by His guiding presence. So, where do we find that guidance, that leading? Let's start by looking at some of the essential prerequisites that help us determine God's will. Thankfully, these are neither ambiguous nor mysterious.

PREREQUISITES FOR FOLLOWING THE WILL OF GOD

First and foremost, you must be a Christian. "For all who are being led by the Spirit of God, these are sons of God" (Romans 8:14).

When you accept Christ as the Savior and Lord of your life, the Holy Spirit comes to dwell within you. Among other things, He is there to reveal the will of God to you. Only the believer has the Spirit's presence within, and we must have this inside help if we are going to follow the will of God.

Second, you must be wise. "Therefore be careful how you walk, not as unwise men, but as wise, making the most of your time, because the days are evil" (Ephesians 5:15–16).

At the beginning of the chapter, I gave you a couple of examples of the foolishness that can occur when people attempt to decipher God's will in the wrong way. God tells us not to be foolish, but wise, making the most of our time, taking every opportunity that comes our way and using it wisely.

Before his twentieth birthday, Jonathan Edwards, the brilliant and godly philosopher-theologian who became God's instrument in the Great Awakening revival of the eighteenth century, resolved "Never to lose one moment of time, but to improve it in the most profitable way I possibly can." That is exactly what he did, using well the intellectual gifts God had given him. He entered Yale at thirteen and at seventeen graduated at the head of his class. At twenty-six he was the minister of one of the largest congregations in Massachusetts.

Scripture says that doing the will of the Lord requires wisdom, for, as Paul writes in the next verse, those who are wise, those who are not foolish, "understand what the will of the Lord is."

Following the will of God requires wisdom, clear thinking, and, yes, even good old garden-variety common sense. Such a mixture helps us understand the Father's will.

Third, you must really want to do the will of God. "If any man is willing to do His will, he shall know of the teaching, whether it is of God, or whether I speak from Myself" (John 7:17).

Your "want to" is a green light: You really will do what He wants you to do. You really want to do the will of God more than anything else. More than completing your education, more than getting married, more than getting your house paid for; more than anything else you want to do the will of God.

Looking back on my own life, I know that there have been times when I said I wanted to do His will but I really didn't. That's a tough thing to confess, but looking back with 20/20 hindsight, I realize that at times I resisted His will. I've learned that serious consequences follow selfish resistance.

The apostle Paul offers words of counsel to those who were enslaved. They have great meaning for us in this context. "Slaves, be obedient to those who are your masters according to the flesh, with fear and trembling, in the sincerity of your heart, as to Christ," wrote Paul, "not by way of eyeservice, as men-pleasers, but as slaves of Christ, doing the will of God *from the heart*" (Ephesians 6:5–6, emphasis added).

Doing the will of God from the heart—that's as deep as it gets. More than pleasing people, more than staying comfortable and safe, you want to please God. You want to follow His will with all of your being.

Fourth, you must be willing to pray and to wait. "Ask, and it shall be given to you; seek, and you shall find; knock, and it shall be opened to you. For everyone who asks receives, and he who seeks finds, and to him who knocks it shall be opened" (Matthew 7:7–8). "And this is the confidence which we have before Him, that, if we ask anything according to His will, He hears us. And if we know that He hears us in whatever we ask, we know that we have the requests which we have asked from Him" (1 John 5:14–15).

Knowing and then following the will of God at times can be a lengthy and painful process. Back in the early 1990s both the president and the chairman of the board of Dallas Seminary asked me to consider becoming the next president of that school. For more than twenty years I had been the pastor of a church in Fullerton,

California. I was not looking for a change, nor did I feel any urgent "push" to entertain their offer. In fact, I spent only a small amount of time in prayer and discussion with my wife before I wrote a letter to the president and the chairman, stating that I had no sense of God's leading me in that direction. As I recall, I listed several "airtight" reasons I should not make such a change in my career. All of these reasons made good sense, which led me to believe I should not consider the issue any further. I wrote a convincing two-page letter that made perfect logical sense . . . but it was wrong!

The Spirit of God would not leave me alone. In subtle yet definite ways He kept bringing the thought back to my mind. I'd shove it aside, only to have Him bring it back. I would ignore the prompting within, but He would not allow me to go very long without another thought returning, prodding me to reconsider. A painful struggle followed. The mystery mushroomed in my mind.

In the meantime, several other events transpired, forcing me to return to the subject. God was going to have His way, whether I was open or not! He refused to leave me alone. There were other phone calls, visits, protracted times spent in prayer and with the Scriptures, conversations with those I respected, and restless nights. Finally, my heart was turned in that direction and I found myself unable to resist any longer. By the end of 1993, I had come full circle: it was the Father's will. I could deny it no longer. Surprised and amazed, I said yes.

Fifth, following the will of God means you must be willing to give up your creature comforts. "And now, behold, bound in spirit, I am on my way to Jerusalem, not knowing what will happen to me there, except that the Holy Spirit solemnly testifies to me in every city, saying that bonds and afflictions await me. But I do not consider my life of any account as dear to myself, in order that I may finish my course, and the ministry which I received from the Lord Jesus, to testify solemnly of the gospel of the grace of God" (Acts 20:22–24).

Here, Paul speaks of the direction in which the Spirit is leading him as being "bound in the spirit." He is caught up in following the will of God, committed to it, bound by it. "I'm leaving you folks here in Ephesus," he says, "and I'm going where it's not going to be as comfortable. In fact, there will be struggles, pressures, discomforts, and afflictions—dangerous risks, even imprisonment. But none of that matters. Even my life doesn't matter."

We're in a process; we're on a journey. If we are to finish the course well, according to the will of our Lord, we must be willing to face some tough things on the journey. Among them will be the loss of things familiar and the need to make some major adjustments.

Now we know some of the essentials that are required before we can even think of following the Lord's will. Yet even if all those are in place, or at least we are committed to them, where do we go next? If we are going to follow, we have to be able to sense the presence and pleasure of our Leader. So, then, how does God lead us into His will today? Without removing all the mystery that often accompanies His will, I have found several absolutes that assist me in following the Lord.

HOW DOES GOD LEAD TODAY?

I could probably list at least ten ways that God leads His children today, but I will limit myself to the four that I think are the most significant methods of God's leading.

First and most basic, God leads us through His written Word. As the psalmist said, "Thy word is a lamp to my feet, and a light to my path" (Psalm 119:105).

Whenever you see the scriptural phrase "This is the will of God," you know for sure that's His will. You also know that to disobey is to break His Word. Other clear indications of His leading are the precepts and principles in the Scripture.

Precepts are clearly marked statements like "Abstain from sexual immorality." That's like saying, "Speed Limit 35." What is speeding? Anything over thirty-five miles an hour. That's a precept.

Then there are principles in the Scriptures, and these are general guidelines that require discernment and maturity if we are to grasp them. Paul writes of "the peace of God" guarding and guiding our hearts and our minds (Philippians 4:7). That's like the sign that says, "Drive Carefully." This may mean forty miles an hour on a clear, uncongested highway, or it may mean ten miles an hour on an ice-covered curve. But it always means that we must be alert and aware of conditions; it always means we have to be discerning. There is no sign large enough to list all the options you have when you're behind the wheel. So you must know the rules of the road, follow the signs that are there, and use all your skill combined with discernment.

There are precepts in Scripture, but mainly God has given us principles to follow. These principles require wisdom and discernment. "Teach me good discernment and knowledge," wrote the psalmist, "for I believe in Thy commandments" (Psalm 119:66).

So often in the emotion of the moment or the pressure of the day, we make a decision that we would never make in the clear, discerning light of God's Word. I recall a couple that came to me for marital counseling several years ago. Their marriage wasn't working, and they had come to the hurried conclusion that what they needed to pull them together was a dog, or maybe a baby. God bless 'em, if the marriage was in trouble, a baby certainly wouldn't fix it, and neither would a dog. Maybe the problem was that one was a believer and the other was not. Perhaps one was not honoring the other. Whatever was needed, I assured them that the principles to follow can be found in the Bible.

You will never, ever go wrong in consulting the Scriptures. Just be sure you take it in context. First Corinthians 7, for example, is all about marriage and remarriage and the struggles in marriage. It's a crucial chapter with very practical advice, but you have to examine all of those verses in their context. Don't use the "open-window method," letting the wind blow across the pages of your Bible and then closing your eyes and pointing to a verse and saying, "This is God's leading on this." If you do that, you could end up with "Judas went away and hanged himself" as your verse for the day! Don't go there.

Would you want to go to a doctor with an ailment and have him say, without ever examining you, "It's your gallbladder?" You ask, "How do you know?" And he'd say, "Well, I sat by the window a few minutes ago and trusted God to blow the pages of my anatomy book to the problem—and the subject on the page was gallbladder." You'd get out of there pretty quick, wouldn't you?

But there are people who make their decisions in life this way—on Philippine Embassies and 747s, on the mood of the moment. And many of them are so sincere that my heart goes out to them. They practice this kind of theological voodoo and then they get in a mess and they say, "Well, God led me" when God had nothing whatsoever to do with their decisions.

So we need to be very clear about the way God leads His people today. God leads us through His written Word. However, keep in mind that this does not mean that we must have a particular Bible verse for every single decision or move we make.

Second, God leads us through the inner prompting of the Holy Spirit. Read the following statement carefully: "So then, my beloved, just as you have always obeyed, not as in my presence only, but now much more in my absence, work out your salvation with fear and trembling; for it is God who is at work in you, both to will and to work for His good pleasure" (Philippians 2:12–13).

Now that you've been born again, Paul says, work out your salvation. In other words, be discerning, think it through, use your head, pay attention, get serious about your Christian walk. For it is God (the Holy Spirit) who is working His will in you. That's why the apostle can say in the next verse, "Do all things without grumbling or disputing" (Philippians 2:14). As the Spirit of God within you engages in various ways of leading you, working out God's will in you, you come to accept it, regardless of the challenges the future brings.

God leads you to a hot, desert-like setting, and you go without grumbling and disputing. You have been married for six months and your spouse is stricken with a debilitating disease that puts her in a wheelchair. You face it "without grumbling and disputing." Though you don't understand how, you trust that it's part of the plan. I could tell you at least half a dozen stories of people who have lived through this kind of trial and come through with magnificent testimonies. One of the most universally recognizable, of course, is Joni Eareckson Tada, whose testimony has touched the lives of multiple-thousands of people. I also think of a young Christian couple who for the past fifteen years have been living through unbelievably difficult circumstances. When they were in their late twenties, parents of four children, the young mother was diagnosed with multiple sclerosis. Now in their thirties, with her condition worsening severely, they are still living witnesses of God's grace "without grumbling and disputing." That is clearly the result of the Holy Spirit's work within.

The inner prompting of the Holy Spirit gives us a sense of God's leading, although that leading is not always what we might call a "feel-good" experience. In my own life, as I mentioned earlier, my decision to accept the presidency of Dallas Seminary was not an easy one. Ultimately, it was an at-peace decision, but it was not what I would have wanted or chosen. Remember my story? I found all kinds of ways to resist when the position was first offered to me. Remember that two-page, airtight letter, carefully thought through, full of Scripture? It should have convinced anybody that I was the wrong person for the job. Except that God was busy convincing them—and, later, me—that I *was* the right person. Although it went against my own wishes at the time, I could not resist the sovereign, all-powerful prompting of the Holy Spirit.

The Book of Jude offers a wonderful example of this: "Beloved, while I was making every effort to write you about our common salvation, I felt the necessity to write to you appealing that you contend earnestly for the faith which was once for all delivered to the saints" (Jude 3). Jude started to write a letter to his fellow Christians about salvation, about the finished work of Christ on the cross. That was his original plan . . . until the Holy Spirit prompted him to do otherwise. "I felt the necessity to do so," Jude admits. I've underlined that phrase in my Bible: "I felt the necessity." That was nothing less than the inner prompting from the Spirit of God.

In similar fashion, I felt the necessity of reconsidering the invitation to Dallas Seminary. So I can testify from personal experience that you can believe you really know God's will, and you may be dead wrong. But if you are, the prompting of the Holy Spirit will be nudging you within. "The mind of man plans his way, but the LORD directs his steps" (Proverbs 16:9).

Nothing wrong with planning. Nothing wrong with thinking it through. Nothing wrong with doing your charts, listing all the pros and cons, talking it over. But as you are moving along, stay sensitive to the quiet, yet all-important prompting of God through His Holy Spirit. It's easier to steer a moving car. Just get the car rolling and you can push it into the filling station to get the gas. But it's hard to get it moving from a dead stop. So you're on your way, you're making your plans, you're thinking it through. Just stay open. By doing so, you may well sense inner promptings that will spur a thought such as, "I can't believe I'm still interested in that. I wonder what the Lord's doing? I wonder where He's going with this?"

As author Henry Blackaby says, "Watch to see where God is at work and join Him!" Just go there. Why do you want to be anywhere God isn't at work?[1]

"I will instruct you and teach you in the way which you should go," says the Lord. "I will counsel you with My eye upon you" (Psalm 32:8). The Spirit of God inside is steering us.

That inner prompting is crucial, because much of the time we just can't figure it out. "Man's steps are ordained by the LORD, how then can man understand his way" (Proverbs 20:24)? (I love that!) When all is said and done, you'll say, "Honestly, I didn't figure this thing out. It must have been God." Talk about mysterious! The longer I live the Christian life, the less I know about why He leads as He does. But I do know that He leads.

The third way God leads us is through the counsel of wise, qualified, trustworthy people. This does not mean some guru in Tibet or serious-looking stranger at the bus stop. This is an individual who has proven himself or herself wise and trustworthy and, therefore, qualified to counsel on a given matter. Usually such individuals are older and more mature than we. Furthermore, they have nothing to gain or lose. This also means that they are often not in our immediate family. (Immediate family members usually don't want us to do something that will take us away from them, or cause us or them discomfort or worry.)

One well-known exception to this is Moses, who listened to the wise counsel of his father-in-law, Jethro (Exodus 18:19–27). "Moses, you're trying to take on too much," said Jethro. "You can't do everything. You need help." Moses listened, and he found that the will of God was that he delegate most of his numerous responsibilities.

At critical moments in my own life, I have sought the counsel of seasoned individuals—and they've seldom been wrong. That's been my experience. But you must choose your counselors very carefully. And just as the best counselors are often not your family, often they are not your best friends either. Wise and trustworthy counselors are persons who want for you only what God wants. Such persons will stay objective, listen carefully, and answer slowly. Often they won't give you an answer at the time you ask for it. They want to sleep on it; they want to think about it.

Finally, God leads us into His will by giving us an inner assurance of peace. "And let the peace of Christ rule in your hearts," Paul writes to the Colossians, "to which indeed you were called in one body; and be thankful" (Colossians 3:15). God's inner assurance of peace will act as an umpire in your heart.

Although peace is an emotion, I have found it wonderfully reassuring as I've wrestled with the Lord's will. This God-given peace comes in spite of the obstacles or the odds, regardless of the risk or danger. It's almost like God's way of saying, "I'm in this decision . . . trust Me through it."

The will of God for our lives is not some high-sounding theory; it is reality. We have discussed some of the prerequisites and requirements for following the will of God, and we have looked at some of the ways God leads us into His will. Now comes the bottom line: We have to live out His will in the real world. In his fine book *Experiencing God,* Henry Blackaby gives some good advice about doing exactly that.

First, doing God's will leads to what he calls a "crisis of belief." That "is a turning point or a fork in the road that demands you make a decision." Doing God's will demands a decision. And that decision requires *faith* and *action.* You can't see the end, so you have to trust Him in faith and then step out. You have to act. Faith and action are like twins; they go together.[2]

Imagine how hard it must have been for Moses to take that first step into the Red Sea. But his faith required action. Before he could get across, he had to take that first step. And as he did, God opened up a dry path through the sea. Blackaby writes,

> God is wanting to reveal Himself to a watching world. He does not call you to get involved just so people can see what you can do. He calls you to an assignment that you cannot do without Him. The assignment will have God-sized dimensions. . . . Some people say, "God will never ask me to do something I can't do." I have come to the place in my life that, if the assignment I sense God is giving me is something I know I can handle, I know it probably is *not* from God. The kind of assignments God gives in the Bible are always God-sized. They are always beyond what people can do because He wants to demonstrate His nature, His strength, His provision, His kindness to His people and to a watching world. That is the only way the world will come to know Him.[3]

Hebrews 11:6 tells us that "without faith it is impossible to please Him, for he who comes to God must believe that He is, and that He is a rewarder of those who seek Him." Following God's will means that we must believe that God is who He says He is and that He will do what He says He will do.

When Cynthia and I started Insight for Living back in 1979, we were total novices. We had no background in radio, no understanding of the world of media, and virtually no money to buy air time. Neither of us even listened to Christian radio. But that was where the Lord's God-sized plan took us. For two uninterrupted decades, we have had to believe that God is who He says He is and will do what He says He will do. We'll be backed into a corner, with seemingly no way out, so we just have to trust Him. And He will move in a special way to give us direction. When it comes time to roll the credits, His name is the name that should be there.

God-sized assignments not only require trust, they also require major adjustments. I have never seen an exception to this rule: *Major adjustments accompany God's will.* Moving from theory to reality in the will of God means risk and release, which spell change. To quote from Blackaby once again:

> You cannot continue life as usual or stay where you are, and go with God at the same time. That is true throughout Scripture. Noah could not continue life as usual and build an ark at the same time. Abram could not stay in Ur or Haran and father a nation in Canaan. Moses could not stay on the back side of the desert herding sheep and stand before Pharaoh at the same time. David had to leave his sheep to become the king. Amos had to leave the sycamore trees in order to preach in Israel. Jonah had to leave his home and overcome a major prejudice in order to preach in Nineveh. Peter, Andrew, James, and John had to leave their fishing businesses to follow Jesus. Matthew had to leave his tax collector's booth to follow Jesus. Saul (later Paul) had to completely change directions in life in order to be used of God to preach the gospel to the Gentiles.[4]

TWO SEARCHING QUESTIONS

Let me ask you two pointed questions as we wrap up our thoughts in this chapter. First: *What makes risk so difficult for you?* Be painfully honest as you answer that question. Blow away the fog in your thinking. Clear out the nettles and overgrown vines of tradition or bad habits or just plain sloth. Change, for most folks, is enormously challenging. Walking with the Lord is a risky path, and everything within us, when we live and lean on our own understanding, screams, "Just keep it like it is. Just leave it alone. If it ain't broke, don't fix it." But sometimes things need to be rearranged even though they aren't broken. Sometimes we need a major change of direction—not because we are necessarily going in an evil direction, it's just not the direction God wants for us. God does not want us to substitute the good for the very best.

Now, here's my second question: *Are you willing to make a major change in your life—assuming that it's the Lord's will?* I'm now convinced that the real issue is not so much "What does the Lord want me to do?" as it is, "Am I willing to do it, once He makes it clear?"

Before moving on into the next chapter, stop and answer those two questions. Not until they are answered are you ready to move ahead, fleshing out the will of God.

4

Fleshing Out the Will of God

The years that lie behind you, with all their struggles and pains, will in time be remembered only as the way that led to your new life. But as long as the new life is not fully yours, your memories will continue to cause you pain. When you keep reliving painful events of the past, you can feel victimized by them.

—Henri Nouwen, *The Inner Voice of Love*

A holy life isn't the automatic consequence of reading the right books, listening to the right tapes, or attending the right meetings. It's the result of a living, loving union with Jesus Christ and a life marked by godly discipline..

—Warren Wiersbe, *On Being a Servant of God*

Chapter Four

Fleshing Out the Will of God

SO MUCH FOR GENERAL INFORMATION. Now it's time for personal involvement. The truth is, our problem is not a lack of knowledge but an absence of passion . . . a reluctance to do what we believe God would have us do. I've met some who excuse their lack of involvement by claiming that God does it all. After all, He is sovereign. He, alone, makes things happen.

In his book *The Knowledge of the Holy,* A. W. Tozer gives this simple but helpful illustration of the will and sovereignty of God.

> If in His absolute freedom God has willed to give man limited freedom, who is there to stay His hand or say, "What doest thou?" Man's will is free because God is sovereign. A God less than sovereign could not bestow moral freedom upon His creatures. He would be afraid to do so.
>
> Perhaps an illustration might help us to understand. An ocean liner leaves New York bound for Liverpool. Its destination has been determined by proper authorities. Nothing can change it. This is at least a faint picture of sovereignty.
>
> On board the liner are scores of passengers. These are not in chains, neither are their activities determined for them by decree.

> They are completely free to move about as they will. They eat, they sleep, play, lounge about on the deck, read, talk, altogether as they please; but all the while the great liner is carrying them steadily onward toward a predetermined port.
>
> Both freedom and sovereignty are present here and they do not contradict each other. So it is, I believe, with man's freedom and the sovereignty of God. The mighty liner of God's sovereign design keeps its steady course over the sea of history. God moves undisturbed and unhindered toward the fulfillment of those eternal purposes which He purposed in Christ Jesus before the world began. We do not know all that is included in these purposes, but enough has been disclosed to furnish us with a broad outline of things to come and to give us good hope and firm assurance of future well-being.[1]

As children of God, our greatest desire should be to do His will. And in our most thoughtful, mature moments, we want to do His will. In fact, we delight in doing His will. And invariably, looking back, we are so grateful for the way He has led us thus far; we are amazed as we see how He has guided us to where He wanted us to be.

And that's what being on the ocean liner of God's will boils down to: going where He wants us to go and being what He wants us to be. This means releasing our own plans and pride and will as we flesh out His plan and purpose. That's what it's all about. In the process, we experience a deep inner peace, a satisfying sense of fulfillment, because we are within the circumference of His plan, moving inexorably toward His destined arrangement for our lives.

In the course of that plan we come under the decreed will of God, which generally covers the things revealed in the Scriptures and leaves unstated the things yet future. We participate in the specific parts of His will wherein we play a part. The latter is where the struggle often comes, because the process of God's will is not passive. It isn't a matter of just lying back and waiting for Him to move us from Plan A to Plan B.

For example, on a very mundane level, you're dressed today

because you dressed yourself this morning. You're full because you fed yourself that last meal. You are clean because you bathed yourself or took a shower. You got to work because you put gas in your car and drove yourself to your place of employment. You arrived on time because you take seriously the responsibilities that are part of your job profile. And had you simply stayed in bed, God would have done none of those things for you.

We cannot assume a slothful attitude that says, "God does it all, and if He wants this done, He'll have to do it." There are times, of course, when we reach a point where we must say, "I now must leave this in God's hands." But that is about coming to terms with what He wants rather than what I want.

In the previous chapter we affirmed that following the will of God requires faith and action, which in turn call for risk and release. This is where things get very personal; this is where we persevere and flesh out the will of God.

I have come to this conclusion: Doing the will of God is rarely easy and uncomplicated. Instead, it is often difficult and convoluted. Or, back to my preferred term, it is *mysterious.* Because we don't know where He is taking us, we must bend our wills to His—and most of us are not all that excited about bending. We'd much prefer resisting. That's why the Christian life is often such a struggle. I don't mean that it's a constant marathon of misery. It's just a struggle between our will and His will. Someday, when we are caught up with the Lord in glory, we will finally be all the things we have longed to be. Until then, we live in this never-ending tension of give and take, push and pull.

At the fork of every road, we need faith and action to follow God's leading. That is the crisis of belief that I mentioned at the end of the previous chapter. It is a turning point, where we must make a decision. It's like those expressway signs that say "Garden Grove Freeway, East, West," with arrows pointing to the two exit lanes. You're rolling along carefree at sixty-five miles an hour and suddenly you have to decide: Which way? East? West? Which is it? Only one way will get you where you want to go. So you have to make a decision. You can try to go in both directions, but it will hurt.

Jonah experienced that kind of crisis of belief when God told him to "Go to Nineveh." Although he was a prophet of God, his prejudice and bigotry got in the way of God's will for him. Nineveh was the capital of Assyria. Jonah despised the Ninevites because they were pagans, filled with idolatry and violence. "Go and proclaim my message there," God told Jonah. His map was clearly marked; God had told him which way to go. But Jonah still had to make a decision—to obey God or not. Jonah thought, "No way," and took the next ship to Tarshish, which was in the opposite direction, which is kind of like living in Texas and going to Berlin by way of Honolulu. (Tempting, isn't it?).

God refused to ignore the prophet's disobedience. He threw a few obstacles in his way—like a violent storm and a near-death experience in the belly of a fish—and gave Jonah another chance.

Jonah was vomited out of the fish, and while he was lying there gasping for breath on the beach, God repeated His will: "Go to Nineveh."

Another person who struggled with a crisis of belief was Sarah, Abraham's wife. "You will have a baby," God promised. Many years passed but she didn't conceive. Finally, she decided to take control of her own destiny. She told Abraham, "Go in to my handmaiden, Hagar, and have the child by her." Dumb decision. Instead of waiting for God's plan and timing, she rushed ahead and pushed Hagar into Abraham's tent. And to complicate things, Abraham foolishly cooperated. The result was Ishmael, and we all know where that led. The conflict that resulted between the descendants of Ishmael and the descendants of Isaac has only intensified through the centuries. Today the Arabs and the Jews are still in conflict with each other.

"To get from where you are to where God is will require major adjustments," writes Henry Blackaby. "These adjustments may relate to your thinking, circumstances, relationships, commitments, actions, and/or beliefs." To this list I would add geography, both physical and spiritual, because, as Blackaby warns, "you cannot stay where you are and go with God at the same time."[2]

It's at this point that we feel the vice tightening a little bit, and a subtle uneasiness sets in. *Well, what about my family?* we think. *What about my mom? She really needs me nearby.* Or, *I've finally found a great church. I don't want to leave this area.*

My mind flashes back to Tom and Sue Kimber, who were a part of our Insight for Living ministry for many years. Then one summer they decided to participate in a short internship in China. While there, they began to wonder, *Is this what God wants us to do? Is this where He wants us to be?* They loved Southern California; their family was there and their church was there. Besides, they didn't know one word of Chinese. Would God really call them and their son, Thomas, to such a distant place and unfamiliar culture?

Well, to cut to the chase, He did. And that's where they are today. Living in a culture that is totally unfamiliar. Reaching out to people who speak a different language. I can hardly imagine a greater adjustment for a couple and their son. But guess what? They are having the time of their lives. Because they made the right turn at the fork in the road, with a terrific attitude, they deliberately released and risked and got on with God's plan and process for their lives.

You may wonder how they could have done it. Easy answer . . . hard to apply: That's where faith comes into the equation. "And without faith it is impossible to please Him, for he who comes to God must believe that He is, and that He is a rewarder of those who seek Him" (Hebrews 11:6).

Faith is believing God is who He says He is and that He will do what He says He will do. Faith is obeying the Lord when I'm unsure of the outcome. Faith is trusting Him when everything in me screams for empirical proof: "Show it to me. Give me the evidence. I want it in a test tube. Put it under a microscope. Prove this. I need the whole picture clearly developed. When I see it, then I'll go with it."

God wants us to walk by faith, not by sight. But we're only comfortable when we can see what's ahead, and what's behind, and what's all around us. We want proof. We want guarantees. That's why we like contracts. Put it in writing, we say; I want a guarantee. We much prefer sight to faith. Extreme faith gives most Christians a rash.

We prefer talk to action. We can talk about the will of God for hours, just so we don't have to do it. While we may not admit it, we secretly cling to the familiar—we're not about to release it. We like the predictable rather than the risky. But God says, "If you're going to please Me, you're going to have to take My Word on this. You're going to have to believe that I am who I say I am, and that I will do what I say I will do." Plain and simple, we gag on that statement!

Seldom do we read the word "impossible" in Scripture. But here God says, "Without faith, pleasing Him is impossible."

God loves it when we trust Him without needing a panoramic picture before us. But trusting Him doesn't guarantee ease and simplicity. Living out the will of God can be difficult and convoluted. Sometimes we are literally at a loss to know what God is up to; but we know that staying where we are is not His plan. That is a tough place to be, because we know He is up to something, we want to be engaged in it, and we find ourselves restless, trying to figure it out. We're back to the mystery of God's will.

Fortunately, God has given us many examples of men and women who lived by faith, not by sight. These are historic models of faith and action, release and risk. They also prepare us for some of the difficulties we will encounter when we flesh out the will of God in our lives.

DOING GOD'S WILL MAY UPSET OTHERS

Hebrews 11, sometimes known as the roll call of faith, records at least a dozen people who modeled faith and action, release and risk. I'd like to look at four of them who offer realistic examples of people who did God's will by faith but found that it was not easy or comfortable or simple. The first is Abel.

> By faith Abel offered to God a better sacrifice than Cain, through which he obtained the testimony that he was righteous, God testifying about his gifts, and through faith, though he is dead, he still speaks. (Hebrews 11:4)

Cain and Abel were sons of Adam and Eve. Abel was a shepherd, and Cain was a farmer. Both brought offerings to God. Cain brought some of his crops, but Abel brought the very best portions from his flock. One commentator says, "The contrast is not between an offering of plant life and an offering of animal life, but between a careless, thoughtless offering and a choice, generous offering. Motivation and heart attitude are all-important, and God looked with favor on Abel and his offering because of Abel's faith." [3]

Infuriated that God had accepted his brother's offering and not his own, Cain violently murdered his brother.

Sometimes when you do the will of God, you will upset or anger your family. This can result in great pressure, relational turmoil, angry words, and perhaps even hostile reactions against you. But remember, you are not on this earth as a child of God to please your family members.

I should also add, however, that we're not here deliberately to make our family members nervous. Motivation has to be the balance wheel here. But of the two, we want to be so committed to our heavenly Father that we know clearly and distinctly what His plan is. We're not here specifically to please our sons and daughters or our mothers and fathers. Sometimes our family can be wrong.

I know this from personal experience. Over forty-five years ago, my parents were not convinced that Cynthia was the best mate for me. They were sincere . . . but on that matter, they were wrong. Had I listened to them, I would not have married the woman I should have married. (We recently celebrated our forty-fourth wedding anniversary. It's still working!)

Now, if they are believers and if they're walking with the Lord, parents are usually good counselors on most things. But they don't walk on water. Sometimes parents can be shortsighted and selfish. This is also true of other family members, and sometimes your immediate family represents the most difficult part of your obeying the will of God. They may even become resentful or angry when they disagree with your life decisions. But when a crisis of belief occurs, faith and obedience must prevail. Releasing and risking will be required. First and foremost, we are to do God's will. That's Obedience 101.

Parents, here's a direct word for you at this point: We have two primary jobs as parents: (1) rearing our children carefully and (2) then releasing them completely. Children don't need our constant oversight or advice when they are grown. Cynthia and I have learned the hard way that our grown children receive our advice best when they ask us for it. At times, we have advice nobody's asking for; we have answers to questions nobody's asking. So we just wait for them to ask. Sometimes they do; often they don't. That's part of parenting, and admittedly, it's a tough part because no matter how old your children are, you don't stop worrying or caring, especially when you think they may be making a wrong decision. But again, faith not sight is what works here. Just turn them over to the Lord and rest in the confidence that He is working out His plan for their lives, just as He is working out His plan for yours.

DOING GOD'S WILL MAY LEAD TO A SURPRISE ENDING

Enoch is the next example of faith. The author of Hebrews says of him: "By faith Enoch was taken up so that he should not see death; *And He was not found because God took him up*; for he obtained the witness that before his being taken up he was pleasing to God" (Hebrews 11:5).

In Genesis 5 we learn that when Enoch was sixty-five years old, he had a son, Methuselah. And from then on, Enoch "walked with God." He walked with God for three hundred years, and "then he was no more, because God took him away." Surprisingly, the man was taken into the presence of God without ever experiencing death.

Now three hundred and sixty-five years may not seem like an early death to us, but in comparison to the length of time people lived in those days (Enoch's son Methuselah lived nine hundred and sixty-nine years), Enoch was a young man when God took him.

Sometimes a remarkable life of obedience is underscored by a premature death. In the mid-1950s, five young men felt God leading them to evangelize the Auca Indians in Ecuador. Jim Elliott, Nate Saint, Roger Youderian, Ed McCully, and Peter Fleming set out on this mission to take the good news of salvation to this hostile tribe of headhunters. All five of the men were found in or near the Curaray River with spears through their bodies. Nearby sat their destroyed plane, like a large bird that had invaded the enemy territory and threatened this tribe. The Aucas didn't understand that these men meant them no harm, nor that they had slaughtered five godly men. Later, Elisabeth Elliott, the widow of Jim Elliot, along with their young daughter and Rachel Saint, sister of the pilot, Nate Saint, returned to this place full of gruesome memories for them and led the very people who had killed their loved ones to the Lord.

In January 1958, I was a young Marine, resentful and disillusioned because I had to go overseas. I was visiting my brother Orville in Pasadena, California, and as I was preparing to return to Camp Pendleton, just prior to getting on the troop ship, Orville said to me, "Charles, here's a book I want you to read."

"I'm not interested in reading." I said.

"I didn't ask if you're interested in reading. I want you to read this book."

"I'm not gonna read the book."

He shoved it in my seabag and said, "Once you start, you'll never be able to put it down."

Later, I sat on the bus, looking out the rain-splattered window at the cold, wet January day. I was lonely, disillusioned, disappointed, and a little despairing of life. The Marine Corps didn't allow wives to accompany their husbands overseas, so Cynthia was back in Houston. How could God allow my wife and me to be separated like this? Turning away from the depressing scenery, and trying to turn away from my depressing thoughts, I pulled out the book my brother had given me.

The book was titled *Through Gates of Splendor,* and the author was Elisabeth Elliott. In it she told the story of those five men and their call to the Aucas. Reading that book absolutely transformed my thinking. My brother was correct. I couldn't put it down. When I got back to Camp Pendleton, I sat in the men's room reading, which was the only place on base that had lights through the night. I sat there all night reading until I finished the book. On the troop ship, seventeen days at sea, I read it again. And while stationed on Okinawa I read it a third time.

Through the years, I've had the privilege of meeting most of the widows of those five men and heard them tell the story, with tears in their eyes. And I've told Elisabeth Elliott that it was that book, and through it the witness of those men, that God used to turn my heart toward ministry and missions. Who knows how many other tens of thousands have been affected by the lives of those five young men whose faith was so deep that they walked with God until He said, "You come on home with Me now."

As I think of this, I think of another young man, Kris Boring, who graduated as one of our top students at Dallas Seminary. Kris was valedictorian of his high school class, top of his class in college, and a splendid student at the seminary. In May of 1997 I handed him his Master of Theology degree at commencement. Kris and his fiancée, thinking God's plan was for them to serve Him on the mission field, went together to look into a particular ministry opportunity. While there, Kris contracted a virus, and in two and a half weeks he was dead. Kris was twenty-eight years old.

I remember his saying to me after graduation, "I just can't wait. Now I can go. I'm all prepared." And surprisingly . . . mysteriously, God took him.

Who knows how many people, because of Kris Boring's premature death, will suddenly be made aware of God's plan for them. I don't know. I can't figure such things out. It's another mystery. But modern-day Enochs like Jim Elliott and Kris Boring still walk with God—and God takes them for *His* purposes.

Sometimes a person's life of obedience is underscored by a premature death. Remember this when it comes close to home. It will help you resist the questions "Why?" and "How could you, Lord?"

While attending Kris's memorial service I heard one student after another tell how this young man's death had riveted into them the importance of serving Christ with even greater devotion. Who knows if they would have seen the will of God so clearly if Kris had not been taken? All I know is that "Precious in the sight of the Lord is the death of His godly ones" (Psalm 116:15).

DOING GOD'S WILL MAY MEAN PERSECUTION

Our next model of faith and action, release and risk, is Noah.

> By faith Noah, being warned by God about things not yet seen, in reverence prepared an ark for the salvation of his household, by which he condemned the world, and became an heir of the righteousness which is according to faith. (Hebrews 11:7)

Noah was not just an ark builder. Before the flood, he was "a preacher of righteousness," and a man who "found favor in the eyes of the Lord" (2 Peter 2:5; Genesis 6:8).

Between the time God told Noah there would be a flood and the first sprinkles of rain, one hundred and twenty years elapsed. So for almost a century and a quarter—that's longer than any of us will live—Noah was building the ark and preparing for God's judgment.

> Then the Lord saw that the wickedness of man was great on the earth, and that every intent of the thoughts of his heart was only evil continually. (Genesis 6:5)

But Noah was different. He was sensitive to God; he heard God's message. God informed Noah of His plan: He was going to destroy the world with a flood. So for one hundred and twenty years, by faith, Noah followed the Lord's leading. He gathered the materials, he built the ark, probably to the ridicule of everyone around him. After all, this was a world that had never known rain; the earth was watered from beneath. And while Noah was building this ark, he was preaching righteousness to those around him. "The flood's coming, judgment's coming." Surrounded and mocked by his depraved, reprobate, wicked contemporaries, this preacher of righteousness, by faith, stood against the tide of his culture. Sometimes our faith is such a rebuke to our peers that we suffer persecution because of it. No extra charge for this simple warning: Don't expect overwhelming approval and affirmation just because you've chosen to walk by faith. History is replete with examples.

Back in the fourteenth century, there was a distinguished professor of divinity at Oxford University who, because of his faith, was "branded an instrument of the devil . . . the author of schism." He was driven into virtual exile by the hypocritical alliance of church and state authorities in the Roman Catholic Church, prompted by the pope's decision. I'm referring, of course, to John Wycliffe, once the pride of Oxford University, the foremost scholar of his day (according to more than one biographer), and clearly the most influential preacher in England at that time. Yet he could no longer stay in his ivory tower of academia knowing that the papacy was corrupt and the people were left in ignorance with no Bible in their own language.

We cannot fathom that. Our shelves are full of a multitude of versions and paraphrases of the Scripture in our own language and countless other languages, in every conceivable type size and binding and format. But in those days there was not one copy of the Bible in English. It was available only in the language of the clergy, Latin, and those were chained to the pulpits of the cathedrals. Unable to read God's Word for themselves, the people were at the mercy of the church leaders, who often relied on the people's ignorance in order to manipulate the public.

Wycliffe said, "This is not right. People should be able to read the Bible in their own language." And like Noah, who drove those nails into that ark while people mocked and scorned him, Wycliffe began the task of translating the Scriptures as a flood of persecution rose around him. He was publicly branded a heretic. When he finally finished the translation of the Scriptures, he wrote these words in the fly-leaf of the first copy of the English Scriptures: "This Bible is translated and shall make possible a government of the people, by the people, and for the people."[4] (Five hundred years later the sixteenth president of the United States, Abraham Lincoln, would borrow that statement for his great Gettysburg Address.)

Thirty years after Wycliffe's death he was again declared a heretic. As a result, his body was exhumed, the bones were burned to dust, and his ashes were cast into a river. A contemporary historian describes the scene like this:

> They burnt his bones to ashes and cast them into Swift, a neighboring brook running hard by. Thus this brook hath conveyed his ashes into (the river) Avon, Avon into Severn, Severn into the narrow seas, they into the main ocean. And thus ashes of Wicliffe are the emblem of his doctrine, which now are dispersed the world over.[5]

In a similar vein, Harry Emerson Fosdick writes these eloquent words: "His enemies, who thought they had now finished him, did not foresee history's verdict: "The Avon to the Severn runs, / And Severn to the sea; / And Wycliffe's dust shall spread abroad / Wide as the waters be.'"[6]

Right now, your life of faith, lived in a culture of contemporary depravity, may not seem all that significant. Living out your faith at the office or in that university dorm or in your high school may feel pretty lonely. Walking by faith and honoring the Lord in your factory or in your profession or in the military may seem futile at times. In fact, in your own lifetime, you may never know the significance of your walk of faith. But God will use you in His special plan for your life, just as he did John Wycliffe and countless others.

I've sat in the castle where Luther hid while he was translating the Scriptures into the German vernacular. I've looked out his window and thought about Luther as he sat in that very room, faithfully discharging his task, knowing that if the church leaders found him they would put him to death. Wycliffe, Luther, Calvin, Savonarola, Knox, Wesley, Whitefield, Edwards . . . on and on the list goes, right up to today. While the world mocked, God honored them. And that still happens.

Just because something is God's will doesn't mean people will understand. On the contrary, most never do. But that's part of the mystery. Faith leads to action, requiring release and risk.

DOING GOD'S WILL MEANS LEAVING THE FAMILIAR FOR THE UNKNOWN

Few epitomize "leaving the familiar" more than Abraham.

> By faith Abraham, when he was called, obeyed by going out to a place which he was to receive for an inheritance; and he went out, not knowing where he was going. By faith he lived as an alien in the land of promise, as in a foreign land, dwelling in tents with Isaac and Jacob, fellow heirs of the same promise; for he was looking for the city which has foundations, whose architect and builder is God. (Hebrews 11:8–10)

Abraham had lived all of his life in Ur of the Chaldeans, as had his father before him. He had deep, long roots in that place. Then, when he was seventy-five-years old (think of it!), God told Abraham to leave his homeland for a "land which I will show you" (Genesis 12:1).

There he is, getting on in years, and he and his wife, Sarah, who is only ten years younger than he is, have settled into their comfortable life together. Suddenly God comes along and invades their nest. His will is clearly stated: "Move out!"

Now, picture the scene: Abraham and Sarah have no children, but they do have a lot of family and friends. And one day Abraham announces to all of them, "We're moving."

"At your age?" they say. "Why would you do that?"

"Well, God told us."

"Right. So where are you going?"

"Well, He hasn't told us that." (Just imagine the reaction).

So they load up the camels and pile everything they own on the carts and start making their way out of Ur. The biblical account makes it clear: Abraham went out "not knowing where he was going" (Heb. 11:8).

Abraham was a relatively wealthy man, and now he found himself dwelling in a tent, living like an alien, because "he was looking for the city which has foundations, whose architect and builder is God" (Heb. 11:10). (I love that description).

Out of the blue, with no details provided, God said, "Go, and I'll show you where later." And Abraham obeyed by going out, "not knowing where he was going." Talk about releasing and risking.

I'm reminded of John Henry Jowett's comment, "Ministry that costs nothing, accomplishes nothing."[7] Remember that, in this era of cheap grace. In fact, I suggest you memorize that line: "Ministry that costs nothing, accomplishes nothing."

Abraham paid the price of comfort and familiarity in order to do the will of God. This is a classic example of the crisis of belief and the need for major adjustment, of faith and action, release and risk.

Discovering and then obeying God's will may require you to leave the familiar and the comfortable.

In my friend Warren Wiersbe's book *Walking with the Giants,* one of the giants he writes about is Hudson Taylor, another of our heroes of faith.

> A Presbyterian moderator in a Melbourne, Australia, church used all his eloquence to introduce the visiting missionary speaker, finally presenting him to the congregation as "our illustrious guest." He was

> not prepared for James Hudson Taylor's first sentence: "Dear friends, I am the little servant of an illustrious Master."
>
> Nearly twenty years before, Hudson Taylor had written in an editorial, "All God's giants have been weak men, who did great things for God because they reckoned on His being with them." As he looked at himself, Hudson Taylor saw nothing but weakness; but as generations of Christians have studied Taylor's life, they have become acquainted with a man who dared to believe the Word of God and, by faith, carried the gospel to inland China—and saw God work wonders![8]

"Want of trust," said Hudson Taylor, "is at the root of almost all our sins and all our weaknesses."[9]

The man was thirty-three when he founded China Inland Mission on June 27, 1865. In doing so, he was the first to take the gospel to the people of that land. Leaving his familiar, comfortable homeland in England, he walked with God as an alien in a land that God had placed on his heart.

Discovering and embracing God's will invariably brings us to a crisis of belief. And that forces us into faith and action.

Obeying and delighting in God's will leads us to make major adjustments. And that requires us to release and risk—releasing the familiar and risking whatever the future may bring. That's the bottom line of fleshing out God's will.

The longer we walk with the Lord, the more we realize that we really don't know what each new day may bring. A phone call can come in the middle of the night shattering our joy. Suddenly, everything changes. It's amazing what a knock at the door can bring or what the opening of a letter can do.

I don't say these things to conjure up fear in our hearts, but simply to remind us that God alone knows our future. And there's no safer, no better, no more rewarding place to be than in the nucleus of His will, regardless of where that may be.

In spite of all our struggling, there's something within us, down in our redeemed hearts, that craves to know His smile, His rewards, and the joy of following obedience. Nothing can be compared to that. No salary offers it; no money can buy it; no possession can replace it . . . just knowing we have pleased our Father is sufficient.

God is not running around hiding from us, mocking us, or delighting in keeping us squirming in a dungeon of confusion. In many ways, His will for us emerges very clearly as we go through this process we've been considering. But we do have to be willing to walk by faith, which means doing His will against seemingly insurmountable odds.

We are only finite human beings. We can only see the present and the past. The future is a little frightening to us. So we need to hold onto His hand and trust Him to calm our fears. And at those times when we're stubborn and resisting and God shakes us by the shoulders to get our attention, we're reminded that we don't call our own shots, that God has a plan for us, mysterious though it may seem, and we want to be in the center of it.

All the risks notwithstanding, that is still the safest place on earth to be.

5

Another Deep Mystery: God's Sovereignty

Let us then learn the rule and the order, which God is in the habit of using in the government of the saints. For I, too, have frequently tried to prescribe certain methods for God to employ in the administration either of the church or of other affairs. Ah, Lord, said I, I should like to have this matter done in this way, in this order, and with this result . . . But God did the very opposite of what I asked.

—MARTIN LUTHER, *What Luther Says*

In many ways, you still want to set your own agenda.
You act as if you have to choose among many things,
which all seem equally important. But you have not fully
surrendered yourself to God's guidance.
You keep fighting with God over who is in control.

—Henri Nouwen, *The Inner Voice of Love*

Control is an illusion, you infantile egomaniac!
Nobody controls anything.

—Nicole Kidman to Tom Cruise in *Days of Thunder*

Chapter Five

Another Deep Mystery: God's Sovereignty

In the summer of 1961 my life was changed. I was already a Christian. In fact, I was between my second and third year in seminary, deeply entrenched in theological studies. I had been invited to intern that summer at a church in Northern California, Peninsula Bible Church, which I did, along with another young man named Gib Martin. During that three-month period, Gib, still single at the time, lived with Cynthia and me.

I was struggling with some of the more profound truths in the Word of God during those days. When you're in graduate study and are doing intensive work in the biblical text, you must wrestle with and to come to terms with certain truths. You can no longer leave them in the "unsettled" realm. One of my major battles at the time was the sovereignty of God.

Candidly, this doctrine frightened me. In seminary I had seen some close friends take God's sovereignty to such ridiculous extremes that they had become unbalanced . . . in my mind, borderline heretical.

On a practical level, I was grappling with several issues in my own life that seemed to relate. Cynthia and I were uncertain about our future. We had been married for over six years, and while our marriage was not weak, it wasn't as strong as it needed to be. And she was carrying our first child, causing both of us to feel somewhat anxious about being parents. Neither of us had come from homes where we had great parenting models to follow. They were good homes and we were loved, but much of the parenting process was lacking, at least from our perspective.

All of this, as well as a few other issues, were troubling me. So that summer I decided I really wanted to dig into a book of the Bible, ideally one with a dozen chapters or so to coincide with the twelve weeks that we would be away from school. I chose the Book of Daniel. I had never seriously studied the book on my own, so I decided to spend a major portion of my morning devotional time in each week's given chapter. It was in our fourth week at Peninsula Bible Church in Palo Alto, California, when I was in the fourth chapter of Daniel, that I came upon the truth that transformed my thinking and, in fact, changed my life.

To give you a little background, Daniel 4 begins with a dialogue and ends with a monologue. The chapter revolves around a dream. Nebuchadnezzar, the king of Babylon, had a dream that disturbed him. None of his wise men could interpret the dream for him, so he ended up consulting a Jewish prophet named Daniel. Daniel not only interpreted the dream; he also exhorted the dreamer.

Nebuchadnezzar was a proud man, a heavy-handed ruler; all he had to do was turn thumbs down and Daniel's life would be history. He was the sovereign monarch of Babylon, humanly speaking. But Daniel had the divine courage to look Nebuchadnezzar in the eye, as all true prophets would do, and tell him the truth. As he interpreted the dream, he challenged King Nebuchadnezzar to do something about the truth that it represented.

> This is the interpretation, O king, and this is the decree of the Most High, which has come upon my lord the king: that you be driven away from mankind, and your dwelling place be with the beasts of the field, and you be given grass to eat like cattle and be drenched

> with the dew of heaven; and seven periods of time will pass over you, until you recognize that the Most High is ruler over the realm of mankind, and bestows it on whomever He wishes.
>
> And in that it was commanded to leave the stump with the roots of the tree, your kingdom will be assured to you after you recognize that it is Heaven that rules.
>
> Therefore, O king, may my advice be pleasing to you: break away now from your sins by doing righteousness, and from your iniquities by showing mercy to the poor, in case there may be a prolonging of your prosperity.'
>
> All this happened to Nebuchadnezzar the king.
>
> (Daniel 4:24–28)

A chill still runs up my spine when I read these words and reflect back on that summer morning in Palo Alto. I remember, as if it were yesterday, taking a pencil from my desk and underscoring two lines that are almost identical. In verse 25, "until you recognize," and verse 26, "after you recognize."

In essence, Daniel says, "All of this will happen to you, Nebuchadnezzar, *until* you recognize that you aren't sovereign over your life, *until* you recognize that the Most High is the ruler. Things will not change until *after* you recognize that it is Heaven that rules."

Recognize. The Hebrew verb is "know." Perhaps the word "acknowledge" is a better translation than "recognize." And the NIV renders it so: "until you acknowledge." You can recognize something and not be involved in it. But you can't really acknowledge something without having some kind of involvement and acceptance—even embracing. I think that's what Daniel has in mind. "Nebuchadnezzar, until you embrace the truth that you aren't sovereign, but God is . . . that you don't rule your life, but God does, you will never break from that insane experience."

Stop and think for a moment about the word "sovereignty." There's a smaller word nestled in the heart of it, the word "reign": sov-*reign*-ty.

Nebuchadnezzar conducted his life as if he were reigning over it, just like he reigned over his kingdom. Then Daniel steps on the scene and says, "God has given you this dream so that you will know that there is another way of viewing life: The eternal God of heaven, your creator, not only made you and gives you breath for your lungs, but He *reigns* over you." This must have been a tough pill for Nebuchadnezzar to swallow.

Now notice the first three words in the next verse:

> *Twelve months later* he was walking on the roof of the royal palace of Babylon. (Daniel 4:29, italics mine)

"Twelve months later." A full year has passed, during which God has patiently allowed Nebuchadnezzar to let that truth wash around in his mind. "Do I reign over my life or does the Creator? Am I sovereign or is He? Is He in control? Are His ways being carried out? Or am I in control, accomplishing my ways?"

Well, his answer emerges in the following verses.

> The king reflected and said, "Is this not Babylon the great, which I myself have built as a royal residence by the might of my power and for the glory of my majesty?"
>
> While the word was in the king's mouth, a voice came from heaven, saying, "King Nebuchadnezzar, to you it is declared: sovereignty has been removed from you, and you will be driven away from mankind, and your dwelling place will be with the beasts of the field. You will be given grass to eat like cattle, and seven periods of time will pass over you, until you recognize that the Most High is ruler over the realm of mankind, and bestows it on whomever He wishes."
>
> Immediately the word concerning Nebuchadnezzar was fulfilled; and he was driven away from mankind and began eating grass like cattle, and his body was drenched with the dew of heaven, until his hair had grown like eagles' feathers and his nails like birds' claws. (Daniel 4:30–33)

Nebuchadnezzar went completely insane. He literally lived out in the fields. Totally removed from the realm of logic and reason, this once-proud sovereign of the land lived in the wilderness like a beast.

But the story isn't over. And this is where the dialogue between Daniel and the king becomes a monologue. I think Daniel gave Nebuchadnezzar the pen and said, "Here, you write the rest of this story."

> But at the end of that period I, Nebuchadnezzar, raised my eyes toward heaven, and my reason returned to me, and I blessed the Most High and praised and honored Him who lives forever;
>
> For His dominion is an everlasting dominion,
> And His kingdom endures from generation to generation.
> And all the inhabitants of the earth are accounted as nothing,
> But He does according to His will in the host of heaven
> And among the inhabitants of earth;
> And no one can ward off His hand
> Or say to Him, "What hast Thou done?"
>
> At that time my reason returned to me. And my majesty and splendor were restored to me for the glory of my kingdom, and my counselors and my nobles began seeking me out; so I was reestablished in my sovereignty, and surpassing greatness was added to me.
>
> Now I Nebuchadnezzar praise, exalt, and honor the King of heaven, for all His works are true and His ways just, and He is able to humble those who walk in pride. (Daniel 4:34–37)

I vividly recall that morning in Palo Alto when I circled six statements in these verses. Verse 34: "His dominion" and "His kingdom." Verse 35: "His will" and "His hand." Verse 37: "His works" and "His ways." Everything the king had experienced and everything that followed his insanity was of God. *All* orchestrated by God, alone.

I sat and stared at that passage of Scripture for who knows how long. My heart beat faster, and I broke out in a sweat as I struggled with what I had read. Finally I told the Lord that I would give up the fight and acquiesce to His plan. I invited Him to take sovereign charge of my life. I gave Him my marriage. I gave Him my wife. I gave Him the birth of our firstborn. In fact, I surrendered my entire future to Him. And I finished the time on my knees weeping in wonder and with a sense of relief. From then on, it would be "God, and God alone."

I don't write this story to sound dramatic or pious; I tell you this story because it changed my life. And I would need a reminder of this moment several years later when Cynthia and I suffered through two miscarriages. The sovereignty of God came to my rescue in those tragic hours. I needed this reminder when we were involved in a terrible automobile collision that broke our son's jaw and injured my wife seriously and totaled our car on the icy streets of Houston. I needed this reminder during the hard times in the years that would follow in various struggles we have endured, from being misunderstood, misrepresented, and maligned. I need it today. Good times and hard times. Happiness and hardship. Gain and loss. Promotion and demotion. Joy and sorrow. Ecstasy and tragedy. Confusion and clarity. His sovereignty covers it all. God, and God alone, is in full control.

That summer morning in 1961, I decided my entire life would be His dominion and His kingdom, not mine. It would be His will shaped by His hand, not mine. It would be His works and His ways, not mine, that I would spend the balance of my life proclaiming and promoting. That decision, I repeat again, totally transformed my life.

I also promised Him that every chance I got when I had a chance to speak of His character, sovereignty would be first and foremost, and that by His grace I would be faithful in promoting that major doctrine every chance I got. Here's another chance to do so.

His way is always right. It doesn't always make sense—in fact, as we are learning, it is often mysterious. It can seldom be explained. It isn't always pleasurable and fun. But I have lived long enough to realize that His way is always right.

And that's what Nebuchadnezzar had to acknowledge. In fact, not until he acknowledged it did true reasoning return to him. Following this example, I believe that not until we embrace God's sovereignty will we have the ability to reason our way through life theologically. Until then we will be too important in the plan. Man's opinion will be too significant to us. And we will churn and wrestle and struggle our way through this Christian life, trying too hard to please people rather than living it relieved and relaxed in His plan.

ONLY GOD IS SOVEREIGN

Long before Daniel said those words to Nebuchadnezzar and Nebuchadnezzar wrote them for himself, God had led Solomon to write this proverb: "The king's heart is like channels of water in the hand of the Lord; He turns it wherever He wishes" (Proverbs 21:1).

Often, when looking upon great kings and great presidents and great governors and great men and women of state, we suck in our breath in awe. Yet God is able to move their hearts like His finger would reach down and retrace the course of a river. It's no problem to Him. He moves as He wills, and He isn't through doing so. Let me add, this isn't limited to kings. It's true of you and me.

Now that's hard to accept if you are a proud person, especially if that pride is connected with stubbornness. (Usually they go together.) You resist that thought because you can name some people who have gone through some awful times, and you say, "You're telling me that God smiled on *that?* He was responsible for *that?* He allowed *that?"* Yes, God, and God alone.

Although I have referred to him before, Job's situation bears repeating. Here was a man who lost everything but wife and life. As we saw earlier, He lost his children, his home, his livestock, his servants, his bankroll, everything! He even lost his health. His body was covered with oozing skin ulcers. You and I can't imagine such pain.

And on top of that, he had to listen to Eliphaz, Bildad, Zophar, and Elihu, his so-called friends, lecture him on why he was getting what he was due. Finally God breaks His silence and addresses Job personally. I would suggest that when you finish this chapter you read through the final five chapters of Job . . . but for now, glance over these highlights slowly and thoughtfully:

Then the LORD answered Job out of the whirlwind and said,

> Who is this that darkens counsel
> By words without knowledge?
> Now gird up your loins like a man,
> And I will ask you, and you instruct Me!
> Where were you when I laid the foundation of the earth?
> Tell Me, if you have understanding,
> Who set its measurements, since you know?
> Or who stretched the line on it?
> On what were its bases sunk?
> Or who laid its cornerstone,
> When the morning stars sang together,
> And all the sons of God shouted for joy?
>
> Or who enclosed the sea with doors,
> When, bursting forth, it went out from the womb;
> When I made a cloud its garment,
> And thick darkness its swaddling band,
> And I placed boundaries on it,
> And I set a bolt and doors,
> And I said, "Thus far you shall come, but no farther;
> And here shall your proud waves stop"?
>
> Have you ever in your life commanded the morning,
> And caused the dawn to know its place;
> That it might take hold of the ends of the earth,
> And the wicked be shaken out of it?

It is changed like clay under the seal;
And they stand forth like a garment.
And from the wicked their light is withheld,
And the uplifted arm is broken.

Have you entered into the springs of the sea?
Or have you walked in the recesses of the deep?
Have the gates of death been revealed to you?
Or have you seen the gates of deep darkness?
Have you understood the expanse of the earth?
Tell Me, if you know all this.

Where is the way to the dwelling of light?
And darkness, where is its place,
That you may take it to its territory,
And that you may discern the paths to its home?
You know, for you were born then,
And the number of your days is great!
Have you entered the storehouses of the snow,
Or have you seen the storehouses of the hail,
Which I have reserved for the time of distress,
For the day of war and battle?

(Job 38:1–23)

"Then the Lord answered Job out of the whirlwind." That's the way the Lord saw all the counsel Job had been getting before He appeared on the scene—a humanistic whirlwind. Ever been in a place like that? Ever been in a quandary and then you've had people volunteer their counsel and push their advice on you? Before very long it's all conflicting and confusing, anything but comforting. It's like a manmade *whirlwind!* And you long to hear God's clear, pristine message.

That's what Job finally gets. And what God says to Job is what we needed to hear: "I am in charge. I know what I'm doing. My way is right. Pain, suffering, and all, I am reigning sovereignly over you."

Then He asks Job a series of rhetorical questions that emphasize the fact that He, and He alone, is in control. Our newspapers report, "Disaster strikes! Blizzard sweeps across the north Midwest." And we say, "What a tragedy." God says, "I had My storehouses all ready and I sent the snow." Yes. Either that or He is *partially* sovereign . . . He is *almost* in control. Impossible. That's like my being *almost* a husband or *almost* a father.

God then talks about the stars, the constellations above us. Do we have any control over that? No, we can make lenses that help us see them, but we can't change the direction of the stars. We can stand back in amazement, and study the heavenly patterns, but we can't change the movement or alter the order of the universe.

Throughout these chapters, God addresses many of the other parts of His creation, until finally Job hears enough.

> Then Job answered the Lord, and said,
> "I know that Thou canst do all things,
> And that no purpose of Thine can be thwarted."
> (Job 42:1–2)

Job got a four-year seminary education in a few fleeting moments with the living Lord! God kept piling it on, until finally Job says, "I've got it. I see it! It's clear . . . it's clear. No purpose of Thine can be thwarted."

"No purpose of Thine can be thwarted." Remember that conclusion. Don't scissor that out of your Bible. Mark it and memorize it. When God says it shall be done, it will be done. If it makes me unhappy? It makes me unhappy. If it hurts? It hurts. If it ruins my reputation? It ruins my reputation. God says it shall be done and His purpose will not be thwarted . . . or He is not sovereign.

You want to know who's in charge around here? The One who called the spaces into being, the One who put the clouds in place, the One who established the atmosphere in which we're able to live, the One who separated the seas and the dry land, who gave you breath for your lungs and the ability to think. The One who placed you here, now, in time, for His purpose, and the One who with the snap of His divine finger will pull you from life into eternity. Mysterious though our lives may seem, God, and God alone, is in charge.

Whoever is sovereign must have total, clear perspective. He must see the end from the beginning. He must have no match on earth or in heaven. He must entertain no fears, no ignorance, and have no needs. He must have no limitations and always know what is best. He must never make a mistake. He must possess the ability to bring everything to a purposeful conclusion and an ultimate goal. He must be invincible, immutable, infinite, and self-sufficient. His judgments must be unsearchable and His ways unfathomable. He must be able to create rather than invent, to direct rather than wish, to control rather than hope, to guide rather than guess, to fulfill rather than dream. Who qualifies? You guessed it . . . God, and God alone.

And that doesn't begin to describe His resumé. He is our God, the One who says "it shall be" and it is done, and "it shall not be" and it is held back.

William Wordsworth, in his poem "Prelude," describes how wonderful it was for him to escape the city where he had been pent up for so long. Now, he says, "I'm free, free as a bird to settle where I will."[1] Free as a bird?

One man put it this way: "The naturalist knows that the supposedly free bird actually lives its entire life in a cage made of fears, hungers, and instincts; it is limited by weather conditions, varying air pressures, the local food supply, predatory beasts, and that strangest of all bonds, the irresistible compulsion to stay within the small plot of land and air assigned it by birdland committee. The freeist bird is, along with every other created thing, held in constant check by a net of necessity. Only God is free."[2]

Certainly you and I know nothing of freedom. We are bound to a very particular planet with a very particular climate and set of conditions in which we can survive. We are bound by relationships.

Bound by gravity. Bound by nature. Relying on God for the very impulses that cause our hearts to beat and our lungs to breathe and our bodies to move and our brains to think. Free? We strut about as though we are free . . . what a joke! The fact of the matter is, we are incredibly dependent people, every one of us.

Only God knows no such dependence. Only He is sovereign.

WHAT IS SOVEREIGNTY?

The apostle Paul developed this topic as well as anyone in Romans 9–11, and I want to challenge you to make your own study of those chapters. And if you don't struggle with those chapters, you're not really studying them. You'll think you have it all solved in chapter 9, and then you'll come upon chapter 10, and you'll struggle with what was said in chapter 9. But when you finally come to that great doxology at the end of chapter 11, perhaps you will, as I did, sigh with a sense of incomprehensible relief, leaving much of the mystery with God. Remember the words? We looked at them earlier.

> Oh, the depth of the riches both of the wisdom and knowledge of God! How unsearchable are His judgments and unfathomable His ways! (Romans 11:33)

Let's revisit the scene of this grand doxology. This brilliant apostle, under the direction of the Spirit of God, extols the Lord our Father as being full of wisdom and knowledge. So whatever is sovereign is bathed in wisdom and knowledge. When He makes His decisions, which here are called "judgments," they are "unsearchable," because we live in a finite realm and He in the infinite. We live in the temporal now. He lives in the eternal forever. So His decisions, His judgments are "unsearchable." Furthermore, His ways, while they are right, are in the final analysis "unfathomable." You cannot get to the bottom of them. You do, however, often come to the place where you say: "I just accept it." And that requires a humility that is very difficult for the educated, intelligent person of today.

All this has led me to a simple definition: Sovereignty means our all-wise, all-knowing God reigns in realms beyond our comprehension to bring about a plan beyond our ability to alter, hinder, or stop.

Let me go further. His plan includes all promotions and demotions. His plan can mean both adversity and prosperity, tragedy and calamity, ecstasy and joy. It envelops illness as much as health, perilous times as much as comfort, safety, prosperity, and ease. His plan is at work when we cannot imagine why, because it is so unpleasant, as much as when the reason is clear and pleasant. His sovereignty, though it is inscrutable, has dominion over all handicaps, all heartaches, all helpless moments. It is at work through all disappointments, broken dreams, and lingering difficulties. And even when we cannot fully fathom why, He knows. Even when we cannot explain the reasons, He understands. And when we cannot see the end, He is there, nodding, "Yes, that is My plan."

> For who has known the mind of the Lord, or who became His counselor? Or who has first given to him that it might be paid back to him again? For from Him and through Him and to Him are *all things.* To Him be the glory forever. Amen. (Romans 11:34–36)

If you want to alter sovereignty and make it temporal or limited, then you have to get rid of "all things," just as you must do in Romans 8:28.

> And we know that God causes *all things* to work together for good to those who love God, to those who are called according to His purpose. (Romans 8:28)

If God says "all things," He means just that.

And "all things" are for His glory forever. "To Him be the glory forever and ever." Our Sovereign is the master and the mover. He is the giver and the receiver. He is the originator, for it says "from Him." He is the enforcer, for it says "through Him." He is the provider, for it says "to Him are all things." And lest we think of this as a blind, bitter fate, remember, it is for His greater glory forever.

Right about now, some of you reading these words are getting really nervous. You've already begun to plan the letter you want to write this author, saying, "Chuck, I think you've gone off the deep end." Let me put your mind at ease. It was the madness of that kind of extremism that kept me from embracing sovereignty. That was why my own wrestling endured so long. And it isn't that I don't still wrestle with these things at times. Believe me, I do. But hear me on this: When people take this doctrine to unbiblical extremes, they become passive and uninvolved. They lack zeal, become irresponsible, and do not strive for personal excellence. All is of God, they say; so God does everything.

I find it interesting that the apostle who writes this grand three-chapter declaration and ends it on such a high note devotes the balance of the Book of Romans to *our* responsibilities. The doctrine of the book is chapters 1 through 11, but from chapter 12 on, it's mainly about duty. "God is in control," the apostle says. "God is in charge," "God is sovereign," "God is responsible." But then . . .

> I urge you therefore, brethren, by the mercies of God, to present your bodies a living and holy sacrifice, acceptable to God, which is your spiritual service of worship. (Romans 12:1)

This command is to the believer, and there's a sense of urgency about it. There's responsibility.

> And do not be conformed to this world, but be transformed by the renewing of your mind, that you may prove what the will of God is, that which is good and acceptable and perfect. (Romans 12:2)

You have a responsibility not to let the world around you squeeze you into its own mold. "Oh, don't worry about that. I believe in sovereignty." Well, so does the one who wrote it. And he says it's our responsibility to guard against that happening.

> And since we have gifts that differ according to the grace given to us, let each exercise them accordingly: if prophecy, according to the proportion of his faith; if service, in his serving; or he who teaches, in his teaching; or he who exhorts, in his exhortation; he who gives, with liberality; he who leads, with diligence; he who shows mercy, with cheerfulness. (Romans 12:6–8)

Look at that! One command after another, one active imperative after another. And it goes on into chapter 13, and into chapter 14, and further into chapter 15.

God's sovereignty does not mean that I am released from responsibility. It does not mean I have no interest in today's affairs, or that I cannot be bothered about decisions, or that I need not concern myself with the eternal destiny of the lost. It doesn't mean that at all. Somehow there has to be a balance.

In his book *The Knowledge of the Holy*, A. W. Tozer writes these very wise words:

> God sovereignly decreed that man should be free to exercise moral choice, and man from the beginning has fulfilled that decree by making his choice between good and evil. When he chooses to do evil, he does not thereby countervail the sovereign will of God but fulfills it, inasmuch as the eternal decree decided not which choice the man should make but that he should be free to make it. [3]

That choice, amazingly, includes our choice of destiny. I personally believe that our Lord God has given us the privilege of choice. We can choose *for* or we can choose *against*. But we cannot choose the consequences. If we choose against the person of Jesus Christ, we thereby step into God's decree of eternal punishment. If we choose in favor of the Lord Jesus Christ, then we inherit all the rewards of heaven—the blessing of forgiven sins and eternity with God. God rules. God reigns. And His way is right.

Where will all of this lead? "To Him be the glory forever. Amen." And don't think that most people think of that. Most of us think: How will I get the glory? What will be the benefits to me? How will I be blessed? In God's sovereign plan, your life may be painful, disappointing, difficult, inexplicably confusing, and downright mysterious. But through it all, God somehow will get all the glory.

I think of that when I read this:

> Then comes the end, when He delivers up the kingdom to the God and Father, when He has abolished all rule and all authority and power.
>
> For He must reign until He has put all His enemies under His feet.
>
> The last enemy that will be abolished is death.
>
> For *He has put all things in subjection under his feet.* But when He says, "All things are put in subjection," it is evident that He is excepted who put all things in subjection to Him.
>
> And when all things are subjected to Him, then the Son Himself also will be subjected to the One who subjected all things to Him, that God may be all in all. (1 Corinthians 15:24–28, italics mine)

We come all the way to the end of time, just before we step into eternity future. And God is setting forth the final plans for this earth and all of its inhabitants. I love this section because it's so final, so clear: "Then comes the end."

Is that great or what? And at the very end we read the ultimate objective: "that God may be all in all." That's what heaven's door will read. "God is all in all!" Even in tragedy? Even in tragedy. Even in loss? Even in loss. Even in joy and sorrow? Yes, even in all of that. Even in earthquakes? Yes. I don't know how. I don't know why. But even in calamity, even in your home that's been split apart, even there "all things are subjected to Him . . . that God may be all in all."

That's the last chapter of the Book:

> And there shall no longer be any curse; and the throne of God and of the Lamb shall be in it, and His bond-servants shall serve Him; and they shall see His face, and His name shall be on their foreheads.

> And there shall no longer be any night; and they shall not have need of the light of a lamp nor the light of the sun, because the Lord God shall illumine them; and they shall reign forever and ever. (Revelation 22:3–5)

God rules. God reigns. God, and God alone. And His way is right. It leads to His glory.

Deep within the hearts of men and women, even though most would never acknowledge it, is this realization that we really don't have the final answer. There is this little hidden clause tucked away in the deep recesses of most thinking minds that says, "There may be a God after all."

When we take this to the ultimate future for humanity, God is sovereignly in charge. One second after they die, the men and women who have rejected and resisted the Lord for years will step into eternity. One second . . . and they will be totally at a loss to determine their future. God's sovereignty steps over their lives and sets forth His decree, "That God may be all in all."

BUT WHAT DOES IT ALL MEAN?

God's sovereignty. A mysterious doctrine at times, but one with great relevance for our lives. Not just something for scholars and theologians to argue over.

First of all, the sovereignty of God relieves me from anxiety. It doesn't take away my questions. It takes away my anxiety. When I rest in it, I am relieved of the worry.

Second, the sovereignty of God frees me from explanation. I don't have to have all the answers. I find ease in saying to certain individuals at critical times, "You know, I don't know. I can't unravel His full plan in this."

The problem with learning a little theology, remember, is that we start thinking we can unscrew the inscrutable. Believing we can fathom the unfathomable. That there's no depth that we cannot plumb. Well, let's face it . . . that's not true. There are some times when those who know the most simply must back off with hands behind their back and say, "It's beyond me. I don't know why God closes some doors and opens others. I don't know why some reject Him and become vessels of wrath. I don't know how that fits in. I don't know how evil can be used for good. And I don't know how the interplay between the two in some way glorifies God. But I know ultimately it does and it will, because God will be all in all. I don't have to explain it.

Third, the sovereignty of God keeps me from pride. Once I got hold of that thought in 1961, it began to revisit me on a regular basis throughout the balance of my education and then on into ministry. I have returned to it again and again and again. And it's helped me face some of the most difficult times of my life. It's kept me on my face before God.

Like every other human being, I have many, many battles. I have numerous sins—recurring sins—that plague me. Sins I wrestle with and confess and bring before God. But I have to tell you, because of my firm confidence in the sovereignty of God, pride is not a major battle for me. I never think of being proud, not even secretly. Sovereignty solves that battle once and for all! Instead, I am grateful that He's given me breath and the ability to think and to minister and to serve.

He's sovereign over my life. And He's sovereign over your life. He's sovereign whether you accept it or not. Nebuchadnezzar discovered that fact. You may not know it right now, but you'll know it a second after you die. God, and God alone, rules. His way is right.

John Oxenham, back in 1613, called this "God's Handwriting."

He writes in characters too grand
For our short sight to understand;
We catch but broken strokes, and try
To fathom all the mystery
Of withered hopes of death, of life,
The endless war, the useless strife—
But there, with larger, clearer sight,

We shall see this—
His way was right.
His way was right.[4]

After all these years, I am still so grateful for that epochal moment in the summer of 1961 when I was forced to come to terms with an issue that had been troubling me. I'm grateful for the comfort it has brought over the years. I'm satisfied that God was directly involved when my eyes fell upon that passage in Daniel. And I thank Him for preserving this account of King Nebuchadnezzar and of Job and the writings of Paul so that we might learn that His rule and His sovereignty is right. His way is right.

Sometimes we struggle. Sometimes the handwriting is difficult to read or hard to accept. But I pray that the Lord will minister in a very special way to you who are struggling, who are coming to terms with His right to rule over you. And I pray that the name of the almighty, sovereign God will be lifted up, and that all the glory will be His . . . despite the mystery of it all.

6

Reading God's Mysterious Lips

All is riddle, and the key to a riddle is another riddle.

—Emerson, *The Conduct of Life*

In human intercourse the tragedy begins.
Not when there is misunderstanding about words,
but when silence is not understood.

—Thoreau, *A Week on the Concord and Merrimack Rivers*

I found Him in the shining of the stars,
I marked Him in the flowering of His fields,
But in His ways with men I find Him not.

—Alfred, Lord Tennyson, *Idylls of the King*

Chapter Six

Reading God's Mysterious Lips

IN THE MID-1970s I had to have tympanoplasty surgery done on my right ear. I was born with a congenital hole in that ear, which, consequently, was susceptible to infection. During my childhood, I suffered some painful bouts with this, and by the time I reached my late thirties, the hole had gotten larger, which meant I was beginning to experience a slight loss of hearing. So my surgeon repaired the damage by using a little bit of my fascia, which is located immediately under the scalp, to rebuild my eardrum.

Tympanoplasty is not a painful surgery, but it does require a somewhat lengthy recovery time. And while I was recovering, I thought quite a bit about what life would be like without hearing. What would be the difficulties, the major adjustments? I decided that one major adjustment would be learning to read lips.

I remembered this last year when I was speaking at a conference and a woman, who always sat on the front row, came up and thanked me for articulating carefully. "I can't hear, so I have learned to read lips," she said. When I asked if this was very difficult for her, she said, "Oh no . . . I watch television, I go to movies, I do all the things that many people think those without hearing could never do." And then she added this insightful thought: "It's great, actually. I really get to study the person who is speaking, really get to watch closely, because I can't take my eyes off the lips. If I do, I don't hear what's going on."

All this ties in beautifully with our walk with the Lord, for God is not only invisible and sovereign, He is also silent. Some of the great hymn writers have scripted eloquent lyrics on this subject. For example, Walter Chalmers Smith's hymn:

> Immortal, invisible, God only wise,
> In light inaccessible hid from our eyes,
> Most blessed, most glorious, the Ancient of Days,
> Almighty, victorious, Thy great name we praise.
> Unresting, unhasting, and silent as light,
> Nor wanting, nor wasting, Thou rulest in might . . . .[1]

"Silent as light." That's our God. We don't see Him; we don't hear Him, at least in a physical sense. Yet we're commanded to be wise and to understand what the will of the Lord is. But He doesn't speak.

Wouldn't it be easier if twice a week He would break the silence, visit us in our prayer closet or at our desk or in some part of our home and say, "This is our time together. I want to give you My will for next week." But if that happened, we'd be walking by sound and not by faith.

And so, since He is invisible and silent, and we can't read His lips, how do we get our messages from God?

LISTENING IN THE SILENCE

First of all, *we need to be sensitive and skilled* because God's will is unpredictable.

In Psalm 32 we find a dialogue between David and the Lord.

By the way, notice that this psalm is not only called "A Psalm of David," it is also called "A Maskil." A *maskil* is an instructive psalm. Also notice that right in the heart of the psalm the word *Selah* appears three times. *Selah* is a bracketed musical hint included by the psalmist, which calls for a pause. When you have a pause in music, you ponder what has just been played or sung as it lingers in the air, and then you anticipate what is coming next. In music, a pause can be very effective. In this case, there are three of them. And right after the third one come these words:

> I will instruct you and teach you in the way which you should go;
> I will counsel you with My eye upon you. (Psalm 32:8)

God is silent. So He does not say, "I will instruct you with My voice." He says, "I will instruct you and teach you and counsel you with My eye upon you." The movement of the eyes is a silent movement. So, like the lip reader, we must be very sensitive and skilled as we study our Lord and then respond to the inner promptings from the Spirit of God.

God's will is not only mysterious, it's also unpredictable. We've certainly established that, haven't we? Often it is not what we would have expected. Recently, a couple who are good friends of ours have been searching for God's will in the area of the husband's vocation. They had made a decision that seemed to be God's will, only to come up against a brick wall. For them to stay in the situation would be a compromise of this man's integrity. "So we're backing away from that," he told me. "For me to stay is to compromise my character. I won't do that." They are being very sensitive to what God is leading them to do, because it is obviously not what they had anticipated.

Second, *we need to be perceptive and patient* because God's plan is continually unfolding. What brought us to where we are right now is all part of His overall plan. But that plan is still in the process of unfolding in our lives, which means that taking us from where we are to His place for us in the future will involve change. And some of those changes are things we would never expect.

LEARNING FROM JEREMIAH THE PROPHET

Let's return to a biblical character we met earlier in this book. Jeremiah was a prophet used by God during some of the most difficult times in Israel's history—the last days of the kingdom of Judah.

> The words of Jeremiah, the son of Hilkiah, of the priests who were in Anathoth in the land of Benjamin, to whom the word of the LORD came in the days of Josiah, the son of Amon, king of Judah, in the thirteenth year of his reign. It came also in the days of Jehoiakim, the son of Josiah, king of Judah, until the end of the eleventh year of Zedekiah, the son of Josiah, king of Judah, until the exile of Jerusalem in the fifth month.
>
> Now the word of the LORD came to me saying, (Jeremiah 1:1–4)

"Now the word of the Lord came to me . . . ." Jeremiah has picked up his pen and begun writing. The pronoun "me" reveals it. I don't think Jeremiah knew he was writing Scripture. I don't think he had any idea that fifty-two of the chapters in the Bible would be entrusted to him. Jeremiah was just writing what the Lord had revealed to him, and God saw fit to guide his writing so that it became an inspired part of the canon of Scripture. So he records "The word of the Lord came to me saying . . ."

> "Before I formed you in the womb I knew you,
> And before you were born I consecrated you;
> I have appointed you a prophet to the nations." (Jeremiah 1:5)

God tells Jeremiah that He had set him apart as a prophet before he was even born. *Before* he was *formed* in the womb, God *knew* him. *Before* he was born, God *consecrated* him and *appointed* him a prophet to the nations.

God's predetermined plan is fixed. Before we were even conceived in our mothers' wombs, God's plans for us had been put into place.

In his book *Run with the Horses,* Eugene Peterson has some marvelous insights regarding this ancient scene. In the chapter titled "Before," he points out several splendid observations:

> Before Jeremiah knew God, God knew Jeremiah: "Before I formed you in the womb I knew you." This turns everything we ever thought about God around. . . .
>
> We enter a world we didn't create. We grow into a life already provided for us. . . . If we are going to live appropriately, we must be aware that we are living in the middle of a story that was begun and will be concluded by another. And this other is God. . . .
>
> Jeremiah's life didn't start with Jeremiah. Jeremiah's salvation didn't start with Jeremiah. Jeremiah's truth didn't start with Jeremiah. He entered the world in which the essential parts of his existence were already ancient history. So do we. "I knew you." . . .
>
> The second item of background information provided on Jeremiah is this: "Before you were born, I consecrated you." *Consecrated* means "set apart for God's side." It means that the human is not a cogwheel, that a person is not the keyboard of a piano on which circumstances play hit-parade tunes. It means we are chosen out of the feckless stream of circumstantiality for something important that God is doing.
>
> What is God doing? He is saving; He is rescuing; He is blessing; He is providing; He is judging; He is healing; He is enlightening. And there is a spiritual war in process, an all-out moral battle. There is evil and cruelty, unhappiness and illness. There is superstition and ignorance, brutality and pain. But God is in a continuous and energetic battle against all of it. God is for life and against death. God is for love and against hate. God is for hope and against despair. God is for heaven and against hell. There is no neutral ground in the universe. Every square foot of space is contested.
>
> Jeremiah, before he was born, was enlisted on God's side in this war.
>
> God did a third thing to Jeremiah before Jeremiah did anything

> on his own: "I appointed you a prophet to the nations." The word "appointed" is, literally, "gave"—I "gave" you as a prophet to the nations. God gives. He's generous. He is lavishly generous. Before Jeremiah ever got it together he was given away.
>
> That is God's way. He did it with his own Son, Jesus. "God so loved the world that He gave . . . ."
>
> Some things we have a choice in, some we don't. In this we don't. It's the kind of world into which we were born. God created it. God sustains it. Giving is the style of the universe. Giving is woven into the fabric of existence. . . .
>
> Jeremiah could have hung on to the dead-end street where he was born in Anathoth. He could have huddled in the security of his father's priesthood. He could have conformed to the dull habits of his culture. He didn't. He participated in the giving, throwing himself into his appointment.[2]

That is what I want for you! Wherever God's will may lead you, and whatever He may call you to do, wherever He requires you to live, whatever must be given up, and whatever must be taken on, DO IT! That is life at its best. The quest for life at its best means we run with the horses, we do His will, which is always the safest and most rewarding place to live—even though it is full of changing and risking and releasing. DO IT!

FIVE GUIDELINES FOR READING GOD'S LIPS

I've heard some Christians say that they pray only once and then they trust God. To pray more than once, they say, is to doubt. I question that. What about Paul, who prayed three times that the thorn in the flesh would be taken from him? Maybe he didn't pray beyond the third time, but he did pray three times, fervently. I don't find anywhere in Scripture that praying more than once is disobedience or doubt. We need to think reflectively, sensibly. God has given us a brain and His Spirit to work in harmony and in concert.

God wants us to understand what His will is. He isn't playing games with us; He isn't playing hide and seek with us. "No, no, no, wrong place, keep looking. You're getting warmer." He wants us to know His will. Though He remains "silent as light," He is engaged in directing our steps. He has created us to do His will. To help us do that, He has given us some guidelines.

To help me remember them, I've come up with an ultra-simple plan. I've used the first five letters of the alphabet: A-B-C-D-E. Frankly, I go through these five myself when I try to read God's mysterious lips.

A: An accepting frame of mind. I call this a "can-do" spirit.

To be in this frame of mind, we need to be relatively free of anxiety and stress. You say, "Well, I can remember two days in my adult life when that was true." And you're right. Most of us live pretty stressful lives. That's why we need an intimacy with the Almighty; we need times of solitude and silence. There's nothing mysterious about that. Some call it mystical. I call it wise.

I know a man who sets aside one day every month to do nothing but be alone, to be silent, and to think. For years, he successfully led an organization because of his commitment to that kind of discipline. On that day, he would eat a good breakfast and then fast at lunchtime. Then he invested the balance of that day alone thinking through, praying about various matters on his mind. Sometimes he took a Bible, sometimes he took a book, sometimes he took nothing. And he would go to different places—there was no sacred meeting place.

You may have a special spot where you like to go to be alone. For others, variety is important. One day it may be a walk on the beach. Another day it may be a trip into the mountains. It may be a long drive. It may be a walk around your neighborhood or just time spent on a park bench. It doesn't matter where, just so you have time to reflect where you're relatively free of stress.

What's important is that you have an accepting frame of mind—regardless. Regardless of where it may be or what it may include, you remain open. Teachable. Sensitive. Available.

Did Jeremiah have an accepting frame of mind? After God told him, "I formed you, and I consecrated you, and I appointed you," his answer was,

> "Alas, Lord GOD!
> Behold, I do not know how to speak,
> Because I am a youth." (Jeremiah 1:6)

Here is a prophet in the making. "I don't know how to speak." What did prophets do? They preached.

> But the LORD said to me, "Do not say, 'I am a youth,'
> Because everywhere I send you, you shall go,
> And all that I command you, you shall speak.
> Do not be afraid of them,
> For I am with you to deliver you," declares the LORD.
> Then the LORD stretched out His hand and touched my mouth, and the LORD said to me, "Behold, I have put My words in your mouth." (Jeremiah 1:7–9)

When we are listening in the silence, we need to be in an accepting frame of mind.

When I was in my freshman year of high school, I stuttered so badly I could hardly finish a sentence. One day our drama teacher, Dick Nieme, stopped me in the hallway at Milby High School and said, "I want you to be a part of our Thespian group." And I go, "Bl, bl, bl, bl, me?" He said, "Yeah, you."

I really thought he had the wrong kid. I thought he meant the guy next to me, who was a star basketball player. "No," he said, "you."

My first thought was, "Oh, I'm so inadequate. You have no idea how embarrassed I am in front of a group. You want me to stand there and st-st-stutter? I'll ruin the whole thing."

But only three years later, I had the lead in our senior play, I was on the debate team . . . and I loved it.

The late, great Dick Nieme, whose picture sits on my desk alongside my other mentors, saw what I couldn't imagine. He saw something within me before it was ever reality. All that happened to me is just an earthly, shadowy picture of the way God sees us.

An accepting frame of mind says, "Me? If you say so, I'm willing."

B: Biblical investigation. By now you know that God's will is never contrary to God's Word. You will never do God's will and then look back and find, "Oh, my goodness, this passage of Scripture condemns what I'm doing." It'll never happen. You're safe.

> O how I love Thy law!
> It is my meditation all the day.
> Thy commandments make me wiser than my enemies,
> For they are ever mine.
> I have more insight than all my teachers,
> For Thy testimonies are my meditation.
> I understand more than the aged,
> Because I have observed Thy precepts. . . .
> Thy word is a lamp to my feet,
> And a light to my path. (Psalm 119:97–100, 105)

God's Word makes you and me wiser than our enemies, gives us more insight than we had from our teachers, and provides us an understanding that's beyond the aged. That's an awfully good set of promises.

Now what does this entail? First of all, in searching God's Word for His will, find the subject that is closest to the area of need. Marriage, suffering, money, occupation, submission . . . there are hundreds of subjects. Get a concordance, which is an alphabetical listing of all the words in the Bible, and locate that word. If it's suffering, look up the word "suffering." There you will find a list of all the references in the Scriptures where the word is mentioned. Then begin your study on that subject.

Obviously, some of the things you might be concerned about

may not be mentioned in Scripture by that specific word, so look for synonyms. That's one way to do biblical investigation.

Second, stay alert to actual precepts and principles that you uncover. Remember the difference between "Speed Limit 35" and "Drive Carefully"? Pay attention in church or Bible study. This is not a time to drift. This is instruction time; this is a time to learn. Take notes. Jot down questions you want to think through.

Another part of biblical investigation is your time with the Lord. It can also be a part of your discussion with Christian friends. Instead of sitting over lunch and talking about the latest movie, discuss subjects of value. Remember, the lowest level of conversation is people. The next level is events. The highest level is truth and ideas. Call a friend for lunch and say, "While we eat, I'd really like to talk about . . ." By stating it, you set the agenda. You'll find you're eating less and thinking more. Pick your lunch partner carefully, though, because you want insight from this other person, and you also want the freedom to be vulnerable.

Finally, when it comes to biblical investigation, at the risk of being painfully elementary, I would suggest that you need a Bible that is a good, reliable translation of the Scriptures. In my estimation, the most accurate translation, although not the most readable, is the New American Standard Bible. The New International Version is also very good. The New Living Translation can give you a fresh slant on passages of Scripture, as does Eugene Peterson's easy-to-read, contemporary paraphrase, *The Message.*

Biblical investigation requires sound, sensible interpretation of the Scriptures. Study passages in context. Don't pick verse 7 and ignore verses 1 to 6. It's sort of like a diamond. Without a setting, a diamond is loose and can get lost. But when you put it in a setting, you can then enjoy the beauty of that gem. So it is with verses of Scripture.

God's Word answers most of our questions, but to find those answers takes time, patience, and effort. It's like a handbook or a manual of instruction for your computer software. You may have to dig to find the answers, but they are there. (When it comes to computers, of course, some of us may have to dig a long time!) You can read God's lips much more easily if you spend sufficient time in His Word.

C: The clarification and conviction from the Holy Spirit. This combination of God's Word and God's Spirit works within us like an inner compulsion. You're drawn, almost as if somebody has grabbed onto your clothing and is pulling you in a certain direction. . . . like an inner magnet, drawing you toward that goal.

When you're walking in the Spirit, and when you're thinking through the Sciprutures reflectively, when you're open to where God's leading, that magnet will start pulling on you, and you will sense a direction. It may not come quickly, by the way, but ultimately it will come. David says in Psalm 40:1, "I waited patiently for the LORD; and He inclined to me, and heard my cry." In *The Message,* Eugene Peterson paraphrases it this way: "I waited and waited and waited for Yahweh. And He inclined to me, and heard my cry."[3]

"I waited and waited and waited . . . and finally He did what He said He would do." Keep in mind, God doesn't operate by a twenty-four-hour clock. His timing is eternal. Furthermore, He knows His plan for us, even when we are so confused that we don't even know what questions to ask.

If you want verification of this, consider these significant thoughts from Romans 8:

> For all who are being led by the Spirit of God, these are sons of God. For you have not received a spirit of slavery leading to fear again, but you have received a spirit of adoption as sons by which we cry out, "Abba! Father!" The Spirit Himself bears witness with our spirit that we are children of God, and if children, heirs also, heirs of God and fellow heirs with Christ, if indeed we suffer with Him in order that we may also be glorified with Him. . . . And in the same way the Spirit also helps our weakness; for we do not know how to pray as we should, but the Spirit Himself intercedes for us with groanings too deep for words; and He who searches the hearts knows what the

> mind of the Spirit is, because He intercedes for the saints according to the will of God. (Romans 8:14–17, 26–27)

Isn't that great? Paul admits, "I am in such an uncertain state that I don't even know how or what to ask, but God understands even my 'groanings.'"

Ever been there? Sometimes in prayer I've only been able to groan, literally. As remarkable as it may seem, somehow the Holy Spirit interprets my "groanings too deep for words" and places them before God's marvelous presence, clearly and correctly. The Spirit of God does that. Take comfort in that, you who want to word everything just so. You really don't have to spell our every detail of your concern. So stop trying!

I'm being totally honest here. There are occasions when I look up from my desk in the midst of some situation I can't see my way through and I simply say, "Help, Lord, help, help." I can't get anything else out of my mouth. "Help." And He does . . . He really does.

When we are willing to wait and let Him take charge of the problem, He will. The trouble comes when I jump up from my desk and say, "I know how to handle this. I'm just gonna take care of it right now." And invariably, I regret such actions prompted by the flesh.

Sometimes, of course, action is what God wants from us at that moment. But usually it's best to wait. As someone has said, "I never felt sorry for the things I did not say." I've rarely regretted times I waited. Often, the bigger the decision, the longer the wait.

D: Determine if peace is occurring. "And let the peace of Christ rule in your hearts, to which indeed you were called in one body; and be thankful. Let the word of Christ richly dwell within you, with all wisdom teaching and admonishing one another with psalms and hymns and spiritual songs, singing with thankfulness in your hearts to God" (Colossians 3:15–16). Let the peace of Christ call the shots. The word "rule" means "to serve as an arbiter," or to use a contemporary term, "to act as an umpire."

An umpire is the final voice in the game. He makes the crucial decisions, calls the fouls, and settles situations before they turn into conflicts. He keeps the game moving. That's the way it is with peace.

If you were to tell me that you were in the midst of a struggle and had just about come to a decision, I would say, "Do you have peace in all of this?" And if your answer was, "You know, I'm really unsettled. Actually, I don't have peace," then I would say, "If you don't have peace, you're still churning. If you're still churning, you're not there yet." Never move ahead into important decisions without peace!

For those of you who are married, let me add this: When it's decision time, your mate should have peace about the matter, too. Resist the urge to drag your husband or wife along against his or her wishes. I've seldom seen that turn out well. Some guys seem to take delight in doing that: "We're doing this whether she's ready or not. She's obviously not open to God." Wait a minute, she knows you better than anybody else on earth. She's part of the project, and she's your partner, which means you're one. In fact, you're so much one, Scripture teaches, if there are conflicts, your prayers will be hindered. "You husbands likewise, live with your wives in an understanding way, as with a weaker vessel, since she is a woman; and grant her honor as a fellow heir of the grace of life, so that your prayers may not be hindered" (1 Peter 3:7).

My dear friend Tom Kimber (whom I mentioned earlier) should never have gone to China if he'd had to pull Sue behind him, dragging her heels. And I know him well enough to say that he would not have done so. They went because they both had peace about the decision.

An extremely reliable theologian of yesteryear named Dr. Lightfoot writes, "Wherever there is a conflict of motives or impulses or reasons, the peace of Christ must step in and decide and prevail." What a great way to put it! When there is a conflict of motives or impulses or reasons, the peace of God must settle things down.

I do not try to talk people into decisions, and I don't talk them out of decisions. Sometimes there is a certain person we really want on our staff, whether at the church or at Insight for Living or at Dallas Seminary, and I feel that he or she is the right person for the job. But if they're unsure about it, I don't intensify the pressure. I've done that in the past, and invariably I've regretted it. If someone comes to me and says, "You know, I sense God is leading me elsewhere," I don't argue with that. Instead, I affirm and applaud the decision.

God doesn't give us His will for another person's life. He gives it to that individual. If a warning is appropriate, we may need to warn them. Or if we see peril in the decision (this could be the "wise counselor" role we talked about earlier), we may want to point that out. But ultimately the decision must be between them and God, who gives that sense of inner peace.

E: Expect struggles and surprises as you experience the results. "Consider it all joy, my brethren, when you encounter various trials, knowing that the testing of your faith produces endurance" (James 1:2–3). Sometimes we step into a situation that is clearly the will of God for us. We have reflected on it, we have gotten counsel from people we respect, and we have peace about it . . . and strangely, we're not in it two weeks before we realize, *This is a can of worms!* This is work! So even within the will of God, there are surprises and struggles. But we still have peace, knowing that we are the one who is supposed to deal with this can of worms. This is God's plan. This is where He wants to use us. But that doesn't mean there won't be mysteries—remember that!

SOME PRACTICAL ADVICE

I'd like to conclude this chapter with a couple of very practical suggestions. One has to do with the secret of knowing God's will, and the other has to do with success that follows it.

First, the secret of knowing God's will means we must get beyond all excuses and rationalizations. Remember Jeremiah's excuse? "'Alas, Lord God! Behold, I do not know how to speak, because I am a youth" (Jeremiah 1:6).

Did he think God didn't know that? God doesn't call you into a situation to be compared to someone else. You're called into it as an instrument. And in that role you are, in God's plan, invincible.

Second, the success that follows doing God's will rests with God, not you. This takes all the strain and the sweat out of the matter. Sometimes in the midst of a situation I'm so over my head that the only peace I have is in saying, "Hey, Lord, here I am again, totally inadequate. This was Your plan from the start."

That's when I go back to my biblical investigation of God's handbook and find things like God's response to Jeremiah's lame excuse:

> But the LORD said to me, "Do not say, 'I am a youth,' Because everywhere I send you, you shall go,
>
> "And all that I command you, you shall speak.
>
> "Do not be afraid of them, For I am with you to deliver you," declares the LORD. Then the LORD stretched out His hand and touched my mouth, and the LORD said to me, "Behold, I have put My words in your mouth. . . .
>
> "Now, gird up your loins, and arise, and speak to them all which I command you. Do not be dismayed before them, lest I dismay you before them.
>
> "Now behold, I have made you today as a fortified city, and as a pillar of iron and as walls of bronze against the whole land, to the kings of Judah, to its princes, to its priests and to the people of the land. And they will fight against you, but they will not overcome you, for I am with you to deliver you," declares the LORD. (Jeremiah 1:7–9, 17–19)

I do not believe that we pull those verses out of context when we claim such things in doing God's will. I believe those verses have been preserved for our meditation and application, because I have seen God do exactly what He says here. I've seen Him take young, fresh-out-of-seminary pastors and place them in situations that call for wisdom and skill and gifts beyond their years, and I have seen them stand like a wall of bronze. I've seen women, because of death or divorce, forced to step into roles and situations they had never handled before. And I have seen them stand like a pillar of iron, surprising even themselves by their ability to handle the pressure . . . surprised that they are not overcome. When we're in the father's will, He steps up!

Please allow me one final return to Peterson's reflections on Jeremiah. Because he says it better than I could, I prefer to have you read his words.

> His strength was not achieved by growing calluses over his highly sensitive spirit. Throughout his life Jeremiah experienced an astonishing range of emotions. His spirit registered, it seemed, everything. He was one of those finely tuned persons who pick up and respond to the slightest tremors around him. At the same time he was utterly impervious to assault and mockery, to persecution and opposition.
>
> The thorough integration of strength and sensitivity, of firmness and feeling, is rare. We sometimes see sensitive people who are unstrung most of the time. They bleed profusely at the sight of blood. Their sensitivity incapacitates them for action in the rough-and-tumble cruelties of the world. In contrast others are rigid moralists, ramrod stiff with righteous rectitude. There is never any doubt about their dogmatically asserted position. But their principles are hammers that crack skulls and bruise flesh. The world makes a wide circuit around such persons. It is dangerous to be in their company for very long, for if they detect any mental weakness or moral wavering in us, we will be lucky to escape without at least a headache.
>
> But not Jeremiah. Educated by the almond rod, his inward responsiveness to the personal, whether God or human, deepened and developed. Educated by the boiling pot, his outward capacity to deal with dehumanizing evil and to resist depersonalizing intimidation became invincible: "a fortified city, an iron pillar, bronze walls." Not bad for someone who started out as "only a youth."[4]

Let me encourage you not to rush in, as Jeremiah did, to rehearse before God your inadequacy. You think He doesn't know? *All of us are inadequate!* If we weren't, we wouldn't need God.

Our comfort comes in knowing that He does all things well—including His plan for our lives. His mercy rushes to our rescue. He is longsuffering and patient beyond our imagination, fully committed to using us, warts and all.

Part II

The Blessings of God's Will

Grieve not, because thou understandest not
life's mystery;
Behind the veil is concealed many a delight.

—Hafiz, *Divan*

The Magnificent Chesed of God

Entrust the past to God's mercy, the present to His love, and the future to His providence.

—St. Augustine, *Confessions*

What value has compassion
that does not take its object in its arms?

—Saint-Exupéry, *The Wisdom of the Saints*

Chapter Seven

The Magnificent Chesed of God

SEVERAL YEARS AGO, my sister Luci asked me a question that I'd never been asked before: "What is your favorite feeling?" Ever thought about that? My answer to her was, "I believe my favorite feeling is the feeling of accomplishment." (Sounds like a driven person's answer, doesn't it?) I like the feeling of getting something done. "Finished" is one of my favorite words.

When I asked her to answer the same question, she said, "My favorite feeling is relief."

I thought that was a great answer. In fact, better than mine! When I checked Webster's later, I found that the feeling of relief means "the removal or lightening of something oppressive, painful, or distressing."

When we are in physical pain, relief means that the pain subsides.

When we are emotionally distraught, relief calms us, gives us a sense of satisfaction.

When guilt assaults us in transgression and we seek God's forgiveness, the guilt that ate like a cancer inside us goes away as God brings relief.

When a relationship is strained, perhaps with someone we were once close to, we do not feel relief until we have worked through the painful process of making things right with that person.

When we are burdened by heavy financial debt, getting that paid off brings the sweet release of relief.

In chapter 5 we learned that the sovereign Most High God is ruler over our lives. So it's obvious that if we ever have the feeling of relief, God has given it to us. He's the author of relief. He is the one who grants us the peace, the satisfaction, the ease. In fact, I think relief is a wonderful synonym for mercy. Mercy is God's active compassion which He demonstrates to the miserable. When we are in a time of deep distress and God activates His compassion to bring about relief, we've experienced mercy.

Mercy. It isn't passive pity. It isn't simply understanding. It isn't mere sorrow. It is a divine action on our behalf through which He brings about a sense of relief. God, our compassionate and caring heavenly Father, is the author of relief. And when it comes to those mysterious, confusing times when doing His will results in the unexpected, there's nothing like mercy to make it bearable.

MERCY: OUR SOURCE OF RELIEF

The beautiful thing about mercy is that it is demonstrated to the offender as well as to the victim. When the offender realizes his or her wrong, God brings mercy. When the victim needs help to go on, God gives mercy.

> And you were dead in your trespasses and sins, in which you formerly walked according to the course of this world, according to the prince of the power of the air, of the spirit that is now working in the sons of disobedience. Among them we too all formerly lived in the lusts of our flesh, indulging the desires of the flesh and of the mind, and were by nature children of wrath, even as the rest.
>
> But God, being rich in mercy, because of His great love with which He loved us, even when we were dead in our transgressions, made us alive together with Christ (by grace you have been saved), and raised us up with Him, and seated us with Him in the heavenly

> places, in Christ Jesus, in order that in the ages to come He might show the surpassing riches of His grace in kindness toward us in Christ Jesus. (Ephesians 2:1–7)

"But God," the apostle writes, "being rich in mercy." The connecting link between a holy God and a sinful person is God's love, which activates His grace, which, in turn, sets in motion His mercy. They're like divine dominoes that bump up against one another. He loves us not because of something in ourselves but because of something in Himself. And in His love He demonstrates His grace, which brings forgiveness. And on top of that, grace prompts mercy . . . and there it is: *relief!*

To make it even more personal, look at Paul's own testimony in 1 Timothy 1:12–13. In Ephesians 2 he writes about everyone. In 1 Timothy 1 he writes about himself.

> I thank Christ Jesus our Lord, who has strengthened me, because He considered me faithful, putting me into service; even though I was formerly a blasphemer and a persecutor and a violent aggressor. And yet I was shown mercy, because I acted ignorantly in unbelief.

Look closely at those three descriptions of Paul's former life. First, he says, "I was a blasphemer." The word means "an insulter." "I insulted God's people. I was angry at Christians. I accused them of crimes against God. I was a blasphemer."

Second, "I was a persecutor." He took every means open to him under Jewish law to hurt, to humiliate, even annihilate, Christians.

And then that terrible admission, "I was a violent aggressor." The Greek word suggests a kind of "arrogant sadism." It describes a person who is out to inflict pain and injury for the sheer joy of inflicting it. "I loved to make them squirm. I loved to watch them cry. I loved to see them removed from this earth!"

We don't usually think of Paul in these terms, but that's the way he describes himself before Christ. And lest you cluck your tongue at

Paul or wag your finger and say, "Shame, shame," realize that the same nature is inside of you. It may not work its way out in these kinds of actions, but it comes out in other ways. Most of us can remember acts of cruelty we've committed. What is true of the apostle is true of us. God showed Him mercy, and He does the same for us. (What a relief!)

Can you imagine what Paul's conscience must have been like when the Lord found him on the way to Damascus? Can you imagine the guilt? Can you imagine what he felt when his life passed in review while he was blind, before he saw God's plan for his life? Can you imagine how he felt? The enormity of the pain of his past? And to hear God say, "I want to use you, Saul, in My service"?

John Newton knew the same kind of anguish, which he revealed when he composed his own epitaph for his tombstone:

John Newton, Clerk,
once an Infidel and Libertine,
a Servant of Slaves in Africa,
was by the Mercy of our Lord and Saviour Jesus Christ,
Preserved, Restored, Pardoned,
and Appointed to Preach the Faith
he had so long laboured to destroy.[1]

Some of you have been Christians so long you've forgotten what you were like before Christ. Could that explain why you're still so proud? Maybe that's why the Lord has to spend so much extra time getting your attention. You've forgotten how undeserving you are of His grace. You've forgotten His mercy.

I love the letter that an old Puritan, Thomas Goodwin, wrote to his son.

> When I was threatening to become cold in my ministry, and when I felt Sabbath morning coming and my heart not filled with amazement at the grace of God, or when I was making ready to dispense

> the Lord's Supper, do you know what I used to do? I used to take a turn up and down among the sins of my past life, and I always came down again with a broken and a contrite heart, ready to preach, as it was preached in the beginning, the forgiveness of sins. I do not think I ever went up the pulpit stair that I did not stop for a moment at the foot of it and take a turn up and down among the sins of my past years. I do not think that I ever planned a sermon that I did not take a turn round my study table and look back at the sins of my youth and of all my life down to the present; and many a Sabbath morning, when my soul had been cold and dry, for the lack of prayer during the week, a turn up and down in my past life before I went into the pulpit always broke my hard heart and made me close with the gospel for my own soul before I began to preach.[2]

The wonderful thing about the writings of the apostle Paul is that he frequently returns to the sins of his past. He reminds me of what Great-heart says to Christian's children in Part II of *Pilgrim's Progress:* "You must know that Forgetful Green is the most dangerous place in all these parts."

Try hard not to forget what life was like before Christ and you will be a frequent visitor at the gate of mercy.

FIVE MISERIES RELIEVED

In the Old Testament the Hebrew term for "mercy" is *chesed.* It is a magnificent word, often translated "lovingkindness" or simply "kindness." When I trace *chesed* through the Old Testament Scriptures, I find at least five different miseries to which mercy brings relief. It's like that Visine commercial: "It takes the red out." Mercy mysteriously takes the red out of the anguish of your life.

The first anguish mercy relieves is the anguish of unfair treatment. For an example of this, we have only to look at Joseph, a great and godly man who was falsely accused.

Potipher's wife comes at Joseph again and again. Each time he rejects her. Finally she corners him alone in her home, with the doors locked and the servants gone and the lights low. Seductively she whispers, "Lie with me." Joseph looks her in the eyes and refuses . . . then makes a mad dash for safety. She is so infuriated that she grabs at him, tears off a piece of his garment, and cries, "Rape!" The word gets to her husband, Potiphar, and Joseph winds up in jail, though he never laid a hand on the woman. The story is found in Genesis 39. Then, at the end of the account, *chesed* appears:

> But the LORD was with Joseph and extended kindness [*chesed,* mercy] to him, and gave him favor in the sight of the chief jailer. (Genesis 39:21)

Where did mercy appear? In a jail cell. In an Egyptian dungeon, the Lord visited Joseph and relieved him of the misery of suffering unfair consequences. God ministered to Joseph's heart and kept him from bitterness. God even "gave him favor in the sight of the chief jailer."

Chuck Colson has told me story after story about life behind bars, both from his own life experience and from the prisons in which he has ministered through the years. And mercy welled up within me all over again as he described each scene that transpired in those dark cells of loneliness and regret.

Here is Joseph in such a place, in great need of encouragement, and God demonstrates *chesed.* God gives him mercy.

You may not be in jail, but you may be going through a time of unjust criticism, even though you obeyed the Lord and followed His lead. You're in His will, but now you find yourself in need of His *chesed.* You may be suffering the backwash of unfair statements made against you. You need the kind of relief only God can give. It's the same kind the Lord extended to Joseph in that Egyptian cell.

Even when you are forgotten by those who should remember you, even when someone doesn't fulfill his promise to you, when you're left alone and you (alone) know your heart is just, God will give you His mercy. He'll bring you relief. He'll meet you in your loneliness.

The second anguish mercy relieves is the anguish of the grief of loss. The Book of Ruth provides a wonderful example of this.

Ruth actually begins with the story of Elimelech and Naomi and their two sons. Almost immediately we read that Naomi's husband dies, apparently at a relatively young age, and she is left to raise her two sons as a single parent. When they are grown, both boys marry Moabite women, Orpah and Ruth. About ten years later, both of Naomi's sons die, and suddenly the family consists of the three widows: a mother-in-law named Naomi and two daughters-in-law, Ruth and Orpah, grieving over the deaths of their loved ones.

Think of it. Naomi is probably still trying to get over the loss of her husband, and now she has to face the loss of her sons. And the daughters-in-law have lost their husbands. That's a lot of deaths in one family; the need for *chesed* is great. People need mercy when grief invades their lives. . . even when they are in the Father's will.

> And Naomi said to her two daughters-in-law, "Go, return each of you to her mother's house. May the LORD deal kindly with you as you have dealt with the dead and with me. May the LORD grant that you may find rest, each in the house of her husband." Then she kissed them, and they lifted up their voices and wept. (Ruth 1:8–9)

Naomi says to them, "May the Lord give you mercy in your grieving. May He help you when the pain is so great and you don't know where to turn and when the lights go out at night you have no one near to put their arms around you."

It's easy to pass over this too quickly, especially if you haven't recently endured a time of grief. But at some time, all of us will. And when you do, remember that God has a special mercy for those who are left as widows and widowers, and for those who are left as grieving parents or grieving children.

It happened on April 20, 1999, in Littleton, Colorado. Heartbroken families were shocked to hear that their sons and daughters and one husband had been shot and killed. That morning they saw them off to school . . . that night they found themselves standing, grief-stricken, in a funeral home. If ever mercy was needed, it was then. Who could ever explain how such a tragic event could be included in God's permissive will? Mercy soothes such harsh times of confusion.

God's will may be for you to be a Naomi. You may be the one to put your arms around the grieving and to bring relief. In those circumstances, people need heartfelt compassion. They need your loving presence. So during times of grief God uses folks like us to extend His *chesed* as the grieving work through their sorrow.

The third anguish mercy relieves is the anguish of struggling with a handicap. To see a wonderful example of this, we only have to turn to the Book of 2 Samuel, chapter 9. It has become one of my favorite chapters in the Old Testament. It revolves around a man with a real tongue-twister of a name: Mephibosheth.

Mephibosheth was a grandson of King Saul. According to some ancient customs, when the king died and a new dynasty began to rule, all of the descendants of the old king were annihilated. So when Mephibosheth's nurse heard that both Saul and Jonathan, Mephibosheth's father, had been killed, she took matters into her own hands.

> Now Jonathan, Saul's son, had a son crippled in his feet. He was five years old when the report of Saul and Jonathan came from Jezreel, and his nurse took him up and fled. And it happened that in her hurry to flee, he fell and became lame. And his name was Mephibosheth. (2 Samuel 4:4)

Now, I don't believe that David would have allowed any harm to come to this child; after all, the lad was the son of David's dear friend Jonathan. However, not knowing this, for years this young man was hidden from the king. Crippled and forgotten, he lived a life of obscurity in a place called Lo-debar, which when translated means "no pastureland." It's a word picture of a place of barrenness.

Then one day, out of the blue, in the midst of all his pomp and prosperity, David remembers his dear friend Jonathan, possibly thinking about how much he still misses him—perhaps even still grieving over the loss of his friend.

> Then David said, "Is there yet anyone left of the house of Saul, that I may show him kindness for Jonathan's sake?" Now there was a servant of the house of Saul whose name was Ziba, and they called him to David; and the king said to him . . . "Is there not yet anyone of the house of Saul to whom I may show the kindness of God?" And Ziba said to the king, "There is still a son of Jonathan who is crippled in both feet." (2 Samuel 9:1–3)

The Scriptures don't tell us what was going through Ziba's mind, but perhaps he was thinking, "I'd better warn the king that Mephibosheth is crippled, because he may want to rethink his request." But if that was what he was thinking, he didn't know David or David's God, who has a special place in His heart for the handicapped.

The king never misses a beat. I love that. He never says, "Oh, really. How bad is the disability?" He doesn't say, "Is the boy on crutches? Can he walk at all?" No, instead, he quickly replies, "Where is he?"

> So the king said to him, "Where is he?" . . . Then King David sent and brought him from the house of Machir the son of Ammiel, from Lo-debar. And Mephibosheth, the son of Jonathan the son of Saul, came to David and fell on his face and prostrated himself. And David said, "Mephibosheth." And he said, "Here is your servant!" (2 Samuel 9:4–6)

Mephibosheth probably expected to be put to death. But David shows him mercy . . . God's magnificent *chesed.*

> And David said to him, "Do not fear, for I will surely show kindness *[chesed*—there's that wonderful word again] to you for the sake of your

> father Jonathan, and will restore to you all the land of your grandfather Saul; and you shall eat at my table regularly." (2 Samuel 9:7)

In fact, David went above and beyond. He not only showed Mephibosheth mercy on behalf of his father (David's friend), but he restored to him all the land that had belonged to his grandfather Saul (David's enemy). And if that weren't enough, David made him part of his family. "There is always a place for you at my table," he said.

It's easy for us in an unguarded moment to treat those who are not whole physically or emotionally with pity or condescension, almost as though they are less than human. Mephibosheth even refers to himself as a "dead dog" (2 Samuel 9:8), reflecting the kind of self-pity or lack of self-esteem that sometimes accompanies one who is disabled. But David saw him differently:

> So Mephibosheth ate at David's table as one of the king's sons. . . . So Mephibosheth lived in Jerusalem, for he ate at the king's table regularly. Now he was lame in both feet. (2 Samuel 9:11, 13)

Isn't that *good!* Better still, isn't that mercy? I love the true story of the man who preached this passage and then he said as he concluded the sermon, "And the tablecloth covered his feet."

Every evening at supper there was stalwart Joab with all his military prowess and handsome Absalom and all the other members of David's household, and then as they waited they heard the crutches and they listened to the shuffling of feet until Mephibosheth sat down. And the tablecloth covered his feet.

God has a special mercy for those who are handicapped, . . . and let me add, also for those who minister to the handicapped. There's a special mercy that it takes, a special mercy that's needed.

Last year I was driving the freeway and I noticed a personalized license on the car ahead of me. It caught my eye because this plate read *"Chesed"*—that Hebrew word for mercy. And then I noticed, because we both took the same exit and I stopped right behind him at the stop sign, that on the dashboard of his car was a handicapped sign. It was as if the license plate was announcing: "I need mercy. Take it easy. *Chesed."* There's a special mercy for those who struggle with handicaps of every kind.

The fourth anguish mercy relieves is the anguish of suffering. No one exemplifies this better than our old friend Job.

> I loathe my own life;
> I will give full vent to my complaint;
> I will speak in the bitterness of my soul.
> I will say to God, "Do not condemn me;
> Let me know why Thou dost contend with me.
> "Is it right for Thee indeed to oppress,
> To reject the labor of Thy hands,
> And to look favorably on the schemes of the wicked?
> "Hast Thou eyes of flesh?
> Or dost Thou see as a man sees?
> "Are Thy days as the days of a mortal,
> Or Thy years as man's years,
> That Thou shouldst seek for my guilt,
> And search after my sin? (Job 10:1–6)

Here's a man we've looked at before . . . a man in tremendous anguish, both physical and emotional. Imagine yourself in a hospital in the cancer ward where a person is dying in intense pain, and in the enormity of his physical pain, out come words like this. "Why do I have to live in this physical anguish? How much better had I never been born." That's how Job felt.

But then look at verse 12:

> 'Thou hast granted me life and lovingkindness *[chesed];*
> And Thy care has preserved my spirit. (Job 10:12)

Even in the midst of Job's struggle with God's mysterious plan, out of his affliction there comes the magnificent presence of divine mercy—*chesed.*

If you have ever been close to someone who is enduring a lengthy time of suffering, or if you have been through such suffering yourself, you know that there are brief breaks in the pain when God's mercy comes over you like a soft-falling rain of relief that washes your sadness and discouragement away. How refreshing!

We are not talking about a handicap here; we are talking about a period of physical affliction. That is what Job is going through. And here he says in his anguish, "You have granted me life and You have given me mercy to continue, to endure."

I have a dear friend who stayed by his wife's side for almost a year as she was dying with ovarian cancer. He told me of such occasions, when the Lord gave merciful relief from pain. He said it was almost as if an angel of mercy hovered over their room.

When we're suffering the consequences of unfair treatment, there is mercy with God. When we're enduring the grief of loss, there is mercy. When we struggle with the limitations of a handicap, there is mercy. When we're hurting and in physical pain, there is mercy. All these earthly struggles that occur are no accidents. God is in the midst of them, working out His sovereign will. Yes, it's a mystery, which means we need special mercy to endure the anguish and misery of the pain.

The fifth anguish mercy relieves is the misery of guilt. And here again, we return to David, who offers us a clear glimpse into the tortured soul of a guilty man. Perhaps the most descriptive section in all of Scripture of the misery of secret sin and the relief of guilt confessed is found in two of David's psalms.

> How blessed is he whose transgression is forgiven,
> Whose sin is covered!
> How blessed is the man to whom the LORD does not impute iniquity,
> And in whose spirit there is no deceit!
> When I kept silent about my sin, my body wasted away

Through my groaning all day long.
For day and night Thy hand was heavy upon me;
My vitality was drained away as with the fever heat of summer. *Selah.*
(Psalm 32:1–4)

When you deceive those around you, you're living a lie. And when the child of God tries to hide his sin, the guilt virtually eats him or her alive. But when you finally come to terms with your sin, and you make your confession, when you declare yourself guilty, God "surrounds you with His lovingkindness"—His magnificent *chesed.*

I acknowledged my sin to Thee,
And my iniquity I did not hide;
I said, "I will confess my transgressions to the LORD";
And Thou didst forgive the guilt of my sin. . . .
Many are the sorrows of the wicked;
But he who trusts in the LORD, lovingkindness *[chesed]* shall surround him.
(Psalm 32:5, 10)

We see this same pattern in Psalm 51. Same context. Same man. Same set of sins. In fact, look in your Bible and you'll see in the superscription, just below the title, that this is "A Psalm of David, when Nathan the prophet came to him, after he [David] had gone in to Bathsheba." So this is months after David had committed adultery and had Bathsheba's husband, Uriah, placed in the fiercest point of battle where he surely would be killed. David hugged his secret sins to himself until that day when Nathan courageously looked him in the eye and said, "You are the man!" And David's response, recorded in this psalm, is "Be gracious to me, O God, according to Your *chesed.*"

Be gracious to me, O God, according to Thy lovingkindness;
According to the greatness of Thy compassion blot out my transgressions. (Psalm 51:1)

"Lord, I'm at Your mercy," David cried. "Lord, I need Your mercy. I plead for Your mercy." And God granted it to him.

Do you remember the last part of David's great Psalm 23?

> Surely goodness and lovingkindness will follow me all the days of my life,
> And I will dwell in the house of the Lord forever. (Psalm 23:6)

God's goodness and lovingkindness—His *chesed.* His mercy.

Some quaint commentator once suggested that since this psalm is written from the viewpoint of a shepherd and his sheep, that last verse could represent God's sheep dogs named Goodness and Mercy.

Sheep of God, do you realize that these two faithful "dogs" watch over you and care for you? Their presence reminds us that relief has come. They nuzzle us back into the shadow of the Shepherd, who graciously welcomes us and forgives us.

TENDER MERCIES

When I am treated unfairly, God's mercy relieves my bitterness. That's what happens when *chesed* comes into my cell. I have been in a dungeon of unfair treatment. Bitterness becomes my enemy, but mercy relieves it. Mercy relieves my heart of bitterness, and I can endure whatever comes my way.

When I grieve over loss, God's *chesed* relieves my anger. Often that's the part of grief we don't want to admit—especially anger against the one who has left us and anger against God for taking our loved one. Mercy relieves our anger. Not instantly, but ultimately.

When I struggle with a handicap, God's *chesed* relieves my self-pity. That can be a major enemy for the handicapped—self-pity. When they finally come to terms with it in God's mercy, they are ready to do great things for God. But it takes mercy to get them over the hurdle of self-pity.

When I endure physical and/or emotional pain, *chesed* relieves my hopelessness. The great fear of those in long-lasting pain is hopelessness, the deep anguish that they cannot go on. That there'll never be a bright tomorrow. Relief seems gone forever.

When I deal with sinful actions, God's *chesed* relieves my guilt. Grace brings me forgiveness, but it doesn't do anything to my guilt. It takes mercy to relieve my guilt.

I love the lines from that old hymn, "Day by Day":

> Ev'ry day the Lord Himself is near me
> With a special mercy for each hour;
> All my cares He fain would bear, and cheer me,
> He whose name is Counsellor and Power.[3]

We often find ourselves in miserable situations . . . mysteriously, yet magnificently, mercy brings the relief that is so desperately needed.

One of my all-time favorite movies is *Tender Mercies.* It's the story of two opposites who marry. Mac is a man who has lost the battle with the bottle. The woman is a young widow whose husband was killed in Vietnam while she was pregnant with their first and only child, a little boy. After they marry, Mac battles with drink, but she never threatens him, never makes enormous demands. She quietly, graciously, and patiently, with tender mercy, trusts God to deal with her husband.

The story reaches its climax when Mac, in a fit of depression, goes out, buys a bottle, and takes a drive in his pickup. You're sure he's going on a binge. But he comes home late at night and finds his wife in bed, quoting verses of Scripture to encourage herself while he's gone. He walks in and says, "I bought a bottle, but I poured it out. I didn't drink anything." And at that point, his life turns the corner.

It is the simple story of a woman who loves God and loves her husband into loving God, and through tender mercies wins him to the Lord. He winds up in the waters of baptism, along with the little boy, his stepson. Tender mercies. Justice is tempered with mercy, and mercy is wrapped in tenderness.

When God commanded the Israelites to build the tabernacle, He had them construct a special piece of furniture for the holiest place of all. Not simply a holy place, but the holiest of all, the Holy of Holies, hidden safely behind the thick-veiled curtain where God's presence rested. This piece of furniture was a sacred box called an ark, in which the Israelites were to place the tablets of the Law and Aaron's rod that budded.

On this ark was a lid, and over this lid they placed two hand-carved golden angels called cherubim, one at each end, their strong solid gold wings reaching out toward each other. And the place over which the cherubim hovered was the most intimate place in the tabernacle because it was the lid over the box where the blood was poured century after century. Appropriately, this most-intimate part has come to be called "the mercy seat." When the blood was poured out onto the ark, God was satisfied. His anger abated as His mercy emerged.

Frances Schaeffer writes, "It was [Martin] Luther, when translating the Old Testament into German, who first used the term 'mercy seat.' It is a beautiful, poetic phrase—but it also accurately communicates what the lid on the ark really was, a place of mercy."[4] It wasn't simply a place of rigid, demanding Law; it became a place of tender, forgiving mercy.

As people of God, we must be people of mercy. Like the wife in the movie, we must lessen our demands and increase our compassion, just as our God so often does with us. His tender mercy so beautifully balances His sovereignty and His justice and His holiness.

What a mystery! God, who has every reason to judge us for our iniquities, graciously grants us His mercy. Mercy full of forgiveness. Mercy wrapped in love. The magnificent *chesed* of God, which we do not deserve . . . but from which we find great relief.

8

God's Mysterious Immutability

Behind the dim unknown
standeth God within the shadows
keeping watch above His own.

—James Russel Lowell, *The Present Crisis*

Only this I know,
that one celestial Father gives to all.
—Milton, *Paradise Lost*

Chapter Eight

God's Mysterious Immutability

No book on the mysterious nature of God's will would be complete without several chapters on the mysterious nature of God Himself. We're in the midst of that as we continue to probe the Scriptures on this fascinating subject.

As we've observed again and again, it's impossible for us to fully understand the One whom we worship and adore, whose will we desire to obey. He is infinite. He is also our sovereign Lord—we've established that fact with clear scriptural evidence. And He is full of tender mercy, even though we sometimes question that, given our shortsighted view of life.

Furthermore, this One whose will often seems confusing and mysterious is faithful to the end . . . consistently and immutably the same. Strange as it may seem, our God stays faithful, constant, and ever-present in and over our lives, even when we cannot sense His presence, even when we question His plan . . . even when we have disobeyed Him, blown it royally and are suffering the consequences.

This is not only true, personally; it's true nationally. A nation can slide into a series of moral compromises that lead to tragic consequences. Those consequences can then escalate to such a degree that everything becomes chaotic. This happened to the ancient Jews. In fact, Hosea the prophet called it "reaping the whirlwind."

For they sow the wind,
And they reap the whirlwind. (Hosea 8:7a)

The prophet is describing his people, who had lost their way. Why had it happened? Moses had made it clear when they left Egypt and entered Canaan: "You're entering a culture that is idolatrous," he warned them. He told them, in effect, "It is a way of living that is opposed to your monotheistic way of life. Stay true. Stand firm. Be distinct. Don't compromise. No idols. No intermarriage. Remember Jehovah. Obey Him. Watch out for the signs of erosion!"

It wasn't long before the Hebrews forgot those warnings. Some kept the Canaanite idols. They may not have worshiped them at first. In fact, they probably just tossed them in a corner somewhere. But why not keep them; after all, they're just artful carvings. Then perhaps one of the children found an intriguing little figure and started to play with it. Later, he showed it to a neighbor who got interested, and before you know it, several people began to spend more time with the idol. And that led to further involvement . . . and more interest . . . until they "sowed the wind" and finally they "reaped a whirlwind."

In fact, if you take the time to make a study of Hosea 8, you'll see a series of things that led up to the whirlwind. "They transgressed My covenant and rebelled against my law" (v. 1). That's not simply Hebrew poetry; that's truth. They looked at God's law and they rearranged things. Can't you imagine their way of thinking? "This seems pretty strict for Canaan life. It made sense when we were in the desert, but we've got to look at things a lot more realistically now. A lot of what Moses said just isn't practical anymore. Our culture requres us to adjust here and tolerate there. I mean, these Canaanite women are not only attractive . . . they're lovely. What's the difference if our son falls in love with one of them? He's been raised right. He's not going to go off the deep end."

And so, in the process of sowing the wind, they "rejected the good" (v. 3). The implication? They embraced the bad. And when it came to deciding about their leaders, they slowly stopped listening to God or seeking His counsel, which led to a major compromise.

> They have set up kings, but not by Me;
> They have appointed princes, but I did not know it.
> With their silver and gold they have made idols for themselves,
> That they might be cut off. (Hosea 8:4)

Can you believe what you just read? These aren't pagan, idol-worshiping Canaanites. These are God's own people, the Hebrews! And it all started with one or two shrug-of-the-shoulders compromises. Something so simple led to so much sin, so much sorrow, so much suffering and, finally, an entire nation in exile. They sowed the wind, and they reaped the whirlwind.

Pay attention to the first few steps down the slope . . . because that's the culprit. And whoever continues downward sets in motion a cycle of complications. That's why God commands Hosea, "Put the trumpet to your lips!" (v. 1). Scream it out, son! Sound the alarm! Tell the people, "It isn't worth it. It isn't worth it!"

When Israel failed to trust God and refused to seek His will, they embraced the godless culture around them, which then drew them into a godless lifestyle. After a time, the godless lifestyle ruined them, as a people and as a nation. Eventually, the Assyrians invaded and conquered Israel, the Northern Kingdom, leading the Hebrews into captivity. At first, God's people lost their distinction . . . then they lost their faith . . . then they lost their freedom! They had reaped the whirlwind. Later, the same thing happened in Judah, when the Southern Kingdom fell into the hands of the Babylonians. Remember the psalmist's account?

> By the rivers of Babylon,
> There we sat down and wept,
> When we remembered Zion.
> Upon the willows in the midst of it

> We hung our harps.
> For there our captors demanded of us songs,
> And our tormentors mirth, saying, "Sing us one of the songs of Zion." (Psalm 137:1–3)

"Let's hear some of those songs of Zion. Let's hear you sing them now." And the psalmist sighs, "How can you sing the Lord's song in a foreign land?" They had lost everything.

They transgressed God's covenant. They rebelled against God's law. They rearranged God's words. The rejected God's will. They no longer listened to the Lord or sought His counsel.

Compromise always complicates our commitments. But never forget: God doesn't leave. Grieved and disappointed, He faithfully ushers in the consequences. God doesn't distance Himself even when He pours on the discipline. Why? Because He is immutable. Amazingly, consistently, and from our point of view, *mysteriously* faithful.

THE CYCLE OF COMPLICATIONS

One of the prophets who watched Judah's transition from compromise to captivity was Jeremiah. He prophesied for forty years, and he wept as he preached, all the while witnessing the erosion of apostasy. We have two of his books in the Old Testament. The first, of course, bears his name, which we have already referred to several times. But the second book, in my opinion, is even more eloquent. It is Jeremiah's journal of woe, called, appropriately, Lamentations.

We rarely use that word nowadays, but it's a great word. To lament is "to cry out with words of grief." It's like a wailing cry in the middle of the night. It represents deep sadness brought on by loss. And Jeremiah, as he stumbles through Jerusalem, once the stronghold of Zion, remembers and records all that they've lost.

Jeremiah remembers when they were a people of God. He remembers the warnings, and now, with a sigh, he records the failures. He reminds his readers that his people had set in motion a cycle of complications. By the way, that cycle is regularly repeated. It isn't limited to the ancients. Disobedience always brings a cycle of complications. God faithfully sets them in motion. I find at least three actions unfolding in that cycle. *First, when we compromise truth, we begin to be afflicted.*

> I am the man who has seen affliction
> Because of the rod of His wrath.
> He has driven me and made me walk
> In darkness and not in light. (Lamentations 3:1–2)

Jeremiah and his fellow Jews have certainly "seen affliction." That's the beginning of the cycle. When you do wrong, when you compromise with the truth, you begin to be afflicted, because God doesn't let His children play fast and loose in the traffic. He faithfully disciplines those He loves. He wants to bring us back. And so, in His mysterious will, He faithfully afflicts us with the rod of righteousness.

> Surely against me He has turned His hand
> Repeatedly all the day.
> He has caused my flesh and my skin to waste away,
> He has broken my bones.
> He has besieged and encompassed me with bitterness and hardship.
> In dark places He has made me dwell,
> Like those who have long been dead.
> He has walled me in so that I cannot go out;
> He has made my chain heavy.
> Even when I cry out and call for help,
> He shuts out my prayer.
> He has blocked my ways with hewn stone;
> He has made my paths crooked.
> He is to me like a bear lying in wait,

> Like a lion in secret places.
> He has turned aside my ways and torn me to pieces;
> He has made me desolate. (Lamentations 3:3–11)

Does Jeremiah's lamentation resonate with you? Have you ever found yourself under that smarting rod of God? You may be there right now. You've walked away from His truth and are now suffering the consequences. Who hasn't been there? The pain is borderline unbearable. And you're supposed to hurt. He loves and cares for you too much to let you play with fire without getting burned.

Second, when we compromise truth, hope flees. Affliction turns to desolation. "He has made me desolate," weeps Jeremiah. "He has walled me in so that I cannot go out." That's desolation, isn't it? You can feel it in every phrase that follows:

> I have become a laughingstock to all my people,
> Their mocking song all the day.
> He has filled me with bitterness,
> He has made me drunk with wormwood.
> And He has broken my teeth with gravel;
> He has made me cower in the dust.
> (Lamentations 3:14–16)

This is serious stuff. Jeremiah, God's prophet, had become a laughingstock to his own people. "Ha!" they said. "You're telling me that's the God we ought to follow? And you told us a few years ago that we ought to repent? And this is the treatment we get from Him? He's the one who brought all this on us. What a sick joke!"

"I'm humiliated, Lord," answers Jeremiah. "They're laughing at me." He records it all in his journal of lamentations.

> And my soul has been rejected from peace;
> I have forgotten happiness.
> Surely my soul remembers
> And is bowed down within me. (Lamentations 3:17, 20)

"My soul remembers and is sunk." That's the meaning of the Hebrew word here—*sunk.* "I am as low as I've ever been. I have forgotten happiness."

I talked to a man sometime ago who said, "I can't remember the last time I laughed, Chuck. I haven't even been able to smile for days." He described rather vividly the compromises that led to the lifestyle he had been living. He had gotten to the point where he was thinking of taking his own life. He had lost his joy; he had forgotten happiness. Then, in the faithful plan of God, I had the privilege of stepping into the man's life, and now he is not only alive, he's back in strong fellowship with God. Not because of anything I did, but because of the faithfulness of God. God was there all along, overseeing faithfully the consequences, waiting for the man to repent, acknowledge his wrongdoing, and humbly return to the joy he had left.

"For who can eat and who can have enjoyment without Him?" asks the wise Solomon (Ecclesiastes 2:25). Isn't that a great verse? Who can enjoy a wonderful meal, who can laugh at life and enjoy his God when he has distanced himself from Him? To have a joyful heart requires fellowship with the living God.

There's nothing worse than being responsible for our own affliction. It's bad enough to be a victim. It's doubly difficult when you've caused it. All of us who have "been there, done that" need no further reminder of those painful days.

F. B. Meyer, in one of his fine devotional books, *Christ in Isaiah,* wrote eloquently of the Hebrews' compromise and how they brought such suffering on themselves. Read the following slowly and with feeling:

> In the case of the chosen people, who for nearly seventy years had been strangers in a strange land, and had drunk the cup of bitterness to is dregs, there was thus added weight to their sorrow—the conviction of their captivity being the result of their own impenitence and transgression. This is the bitterest of all—to know that suffering need not have been; that it has resulted from indiscretion and inconsistency; that it is

> the harvest of one's own sowing; that the vulture which feeds on the vitals is a nestling of one's own rearing. Ah me! this is pain! There is an inevitable Nemesis in life. The laws of the heart and home, of the soul and human life, cannot be violated with impunity. Sin may be forgiven; the fire of penalty may be changed into the fire of trial; the love of God may seem nearer and dearer than ever—and yet there is the awful pressure of pain; the trembling heart; the failing of eyes and pining of soul; the harp on the willows; the refusal of the lip to sing the Lord's song.[1]

Finally, when we compromise truth, God doesn't move. We do.

That's what happens when we deliberately walk away from the will and ways of God. Like the Israelites, if we sow the wind, we reap the whirlwind. The fact is, you see, God hasn't moved at all. He remains faithfully by our side, grieved over our condition. We're the ones who moved.

This reminds me of the couple who were driving home on their twenty-fifth wedding anniversary after a celebration at a fine restaurant. She was sitting over against the door on the passenger side. He was behind the wheel as she began to lament, "Oh, honey, remember when we were so close? I mean, I remember when we first got married. We sat so close that you could hardly shift the gears. And look at us now." To which he responded with a shrug, "Well, I never moved."

That's the way it is with our living God.

"Lord, I remember when we used to be close."

"I never moved."

"I remember when You and I were on speaking terms."

"I never moved. I'm still listening. I'm still here."

"I remember when I used to talk to You in very private moments and You meant something to me."

"I never moved! I never went anywhere when you chose to distance yourself from Me. You're still important to me."

Now, we've heard the bad news. It's time for the good news. And the good news is hope.

BECAUSE GOD IS FAITHFUL, HOPE RETURNS

We begin to see the hope in these hinge verses of Lamentations. They mark the turning point in Jeremiah's journal of woe.

> This I recall to my mind,
> Therefore I have hope.
> The LORD's lovingkindnesses indeed never cease,
> For His compassions never fail.
> They are new every morning;
> Great is Thy faithfulness.
> "The LORD is my portion," says my soul,
> "Therefore I have hope in Him."
> The LORD is good to those who wait for Him,
> To the person who seeks Him. (Lamentations 3:21–25)

"This I recall to my mind." I love that. Jeremiah is in the midst of sadness and affliction, remembering the bitterness of days gone by . . . lamenting over the "whirlwind" of current consequences. He is walking through the remains of the city he loves, kicking the debris and wondering how in the world this could have happened . . . and suddenly it dawns on him. "This I recall to my mind." The "this" points ahead. In my Bible I've circled "this" and then drawn a little arrow that goes right down through verse 32—which is the "this" that's coming; it's what he remembers. "This I recall to my mind, therefore I have hope."

When you are at the very bottom, hope will flee. And when hope leaves, a part of you shuts down. You can't even recall those verses that you learned as a child. You can't remember one line of one song. You can't remember one prayer you ever memorized, because your hope's gone. It was in the midst of that kind of bottoming out, that Jeremiah got hope.

What is that hope? It consists of three things, and I want you to write them down. In fact, I suggest you put them on a 3-x-5 card and prop that little card up where you can read it every morning. I'll tell you why in a minute.

Here are the three lines. They're right from the Scriptures:

First, The Lord's lovingkindnesses never cease. (If you like the word "mercies," you can put it in place of "lovingkindnesses." This is that same magnificent word, *chesed,* we discovered in the previous chapter.) "The Lord's mercies never cease." Let that seep into your busy mind. Some of you have been in such a hurry that not much has seeped in during the last fifteen or twenty days—not much, that is, from God. This glorious statement shouts from the heavens. It comes directly to you, personally delivered with your name on it. "My mercies never cease."

Remember the last lines of Psalm 23? God's two sheep dogs, Goodness and Mercy, follow us all the days of our life. They work to keep us in bounds, but sometimes we run. Yet even when we run, Mercy stays at our heels. Why? Because God is immutable. That's what this passage says. "The Lord's mercies never cease." Isn't that good? Aren't you glad He isn't fickle? Aren't you grateful that He doesn't turn away when you yell back at Him, or when you ignore His commands, or when you deliberately misread and misjudge His mysterious will? His mercies never cease.

Second, "The Lord's compassions never fail." (Here's the second line to write on your 3 x 5 card.) Interesting word, *compassion.* It means "sympathetic love, concern for the helpless." His compassions are unalterably the same. His heart keeps going out to the one who is running from Him.

This reminds me of the father of the prodigal son in Luke 15. The boy wanted all the inheritance that was coming to him, and as soon as he got it, he left home. Without an argument, the father let him go, just like our Father does. How long he was gone, we're never told. But when the son ran out of money, ran out of fun, ran out of food, and ran out of hope, he finally came to his senses. Everything he had looked for in all his "loose living" in "a distant country" could only be found back home. Somehow, when you're ankle deep in the filth of the pigsty, you get a different perspective than when you're fat and sassy at home, resenting the rules.

So when the prodigal "comes to his senses," he returns home. And his father, seeing him while he is still a great distance away, runs to him. Now, he does not angrily confront his son and say, "What have you been doing? Give me an account of your time. Where in the world is all the money? And look at the mess you've made of yourself . . . you stink! You're a disgrace to this family." No, no. None of that. Instead, he embraces his boy and repeatedly kisses him as he announces, "Kill the calf! We'll have a barbecue. We're gonna have a first-class family celebration! My son who was lost has been found. He ran away from me, but now he's back." This father is filled with compassion for his wayward son. He remained faithful, full of compassion.

So it is with our Father-God. When you come home, He says, "I forgive you . . . I missed you. I'm so glad you're back."

Finally, *the Lord's faithfulness never diminishes.* (There's the third line for your card.) Don't miss the progression here: The Lord's mercies never cease. The Lord's compassions never fail. The Lord's faithfulness never diminishes.

Even when you blow it? Yes, even when you blow it. Even when you make several stupid decisions? Even when you make several stupid decisions. Even when your marriage fails? Even when your marriage fails. Even when you knew better? Even when you knew better. His faithfulness never diminishes. See how Jeremiah expresses it? "Great is His faithfulness."

Now, when you've written those three lines on the card, set it by your bed. Read it every morning. Before you put your feet on the floor, look at that card, and read it aloud.

The Lord's mercies never cease.

The Lord's compassions never fail.

The Lord's faithfulness never diminishes.

That defines God's immutability, which is a four-bit word for "He doesn't change." He has to remain faithful. Being immutable, He not only will not change in His faithfulness, He *cannot* change. He never cools off in His commitment to us. He never breaks a promise or loses enthusiasm. He stays near us when we are zealous for the truth, and He stays near us when we reject His counsel and deliberately disobey. He remains intimately involved in our lives whether we are giving Him praise in prayer or grieving Him by our actions. Whether we are running to Him or from Him, He remains faithful. His faithfulness is unconditional, unending, and unswerving. Nothing we do can diminish it, and nothing we stop doing can increase it. It remains great. His immutability never diminishes. Mysterious though such incredible constancy may seem, it's true.

Why is it when we lose all hope the enemy says, "Take your life"? Why is it that the enemy's favorite option for desperate, hopeless people is suicide? Why, in the dark night of the soul, does he prompt, "Put an end to it"?

I think the prophet provides part of the answer. Back in the Lamentations passage where we find our three promises of hope, there is another important line:

> The LORD's lovingkindnesses [mercies] indeed never cease,
> For His compassions never fail.
> They are new every morning;
> Great is Thy faithfulness; (Lamentations 3:22–23)

The Lord's mercies, compassions, and faithfulness are *new every morning.*

I don't know about your life, but I can tell you about mine. My hardest time is late in the evening. If I'm going to get low, if I'm going to get a little depressed, it will be when the sun goes down. If I'm going to have a battle that day, it will usually occur somewhere between sundown and bedtime. It will rarely be in the morning. There is something about the fresh dawn that brings back the hope that I'd lost sight of the night before. Are you like that?

There is a reason they call it "the dark night of the soul." In my forty-plus years of ministering to troubled souls, I've observed that very few people take their lives in the early hours of dawn. Most suicides I've had to deal with take place when the sun goes down—at night, in the darkness, when life just caves in and hope disappears.

Do you know what God's fresh, new morning message is to us? Whether the sun is shining brightly or whether it's pouring down rain? Whether the morning is bright or whether it's gray and overcast? His promise is the dawn itself. "Every morning," He says. Not every time you see the sun. The weather is insignificant. Every morning the Lord comes through with His encouraging message, "We're still on speaking terms, you know! I'm here. I haven't moved. Let's go together today." That's why I suggest you read those three lines every morning. It's a reminder from God that "we're still in business."

Trust God to remember you. He won't forget your name, He won't forget your circumstance, He certainly won't forget your prayers. He's not on the edge of heaven frantically trying to figure out who you are, or thinking, "What am I gonna do with her?" He's faithful to know exactly where you are. Trust Him, He remembers you. His immutability won't let Him forget.

I recall a wonderful promise that verifies this, written by the prophet Isaiah:

> But Zion said, "The LORD has forsaken me,
> the Lord has forgotten me."

> "Can a mother forget the baby at her breast
> and have no compassion on the child she has borne?
> Though she may forget,
> I will not forget you!
> See, I have engraved you on the palms of my hands;
> your walls are ever before me. (Isaiah 49:14–16, NIV)

Amazing! We are engraved on the palms of God's hands.

TRUST GOD TO REMEMBER YOU

How do we do that? Well, that's why God gave us the rest of this section of Jeremiah's journal.

> The LORD is good to those who wait for Him,
> To the person who seeks Him.
> It is good that he waits silently
> For the salvation of the LORD.
> It is good for a man that he should bear
> The yoke in his youth.
> Let him sit alone and be silent
> Since He has laid it on him.
> Let him put his mouth in the dust,
> Perhaps there is hope. (Lamentations 3:25–29)

If you want to trust Him to remember you, *stop running and start waiting!* "The Lord is good to those who wait for Him" (v. 25a). Stop running! Wait patiently.

Second, start seeking Him again. "The Lord is good to those who seek Him" (v. 25b). So, instead of ignoring Him, return to His open arms and start seeking Him again.

"Lord, I'm back. I know You've heard it before, and I know You remember me. I'm ashamed to tell You what I've been doing (as if

You didn't know), but it's good for me to rehearse it. Here's where I've been, here's what I've done; here are the things that brought shame to Your name and that hurt me as well as other people. I want to tell You today, as I come back to You and seek You diligently, that I come on the merits of my Savior, Christ. I haven't any merits of my own. I'm under His blood. I'm one of Your children, and I've been away from You far too long. I've acted stupidly. I've acted ignorantly. At times I've been both vile and vicious. But I'm back and I diligently seek You. I'm not going to ignore You any longer." Just dump the full load of your guilt on Him. He can handle it.

Then, stop talking and sit silently. "Sit alone and be silent since He has laid it on him" (v. 28). Wait patiently, seek diligently, sit silently. That means you need to stop talking. After you've poured out your heart, deliberately be quiet.

Spend a full day in quietness. Sundays are great days to do that. Set aside at least part of the afternoon to be completely quiet. Meditation is a lost art in this modern, hurry-up world. I suggest you revive it. Not by endlessly repeating some mantra to get into some other frame of mind. Not that. Simply and silently wait before your faithful God. Read a passage of Scripture, perhaps a psalm, and let it speak. Say nothing. Just sit silently. Let Him talk. Let Him reassure you that you are fully and completely forgiven and that your shame is gone. Feel His arms reach around you. Understand the cleansing that He's bringing. Feel again the freshness and relief of His presence.

Finally, submit willingly. "Let him put his mouth in the dust, perhaps there is hope" (v. 29). To me, this suggests no rationalizing, no excuses. Shove your mouth to the ground if that'll help. Stop trying to get around the heinousness and horror in your life. Face it. Submit willingly.

> Let him give his cheek to the smiter;
> Let him be filled with reproach.
> For the Lord will not reject forever,

> For if He causes grief,
> Then He will have compassion
> According to His abundant lovingkindness. (Lamentations 3:30–32)

Like dominoes standing on end, those actions bump up against one another. It starts with love, leads to mercy, and then compassion; then grace washes over you as your immutable God gives you a fresh start. Stop fighting and submit to Him. It works. I know. I've been there . . . more times than I want to remember.

The beautiful part of this is that God will fulfill every one of those three lines. He'll show you that His mercies haven't ceased, His compassions haven't failed, and His faithfulness hasn't diminished.

David Redding speaks to this in a wonderful little book I've enjoyed for years, called *Jesus Makes Me Laugh.* He tells about starting a little flock of Shropshire sheep when he was a boy, which was how he got his dog. Read his words slowly. Picture the scene he portrays so vividly.

> I had a beautiful ram. The poor man next door had a beautiful dog and a small flock of sheep he wanted to improve with my ram. He asked me if he could borrow the ram; in return he would let me have the choice of the litter from his prize dog.
>
> That's how I got Teddy, a big, black Scottish shepherd. Teddy was my dog, and he would do anything for me. He waited for me to come home from school. He slept beside me, and when I whistled he ran to me even if he was eating. At night no one would get within a half mile without Teddy's permission. During those long summers in the fields I would only see the family at night, but Teddy was with me all the time. And so when I went away to war, I didn't know how to leave him. How do you explain to someone who loves you that you're leaving him and you won't be chasing woodchucks with him tomorrow like always.
>
> So coming home that first time from the Navy [during World War II] was something I can scarcely describe. The last bus stop was

> fourteen miles from the farm. I got off there that night about 11:00 and walked the rest of the way home. It was two or three in the morning before I was within a half mile of the house. It was pitch dark, but I knew every step of the way. Suddenly Teddy heard me and began his warning barking. Then I whistled only once. The barking stopped. There was a yelp of recognition, and I knew that a big black form was hurtling toward me in the darkness. Almost immediately he was there in my arms.
>
> What comes home to me now is the eloquence with which that unforgettable memory speaks to me of my God. If my dog, without any explanation, would love me and take me back after all that time, wouldn't my God? [2]

Yes, a thousand times yes. Why? Because He is immutable.

He's faithfully there. And hurtling through the darkness of your life will come this magnificent truth, which will wrap itself around you: God will keep His promise to forgive and welcome you home. His mercies are new every morning.

Remember that when the sun goes down tonight.

9

Can God's Will Make Us Holy?

Character cannot be developed in ease and quiet. Only through experience of trial and suffering can the soul be strengthened, vision cleared, ambition inspired, and success achieved.

—*Helen Keller's Journal*

I believe that today in the west, and particularly in America, the new barbarians are all around us. We have bred them in our families and trained them in our classrooms. They inhabit our legislature, our courts, our film studios, and our churches. Most of them are attractive and pleasant; their ideas are persuasive and subtle . . . Today's barbarians are ladies and gentlemen.

—Chuck Colson, *Against the Night*

Chapter Nine

Can God's Will Make Us Holy?

It's time to dig deeper into the mysterious will of God. In doing so, we must come to terms with our age-old, inescapable battle with sin. Can God's will result in our being holy?

We've just learned some things about the faithfulness of God from the journal of Jeremiah. Now, let's look into the writings of another great prophet of God, who was the most prolific and eloquent of all God's prophets. His name was Isaiah. Many consider him the most noble of them all. Certainly God spoke mightily through the man. What's more, God gave Isaiah eyes to see the invisible.

> In the year of King Uzziah's death, I saw the Lord sitting on a throne, lofty and exalted, with the train of His robe filling the temple. Seraphim stood above Him, each having six wings; with two he covered his face, and with two he covered his feet, and with two he flew. And one called out to another and said,
>
> "Holy, Holy, Holy, is the Lord of hosts,
> The whole earth is full of His glory." (Isaiah 6:1–3)

Isaiah sees and records something that appears nowhere else in the Bible: the seraphim, a body of worshiping angelic creatures, surrounding the Lord. Seraphs, mentioned only here in Isaiah 6:2 and 6:6, are heavenly beings that resemble flaming fire in their person. I say that because the Hebrew word *sarap* means "to burn." It's the same word that is used to describe the fiery serpents that bit the children of Israel in the days of Moses (see Numbers 21:4–9). So these are hovering angels, perhaps blazing like fire, or so full of zeal they become firelike in their worship. They surround the throne of God, ministering to Him in continual praise.

Isaiah does not tell us how many there were. Maybe there were hundreds, maybe dozens, maybe only a few, but "each had six wings" and stood above the Lord, swarming about His throne with their zealous and dramatic expressions of praise.

In this amazing scene, Isaiah is allowed to draw back the curtain of heaven and catch just a glimpse of the angelic creation and their activities. These are activities that go on incessantly in the highest heaven, which we never see—their adoration and praise of a holy God.

Not only could Isaiah see all this, he could hear the antiphonal voices in which they were worshiping, one calling out to another, back and forth: "Holy, Holy, Holy." Some have interpreted this to mean the Trinity: God the Father, God the Son, God the Spirit. I think, rather, it is a reference to the Lord's infinite holiness. When words are repeated in the Hebrew text, it is for emphasis, and rarely are words repeated three times. Here, this repetition conveys infinite exaltation. "Incredible holiness is due Your Name, O Lord God of Hosts. The earth is full of Your glory." Again and again, these mysterious seraphim called out such praises to one another.

In earthly terms, with the Israelites burning incense on the high places, worshiping like their pagan neighbors, the earth was not marked by evident glory. But from the seraphim's viewpoint in the throne room of God, the earth is full of God's glory. Don't forget that. Our newspapers will never report angelic praise. They tell nothing of the glory of God. They only tell what is occurring on the horizontal plane, and as you know, they focus mainly on the bad news. But the earth will one day be full of God's glory. Don't doubt it. Our current surroundings will ultimately be removed, and they will be replaced by that which evidences the glory of God. But for a moment, Isaiah was caught up in a scene that other people couldn't see:

> And the foundations of the thresholds trembled at the voice of him who called out, while the temple was filling with smoke. (Isaiah 6:4)

The temple foundations trembled at the overwhelming, thunderous praises of that angelic choir. The place was filled with smoke and with adoring, worshiping praise. And then, for the first time in the account, Isaiah records his own response.

Up until now he's only been an observer. I think if it had happened to you or me, the same would be true. We would be stunned. We would also be mute as we listen and gaze on this unique angelic scene. The first words out of Isaiah's mouth are,

> "Woe is me, for I am ruined!
> Because I am a man of unclean lips,
> And I live among a people of unclean lips;
> For my eyes have seen the King, the Lord of hosts."
> (Isaiah 6:5)

Isaiah's response to this scene of supreme, complete, infinite holiness is, "I am not even worthy to be in the presence of such a scene." *The Living Bible* paraphrases it this way: "My doom is sealed, for I am a foul-mouthed sinner, a member of a sinful, foul-mouthed race; and I have looked upon the King, the Lord of heaven's armies."

Isaiah sees the Lord in all of His glory, and then he suddenly views his own sinful self in contrast, and responds, in effect, "I am completely unworthy to be in His presence." God's pristine perfection was an eloquent and humiliating rebuke to the prophet. Gifted though he was, his sin-soaked humanity was painfully exposed as he found himself in the presence of pure holiness.

THE TRUTH ABOUT HOLINESS

Both the original Hebrew and Greek terms that are translated "holy" in the Scriptures convey the idea of "separateness" or "separation, a setting apart." In the Bible, when something is said to be "holy," that something is set apart for God, like our two words "dedicated" and "consecrated." The furniture in the tabernacle was "dedicated" furniture; the robes worn by the priests were "consecrated" robes. They were holy, in the sense of being set apart for the purpose, the work, and the glory of God. "Holiness" carries the concept to its maximum expression, indicating a total separation from all that is sinful, impure, and imperfect. Moral wholeness is encompassed within the word holiness, meaning that God is absolutely separate from any and all contamination.

To the surprise of many, it is the will of God for us to be holy, too. Remember Peter's words?

> As obedient children, do not be conformed to the former lusts which were yours in your ignorance, but like the Holy One who called you, be holy yourselves also in all your behavior; because it is written, "YOU SHALL BE HOLY FOR I AM HOLY." (1 Peter 1:14–16)

But because the human race is contaminated by sin (thanks to Adam and Eve's fall in the Garden), we, during our earthly lives, cannot ever know complete holiness. At salvation, we are made holy before God by our position in Christ, but we can never know a complete sinless experience during our earthly existence. That's why Isaiah responds the way he does. By witnessing infinite holiness before his very eyes and hearing the deafening antiphonal angelic praises, he is reminded of the incredible contrast between his holy God and his own sinful self.

Why is it important for us who seek His will to know that our God is holy? First of all, *His holiness assures us that He is absolutely trustworthy.* Being holy, He will never take advantage of His children; He will never abuse us, He will never manipulate us, and He will never lead us astray. His will may seem mysterious, but it's never wrong. This holy Being who is sinless cannot do wrong. You and I can trust Him to do only what is right at all times.

Second, *His holiness guarantees that He has no deceitful agenda, no questionable motives.* When God leads you into His will, you never have to wonder: Will this backfire? Will this somehow work against me? His holy will is free of question.

Third, *His holiness represents a model of perfection.* Our God has not one flaw, hidden or observed, unwritten or recorded. Not even indirectly.

In an earlier chapter I mentioned that God will never tempt us to sin, not even indirectly. A person who sins will sometimes rationalize his actions by saying, "God set me up. I mean, after all, if it hadn't been for His plan, I wouldn't have a sinful nature. And if it hadn't been for the events—events that He's sovereignly in charge of, I might add—I wouldn't have been drawn into that whole mess in the first place . . . I wouldn't have been enticed." But mark this down: Because God is perfectly holy, He is never involved in our acts of sin, not even indirectly. It's not possible. Not only can He not be tempted, He also cannot tempt. That's right . . . *He cannot.* His holiness keeps that from happening.

So, what's the significance here? Well, consider this: What if holiness were limited to God and kept from us?

First, if we were not given holiness from God, we could not have fellowship with Him.

> And this is the message we have heard from Him and announce to you, that God is light, and in Him there is no darkness at all. If we say that we have fellowship with Him and yet walk in the darkness, we lie and do not practice the truth; but if we walk in the light as He Himself is in the light, we have fellowship with one another, and the blood of Jesus His Son cleanses us from all sin. (1 John 1:5–7)

Light, here, is a symbol of purity. God is absolutely resplendent purity. As Isaiah observed, He is flawless in His holiness. "In Him is no darkness at all." Imagine, not one dark thought, not one dark motive, not one deceitful statement or act. In His nature and in His will there is no darkness at all.

And when we lay our sins before Him, He cleanses us. As His children, He gives us a purity that matches His own, and thus we can fellowship with Him. Imagine that. Sinful creatures though we are, when walking His will, basking in the light of His purity we have intimate communion with our God.

Second, if we were not given holiness by God, we would live our entire lives driven by evil motives, unable ever to be free of the darkness of sin. That's why Isaiah said in a sudden burst of spontaneous humiliation, "Woe is me! There's no hope. I can't connect, because of my condition and of what I see of Him. Woe is me!" And that would be true . . . except that God graciously transfers His holiness to us when we are walking in the light. Talk about grace!

Third, if we were not given holiness by God, we would not have the hope and assurance of seeing the Lord in heaven.

> Pursue peace with all men, and the sanctification without which no one will see the Lord. (Hebrews 12:14)

The same word rendered "holy" elsewhere is here rendered "sanctification" here. If it were not for holiness being transferred to our account through the righteousness of our God, we would never see the Lord. That means we would never receive the promise of heaven.

I'll be honest with you here: That term "holiness" used to seem a little spooky to me. I thought I was alone in that concept until I came across a similar admission in John White's work, *The Fight,* in which he writes this:

> Ever gone fishing in a polluted river and hauled out an old shoe, a tea kettle or a rusty can? I get a similar sort of catch if I cast as a bait the word "holiness" into the murky depths of my mind. To my dismay I come up with such associations as: thinness, hollow-eyed gauntness, beards, sandals, long robes, stone cells, no jokes, no sex, hair shirts,

> frequent cold baths, fasting, hours of prayer, wild rocky deserts, getting up at 4 A.M., clean fingernails, stained glass, self-humiliation.
>
> The list is a strange one. Some items suggest you can only achieve holiness by a painful and rigorous process. Yet many teachers claim that your most intense efforts will be in vain since holiness is something God gives, not something you achieve. Again, my juxtaposition of items lends an air of frivolity to a subject which none of us dare take lightly. If the means by which men and women have sought holiness seem ridiculous, we should weep rather than laugh.[1]

Some people give the impression that we'll never be able to work hard enough to be holy enough. We'll never give up enough things to be holy. At the opposite extreme are those folks who see holiness as entirely passive. God distributes it. He dumps it on you. You enjoy it, take advantage of it, but you're just a passive part of the process.

Let me correct both of these extremes. First of all, we must be holy. Holiness always suggests, as I said earlier, separateness and difference. God, being holy, is different and separate from all other gods. And we, as His children, must be separate and different as well. We must live holy lives. We must live lives of ethical integrity and moral excellence. If that were impossible for us, God would never require it of us. But He does.

> For I am the LORD your God. Consecrate yourselves therefore, and be holy; for I am holy. And you shall not make yourselves unclean with any of the swarming things that swarm on the earth. For I am the LORD, who brought you up from the land of Egypt, to be your God; thus you shall be holy for I am holy. (Leviticus 11:44–45)

Those who walk in the light, obeying God's will, are actively engaged in a holy—different kind of—walk. Second, holiness is not passive. It isn't all up to God. We are active participants in the process. Holiness is part of the process of the will of God for us, His children.

> Who may ascend into the hill of the LORD?
> And who may stand in His holy place?
> He who has clean hands and a pure heart,
> Who has not lifted up his soul to falsehood,
> And has not sworn deceitfully.
> He shall receive a blessing from the LORD
> And righteousness from the God of his salvation. (Psalm 24:3–5)

Notice the involvement on the part of men and women as the psalmist described it: "Those who stand in God's holy place are the ones who have clean hands and a pure heart, those who do not lift up their soul in falsehood and do not swear deceitfully."

I think it is interesting that this Scripture mentions both our hands and our heart. Sometimes we think it is just enough to have clean hands. After all, people can see dirty hands. If we are unjust or unfair, people can see our unclean actions . . . our soiled behavior. That's obvious. So we "keep our hands clean," as the saying goes. But a deceitful heart—now, that's something else. We get good at deceit. We find ways to hide our true motives. A deceitful heart has no part in modeling the holiness of God. Remember Paul's strong injunction in his words to the Romans?

> Therefore do not let sin reign in your mortal body that you should obey its lusts, and do not go on presenting the members of your body to sin as instruments of unrighteousness; but present yourselves to God as those alive from the dead, and your members as instruments of righteousness to God. For sin shall not be master over you, for you are not under law, but under grace.
>
> What then? Shall we sin because we are not under law but under grace? May it never be! Do you not know that when you present yourselves to someone as slaves for obedience, you are slaves of the one whom you obey, either of sin resulting in death, or of obedience resulting in righteousness? But thanks be to God that though you were slaves of sin, you became obedient from the heart to that form

> of teaching to which you were committed, and having been freed from sin, you became slaves of righteousness. (Romans 6:12–18)

Shall we sin? "What a ghastly thought!" says J. B. Phillips in his paraphrase. And yet many choose to live that way. "I've heard about grace," they say. "I understand it's full of understanding and forgiveness, and I know that God always deals with me in grace, so I will sin, knowing that He will respond to my actions with grace." May I respond to that statement in all truthfulness? That is heresy. "May it never be!"

Now, it's time to learn a major lesson in theology here. Without Christ we are slaves to sin; without Christ, sin is our overlord, our enslaving master. We can make all the New Year's resolutions we wish, all the promises to ourselves, we can give all the assurances imaginable to our accountability group, but unless we have God's power within us that overcomes and conquers sin for us, we cannot keep from serving it. That power is Christ's power, available to us only after we have been converted.

When we come to the cross and give ourselves to the Savior alone by faith alone . . . at that moment, the slavery to sin is canceled, and we become enslaved to God. However, there still dwells within us this tendency to do wrong. Because we're "bent" in that direction within, so it keeps rearing its ugly head, keeps coming back, keeps revisiting us. Even though we are right with God, we still must fight the good fight—stay engaged in the battle against sin. Whoever denies this is simply denying reality.

Let me explain how it works. God sees us in Christ when we come as believing sinners at salvation, and He justifies us before himself. (Justification is the sovereign act of God whereby He declares righteous the believing sinner while we are still in a sinning state.) Even though we still live our earthly lives in a sinning state, God says, "On the basis of your faith in Christ, you are in Christ, you belong to My family, I declare you righteous." At that epochal moment God credits His righteousness to our spiritual account.

What a wonderful transfer! What a great relief of debt! Here's the great benefit: The hold that sin once had over you all your life before Christ is instantly released. You are no longer a slave to sin, unable to break its grip. Before, you had no choice. Now, you do. And the deep-down result is peace. Peace within. Peace with God.

> Therefore having been justified by faith, we have peace with God through our Lord Jesus Christ. (Romans 5:1)

And with peace comes holiness. He grants us not only forgiveness, not only righteousness, not only peace, but the capacity for personal holiness. Now the point Paul makes here is, "Since you have been declared "not guilty," what are you doing serving sin? It's no longer your master. Up until now, outside of Christ, you have been yielding yourselves as instruments of unrighteousness to sin. You couldn't help yourself. Do that no longer! Yield yourself to God. Walk in the light of His will. In doing so, you can take advantage of His gift of holiness."

Once again, this is where the issue of passivity must be addressed. Some say, "Well, when you do that, when you yield, you become totally passive. God does it all. You simply believe, and the rest is up to God." And I repeat, no! These folks who teach that may be well-meaning, but they are misled.

Look at these familiar verses and tell me to whom the commands are addressed? To God? No!

> I urge you therefore, brethren, by the mercies of God, to present your bodies a living and holy sacrifice, acceptable to God, which is your spiritual service of worship. And do not be conformed to this world, but be transformed by the renewing of your mind, that you may prove what the will of God is, that which is good and acceptable and perfect. (Romans 12:1–2)

The problem with a living sacrifice is that it keeps wanting to crawl off the altar. So when you crawl off the altar, my advice is simple: Get back on the altar. And you may have to do it every morning. Frankly, I do it most mornings of my life. I start my day with words like "Lord, today is Your day. Today is going to include temptation, and I know my tendency is to act in the flesh. I don't want to do that. I want to walk in the light . . . in Your will. I want to act in Your Spirit. I want to respond as You would have me respond. So I place myself on Your altar, and I ask You to assist me as I accept Your power to hold me in Your will. Help me to live like that moment by moment, all through this day."

It isn't all up to God. It is up to God to give us the strength. It is up to us to claim it and obey. When we do, His holy will becomes our delight. Remarkably, by walking in His will, we, sinful creatures though we are, experience what it means to be holy—set apart for God's glory. And the good news is this: When we let go, He takes charge and pours His power into us.

When I was younger, I worshiped in a church in East Houston. Inside that church, above the choir loft, was a large white sign with bold black letters that read, "Let go and let God." As a teenager I looked at those words every Sunday for several years. "Let go and let God." They sounded really great, and I'm sure whoever put them up there wanted them to convey that message to everybody.

Since then, I've learned the origin of the words on that sign—at least this is what I've been told. Back in the nineteenth century, a Christian college student took six postcards and wrote a large letter on each one of the cards: L-E-T G-O-D. "Let God." And he put them on the mantelpiece in a room in his dormitory at school. One evening a gust of wind blew through the room and the "D" blew away, leaving him with L-E-T G-O. "Let Go." The student took that as a message from God. He believed God had given him the secret of the Christian life: Only by letting go can you let God. I guess the end of the sentence would be "have His way" or "carry out His will in your life."[2] It's not a bad thought, but taken to an extreme, let me warn you, it could lead you into a rather passive mentality.

Nowhere in any of the wonderful biblical passages directing us to live a life of holiness do I see instructions to let go. Unless it's letting go of the former lusts (and that certainly is needed), or letting go of wayward thoughts so that we gird our minds for action. It isn't that God does it all and I do nothing. It's that God does His part, and then I do mine. God sends the signals, and as I read them, I respond in obedience . . . and that simple plan results in my experiencing His holy will.

My car has warning lights on the dashboard. Every once in a while when I am driving, one of them flashes bright red. When it does, I do not respond by pulling over and getting a little hammer out of the glove box and knocking out the light so that I can drive without being distracted. No, I stop and turn the engine off. In fact, I've had mechanics say, "Never just keep driving when your warning lights light up. Stop and find somebody to give you some help."

God has His own warning lights, and at times He flashes them, saying to us, "Stop, stop, don't, don't, don't, don't!" And if we're wise, we stop. We don't just let go and say, "Well, He's gonna have to take care of it." We take care of it. "We confess our sins and He is faithful and just to forgive us our sins." We use the necessary disciplines that keep our minds pure, and He does His part in honoring that obedience.

We don't passively yawn our way through life hoping by the grace of God that we'll somehow make it. We get actively involved in a life of holiness. In His strength, we supply self-control, we supply perseverance, and in our perseverance, godliness. (2 Peter 1:5–8).

We yield and place ourselves at God's disposal. Once we are yielded, He pours out the power, and we declare war on everything that is evil within and without. We live a life that is different—morally excellent, ethically beautiful. It's called a holy life. And He honors that. Because it's like He is. And according to Ephesians 5:1, we are to mimic God, living as He lives.

God has called us to be holy, so let's be holy. Take a really honest look at your walk. Are there any areas where old sins have begun to take control again? Those things you battled with for so long and finally got control of through the power of Christ? This would be a wonderful time to allow Him to bring fresh order out of longstanding chaos.

All of our Christian lives we have sung the old hymn "Take Time to Be Holy." Those words are true. It does take time to be holy. It certainly takes time to be mature. It takes time to cultivate a walk with the Lord that begins to flow naturally, because the enemy is so much more assertive and powerful than we . . . and so creative, so full of new ideas on how to derail us and demoralize us.

We need to lock onto that power that comes from God's throne. It's time we learned a never-to-be-forgotten lesson from old Isaiah the prophet. As he was willing to do, let's quickly and openly confess our human condition. Then, let's bow before our holy God's presence and invite Him to cleanse our thoughts, to correct our foul speech, to forgive us completely, and make us holy vessels who, like those winged seraphim, spend our days bringing glory to His holy name.

Can God's will make us holy? Absolutely.

10

Surprised by God

God is full of surprises. Mere superficial pressures never determine life's outcome . . . If you are intimately linked with the living God of the universe, you don't need to worry about what the crowd is doing—or even what the king is doing. The same God who created the world is able to carry you through and to work out every situation of your life, no matter how impossible it may seem.

—Ray Stedman, *Adventuring Through the Bible*

To be surprised, to wonder, is to begin to understand.
—José Ortega y gasset, *The Revolt of the Masses*

Chapter Ten

Surprised by God

IT IS ONE THING to sit in a comfortable place and read about being surprised by God. It is quite another to be in the midst of a situation that touches us personally and deeply because it came as a total surprise. But I have come to the settled that surprises are among God's favorite things. They are often the very best tests of how willing we are to obey Him.

Consider the day God surprised Abraham, who was well over one hundred years old at the time.

> Now it came about after these things, that God tested Abraham, and said to him, "Abraham!" And he said, "Here I am." And He said, "Take now your son, your only son, whom you love, Isaac, and go to the land of Moriah; and offer him there as a burnt offering on one of the mountains of which I will tell you."
>
> So Abraham rose early in the morning and saddled his donkey, and took two of his young men with him and Isaac his son; and he split wood for the burnt offering, and arose and went to the place of which God had told him. On the third day Abraham raised his eyes and saw the place from a distance. And Abraham said to his young men, "Stay here with the donkey, and I and the lad will go yonder; and we will worship and return to you."

> And Abraham took the wood of the burnt offering and laid it on Isaac his son, and he took in his hand the fire and the knife. So the two of them walked on together. And Isaac spoke to Abraham his father and said, "My father!" And he said, "Here I am, my son." And he said, "Behold, the fire and the wood, but where is the lamb for the burnt offering?" And Abraham said, "God will provide for Himself the lamb for the burnt offering, my son." So the two of them walked on together. (Genesis 22:1–8)

Put yourself in Abraham's sandals. Try to imagine being that faithful. What kind of obedience did it take to bring Abraham to this point? What must have gone through his mind as he prepared to sacrifice his own son? It's unfathomable. I honestly cannot even imagine the emotions the old man had to work through.

> Then they came to the place of which God had told him; and Abraham built the altar there, and arranged the wood, and bound his son Isaac, and laid him on the altar on top of the wood. And Abraham stretched out his hand, and took the knife to slay his son.
>
> But the angel of the LORD called to him from heaven, and said, "Abraham, Abraham!" And he said, "Here I am." And he said, "Do not stretch out your hand against the lad, and do nothing to him; for now I know that you fear God, since you have not withheld your son, your only son, from Me."
>
> Then Abraham raised his eyes and looked, and behold, behind him a ram caught in the thicket by his horns; and Abraham went and took the ram, and offered him up for a burnt offering in the place of his son.
>
> And Abraham called the name of that place The LORD Will Provide, as it is said to this day, "In the mount of the LORD it will be provided." (Genesis 22:9–14)

Again, what kind of agony must Abraham have experienced as he bound his own son, placed him on an altar, and lifted the knife to kill him—all of this, if you can believe it, in obedience to the will of

God. And then. *Surprise!* God not only stopped Abraham from going any further, He also told him He now knew Abraham feared Him . . . and He provided a ram in a nearby thicket for the sacrifice. What a strange set of affairs! What an unusual process to take Abraham (and Isaac) through!

Have you ever been surprised by God? Years ago, C. S. Lewis wrote his testimony in a book called *Surprised by Joy,* where he told of his unusual conversion to Christ. But I'm not talking about the surprise of joy we experience when we come to Christ; I'm talking about being surprised, really stunned, with God's will for your life. If you are honest, I think you would have to say, "Who hasn't been? Who hasn't endured God's surprises?"

You lay yourself before Him. You pray. You ask for counsel. You seek His Word. You are willing to give up whatever you need to give up, and you move through the door, the door closes behind you, it is locked, and you know that God led you there, and then . . . boom! . . . your surroundings are a total surprise. You thought it would be one way, and it turned out to be another. Talk about unfathomable. Talk about unsearchable and infinite. Surprises—especially those that disappoint us—are all of the above.

CONSIDERING SOME GENERAL EXAMPLES

Several common examples come to mind. You get word that a dear friend, a middle-aged woman who has been healthy all of her life, is in the hospital. You go to visit her at County General. The illness is not considered life threatening, but she is running a high fever, and the doctor is taking her through several tests to pinpoint the cause. You leave the hospital, and on the way home you pray, "Lord, I love this person. She has lived a remarkable life of faith and has been a real example to me. I pray that You will give recovery and relief. Please release her from whatever is causing this fever." You drop off to sleep that night, peacefully confident that God has heard and will honor your request. You sleep well.

Morning comes early as the shrill ring of the phone wakes you. Another friend, who has been at the hospital through the night, tells you that your friend has died. You prayed, but she did not recover. And there is no way to explain why death happened to this healthy, godly, middle-aged friend who had many years of productive life ahead of her (from your perspective). You have been surprised by God.

Here's another. You're working at a job you love. Your diligence has been rewarded with promotions and raises. You're making a good living and your family is delighting in the benefits. You're enjoying where you live and you feel confident you're there to stay. Suddenly, you begin to have little squiggly feelings inside, a sense of uneasiness, restlessness. And you think, *Why? Everything is going so well.*

And then, out of the blue, you get a job offer. You didn't expect it, you didn't seek it, but you have to admit, it sounds appealing. There are new dimensions, new challenges to it. There's a sizable promotion involved, more money, but you would have to move to another state. The good news is, the climate is better there, and you've got long-time friends who live in that area.

You begin to seek guidance from the Word of God. You talk to people you admire whose walk with the Lord is more mature than yours. You pray. You wait. Ultimately, you think, "Why sure, this is the way God does it—He's providing a whole new and exciting opportunity. Why Not?" You are at peace about the decision. So you resign, and move. It isn't three months before you realize, *I don't fit here.* This isn't what you expected. You try to make it work. You think, *If I just work harder and longer, and if I just give it more time, then it'll turn around.* But it doesn't. Things only get worse. And within a few months, you've lost that job. His unsearchable, unfathomable, infinite plan that you can't explain, results in your being surprised by God.

In the mystery of God's will we sometimes come to a place where we cannot explain why things turned out as they did; yet, amazingly, we are still right in the middle of His will. It's not that you or I created a problem; it's that God is in the process of surprising His people on a regular basis. As we've illustrated throughout this book, the Scriptures are full of stories like this.

Now before we go any further, let me answer the skeptic who is thinking, *Well, maybe God isn't really involved in all these 'surprises' at all. This is just life happening, running its random course. Maybe God just operates from a distance. He's a big picture God. He's sort of involved in the nations and the international scene and wars and those kind of things, but when it comes to daily living, He's not really that connected.*

Oh, no. The Bible includes numerous statements that refute that idea. Here are only three of them:

> For He looks to the ends of the earth,
> And sees everything under the heavens. (Job 28:24)
>
> Thou dost scrutinize my path and my lying down,
> And art intimately acquainted with all my ways. (Psalm 139:3)
>
> For the ways of a man are before the eyes of the Lord,
> And He watches all his paths. (Proverbs 5:21)

Doesn't sound to me like a distant Deity. He is exacting in His knowledge. As we have already learned, He is sovereign over all the events of our lives. Not one detail escapes His attention. The very hairs of our head are numbered. He knows everything about us. We are an open book before Him. Furthermore, He is immutably faithful. And yet He deliberately surprises us with difficult assignments, premature or unexpected deaths, lost jobs, and disappointing circumstances along the journey, even while we're in the nucleus of His will. Let's face it, it's a mystery.

RETURNING TO A SPECIFIC EXAMPLE

Let's go back and dig a little deeper into Abraham's test, recorded in Genesis 22. There we see God speaking clearly and forthrightly. He does not stutter, nor hesitate in His command: "Take your son, your only son, Isaac, whom you love . . . ."

Ishmael and Hagar have been sent away by this point in Abraham's life. But lest Abraham be tempted to search for Ishmael and offer him, God states specifically, "I want Isaac on that altar. Offer him up as a burnt offering." The Hebrew word is *olah,* which means "a whole burnt offering." If it were used of an animal, it would mean from hoof to head, all of it. "I want Isaac on an altar, consumed in fire, and the aroma coming up to Me will be an act of worship on your part, Abraham."

You know what's remarkable to me? We don't read of an argument or even a moment's hesitation on Abraham's part. And in case you think Isaac is just a little boy, a toddler, note that when they get to the mountain, he carries the wood for the fire. So Isaac is probably in his mid- to late-teen years, at least.

And on the way, there is this dialogue that touches me every time I read it. Isaac says, "Father!" And Abraham answers, "Yes, son." Isaac continues, "We've got the fire and the wood, but where's the lamb? Where's the sacrifice?" Isaac has seen his father offer sacrifices before. He's knows the drill. "Dad, . . . what do you plan to use for a sacrifice?"

Abraham's answer is nothing short of magnificent: "God will provide, my son . . . God will provide the sacrifice."

God is not like us. We have established that at length in the previous chapters. His ways are higher than our ways, and His will is different than our wills. God has a plan that's deeper than anything you and I can envision, let alone figure out.

This is a checkpoint of Abraham's faith. "Is your fear of Me greater than your love for your boy? Is your confidence in Me stronger than your affection for your very own son?"

And Abraham passes the test. Totally and stoically obedient, the man builds the altar, arranges the wood, and binds his son. On Isaac's part there's no wrestling to get free. Isaac now gets the picture. Abraham places him on the altar on top of the wood. And I'm convinced he would have brought the knife right down into his son's chest had God not intervened with another surprise.

But the Lord calls out, "Abraham! Abraham!"

And he says, "Here I am."

And the Lord says, "Don't strike that blow. Don't sacrifice your son. You have feared and obeyed Me above all—even your precious child."

You talk about being surprised. This is a wonderful surprise. This is what I call a domestic crisis surprise. Words fail to convey how precious children are to their parents. Yet in the plan of God, who plants that parental love deep in our hearts, He also, in one way or another, has ways that help us release them to Him one by one. It is one thing to love our children and care for them, watch over them and provide for them; it's another thing to place them on a level of adoration above our adoration of God. It is one thing to be grateful for them, to nurture them, and to train them; it is another thing to make idols out of them.

Someone said to me recently that God provides us with things, it seems, only for the purpose that we might learn to release them back to Him. He wants us to hold all things loosely. To release all things to Him.

Is the Lord going to use you in a great way? Quite probably. Is He going to prepare you as you expect? Probably not. And if you're not careful, you will look at the trials, the tests, the sudden interruptions, the disappointments, the sadness, the lost jobs, the failed opportunities, the broken moments, and you will think, *He's through with me. He's finished with me,* when in fact He is equipping you.

"It's doubtful God can use anyone greatly till he's hurt him deeply," said A. W. Tozer.[1]

Why do I dwell on this so deliberately? Why have I returned to it throughout this book? Because I'm convinced that these experiences are not the exception; they are the rule. Our idea of the will of God is that He leads as we would lead and plans as we would plan. But that's not the case. His will is not like that at all. In fact, here are four simple principles we need to keep in mind regarding God's leading.

First: God's preferred method is surprise. So expect surprises. I repeat, surprises are the rule, not the exception.

Second: His surprises require flexibility and adaptability. When you get in a situation that you didn't expect, you have to adapt; you are forced to adjust. God hasn't made a mistake. You haven't made a mistake. You're just going through the process of internal development that is all part of God's arrangement of events, painful though that may be.

In our home, Cynthia calls these changes "Plan B" arrangements. "Well, we go to Plan B today," she'll often say. We expected Plan A; it seemed so clear. Then, out of the blue comes a surprise, and we're left with another whole series of plans. Plan B kicks in as we flex to our Father's surprising will.

Third: Behind God's surprises are purposes we are not aware of. Evaluate them. Remind yourself that this is no mistake. This is no accident. God has deliberately planned this. Rather than feeling sorry for yourself, pray, "Lord, give me some insight here. Help me to understand why my job isn't what I thought it would be. Help me learn what I can learn through this loss, through this whole rearrangement of events. Why did You disrupt my plans and move me so obviously from there to here? Why is it that after I prayed Your answer was no? What is it You want me to learn in this process? Rather than becoming embittered, angered, and disillusioned, rather than calling the whole thing "a mistake," ask, "What can I learn from this?"

Fourth: When God surprises us, He supplies sufficient grace to handle the unexpected. As we lean on Him, He supplies what we need to endure whatever His will encompasses for us.

When I spoke of this in a sermon recently, a member of our congregation, who is going through a difficult test with two of his children, handed me this note: "Thanks, Chuck. Grace is sufficient, but sometimes the process is scary." And it is.

God's surprises can be very scary, very unsettling. They can push you to the absolute limit. But you know what you're learning to do in this process of dealing with God's surprises? You're learning to think theologically. . . . to view life from a vertical perspective. By doing so, you can release your child. You can even accept mistreatment without becoming bitter. You can handle delayed gratification and learn patience. The list goes on and on.

The sovereign God of surprises still reigns supreme. How grateful I am for that. And it could be the biggest surprise of my life, or your life, is just ahead. Or perhaps you're right in the midst of one of those surprises.

It's possible that God's surprise is intended to help you to see for the first time in your whole life your great need for Him. Maybe you have gone your own way throughout your years. And now, through a chain of events too complicated to describe, you are realizing, "There's never been a time in my life when I've really surrendered anything to this invisible God you're talking about."

Wherever you are in this journey called life, wherever you may be employed, wherever you may be in your domestic situation, wherever you may be in your age, your health, or your lifestyle, God may be preparing you for a great surprise in order to find you faithful. Rather than running from Him, let me suggest the opposite: Run *toward* Him. And rather than looking for someone to blame for the pain that you're now enduring or the change that's on the horizon, look heavenward and realize that this arrangement is sovereignly put together for your good and for His glory.

It's a wonderful thing when we learn how to turn His surprises into opportunities to surrender whatever we've been clinging to these many years. But I need to warn you: It is never easy.

For Abraham, it was Isaac. What is it for you?

11

Closed Doors, Open Doors

Ah, what a dusty answer gets the soul when hot for certainties in this our life!

—George Meredith, *Modern Love*

When the oak tree is felled, the whole forest echoes with
it; but a hundred acorns are planted silently by
some unnoticed breeze.

—Thomas Carlyle, *On History*

Chapter Eleven

Closed Doors, Open Doors

YOU AND I have traveled quite a ways together through these pages. We've been reminded of some things we'd forgotten, and we've learned some things we didn't know before. I can't speak for you, but I can say it's been a helpful journey for me. I needed this trip, having spent these last five-plus years where I never thought I'd be. But I had no other choice. God slammed all the other doors shut.

A slammed door is a harsh sound. It's not an easy sound to listen to. And it's an even harder thing to experience, especially if you have genuinely sought God's will.

You've prayed, you've sought the counsel of people you admire, you've studied sections of His Word that might very well lead you into the way you ought to go, you've spent time alone, weighing the pros and cons, your heart is willing, your spirit is ready, your soul is soaring. And about the time you get near it, bang! . . . the door slams shut.

That can be very disillusioning. Painfully disappointing.

I'm not saying it closed because you were living in sin or because your heart was turned against what God wanted or because you were selfish in some way. It just closed. Nobody can explain why. And you sort of reel and step back. You talk to the Lord and it's as though the heavens are brass. The door has closed. Period. End of story. Or is it?

You cultivate a relationship with this fine individual, and you go together for months, sometimes more than a year, and you fall deeply in love with that person. And just before you get to the subject of marriage, bang! . . . the romance cools and the relationship ends. Closed door.

You've got your heart set on a particular school. You've got the grades, you've got a good resumé, and you've got the background to do the work academically. But they can take just so many, and when the final cut comes, bang! . . . you're not chosen. You can almost hear the door slammed shut. No explanation, no reason. You're disillusioned.

I want to tell you that Cynthia and I, in almost forty-five years of marriage, have encountered a few closed doors that to this day we still cannot explain. With all our hearts we sought to do what we believed to be the will of God. We asked for guidance, we laid ourselves before Him, we held nothing tightly, willing to give up whatever needed to be given up to make it happen. Bang! Closed door.

By now, we hardly need the reminder that the Christian life is not a cloud-nine utopia. And if you still think it is, after all we've dealt with in these chapters, then I am going to burst that balloon once and for all. Because that's not only a terribly unrealistic view, thinking that Christ helps you live happily ever after; it's downright unbiblical! Once we're in heaven, sure, that's a different story. But until then, there are not many days you could write in your journal as fantastic, unbelievable, incredible, or remarkable. Most of life is learning and growing, falling and getting back up, forgiving and forgetting, accepting and going on.

Dr. Bruce Waltke, one of my mentors in the Hebrew language at seminary, used to say, "The longer I live and the closer I walk with Christ, the more I believe He does not take the time to explain why. So we trust Him through our lives without expecting the 'why?' to be answered."

I find a similar kind of comfort in the third chapter of Revelation. This chapter not only has something to say about who's in charge of closed doors, it also puts the responsibility where it belongs: squarely on the Lord.

Earlier, I mentioned the sovereign Potter doing with the clay as He pleases. I've watched a few potters at work. And it's a funny thing. I have seen them suddenly mash the clay down and start over again. Each time they do this, the clay comes out looking entirely different. And with gifted potters, they can start over and over—each time it's better and better.

He is the Potter, we are the clay. He is the one who gives the commands; we are the ones who obey. He never has to explain Himself; He never has to ask permission. Nor does He predict ahead of time that we're just about to encounter a closed door. He is shaping us into the image of His Son, regardless of the pain and heartache that may require. Those lessons are learned a little easier when we remember that we are not in charge, He is. That very thought is underscored in the last book of the Bible.

WHO HOLDS THE KEY?

In Revelation 3, as John writes under the direction of the Holy Spirit, the Lord Jesus Christ has the floor and is telling John to write to the messenger of the church at Philadelphia.

> And to the angel of the church in Philadelphia write:
>
> He who is holy, who is true, who has the key of David, who opens and no one will shut, and who shuts and no one opens, says this: "I know your deeds. Behold, I have put before you an open door which no one can shut, because you have a little power, and have kept My word, and have not denied My name." (Revelation 3:7–8)

Here our Lord defines Himself as the one "who is holy," . . . that is, sinless, the one "who is true." And by that He means He hates evil, and He does not counsel in error or engage in erroneous activities. He is "holy," He is "true," and He "has the key of David," which is symbolic for authority.

Someone who has the key to the safe has the authority to open the safe. You have a key to your home. That gives you the authority to go into the home. Whoever doesn't have the key has no right to invade a home.

Since Jesus "has the key of David," clearly He has the authority. And look at the description of that authority: He describes himself as the one "who opens and no one will shut, who shuts and no one opens." He alone has the right to open a door of opportunity and escort us through it. And we enjoy the benefits as well as endure the tests. As He walks with us, we persevere through the doors He opens. He also has the right to slam doors without explanation. And more often than not, when a door of opportunity is shut, it is to lead us through a better door with greater opportunities. Closed doors . . . open doors: Either is God's prerogative.

You don't live very long in the Christian life before you realize that both happen regularly. As profoundly as we may pray and as consistently as we may make ourselves available to do the Lord's will, there are times that His answer is no. That's right . . . no. Closed door.

Now it's our tendency, being only human, to use a little force when we encounter a closed door. After all, we've worked pretty hard for this plan. I mean, we gave up what we had over there and we moved over here, and we're not going to take a closed door sitting down. So we get out the crowbar of ingenuity, or we use some dynamite of carnality, and we start working on the door, because we're gonna get that door open.

Stop . . . stop. Take it from one who's done that too many times. Anytime you force a door, thinking you'll get your way, ultimately you will regret it. Leave it closed, back away, accept it. In acceptance lies peace.

A CLASSIC EXAMPLE

In Acts 16 we find an example of how this occurred in the lives of some of God's true servants. Here we find two missionaries on their way across Turkey, which is called Asia in this biblical account. They travel from the southeastern part of the country to the westernmost region, and it is remarkable what they encounter. Understand, Paul and Silas have great hearts. They desire to make Christ known; they have no selfish motives; they are not in this for themselves. Paul has already had one successful missionary journey. Oh, it had its trials, but what a success it was! And the church at Antioch that sent them out before has now sent them out again. This time, though, rather than crossing the Aegean Sea, they are going by land.

So they come "to Derbe and to Lystra," where they were before, and while in Lystra, the Lord leads them to the young man named Timothy (Acts 16:1). So Paul and Silas link arms with young Timothy and he begins to travel with them. And "the churches were being strengthened in the faith, and were increasing in number daily" (Acts 16:5).

This is remarkable. They are in a pagan region. This is idolatrous country. Yet all across the area, people are coming to Christ, churches are being founded. *Why,* they must have thought, *we are in for the time of our lives.* So they leave the familiar area and move on toward the Phrygian/Galatian region with high hopes. Read what happened.

"And they passed through the Phrygian and Galatian region, having been forbidden by the Holy Spirit to speak the word in Asia; and when they had come to Mysia, they were trying to go into Bithynia, and the Spirit of Jesus did not permit them" (Acts 16:6–7).

Now wait a minute. They've had success, open doors, green lights. It's working. But when they move into the more central and southern regions, God closes the door. It's another of His surprises. Understand, there are people who don't know Christ in those parts of the country. There are many who may never hear of Christ. Nevertheless, God closes that door. So they think, *Obviously the Lord is leading us more toward the central and northern regions.* And so "when they had come to Mysia, they were trying to go into Bithynia."

Let's use our own geography to get a better sense of their journey. They start in South Carolina, make their way over into Tennessee, and there's a closed door. So they go down to Alabama, Mississippi, and Louisiana. "Maybe we can do it there." Nope, another closed door. " Well, let's go up to Kansas and on into Nebraska. How about North Dakota?" Slam, slam . . . closed door. One closed door after another.

No opportunity. They couldn't speak of Christ. In fact, it says, "the Spirit of Jesus did not permit them." And later, they were "forbidden by the Holy Spirit."

So they wound up at Troas. That's like trudging all the way to San Francisco. I mean, the next step, you get wet, okay? You walk right into the ocean. You can't go further than San Francisco. In Turkey, you can't go further than Troas. It's the northwesternmost point of the continent!

They went all the way to Troas. And as they looked at the Aegean, Paul must have thought, "Lord, what is this about?" He, Timothy, and Silas must have sought the Lord for hours, asking God, "What are You trying to do? What are You trying to tell us? I mean, look at the people we've left unevangelized. You've not allowed us to speak one word to them."

We don't know how long they were in Troas before the night vision appeared to Paul. I've been taught that the vision appeared their first night. But the narrative doesn't say that. Maybe they'd been there a week. Maybe they had been there a month, waiting and praying.

You see, because we like action, movement, it's our tendency to jump ahead to what happened. But pause and entertain the emotion of their disappointment. They couldn't preach in either Phrygia or Galatia, nor were they permitted to share Christ in Mysia or Bithynia. They had to pass by those populated places where the good news was sorely needed and come all the way to Troas. And apparently they weren't going to do much preaching there. It was a major city at that time. The harbor has now silted up quite a distance, leaving Troas inland today, but back then it was located at the sea. And some historians teach that it would have been the capital of the continent before too many more years. This is a significant metropolitan center . . . and they're not going to preach here? Paul and his companions must have been trying to figure out what God was saying.

You've been there, haven't you? This looked like what you ought to do, and you threw yourself into it, and you invested in it, whether it was time or money or gifts or effort, and . . . bang! . . . to your shock, the door slammed shut. It's often difficult to know why.

Sometimes it's to teach us an invaluable lesson. Several months ago I was speaking with a man who went through the lean years in Dallas. Like many through the 1970s and early 1980s, he had done well in the real estate market. I mean *really well.* Then, he said, "When it crashed, it was like you could hear the doors slamming. Banks under investigation suddenly called in their loans, and everything just dried up." This man said, "Back then, in the heyday of prosperity, I was driving a brand-new Porsche. Almost overnight I found myself driving a used, borrowed Chevy. One morning when I drove up to the tollway booth, I realized I didn't even have a quarter to put in the basket." From this enormous high to this closed-door low, the one-time high roller told me, "I lived in a bathrobe in my home for the better part of two years. Thankfully my wife was able to work and get us through it." The wide-open door suddenly slammed shut, leaving the man depressed for almost two years.

I don't know how long Paul was in Troas, but one night things changed. And aren't we grateful when there's a breakthrough. Isn't that a great moment? Imagine Paul's joy!

And a vision appeared to Paul in the night: A certain man of Macedonia was standing and appealing to him, and saying, "Come over to Macedonia and help us" (Acts 16:9).

But wait just a minute. Don't go any further. Stop right there. People read this and they think, *That's what I need, a night vision.* You don't. As I emphasized very early in this book, it's not dreams and visions we need in order to determine and follow God's will. If we didn't have a Bible, we would. If we didn't have the completed Scriptures, we would certainly need some phenomenal, Spirit-guided evidence that God wants us to do such-and-such.

As we discussed earlier, He has limited the revelation of His will to the pages of His Word. Look at it this way: When you exhaust the Scriptures, then you can start trusting in visions. But, obviously, no one can exhaust the inexhaustible Word of God. We have prayer, we have the Word of God, we have the Spirit of God dwelling within us, we have the counsel of wise friends, and with that, we have all we need. We don't need night visions. What we need most of all are scriptural insights and willing hearts.

But at that time Paul needed the Lord to reveal His plan visibly. And in this vision he saw "a certain man of Macedonia was standing and appealing to him, saying, 'Come over to Macedonia and help us.'"

Now if you don't know your geography, you can't appreciate what that call would require of Paul and his companions. They were in Troas, which is in westernmost Asia. Macedonia is all the way across the Aegean Sea, on the European side. And that man in Macedonia is saying, "Come over and help us." In other words, he invites them to another culture, another language, another continent. Closed door on one side. Open door on the other. And Paul was ready. Look at how he responded.

> And when he had seen the vision, immediately we sought to go into Macedonia, concluding that God had called us to preach the gospel to them.
>
> Therefore putting out to sea from Troas, we ran a straight course to Samothrace, and on the day following to Neapolis; and from there to Philippi, which is a leading city of the district of Macedonia, a Roman colony; and we were staying in this city for some days. And on the Sabbath day we went outside the gate to a riverside, where we were supposing that there would be a place of prayer; and we sat down and began speaking to the women who had assembled. And a certain woman named Lydia, from the city of Thyatira, a seller of purple fabrics, a worshiper of God, was listening; and the Lord opened her heart to respond to the things spoken by Paul. (Acts 16:10–14)

We aren't told many things. How long they tried the other regions, we're not told. How they responded when the doors closed, we're not told. How soon the vision came once they got to Troas, we're not told. We're not even told the identity of the man from Macedonia. But it doesn't matter who the person was. It was a vision miraculously sent from God. And the man said, "Come over." So they concluded that God had called them to preach the gospel over there, and immediately that's where they went.

This is the first work of evangelism in Europe recorded in the New Testament. This will mean the beginning of the church at Philippi, the church at Thessalonica, and the church at Corinth. God's at work. The door has now swung wide open. It had been closed, and now it's open. God did both without asking permission, without a warning, and without any explanation.

CLOSED AND OPEN DOORS STILL HAPPEN

Several years ago I was asked to speak at a reunion of the Navigators at Estes Park, Colorado. At the end of the week, one of the men drove me back to Denver so I could catch my plane. And on the way, he said, "Can I tell you my story?"

"Sure," I said.

"Actually, it's a story of closed doors and open doors."

"Great," I said, "I've had a few of those, so tell me what yours were."

"Well," he began, "my wife and I could not find peace, in any manner, staying in the States. And while at a conference years ago with a number of the leaders of the Navigators, I was offered the opportunity to open our work in Uganda.

"Uganda," he said. "I could hardly spell it when they pointed to me and said, 'Perhaps that's where the Lord would have you and your family go.'

"I went home, I told my wife and our children, and we began to pray." I believe he said they had three small kids at the time, and their oldest son was just about to start school. And he said to his wife, "Honey, are you ready to take on the challenge of Uganda?" And she said, "If that's the door God has opened for us, I'm ready for the challenge." Wonderful response.

So they flew to Nairobi, Kenya, where he put his family up in a hotel while he rented a Land Rover and drove across the border into the country of Uganda to check out the situation.

This was just after Idi Amin's reign of terror. My friend said, "One of the first things that caught my eye when I came into the village where I was going to spend my first night were several young kids with automatic weapons, shooting them off in the sky. As I drove by, they stared at me and pointed their guns." Nothing happened, but it was that kind of volatile setting. And he thought, *Lord, are You in this?* His heart sank as the sun began to set.

By now the streets were dark, and he pulled up at a little dimly lit hotel. Inside, he went up to the registration counter. The clerk, who spoke only a little English, told him there was one bed available. So he went up two flights of stairs and opened the door and turned on the light—a naked light bulb hanging over a table. He saw a room with two beds, one unmade and one still made up. And he realized, "I am sharing this room with somebody else."

That did it. He needed the kind of encouragement only God could provide. "I dropped to my knees and I said, 'Lord, look, I'm afraid. I'm in a country I don't know, in a culture that's totally unfamiliar. I have no idea who sleeps in that bed. Please, show me You're in this move!" And then, he said, "Just as I was finishing my prayer, the door opened and there stood this six-foot five-inch African frowning at me, saying in beautiful British English, 'What are you doing in my room?' "

"I stood there for a moment, and then I muttered, 'They gave me this bed, but I'll only be here one night.' "

"What are you doing in my country?" the African asked.

"Well, I'm with a little organization called the Navigators."

"Aahh! The Navigators!" And the African broke into this enormous grin, threw his arms around his new roommate, and laughed out loud.

"He lifted me up off the floor and just danced around with me."

"Praise God, praise God," said this African.

Finally they sat down at the table, and this brother in Christ, this African fellow Christian, said, "For two years I have prayed that God would send someone to me from this organization." And he pulled out a little Scripture memory-verse pack, and at the bottom of each of the verses it read, "The Navigators, Colorado Springs, Colorado."

"Are you from Colorado Springs, Colorado?" the African asked.

"I was," said the man. "But I'm coming to Uganda to begin a work for the Navigators in this country."

The door of new hope flew open in my friend's life. That African became a member of the man's board, helped him find a place to live, helped him rebuild a section of his home, taught him all about the culture, assisted him with the language, and became his best friend for the many years they were there, serving Christ . . . who "opens and no one will shut, and who shuts and no one opens."

Doors are closed. Doors are opened. Lives are changed.

FOUR GUIDELINES THAT WILL HELP

If you're still struggling with a closed door, I have four guidelines to share with you—guidelines that have helped me in my own process of dealing with the doors Christ has opened and closed.

1. *Since God is sovereign, He is in full control.* May I repeat that statement in Revelation 3? "I am the one who opens and no one shuts, I am the one who shuts and no one opens."

2. *Being in full control, God takes full responsibility for the results.* Don't try to carry that burden. It's not up to you to make the divine plan work; it's up to God. Your job is to walk in His will, regardless; it's God's job to make His will work.

3. *The closing of a good opportunity occurs in order to lead you to a better one.* Consider the story you just read. A good door closed in the States for that dear family; a better door opened in Uganda.

I've heard countless stories like this through my years of ministry. "I hit the closed door . . . I got to the end of my rope, I tied a knot and hung on . . . I trusted the Lord through this, and you can't believe what happened as a result of my not pushing my way in the direction I thought I was supposed to go." God took over and turned a jolt into joy.

4. *Not until we walk through the open door will we realize the necessity of the previously closed one.* As a result of obeying God, doing His will, accepting the closed doors, and walking through the open ones, God will honor you with a perspective you would never otherwise have.

Let me go back to my Uganda story. After more than a dozen years, the Navigator work was well established and the man's work there was finished. Another person from the staff of the Navigators came and picked up the work as my friend and his family returned to the States.

They had not been back quite a year, when his son's high school class went to Washington D.C. for their senior field trip. The father said to his boy before he left, "Son, here's forty dollars. I want you to buy something for yourself that will be a great memory for you of this trip to our nation's capitol."

So his son went to Washington, D.C., for several days. When he got back, he had a package with him. He said, "I want to surprise you, Dad." So the father waited until his son called him into his bedroom. As my friend walked into the room, he saw, hanging over the bed, a huge Ugandan flag. "This is what I bought with the money you gave me," said the boy. "Those years in Uganda were the best years of my life, Dad."

Talk about perspective. The man feared that by going to Uganda he might hurt or hinder his family, when, in fact, his son now had an abiding passion for God's work outside the borders of these United

States. It was a passion he would never have had if that man had not obeyed and walked through the open door.

God is full of surprises, isn't He?

Perhaps you've come to a closed door, and you've been resisting it, you've been pushing it, you've been fighting it. You've looked for someone to blame. You've determined that this is what you're supposed to be doing, and it's hard for you to accept the fact that the door is truly closed.

Accept it, give up the fight, let it be, my friend . . . let it be.

You've come to your own Bithynia or Phrygia, Galatia or Mysia, and to your surprise the door has closed. Ask the Lord to meet with you at your own personal Troas as you look out across that vast sea of possibilities. Ask Him to give you peace in a whole new direction. And be open, be willing. . . . be ready for a surprise!

It is easy to be disillusioned and discouraged and to think we have missed His will, when, in fact, we are in the very nucleus of that will. It is hard to have dreams dashed, to have hopes unfulfilled, to face a future that is unknown and unfamiliar and sometimes, if the truth were known, unwanted. But God has a way of guiding us unerringly into the path of righteousness for His name's sake.

Isn't it about time you stopped trying to figure it all out? Then let it be, my friend . . . let it be. You'll exchange a lot of intensity and worry for tranquility and relief. That's a pretty good trade, if you ask me. Or ask my friend who walked through that open door into Uganda.

12

A Better Way to Look at God's Will

Penetrating so many secrets, we cease to believe in the unknowable. But there it sits nevertheless, calmly licking its chops.

—H. L. Mencken, *Minority Report*

God's will alone matters, not my personal wants or needs.
When I played tennis, I never prayed for victory in a match.
I will not pray now to be cured.

—Arthur Ashe, *Former Professional Tennis Player*

Chapter Twelve

A Better Way to Look at God's Will

As I have been saying since we started this journey together, God usually works His will in unexpected ways. Those ways are full of surprising twists and turns. But let me assure you of this: While none of us can guess the future, God is up to something great. And if we can ever figure it all out, it'll be terrific, right?

Well, don't get your hopes up. You never will. As we've repeated again and again, His decisions are unsearchable, and His ways are unfathomable, which brings us full circle to where we started: the mystery of God's will.

Recently I was in Israel, sitting on the southern steps of the temple in Jerusalem with our Insight for Living tour group while Steve Green sang "I Walked Today Where Jesus Walked." The thought crossed my mind, *Not only am I walking where He walked, I am walking with Him. As best I can tell, I am in the nucleus of God's plan for my life. Being in the center of where He has placed me, right here near the ancient wall of Zion, I'm contented.* (Who wouldn't feel that way, sitting there and listening to Steve's beautiful voice?)

But unlike that tour, where we knew every destination ahead of time, every hotel room, every lunch stop, I have no idea where this lifelong journey I am on with Him is going to take me. I really haven't a clue. The same is true for you, as a child of God. You have no way of knowing what you will experience even one minute from now. You don't know what lives you are impacting. You don't know where tomorrow will take you. You don't know the day of your death or how the Lord plans to call you home. All of this is part of His profound plan, His mysterious will. Only He knows all the details. The older I get, the more I like it that way.

At the moment, I am involved in a new church start-up north of Dallas in the once-farming community named Frisco . . . a town that is growing like Topsy. Now if anyone had told me a couple of years ago that I would be involved with a new church in Frisco, Texas, I would have responded, "Where's that?" But here I am, in the midst of another one of God's surprises! And two years ago I would have sworn that Insight for Living would be located in the Dallas area by now. Not so. Not yet. Maybe next year. Maybe never. Who knows?

I have two enduring goals in life. First and foremost, *I desire to learn how to think biblically.* I want to see life through the lens of God's eyes for the rest of my days. I don't want to argue with Him, I don't want to fight Him, I don't even need to understand Him, but I desperately desire to obey Him. And so I want to see life, whether it be struggle or joy, whether it be loss or gain, through God's perspective.

I want to be able to turn to the Scriptures and find direction and help. And when I can't find answers, I want to trust and to wait for God, even when I can't understand the reason behind where I'm going. And I want to have inner peace through all of that. . . . True contentment, like I felt sitting on those ancient steps of Jerusalem's temple.

And coming in a close second, *I want to encourage other people to do the same thing.* I want to help them know how to do what I am learning to do. That's why I'm writing this book.

I'm convinced that everything within us screams against that way of thinking and that way of living. From the time we were very small children, we have been self-centered. Our world revolves around what we want when we want it. And if someone else has it, we want it even more. And then when we get it, we want to keep it. But it doesn't satisfy, so we go looking for something else. Something more . . . always more. And so, unless something drastic takes place to change that ego-centric perspective, we spend our lives focused upon ourselves rather than upon God.

The result of all this is that we view God through human eyes. We think that He's really a lot like us, except He's older and He's stronger. We think His will is pretty much like our will, except His is smarter and has a longer view. We read our human style into God's character, so that when He throws us a curve, we view Him as unfair or untrustworthy. Or, worse, our faith gets shattered when bad things happen to people we admire. Or little children. Or whole countries.

For example, if I were God—which is a frightening thought in and of itself—I would never have allowed Dietrich Bonhoeffer to die at age thirty-nine in a concentration camp. I would have helped someone get rid of Hitler and then given Bonhoeffer at least fifty or sixty more years to live and to model, as well as to write more about the great life of faith.

If I were God, I would never have let Jim Elliott and those other fine young men be slain by the Auca Indians back in the mid-1950s. Never. I would have used them in ways that I considered worthwhile for many, many years.

If I were God, I would never have put Corrie ten Boom and her family through what they went through. Never. Because that's not fair to treat such godly people that way. I can think of some people I might put through that, but it wouldn't have been Corrie ten Boom, and it wouldn't have been Dietrich Bonhoeffer. It would have been people I felt deserved it, because that's the human way to do things . . . and so that's the way I think.

If I were God, I wouldn't have had Chuck Swindoll's mother die at age sixty-three, and I wouldn't have had his dad die a slow, painful death nine years later. I wouldn't have done it like that. My mother was fifteen years younger than my dad. She should have outlived him by fifteen years. I mean, that makes logical sense, doesn't it? Certainly from our perspective.

And if I were God, I wouldn't have had you go through the tough things you've gone through these last twelve months. You deserve better than that. Well, most of you anyway.

That may be sensible, logical, horizontal thinking . . . but that's not thinking biblically. That's putting God in human garb and giving Him our human emotions. That's calling fair what I consider fair, right what I consider right, wrong what I consider wrong. Only one major fly in this ointment: God cannot be put in our human framework. This brings us back to square one, which, again, is why I decided to write this book. There is a mystery, an aura, about the living God that is designed to force us to trust Him, even when we cannot figure Him out (which is most of the time). Why? Because, as we've learned in these chapters, He is inexplicable, He is unfathomable, He is infinite.

The mystery is purposeful, because His overall plan is profound. And let's not forget that His plan is not designed to make us comfortable; it's designed to make us more like Christ, to conform to His will. Nor is it intended to make human sense. In fact, more often than not, *God's will is downright humanly illogical.* There, I've said it.

In this life, we have focus choices. We can focus on ourselves, we can focus on our circumstances, we can focus on other people, or we can focus on God. When you think biblically (which is another way of saying theologically), you focus first on God. Regardless of what you want, regardless of the circumstances you're under (what are you doing under there anyway?), regardless of what others say or think, regardless of how you feel, God and God alone is working out His great plan. And in the final tally, it will be fabulous!

But wait. In the course of all this unfathomable mystery, we must not turn God into a cruel and unfair kind of peeved Deity. As I said, He has a divine purpose in mind. But that doesn't mean that He just carelessly tosses people into the winds of fate and then stands back with arms folded, thinking, *Ah, now let's see if they can make it through that.* God is not like that. As we've learned, He is full of tender mercies, faithful to the end, dripping with compassion.

As we discussed at the beginning of the book when we talked about Job and Jeremiah, we saw that even before the foundations of the world, He designed and put together the plan that would include the martyred missionaries, the Corrie ten Booms, the Dietrich Bonhoeffers, and millions of other names I could bring before you whose lives (and deaths!), in human terms, did not make sense.

That's a tough concept for us to grapple with, let alone grasp, because such knowledge is beyond our human way of reasoning. We never know anyone before they are born. We can't. We're finite. We do well to learn a little from history, looking back with 20/20 hindsight.

We take care of ourselves. We watch out for number one. We're focused far too much on how we look and what people are thinking and saying about us. If we have one button missing on our shirt or blouse, it's all we can do to exist until we can get alone and repair it.

Why? Because, bottom line, we don't think theologically. We think humanly. We're not nearly as concerned about what Scripture teaches as we are about what other people think and how they feel about us. If you and I genuinely believed the promises of God, we would not have worried this past week as we have worried. We would not have tried to shoulder that enormous load that is beyond our ability to carry. We would not have rationalized wrong or made up an excuse to cover our tracks. We would have flat-out told the truth and let the chips fall where they may. How very difficult it is to be totally and completely authentic!

Meanwhile, however, God is working His will in us. He is shaping us into the image of Christ, which means His Son's discipline, His endurance, His faithfulness, His purity, His attitude, His whole philosophy of life. God's goal is to make us like His dear Son. And that is a lifetime task . . . our lifetime, that is.

WHAT TO DO WITH THE UNEXPLAINABLE

It's a completely new way to look at God's will. Meaning? Do you know what I would suggest we do? Spend less time analyzing God and more time obeying Him. You say, "What are the practical ramifications of that?" That means this: When you follow His will and find yourself in a situation that you cannot explain, *don't even try.* If you do, you'll use human wisdom, and you'll just mess things up. Call it like it is. It's another of His mysterious surprises. Practice using words like "I don't know." "I don't understand." "This is beyond me." "It doesn't make sense to me . . . but that's okay. God knows."

Some young father has been diagnosed with a brain tumor. Why? I don't know. I cannot explain that. If I know that person, I want to comfort him and his family. I want to put my arms around them, and assure them of my prayers and love and confidence that nothing is a mistake with God. But that's the only answer I have. That's the limit of my understanding. And so I wait with them.

You and I could name things, specific things that we've gone through in the last several years, that make no logical sense whatsoever . . . but that's okay. We can't figure them out. But let me assure you, God is at work doing His mysterious plan (mysterious to us) which defies human logic. *So quit trying to make it humanly logical.* Trust Him. When we do, we begin the vital process of thinking biblically . . . thinking theologically.

Do you realize what a peaceful life you can live if you decide to live like this? Do you realize how relaxed you can be, how free of stress? Honestly. It is so helpful for me to remind myself: He is the One who is unfathomable. He is unsearchable. I'm neither.

So, how can we understand His ways? Face it, we cannot. That's precisely what Solomon wrote thousands of years ago:

> Man's steps are ordained by the LORD,
> How then can man understand his way? (Proverbs 20:24)

What a great line. How absolutely arrogant of us to think we could possibly understand the ways of the Almighty!

Job, in one of his many moments of struggle with the mysteries will of God, said,

> When He acts on the left, I cannot behold Him;
> He turns on the right, I cannot see Him. (Job 23:9)

"Lord, I am at a loss," said Job. Ever feel like that? I have . . . and very recently.

Cynthia and I were struggling for the longest time with a situation. I finally admitted to her, "I feel like the heavens are brass. It's like we can't get through." A little later she said to me, "I feel like we're just muttering words together here in our room." We prayed and waited and trusted and prayed some more. Nothing happened. We're still waiting. We still don't understand.

Have you ever felt that way? Job did. "I can't find Him," he admitted. "I look for Him and He's not around. If only He could just appear and I could reason my way through this, it would help so much." Sounds to me like Job's faith is getting a little thin. But then he says,

> "But He knows the way I take;
> When He has tried me, I shall come forth as gold. (Job 23:10)

Great, great insight! The overarching will of God is not about geography. (Where should I go?) It is not about occupation. (Where should I work?) It is not about exactly what car I should drive. (What color do you prefer?) The overarching, big-picutre will of God is not centered in the petty details of everyday life that we worry over. The will of God is primarily and ultimately concerned about our becoming like Christ. And in that sense, the will of God is a test. When He's tried us, and we have responded in obedience (even though we didn't understand why), we will come forth as gold.

"But I still don't understand," you say. "I don't understand why He's doing all this." Guess what? That's perfectly fine with Him. And so it's okay to admit it. It's all part of the gold-making.

Does it make the journey easy? It does not. Does it make it simple? It does not. Does it make everything that happens logical? You know that answer by now. Then what does knowing this do for you and me? It makes it bearable, especially when we call to mind that God makes no mistakes.

THINKING THEOLOGICALLY

We are riveted to earth, and we don't like things dangling. We don't even like dangling participles. We don't like dangling stories. Don't you hate it when the movie credits start to roll and you're still saying, "What? Wait a minute. Wait just a minute. I want to know who won. Who got the girl? What happened?" I hate that, when the movie just ends.

Well, a lot of things in life "just end." The credits roll before you get the final details figured out. You lost the romance that you thought was leading to marriage. It just ended. He or she just walked away from you. You lost a marriage that you thought God had put together forever. Our lives are full of stories like that—"a riddle wrapped in a mystery inside an enigma," to use a phrase coined by Sir Winston Churchill.

We don't know. And it's okay. See, it's the "okay" part that requires thinking theologically. It's also where the peace comes from, because we can relax as we leave it with God.

Which is another way of saying that we leave it with Romans 8. When things are dangling, when you can't figure out the ending and the credits are rolling, when things are not ending as you'd expected, it's time to turn to Romans 8. That works every time. I don't know what I would have done through much of my life if I hadn't had Romans 8 as my stabilizer.

When we think theologically, we find comfort in four things.

1. *We wait and persevere.* "But if we hope for what we do not see, with perseverance we wait eagerly for it" (Romans 8:25). Let that truth sink in. Read the verse once again. When we don't see what we had hoped to see, think theologically! Don't run. Don't panic. Don'r doubt God's love. Don't fight. Wait and persevere.

When you get the results of your physical exam from the doctor, you wait, you persevere through it. You may get sick to your stomach, you may feel your head spin when the negative report comes, but you still wait. You persevere. Mentally, you connect with your Lord and express your willingness to trust Him entirely.

That takes faith. "Lord God, I don't know how to explain it. I don't know why this happened . . . why now, why me, why this? But I wait for You. I am determined, by Your grace and in Your strength, to persevere through this time. Because You make no mistakes, You don't have to explain it to me. I'm trusting in You right now." We risk trusting Him, not knowing how it's going to come out. He's trustworthy, so the "risk" is minimal!

2. *We face the test head-on but on our knees.*

> And in the same way the Spirit also helps our weakness; for we do not know how to pray as we should, but the Spirit Himself intercedes for us with groanings too deep for words; and He who searches the hearts knows what the mind of the Spirit is, because He intercedes for the saints according to the will of God. (Romans 8:26–27)

You've been there, haven't you? "I just don't know how to pray about this." Of course . . . you and I have been there a hundred times. What happens? He tells us that "the Spirit Himself intercedes for us with groanings too deep for words." (We looked at this earlier, but it's worth a second glance.)

Oh, how we groan at times like this. Our soul is so troubled that we have no words to express our anguish. We fall to our knees, and, reading our inability to say what we're feeling, the Holy Spirit interprets our wordless mumblings and verbal stumblings as He intercedes for us. The Spirit intercedes as we groan on our knees: "I don't know why I lost my job, now of all times." "I don't know why I've been left to raise these four children on my own without the help of my partner." "I don't know why, Lord. All I can do is groan before You." And the Spirit intercedes for us, "according to the will of God."

To wait and persevere takes faith. Confident faith. To face the test head-on but on our knees takes humility. Submissive humility.

Humility says, "I'm willing to surrender." I'm willing to surrender my child. I'll weep as long as my grief lasts. I'm doing all I can to get the medical help we need. But ultimately, I am surrendering it all to You, dear Father. And if death comes, Lord, I accept it as part of Your plan."

This is serious stuff, folks. And I need to repeat myself, it works against our human nature to release anything. Everything in our flesh tempts us to clutch and cling. Remember? But here we humbly release as we face this test head-on . . . kneeling in full submission.

3. *We rest in our sovereign God and His plan.*

> And we know that God causes all things to work together for good to those who love God, to those who are called according to His purpose. (Romans 8:28)

Sometimes I say out loud to myself, "This is for my good and for God's glory, even though I cannot begin to explain it."

Several weeks ago our youngest grandson, Jonathan, became very sick. As Cynthia and I were driving home from the hospital, I was thinking of that tiny, precious body lying there in his hospital crib . . . and I quietly said to Cynthia, "I think we're going to lose him." Those words got almost stuck in my throat . . . I could hardly get them out of my mouth. And then the next thing I said was, "Lord, I rest in You. You know what's best. You know the reason for this. You know how much we love that little boy. But he's Yours. He was Yours before he was ever his parents or ours." Cynthia and I wept as we drove the rest of the way home in silence. I turned Romans 8:28 over in my mind for the next several hours.

We rested in our sovereign God. We know that God causes "all things to work together for good" to those who love Him. Our little Jonathan is included in that. And let me add here, your situation is included in that, too.

In this situation, God graciously chose to bring healing. As I played with Jonathan yesterday afternoon, I gave Him thanks all over again. His tender *chesed* ministers to Cynthia and me in our sorrow and struggle.

I am learning that if you think theologically, you won't put a border around "all things." You'll let it be "all things." Your loss, your gain. Your prosperity, your bankruptcy. The accident, the fall, the loss, the disease, the disappointment. And yes, the relief, the success, the healing, the cure, the promotion. "All things work together for good . . . regardless. So we rest in our sovereign God. We rest in His plan, in what He considers best for us.

4. *We remember we're being conformed to the image of Christ.*

> For whom He foreknew, He also predestined to become conformed to the image of His Son, that He might be the first-born among many brethren. (Romans 8:29)

Waiting and persevering takes faith. *Confident faith.* Facing the test head-on but on our knees takes humility. *Submissive humility.* Resting in our sovereign God and His plan takes flexibility. *Unguarded flexibility.* And being conformed to the image of Christ takes sensitivity. *Willing sensitivity.*

"It's Your plan that's important, Lord, not my desire. I didn't bring myself into this world, and I can't take myself into heaven. Furthermore, I really don't know what is best for me or for those I love. That's Your call, Lord. Make me sensitive to the reality that You are in control, and You are using this—even this—to conform me to the image of Your Son. I want that most of all."

Together let's learn to think biblically—theologically.

I had a dear friend, who has now passed into glory, whom I loved and enjoyed being with. He was a classmate during our student years at Dallas Seminary. After he finished seminary, he and his wife and their firstborn child, a son, moved to Southern California, where my friend earned his doctorate. While they were there, they had two more children, two little girls. Then, one dark day, their little boy wandered into a neighbor's backyard, fell into their swimming pool, and drowned. On that tragic afternoon, they lost their adorable little boy.

My friend was grief stricken. This fine man of God got into his car and drove the freeways of Los Angeles for hours that night, screaming out to God about the loss of his boy. "And the things I said to God on the freeway," he later told me, "I would never repeat to another soul." Finally, hours later he pulled back into his own driveway, wet with sweat and tears, and turned his car off. He rested his head on his steering wheel and finally stopped sobbing. "It then dawned on me," he said, "that God could handle all of this. He could hear me, and He could understand where everything inside me was coming from. I finally came to terms with my loss . . . and grew closer to God than I'd ever been before." Ultimately, he found peace by forcing his mind to accept what occurred. He acknowledged that even the death of their little boy must be included among the *"all things"* in Romans 8:28.

That is thinking theologically.

If you counsel, counsel people theologically. If you advise, advise them theologically. If you're going through a trial, go through it theologically. Train your mind to acknowledge God's hand in *whatever* it is you're living with.

We've had enough humanistic reasoning. We've had enough of horizontal thinking. Let's just stop it and begin practicing words like, "I don't know," "I will trust," "I can't explain," "I release it all," because the star of the show is God. He is the beginning, He will be the ending, and in between, by His grace, He lets us be part of His perfect plan. . . . for His glory and for our good.

In the meantime, expect a mystery.

Conclusion

Here, we see through a glass darkly, but there face to face . . . There, riddles shall be unraveled, mysteries made plain, dark texts enlightened, hard providences made to appear wise. The meanest soul in heaven knows more of God than the greatest saint on earth . . . Not our mightiest divines understand so much of theology as the lambs of the flock of glory. Not the greatest master-minds of earth understand the millionth part of the mighty meanings which have been discovered by souls emancipated from clay.

—Charles Haddon Spurgeon, *Spurgeon's Gems*

Conclusion

As you can tell, I'm standing in awe of mysteries these days. It's because they comprise so much of life.

Some are deeply serious. Others are lighthearted and humorous.

The washing-machine-in-our-laundry-room mystery comes to mind. Every family experiences it. You drop eight perfectly matched pairs of socks in the same load, only to pull out six matched pairs and a couple of individual socks that don't match anything. Not only do you not remember putting those two in . . . the others you did put in never show up again.

Then there's the mystery of traffic lanes. The one you find yourself in is invariably the slowest. Change lanes, and that one immediately slows to a crawl. Go figure.

Also, there's the peanut-butter-and-jelly sandwich mystery. Now, there's a tough one. Why, when accidentally dropped during the hand-held construction process, does it usually fall face down? (It has been suggested that whether it falls face down or face up is in direct proportion to the cost of the carpet.)

And how about the auto-trouble mystery? For three weeks you struggle with the same nagging problem with your car. So, early one morning you finally squeeze in time to run it by the shop. As soon as the mechanic lifts the hood, that baby purrs like a kitten. Not even the slightest miss in the engine. The guy in the overalls stares at you like *you're* the one needing to be fixed. You drive off puzzled—and halfway to work, it stalls on the freeway. Mysteries abound.

On a more serious note, there's the mystery of the sea, especially the tide, with its unusual marriage to the moon. Or the consistent, absolutely precise movement of the stellar spaces and the mind-stretching enormity of outer space. At the other extreme, a casual glance through a microscope reveals an otherwise invisible world buzzing with life.

And talk about tiny! Did you realize that if an electron could be increased to the size of an apple, and if a human being could be enlarged by the same proportion, a person could hold the entire solar system in the palm of his hand . . . and would have to use a magnifying glass in order to see it?

If you think those things are amazing, join me in trying to figure out what God is up to. We've spent twelve chapters together addressing this one. He gives; He takes. He starts; He stops. He grants us our desire; He abruptly says no. He surprises; He disappoints. He seems distant and uncaring; He surrounds us with His comforting presence.

He gives a dream, full of excitement and hope; He stops us short of fulfillment without one word of explanation. We lose.

On the other hand, we encounter a situation that appears hopeless, totally beyond our ability to handle . . . then He removes one obstacle after another, most of which we cannot explain, as we enjoy remarkable success. We win.

It's called God's inscrutable plan. I suggest it's time we stopped trying to unscrew it. Face it. It's beyond us. So? Deal with it. That's my advice, plain and simple.

Having walked with Him now for over fifty years, I've finally worked up the courage to say it publicly, loud and clear: God's will—from our finite, human standpoint—is a mystery. That's right, M-Y-S-T-E-R-Y.

Remind yourself of that two or three times a day. Before you know it, you'll really start to believe it and live it. When that happens, you cannot imagine how relaxed and relieved you'll be, filled with anticipation and adventure . . . for the rest of your life.

Endnotes

Chapter One
A Process and a Puzzle

1. Elisabeth Elliot, *Keep a Quiet Heart* (Ann Arbor, Mich.: Vine Books, 1995), as quoted in *Christianity Today*, 6/14/99 issue, p. 84.
2. Origen, *On First Principles* (New York, N.Y.: Harper & Row, Publishers, 1966), n.p.

Chapter Two
God Decrees . . . God Permits

1. Grant Howard, *Knowing God's Will—and Doing It* (Grand Rapids, Mich.: Zondervan Publishing House, 1976), p. 14.
2. Ibid., pp. 14–15.
3. Garry Friesen with J. Robin Maxson, *Decision Making and the Will of God: A Biblical Alternative to the Traditional View* (Portland, Ore.: Multnomah Press, 1980), p. 244.

4. John R. W. Stott, *The Preacher's Portrait* (Grand Rapids, Mich.: William B. Eerdmans Publishing Co., 1961), pp. 11–13.

Chapter Three
Moving from Theory to Reality

1. Henry T. Blackaby and Claude V. King, *Experiencing God* (Nashville, Tenn.: Broadman & Holman Publishers, 1994), p. 44.
2. Ibid., p. 133.
3. Ibid., pp. 36 and 138.
4. Ibid., pp. 147–148.

Chapter Four
Fleshing Out the Will of God

1. Excerpts, as submitted from *The Knowledge of the Holy, The Attributes of God: Their Meaning in the Christian,* by A. W. Tozer, p. 111. Copyright © 1961 by Aiden Wilson Tozer. Copyright renewed. Reprinted by permission of HarperCollins Publishers, Inc.
2. Henry T. Blackaby and Claude V. King, *Experiencing God* (Nashville, Tenn.: Broadman & Holman Publishers, 1994), p. 38.
3. Footnote on Genesis 4:3–4, NIV *Study Bible,* (Grand Rapids, Mich.: Zondervan Publishing House, 1985), p. 11.
4. Stuart P. Garver, *Our Christian Heritage* (Hackensack, N.J.: Christ's Mission, 1973), p. 59.
5. Philip Schaff, *History of the Christian Church* (Grand Rapids, Mich.: William B. Eerdmans Publishing Co., 1910), p. 325.
6. As quoted by Harry Emerson Fosdick in *Great Voices of the Reformation* (New York, N.Y.: Random House, 1952), p. 8.
7. As quoted by Warren W. Wiersbe and David Wiersbe in *Making Sense of the Ministry* (Grand Rapids, Mich.: Baker Book House, 1983), p. 36.

8. Warren Wiersbe, *Walking with the Giants* (Grand Rapids, Mich.: Baker Book House, 1976), p. 61.
9. As quoted by Warren Wiersbe in *Walking with the Giants,* p. 61.

Chapter Five
Another Deep Mystery: God's Sovereignty

1. As quoted by A. W. Tozer in *The Knowledge of the Holy* (San Francisco, Calif.: Harper & Row, Publishers, 1961), p. 115.
2. Tozer, *The Knowledge of the Holy,* pp. 115–116. Used by permission.
3. Tozer, *The Knowledge of the Holy,* pp. 117–118. Used by permission.
4. John Oxenham, *Bees in Amber* (New York, N.Y.: American Tract Society, 1913), n.p.

Chapter Six
Reading God's Mysterious Lips

1. Walter Chalmers Smith, "Immortal, Invisible," (n.d.)
2. Eugene Peterson, *Run with the Horses.* Copyright © 1983 InterVarsity Christian Fellowship of the USA. Used by permission of InterVarsity Press, P. O. Box 1400, Downers Grove, Il 60515, and HarperCollins Publishers Ltd.
3. Peterson, *Run with the Horses.* Used by permission.
4. Ibid.

Chapter Seven
The Mysterious *Chesed* of God

1. As quoted by William Barclay in *The Letters to Timothy, Titus and Philemon* (Edinburgh, Scotland: The Saint Andrew Press, 1956, 1960), p. 53.

2. Barclay, *The Letters to Timothy, Titus and Philemon,* pp. 53–54.
3. Carolina Sandell Berg, "Day by Day," trans. Andrew L. Skoog (n.d.)
4. Francis A. Schaeffer, *No Little People* (Downers Grove, Ill.: InterVarsity Press, 1974), p. 112.

Chapter Eight
God's Mysterious Immutability

1. F. B. Meyer, *Christ in Isaiah* (Fort Washington, Penna.: Christian Literature Crusade; London: Morgan and Scott, [n.d.]), pp. 9–10.
2. David A. Redding, *Jesus Makes Me Laugh* (Grand Rapids, Mich.: Zondervan Publishing House, 1977), pp. 101–102.

Chapter Nine
Can God's Will Make Us Holy?

1. John White, *The Fight* (Downers Grove, Ill.: InterVarsity Press, 1976), pp. 179–180.
2. Paul Lee Tan, ThD, from "Gospel for the Youth," in *Encyclopedia of 7,700 Illustrations: Signs of the Times* (Chicago, Ill.: Assurance Publishers, 1979), p. 1404.

Chapter Ten
Surprised by God

1. A. W. Tozer, *The Root of the Righteous* (Camp Hill, Penna.: Christian Publications, 1955, 1986), p. 137.